Irma Dreyfus

Lectures on French Literature Delivered in Melbourne

Irma Dreyfus

Lectures on French Literature Delivered in Melbourne

ISBN/EAN: 9783337205256

Printed in Europe, USA, Canada, Australia, Japan

Cover: Foto ©Thomas Meinert / pixelio.de

More available books at **www.hansebooks.com**

LECTURES

ON

FRENCH LITERATURE

DELIVERED IN MELBOURNE

BY IRMA DREYFUS

WITH PORTRAIT OF THE AUTHOR

LONGMANS, GREEN, AND CO.
LONDON, NEW YORK, AND BOMBAY
1896

THE SPRING AND SUMMER

OF

FRENCH LITERATURE

A SERIES OF LECTURES DELIVERED IN FRENCH

BY

IRMA DREYFUS

TRANSLATED BY JAMES SMITH

LONGMANS, GREEN, AND CO.
LONDON, NEW YORK, AND BOMBAY
1896

ERRATA.

Page	9,	line	27,	*for* Villeneuve	*read*	Villemain
,,	12,	,,	last,	,, excited	,,	excites
,,	31,	,,	1,	,, Kempis	,,	Gerson
,,	39,	,,	6,	,, Monstrelet	,,	Commynes
,,	45,	,,	13,	,, the	,,	his
,,	99,	,,	35,	,, la	,,	ta
,,	103,	,,	26,	,, craignant	,,	craignent
,,	119,	,,	35,	,, Scarrou	,,	Scarron
,,	120,	,,	27,	,, Charles X.	,,	Charles IX.
,,	132,	,,	16,	,, 1553	,,	1573
,,	137,	,,	22,	,, 1604	,,	1634
,,	138,	,,	6,	,, cuve	,,	cave
,,	139,	,,	6,	,, 1597	,,	1594
,,	189,	,,	6,	,, eighteenth	,,	XVII.
,,	191,	,,	9,	,, and his	,,	in the
,,	222,	,,	6,	,, Stency	,,	Stenay
,,	237,	,,	20,	,, his	,,	this
,,	243,	,,	29,	,, must	,,	most
,,	248,	,,	last,	,, l'aurait	,,	l'aurais
,,	266,	,,	35,	,, Juba's	,,	Julia's
,,	280,	,,	6,	,, Monturar	,,	Montufar
,,	282,	,,	1,	,, 1645	,,	1630
,,	326,	,,	32,	,, de Rude	,,	de Lude
,,	326,	,,	35,	Chateaubriand	omit	
,,	336,	,,	13,	*for* la fis	*read*	le fis
,,	354,	,,	24,	,, dieux	,,	deux
,,	359,	,,	39,	,, C'est le roi et Mme. de Montespan que tient la carte	,,	Le roi est auprès de Mme. de Montespan qui tient la carte
,,	443,	,,	13,	,, fourth	,,	fifth

,, 453 from line 3 to line 44 to be read as following line 35 on page 454.

INTRODUCTION

THE book now submitted to the public is merely a collection of lectures delivered by me at Melbourne during the years 1893–5. The kindly reception which these modest studies met with from the Australian public has encouraged me to have them rendered into English, the Professors of the University, as well as my Translator, having been good enough to regard these unpretentious notes as giving a faithful abstract of the principal epochs of French literature, up to the time of Molière, such as might usefully be brought under the notice of a wider circle.

The difference between a lecture delivered *viva voce* and the same lecture set down in writing is so great that I long hesitated to publish this collection ; and I should never have taken what I consider a very bold step, had it not appeared to me that the difficulties of writing in one language what was spoken in another have been overcome by my Translator, who has a thorough knowledge of both languages and their respective literatures.

After all, why should not these short lectures be worthy of perusal ? Those who are familiar with the subject of which they treat will certainly not derive instruction from the book ; nevertheless, they will find in it a correct classification, which may be consulted with advantage. As for those to whom the French authors of the sixteenth and seventeenth centuries are mere names—vague recollections of their college days—to such the book may serve as a guide in their reading. I had no other end in view in the composition of these Lectures, which constitute simply a conscientious compilation.

My criticisms have been dictated by my taste, which has also guided me in my selection of authors from the various periods; and my readers will be able to form their own judgments without finding their ideas hampered by bias or a 'tendency.'

I have consulted Villemain, Sainte-Beuve, Nisard, Taine, Geruzez, Walter Besant, Henry Hallam, Buckle, and many other French and English critics. Where I have borrowed from them I have been careful to indicate the fact by notes.

I believe that I have succeeded in popularising French literature in Melbourne by these Lectures, and I can only hope that the success which they met with here, delivered in the French language, will attend this translation of them in all English-speaking countries.

IRMA DREYFUS.

MELBOURNE: 1896.

CONTENTS

LECTURE I

Origins of French Literature.—'Chansons de Geste' (3).—Analysis of the 'Chanson de Roland' (middle of the eleventh century) (3-6).—Cycle of Arthur and the 'Round Table' (twelfth and thirteenth century) (7).—Romance of 'Brut' by Wace (8).—Chrestien de Troyes: romance of the 'Chevalier au Lion' (8).—'Tristan and Iseult' (10). Third Epic Cycle: Benoit de Sainte-Maure (middle of the twelfth century) (10).—Adam Adenez, or Adam le Roi (11).—'St. Peter and the Juggler' (11).—'Roman de la Rose:' Guillaume de Loris, Jean de Meung (end of the reign of St. Louis, 1270) (12).—'Roman de Renard' (1236) (13).—Literary fecundity in France in the thirteenth century (14).—Analysis of the farce of 'L'Avocat Pathelin' (1470) (14-19).

LECTURE II

Guyot de Provins (thirteenth century) (20).—Analysis of several fabliaux of the twelfth and thirteenth centuries (21-26).—Thibault de Champagne (26).—Rutebœuf (27).—Marie de France (28).—Christine de Pisan (29).—Jean Gerson (30).—Alain Chartier (31-33).—Eustache Deschamps (33).—Basselin de Vire (end of the fourteenth century and beginning of the fifteenth) (34-36).—Le Houx (end of the sixteenth century) (36).—Clotilde de Surville (36-38).

LECTURE III

Villehardouin (1160-1213) (39-44).—Joinville (1223-1319) (44-51).—Froissart (1333-1410) (51-61).—Monstrelet (1390-1453) (61).

LECTURE IV

Philippe de Commynes (1445-1509) (63-68).—Charles d'Orléans (1391-1465) (68-73).—François Villon (1431 ?-1485 ?) (73-81).—Of the Great Testament of Villon (1461) (79-81).—Budé (1467-1540) (84). Erasmus (1467-1536) (84).

LECTURE V

Clément Marot (1495-1544) (86-92).—Marguerite de Valois (1492-1549) (92).—Mellin de Saint-Gelais (1491-1558) (93).—Joachim du Bellay (1524-1560) (96-103).

LECTURE VI

Ronsard (1524-1585) (104-110).—Remi Belleau (1528-1577) (110).—Baïf (1552-1591) (111).—Jodelle (1532-1573) (111-114).—Alexandre Hardy (1560-1630) (115).—Robert Garnier (1524-1590) (115).—Guillaume de Salluste, Sieur du Bartas (1544-1590) (116-119).—Théodore d'Agrippa d'Aubigné (1550-1630) (119).

LECTURE VII

Desportes (1545-1606) (123-127).—Bertaut (1552-1611) (127-129).—Régnier (1573-1613) (129-133).—Malherbe (1555-1628) (133-137). Racan (1589-1670) (137-139).—Gombauld (1570-1666) (139).—Maynard (1583-1646) (139-141).—Malleville (1597-1647) (141).

LECTURE VIII

Rabelais (1495-1553) (142-156).—Amyot (1513-1593) (156-158).—Montaigne (1533-1592) (158-170).

LECTURE IX

La Boëtie (1530-1563) (171-178).—Pierre Charron (1541-1603) (178-181).—Michel de l'Hôpital (1503-1573) (181-184).—Cujas (1522-1590) (184).—Bodin (1530-1596) (185).—Calvin (1509-1564) (185-187).—Costar (1603-1660) (188).—Vaugelas (1585-1650) (189).—La

CONTENTS

Mothe le Vayer (1588-1672) (189).—Le Maistre (1608-1658) (190).—Patru (1604-1681) (190).—Tallemant des Réaux (1619-1692) (190). Descartes (1596-1650) (191-195).—Pascal (1623-1662) (195-203).

LECTURE X

La Satyre Ménippée (1593) (204-210).—Jean Passerat (1534-1602) (210-213).—Louise Labé (1526-1566) (214-217).—Madame de la Fayette (1634-1693) (217-220).—Madame de Longueville (1619-1679) (220-225).—Madame Deshoulières (1634-1694) (225-232).—Madame de la Sablière (1636-1693) (232).

LECTURE XI

' L'Astrée ' of D'Urfé (1568-1625) (233).—Balzac (1594-1655) (234-236). Voiture (1598-1648) (236-240).—Mademoiselle de Scudéry (1607-1701) (242-248).—La Rochefoucauld (1613-1680) (248-256).—Select ' Maxims ' (251-255).

LECTURE XII

Hôtel de Rambouillet (257-262).—La Calprenède (1610-1663) (262).—Giles Ménage (1613-1692) (263).—Isaac de Benserade (1612-1691) (264-266).—Godeau (1605-1672) (266).—Segrais (1624-1701) (267). Brébeuf (1618-1661) (268).—Académie Française (1634) (270).—Sarrazin (1605-1654) (271).—Saint-Evremond (1613-1703) (272).—Charles Perrault (1628-1703) (273).—Théophile Viaud (1590-1626) (275).—Saint-Amant (1594-1661) (275-277).—Cyrano de Bergerac (1620-1655) (277).—Paul Scarron (1610-1660) (277-280).—Father Bouhours (1628-1702) (280).

LECTURE XIII

La Bruyère (1645-1696)—Selected ' Characters ' (282-321).

LECTURE XIV

Madame de Sévigné (1626-1696) (322-872).

LECTURE XV

La Fontaine (1621-1695) (373-406).

LECTURE XVI

Molière (1622-1673)—'Les Précieuses Ridicules' — 'L'Ecole des Femmes' (407-435).

LECTURE XVII

Molière : 'Le Misanthrope'—'Les Femmes Savantes' (436-471).

LECTURES

ON

FRENCH LITERATURE

LECTURE I

Origins of French Literature—'Chansons de Geste'—Analysis of the 'Chanson de Roland' (middle of the eleventh century)—Cycle of Arthur and the 'Round Table' (twelfth and thirteenth century)—Romance of 'Brut' by Wace—Chrestien de Troyes : Romance of the 'Chevalier au Lion'—'Tristan and Iseult'—Third Epic Cycle : Benoit de Sainte-Maure (middle of the twelfth century)—Adam Adenez, or Adam le Roi—Peter and the Jugglers—'Roman de la Rose : '—Guillaume de Loris, Jean de Meung (end of the reign of St. Louis, 1270)—'Roman de Renard' (1236)—Literary fecundity in France in the thirteenth century—Analysis of the farce of 'L'Avocat Pathelin' (1470).

MY first emotion is that of gratitude ; my first words must be those of thankfulness, for the distinguished patronage which has enabled me to make my *début* this evening under such favourable auspices. The kindly reception which I met with at your hands, when I ventured to submit an outline of the plan of my modest literary lectures, will remain for ever engraven in my memory and my heart. It is your goodness which has encouraged me to give practical effect to an idea I have entertained for many years past ; and if my work should hereafter be found to possess any merit whatsoever, it will be to you my gratitude will be due, because I have endeavoured by every means in my power to render it worthy of so generous and intelligent an audience.

Let me premise, at the outset, that I have no intention of indulging in pedantic and wearisome dissertations, but that my aim is to treat my subjects in a light and familiar spirit. And to gratify my own feminine predilections, I have selected from among our French authors those who, having been recognised as really meritorious by many generations, may be recalled to your recollection with the certainty of interesting, without any pretensions on my part to instruct you.

What is intrinsically beautiful is not confined to any epoch or any school of letters; and I have therefore sought, and trust I have succeeded in disengaging it, as well in the earliest productions of our old authors, struggling against a rebellious language, as in our classic writers employing a polished and refined vocabulary.

Of all literatures, it has been said, the French is the only one which no foreigner can afford to ignore. Indeed, it has been often remarked that every one who comes into the world has two countries—his own and France.

But whether this kind of baptism be accepted or declined is immaterial. This, at least, is obvious, that the acquisition of a foreign language and a knowledge of its literature confer upon a person something like a second existence; or, as Charles V. said, 'He who knows two languages is twice a man; he who knows three is thrice a man;' and so on. And this is all I wish to prove. In fact, is it not to live twice, to have studied the languages of two great peoples, and to have divined, in the literature of both, the development of the human mind? What I propose, then, is to converse with you modestly on the great writers of my country, and to try to bring you to like them by familiarising you with their works. I neither intend nor pretend, as I have already said, to increase your literary acquisitions in my own language. I aim only at inducing you to take pleasure in reading our authors; and so, without further preface, I will plunge into the heart of my discourse.

The limits of my lectures having been thus clearly defined, you will not expect, on my part, any elaborate disquisition on the origin of French literature. Every library will be found to contain treatises on this subject, and these are easily accessible to those who wish to pursue deeper researches than are now practicable for me. At the same time I perceive that, in order to render my task more complete, I must briefly glance at the dawn of our literature, its renaissance, its classic period, and its later developments.

'France,' said Henry Martin, 'whose epic genius was disputed during the long oblivion in which our old poetry was enshrouded, is precisely the nation which revived the *épopée* in Europe ; and it was in its two mediæval languages which combined to constitute our mother tongue, that the ' Chanson de Geste ' (the historic and chivalrous ballad) had its birth. Mediæval Europe openly recognised this by designating this kind of heroic poem the 'Chanson à la Française,' just as it called our jousts and tournaments 'Jeux Français.'

The epic productions of the North are generally divided into three cycles. The first turns principally upon the recollections of Charlemagne and his race.

The rising chivalry, largely preoccupied by its wars against the Moslems in Spain, which were a prelude to the Crusades, was attached almost exclusively to narratives of deeds of war and love. And this is called the second cycle, the cycle of Arthur and the Knights of the Round Table.

In the third cycle the names of Greek antiquity cropped up for the first time.

It was in the middle of the eleventh century that the 'Chanson de Geste' burst forth to the north of the Loire. The date is certain. At the Battle of Hastings in 1066, in front of the army ready for the attack, Taillefer, the Norman *jongleur*, intoned the animated strophes of the 'Chanson de Roland.' Only a few years ago that very poem, the composition of the *trouvère* Theroulde, was rediscovered, if not in its primitive text, at any rate in one somewhat enlarged, and certainly anterior to the First Crusade ; and, at the end of the eleventh century, a cry of admiration arose when the 'Chanson de Roland' emerged, in all its vigour and native originality, from beneath the successive layers of imitations under which it had been buried for five centuries. How powerful in its simplicity ! What elevation of sentiment expressed in that still unformed language ! What grandeur of construction ! What unity in the plan and progress of the poem ! What majestic figures those of Charlemagne, Roland, Oliver, and Ganelon ! And how different the last-named from the vulgar traitor of later romances !

Has the heroic poetry of any age or of any country anything more touching or more grandiose than the picture of the death of Roland and the eleven peers? 'It wants, no doubt,' observes Henry Martin, 'the language of Homer; but, as regards the art of composition, Theroulde acquired at a bound the genuine epic form, which the romance of the middle ages never succeeded in regaining after him; and as to its spirit, the *trouvère* of the eleventh century is abreast of all. To read it is, surprising to relate, an elevation of the soul. Patriotism is the very breath of the poem, and this at the very time when there was as yet only a simple community of manners and of language, and when there was really no political country!' The mind of the poet created in that far-off time that which was reserved for the hereafter, a true France, that 'sweet France,' for which her heroes expressed such a touching tenderness, and it is Charlemagne who constitutes its majestic personification.

A few words will suffice for the analysis of the poem.[1] Spain is conquered; Saragossa alone holds out, defended by the African king, Marsile, but he proposes to surrender. Blancerdin presents himself in his name before Charlemagne, who sends Ganelon to negotiate conditions of peace; Ganelon, who, at the instigation of Roland, has reluctantly undertaken that dangerous mission, and already a traitor in his mind, promises to cause Roland and the *élite* of the army of Charlemagne, forming his rear guard at the moment of retreat, to fall into an ambuscade. The plot thus contrived is executed. The bulk of the army has already reached the other side of the Pyrenees, when the rear guard enclosed in the Valley of Roncevaux hears the sound of a formidable army, of which the numerous battalions are advancing upon it. A combat is thenceforth inevitable. Thereupon, Roland blows a terrible blast upon his 'olifant.' Charlemagne, warned by the sound, retraces his steps, and arrives in time to repulse the Saracens. But Roland rejects, as an unworthy weakness, the advice given him by the brave Oliver, and flatters himself that he can make head against the enemy and exterminate him without the help of the emperor. The combat commences; and who shall relate and enumerate the exploits of Roland, of

[1] Geruzez, i. 35.

Archbishop Turpin, and of Oliver? There all is on a grand scale, both the field of battle and the heroes. That indomitable phalanx, which never recoils, bestrews the ground with corpses; but it will perish beneath the blows of an enemy constantly returning to the charge. It is then that Roland awakens the echoes of the mountains with the blare of his ivory horn. The combat continues more desperately than ever, while the army of Charlemagne, at length alarmed, hastens to the spot.

Succour approaches, but the danger redoubles. Oliver, Roland's comrade in arms, is slain. Two warriors alone survive the carnage, Archbishop Turpin and Roland. Their last exploits have struck terror to the hearts of the Saracens, who are still further dismayed by the increasing sound of Charlemagne's clarions. They take flight. The archbishop is mortally wounded, and Roland summons up just sufficient strength to collect the dead bodies of his friends and lay them at the feet of Turpin, who dies in blessing them. Roland alone survives, but the blood is streaming from his veins, and he is at the point of death. He vainly endeavours to break his sword. He lies down upon the sward with his eyes turned towards Spain, and angels descend to receive the hero's soul. It is borne towards heaven, just as Charlemagne appears upon the scene with his army.

Such, in broad outline, is the analysis of that celebrated 'Chanson de Roland,' which reveals the heart and the imagination of a great people; relating the death of an invincible captain by treason, while compensating it, in defiance of history, by a sudden and glorious revenge. That idea of the country, so vivid in the 'Chanson de Roland,' will be obliterated from that poesy with the rising grandeur of the national monarchy, and the feudal poets, moving in a direction opposed to facts, will no longer celebrate local heroes or the exploits of knight-errantry. But the popularity of such a personage as Roland will not undergo those vicissitudes to which the memory of Charlemagne has been subjected. That French Achilles invades all languages, all literatures, and the imagination of the whole of Christendom. We meet with legends of Roland among the Turks of Asia Minor, and in the heart of the Caucasus. Dante, in his 'Inferno,' compares the voice of Nimrod to the sound of the dying Roland's olifant. Pulci describes the battle of Roncevaux in his 'Morgante Maggiore.' Roland is also the hero of the 'Orlando Innamorato' of Berni. Boiardo has done the same in his serio-comic epic, and Ariosto has immortalised the name of the French Achilles in his 'Orlando Furioso.' Milton alludes to the battle of Roncevaux in 'Paradise Lost;' and Cervantes relates how Don Quixote met a peasant carolling the 'Chanson de Roland' as he walked along. It is thus that when a man of genius kindles a fire, twenty poets who have been inspired by his example hasten to light their own torches by its flame.

I have dwelt at some length upon this old *chanson de geste*, because it is by far the most beautiful production of the cycle to which it belongs, and therefore I can only casually refer to the romance of the 'Loherains,' and enumerate the titles of the principal chansons founded on the feudal relations of Charlemagne with his vassals. These are the 'Chronicles of Turpin,' the 'Four Sons of Aymon,' 'Maugis d'Aigremont,' 'Huon de Bordeaux,' and 'Doolin de Mayence.' The four last chansons were written by Huon de Villeneuve. Then came the 'Roman de Viane' (Vienne), by Bertrans; 'Beuves de Hanstone,' by an unknown author; 'Augier le Danois,' and 'Raoul de Cambrai.'

'It is in these long narratives,' observes M. Quinet, 'that we meet with the monastery, the ladies of the clear complexion gathering the flowers of May, or watching from their balconies the approach of messengers with news; the hermit poring over his illuminated missal in the depths of the forest; the young lady mounted on her dappled palfrey; the messengers; the pilgrims seated at table and conversing in the great chamber; the townsfolk loitering under the postern; the deer in the glade; the banners fluttering in the wind; the embroidered flags unfurled; the sports of falconry; the trials by fire, water, and the duel; pleadings; the joustings; the heroic swords; the Durendal; the neighing steeds, each with his own name, as in Homer; the "Bayard" of the Sons of Aymon, the "Blanchard" of Charlemagne, and the "Valentine" of Roland.

'It is in these *chansons de geste* that we may behold the entire spectacle of that noisy, silent, diversified, monotonous, religious and warlike life, where all extremes met; so that these poems, which seem so extravagant at first, very often conclude by presenting you with a truth of details and of sentiments more real and striking than history itself.'

Every subject which the Middle Age could supply was thus treated by these *trouvères*; but among the numerous themes they most affected there were two to which they incessantly reverted. They could neither exhaust them nor lay them down when they had taken them up. These were jousts and battles.

The poems of the Carlovingian cycle were purely feudal. They were to become chivalrous. In the second cycle, known as that of Arthur and the Round Table, the poets would continue to sing of knights and arms, but would add to them lays of love and ladies. According to the generally accepted theory, the Round Table was an association composed of twelve knights, chosen by King Arthur from the worthiest of those who attended his court, in order to form a secret brotherhood, whom he used to assemble at a round table in order to abolish all differences of rank among them. Nothing can more clearly prove the strength of the popular belief in the historical truth of these Arthurian legends than the fact that in Winchester Castle, ever since the thirteenth century, a table has been carefully preserved as that which has been rendered famous in connection with King Arthur.

In the North of France there has arisen a cloud of epic poems which relate, in the prevalent style of the period, the deeds and gestes of the Knights of the Round Table. These poems were all very successful, and spread far beyond the limits of France; and the same continually acquired by accretion new ideas and foreign elements. 'Merlin,' 'Tristan,' 'Lancelot du Lac,' and 'Perceval,' are the principal poems of that cycle. The author of the last two is Chrestien de Troyes, who wrote, moreover, 'Le Roman du Chevalier au Lion,' that of 'Guillaume d'Angleterre,' 'Erec et Enide,' and 'Cliget.'

I cannot invite you to launch out with me upon the ocean of French romances of the Round Table, romances which were imitated in their turn in every language of Europe, and which, like the epic traditions of Roland, penetrated as far as Greece and Asia. Love, scarcely hinted at in the most ancient poems of the cycle of Charlemagne, reigned supreme in the Armorican cycle, or that of Arthur, with characters entirely new. The heroism associated with love has equally novel incentives: primarily, that of the passion itself; and, secondarily, the thirst for adventure, the craving for the unknown and the marvellous, the pursuit of emotion for its own sake, replacing the eagerness for conquest and the enthusiasm of the religious wars. To the conquering and political knight, the son of France, succeeded the knight errant, the son of Gaul, pursuing through the world the poetry of danger and the ideal of love; having the entire field of nature for his exploits, animated and illuminated as it were by elfin creations, among birds of evil omen, dwarfs, giants, benevolent fairies, hostile monsters, and animals acting as brethren in arms to man. An entirely enchanted world encompassed the Knights of the Round Table, and versions in verse and in prose—'Luces de Gast,' 'Gautier Map,' 'Robert,' and 'Helie de Barron' among the latter—filled the second half of the twelfth and the whole of the thirteenth century with a long series of *romans*, commencing with the 'Brut' of Wace, which embodies the whole, or at least the greater part, of the traditions current; then each of the Breton heroes furnished a theme for vast compositions, all of which connected themselves with the general cycle, and revolved around the Round Table.

All the poems of that cycle adopted a new rhythm, the octosyllabic couplet, a graceful, facile, and agreeably harmonious form of versification, well adapted to the expression of tender sentiments and delicate shades of feeling, and calculated to impart an animated movement to a narrative, but, at the same time, so easy of acquirement as to tend to laxity and diffuseness. These are, in fact, the qualities and defects of the Champenois *trouvère*, Chrestien de Troyes, who dominates French poetry during the second half of the twelfth century by the number and lustre of his productions—a writer distinguished rather by the fertility, elegance, suppleness, and variety of his productions than by their genius. 'He develops, occasionally enlarges, and in no wise invents.'

I must not leave Chrestien de Troyes without borrowing from him something to give you an idea of the style of this *trouvère*. In the 'Chevalier au Lion,' of which Yvain or Owenn is the hero, and the Lady of the Forest of Broceland is the heroine, an old Armorican legend has been woven into the following story. Yvain, who has been the means of widowing the lady, has to console her later on by becoming her husband. Thanks to a magic ring, which renders him invisible, he has witnessed her transports of grief and listened to her threats of vengeance. She does not know, observes the poet, that she is already avenged; for, to quote the words of Chrestien de Troyes, the wounds inflicted by love are deeper and more incurable than those occasioned by a lance. For these yield to the treatment of the surgeon, but those become more acute when the sufferer approaches more nearly to the only person capable of healing them.

What is most surprising about this poem is the modernity of the character and language of the lady's waiting-maid, who resembles a saucy *soubrette* of modern comedy, and tells her mistress that a live dog is worth more than a dead lion; or, in other words, that the living victor is greatly to be preferred—because he is living—to the unfortunate husband, who is now a mere corpse.

None of these poetic jewels will bear translation, for their charm is inseparable from their form. Nor is it necessary for me to dwell upon the numerous *romans* of the Armorican cycle. It will suffice to indicate their general characteristics. The Breton supplants the Celtic legend. Arthur succeeds Charlemagne. A chivalrous worship of woman replaces the rough deeds of war. 'The sweet vision of the Holy Grail' inspired Sir Galahad, Sir Perceval, and Sir Bois to set out in quest of it, and we are launched into that region of romance which has been rediscovered and almost recreated by the genius of Alfred Tennyson.

As Villeneuve has so perspicuously pointed out, the Middle Age has taken advantage of three mythologies—the chivalrous, the allegorical, and the Christian. The first gave birth to a swarm of enchanters, fairies, dwarfs, and magicians; from the second, which was the natural offspring of the first, sprang the personification of every possible virtue, and of the vices and evil thoughts; and it is to that allegorical mythology that the world is indebted for the 'Roman de la Rose,' that teeming storehouse of allegory upon which the writers of later centuries have largely drawn.

Nor can I quit this cycle without saying a few words about an unknown Norman, whose work has reached us perhaps in a mutilated condition, but who seems to me to surpass Chrestien de Troyes in simplicity, sobriety, rapidity both of action and of style, in warm colouring and deep sensibility. His 'Tristan,' fragmentary as it is, is one of the most perfect compositions of the Armorican cycle; and the beauty of the *dénouement*, narrating the death of the hero and heroine—both of whom are said to have lived in the sixth century—is unequalled. Nothing more touching is to be found in any poetry. What the catastrophe of Roland is in the purely warlike chivalry of the Carlovingian *épopée*, it has been well observed, is this incident in the amorous chivalry of the later cycle.

We have now arrived at an epoch when the memory of Charlemagne and of his great deeds is entirely effaced—at an epoch in which the exploits of war and tales of love no longer suffice for the imagination of the *trouvères*. The Round Table, together with Arthur and his Knights, undergoes the fate of Charlemagne and his Paladins. A new field is discovered in the records of antiquity, and we begin to hear of the Siege of Troy, of Ulysses and Helen, of Alexander, and of Hector.

It was towards the end of the twelfth century that French poetry began to repeat those glorious names in the confused recollections of antiquity, to satisfy the curiosity of their auditors. The first among those who treated of the Trojan war was Benoit de Sainte-Maure, an Anglo-Norman poet who lived in England for some time during the reign of Henry II., and composed a history of the Dukes of Normandy in 23,000 verses, of which the following may be quoted as a fair specimen:

> Quand vint le temps qu'hiver dérive,
> Que l'herbe verd point à la rive,
> Lorsque florissent les ramel,
> Et doucement chantent oisel,
> Merle, mauvis et loriol,
> Et estornel et rossignol,
> La blanche flor pend à l'épine,
> Et reverdoie la gaudine;
> Quand le temps est doux et soeufs [suave]
> Lors sortirent del port les nefs.

These descriptions of the Spring, in the still youthful language of the Middle Age, have all the freshness of the season they aspire to paint. The *trouvères* seem to have felt, as some one has remarked, the analogy between the spring time of the year and that of their mother tongue. They loved to expatiate on the *primavera dell' anno*; even as Chaucer did, when he characterised the colour of the tender leaves on their being first unfolded to the tender sunshine of April and May as 'a *glad* light green.'

Another *trouvère*, the most celebrated of his time, 'the King of Minstrels,' Adam Adenez, otherwise Adam le Roi, minstrel of Henry III., Duke of Flanders, achieved great distinction among the poets of chivalry composing the poetic era which opened with the 'Chanson de Roland.' His chief work, written in honour of his protectress, Mary of Brabant, bore the uncomplimentary title of 'Berte aux grands piés.' He also wrote the 'Roman de l'Enfance d'Ogier le Danois,' and the 'Roman de Pepin et de Berte sa femme.' Both are taking poems, noble in sentiment, felicitous and sometimes dramatic in expression, and harmonious in versification, although encumbered by the Alexandrine metre.

Adenez seems to have been almost the last of his class. The troubadours of the *langue d'oc* had disappeared, and the *trouvères* of the *langue d'oïl* presently followed them. The soil which had been so fertile in poetic growths during the first half of the thirteenth century lay fallow during the second. But in the meanwhile the seed of a new flower was germinating beneath the surface, which presently sprang up and budded and blossomed as the *fabliaux*. These superseded the old heroic poetry. The poems themselves were imitations, in the first instance, of Eastern stories adapted to Western modes of thought and expression. Popular satire found a voice for the first time in this new form of composition; and we may trace in some of the *fabliaux*, perhaps, the dawn of that satirical and mocking spirit which reached its climax in the writings of Voltaire. Not only so, but these early examples of sarcasm, and of sly jests at the religious abuses of the period, anticipated Rabelais to some extent. Might he not have written the pleasant story of 'St. Peter and the Juggler,' which tells us how the Devil, wishing to enjoy a cooler temperature, took a trip into the country, and left the keys of Hell in charge of a fiddler, who was an inveterate gamester? St. Peter, happening to stroll in that direction, challenged the fiddler to have a game at dice. So they sat down and played for lost souls. All the luck was on the side of Peter, who went on doubling the stakes until his infatuated opponent had emptied Hell, and Peter had drafted off its entire population to Paradise. What the Devil said when he came back from his country walk, and discovered the trick which had been played upon him by the Apostle, is altogether inconceivable. We may be sure that the fiddler 'caught it hot.'

The 'Roman de la Rose,' a model and masterpiece of this artificial kind of composition, has left its impress upon the greater part of the literary productions which made their appearance between its date and the Renaissance, if not afterwards. It also gave the final blow to heroic poetry. It was begun by Guillaume de Loris towards the end of the reign of St. Louis, and was continued by Jean de Meung. By these two a gallant allegory, which might have furnished a troubadour with the subject of a graceful and subtle little poem, was expanded into an immense mass of versification, in which they broke away completely from the poetical precedents and traditions of the past.

To pass from the old *trouvères* to Loris and Jean de Meung is like passing from a green lane bordered by sweetbrier and honeysuckle to a shop full of artificial flowers; or from a green meadow, in which children are making holiday, to a cemetery full of stiff statuary. Nevertheless, this kind of romance has played such an important part in French literature that I must offer a brief analysis of it.

The 'Roman de la Rose,' a long, learned, and wearisome allegory of more than 20,000 verses framed in a dream, all turns upon whether the hero of it shall succeed in picking a rose which he has seen in a garden, and is forbidden to gather by twenty personified abstractions, such as Danger, Baseness, Hatred, Avarice, and so forth. He has for his auxiliaries Kindly-welcome and Sweet-face. Dame Idler conducts him to the Château of Enjoyment—did Thomson borrow his 'Castle of Indolence' from the 'Roman de la Rose'? —and there he finds Love with all his retinue of Jollity, Courtesy, Freedom, and Youth. Need I dilate upon anything so frigid and inanimate as this symbolical mythology? The smallest adventure of a real living being excited more interest than all the fantastic proceedings of these bodyless shadows. Guillaume de Loris might have said all he had to say by way of conclusion in a few hundred lines; but his unfinished work fell into the hands of Jean de Meung, who had, like Dogberry, the gift of tediousness, and he tacked on to it his crude ideas of science, his profane ethics, and his political theories and opinions.

I think I have said enough of the 'Roman de la Rose,' which must not be confounded with another celebrated poem, also allegorical in character, the 'Roman de Renard,' belonging to the second half of the twelfth century. But an apologue is not an allegory; the first is living, the second is dead. 'Renard' is a masterpiece of satirical poetry, and while differing in form from the *fabliaux* of which we shall presently speak, its spirit is essentially the same. It has been justly styled an analysis of human life, where all the world is figuring in masquerade, and each of the more prominent divisions of society is typified by an animal, who embodies its salient characteristics. All the conclusions of modern science with respect to the descent of man seem to have been anticipated in this really wonderful satire, which is supposed to have been written between the First and Second Crusades, and has since found its way into all countries and all literatures. By successive accretions it grew into a poem of 80,000 lines; and people of all classes derived exquisite enjoyment from the diverting adventures of the fox, the wolf, the lion, and the ass. Especially did the disinherited of fortune enjoy the sly gibes indulged in at the expense of the nobility and clergy. In an age when authority and force were paramount, the helots of society rejoiced to think that cunning and craft were sometimes stronger than either. Nor, we may be sure, did they view with regret the disparagement or denial of the spirit of chivalry, identified as this was in their minds with the domination of an arrogant and oppressive class. Is it not just possible that the 'Roman de Renard' may have dropped into the hearts of the people the seeds which afterwards bore fruit in the Jacqueries and the Huguenot movement? But versified allegories falling into disrepute by reason of their general impotence and frigidity, there then arose the *fabliau*, also a product of the thirteenth century, which, representing the critical side of the French genius, contained the elements of an enduring nobility.

The epoch was one of amazing literary fecundity. France alone produced a hundred poets, and the age, as Sir Walter Besant has pointed out, was fruitful of great rulers— Innocent III. in Rome; Philippe-Auguste, St. Louis, and Philippe le Bel in France; Edward I. upon the throne of England, and Barbarossa and Frederick II. on that of Germany, while the Italian cities were springing up into power and importance. Professor Morley has remarked that France was the nursing mother of the imagination of two nations, England and Italy. Chaucer, who translated the 'Roman de la Rose' into his own tongue, owed quite as much to French influence as to that of Petrarch, while the obligations of Dante and his precursors to the same source are undeniable. Both Boccaccio and Chaucer derived the story of Griselda from an old *fabliau*; and the English poet's 'House of Fame' appears to me to have been suggested by one of the French allegories I have previously spoken of.

I now come to speak of an important literary event—the birth of the first French comedy, 'Maître Pierre Pathelin,' a modern version of which was produced upon the London stage, a hundred years ago, under the title of 'The Village Lawyer,' with John Bannister as Scout (Pathelin). And I introduce it in this place out of its chronological order for the sake of relieving by a note of gaiety the unavoidably dry and perhaps heavy matter by which I have preceded it.

The original is undoubtedly the oldest and most curious monument extant of the comic gaiety of our ancestors. When it was written and by whom are extremely doubtful. The earliest manuscript of it known was copied from a document of the time of St. Louis. Hence it dates back to the middle of the thirteenth century, but it was not until about the year 1470 that we hear of its first presentation on the stage, and a little later we find a Latin version of it performed by the students at Heidelberg.

An English critic has acknowledged its incontestable superiority in language, versification, and comic sentiment over the first efforts of the humorous muse translated in England, such as 'Gammer Gurton's Needle,' 'Ralph

Roister Doister,' although these appeared three centuries later, and it really appeared as if French comedy sprang into existence not so much an infant as a full-grown goddess six centuries and a half ago. But pleasantry is in the blood of the French people. To laugh is a national and individual necessity, and thus 'l'esprit gaulois,' which animated the old *fabliaux*, found jovial expression in this very ancient farce, or farcical comedy, at the time the rest of Europe was patiently enduring the solemn mysteries and dreary moralities which were then in vogue.

'L'Avocat Pathelin' has given birth to innumerable proverbs, and the very name has become synonymous with a crafty knave and an arrant trickster. *Pateliner* and *patelinage* are convertible terms with cozenry and imposition, and there are few phrases which have passed into such universal use as that employed so often by the judge in order to recall the witness to the matter in contention— *Revenons à nos moutons*.

The comedy is divided into two acts, and it opens in the poorly furnished cottage of Pierre Pathelin, advocate, and Guillemette, his wife. Pathelin bewails his ill-luck. He has tried to do his best, has worked hard, and has even deceived the public, and is, nevertheless, as poor as ever he was. Guillemette confirms all he says, and adds that the neighbours declare he is by no means so clever and sharp a practitioner as he was. Pathelin rejoins that in point of skill and knowledge he is without an equal. 'What's the good of all your learning,' exclaims Guillemette, 'if it won't fill the cupboard? We are literally without food ; and look at our clothes—they are falling to pieces !'

Pathelin, who is growing rather tired of his wife's querulous complaints, asserts that he has hit upon an idea. 'Hold your tongue!' he cries. 'On my conscience, if I wished to put my ability to the test, I should know where to find a cap and gown.'

Guillemette does not believe him, and says, 'You've neither pence nor farthings—what are you going to do?'

Pathelin, full of self-reliance, sets out for a neighbouring fair, where he calculates upon obtaining credit from a merchant, by means of a ruse, for six yards of cloth, which will suffice for a robe for himself and a gown for his wife. Then follows a deliciously comic scene between Pathelin and the merchant at the fair. The former professes to have known the clothier and his father, and flatters the simple vanity of the trader by singing the praises of the incomparable family from which he descends. 'What a man your father was! What a head for business he had! Do you know, you are as like him as two peas! Isn't it extraordinary that nature should have been capable of producing two men so perfectly resembling each other? And your Aunt Lawrence! she was one of the beauties of her day—upright, graceful, and just your figure! Ah, you come of a fine old stock! I don't know anything like it in all the country-side!' And while he is speaking, and as if by mere chance, his hand glides among the folds of a bale of cloth, of which he extols its soft, silky touch. In fact, he has never met with such a beautiful fabric before. The merchant explains that it has been made from the wool of his own sheep. Thereupon Pathelin piles up fresh panegyrics of the business qualities of the trader.

'Bah!' he observes, 'I had saved up eighty crowns, but I see very plainly that some of them will find their way into your purse, for I cannot possibly resist the sight of that splendid cloth. Cut me off six yards; the price is no object.' This having been done, he will not give the merchant the trouble even of sending it home, but will carry it himself, adding, 'Will you come by-and-by, just in a friendly sort of way, and take pot luck with us? No ceremony, you know. My wife has got a goose on the spit. And I will pay you for the cloth at the same time.' Pathelin goes home in triumph, and explains to Guillemette how he has obtained the cloth. But she reminds him of the old fable of the crow and the cheese; and my readers will probably be interested to find in the farce of Maître Pathelin one of the models, or, at any rate, the antecedents, of La Fontaine's charming fable:

> Il m'est souvenu de la fable
> Du corbeau qui était assis
> Sur une croix de cinq ou six
> Toises de haut, lequel tenait
> Un fromage au bec. Là venait
> Un renard qui vit le fromage ;
> Pensa en lui : ' Comment l'aurais-je ? '

> Lors se mit dessous le corbeau :
> 'Ah !' fit-il, 'tant as le corps beau,
> Et le chant plein de mélodie !'
> Le corbeau, par sa couardie,
> Oyant son chant ainsi vanter,
> Si ouvrit le bec pour chanter,
> Que son fromage choit à terre :
> Et maître Renard vous le serre
> A bonnes dents et si l'emporte.

Another excellent scene succeeds. It is that in which Guillemette, instructed as to the part she has to play, receives the merchant and begs of him to speak low, because Master Pierre Pathelin is suffering a perfect martyrdom on a bed of sickness, from which he has not arisen for the last six weeks. The merchant does not believe a word of it; but, on a second visit, he arrives at the conclusion that Pathelin is really lying at the point of death; and he beats a hasty retreat, imagining that it must be the very devil himself who has robbed him of his six yards of cloth, because he has heard Pathelin raving first of all in the Limousin patois, because, as Guillemette explains to him, her husband has an uncle in that district; then in the dialect of Picardy, because his mother came from that region; then in Flemish and in Norman, because he went to school in Normandy; then in Breton, because his mother originally lived in Brittany; and finally in Latin.

Some of the scenes in the second act are even more really comic than those which have gone before. The merchant has already apprised us that he grows his own wool; and we presently make the acquaintance, first of all in his shop, and afterwards before a judge, of the faithless shepherd who has killed and eaten his master's sheep. This man, Aignelet by name, is defended by Pathelin, who recommends him to feign idiocy and to bleat out 'Baa,' like a sheep, in reply to every question put to him by the judge. I should only spoil what follows, if I were to analyse or translate it. The comicality of the situation reaches its climax when the merchant finds himself confronted by the man who has cheated him out of his cloth, and in the excitement of his feelings he continually mixes up his lost goods and his purloined sheep. This is part of the plaintiff's case, whom the magistrate incessantly recalls to his 'muttons:'

> *Drap.* Or, çà, je disais,
> A mon propos, comment j'avais
> Baillé six aunes . . . Je veux dire
> Mes brebis (je vous en prie, sire,
> Pardonnez-moi). Ce gentil maître,
> Mon berger, quand il devait être
> Aux champs, il me dit que j'aurais
> Six écus d'or quand je viendrais. . . .
> Dis-je, depuis trois ans en ça
> Mon berger me convenança [promit]
> Que loyaument me garderait
> Mes brebis et ne m'y ferait
> Ni dommage ni vilenie :
> Et puis maintenant il me nie
> Et drap et argent pleinement.
> Ah ! Maître Pierre, vraiement
> Ce ribaud-ci m'emblait [volait] les laines
> De mes bêtes ; et toutes saines
> Les faisait mourir et perir
> Par les assommer et ferir
> De gros bâton sur la cervelle. . . .
> Quand mon drap fut sous son aisselle
> Il se mit en chemin grand erre [très vite] ;
> Il me dit que j'allasse querre
> Six écus d'or en sa maison.
>   *Le Juge.* Il n'y a rime ni raison
> En tout ce que vous rafardez.
> Qu'est-ceci ? vous entrelardez
> Puis d'un, puis d'autre ; somme toute,
> Par le sang bleu ! je n'y vois goutte !
> . . . Revenons à nos moutons. . . .

Aignelet having succeeded in passing himself off as an idiot, thanks to his bleating, quits the tribunal, and pays off Pathelin in his own coin, when the latter, exulting in the success of his stratagem, asks for his fee.

'Baa!' cries Aignelet. 'Come, come ; we've had enough of this.' 'Baa!' 'Yes, yes ; the case is over. Drop it, now. Didn't I work the dodge well? wasn't I wide awake?' 'Baa!' 'Look sharp ; I want to go. Stump up!' 'Baa!' and so on, to the end ; the advocate becoming more and more importunate, and his client bleating more and more idiotically. Ultimately the cunning shepherd beats a retreat, pursued by his angry dupe, venting all sorts of impotent maledictions upon Aignelet who has profited so well by the lawyer's lesson in dissimulation.

It has been justly remarked that there is nothing in Molière more delightfully comic than the last scene but one of the second act of 'L'Avocat Pathelin,' where the doubly wronged merchant confounds in his pleadings the two robberies of which he has been the victim. But the unknown author of the comedy sought for his materials, as Jean-Baptiste Poquelin did for his, in human nature; and so also did Shakespeare, when he caused Shylock, writhing under the twofold loss he had sustained, to exclaim :

> My daughter! O my ducats! O my daughter!
> Fled with a Christian! O my Christian ducats!
> Justice! The law! My ducats and my daughter!

LECTURE II

Guyot de Provins (thirteenth century)—Analysis of several fabliaux of the twelfth and thirteenth centuries—Thibault de Champagne—Rutebœuf—Marie de France—Christine de Pisan—Jean Gerson—Alain Chartier—Eustache Deschamps—Basselin de Vire (end of the fourteenth century and beginning of the fifteenth)—Le Houx (end of the sixteenth century)—Clotilde de Surville.

I WILL now revert to the chronological order of my subject-matter, from which I deviated at the end of my last lecture.

Our worthy forefathers, although well inclined to lend an ear to the heroic and chivalrous lays of their poets, did not disdain the reading of playful compositions. After the tragic muse came the *Jongleurs*, to serve up to those laughter-loving ancestors of ours a dish of lighter verse, the indulgent auditors of which welcomed an outburst of simple hearty gaiety as a relief from, and contrast to, the more sombre emotions awakened by sterner themes. In that extraordinary epic, 'Renard,' the satire, truth to say, was only indirect, and the main, if not the only, purpose of the authors was to amuse their audience. But, as M. Geruzez has said, the Middle Age was not without its malcontents and its soured bilious spirits; and their moroseness found vent in invective. At their head may be noted Guyot de Provins, who, towards the end of his life, at the close of the twelfth or the beginning of the thirteenth century, wrote a satire of about 3,000 lines, in which, although he belonged to the Benedictine Order and died in the monastery of Cluny, he attacked the Pope and the College of Cardinals with extreme virulence, just as Robert Langland did, in England, many years later, in his 'Vision' and 'Creed of Piers Plowman.' He was no common versifier, this Guyot de Provins, but a man who had travelled much, both in France and Germany, had been a guest in the courts of kings, the palaces of prelates, and the châteaux of noblemen; was an acute observer of the follies and vices of the great, and knew how to lash them with an unsparing hand. In the then state of society he found endless provocatives of scathing sarcasm. Profligacy reigned supreme in all the higher walks of society, both lay and ecclesiastical, and the very name of priest had become so odious in public estimation that those who had received the tonsure covered their heads in order that their profession might not be recognised; and we read of a Bishop of Cambrai, who, making war upon Sivard de St. Aubert, otherwise called Maufilatre, caused the eyes to be gouged out of all the serfs of his enemy who fell into his hands.[1]

No wonder this keen-sighted monk, with his rare gift of satire, denounced, in caustic language, the vices of men in high places, who were guilty of practices so infamous and abominable that I dare not even hint at them. Nor did such invectives emanate from churchmen only; for laymen, like the Seigneur de Berze and Gautier de Coinsy, outdid the Benedictine monk in the severity of their animadversions on the dissolute manners and morals of the age. Nor would it be difficult to find, in the narratives of the *trouvères* of the period, the materials for a terrible bill of indictment against the Middle Age, involving the nobility and clergy and both the learned professions. In fact, the 'good old times' continually recede farther and farther backward, the more closely we examine the political and social life of any given period.

But at this very epoch, when lengthy chivalrous epics, such as aroused the admiration of our ancestors, were enjoying the height of their popularity, and when malcontents, like Guyot de Provins and others, were revealing the purulent sores of society, there arose another form of poetical composition which combined brevity with bonhomie, a certain elegance of narrative with a malicious naïveté of expression, and aimed at blending amusement with instruction, and at presenting more variety than was to be found in the poems of an earlier time. This was the *fabliau*, which is admittedly one of the most valuable bequests we have received from the thirteenth century. Sometimes it related

[1] *Recueil des Historiens de France*, xi. 299.

an anecdote, sometimes a diverting incident, and sometimes a *bon mot*. Gaiety was its dominant note, but it was not always free from grossness. The art of narrative was pushed to its utmost limits. The genius of the nation seemed to find itself perfectly at home in these familiar stories, and it already revealed in man some of his finest qualities. And the influence of the *fabliaux* upon the English and Italian imagination was, as I have already hinted, very great indeed. Chaucer, Boccaccio, and Petrarch freely appropriated the inexhaustible resources they discovered in them; and French authors, in later centuries, took advantage of them just as freely. Molière was indebted to them for his 'George Dandin,' his 'Médecin malgré lui,' and probably for other borrowings; and La Fontaine derived from them the groundwork of many of his fables and stories. To the people of the nineteenth century these *fabliaux* are chiefly interesting on account of the strong light they throw on the manners and customs of the *bourgeoisie* and the lower classes in the Middle Age; although some of the stories are borrowed from much older sources. Take, for example, 'Le Vilain Mire,' which suggested 'Le Médecin malgré lui,' and is derived from a Latin legend, which may be thus translated: ' A certain woman who had been beaten by her husband waited upon a gentleman who was ill, and informed him that her husband was a doctor, but that he would never consent to prescribe for his patients until he had been well cudgelled; and by this means she caused her better half to receive a sound thrashing.' The author of the *fabliau* has expanded this brief sketch into a large canvas. He marries a rich peasant to the daughter of an old knight who has nothing to boast of but his high descent. The peasant fustigates the poor woman before he goes out to his work in the morning, and begs her pardon for his ill-usage of her when he comes home at night. This being his daily practice, it becomes rather monotonous—to her, at any rate. She reflects upon the reason of his brutality, and a happy thought strikes her. He beats her from sheer inexperience. He has never felt the weight of a cudgel himself, and the one thing needful is to procure for him that sensation. But how? As good luck would have it, the prince who rules the country sends out his messengers far and near to find a doctor capable of healing his own daughter who is lying at the point of death, owing to a fish-bone having stuck in her throat. The peasant's wife points out her husband as a medical expert, but whispers to them that he will only exercise his art under constraint. So they give him a preliminary pommelling, and when he reaches the court the king orders him another. Introduced to his patient he writhes and wriggles so much under the beating he has received, that the princess is seized with a violent fit of laughter, and coughs up the recalcitrant bone. After this he tries to sneak away, and is again cudgelled for making the attempt. Patients come from far and near, and, at his request, a spacious hall is fitted up for their reception. He causes a great fire to be lit; and presently the king, who has been waiting at the door to see what will happen, perceives the sick folk rushing out one after another, protesting that they have been perfectly cured. How has the fellow operated upon them? By a very simple device. He required the greatest of the sufferers present to submit to be calcined in the huge wood fire, because the powder of his bones would supply the medicine indispensable for the successful treatment of the rest. The king was so much pleased with the shrewdness of the peasant that he loaded him with presents and sent him home to his wife, against whom he never more lifted his hand.

Here, then, we have the skeleton of one of our most delightful comedies; just as Shakespeare went to the old story-tellers—to Bandello, Montemayor, Cinthio, and others —for the plots of his dramas.

Side by side with 'Le Vilain Mire' may be placed the 'Vair Palefroi,' which is not less ingenious in its construction, and owes its interest even more to the delicacy of its sentiment than to the lively fancy of the narrator. A young, courteous, brave, and good-looking knight, with a light purse and an excellent *palefroi* (*anglice* palfrey), lives near an old gentleman, who has a very beautiful daughter. Naturally, the two young people have 'met by chance, the usual way,' and have fallen in love with each other. Naturally also the young knight asks the old gentleman for his daughter's hand, but is politely shown the door on account of his straitened circumstances. The lovers are not going to be

discouraged by a rebuff of that kind. Romeo has an uncle
—everybody in distress flies to an uncle—and as he is that
relative's sole heir, Juliet recommends that an application
be made to him for assistance. The uncle promises to
advance him something on account, and calls upon Juliet's
father, who happens to be an old crony of his. Meanwhile
the lover rides off to a tournament, and the uncle asks for
and obtains the young lady's hand. It is for himself, however; and preparations are made for the nuptials. The
knight returns home from the tourney, full of hope, and
does not receive the news of his uncle's treachery until somebody comes to ask him for the use of his handsome *palefroi*,
whereon to conduct the bride from the residence of her
father to the church. The unhappy lover, in spite of his
grief, consents to the sacrifice, and the fair lady mounts the
saddle. The cortège sets out before daybreak, and when it
reaches a four-cross way in the forest, the horse, recognising
a familiar track, sets off at full gallop, not checked, we may
be sure, by his rider. It will be readily guessed whither his
instinct conducted him. Arrived at the château of the
knight, the young lady finds a chaplain there—quite by accident, of course—who joins their hands in holy matrimony;
and when the two old folks come to claim the fugitive, they
find it is too late, and nothing remains but to give their
reluctant assent to a union consecrated by affection and
religion. Let us add that this *fabliau*, so cleverly conceived
and worked out, is naturally and gracefully related. It was
written by Huon le Roy, who must not be confounded with
the more celebrated Huon de Villeneuve; the authorship
of 'Le Vilain Mire,' however, as well as of 'St. Pierre et le
Jongleur,' already referred to, is quite unknown. St. Peter,
by the way, figures conspicuously in the *fabliaux* of the
Middle Age. One of the best of the stories relating to him
has a blacksmith for its hero. The Virgin Mary, in requital
for some good deed he had performed, had promised him
that whenever he sat himself down upon an old cap he
wore, no power, human or divine, should remove him thence.
After his death, on arriving at the gates of Paradise, he
begged of the saint just to allow him one peep into the
realms of bliss, and Peter good-naturedly opened the portals
for a foot or so, and thereupon the blacksmith flung his

smoke-blackened cap inside. 'At least you will allow me to step inside and pick it up, won't you?' said the blacksmith in his most insinuating manner. St. Peter nodded assent, and the crafty blacksmith, gliding into Paradise, squatted down upon his cap, from whence neither saint nor angel could ever dislodge him.

In many of these *fabliaux* we may detect, on the part of the writers, a deep undercurrent of sympathy with the poor and the oppressed; and at that time the words were almost synonymous, for the peasants were serfs and chattels, and the nobles, who inhabited the 4,350 castles scattered over the surface of France, looked upon them as no better than so many beasts of burden, and inflicted on them far worse treatment. 'So many châtelains, so many tyrants,' said the old French proverb. But the poet, who witnessed the burdens of the people and the arrogance of their oppressors, often took care to let Jacques Bonhomme have the best of it in the next world, where his mother-wit stood him in excellent stead, as for example in the *fabliau* of 'The Vilain who conquered Paradise by his pleadings.' It is a delightfully naïve story, and illustrates the quaint spirit in which sacred subjects were dealt with by these mediæval versifiers. It was this:

A vilain died, without either angel or devil concerning himself about him; but his soul, looking straight up to heaven, saw the Archangel Michael conducting one of the elect to Paradise, and followed him. St. Peter opened the gate to the new comer, but repelled the other spirit, swearing by St. Guilain that heaven was no place for such as he. 'Good, Sir Peter,' said the rejected soul, 'God made a great mistake when He chose you for an apostle, and afterwards for a door-keeper—you who denied Him thrice. Stand aside, and let a more loyal man than you come in.' St. Peter, somewhat abashed, went to complain of the intruder to his colleague St. Thomas, who also tried to keep the intrusive stranger out. 'A deal you have to be proud of, Master Thomas,' said the vilain, 'when you wouldn't believe in God until you had felt His wounds.' The discomfited saint then fell back upon St. Paul, whose interference drew down upon him this rebuke: 'Was it not you, Don Paul the Bald, who stoned St. Stephen, and to whom the good God gave a stinging blow?' As neither Peter, Thomas, nor Paul could utter a word in reply, they carried the case to the judgment seat of the Most High, before whom the enfranchised serf justified himself by his pleadings, and was admitted into heaven.

There was nothing irreverent in these old *fabliaux*. They simply displayed what Mrs. Barrett Browning described as one of the characteristics of Chaucer—namely,

> An infantine
> Familiar clasp of things divine.

At the same time, the *trouvères* and *jongleurs*, and the *jongleurs* more particularly, were by no means saints. They were, by inclination and by natural frailty, fond of the good things of this life—when they could get them—light-minded, light-hearted, and light-spoken. Clément Marot claims for them that they were the best fellows in the world. One of them imagined and described the Utopia of gluttons, or, in other words, the Land of Cocagne; a country in which everybody has a great appetite and can always find an abundance of succulent and savoury dishes. The realm itself is a pure invention of the *trouvères*; and the word is said to be derived from *coquina*, which is identical with *cuisine*. In England it signified 'Lubber-land;' and the modern word Cockney, as applied to a native of London, means, according to certain etymologists, an inhabitant of the Land of Cocagne.

And thus, as will be seen, these merry story-tellers, during the second half of the twelfth and the whole of the thirteenth centuries, amused themselves and their hearers at the same time. I must mention in passing the names of some of the ablest of the poets of that epoch. Thibault de Champagne, who was born in 1201, was protected by Philippe-Auguste, took part in one of the Crusades, returned safe and sound, cultivated letters, wrote poetry, and died in 1253. These few words summarise his life. He has been sometimes styled the first of the French poets, although upon this point the critics are not unanimous; and it may be remembered that a similar title has been conferred on Charles d'Orléans, Alain Chartier, Villon, Clément Marot, Chrestien de Troyes, Eustache Deschamps, and Marie de France.

Thibault de Champagne wrote *chansons, tensons*, sonnets, and *reverdies*; the latter, as the name implies, were composed in honour of the spring and of the return of the flowers. Marot describes them as May-songs. But

Thibault's style and language are so antiquated that I should scarcely venture to quote one of his *reverdies*. You will find something very like them, only more modern, in Robert Herrick's poems. One can hardly speak of Thibault as having written after the manner of the *fabliaux*, which were really a form of composition that nobody invented and everybody adopted; and if I have introduced his name, it is in order not to omit him in the chronological order.

Rutebœuf, one of the continuators of the 'Roman de Renard,' is one of the most daring and one of the ablest of the *trouvères* who versified their stories. His works may be easily read, with a little practice, and are well worth consulting by any one interested in the language and literature of France. His life and his poems might serve me as types of those of very many of the *trouvères*; for the first oscillated between extravagance and penury, debauchery and privation, sometimes reciting his poems at bridals and other festivities in the castles of the nobility, and at other times declaiming them to gaping rustics at country fairs. He was a gambler and a spendthrift; and while some of his compositions were remarkable for their elegance of expression and the harmony of their versification, others were coarse and indecent to excess and were written down to the level of a boorish auditory. In one of his poems he writes: 'I am without a coat, without victuals, and without a bed. I am shivering with cold and gaping with hunger.' But this did not prevent him from marrying twice, and he thus describes his second wife: 'When I married her, she was as poor as Job; and odd to relate, I was as destitute as herself. She is neither comely nor pretty. She is meagre and wizened. She has fifty years on her shoulders, and is, therefore, not likely to play me false.' Rutebœuf seems to have died in indigence about the year 1286. Two of his best *fabliaux* were the 'Testament de l'Ane' and the 'Moine Sacristain.' Of the other *trouvères* who were his compeers, it is only necessary to mention Guérin, Baudouin, Jean de Condé, and Jean de Boyes. But I must not omit to allude to one versifier, named Hans Helinand, who was historiographer and also poet laureate to Philippe-Auguste, an office, it will be seen, which existed in the court of France more than two hundred years before it was introduced into

England. Helinand's duty was to amuse the king after dinner by reciting original narratives of love and warfare. Towards the close of his life he entered the monastery of Froidmont, belonging to the Cistercian order, and the only poem of his extant is entitled 'Vers sur la Mort.' It bristles with pungent sallies against the court of Rome, but has come down to us in an imperfect condition, and is very hard reading.

If there were many starvelings, like Rutebœuf, among the *trouvères*, there were also some royalties—Richard Cœur de Lion (1157–1199) and Charles of Anjou (1220–1285) among the number; both of whom left behind them poems which are still held in remembrance. Many princes and nobles also loved and cultivated the muse in France during the twelfth and thirteenth centuries. It is only necessary for me to enumerate the most conspicuous—Pierre, Duke of Brittany, Jean de Brienne (1237), Guillaume de Ferrier, Vidame de Chartres, the Comte de Chalons, and Hugues de Lusignan (1361).

Marie de France, as her name indicates, was born in that country, but the date and place of her birth are alike unknown. She went to England during the reign of Henry III., where she made a great reputation by her poems, which included a collection of 103 fables, under the title of 'Ésopet,' numerous 'lays' illustrating the legends of the Armorican cycle, which are masterpieces of poetical narrative; and a romance of the marvellous in verse, entitled 'Le Purgatoire de St. Patrice.' Her French reached the highest point of perfection, as regards the old language, before it underwent the gradual modifications which resulted in the formation of our present tongue. I should like to quote one or two of her charming 'lays,' but their diction, like that of Rutebœuf's poems, is of too antiquated a character to render it easily intelligible to modern readers.

Many of the French kings, and more particularly the Charleses, were munificent patrons of letters. Thus Charles V., by his example and his liberality, encouraged the cultivation of ancient literature, and assisted in the formation of many able writers; foremost among whom were Christine de Pisan, Jean Gerson, and Alain Chartier. When Andrelin recited his poem on the Sack of Naples before Charles VIII., that monarch rewarded him with a sack so full of silver coin that he staggered under its weight as he carried it home. Charles IX. was more judicious in his bounty, because he used to say that poets resembled racehorses, and should be fed not fattened; and Marot, of whom I shall speak hereafter, was called 'The poet of princes and the prince of poets.'

Besides Christine de Pisan, Jean Gerson, and Alain Chartier, other writers were associated with himself by that enlightened monarch—who laid the foundation of the Royal Library, and extended the privileges and jurisdiction of the University of Paris—in his efforts towards the restoration of letters; and this, too, at a time when France had been dismembered by the Treaty of Brétigny, was crushed beneath the weight of an enormous debt; and was convulsed by civil war. His son's tutor, Nicholas Oresme, whom he created Bishop of Lisieux, was at once an eminent statesman, a learned divine, a distinguished economist, a good geometrician, and an accomplished scholar, whose 'Traité des Monnaies' was the means of placing the French currency on a sound basis, and who gave us a masterly translation of the 'Ethics' and 'Politics' of Aristotle. He it was who enriched the French language with a number of new words, such as *actif, action, aristocratie, barbare, contemplation, démagogue, démocratie, despote, héros, économie, illégal, incontinent, législateur, législation, mélodie, harmonie*, and many others. Philippe de Maizières, whom 'Charles the Wise' appointed governor to the Dauphin, was the author of the 'Songe du Viel Pèlerin,' which is, in reality, a complete treatise on morality; while the 'Songe du Vergier,' sometimes attributed to him, but probably written by Raoul de Presle, a great work of jurisprudence, written in the form of a dream, is one of the most remarkable productions of the period, and powerfully vindicates the privileges and prerogatives of the French crown as against the pretensions of the Roman Curia.

Christine de Pisan, daughter of Thomas Pisan, astrologer to Charles V., was taken to the court of France by her father in 1368. After receiving a good and solid education she was married at an early age to a gentleman of Picardy, who left her a widow with three children when only twenty-five; and it was then that she began to write. One of her children was adopted by the Earl of Salisbury and taken to England. Two portraits of her are still extant: one in the National Library in Paris, and the other in the British Museum. She wrote some pretty ballads and other poems, much in the diction of Alain Chartier; and the estimation in which the former were held may be judged of by the fact that Jean, Duc de Berry, gave her 200 golden crowns for the manuscript of them. Her 'Pucelle' and her 'Hundred Tales of Troy' were the most important of her poetical works, as her 'Life of Charles V.' was certainly her best prose production. That monarch had been her protector and friend, and on his death she was persuaded by Philip the Good, Duke of Burgundy, to prepare his biography; and she executed the task so conscientiously and well that, as M. Geruzez has observed, she 'ennobled the profession of letters.' A later writer, Martin le Franc, declared that she rivalled Cicero in elegance and Cato in wisdom; while Clément Marot thus summarises her merits:

> D'avoir le prix en science et doctrine
> Bien mérita de Pisan la Christine.

Although it would be impossible to replace Christine de Pisan on the high pedestal raised for her by her contemporaries, which she retained until the sixteenth century, yet she does not deserve the oblivion into which she has fallen. More of a scholar than a poet, she nevertheless stood out from among the singers of her time by reason of the intense spirit of patriotism which breathed through her writings; and a letter which she addressed to Isabeau of Bavaria, on behalf of her beloved France, palpitates with pathetic emotion, and with a deep womanly sympathy for the afflicted widows and the famishing orphans upon whom civil discord inflicted such severe and undeserved sufferings.

Jean Chartier, commonly called Gerson after his native village, was originally a farmer's son, and rose to be Chancellor of the University and Church of Paris. He was a mystic in religion, and a Neo-Platonist in philosophy. Whether he wrote the famous 'Imitation de Jésus-Christ,' or whether it was the work of Thomas à Kempis, is still a moot-point. On the whole the balance of evidence seems to incline in favour of Kempis. It was largely owing to his influence that the Council of Pisa, in 1409, deposed the rival Popes, and seated Alexander V. in St. Peter's chair. It was reserved for himself and for Christine de Pisan, towards the close of their lives, to witness that glorious outburst of religious and patriotic inspiration, in the person of Jeanne d'Arc, to which France was destined to owe her emancipation from the yoke of the stranger; and both rendered homage to her simple piety, her lofty devotion, and the purity and nobility of her character. Christine, who only beheld her first successes, never doubted and confidently predicted her ultimate triumph.

Alain Chartier (1386-1458) was secretary to Charles VI. and Charles VII. successively. His numerous works exist for the most part in manuscript only, and are so voluminous that it would consume a little fortune to print and publish them, and a lifetime to read them when published. He was said to be the ugliest man in France, which did not prevent Marguerite of Scotland, the first wife of the Dauphin, afterwards Louis XI., from kissing him in the presence of the ladies of her Court as he lay asleep; observing, as she did so: 'It is not the man I have kissed, but the mouth from whence have issued so many golden words, both gay and grave.' His poetical works have not been reprinted since 1617, and comprise 'Le Débat du Reveil-matin,' 'La Belle-Dame sans Merci,' 'Le Bréviaire des Nobles,' and 'Le Livre des Quatre Dames.' The latter was composed shortly after the disaster of Azincourt, in which one of the ladies has lost her lover, whose death she bitterly bewails, and whose character she extols; the second has heard that her lover has been taken prisoner; the third knows nothing of the fate of hers; and the fourth claims to be the most wretched of the group, because her lover has proved to be a coward, and has basely fled from the field of battle; so that she would a hundred times rather he had died than live thus dishonoured. The poem affords Chartier an opportunity of expressing his own patriotic grief at the reverse which his country has just sustained, and I cannot resist the pleasure of quoting some passages from this his best work. Here is a description of the place in which the four ladies assembled:

> Tout autour oiseaulx voletoient,
> Et si très-doucement chantoient
> Qu'il n'est cuer [cœur] qui n'en fust joyeux :
> Et en chantant en l'air montoient,
> Et puis l'un l'autre surmontoient
> A l'estrivée, à qui mieulx mieulx.
> De bleu estoient vestus les cieux
> Et le beau soleil cler luisoit ;
> Violettes croissoient par lieux
> Et tout faisoit ses devoirs, tieux
> Comme nature le duisoit.

With all our earliest poets the springtime, love, joy, grief, and old age, were the themes they preferred; and when they had exhausted these fundamental topics they condescended to give us some good advice, as Alain Chartier did in a ballad with the refrain 'You had nought of these when you were born.' Here is a sample :

> Or fols de fols, et les fols mortels hommes
> Qui vous fiez tant ez biens de fortune,
> En celle terre et pays ou nous sommes,
> Y avez-vous de chose propre aucune ?
> Vous n'y avez chose vostre nesune,
> Fors les beaux dons de grâce et de nature.
> Si fortune donc, par cas d'aventure,
> Vous toult les biens que vostre vous tenez,
> Tort ne vous fait, ainçois vous fait droiture ;
> Car vous n'aviez rien quand vous fûtes né.

This ballad, which is an exceedingly lengthy one, concludes with an excellent moral :

> Si fortune vous fait aucune injure,
> C'est de son droit, jà ne l'en reprenez,
> Perdissiez-vous jusques à la vesture ;
> Car vous n'aviez rien quand vous fûtes né.

Of course the philosophy of the poem is as old as the days of Job : 'We brought nothing into this world, and it is certain we can carry nothing out.'

I have only spoken of Alain Chartier as a poet, and something remains to be said of him as a prose writer, and more particularly of his 'Quadriloge Invectif.' It is really a splendid appeal on behalf of national unity to the whole people of France, during a temporary period of national eclipse. The interlocutors are France, the People, Gentry, and Clergy. Cruelly tortured by civil war, and dismembered by foreign invasion, France was passing through the same throes in 1415 which she underwent in 1871, and the voice of Alain Chartier seemed to anticipate that of Gambetta at the later period. 'Awake! Arise! Combine! France is not lost; her resources are not exhausted; her people, though defeated, are not dismayed. Trample faction under foot; let all classes clasp hands; and the nation shall arise greater than ever.' This was the burden of Chartier's message to his countrymen, and it was worthy of his great and noble heart; worthy of one of the best rhetoricians, moralists, orators, poets, and philosophers, and one of the truest patriots of his time.

His literary style, like that of Christine de Pisan, was characterised by a certain stately gravity and by a dignified movement, altogether unknown to the writers who preceded him. Both of them resembled the first pallid rays of the dawn which heralded the approach of the classic renaissance in France.

I have now to speak of Eustache Morel, or Deschamps, a name which he took from a country house near Orleans, in which he spent the latter years of his life. His was an adventurous and remarkable career. He had travelled much in Europe, Asia, and Africa; had been taken prisoner, like Cervantes, by the Moors, by whom he was treated as a slave; and he escaped from captivity in time to take part in the war against the English, in the course of which the defence of two important places was entrusted to him. Writing somewhat earlier than Froissart and Charles d'Orléans, he may be regarded as the precursor of the latter poet.

Deschamps' original manuscripts, containing 1,175 ballads, 171 rondeaux, 80 virelays, 14 lays, and 28 farces and 'Complaints,' remained undisturbed in the National Library, Paris, until the year 1832, when they were discovered by M. Crapelet, who then published a selection from the works of this poet of the fourteenth century. It may be said of Eustache Deschamps that he was the creator of the ballad, which he handled with a grace and a finesse equal to those of Clément Marot, who wrote two

D

centuries later. We may also attribute to him the invention of the drinking-song, a kind of composition eminently French, afterwards perfected by Oliver Basselin, the jolly fuller of Vire, in Normandy, to whom we owe the 'Vau-de-Vire,' from whence, it is said, the word Vaudeville was derived. Deschamps, who was ruined by the ravages of the English, wrote bitterly against what he called *ce peuple maudit*; and his indignation found vent in many poems, and notably in one entitled 'Ballad of the Prophecy of Merlin on the Destruction of England.' Worse than all perhaps, he made an unhappy marriage, which caused him not only to rail against all womankind, but to stigmatise the institution itself as 'a trap and a fraud,' in his 'Mirror of Marriage.' His poems in general are precious monuments for the antiquary and the historian, reflecting, as they do, the manners and customs of our ancestors. Their pastimes, their sports, tourneys, festivals, weapons, diet, household utensils, furniture, and fashions, are all described with artistic fidelity; and thus you may perceive that Eustache Deschamps is well worthy of mention. I greatly regret, indeed, that the space at my disposal compels me to deal so briefly with a poet who seems to have been the precursor of the contemporary school of realists in literature, both in France and in Great Britain.

And now there rises before me the jovial figure of that portly Oliver Basselin, the remains of whose fulling-mill still bear his name, although four hundred years have elapsed since he used to 'set the table in a roar' with his merry and convivial songs. He had been a soldier, had seen some travel, knew Latin, and was, it must be confessed, too much addicted to good cheer. Perhaps he found in the exhilaration of the cider cup forgetfulness of the disaster which overtook him when his mill became a heap of ruins at the siege of Vire. His songs are distinguished by their verve, buoyancy, and gaiety; and after passing from mouth to mouth for upwards of half a century, they were first collected and printed in 1610 by Jean Le Houx, a song-writer like himself.

In reading the following one wonders whether Shakespeare knew anything of Basselin, and if so, whether he remembered these lines when he put into the mouth of

Falstaff his delightful description of the jewelled wealth and luminosity of Bardolph's nose:

> Beau nez! dont les rubis ont cousté mainte pipe
> De vin blanc et clairet
> Et duquel la couleur richement participe
> Du rouge et violet.
>
> Gros nez! qui te regarde à travers un grand verre
> Te juge encore plus beau:
> Tu ne ressembles point au nez de quelque hère
> Qui ne boit que de l'eau.
>
> Un coq d'Inde sa gorge à toi semblable porte:
> Combien de riches gens
> N'ont pas si riche nez! Pour te peindre en la sorte
> Il faut beaucoup de temps.

Basselin, the putative father of the Vaudeville, wrote sixty-two drinking songs; and in the three stanzas subjoined, written at the time the English were besieging Vire, in 1417, the poet shows us that his heart was in the wine-cellars of his native town:

> Tout alentour de nos remparts
> Les ennemis sont en furie;
> Sauves nos tonneaux, je vous prie!
> Prenes plustost de nous, souldars,
> Tout ce dont vous aurez envie,
> Sauves nos tonneaux, je vous prie!
>
> Nous pourrons après, en buvant,
> Chasser notre mérencolie;
> Sauves nos tonneaux, je vous prie!
> L'ennemi qui est cy-devant
> Ne vous veult faire courtoisie,
> Vuidons nos tonneaux, je vous prie!
>
> Au moins, s'il prend notre cité,
> Qu'il n'y trouve plus que la lie:
> Vuidons nos tonneaux, je vous prie!
> Deussions-nous marcher de costé,
> Ce bon sildre n'espargnons mie,
> Vuidons nos tonneaux, je vous prie!

Before quitting Basselin I cannot refrain from quoting a pleasantry with which his name is associated. Sacred history relates how a curse was pronounced upon the human race on account of Adam having eaten that tempting apple. If he had shown a preference for drinking, our author thinks the course of mundane affairs might have been very different. At any rate, this is how the poet puts it :

> Adam—the fact is too well known—
> Would not have caused us so to rue 't
> If he, for liquor over fruit,
> An early preference had shown.

I must depart for a moment from the chronological order of my lecture to speak of Jean Le Houx, who was also a native of Vire, where he died in 1616.

The mantle of Basselin fell upon his shoulders, and the examples of the songs of both writers, given by Mr. Walter Besant, are excellent, full of gaiety and good feeling, untainted by immorality, and so cheerful and jocund in sentiment that it is a pleasure to read them. There are few modern jocularities on the subject which may not be traced back to the songs of these two topers, the later of whom was a lawyer of more than ordinary ability and in very good practice ; but he often penned a stanza when he should have been pleading a cause.

For some time the name of Clotilde de Surville figured among the poetesses of the fifteenth century, until the publication of her alleged works by Vanderbourg in 1803 aroused suspicion as to their authenticity. Nodier and Villemain, among others, detected their modernity, and the artificiality of their antique language ; while others, and notably Mr. Ainger, Mr. Besant, and M. Macé, contended that they were early poems which had been retouched by a modern hand. Hallam, one of the most judicious of critics, treats the poems as forgeries, ' by no means so gross as that of Chatterton ; ' and adopting a vein of gentle sarcasm, speaks of them and of their imaginary author thus : ' The muse of the Ardèche warbled her notes during a longer life than the monk of Bristow (Thomas Rowley), and having sung the relief of Orleans by the hand of Arc in 1429, lived to pour her swan-like chant on the battle of Fornova in 1495. Love, however, as much as war, is her theme ; and it was a remarkable felicity that she rendered an ode of her prototype Sappho into French verse many years before any one else in France could have seen it.' Then, again, Clotilde de Surville undertakes a refutation of a fragment of the 'De Rerum Natura' by Lucretius, which was not discovered until long after her death. Her poems abound in other anachronisms, and there can be very little doubt, I think, that Clotilde de Surville was just as mythical a personage as the Mrs. Harris of 'Martin Chuzzlewit;' and that, as Sainte-Beuve contends, the poems which have been published under her name were the work of the Marquis de Surville, from whom Vanderbourg received them.

As a work of fiction the story of her life is a very pretty one, and it is a pity it should have been invalidated by the application to it of a rigorous criticism. Born at the château of Vallon in 1405, she is said to have written exquisite poetry at the age of twelve ; to have been married at sixteen to a husband whom she adored ; and to have gone on composing verses until she was past the age of ninety. 'Une Héroïde' in honour of her husband ; 'Songs of Love,' for the four seasons ; a sketch of a poem entitled ' Nature and the Universe ; ' the 'Phélypéide,' which is only a fragment ; and the 'Trois Plaids d'Or,' an adaptation of one of Voltaire's stories. One of the compositions which bear her name is so feminine in tenderness of feeling and beauty of expression, that it is difficult to believe it was written by a man. All women, and all mothers more especially, will appreciate the beauty and the charm of the following 'Verselets to my Firstborn,' notwithstanding it is a palpable imitation of Berquin's romance, 'Dors, cher enfant, clos ta paupière : '—

> O cher enfantelet, vrai portrait de ton père,
> Dors sur le sein que ta bouche a pressé !
> Dors, petit ; clos, ami, sur le sein de ta mère,
> Ton doux œillet par le somme oppressé.
>
> Bel ami, cher petit, que ta pupille tendre
> Goûte un sommeil qui plus n'est fait pour moi !
> Je veille pour te voir, te nourrir, te défendre . . .
> Ainsi qu'il m'est doux ne veiller que pour toi.
>
> Dors, mon enfantelet, mon souci, mon idole !
> Dors sur mon sein, le sein qui t'a porté !
> Ne m'esjouit encore le son de ta parole,
> Bien ton souris cent fois m'aye enchanté.
>
> Etend ses bracelets ; s'épand sur lui le somme ;
> Se clost son œil : plus ne bouge. . . . Il s'endort. . . .
> N'était ce teint fleuri des couleurs de la pomme,
> Ne le diriez dans les bras de la mort ?

> Arrête.... Cher enfant.... J'en frémis tout entière !
> Réveille-toi ! Chasse un fatal propos !
> Mon fils ! pour un moment.... Ah ! revois la lumière !
> Au prix du ton rends-moi tout mon repos....
>
> Douce erreur ! il dormait.... c'est assez : je respire.
> Songes légers, flattez son doux sommeil :
> Ah ! quand verrai celui pour qui mon cœur soupire,
> A mes côtés, jouir de son reveil !
>
> Je parle et ne m'entends ... eh ! que dis-je ? ... insensée !
> Plus n'oiroit-il qu'en fut moult éveillé,
> Pauvre cher enfançon ! ... Cher fils, de ta pensée
> L'échevelet n'est encore débrouillé.
>
> Tretous avons été, comme es toi, dans cette heure :
> Triste raison que trop tôt n'adviendra !
> En la paix dont jouis, s'est possible, ah ! demeure !
> A tes beaux jours même il en souviendra.
>
> O cher enfantelet, vrai portrait de ton père,
> Dors sur le sein que ta bouche a pressé !
> Dors, petit ; clos, ami, sur le sein de ta mère,
> Ton doux œillet par le somme oppressé.

By whomsoever written, this is surely admirable in sentiment and diction. The picture of the happy mother bending over her little one, with such anxious affection that even when the child is sleeping she is alarmed by the resemblance which slumber presents to death, and would fain awaken him in order to be convinced he lives, is as beautiful in its way, I think, as some of those divine images of maternal love which Fra Angelico, Botticelli, Gian Bellini, and Del Sarto portrayed upon their canvases for the admiration and delight of after generations. For delicacy of detail, natural truth, simplicity, and grace, this Madonna and Child of the French nursery is not far from perfect; and when we arrive at the study of the poets of the eighteenth century, and observe the analogies between the methods of expression adopted by André Chénier and Berquin, for example, we shall find how faithfully the Marquis de Surville copied the admirable models which they presented for his imitation. Meanwhile, the imaginary Clotilde de Surville has, to quote the words of Hallam, 'fallen into the numerous ranks of the dead who never were alive.'

LECTURE III

Villehardouin (1160-1213)—Joinville (1223-1319)—Froissart (1333-1410)—Monstrelet (1390-1453).

HAVING, in the first two lectures, examined the works of the earlier French poets exclusively, I devote the present one to the study of prose, which is a later formation than poetry, and of which we may watch the development in our four chroniclers—Villehardouin, Joinville, Froissart, and Monstrelet, whom I have grouped together for the purpose of exhibiting the differences of their respective styles and language, deferring, for the moment, the further consideration of the other branch of French literature. The first of the chroniclers is Villehardouin (1160-1213), Marshal of Champagne, who has left us a narrative of the Fifth Crusade, of which he was the actual promoter. His work marks the transition from the epic poem to history; his account of the conquest of Constantinople appearing to constitute, by the grandeur of its subject, and the rude and warlike manners of the personages who figure in it, a sequel to those *chansons de geste* which sang the exploits of Charlemagne.

The merit of the French historian is that he identifies himself so thoroughly with this theme that it is impossible to separate the one from the other. Villehardouin is not only the chronicler, but the most solid hero of the exploits he relates, in which he successfully doubles the parts of soldier and negotiator. The Fifth Crusade (1202-1204), of which he is the narrator, is an historical and not a literary subject. It is written, as Demogeot has said, in a style that is both grave and concise. There is a certain military stiffness about it, which is characteristic both of the man and of the infancy of the language. The phrases are short and sharp, quick in movement, and little varied. They have something of the brusque and angular carriage of the soldier. The worthy Marshal has few formulas at his command. He is always inviting us to hear one of the greatest of wonders, and to behold the miracle of our Lord. The fleet or city he describes is uniformly the finest that has ever been seen since the world began.

An historical monument of this kind gives one a perfect idea of feudal society, of that organised anarchy which was held together only by community of religious faith. The work of Geoffroy de Villehardouin is simply the faithful reflection of passing events. It accompanies them step by step without ever co-ordinating them. It is not yet a modern history, but it is already more than a monkish chronicle. Villehardouin is, according to Henry Martin, the first French warrior who has written an historical work, and his history is the oldest we possess in French prose. With it begins the long series of our historical memoirs, one of the most original and most national branches of our literature.

Villehardouin was, as I have said, the actual promoter of the Fifth Crusade. Sent, in the first instance, to Venice, to obtain vessels, it was he who addressed the Doge in the Basilica of St. Mark, and who concluded the treaty between the Republic and the Crusaders. Here is the text of his speech : 'Signori,—The most high and mighty barons of France have sent us to you. They appeal to your mercy. They implore you to take pity on Jerusalem now in bondage to the Turks, and that God may move you to accompany them in order to avenge the shame done to Jesus Christ. They have made choice of you, because they know of none so powerful on the sea as you are. We have been commanded to throw ourselves at your feet, and not to arise until you shall have granted our petition, and taken pity on the Holy Land beyond the sea.'

On his return into Champagne Villehardouin learned the death of his Seigneur, Thibault, who was to have taken command of the crusade. The expedition was dissolved, but he was resolutely determined to find a chief for it. His choice fell upon the Marquis de Montferrat, who was accepted, and sent forward on the way to Venice, Louis, Comte de Blois, one of the most powerful leaders engaged in the crusade, who wished to reach Palestine by another route.

In the month of October 1202 all was ready for the departure. The Marquis de Montferrat had been nominated commander-in-chief of the army by the French barons, and it only remained to designate the admiral of the fleet. Prayers having been offered up for the success of the expedition—and here I follow Daru—the Doge ascended the pulpit of St. Mark's and entreated the Republic to permit him to assume the cross, declaring that he was ready to place himself at the head of the Venetian army, and to accompany the crusaders, not only to Zara, but whithersoever their zeal might lead them, thankful if his already long life should come to a close in fighting for the deliverance of the Saviour's tomb. Such a resolution on the part of an old man, ninety-four years of age, who preserved all the energy of his maturity, could not fail to excite a mingled feeling of admiration and tenderness. He descended from the tribune amidst the acclamations of the crowd, knelt before the high altar, and placed the cross upon his ducal cap. His son, René Dandolo, was appointed his deputy during his absence.

Picture the brilliant and impressive scene which presented itself in the Basilica of St. Mark on a beautiful autumnal Sunday in the month of October 1202, as the venerable Doge, lifting up his voice in the pulpit of that Byzantine Cathedral, addressed an immense assemblage of men gathered together from all parts of Europe and exclaimed: 'I am a very old man, my health is tottering, and I have greater need of rest than glory; nevertheless, if it be your good pleasure that I should take up the cross to watch over and direct you, leaving my son as the protector of our country, I will accompany you with all my heart, and will live and die with you and the pilgrims.' Then the Venetians, with one accord, lifting their eyes towards heaven, cried out with a loud voice, 'In the name of God, we adjure you to come with us.' Then the Doge, descending the pulpit stairs, while a ray of sunshine fell like a golden aureole upon the head of Christ in the rood-loft, knelt down, his face moistened with tears of joy, and adopted the symbol of the crusaders, while all hearts were touched by the solemnity of this imposing spectacle.

Then from the five porches of the holy edifice, and beneath the resplendent frescoes of the Oriental façade, poured forth into the great Piazza, even then ennobled by the rare beauty of its architecture, five cataracts of human beings, brilliant in the many-coloured costumes of the period, and resembling so many torrents of glittering jewels; while the sun flashed on blazoned shields, on finely chiselled helmets adorned with precious stones, upon embroidered surcoats, and upon armour and weapons of polished steel, while the most beautiful daughters of Venice lent the charm of their loveliness to the imposing grandeur of the dazzling ceremonial; and high above that thronging multitude floated from the summit of the cathedral the glorious gonfalon of Venice, with the winged lion of St. Mark's emblazoned on its folds. And there, at the end of the Piazzetta, and along the Molo to the island of San Nicolo, and stretching away to the Lagunes, were to be seen the five hundred vessels prepared for the transport of the crusaders to the Holy Land, the national ensigns of the warriors of the Cross fluttering in the wind from their ornamental turrets, with the great galley 'Il Mondo' towering above them all. Villehardouin might well exclaim in a transport of admiration, 'Par Dieu, it was the finest spectacle the eye of man ever looked upon.'

I pass over the siege and capture of Zara by the crusaders for the benefit of the Republic of Venice, and hurry on to the end of June 1203, when the expedition assembled before Abydos, at the entry of the Dardanelles. The 500 vessels sailed through the straits and blackened the waters of the Hellespont. Then, with flags flying, they approached so closely to the walls of Constantinople that many of the ships received and returned flights of arrows and of other missiles.

On beholding that superb city, with its domes and palaces, its high walls, the four hundred towers which flanked them, and the masses of people by which they were covered, Villehardouin cries out, ' There was no heart, however stout and bold, which did not tremble, and not without cause, inasmuch as, since the creation of the world, never had so great an enterprise been undertaken by so small a number of people; and each one cast his eyes upon the army.'

The flotilla of the crusaders was composed of fifty galleys, 250 transports carrying troops, seventy laden with provisions and munitions of war, and 120 *palandries*, with from 4,000 to 5,000 horses on board. We know what that small force of about 40,000 men accomplished, and what were the principal achievements of that epical enterprise: the re-establishment of Isaac the Angel, the quarrels of the crusaders with young Alexis, the usurpation and dethronement of Murzuphle, the occupation and pillage of Constantinople in 1204, the installation of Baldwin as Emperor, the combats which had to be sustained with the Greeks and Bulgarians, until the day of Adrianople, when he was made prisoner; the Regency and the first two years of the reign of Henry, Baldwin's brother, and the death of the Marquis of Montferrat in 1207. Henry Martin gives us a magnificent description, after Villehardouin, of the capture of Constantinople by that handful of foreigners, whom the cowardly populace of the city might have annihilated, if only by raining down upon their heads the paving-stones of their terraces, but who laid down their arms and surrendered the capital of the Empire to pillage. The Rome of the East was treated by the men-at-arms of France and Italy just as the Western Rome had been by the hordes of Goths and Vandals. The victors and the vanquished had equal reason to feel ashamed and disgraced. The rapacity of the former inspires no less indignation than the poltroonery of the latter. The knightly crusaders of France and Italy displayed a brutality worthy of the followers of Genseric or of Attila. They destroyed numberless masterpieces of ancient art gathered together in the city of Constantine. The marbles of Pentelicus were hewn to pieces by axes and hatchets; statues of bronze were broken up and converted into money, and the taking of Constantinople by the Latins was one of the most fatal events in the history of art; for, as our military chronicler observes in his customary phraseology, 'never since the world was created was there so much booty obtained in any one city.'

Villehardouin is perhaps the most substantial hero of that epic—the work of his own persistent firmness, and where he played the part, by turns, in decisive moments, and with a success of which he is less boastful than the heroes of Homer, of a diplomatist and of a captain. His memoirs are brought to a close with the death of the Marquis of Montferrat in 1207. It may be said that the old Gallic orthography alone disappears in the language written by Villehardouin. On the other hand, the order and succession of his facts, and the naturalness of his narrative, could scarcely be changed, even to perfect them, without injury to the recital. But one must not look to find in Villehardouin any more depth of thought than literary art. Although entrusted on various occasions with delicate messages with respect to personages who were by no means gifted with his chivalrous loyalty, it does not appear that his penetration ever went beyond that instinct of the heroic ages, in which everything was the result of the first impulse rather than of calculation, and when men could not comprehend the passions which betrayed them. What one must look for, therefore, in the narratives of Villehardouin is the frankness of the knight and the simplicity of the Christian. His is the sincerity of an analyst who only speaks of what he has seen, and who gives his authorities when he recounts only what he has heard. His morality is the will of God, who punishes sins by reverses, and who bestows success upon all those whom He deigns to assist. A practical mind going straight to his aim, Villehardouin, if he has not the depth of vision which we should demand from the historian of a more advanced condition of society, has no more illusions than it should surprise us to find in an historian of his own epoch.

It has been said that Villehardouin is for history what Théroulde is for the epic; for the conquest of Constantinople, like the 'Chanson de Roland,' is the sketch of a master.

Between Villehardouin and Joinville, of whose chronicles I am about to offer a summary analysis, an entire century intervenes. More personal than his predecessor, he is at the same time the admirer of a magnificent and royal hero. He writes, moreover, in a language more cultivated and in a style more modern than that of Villehardouin. The grandeur of the events and of the men, and the relative delicacy of the manners of his epoch, have impressed on him a particular character. Villehardouin represents certain qualities of the French mind; Joinville certain others; and it may be said of both that they mark two epochs of the same language.

Joinville is the inventor of that kind of historical writing which is peculiarly French, and is known as 'Memoirs.' Born towards 1223, he died about 1319. He was the contemporary and historian of Louis IX. (1226-1270) and of Innocent III., who was Pope from 1198 to 1216. Joinville brings to a worthy close the chivalrous period of the Middle Ages, the virtues of which he purified and softened; St. Louis and his historian aptly typifying the warlike and religious heroism of the feudal king and the loyalty of the faithful vassal. Up to the time of his accompanying St. Louis in the first crusade, we know nothing of the life of Joinville. He seems to have succeeded his father, about the year 1240, as Seneschal of Champagne, and he himself tells us that at a grand court held by Louis IX. at Saumur he carved; that is to say, he was gentleman carver to the king. Some days before his departure for the crusade, a son was born to him, and from Easter Monday to the following Friday fêtes were given at the Château de Joinville in honour of the new comer. Nor was it until that Friday that he spoke of his departure. He told those who were there that, as he did not wish to carry away a single coin that did not belong to him, if there was any one present to whom he had done wrong, he was prepared to offer him reparation. Some days afterwards he made confession, assumed the scrip and staff of a pilgrim, performed a pilgrimage barefooted to the neighbouring churches, and when he retraced his steps to the Château de Joinville, in which he had left his wife and children, he said, ' I will not turn my eyes towards Joinville, because my heart would melt at the sight of the fair home in which I leave my two children.'

That paternal tenderness, that regret for the fair home, savouring rather of the man of peace than of the warrior, are delicate sentiments which we must not look for in the Memoirs, nor under the iron breastplate which covered the heart of Villehardouin. And it is by no means astonishing that the same man who turned his eyes away from the abode of his little ones, for fear of being overcome, embarked without enthusiasm, and recalled to mind how he suffered from sea-sickness as he crossed the Mediterranean. Joinville thought more of the land he had quitted than of that which he was going to conquer.

'In a short time,' he writes, 'the wind filled our sail, and we lost sight of the shore, so that we saw nothing more than sea and sky; and every day took us farther and farther from the land of our birth. . . . And I relate these things, because such a one is very rash and foolish who dares to confront a like peril with the wellbeing of others or with a mortal sin upon his conscience; for when you fall asleep in the evening there, you know not whether you may not be found at the bottom of the sea on the morrow.'

Quoting this passage from Joinville, who shrank from looking back on the familiar scenes he had quitted, Chateaubriand in his 'Itinerary from Paris to Jerusalem,' where he professes to go as a pilgrim also, and as the last of the Crusaders, whereas he only proceeds thither as the first of the tourists—to quote the words of Sainte-Beuve—has said:

'In quitting my country even, on July 13, 1806, I was not afraid to turn my head, like the Seneschal of Champagne, because, almost a stranger in my own land, I forsook neither castle nor cottage.' 'The illustrious author,' adds Sainte-Beuve, 'touches me less than he wishes to do by his reasonings. It is very true that to possess a château or a simple residence disposes one to weep at parting, but even if possessing nothing on one's native soil, there are places, the sight of which touches and penetrates one at the moment of separation when our last look rests upon them. Both these departures suggest to the critic the recollection of a third, described in the First Canto of "Childe Harold:"

> The sails were filled, and fair the light winds blew,
> As glad to waft him from his native home;
> And fast the white rocks faded from his view,
> And soon were lost in circumambient foam;
> And then, it may be, of his wish to roam
> Repented he, but in his bosom slept
> The silent thought, nor from his lips did come
> One word of wail, while others sat and wept,
> And to the reckless gales unmanly moaning kept.

'This is altogether the opposite of Joinville; for if a tear is ready to start, pride dries it up upon the instant. Byron surpasses Chateaubriand. He feels the passion of travel, the ironical gaiety of departure. He utters a cry of wild joy in severing himself from his native land, and boasts that he leaves nothing to regret. But he is presently brought back to natural emotion by the sight of his page and his yeoman, who offer a contrast to his own insensibility, and we are thus made to perceive that he is by no means a stranger to tears himself. He shows the boy and man weeping like ordinary mortals, the one for his father and mother, and the other for his wife and children. In a word, he exhibits all the art and all the refinement of a great poet who is *blasé*. He enjoys the pleasure of having two Joinvilles by his side, while playing the Chateaubriand at his leisure; and with an excess of verve and rapture, his egotism is assisted by two sensibilities.'

Marvellous incidents succeed each other on the way, and we at length arrive at Cyprus, the port of rendezvous. All the vicissitudes of the voyage are recounted by Joinville, with that credulous, fertile, and ignorant imagination which Villemain has so well defined. 'For Joinville, all is new, all is extraordinary. Cairo is Babylon, the Nile a river which arises in Paradise. He has his own private notions about many things; but as to actual facts, one does not know where to find so *naïf* a witness. One might say that the objects had been born into the world the day he saw them.'

St. Louis and his army set sail from Cyprus on Saturday, May 24, 1249. 'It was a fair sight to see,' writes Joinville, 'for it seemed as if the whole sea, as far as the eye could behold, was covered with the canvas sails of the vessels, which were reckoned to number 1,800 both great and small.' The arrival and disembarkation in sight of the enemy is related by Joinville. On Thursday after Pentecost the king reached Damietta, and found the entire army of the Sultan on the shore; a goodly host to look upon; for the Sultan's panoply was of gold, and the sun shining on it made it quite resplendent. 'The din which they raised with their cymbals and their Saracenic horns was terrible to listen to.'

We have still the proclamation which St. Louis addressed to his barons before disembarking, and it ran thus :

'My faithful friends, we shall be insurmountable so long as we remain united in charity. It is only by permission of God that we have arrived here so promptly. It is not I who am King of France, nor am I the Holy Church. I am but a single man whose life will pass away like that of any other man when it shall please God. All things are possible to us. If we are conquered, we shall rise to heaven in the quality of martyrs; and if we are victorious, we will proclaim aloud the glory of the Lord, and that of all France, or rather of all Christendom, will be aggrandised. God who foreseeth everything has not upheld me in vain. It must be that He has some great design in view. Let us fight for Jesus Christ, and He will triumph in us; and to Him, and not to ourselves, will we ascribe the glory, the honour, and the benediction.'

On disembarking, lighter craft were employed, and there

was an emulation as to who should be the first to spring to land. But he who nobly outstripped the rest was the Comte de Jaffa; 'for his galley,' writes Joinville, 'was painted inside and out with his coat of arms—a red cross on a field of gold. He had quite three hundred rowers in his galley, and to the right of each was a shield blazoned with his arms, and above each shield a small pennon, with the same blazon in raised gold. As it drew near the land, it seemed as if the galley flew beneath the arms of the rowers, who lifted it up by the power of their oars; and it seemed as if a thunderbolt fell from the heavens; such was the sound occasioned by the pennons as well as the cymbals, drums, and horns of the Saracens within.'

The debarkation of the king is thus described by the historian:

'He sprang into the sea, and the water rose up to his armpits, his shield about his neck, his helm upon his head, his gauntlets upon his hands, and he was one of the first to reach the land. No movement,' as Sainte-Beuve observes, 'could be more prompt or better rendered; it is vivacity itself. Froissart, the literary historian of chivalry, will amuse us one day by describing the shock of arms, the luxury of colours, the dazzling glitter of the casques and halberts in front of the battalions. With Joinville it is not yet a sport nor an art, it is only the natural and rapid flash of the memory, the preserved reflection of that hour of joyousness and sunshine, when one is young, brilliant, and victorious. We have not to follow the history of that crusade of St. Louis, but only to indicate the facts which characterise the *naïf* historian of that century. Damietta was taken almost without striking a blow; and the burning of the bazaar caused Joinville to make the following *naïve* comparison:—" And thus it happened just as if some one were to set fire to-morrow—which God forbid!—to the Little Bridge in Paris."'

The description which Joinville gives us of the Nile is remarkable at once for some faithful strokes and for a mixture of ignorance and credulity, 'It is expedient in the first place,' he says, 'to speak of the river which comes from Egypt and from the terrestrial Paradise.' He makes mention also of the Bedouins and the Mamelukes, but all we meet with in the historian is unmethodical and disorderly. His narrative moves on like the war itself. The arrival of the king upon the battlefield of Massoura is painted by Joinville with a brilliant vivacity in which affection and admiration are closely blended. 'There, when I was on foot with my knights, wounded, as I have said before, came the king with all his battle array and a great flourish of trumpets along a causeway. Never was beheld so goodly a man-at-arms. He appeared to be a head and shoulders above all the rest, with a gilded helmet on his head, and a German sword in his hand.' That day of Massoura was a rough one, and, as was said, a very fine feat of arms; but, from thenceforward, misfortunes and reverses did nothing but follow each other and accumulate. Joinville has little else to do then, but to record the number of the sick and the dead; and famine was soon added to the list of the calamities of an army sorely pressed on all sides by the Saracens.

The historian continues to narrate to us the capture of St. Louis and himself; and presently the negotiations which led to an understanding, arrived at after many uncertainties and vicissitudes, between St. Louis and the Saracens in relation to the king's ransom and that of the numerous Christian captives. During the four years which the king had yet to spend in the East, Joinville will never quit him.

I am obliged to omit many other anecdotes of that Crusade, which Joinville has rendered famous; but I must devote some little space to show you how the historian has portrayed St. Louis, in the midst of his people, during the sixteen years which followed his return to France, 1254–1270. Joinville often saw the king, and it was during his hours of free intercourse that he gathered together most of the anecdotes which compose the first part of his 'Memoirs.'

The portrait traced by Joinville of St. Louis, as a judicial and paternal monarch, will remain for ever that which posterity will be pleased to revere.

'It is impossible,' observes Sainte-Beuve, 'to avoid quoting—even if it be for the hundredth time—that page which is his greatest glory:—" It often happened in the summer time that the king, after hearing Mass, repaired to the wood of Vincennes, and leaning against an oak tree bade us be seated around him. And all those who had any business with him came and spoke to him without the obstruction of any functionary; and when he asked them with his own mouth if there was any one who had a cause to plead, and those rose up who had, he said to them, 'Keep quiet, all of you, and let me hear each in his turn.' And then he called Monseigneurs Pierre de Fontaines and Geoffrey de Villette, and said to one of them, 'Despatch this cause.' And when he saw something to amend in the discourse of those who undertook the pleadings, he corrected it out of his own mouth. I saw him sometimes in summer come to the Paris Garden to render justice to his people, clad in a camlet robe and a linsey-woolsey overcoat without sleeves, with a black mantle round his neck, his hair well combed, but not dressed, and a hat with white peacock's feathers on his head. He caused a carpet to be spread for you to sit upon around him, and everybody who had business with him stood up outside. Then he caused them to be judged and sent away, in the manner I have already described to you in the wood of Vincennes."'

Fifteen years afterwards, when St. Louis experienced a new desire to fight once more beneath the cross (1270), Joinville, in spite of his devotion to his master, resisted and opposed him, adducing the most legitimate reasons for declining to follow him—reasons connected with the well-being of his vassals and his people. It is a final touch which completes the portrait of that frank and upright nature. Joinville survived St. Louis by about forty-seven years, and persisted to the last in his belief that those who had persuaded the king to set forth again had been guilty of a mortal sin. In the course of his long career the Sire de Joinville witnessed the reign of six kings, from Louis VIII. to Philip the Long. Joinville's work is certainly not that of a learned historian. Modern criticism would easily find much to reproach the *naïf* chronicler with. Doubtless he plunges into a mass of often trivial details; but these details are so true, so frankly, simply narrated, and so characteristic as to become really instructive, while they confer upon the recital of the brave knight all the interest of a romance. I will not undertake to relate in detail the part which he played under the various kings of France whom I have enumerated above, and will confine myself, in concluding this lengthened study of him, to a summary of the last years of his life. Under Philip the Handsome, we find him now replying to the commissioners charged with inquiries relative to the canonisation of Louis IX., and now entering into a league of nobles confederated to resist the imposition of a tax upon the province. At length, summoned to the royal standard by Louis X., in an expedition against the Flemings, he once more donned his breastplate, at a very advanced age; for he could not have been less than ninety-two years old.

Jean Froissart (1333-1410), the most celebrated of the chroniclers, is the principal representative of French prose in the fourteenth century. He composed numerous poems, but he is best known by his 'Chronicle of France, England, Scotland, and Spain,' which is an almost universal reflection of events in Europe from 1322 to the end of the fourteenth century. But while Villehardouin and Joinville are important personages, who dictate memoirs of the events in which they have played a prominent part, Froissart is a simple priest and a chronicler by profession, who relates the exploits of others. 'His work is a vast historical picture,' observes Demogeot, 'full of movement, brilliant in colour, splendid in costumes, battles, fêtes, tourneys, sieges of cities, captures of castles, imposing cavalcades, skirmishes, daring deeds, noble acts and feats of arms, entries of princes, solemn assemblies, court balls and robes. All the military and feudal life of the fourteenth century crowds upon and accumulates in his pages in magnificent profusion.'

Froissart is the Walter Scott of the Middle Ages, as well as the father of the war correspondent and the 'interviewer' of modern journalism. It was by perpetual travel that he gathered together the materials of his work. He spent five years in England, where in 1362 he was secretary to Philippa of Hainault, wife of Edward III. He visited Scotland; then attached himself to the Black Prince and to the Duke of Clarence, accompanying the first into France and Spain, and the second into Italy. He travelled over all parts of France and was often in Paris. Everywhere he questioned, with an eager curiosity, his travelling companions or his noble hosts, and wrote sometimes, in the form of conversations, the narratives just as they were related to him. He had learned Latin and possessed some literary culture. His talent for narration is admirable, but he had no critical faculty, nor any power of methodical arrangement.[1]

Froissart, as I have already said, also wrote numerous poems, which are graceful and spirited, and show a great

[1] Walter Besant.

advance in the language over that written by Gaston de Foix and Thibault de Champagne. The subjoined example has been modernised, however :

> Le corps s'en va, mais le cœur nous demeure,
> Très chère dame, adieu jusqu'au retour,
> Trop me sera lointaine ma demeure.

And then he repeats the first and second lines. Most of his poetical pieces resemble the foregoing in form and metre. Might we not fancy it is La Fontaine who is speaking to us in the poem of 'Psyche,' rather than Froissart when he says :

> Mais je passois à si grande joie
> Ce temps. . . .
> Que tout me venoit à plaisir,
> Et le *parler* et le *taisir*,
> Le aller et le être coi.

Froissart greatly liked the spring. His heart always went out where there were roses and violets; but in the winter he also knew how to accommodate himself to the season, and, remaining snugly at home, his especial reading consisted of 'treatises and romances of love.' Adenès, the *trouvère*, was his favourite poet. The first care of Froissart at the English court, and his greatest pleasure, while frequenting the society of the great nobles, and the knights and their squires, was to ascertain the details of every memorable event, and of all the particulars which were capable of being worked up into history. In writing the first part he took for his guide, as he states himself at the outset, the Chronicle of Jean le Bel, Canon of St. Lambert in Liège. Froissart has informed the somewhat dry canvas of Jean le Bel with his animated narrative, his easy and natural abundance. In some passages, even as, for example, in the celebrated siege of Calais, he seems to have entirely recast and renewed, by his own richness, the primitive text of his forerunner, upon whom he has but slightly depended, and only for the primary facts. As regards the years which followed that siege, he has collected his information on his own account, composing his own materials, and flying with his own wings.

The battle of Poitiers (1356), presently to be described, is, in all respects, a masterpiece. But, first of all, we remark that Froissart comprehends to an astonishing degree what was the true rôle of the historian in his days. What was required at this epoch in history was not criticism but philosophy; what was chiefly important was the accumulation of materials and the judicious disposal of them; and this he has done with a zeal and indefatigable ardour, and with an elevated sentiment of the service which he was rendering to posterity by preserving the records of great events and noble deeds.

M. de Barante has said of Froissart:

There is no historian who possesses a greater charm or is more truthful. His book is a living witness of the time in which he lived. No art is required to make it visible. The candour of the sentiments is equal to his *naïveté* of expression. We recognise in it the colour and the charm of the romances of chivalry: the same admiration for valour, loyalty, brave deeds of arms; for the love and service of ladies; and, at the same time, the disorders, the cruelty, the rough manners of those barbarous times, the still-beginning, never-ending wars, the conflagration of cities, the massacres of peoples, desolated provinces, companies of armed men who have become estranged from all countries, and subsisting only on rapine; and nevertheless, in the midst of so many horrors, men appearing to be full of grandeur, freedom, and force. They are cruel, they are fickle in their political affections, but they are sincere and the slaves of their word.

One of the essential points in dispute concerning Froissart is his impartiality. Lengthened sojourns at the English court, and the benefits lavished on him by Queen Philippa of Hainault, seem to have rendered him partial to that country. In fact it seems difficult for a chronicler, resting under an obligation to so many nobles, not to requite the favours received from them by according them great prominence in his writings. 'These are inevitable inconveniences,' observes Sainte-Beuve, 'but the extreme and passionate curiosity of Froissart was a sort of remedy for, and guarantee against, partiality, even if he had been inclined thereto; but he was not the man to close one ear, nor to keep to himself a report once related to him, even if that account should contradict a previous version in some particular. He was eager to listen to all sides.' Observe him hastening to Bruges, and then to Zealand, on learning that a Portuguese knight was there who could give him some information with respect to the affairs of Spain, which would be the counterpart of what he had already obtained from the Gascons and the Castilians. It was this which led Montaigne, when speaking of simple historians who pick up everything that comes in their way, and who record in good faith all things without choice and without discrimination, to say: 'Such, for example, among others, is worthy Froissart, who moves along in his enterprise with such a frank *naïveté* that, having once committed a fault, he has no hesitation in correcting it, so soon as he finds it out, and who acquaints us even with the different rumours current and the various stories in circulation. It is crude and naked history, from which each can derive as much profit as he has understanding.'

To judge Froissart properly, we must take into account the then state of the chivalry, of which he is really the historian, without regard to cause or nation. His ideal is that sort of universal brotherhood which embraces everything that is noble and valiant, and comprehends within its ranks the fine flower of the chivalry which knew how to crown the victor while respecting and honourably raising up the vanquished.

He is, by turns, the countryman of all who act valorously and deserve renown and honour. In a word, he is, strictly speaking, the organ of chivalry. England has been grateful to Froissart for the regard he has entertained for her and which he has always maintained. He has been, at all times, appreciated there, and has found readers and admirers among the *élite*. The poet Gray, writing in 1760, said: '"Froissart" is one of my favourite books. It seems strange to me that people who buy, for their weight in gold, a dozen original portraits of that epoch, to adorn a gallery, never cast their eyes upon so many moving pictures of the life, the deeds, the manners, and the thoughts of their ancestors, painted on the spot in such simple but strong colours.' 'But,' adds Sainte-Beuve, from whom I have borrowed freely for this study of Froissart:

> The one of your authors who has offered him the finest homage is a facile genius, a painter who wields a broad, free pencil, and who is not without a great family resemblance to him. I speak of Walter Scott in his 'Old Mortality.' On the day after the victory which Claverhouse has won over the fanatics, and which he

has sullied in his turn by his pitiless cruelties, Morton, a prisoner, and treated with distinction by the General, accompanies him on his way. Struck by his courage, urbanity, and generous and chivalrous demeanour, he is unable to reconcile such high and estimable qualities with his contempt for men's lives, and especially for those of an inferior class, and he cannot help contrasting him in his heart with the fanatical Balfour of Burley. Some words which he lets fall betray what he is thinking of.

'You are right,' said Claverhouse, with a smile, 'you are very right, we are both fanatics; but there is some distinction between the fanaticism of honour and that of dark, sullen superstition.' And it is then that, after some other talk on the same subject, he abruptly asks Morton, 'Did you ever read Froissart?' 'No,' was Morton's answer. 'I have half a mind,' said Claverhouse, 'to contrive you should have six months' imprisonment in order to procure you that pleasure. His chapters inspire me with more enthusiasm than even poetry itself. And the noble Canon, with what true chivalrous feeling he confines his beautiful expressions of sorrow to the death of the gallant and high-bred Knight, of whom it was a pity to see the fall; such was his loyalty to his king, pure faith to his religion, hardihood towards his enemy, and fidelity to his ladylove! Ah! benedicite! how he will mourn over the fall of such a pearl of knighthood, be it on the side he happens to favour or on the other. But, truly, for sweeping from the face of the earth some few hundreds of villain churls, who are born but to plough it, the high-born and inquisitive historian has marvellous little sympathy, as little, or less perhaps than John Grahame of Claverhouse.'

We will not go so far as Claverhouse, and will only say that Froissart had the morality of his time, that of the nobles and knights with whom he consorted and whom he served. He is a Paul Pry, and his curiosity is appropriate, open, and pleasant. He will never be a philosophical historian like Gibbon, but his work, confined to curious inquiry and the vivid representation of facts, appears to stand out in even greater relief.

The conversation of Froissart with Henry Castide, an English squire, during one of his last journeys to England, will furnish us with a perfect example of the way in which our historian gathered together the materials for his chronicles. The squire speaks first:

'Messire Jean, have you not yet found any one in this country, or in the court of our lord the king, to tell you of the expedition which the king made into Ireland last season, and how four of its kings, great potentates, came to render fealty to the English sovereign?' And I replied, in order to draw him out, 'No, indeed.' 'Then I will tell it you,' said the squire, 'so that it may find a lasting place in your memoir when you go back to your own country, and when you will have leisure and pleasure. Whereupon I was greatly pleased, and replied, 'Many thanks.'

Observe that, on the first question addressed to him by the squire, Froissart, even if he had already heard tell of that journey, made believe to know nothing of it, the better to learn all. And when the squire related to him in detail the submission of those four kings, and when he had shown how they were gradually led to accept knighthood at the hands of King Richard, Froissart adds :

There is one thing I want to ask you, which has not failed to excite my wonder greatly, and which I should much like to know, if you are acquainted with it—as I can scarcely doubt you are—and that is, how it was these four kings of Ireland were so quickly brought to obey the king of England, while his royal grandsire, who was such a valiant man, and so widely dreaded and renowned, could not bring them into submission, and incurred their constant enmity. You have said that it was by treaty and by the grace of God. Well, the grace of God is an excellent thing, when we can obtain it, and certes, it has its price; but one sees very few earthly lords at present enlarging their estates except by strength and might, and when I get back again to the country where I was born, and begin to talk about these things, you must know that I shall be very much questioned and catechised about them.

Thus, Froissart was not satisfied with what contented Joinville. There were occasions when he wanted to ascertain the secondary causes of events. Not only so, but his natural piety was tempered by his worldly experience; for while he did not undervalue the grace of God, he had found that sword and spear were potent elements in worldly affairs, just as Cromwell, in later times, when charging his soldiers to 'put your trust in God,' significantly added, 'and keep your powder dry.'

A century after Froissart, Commynes will go back to political principles and to the first causes of events. 'Note the gradation,' observes Sainte-Beuve. Froissart goes halfway, and there is with him what I would willingly call some remains of the devout *fabliaux*, à la Joinville. His chronicles cover the events of three-quarters of a century, from 1325 to 1400—from the coronation of Edward III. of England to the deposition and death of his grandson, Richard II. And one finds in them the history of everything that took place in all the provinces of France, and of every considerable event in England, Scotland, Ireland, and Flanders, an infinitude of particulars concerning the affairs of the Popes of Rome and of Avignon, as also respecting those of Spain,

BATTLE OF POITIERS

Portugal, Germany, Italy, and sometimes even of more distant countries, such as Hungary, Turkey, and realms beyond the sea. But when our worthy Froissart travels so far afield, he is not always to be depended upon, and mistakes, and even fables, are plentiful. In the midst of that vast and somewhat confused work, England and France occupy the first place. In his Chronicles we meet with three episodes most impressively depicted. The first, King Edward's affection for the Countess of Salisbury, is purely graceful and romantic. The second is pathetic and dramatic —the incident of the siege of Calais and of the six citizens for whom the queen of England successfully interceded. The third is entirely epic and grandiose—the battle of Poitiers, of which I will endeavour to offer you an epitomised narrative.

On the death of King Philip of France, in 1350, his eldest son John succeeded to the throne, was crowned at Rheims, and held high festival in Paris for a whole week. But all this time the Prince of Wales was harrying some of the fair provinces watered by the Loire, which provoked the king into swearing a great oath that he would do battle with his English adversary. Accordingly, in 1356, he marched a large army, consisting of 48,000 men, towards the city of Poitiers, while the enemy was so much inferior in point of numbers that the French exceeded them by six to one. ' God help us ! ' said the Black Prince, when he heard of this enormous disparity. ' We will now consider which will be the best manner to fight them most advantageously.' And he posted his men in a strong position among vineyards and hedges. It was in the middle of the vintage and on a bright autumnal morning, when the bells of the beautiful cathedral were sending their Sabbath music across the fertile plains dominated by the picturesque hill-city of Poitiers, that the French king caused mass to be celebrated in the presence of his chivalry, nineteen of the noblest in the realm wearing the same royal armour as himself, so that the sovereign might not be singled out for special attack. It must have been a splendid spectacle as the early sun flashed and glittered on the brilliant suits of mail, on the embroidered surcoats, on the banners and pennons, on the crimson hat and robe of Cardinal Périgord, and on the albs and stoles of the ecclesiastics. The conflict did not take place on that day, because the Cardinal passed from camp to camp bearing the olive branch of peace; but all his negotiations were ineffectual, seeing which the Black Prince, bating no jot of heart or hope, addressed his followers thus :—'Now, my gallant fellows, what though we be a small number compared with our enemies? Do not be cast down. Victory is not always to the stronger side. It is the Almighty who bestows it. I entreat you to exert yourselves and to combat manfully, for if it please God and St. George, you shall see me act this day like a true knight.'

On the part of the French, when the sun rose on that fateful morning, the preparations for the attack were vigorously commenced. A little patience on their part would have delivered the adversary into their hands, as he was short of provisions and of forage, but it was believed to be dishonourable to delay the assault. It has been ever thus with the posterity of the Franks of the old Carlovingian race, who, on various occasions when a great and deadly duel had to be engaged in, discounted the advantages which courage and ability might have procured for them.

Lord James Audley seems to have had the ordering of the battle; and he masked his men so well behind the hedgerows and the vines, that when the English archers began to open a galling fire of arrows on the French cavalry, the horses, smarting with the pain, threw their riders, and caused the greatest confusion, which reached its climax when the battalion of the marshals was routed by the bowmen, and the men-at-arms rushed upon the discomfited host 'and slew them at their pleasure,' as Froissart says. It was a moment of disaster and dismay, and the bravery of the horsemen was rendered impotent by the wild stampede of their wounded and ungovernable chargers. 'They fell back so much on each other,' writes the chronicler, 'that the army could not advance, and those who were in the rear, not being able to get forward, fell back upon the battalion commanded by the Duke of Normandy, which was very thick in the front, though it was soon thin enough in the rear, for when they learned that the marshals had been defeated they mounted their horses and rode off.'

'In reproducing these words five centuries later,' observes

Sainte-Beuve, 'it must not be forgotten that they are those of an adversary concerning a day which was then one of great mourning for France; but France is so rich in glory that she can afford to honour a victorious enemy so endowed with generosity, as he himself honoured an opponent so full of valour.'

In simple truth, the battle of Poitiers was won upon the village greens of England, where from time immemorial the rustic folk had been accustomed to assemble on summer evenings and on Sunday afternoons to practise archery, and had thus acquired that strength of arm and that precision of aim which told so fearfully upon their brave antagonists who encountered them near the homestead of Maupertuis, to the eastward of Poitiers.

On beholding the retreat of the battalions of the marshals, the English men-at-arms mounted their horses, which were close at hand, and raised a lusty shout of 'St. George for Guienne!' 'The day is ours!' cried Sir John Chandos to the Black Prince. 'Let us make for our adversary the king of France, for he will be in the thick of the battle. I well know that his valour will not let him fly, but he must be well fought with.' And presently the two gallant opponents joined issue, the French raising the thrilling war-cry of 'Montjoye St. Denis!' and the English replying with a loud 'St. George for Guienne!'

In the shock of arms King John gave proofs of splendid prowess, and so did the knights and nobles who rallied round his standard. Most of them, indeed, were slain or taken prisoners; the Duke of Bourbon, the Duke of Athens, Constable of France, and the Bishop of Chalons being among the dead, and the flower of the French chivalry passed into captivity upon that memorable day, as many as two hundred knights and squires having been either killed or taken. The English pursued their foemen to the gates of Poitiers, which were barred against them; and the result was a great slaughter of men and horses under the very walls of the city.

Meanwhile what had become of the brave but defeated king?

His banner-bearer, the Sire de Chargny, was slain with the royal standard in his hand; and a young knight in the

English service, addressing the king, in irreproachable French exclaimed, 'Sire, sire, surrender yourself!' The king, turning sharply round, rejoined: 'To whom shall I surrender myself? Where is my cousin, the Prince of Wales?' 'Sire,' replied Sir Denys, 'he is not here; but surrender yourself to me and I will lead you to him.' 'Who are you?' said the king. 'Sire, I am Denys de Morbèque, a knight from Artois; but I serve the king of England because I cannot belong to France, having forfeited all I possessed there.' The king gave him his right-hand glove, and said, 'I surrender myself to you.'

Brought into the presence of the Earl of Warwick and Lord Cobham, who had been despatched in search of him, the captive king was received with the greatest courtesy, both barons dismounting and standing bareheaded before him. He was then conducted to the Black Prince, to whom he was presented by his noble escort; and wine and spices were brought, the victorious Englishman waiting upon his prisoner with chivalrous hospitality, and, as Froissart quaintly puts it, 'giving all the comfort he could.'

The royal pair travelled to Bordeaux together, and wintered there, for the whole of south-western France was at that time under English rule, and they sailed for England in the spring. Landing at Sandwich, they proceeded to Canterbury, from whence the Prince despatched a messenger to London, directing that magnificent preparations should be made for the reception of his royal prisoner. Indeed, the latter was the hero and the central figure of the brilliant pageant.

For thus writes Froissart concerning the entry of these two heroic men into the English capital:

> The prince and his royal charge remained one day at Canterbury, where they made their offerings to the shrine of St. Thomas, and the next morning they proceeded to Rochester, the third day to Dartford, and the fourth to London, where they were received with much honour and distinction. The king of France, as he rode through London, was mounted on a white steed, richly caparisoned, and the Prince of Wales on a little black hackney by his side. The palace of the Savoy was first appropriated to the French king's use; but soon after his arrival, he was removed to Windsor Castle, where he was treated with the greatest possible attention, and hunting, hawking, and other amusements were provided for him.

It was from the period at which the battle of Poitiers was fought that Froissart, as Sainte-Beuve has pointed out, began to rely upon his own resources as an historian, and from the first pages he sets out by presenting a great picture worthy of a master. Indeed, the most distinguished critics of our times, Villemain, Ampère, and Nisard, as well as Sainte-Beuve, have exhibited a special predilection for him, and have accorded him the highest praises; while Hallam considers that his picturesque descriptions and fertility of historical invention entitle him to be regarded as the Livy of France, Philippe de Commynes being the Tacitus. Froissart found a continuator in Monstrelet, who did not possess the gift of 'invention' ironically attributed to his predecessor, nor his pictorial style, but is more trustworthy perhaps, if occasionally dull. But of him we shall presently have occasion to speak.

Froissart has been sometimes styled the creator of French prose, but such a statement cannot be accepted without reserve, inasmuch as Joinville, and the authors of the oldest and best prose versions of the romances of chivalry, had written before Froissart. What is indisputable is that he holds a foremost place among the primitive prose writers; and that, after him, French prose, far from exhibiting a continuously progressive development, retrograded and was disorganised in the midst of the calamities which disturbed the French mind, overturned the society of the fifteenth century, and signalised the end of the Middle Ages. The French language and French literature only rose again when transformed by the Renaissance. Froissart's poetry has not retained the same celebrity as his prose, and has not the same originality. At the same time it contains enough of sensibility, elegance, and delicacy, to justify the high esteem in which it was held by his contemporaries.

Enguerrand de Monstrelet is said to have been the natural son of a gentleman of good family in the county of Boulogne, and to have been rather wild in his young days. In fact, he appears to have taken to the road, and to have got into trouble for robbing a merchant on the highway near Abbeville. But he was pardoned by King Henry VI. of England in 1424, and a few years later he was taken into the service of John of Luxembourg, and we hear of him as present at the interview which took place between Joan of Arc and the Duke of Burgundy, and afterwards as Provost of Cambrai. He also took part in the siege of Compiègne in 1430. Taking up the thread of Froissart's narrative where he dropped it, Monstrelet chronicles the principal events which occurred between 1400 and 1444; and he tells us that he collected his information at first hand from all manner of trustworthy people; that he endeavoured to record what he had learned with fairness and impartiality; and that his chief desire was to be accurate and truthful to the best of his knowledge and belief.

The principal events related by Monstrelet are the wars which were waged between the Houses of Orleans and Burgundy, the occupation of the city of Paris, and the conquest of Normandy by the English. Exact and conscientious in his statements, laborious in the collection of authentic documents to corroborate the truth of his narratives, he is one of the safest and best guides we possess to a knowledge of all the more important events of the first half of the fifteenth century.

I have left myself still very much to say about Froissart, even from a merely literary point of view, if I had undertaken to exhaust my subject; but I perceive that I have already devoted much more space to the study of this author than to that of all the rest, and I begin to fear that I have put your indulgence to too severe a test. I will commence my next lecture with Commynes.

LECTURE IV

Philippe de Commynes (1445–1509)—Charles d'Orléans (1391–1465)—
François Villon (1431?–1485?)—Of the Great Testament of Villon
(1461)—Budé (1467–1540)—Erasmus (1467–1536).

HAVING spoken of Villehardouin, Joinville, and Froissart, I will now endeavour to present to you the fourth of our oldest chroniclers, namely, Philippe de Commynes, although the title of chronicler is scarcely applicable to one who is really the first of the moderns who placed himself on the track of the political authors of classic antiquity. He is the first actually modern writer, and every reader who does not want to go too far back, nor to gratify an erudite curiosity, but wishes merely to form an entirely modern French library, must needs admit into it the works of Montaigne and of Commynes.

'These are men,' observes Sainte-Beuve, 'who have our ideas, and who have them to the extent and in the sense it would be good for us to have them—men who understood the world and society, and more particularly the art of living in it, and of daily conduct, as we should only be too happy to understand it in the present day. They are counsellors and conversationalists who are as pleasant to listen to after three or four centuries as when they first spoke; Montaigne on all subjects and at all hours; Commynes upon affairs of state, upon the secret springs of great actions, upon what from that time one calls modern political interests; and upon so many of the incentives which actuated men in his day, and have not ceased to move them in our own.'

The historian has been so much studied, men the most deeply versed in literary and historical criticism have so repeatedly explored the 'Memoirs' of the writer who has earned for himself the title of the French Tacitus, that they have left very little to be gleaned by any one wishing to speak of him at the end of the nineteenth century. If, in the case of some of the poets and prose writers of whom I have previously spoken, I have ventured to offer my own thoughts, to look at them from my own point of view, and to select the extracts I have quoted, I must humbly confess that, in the case of Commynes, I must faithfully follow what writers of great authority have said of him, and can only presume to present to you a compilation seriously undertaken, and an exact summary of what has been written with respect to the man and his work. Commynes was born about the year 1445, at the château of Commynes, a place which is to-day a very busy town a few miles from Lille. 'When I had emerged from childhood,' he says, 'and was old enough to mount a horse, I was taken to Lille to see the Duke Charles of Burgundy, who was about to become Charles the Bold;' and he followed him in the war of the League for the Public Good, formed by the great vassals on the eve of giving battle to the new king, Louis XI., a few leagues from his capital, at the foot of the hill of Montlhéri. It was the first battle at which Commynes had been present, and nothing can be more piquant than his narrative of it; and if in narrating that encounter he has endeavoured to parody that of Poitiers, so broadly and clearly depicted by Froissart a hundred years previously, which I have sketched in the last lecture, he could scarcely have done otherwise. The battle in this instance was engaged in by all at cross purposes, and contrary alike to the original plan and to common sense. Louis XI. wished to elude the combat, and what happened was the very opposite. There were traitors on both sides, and when the battle began the Burgundians did the very reverse of what had been decided upon in the council of war. Commynes kept close to the side of Charles the Bold all day, 'having less fear,' he said, 'than he had ever felt in any place since then,' the reason given being that he was young and had no idea of danger. And as he showed himself at Montlhéri so he will be later on at Fornova : full of sangfroid, making very little account of military heroism, and being of opinion with his future master, Louis XI., that he who has the profit of war has the honour of it. The irony of Commynes breaks out in that first narrative, and it is to that irony I seek to call attention, and not to relate the battle, which is of small importance. At a certain moment each side believed itself beaten. On that of the king there was a great personage who fled full gallop to Lusignan without drawing bridle; and on the side of Burgundy another great personage escaped not less quickly to Quesnoi. 'Those two,' remarks Commynes, 'cannot snarl at each other.' A complete analysis of the 'Memoirs' of Commynes would be equivalent to a history of the reign of Louis XI., of his quarrels with his great vassals, and more particularly with Charles the Bold, Duke of Burgundy, as also of the reign of Charles VIII. and of his campaign in Italy, not stopping until we come to Louis XII., who, not requiring the services of Commynes, left him the leisure to write those 'Memoirs' which are engaging our present attention. At the same time I cannot altogether lose sight of the events while analysing the record of them, but I will be as brief as possible.

Commynes, as we have seen, entered at first the service of the Duke of Burgundy, that sanguinary madman who ravaged with fire and sword so many of the fairest provinces of France, and met with his death at the siege of Nancy, when he was not yet forty years of age, after having sustained at the hands of the Swiss the two reverses of Granson and Morat, the glorious anniversaries of which are commemorated to this day by the Helvetic Confederation.

It was at the interview of Péronne, when he was twenty-one years of age, and already wise and prudent, that he attracted the attention of Louis XI., to whom he appears to have rendered a signal service by making known to him the intentions of Charles the Bold, and thus enabling the king to extricate himself as well as he was able from the dangerous position in which he was placed. The king, we do not know exactly how, found himself in the power of Charles the Bold, and he dreaded the jokes of the Parisians about the 'fox captured by Isengrin.' Later on, indeed, to avoid the sarcasms to which he has been habituated, he will give orders to deliver up to one of the king's officers all the chattering birds, magpies or jackdaws, crows or starlings, which have made the streets ring with allusions to the misadventure of Péronne.[1] Charles the Bold, by his trans-

[1] Henry Martin, vii. 47.

ports of rage, his obstinacy, and his cruelty, found himself successively abandoned by the wisest of his servants. It was after his devastations in the district of Caux, and the checks he sustained before Dieppe and Rouen, that his service was forsaken by his chamberlain, Philippe de Commynes. Still young, he was already the politician who was to lead the way among moderns in writing history as a thinker and as a statesman.

He could no longer put up with the freaks of a brutal and fantastic master, and he decided on attaching himself to the king, Louis XI., who was more capable of appreciating the shrewdness of his spirit, and whom he had known ever since the forced sojourn of that monarch at Péronne. Commynes was now only twenty-five, and he served Louis XI. faithfully as counsellor and chamberlain until the king's death in 1483, when he was still not more than thirty-six. 'Commynes,' observes Sainte-Beuve, 'grasped like Machiavelli and Montesquieu the scope of his times, the various forms of government, their principles, and the remote consequences flowing from them. He was also a partisan of the English system of government.'

And at that remote epoch Commynes was an advocate of the principle of self-government; his views upon which will be found set forth in a chapter entitled 'Character of the French People, and of the Government of its Kings'—views denoting his sagacity and his breadth of outlook. Commynes was extremely indulgent in his judgment of Louis XI., as, of all the princes of his time, he was the one of whom he had the most good and the least evil to say; and, as Henry Martin has shrewdly remarked, it would be difficult to pronounce a more cutting satire on the monarchs of the fifteenth century. At the same time it must be remembered that the king was labouring for the unification of the kingdom, completely open to attack up till then (as Michelet observes), when he closed it up for the first time, and gave a lasting peace to its central provinces.

The incomparable details, given by Commynes, of the life of the king after his retirement to Plessis-les-Tours, render that portion of his history a most eloquent picture of royal and human history. No historian conveys so vividly as he does a deep conviction of the wretchedness of royalties and grandeurs, of the mighty and the 'happy' ones of the earth. Listen to what he says of Louis XI. : ' Would it not be far better for him, and for all other princes, and men of middle estate, who have lived under the great, or will live beneath the rule of kings, to choose the *via media*; .... to have less knowledge, less care, and less labour, and to undertake fewer things, to have more fear of offending God and of persecuting the people and their neighbours in so many cruel methods, and to enjoy more ease and honest pleasure? Their lives would be longer, sickness would not overtake them so soon, and their death would be more generally regretted and less desired.' One recognises here, observes Sainte-Beuve, 'the man who has watched the sleepless nights and evil dreams of kings, and who, from the flower of their age until their death, has failed to detect in their envied destinies one single happy day.' In the reflections of Commynes we may hear the stern voice of experience confirming the impressive words which Shakespeare has placed in the mouth of Anne Bullen :

> I swear, 'tis better to be lowly born,
> And range with humble livers in content,
> Than to be perk'd up in a glistering grief,
> And wear a golden sorrow.

From the death of Louis XI. the memoirs of Commynes undergo a sensible diminution of interest. The conquest of Italy by Charles VIII., and his march to Naples, as related by him, belong rather to the domain of history; and it will suffice to mention that Commynes' life was not untroubled, that he passed eight months in one of those iron cages invented by Louis XI., the use of which he taught to his daughter, Anne of Brittany; that he was employed as ambassador by Charles VIII.; and that he apprised him, from Venice, of the Italian coalition, which all his efforts had failed to restrain the Republic of the Adriatic from joining. I will conclude by quoting a *mot* of Vauvenargues, which, observes Sainte-Beuve, Commynes entirely justifies : ' True politicians know men better than those who cultivate philosophy. I might say they are the truer philosophers.' But in order to be so, adds the essayist, they must be genuine politicians, and there are very few who can lay so good a claim to that title as Commynes.

Henry Hallam, in his 'Introduction to the Literature of Europe,' has judged him thus: 'An acute understanding and much experience of mankind gave Commynes this superiority; his life had not been spent among books; and he is consequently free from that pedantic application of history which became common with those who passed for political reasoners in the next two centuries. Yet he was not ignorant of former times, and we see the advantage of those translations from antiquity, made during the last hundred years in France, by the use to which he turned them.'

Commynes has been read, and is still read occasionally, in England, although not to the same extent as our old chronicler, Froissart, who was and is the favourite historian. But Sir Walter Scott has given him a fame as enduring as his own; for one of his best romances, containing an inimitable picture of the Middle Ages, 'Quentin Durward,' is based on the memoirs of Commynes. A French poet, Casimir de la Vigne, has also drawn upon him for the materials of his historical drama of 'Louis XI.,' a character so admirably embodied on the French stage by Ligier and Beauvallet, on the English boards by Charles Kean and Henry Irving, and in the Australian theatres by G. V. Brooke. Théodore de Banville also went to the same source for his comedy of 'Gringoire.'

After having thus studied French prose in its four principal historians, I return to our poetry, and the author who presents himself as next in succession to those already treated of is Charles d'Orléans. Born in Paris, at the Hôtel St. Pol, in May 1391, he was the most gallant knight and accomplished gentleman of his time. It was he who, in 1409, married Isabel of Valois, whom Richard II. of England had espoused at the age of eight, and left her a widow three years afterwards. Made prisoner at Agincourt, he spent twenty-five years of captivity in England, where he wrote several poems in the language of his conquerors: poems which furnish an additional proof of the truth of Shelley's lines:

> Most wretched men
> Are cradled into poetry by wrong;
> They learn in suffering what they teach in song.

Nor was he liberated until 1440, on paying a ransom of 200,000 golden crowns. Some time after his return to

France he retired to his château at Blois, and gave himself up entirely to poetry. The impulse which he imparted to letters in France made itself felt very early in the following century, and he died in 1465. He hospitably opened his home and his heart to the writers of his time, among whom he was undoubtedly the best. For two centuries his name as a poet has been forgotten, and has been only mentioned as that of a French prince who was taken prisoner by the English at Agincourt. Louis XI., his royal cousin, appears to have been jealous of the popularity he acquired on his return from captivity, and it is even said that he died of chagrin on account of the suspicions entertained of him by the king on that account. It is at least probable that a great politician like Louis XI. could not have seen, without protestation, Charles d'Orléans occupying himself exclusively in his château at Blois with his insipid loves, while preoccupations of an entirely different kind absorbed all his own attention.

It was not until 1734 that the Abbé Sallier acquainted France with the name of another forgotten poet, a poet described by Villemain as the only one of the fifteenth century. With respect to Charles d'Orléans we may consult the criticisms and notices written by Sallier, Goujet, Angis, and Villemain. The last-named critic, when speaking of him, dwells on the ingenuousness and homeliness of his diction, his aristocratic and chivalrous good taste, and that elegance of manner, and that fine vein of pleasantry in relation to himself, which one looks for only in an epoch of greater cultivation than his own. He further remarks that one meets with expressions in his poems which belong to no date, and which being always fresh are neither effaced from the memory nor from the language of a people. One can only attribute the oblivion into which the poems of Charles d'Orléans fell, during a couple of centuries, to the invention of printing of which he was the contemporary; for it was the old and not the living authors whose works passed through the press. The earliest book printed in the French language, for example, was the 'Recueil des Histoires de Troye,' produced by Caxton somewhere in the Duchy of Burgundy.

Charles d'Orléans is, undoubtedly, the first *trouvère*

who has written French, and he is much more easy to read than Lydgate in English, for example. At the same time we may call him the last of the *trouvères*, in spite of the opinion of M. Villemain. We do so because he possessed too much in common with the versifiers who were then disappearing to entitle him to the name of poet. He continued, like the *trouvères* who preceded him, to use and abuse allegorical figures, borrowing them more particularly from the 'Roman de la Rose,' of which the influence was still to make itself felt up to the time of the writers of the Hôtel de Rambouillet. Faux-danger, Bel-accueil, Souscy are the personages he selects; and, although allegory was carried to still greater lengths and with even worse taste after him, he really belonged to the period of allegorical versifiers.

His style and his ideas are pure; but, on the other hand, his imagination is weak. He presents us with nothing new, nothing original; and the sole praise due to him is that he abstained from the coarseness in which his contemporaries took delight, but which he felt to be unbecoming his own position as a French prince. The poet Villon, who was not restricted by any considerations of the same kind, availed himself very largely of that licentious freedom which was so liberally taken advantage of by the writers of that time.

In the eyes of Charles d'Orléans personal respect could not exist unless in a man of noble blood, and he showed that he was quite unable to comprehend the possibility of a churl or a bourgeois ever possessing the chivalrous virtues. He never said so explicitly, but all his poems breathe these class prejudices. It was only natural, therefore, that he should entirely have failed to perceive, and should never even have suspected, that gradual elevation of the middle class which began in the fifteenth century; which was more obvious in France than elsewhere, and was taking place everywhere around him. He did not understand that the age of chivalry was coming to an end. No doubt Louis XI. did so, as I have already said, and observed the crumbling to pieces of the old social fabric and the motive forces at work so repugnant to his own ideas. A poet who, notwithstanding he was his own cousin, only looked at things through the prison furnished by Apollo, and abode in the castle of Loyalty, conducted thither by Honour and Fidelity, and loyally defended its ramparts against Recreancy and Treachery, sustained by their minions Deceit, Treason, and Calumny, must have appeared insupportable to a politician of the strength of Louis XI.

It is difficult to make extracts from the poems of Charles d'Orléans; they are all short and generally embody a single idea, agreeably expressed, although often insignificant and insipid; but it is always admirably finished, and one does not really see how a punctilious author could render anything in better form.

Here is a passage by way of example:

> France, jadis on te souloit nommer
> En tous païs, le trésor de noblesse;
> Car un chacun pouvoit en toy trouver
> Bonté, Honneur, Loyauté, Gentillesse,
> Clergie,[1] Sens, Courtoisie, Proesse:
> Tous étrangers amoient[2] te suir
> Et maintenant voy, dont j'ay desplaisance,
> Qu'il te convient maint grief soustenir,
> Très Crestien, franc royaume de France.

In the following verses we find the poet exhorting the people to pray for peace:

> Priez pour Paix, doulce vierge Marie,
> Royne des cieux et du monde maîtresse,
> Faictes prier, par votre courtoisie,
> Saints et Saintes, et prenez vostre adresse
> Vers vostre fils, requérant sa hautesse
> Qu'il lui plaise son peuple regarder
> Que de son sang a voulu racheter
> En desboutant guerre qui tout desvoye
> De prieres ne vous veuilliez lasser:
> Priez pour Paix, le vrai trésor de joye.

And here we have a description of the spring which well deserves quotation:

> Le temps a laissié son manteau
> De vent, de froidure et de pluye,
> Et s'est vestu de broderie,
> De soleil riant, cler et beau;
> Il n'y a bête, ne oiseau
> Qu'en son jargon ne chante ou crye;
> Le temps a laissié son manteau
> De vent, de froidure et de pluye.

---

[1] Instruction.   [2] Aimaient.

> Rivière, fontaine et ruisseau
> Portent, en livrée jolye,
> Gouttes d'argent, d'orfèvrerie ;
> Chacun s'habille de nouveau ;
> Le temps a laissié son manteau
> De vent, de froydure et de pluye.

It is impossible to offer you an analysis of the allegorical poems of Charles d'Orléans, nor would they interest you if I did. One might as well dissect the whole of the 'Roman de la Rose;' in which all the virtues, all the vices, ideas and sentiments of humanity are personified; and even to indicate to you, though ever so briefly, how all these personages speak and move, is really beyond my power; while I believe it would be equally beyond the patience and endurance of my indulgent hearers. The chief reproach to be directed against this last and best of the *trouvères* is on account of his almost entire lack of patriotism in the terrible times which France was then passing through. His muse was not made to bewail the woes of his country. His thoughts were less elevated. In the midst of the frightful disasters of the invasion he found nothing better to sing of, as his predecessors did, than love, the seasons, the flowers, and the green fields. In his critical estimate of Charles d'Orléans Sainte-Beuve remarks that 'when he addresses himself to his lady, it is with a decorous gallantry which shows the knight beneath the *trouvère*. Sensitive as a captive to the beauties of nature, he paints the spring with a gracefulness of imagination and a freshness of drawing which have not yet become antiquated.' Often when the mood takes him, a delicate sentiment of harmony suggests to him that regular coupling together of feminine and masculine rhymes which was an elegance of style before it became a rule of versification.

Henry Martin says that the consolations which he sought in letters have served to render his name second only to those of Thibault de Champagne and of our most celebrated *trouvères*. The prolonged weariness of captivity had developed in him, observes the same writer, a poetic talent which, though wanting in power, was distinguished by a melancholy sweetness of grace. I must cite one more passage from that well-known ballad which he addressed 'To Fortune :'

> Fortune, veuillez-moi laisser
> En paix une fois, je vous prie.
> Trop longuement, à vrai conter,
> Avez eu sur moi seigneurie.
> Toujours faite la renchérie
> Vers moi et ne voulez ouïr
> Les maux que m'avez fait souffrir,
> Il y a jà plusieurs ans passés,
> Dois-je toujours ainsi languir ?
> Hélas ! et n'est-ce pas assez ?

I forbear from quoting any of the English poetry of Charles d'Orléans because the language in which it was written is much further removed from that of Shakespeare than is that of his French compositions from the language of Moliere.

> Villon sut le premier dans ces siècles grossiers
> Débrouiller l'art confus de nos vieux romanciers.

It was in these terms that Boileau, the arbiter of Parnassus, spoke of the poet whom we have now to consider.

Villon was the most remarkable as well as the earliest of the poets belonging to the epoch at which we have just arrived. A student at the University of Paris, a wild roysterer, a reckless ne'er-do-well, a brawler, a libertine, and, it is to be feared, a thief, he was the first to fling aside the chivalrous gallantry, the metaphysical abstractions, and the dreary allegories imitated from the 'Roman de la Rose.' In short, Villon was the first who drew his poetry from himself: the first to write in a style that was vivid, original, and French; and who went to the people itself as the true source of the national muse. That which especially distinguishes his poetry is that it is a mixture of light-hearted gaiety, of sardonic sarcasm, of frolicsome waggery, satirical and clownish sallies, of delicate grace, and of a melancholy that is always touching. Many of his verses are still quoted. Who does not know that tender poem on the beautiful women of bygone days, that charming ballad on the fragility of their destinies, with its pathetic refrain, *Mais où sont les neiges d'antan ?*[1]

I cannot deny myself the pleasure of quoting that delicious composition, because I am sure it will give my hearers pleasure:

[1] *Ante-annum.*

> Dites-moi où, en quel pays,
> Est Flora, la belle Romaine,
> Archipiada, ni Thaïs
> Qui fut sa cousine germaine ;
> Echo, parlant quand bruit on mène
> Dessus rivière ou sur étang,
> Qui beauté eut trop plus qu'humaine ?
> Mais où sont les neiges d'antan ?
>
> Où est la très sage Héloïs,
> Pour qui fut blessé et puis moine
> Pierre Abélard, à St. Denis ?
> Pour son amour eut cette essoine [malheur].
> Semblablement où est la reine
> Qui commanda que Buridan
> Fût jeté, en un sac, en Seine ?
> Mais où sont les neiges d'antan ?
>
> La Reine Blanche comme un lys,
> Qui chantait à voix de sirène ;
> Berthe aux grands pieds, Biétrix, Allis,
> Eremburges qui tint le Maine,
> Et Jeanne la bonne Lorraine,
> Qu'Anglais brulèrent à Rouen ?
> Où sont-ils, vierge souveraine ?
> Mais où sont les neiges d'antan ?

Sainte-Beuve has devoted to this remarkable ballad so eloquent a page, and one so powerfully impressed by that poetry of feeling which inspired the original, that I need not apologise for translating it in full:

'We re-read and re-read aloud the entire piece. . . . Happy is he who has thus known how to find an accent for an immortal and perpetually renewed situation of human nature. He may live, perchance, as long as itself, as long, at least, as the nature and the language in which he has uttered that cry of genius and sentiment. Evermore, when the question arises of the rapidity with which generations of mankind pass away, resembling, as old Homer says, the leaves of the forest; evermore, when one considers the brief duration assigned to the noblest and most triumphant destinies; but, above all, when the mind reverts to those smiling and fugitive images of vanished beauty, from Helen to Ninon; to those transient groups which seem to be swept into the abyss, one after another, in the light whirl of a dance; to the women of the Decameron, of the Heptameron, of the fêtes of Venice, or of the court of Ferrara; and to the cavalcades of Diana (the Diana of Henry II.), who animated the gallant hunting parties of Anet, Chambord, or Fontainebleau ; when we call up the period of the pompous, of the tender rivals who encircled the youth of Louis XIV. as with a garland—

> Ces belles Montbazons, ces Chatillons brillantes,
> Dansant avec Louis sous des berceaux de fleurs ;

when, nearer to us still, although already distant, we recall the name which had such a fresh and pleasant sound in our youth, the then queens of elegance, the Juliets, the Hortenses, and then the Delphines, the Elviras, and the Lisettes of the poets; and when one asks, with a touch of sadness, 'Where are they?' what more natural or more appropriate response arises to our lips than the tuneful refrain which has found its way to every tongue, 'Mais où sont les neiges d'antan?'

An exquisite image of mutability, it must be allowed; and yet one that has been excelled by the incomparable lines of the poet-peasant of Scotland:

> Like the snow-falls in the river,
> A moment white, then melts for ever.

The pretty trifle which follows conceals beneath the playfulness of its form the same tender melancholy, which the poet has so freely infused into the verses I have already quoted, and, indeed, into his works in general. It bears the individual impress of his genius:

> Je congnois bien mouches en laict;
> Je congnois à la robe l'homme;
> Je congnois le beau temps du laid;
> Je congnois au pommier la pomme;
> Je congnois l'arbre à voir la gomme;
> Je congnois quand tout est de mesme;
> Je congnois qui besongne ou chomme;
> Je congnois tout, fors que moy-mesme;
>
> Je congnois pourpoinct au collet;
> Je congnois le moine à la gonne [robe];
> Je congnois le maistre au valet;
> Je congnois au voyle la nonne;
> Je congnois quant piqueur jargonne;
> Je congnois folz nourriz de cresme;
> Je congnois le vin à la tonne;
> Je congnois tout, fors que moy-mesme.
>
> ENVOI
>
> Prince, je congnois tout en somme;
> Je congnois coulorez et blesmes;
> Je congnois mort qui nous consomme;
> Je congnois tout, fors que moy-mesme.

Commenting on these charming lines, Nisard extols the 'neatness of the idea, the vivacity of form, the force of expression, and the deep yet sportive philosophy' they disclose, 'all which,' he observes, 'are superior to the careless facility of Charles d'Orléans. What acquisitions,' he exclaims, ' for the French intellect, and for our poetical language !'

Villon was a Bohemian of the Bohemians, a literary Ishmaelite of the fifteenth century, a Guzman d'Alfarache, doubled by a poet. His real name was Montcordier. His father died when he was a mere child ; his mother was quite illiterate ; and a kind-hearted priest took the poor boy by the hand, sent him to school, and paid his fees at the University of Paris. The priest's name—all honour to his sterling goodness—was Guillaume de Villon, and the young student adopted it in preference to his own. At college François was the gayest of the gay, the wildest of the wild ; foremost in all the practical jokes and boisterous fun that youth and high spirits prompted the students at that period, as of every other, to indulge in. In old Paris there were blocks of stone at convenient intervals, by the aid of which ladies used to mount their palfreys, at a time when carriages were almost unknown. By way of frolic, Villon and his companions removed two of these to what were then known as Mont St. Hilaire and the Montagne Ste. Geneviève. The *sergents de ville* laboriously carried them back again, but the collegians once more transported them to those eminences, danced round them to the merry music of a flute, and celebrated a grotesque marriage between the two blocks of stone.

Another of the freaks of these rollicking youngsters was to detach the large flesh hooks from the butchers' stalls, and to take down and conceal the signs which then hung in front of all manner of shops. One day—it was on June 5, 1455, that being the Fête-Dieu—Villon was conversing with a priest named Gilles and a pretty woman named Isabeau— for, being a poet, he admired pretty women—when another priest, named Philippe Sermoise, came up and picked a quarrel with him. From high words they came to blows, and Sermoise stuck Villon across the mouth with his dagger. The poet picked up a stone and knocked his assailant down. The latter fell so heavily on the pavement as to produce concussion of the brain, from the effects of which he died next day. Villon was tried, convicted of murder, and sentenced to be hanged ; and it was then that the poet wrote the verses beginning :

> Je suis François, dont ce me poise,
> Né de Paris emprès Pontoise,
> Qui d'une corde d'une toise
> Saura, etc., etc.

His sentence was commuted to banishment for life, but with the help of his good friend the priest, who had grown to be very fond of the scapegrace, Villon hid himself in one of the most disreputable purlieus of Paris, and there he enrolled himself in a band of thieves calling themselves *Les Coquillarts*, nearly a thousand strong, owning allegiance to a chief whom they called the King of La Coquille, and having laws and a secret language, or jargon, of their own. Villon not only mastered this argot, but he wrote seven ballads in it. Sad to relate, two of the poet's dearest friends in this band, Regnier de Montigny and Colin de Cayeux, were hanged! Probably he would have shared the same fate, if strong interest had not been used to procure his pardon for killing the priest; for, when this had been obtained, Villon was enabled to return to civilised society; and the good old priest, who held that a true Christian should forgive his erring brother until seventy times seven, received the outlaw and prodigal with open arms, and killed the fatted calf for his better entertainment.

What did the poet do next? He fell in love with a young lady in prosperous circumstances, named Catherine de Vaulselles, who rather discouraged the attentions of the penniless scamp and poet; and one evening her guardian gave Villon such a cudgelling that he went back home with a sore heart and sorer shoulders, to meditate on all the great men of antiquity who had been similarly crossed in love, though not, perhaps, similarly beaten. Towards the end of 1456 he quitted Paris very abruptly. I am sorry to say he had fallen in with some of his old companions, the Coquillarts, and they and he broke into the sacristy of the College of Navarre and stole a coffer containing 500 golden crowns. One-fifth of the booty fell to the share of Villon, who fled from Paris and afterwards turned up at Blois, where he took part in a sort of poetical tournament instituted by the Duke of Bourbon, who gave, as the theme of a competitive ballad, the words, 'Je meurs de soif auprès de la fontaine.' We next find him in prison at Blois, probably for theft

But there was a gaol delivery in honour of Marie de Clèves having given a daughter to her husband, and Villon was liberated with the rest. After many wanderings we meet with him again as a prisoner at Meung-sur-Loire; but, as good luck would have it, Louis XI. passed through there, on his way back from his coronation, and once more the gaol doors were flung open, and the poet crept back to Paris after an absence of five years, still young, according to the calendar, but old in constitution. And there stood the dear old priest, in the cloister of St. Benoit, with a sweet smile on his angelic face, and words of love and tenderness, compassion and forgiveness, on his aged lips. Villon is believed to have died about 1489, and is supposed to have been, at the time, a member of a strolling company for whom he had written a Passion play in the dialect of Poitou, and to have taken part in the performance of it. With all his faults, his heart was as tender as that of a little child, and his character singularly sweet and pious. Strange medley of qualities! Who shall solve the enigma of such a nature and of such a life?

We learn from the cynical admissions of the poet himself that he was a man of many vocations; but one day, in the midst of those ignominies, which only served to furnish matter for his merriment, there broke from him an accent of genuine patriotism, and he launched against the enemies of ' French honour ' a ballad whose energetic refrain still finds an echo in the hearts of his countrymen. He bans and brands, through the whole gamut of malediction, those 'who wish evil to the realm of France.' 'A strange thing,' it has been observed, ' that at a time, above all, when the patriotic sentiment was still so rare, there was at least one Frenchman, and he a regular vagabond, who had neither hearth nor home.'

As I have already said, Villon was a student of the University, but a Bohemian of Bohemians, of whose wild life he has left an animated record in his ' Free Feeds.' The epithet lives, and so does the thing itself; yes, and the author of the poems likewise. There are always Villons in the world, although few of them possess his genius. To eat, drink, and be merry, at the expense of other people; to incur debts without the expectation or intention of ever paying them; to laugh at duns and break a jest upon importunate creditors; to live from hand to mouth, and never to deny himself a single pleasure that could be procured at anybody else's cost: these were Villon's rules of conduct, and they are those of scores of gentlemanly fellows at the present moment in every great city in Europe, America, and Australia.

St. Marc Girardin says that if Villon had lived in our days he would have been as fond of good cheer as ever he was, but that he would have been an honest man. Nothing of the sort. He would probably have thrown an air of refinement over his swindling propensities, and sipped champagne and eaten truffles in a sumptuous hotel, leaving behind him a portmanteau full of bricks in satisfaction of his credulous landlord's bill, instead of cheating the keeper of a wine shop or of a *cabaret*, as the earlier Jeremy Diddler did; but François Villon would be the same man, *au fond*, at the end of the nineteenth century that he was in the second half of the fifteenth.

Irrespective of his ballads, this roystering poet wrote two other pieces: 'The Little Testament,' in 1456, which contained his farewell and his legacies to his friends; and his 'Great Testament,' composed in the maturity of his powers and of his life, and comprising a long succession of satirical bequests, more or less autobiographical in character, and reflecting, as in a mirror, the wayward moods and variable emotions of his highly gifted but perversely erratic mind. He is by turns remorseful and tender, savage and pathetic, a penitent in the confessional and a satirical jester in his cap and bells. Sometimes his strains are those of a lyric poet, delicately touching in sentiment, as in the following bequest:

> Item, donne à ma bonne mère,
> Pour saluer notre maîtresse,
> Qui pour moi eut douleur amère,
> Dieu le sait, et mainte tristesse;
> Autre château ou forteresse
> N'ai où retraire corps et âme
> Quand sur moi court male détresse,
> Ni ma mère, pauvre femme!

There is only one poem in the English language characterised by such an extraordinary versatility of thought and style, by such a strange mixture of seriousness with merriment, by such an amalgam of gold, silver, and clay, by such pathos and buffoonery, as the 'Great Testament;' and that is the 'Don Juan' of Lord Byron. But in his pensive and sombre reflections on a past which can never return, on the brevity of our mortal life, and on the fugitive character of earthly greatness and of earthly glory, Villon reminds us by turns of Bossuet, of Hamlet in the graveyard at Elsinore, and of Thomas Gray moralising among the little green mounds beneath which 'the rude forefathers of the hamlet sleep.' Listen to the French poet discoursing

SUR LA MORT.

Quand je considère ces têtes
Entassées en ces charniers ;
Tous furent maîtres des requêtes,
Ou tous de la chambre aux deniers,
Ou tous furent porte-paniers :
Autant puis l'un que l'autre dire ;
Car d'évêques ou lanterniers,
Je n'y connais rien à redire.[1]

Et icelles qui s'inclinaient
Unes contre autres dans leurs vies ;
Desquelles les unes régnaient,
Des autres craintes et servies ;
Là les vois, toutes assouvies
Ensemble en un tas pêle-mêle,
Seigneuries leurs sont ravies :
Clerc ni maître ne s'y appelle.

De pauvreté me guermentant,[2]
Souventes fois me dit le cœur :
Homme, ne te doulouse tant,
Et ne démène tel douleur,
Si tu n'as tant que Jaques Cœur :
Mieux vaut vivre, sous gros bureaux [3]
Pauvre, qu'avoir été seigneur,
Et pourrir sous riches tombeaux.[4]

Mon père est mort, Dieu en ait l'âme,
Quant est du corps, il gît sous lame :[5]

---

[1] Je ne saurais faire la distinction.   [2] Plaignant.   [3] Gros-drap.
[4] Lafontaine a exprimé cette pensée de Villon par cette phrase qui a passé en proverbe: *Mieux vaut goujat debout qu'Empereur enterré*, et vous avez en Anglais un proverbe qui pourrait bien aussi être tiré de là : 'A live dog is better than a dead lion.'
[5] Tombeau.

J'entends que ma mère mourra ;
Et le sait bien la pauvre femme :
Et son fils pas ne demourra.

Je connais que pauvres et riches,
Sages et fous, prêtres et lais,[1]
Noble et vilain, larges et chiches,
Petits et grands, et beaux et laids,
Dames à rebrassés collets,[2]
De quelconque condition,
Portant atours et bourrelets,
Mort saisit sans exception.[3]

Et meure Paris et Hélène !
Quiconque meurt, meurt à douleur,[4]
Celui qui perd vent et haleine,
Son fiel se crève sur son cœur,
Puis sent Dieu sait quelle sueur !
Et n'est de ses maux qui l'afflige ;
Car enfants n'a, frère ni sœur,
Qui lors voulut être son piège.[5]

La mort le fait frémir, pâlir,
Le nez courber, les veines tendre,
Le col enfler, la chair mollir,
Jointes et nerfs, croître et étendre.
Corps féminin, qui tout es tendre,
Poli, suave, si gracieux,
Te faudra-t-il ces maux attendre ?
Oui, ou tout vif aller aux cieux.

We have now arrived at a period of transition in the literary history of France. The Middle Ages are disappearing, and the Renaissance is about to impress the stamp of beauty upon all our intellectual productions. But before quitting the arid epoch of which I have been offering an imperfect study, I will take a passing glance at those writers who, from the middle of the eleventh century, and expressing themselves in a language becoming less and less barbarous, have been the pioneers of the route along which we shall henceforth travel, without further hindrances or impedi-

---

[1] Laïques.   [2] Hauts collets plissés.
[3] Dans ce passage encore Villon devance Shakespeare, qui a exprimé une pensée analogue dans les deux vers suivants :

'Golden lads and girls all must,
As chimney sweepers, come to dust.'

[4] Avec douleur.   [5] Sa caution.

ments. When we take into consideration all the virile poetry embodied in the 'Chansons de Geste' of the first two cycles; when, among our early chroniclers, one recognises so much vigour of style, and such a comprehensive treatment of the subjects taken up; when we come to admire, in those poets of the thirteenth, fourteenth, and fifteenth centuries, of which Charles d'Orléans and Villon close the list, the ideas, thoughts, sentiments, and originality which they disclose; may we not reasonably ask ourselves whether men like these might not have made of our French literature, many centuries earlier, that which it became in the sixteenth and seventeenth, if only the imperfect instrument of which they availed themselves in their time had been as refined as that of which their more fortunate successors were able to take advantage?

The multiplication of books in France in the sixteenth century, coinciding with the unification of the kingdom, naturally communicated a powerful impulse to letters and led to the creation of a national literature. Thenceforth books were no longer considered as articles of luxury, but became objects of necessity. They passed from the château and the monastery into the sitting-room of the middle-class citizen and the workshop of the artisan. The sun of knowledge, which had hitherto shone only upon the eminences of society, began to flood the valleys with its golden light. It was like Moses descending from the heights of Mount Sinai with the glow of inspiration enveloping his illuminated figure.

Let us take a rapid survey of the literary productiveness of the period which intervened between the 'Great Testament' of Villon, in 1461, and the earliest writings of Clément Marot, in 1515. Guillaume Cretin, whose real name was Dubois, satirised by Rabelais under the epithet of Raminagrobis, wrote, at the request of Francis I., twelve books of rhymed chronicles, beginning with the siege of Troy and coming down to the Carlovingian kings of France. George Chastelain, the friend and 'pantler' of Duke Philip the Good, was both a poet and the chronicler of the House of Burgundy. Of his best work, containing his reminiscences of his own time, only three fragments have come down to us. He was succeeded as historiographer to that ducal family by Jean Molinet, who was librarian to Margaret of Austria. He was a facile writer, both of prose and verse, but destitute of imagination. He was the first, I believe, to introduce double rhymes at the end of his verses: a grotesque fancy so humorously caricatured by Hood in the following lines:

> Nursemaid in a night-mare rest chest pressed
> Dreameth of one of her old flames, James Games,
> And that she hears—what faith is man's !—Ann's Banns
> And his from Reverend Mr. Rice, twice, thrice;
> White ribbons flourish and a stout shout out
> That upward goes shows Rose knows those bows' woes!

Jean Maschinot, who seems to have been court poet to the Dukes of Brittany, is chiefly known by a collection of twenty-five ballads, called the 'Lunettes des Princes,' and was very fond of throwing his verses into extremely fantastic forms. His early years were spent in splendour, and his declining days in comparative poverty. Guillaume Alexis is referred to in terms of praise by Sainte-Beuve; and Martial de Paris, better known as Martial d'Auvergne, is spoken of by the Abbé Goujet as one of the ablest writers in the second half of the fifteenth century. His 'Vigiles de la Mort du Roi Charles VII.,' narrating the principal events of his reign in verse, had an immense vogue at the time it was written. Nor must I omit to mention Guillaume Coquillart, who is believed to have been a native of Reims, and wrote a poem on the entry of Charles VIII. into that city on the occasion of his coronation. The poet is reported to have lost his fortune at the game of *morre* (the game still played in Italy as *morra*), an incident commemorated by Clément Marot in a punning quatrain.

Jean Marot, whose real name was Desmaret, was secretary to Anne of Brittany, wife of Louis XII., and acquired some distinction at her court as a poet; but his reputation was cast into the shade by that of his son, just as the celebrity of Bernardo Tasso was eclipsed by the fame of the illustrious Torquato. Jean le Maire, the instructor of Clément Marot, and gentleman of the chamber to Louis XIII., was not only an accomplished versifier, but a master of many languages, arts, and sciences; and his ideas and inventive faculties were greatly in advance of the age in which he lived. There were also two poets of the name of Saint-Gelais, Octavian and Mellin, father and son, or uncle and nephew—it is uncertain which. The elder was an elegant writer, if a dissolute ecclesiastic. Besides composing some amorous poetry, he translated the 'Æneid' of Virgil and the 'Epistles' of Ovid into French; and, having been appointed Bishop of Angoulême, he renounced the dissolute pleasures of the court of Charles VIII., and devoted himself to the discharge of his episcopal duties. Mellin de Saint-Gelais, educated at the University of Padua, was a man of various gifts and of an estimable character. Music, poetry, philosophy, astrology, and the Greek, Latin, and Italian classics equally engaged his attention. Francis I. gave him the Abbey of Reclus, and Henry II. made him librarian at Fontainebleau. The sweetness of his disposition endeared him to all his friends, and when the hour of his death arrived, and his physicians were hotly arguing about the nature of his malady, he smilingly remarked, 'Gentlemen, I will relieve you from this difficulty,' and turning his face to the wall he breathed his last.

Before proceeding to speak of Clément Marot, who was the first poet of the Renaissance, and of Marguerite d'Angoulême, who was its first romance writer, I must not omit to say something of two famous *savants*—Guillaume Budé and his friend and rival, the learned Erasmus. The former, who induced Francis I. to found the College of France, was the greatest Hellenist of his time. He wrote Greek with equal ease and elegance; and Erasmus designated him 'The Prodigy of France.' His erudition was vast as well as varied, and his devotion to study was so ardent and absorbing that when his servant came to tell him his house was on fire, he calmly remarked, 'Go and tell my wife; you know it is no business of mine.'

Although Erasmus was a Dutchman by birth, we may regard him as a Frenchman by adoption; he spent so many years in Paris, and was so thoroughly French in character. Most of his writings relate to theological questions, and the subject is one so provocative of controversy that I prefer to pass over it in silence. But his influence on the literature of the sixteenth century was so great, and the part he played in the revival of a love for the great masters of antiquity was so important, that he will always stand out as one of the beacon lights of his century. His 'Eloge de la Folie' created a prodigious sensation at the time of its first appearance, and it is still an historical document of the highest value, as enabling us to comprehend the condition of Europe at that epoch, besides being an almost incomparable example of the finest raillery.

LECTURE V

Clément Marot (1495–1544)—Marguerite de Valois (1492–1549)—Mellin de Saint-Gelais (1491–1558)—Joachim du Bellay (1524–1560).

I DEVOTE this chapter to the study of the writers known as the literary *Pléiade* of the sixteenth century, of which Joachim du Bellay was the organiser and Ronsard the most brilliant star, but before doing so I must speak of Clément Marot and must add something to what I have already said of Mellin de Saint-Gelais.

Clément Marot, born at Cahors in 1495, was one of the most striking and picturesque figures of a picturesque epoch. Liberally educated, he began life as page to the Seigneur de Villeroy, and was promoted to be one of the gentlemen in waiting on Marguerite d'Angoulême, 'the pearl of the Valois.' He accompanied her brother, Francis I., on his disastrous expedition into Italy, and, like him, was wounded and made prisoner at the battle of Pavia. Obtaining his release, he returned to France, where the freedom of his religious ideas led to his being accused of heresy and thrown into the prison of the Châtelet, and the rest of his life reflected some of the most characteristic aspects of the period. It was a period in which society and those who governed it tolerated, in both men and women, the utmost licence of conduct; and the more brilliant the sinner, the more indulgent his judges, but woe to those who dared to think for themselves upon any question of faith or religious practice. To break one of the Ten Commandments was a venial offence, but to dispute an article of belief or to doubt a dogma was an unpardonable crime. In his poem entitled 'L'Enfer' Marot tells us that he was denounced by a young lady to whom he was tenderly attached, because he had been guilty of the enormous crime of eating some bacon in Lent! At the

same time, he says that if he were to describe the depraved
life of the monastic orders he could scarcely hope to escape
the scaffold or the stake. At one time, while residing in
Ferrara, which was then a place of refuge for all who had
the audacity to think for themselves, Pope Paul III. induced
the Duke to expel the poor poet who was suspected of
heresy. From Ferrara Marot proceeded to Venice; and
Francis I., extending his protection to his old comrade in
arms, invited him to return to the court of France; for the
king entertained a great predilection for the joyous humour,
the careless gaiety, and the large-hearted tolerance of the
much-abused poet, whose destiny appeared to be to fall
under the ban of the Sorbonne. And he did so, once again.
Struck by the beauty and the religious fervour of the Psalms
of David, he translated those noble compositions from the
original Hebrew into French. His ecclesiastical enemies
scented heresy in this new version of the sublime language
of the Shepherd King, and the book was suppressed by
royal authority! In order to evade pursuit, Marot once
more became an exile and found an asylum in Geneva; but
even here he was not allowed to rest. Wherever he went
and whatever he did, the imputation of heresy followed him
and clung to him like the poisoned shirt of Nessus. This
time it was the austere Calvinists who frowned upon him.
They did more. They denounced him as abandoned by
heaven and guilty of a deadly sin. I almost shrink from
declaring the wickedness of our unfortunate poet. Yet I
must conceal nothing. He was in the habit of beguiling his
leisure hours by playing at trictrac—a very harmless game
identical with the 'tables' of which Shakespeare speaks
in 'Love's Labour's Lost,' and resembling the modern
backgammon, I believe. To escape the penal consequences
of this terrible depravity, Clément Marot fled from Geneva,
turning his back upon that diminutive state of which
Voltaire used to say that, when he shook his wig, he powdered
the whole republic. The poet took refuge finally at Turin,
where he died in poverty in the year 1544. The poor poet,
whose chief fault was that he held ideas of religious tolerance
which were 300 years in advance of his time, found rest at
last in the tomb, and his epitaph might have been that which
Macbeth pronounced upon Duncan:

> After life's fitful fever, he sleeps well . . . .
> Malice domestic, foreign levy, nothing,
> Can touch him further.

Marot's place in French poetry is that of a fixed star, even although his brilliancy should be somewhat dimmed in proportion as the age in which he lived recedes farther and farther from the lifetime of each generation. Demogeot has made the felicitous remark that it seemed as if the poetry of the fourteenth and fifteenth centuries, about to be eclipsed by the rising splendour of the Renaissance, had accumulated all its wealth for the endowment of that fortunate hero of the *trouvères*, combining, as he did, the colour of Villon with the naturalness of Froissart, the delicacy of Charles d'Orléans, the good sense of Alain Chartier, and the caustic humour of Jean de Meung. As regards his language, it will be enough to say that Marot edited the works of Villon with explanatory notes, showing that the elder poet was already regarded as somewhat out of date.

After some youthful compositions, in which Marot revived the allegories of the Middle Ages, he surrendered himself entirely to his own fancies. Various *spirituel* and graceful epistles; elegies in which sensibility seasoned the wit; epigrams full of humour and malice—such were the poetical compositions dear to his lighter moods of thought. The language at his command sufficed for his works. For the use of a brilliant court he polished the poetry of the *fabliaux* and availed himself of that decasyllabic verse which seems to have been invented for gay and piquant narratives. The 'Marotic style' is still spoken of in France, but it is one which bad taste has frequently abused. It is permissible to regret, in our own days, the naïve grace of our old phraseology, words which have become obsolete, and some inversions which have fallen into disuse; but, as Marmontel has said, in order to gracefully handle a naïve style one must be naïve oneself. I think I have sufficiently indicated the kind of style which has derived its name from Marot and which La Fontaine has excelled in imitating. In his epigrams Rousseau has left some admirable specimens of the Marotic style. Voltaire has occasionally used it with exquisite taste, appropriate to each subject.

Among the more notable writings of Marot are 'L'Enfer,'

which is a satire against the judiciary; an 'Epître au Roi,' urging him to release him from prison; his translation of the Psalms of David, and quantities of fables and minor poems. Here are three examples of his versification—the first octosyllabic and the other two decasyllabic. In the following he is speaking of a woman who is vainglorious:

> Vous êtes belle, en bonne foi :
> Ceux qui disent que non, sont bêtes.
> Vous êtes riche, je le voi ;
> Qu'est-il besoin d'en faire enquêtes ?
> Vous êtes bien des plus honnêtes ;
> Et qui le nie est bien rebelle.
> Mais quand vous vous louez, vous n'êtes
> Honnête, ni riche, ni belle.

In the next the poet solicits a loan from his royal protector, on account of the dishonesty of his own valet:

> J'avais un jour un valet, de Gascogne,
> Gourmand, ivrogne, et assuré menteur,
> Pipeur, larron, jureur, blasphémateur,
> Sentant la hart de cent pas à la ronde ;
> *Au demeurant, le meilleur fils du monde.*

Our poet combined wit with elegance, and the French language contains nothing more piquant, naïve, and dexterous than the epistle to the king in which Marot solicits a loan by implication rather than by direct request. I must quote a few lines of this adroit production :

> Je ne dis pas, si voulez rien prester ;
> Que ne le prenne. Il n'est point de presteur,
> S'il veut prester, qui ne fasse un debteur.
> Et sçavez-vous, Sire, comment je paye ?
> Nul ne le sçait si premier, ne l'essaye.
> Vous me debvrez, si je puis, du retour.
> Et vous feray encores un bon tour
> A celle fin qu'il n'y ait faulte nulle,
> Et vous feray une belle sédulle
> A vous payer, sans usure s'entend,
> Quand on veoirra tout le monde content :
> Ou si voulez, à payer ce sera
> Quand vostre los et renom cessera.

The life led by our poet rendered it indispensable that he should make frequent demands for money upon his protectors, his friends, and people generally ; and in a reply to Margaret he thus pleasantly alludes to his financial embarrassments·

> Mes créanciers, qui de dizains n'ont cure,
> Ont lu le vôtre ; et sur ce, leur ai dit :
> ' Sire Michel, Sire Bonaventure,
> La sœur du roi a pour moi fait ce dit.'
> Lors eux, croyant que fusse en grand crédit,
> M'ont appelé *Monsieur* à cri et cor,
> Et m'a valu votre écrit autant qu'or ;
> Car promis ont non-seulement d'attendre,
> Mais d'en prêter, foi de marchand, encor ;
> Et j'ai promis, foi de Clément, d'en prendre.

To a lady, who inquired if he had burnt a certain letter, as she had begged him to do, Marot wrote in reply :

> Aucune fois au feu je la mettais
> Pour la brûler, puis soudain l'en ôtais,
> Puis la remis, et puis l'en reculai ;
> Mais à la fin, à regret—la brûlai,
> Disant :—ô lettre !—après l'avoir baisée,
> Puisqu'il le faut, tu seras embrasée ;
> Car j'aime mieux deuil en obéissant
> Que tout plaisir en désobéissant.

These agreeable pleasantries expressed with so much grace justify the opinion on Marot pronounced by La Harpe. Certainly there is something in that poet which we do not find either in Charles d'Orléans or in Villon. The lady to whom he addressed the verses just quoted was no less a personage 'than the king's' sister, to whom he gave the name of 'Sister in Poetry; ' and to Francis I. himself Marot offered one of his earliest compositions, ' Le Temple de Cupidon,' into which the poet introduced the old mythological personages which had been such favourites with his predecessors. They breathe the same atmosphere of gallantry, and they have the same allegorical names, but a new life has been infused into them by the vivid imagination of the poet, and they are less mannered and less artificial than the exceedingly unreal men and women, or rather personified abstractions, so dear to the hearts of earlier versifiers. Bel Accueil, in a green robe, officiates as porter to the Temple of Cupid, of which Beau-Parler, Beau-Aimer, and Beau-Servir are its joyous and right glorious patrons ; and the Amorous Pilgrim adroitly evades Refus, who is walking in the nave, and by favour of Bel Accueil glides into the choir where Ferme Amour is to be found reposing.

There must have been something very fascinating about these allegories to both writers and readers in those days, not in France alone, but in England, for do we not find Edmund Spenser towards the end of the same century creating his 'House of Holiness' and his 'House of Alma,' and Bunyan, a hundred years afterwards, taking us into the 'House of the Interpreter' and the 'City of Mansoul,' and James Thomson building for us 'The Castle of Indolence' in the first half of the eighteenth century?

Sainte-Beuve does not hesitate to dwell at some length upon Marot's 'Temple of Cupid,' not only because it is the longest of his poems, but because he has also lavished on it such a wealth of imagination. Yet he declines to credit the poet with the possession of genius, inasmuch as 'he had not one of those vigorous talents which place a man in advance of his age and equip him with wings to outstrip it.'

The critic seems disposed, indeed, to take a disparaging view of one whom an English writer has styled 'the greatest poet, in some points, that France ever had;' whose elegance, lucidity, and grace were the admiration of the writers of the seventeenth century, and in whom, as a recent French critic has said, 'Racine and Boileau were contained as Ronsard was in Victor Hugo.' Nor should it be forgotten that Boileau himself has bracketed his name with that of three immortals in the line:

Arioste, Marot, Boccace, Rabelais.

'If his mind had taken a more ambitious aim,' observes Sainte-Beuve, 'there is reason to believe that he might have winged his flight somewhat earlier than Ronsard did towards those poetic heights, as yet inaccessible, which Malherbe had the honour of being the first to reach and to retain. Happily for Marot, his intellect was better suited to the mediocrity of the times. In poetry as in other respects, taking life easily, and prompt to enjoy, he derived something from all he found, without any regrets and without discerning what he wished. One likes to see him taking things easily amidst so many troubles, and in that perfect harmony between the man and his surroundings we recognise the poet of his age *par excellence*.... Having been a page at court, he acquired in his intercourse with the great that delicacy to which Villon was a stranger.... Most of the minor kinds of poetry embraced by our literature found an echo in him without the effort of invention, and with all the charm of their primitive simplicity. The familiar epistle, the epigram, the story, and the song sparkle often with an original grace which has not suffered effacement. And if we are not mistaken, entirely secondary although these have become, they constituted for a long time the chief, if not the unique, substance of our poetry. For a considerable period they formed the warp and woof of the web, whereof to-day they appear to be only an elegant embroidery, and beneath those thin coverings which age has not yet withered was concealed the germ of nearly all our literary future.'

Marot represents the old French poetry in its greatest purity, and one perceives in him the legitimate and direct descendant of Guillaume de Loris, Jean de Meung, Alain Chartier, and François Villon. With the latter Marot had much in common; like him, he sang of his amours and of his imprisonment, but his amours were more delicate and his imprisonment more honourable. 'Marot,' said Nisard, 'is Villon rescued from poverty, Villon at court, page to a king, and valet de chambre to a queen. Villon and Marot were both poets sprung from the people.'

The lady to whom Marot addressed the epistle previously quoted was no other than Marguerite de Valois, who, in her widowhood, espoused the king of Navarre, and gave birth to Jeanne d'Albret, mother of Henry IV. Her court was the refuge of the independent thinkers of her time; so that the little city of Alençon became another Athens. She saved the life of Calvin, and she protected Marot from the malice of his persecutors. She was the Egeria of her brother Francis I.; and without her, it has been said, the brightest ornaments of the Renaissance in France must have perished at the stake of the Inquisition. A singularly accomplished woman, she had mastered Greek and Hebrew, and could converse with equal facility in French, Italian, Spanish, German, and English. She was more than suspected of heresy, because she hated ignorance, fanaticism, and intolerance with all the strength of her generous nature; and when she wrote her mystical poem entitled 'The Mirror of the Sinful Soul,' the Sorbonne included it in the Index Expurgatorius. Living in an age of loose morals and dissolute manners, she preserved 'the white flower of a blameless life' unspotted from the world. All that can be urged against her is, that some of the stories in her 'Heptameron' were tainted by the grossness of the time. But it must be remembered they were written to beguile the weary hours of Francis I. when stretched upon a bed of sickness, and that something had to be conceded to the licentious tastes of her royal brother. In extenuation of their faults, let it be borne in mind that the ideal standard of religion and virtue which was set up in them was higher than that of the period, and that they asserted the rights of conscience at a time when no little moral courage was required on the part of any one, however highly placed, who dared to breathe a word against bigotry and persecution.

Her 'Heptameron,' if not a masterpiece of French literature, is a work which did much to form and fix the language in which it is written; and, as M. Nisard has said, 'it is the first prose composition that one can read without the aid of a vocabulary.' Its title and its idea were obviously borrowed from the 'Decameron' of Boccaccio; but its execution was quite original. Other writers towards the middle of the fifteenth century had been similarly indebted to the Italian story-teller, thus reclaiming from Italy the loans which its writers of fiction had borrowed from our *fabliaux*; but they were destitute of that liveliness of manner and that gift of clear and facile expression which Marguerite of Valois enjoyed. Her narratives cannot be recommended for perusal in our day, in spite of the dictum of Nisard that 'decency without prudery constitutes their original feature and their charm.' After the lapse of three centuries, the French language has no other words for the same ideas, and we can comprehend the agreeable writer of the 'Heptameron,' just as we comprehend our contemporaries. With it commences the history of our prose literature. Her poetry is of a mediocre character; and her best title to our esteem rests upon the work just mentioned, and upon her correspondence, mainly consisting of letters to her brother.

Of Mellin de Saint-Gelais I have already spoken in connection with the older poet of the same name; but chronologically his place is here, for he died in 1558. He may be regarded as one of the best poets of the school of Marot. By M. Viollet-le-Duc he is characterised as the first epigrammatic writer in France. Here are some of his productions:

A UN POËTE VANTARD

Tu te plains, ami, grandement,
Qu'en mes vers j'ai loué Clément,[1]
Et que je n'ai rien dit de toi :
Comment veux-tu que je m'amuse
A louer ni toi, ni ta muse ?
Tu le fais cent fois mieux que moi.

And here is a small piece entitled 'Folie,' which was then synonymous with epigram :

Notre Vicaire, un jour de fête.
Chantait un Agnus gringotté,[2]
Tant qu'il pouvait, à pleine tête,
Pensant d'Annette être écouté.
Annette, de l'autre côté,
Pleurait, attentive à son chant ;
Donc le Vicaire, en s'approchant,
Lui dit : Pourquoi pleurez-vous, Belle ?
Ah ! Messire Jean, ce dit-elle,
Je pleure un âne qui m'est mort,
Qui avait la voix toute telle
Que vous, quand vous criez si fort.

Of the writers who succeeded Marot and Saint-Gelais, and who chose verse as the vehicle for the expression of their thoughts, only a passing mention need be made, for they were merely poetasters. Etienne Dolet, the great printer, who was hanged and his body burned, for no other offence that that of having faithfully translated a passage which Plato puts into the mouth of Socrates, is not remembered by any of his writings but by the *jeu de mots* which he uttered on the way to the scaffold :

Non dolet ipse Dolet, sed pia turba dolet.

('It is not Dolet who grieves, but the sympathetic crowd.') Passing over Thomas Sibilet, Jacques Gohorry, Pelletier du Mans, and Etienne Pasquier, we pause for a moment at the name of Victor Brodeau, whom Marot spoke of as his intellectual child, and of whom the elder poet has preserved the following stanza addressed to two minor friars :

[1] Marot. [2] Twittering.

> Mes beaux pères religieux,
> Vous disnez pour un grand merci.
> Ô gens heureux! Ô demi-dieux!
> Plust à Dieu que je fusse ainsi!
> Comme vous, vivrai sans sousci;
> Car le vœu qui l'argent vous oste,
> Il est clair qu'il défend aussi
> Que ne payez jamais vostre hoste.

Of Louise Labé, the beautiful ropemaker of Lyons, I shall have occasion to speak hereafter; and it may be remarked, in passing, that the same city produced Maurice Scève, one of the most versatile men of his time. An advocate by profession, he was also a poet, musician, painter, architect, and antiquary; his poems winning for him the enthusiastic praises of Marot, Dolet, and Du Bellay.

Towards the close of the reign of Francis I. (1547), there was a lull in the poetical productiveness of France, which seemed to revive on the accession of his successor, Henry II., who was fond of letters and even cultivated them. Mellin de Saint-Gelais, the friend of Marot, was his almoner, and his titular poet was François Hubert, the disciple of both, and the translator of the 'Metamorphoses' of Ovid. Meanwhile the French language was gaining ground, thanks in no small degree to the influence and authority of the late king, who had commanded it to be taught by the professors of the College of France, and had upon all occasions lent it the weight of his sanction. Guillaume Budé, in his old age, had applied himself to write the 'Institution du Prince' in the vernacular; and the classic languages of antiquity no longer monopolised the exclusive devotion of scholars.

Before taking final leave of the reign of Francis I., I must just glance at a few of its literary celebrities, in addition to those already touched upon. Among these was Lazare de Baïf, who translated the 'Electra' of Sophocles, and the 'Hercules' of Euripides, into French verse; Guillaume Cop, one of the restorers of the science of medicine in France, and the translator of the works of the most illustrious Greek practitioners; Jean Ruel, physician, botanist, and canon of Notre-Dame, whose translations from the Greek and Latin caused Bishop Huet to style him 'the eagle of interpreters;' and last, but not least, Jean Grolier, a name dear to the heart of every book-collector, at once the father and the prince of French *bibliophiles*, a scholar and a man of letters, as well as a farmer-general, a foreign ambassador, and a minister of finance under Charles IX. He should never be forgotten, were it only for the device upon his book-plate—*Grolierii et amicorum.*

Towards the close of the fifteenth century, our French *savants* had begun to exhume the literary treasures of antiquity; while, on the other hand, our expeditions into Italy had made us acquainted with Dante, Petrarch, and Boccaccio; and the result of these studies made itself felt at the epoch at which I have now arrived, and of which I must now speak. For a powerful impulse and a novel direction were thus imparted to our poetry by young and enthusiastic men of letters brought up under classic discipline. The savour of our old poets, the elevation of their language, and the nobility of their ideas, were looked upon as pretty nothings by these innovators, who endeavoured to substitute for the naïve and often mannered virelays and rondeaux the masculine beauties of classic compositions.

You will have guessed that I am about to touch upon that association of poets known as the Pléiade, and composed of Ronsard, Daurat, Du Bellay, Remi-Belleau, Baïf the younger, Pontus de Thiard, and Jodelle.

Its manifesto was published by Du Bellay in 1549, under the title of 'The Defence and Illustration of the French Language.' The literary movement thus commenced was prolonged for nearly half a century, under the auspices of Ronsard, its intention having been not only to defend the French language against the attacks and the contempt of the learned men of the epoch, but to show that it was capable of acquiring the very qualities in which it was said to be deficient. Nor can I do better than quote the introduction to Du Bellay's compendious analysis of his own 'Illustration :'

'Languages,' said he, 'do not spring up like plants, some weak and sickly, others healthy and robust. All their virtue lies in the will and determination of mortals. To condemn a language as being struck with impotence is to adopt a tone of arrogance and temerity; as certain of our fellow-countrymen do to-day, who, being nothing less than Greeks or Latins, regard with a more than stoical superciliousness everything written in French. If our language is poorer than the Greek or Latin, this is not attributable to our own inability, but to the ignorance of our own predecessors who have bequeathed it to us in so meagre and so bare a form that it stands in need of ornament, and, so to speak, of plumage from other sources.'

This is the keynote of his argument; and then he goes on to point out that the Greek language was not originally that which it had become in the time of Demosthenes, nor the Latin that which was employed by Cicero in his orations. Thence he proceeds to speak of the unsatisfactory character of all translations from the classic languages of antiquity; especially as regards those compositions which depend for so much of their effect upon the living voice, so that, as he observes, 'when you pass from the text to the translation, you seem to travel from the burning mountain of Etna to the icy summit of Caucasus.' As regards the Greek and Latin poets, he considers that to translate is to betray and profane them. He then makes a remark full of sagacity and practical wisdom. It is as follows: 'The Romans well knew how to enrich their language without applying themselves to the labour of translation. They imitated the best Greek authors, transforming themselves into them, devouring them, and after having well digested them, converting them into blood and tissue. In like manner we must imitate the Greeks and Latins,' and also, he adds, borrow from foreign languages such words and phrases as may be legitimately and advantageously incorporated with the mother tongue. And it is by this means, it may be observed, that the English language has become such a copious and expressive vehicle of thought, having grown by successive accretions from Celtic, Roman, Scandinavian, Norman-French, and other foreign sources, annexing and adopting any word which appeared to be desirable of acquisition and suitable for use.

After observing that, of all our old poets, there are scarcely any but Guillaume de Loris and Jean de Meung who deserve to be read, and these rather out of curiosity than for profit, Du Bellay continues:

> Thou, then, who devotest thyself to the service of the Muses, turn thee to the Greek, Latin, and even Spanish and Italian authors, from whence thou mayest derive a more exquisite form of poetry than from our French authors. In no way trust to the

examples of such of our own as have acquired a great renown, with little or no science; and do not allege that poets are born, for this would be too easy a method of achieving immortality. Therefore read and re-read day and night Greek and Latin models, and leave to me all those old French poems for the Floral Games of Toulouse and the Puy de Rouen, such as rondeaux, ballads, virelays, chants royal, *chansons*, and other suchlike sweetmeats, which corrupt the taste of our language, and only serve to testify to our ignorance.

And so he continues in the same strain, winding up with a recommendation to French poets to select, as Ariosto did, some one of the beautiful old romances in the national literature, such as 'Lancelot' or 'Tristan,' and make it the groundwork of a new 'Iliad' or another 'Æneid.'

This 'Defence,' the only prose work of Du Bellay, constituted in point of fact the programme of the school which made so much noise in the second half of the sixteenth century. 'It was a fierce war which was then undertaken against ignorance,' observes Pasquier in his 'Recherches,' wherein his mind kindles at the recollections of his youth, and in imagination he recalls and depicts Pierre de Ronsard, Ponthus de Thiard, Remi Belleau, Etienne Jodelle, and Jean-Antoine de Baïf, advancing in the order of a brigade and sustaining the brunt of the battle. That brigade is still further reinforced by Jacques Tahureau, Guillaume des Autels, Nicolas Denisot, Louis le Caroud, Olivier de Magny, Jean de la Péruse, Marc-Claude de Buttet, Jean Passerat, Louis des Mesures, and finally himself, who had only just donned his first armour. But to determine with anything like exactitude the number of the writers associated in the ideas of and efforts towards the reform started by Du Bellay would be as difficult as to enumerate the stars forming the constellation from which they took their name. Some of these are visible to the naked eye, while others are discernible only through a telescope. But it is high time we said something of the author of the movement.

Joachim du Bellay, nephew of the famous general, and of the equally distinguished cardinal of the same name, was born at Liré, in Anjou, in the year 1424. In early life he was confined to his bed for two years by a severe illness, and having no other pastime but reading, he devoured every book he could lay his hands on, so that when he regained his health his mind was filled with stores of knowledge. Moreover, he had discovered that he was a poet; and his verses found great acceptance in the brilliant court of Francis I., and discerning appreciation at the hands of Marguerite of Valois. They were so smooth and harmonious as to earn for him the appellation of the French Ovid; while some of his admirers compared him to Catullus. At the age of twenty-five he accepted an invitation from his uncle, the cardinal, to visit him in Rome, where he remained for three years. The condition of society both lay and ecclesiastical in the Eternal City at that time was so scandalous as to inspire him with scorn and indignation, and these found expression in some sonnets replete with caustic satire. The young poet had already entered the Church, and when he returned to France, his cousin Eustace, who was a prelate, presented him with an archdeaconry in the diocese of Paris, as also a canonry in the cathedral of Notre-Dame. He was a welcome guest at the court of Henry II.; but afflicted with deafness, and having relapsed into ill-health, he retired into privacy, solaced himself with poetry, and died in Paris at the early age of thirty-six, leaving behind him 115 sonnets, and numerous odes, elegies, and lyrical compositions. These were first collected and published seven years after his death, and among them are two really beautiful odes. From one of them, addressed to Madame Marguerite, I select the following lines :

> Princesse, je ne veux point suivre
> D'une telle mer les dangers,
> Aimant mieux entre les miens vivre
> Que mourrir chez les étrangers.
>
> Mieux vaut que les siens on précède,
> Le nom d'Achille poursuivant,
> Que d'être ailleurs un Diomède,
> Voire un Thersite bien souvent.
>
> Quel siècle éteindra la mémoire,
> O Boccace ! et quels durs hivers
> Pourront jamais sécher la gloire,
> Pétrarque, de tes lauriers verts ? . . .

The poet, as it seems to me, strikes a note in the foregoing not audible in the poetry of his predecessors. In the second ode, addressed to the Seigneur Bouju, Du Bellay appears to have borrowed his inspiration from Horace; and the composition will be found to repay perusal. From an ode on 'Immortality,' one of his most lyrical productions, I must quote a few lines :

> L'un aux clameurs du Palais s'étudie ;
> L'autre le vent de la faveur mendie :
> Mais moi, que les grâces chérissent,
> Je hais les biens que l'on adore ;
> Je hais les honneurs qui périssent
> Et le soin qui les cœurs dévore :
> Rien ne me plaît, fors ce qui peut déplaire
> Au jugement du rude populaire.

As an example of Du Bellay's sonnets, the following is extremely characteristic :

> Heureux qui, comme Ulysse, a fait un beau voyage,
> Ou comme celui-là qui conquit la toison,
> Et puis est retourné plein d'usage et raison
> Vivre entre ses parents le reste de son âge !
>
> Quand reverrai-je, hélas ! de mon petit village
> Fumer la cheminée, et en quelle saison
> Reverrai-je le clos de ma pauvre maison,
> Qui m'est une province et beaucoup d'avantage.
>
> Plus me plaît le séjour qu'ont bâti mes aïeux
> Que des palais romains le front audacieux ;
> Plus que le marbre dur me plaît l'ardoise fine,
>
> Plus mon Loire gaulois que le Tibre Latin,
> Plus mon petit Liré que le mont Palatin,
> Et plus que l'air marin la douceur angevine.

A chanson addressed to the Zephyrs is written in a lighter vein, appropriate to the subject :

> A vous, troupe légère,
> Qui d'aile passagère
> Par le monde volez,
> Et d'un sifflant murmure
> L'ombrageuse verdure
> Doucement ébranlez,
>
> J'offre ces violettes,
> Ces lis et ces fleurettes
> Et ces roses ici,
> Ces vermeillettes roses
> Tout fraîchement écloses,
> Et ces œillets aussi.

> De votre douce haleine
> Eventez cette plaine,
> Eventez ce séjour,
> Cependant que j'ahanne[1]
> A mon blé que je vanne,
> A la chaleur du jour.

'Les Regrets,' a collection of short pieces, was written during the poet's residence in Rome, where, although he was no puritan, he saw much that shocked and disgusted him. And at the same time his thoughts wandered regretfully across the Alps, and a feeling of sadness and weariness crept into his verse. In the subjoined sonnet he reproached himself for having sacrificed his studies and his hopes of fame to the pursuit of fortune:

> Las! où est maintenant ce mépris de fortune?
> Où est ce cœur vainqueur de toute adversité,
> Cet honnête désir de l'immortalité
> Et cette belle flamme au peuple non commune.
>
> Où sont ces doux plaisirs qu'au soir, sous la nuit brune,
> Les muses me donnaient, alors qu'en liberté,
> Dessus le verd tapis d'un rivage écarté
> Je les menais danser aux rayons de la lune?
>
> Maintenant la Fortune est maîtresse de moi,
> Et mon cœur, qui soulait être maître de soi,
> Est serf de mille maux et regrets qui m'ennuient;
>
> De la postérité je n'ai plus de souci;
> Cette divine ardeur je ne l'ai plus aussi,
> Et les muses de moi, comme étranger, s'enfuient.

In his 'Olive'—an anagram of Viole, a fair young Angevine, whom he really admired—he extols her beauty and analyses its specific features, comparing them with natural objects. 'It is this poetry of sentiment and imagery,' observes Sainte-Beuve, 'which came at an opportune time to temper the gaiety of the cabaret, and to infuse into our language decency as well as sparkle.'

Amidst the ruins of Rome Du Bellay found the same inspiration as Byron did in a later century, and his 'Antiquités de Rome,' consisting of forty-five sonnets, descriptive of its most famous monuments, takes rank with 'Regrets,' as the best of his poems. In them he often displays an energy and uses expressions such as we meet with afterwards

[1] Breathe with difficulty.

in Corneille. It is honourable to the character of the poet that he quitted the palace of his uncle the cardinal as poor as when he entered it. In an era of simony and corruption, he neither soiled his fingers with bribes nor his soul with the sins of a traffic which was not the less infamous because it was so very general. The members of the Pléiade welcomed his return to France with genuine enthusiasm; but he only lived to reach what has been often called 'the fatal age of genius,' and died, as we have said, at thirty-six. His uncle the cardinal had preceded him into the other world by six weeks. All the poets of the time sincerely bewailed the loss of one so young and gifted; and his remains were buried in the cathedral of Notre-Dame.

His 'Antiquities of Rome' were translated into English by Edmund Spenser. Let me not omit to add that the French language is indebted to Joachim du Bellay for that beautiful word *patrie*, for which there was no equivalent in the earlier tongue. Henry Martin says of him that he was at once the initiator of his school and the most discreet and best inspired of its adepts.

The 'Poet Courtier,' another production of Du Bellay's, is remarkable in many respects. It is one of our best classic satires. It is directed against the court poets, whose fatuity and ignorance he makes merry over, and the flimsy character of whose compositions he exposes with the utmost pleasantry. No doubt many of his gibes were directed against Mellin de Saint-Gelais, towards whom he was often unjust, as indeed he was rather apt to be towards the whole of the school of Marot. From another point of view this epistle is a striking one, for in it the Alexandrine line of twelve syllables is managed with gravity and ease. 'This primitive Alexandrine, with its variable *cæsura*, its free flow of sense from one line into the other, and its rich rhymes, was habitually that of Du Bellay, Ronsard, D'Aubigné, and Régnier; that of Molière in his versified comedies, of Racine in his "Plaideurs;" that which Malherbe and Boileau had the misfortune to misunderstand and to persistently combat, and which André Chénier at the end of the last century recreated with incredible audacity and unheard-of good fortune; that Alexandrine,' wrote Sainte-Beuve in 1830, 'is the same as the younger school of poets feels an affection for and cultivates, and which quite recently Victor Hugo in his "Oliver Cromwell," and Emile Deschamps and Alfred de Vigny in their versified translation of "Romeo and Juliet," have aimed at re-introducing into dramatic compositions.'

In the seventeenth century the name of Du Bellay still retained its vogue; but dying so young, his reputation paled before the rising glory of Ronsard, before both of them were enveloped in the same eclipse. By way of conclusion to my study of this standard-bearer of the Pléiade, I will append one of the sonnets from his 'Regrets,' in which he shows how tenderly he loved that France from which he was so far removed, that dear motherland upon which he was the first to bestow the epithet of *Patrie*:

> France, mère des arts, des armes et des lois,
> Tu m'as nourry long-temps du lait de ta mamelle;
> Ores, comme un agneau qui sa nourrice appelle,
> Je remplis de ton nom les antres et les bois.
>
> Si tu m'as pour enfant advoué quelquefois,
> Que ne me respons-tu maintenant, ô cruelle?
> France! France! respons à ma triste querelle:
> Mais nul, sinon Écho, ne respond à ma voix.
>
> Entre les loups cruels j'erre parmi la plaine,
> Je sens venir l'hyver, de qui la froide haleine
> D'une tremblante horreur fait hérisser ma peau.
>
> Las! les autres agneaux n'ont faute de pasture,
> Ils ne craignant le loup, le vent ny la froidure,
> Si ne suis-je pourtant le pire du troupeau.

LECTURE VI

Ronsard (1524-1585)—Remi Belleau (1528-1577)—Baïf (1552-1591)—Jodelle (1532-1573)—Alexander Hardy (1560-1630)—Robert Garnier (1524-1590)—Guillaume de Salluste, Sieur du Bartas (1544-1590)—Théodore Agrippa d'Aubigné (1550-1630).

I CONCLUDED the last lecture with Joachim du Bellay, and, continuing the study of the same group of authors, I will now speak of Ronsard, and pass from the standard-bearer of the Pléiade to its earliest and most energetic combatant. This famous writer—the 'French Homer,' as he has been styled—of whom we are about to treat exercised in fact an immense sovereignty over the literature and poetry of his epoch: an influence, as Sainte-Beuve has remarked, which lasted for half a century and admitted of neither rivalry nor opposition. Of himself, his family, his birth, his education, and his early adventures, Ronsard has furnished us with detailed and exact particulars, in an epistle addressed to Belleau. It appears from the personal information thus supplied that he was born on September 11, 1524, in the Vendômois; that he spent nine years at the College of Navarre; that he left it, at an early age, to enter the service of the Duc d'Orléans, son of Francis I.; that he quitted it for that of James V. of Scotland, and resided for nearly three years in North Britain. James dying, Ronsard resumed his former position; afterwards became page to the Dauphin; and was secretary to a foreign embassy; acquiring during his absence from France a knowledge of the English, German, and Italian languages. He also obtained what was still more valuable, a knowledge of men and affairs while he was yet a youth. For he was only eighteen when he was compelled to relinquish a diplomatic career by a serious illness which afflicted him with deafness, and proved a blessing in disguise, since it was the means of withdrawing him from the court, and of impelling him to embrace a career of study and of comparative seclusion, for he entered the college at Coqueret, where for seven years he enjoyed the benefit of Jean Dorat's tuition, and had for his fellow students Jean-Antoine de Baïf, Remi Belleau, Lancelot de Charles, and Marc-Antoine Muret, each of whom was destined, like himself, to acquire celebrity in letters in after life. They were all struck, like his tutors, by the daring of his intellect, and it was at that time that Ronsard laid the foundations of the literary revolution which changed the future of the French language and its poetry.

It was about a year after quitting Coqueret that Ronsard met with Du Bellay, and associated himself with him in his pursuits. Their first works were published within a year of each other, and the maiden efforts of these innovators were violently attacked at court by Mellin de Saint-Gelais and his coterie, but their opposition was soon silenced, and the success of Ronsard was rapid, unanimous, and something like a triumph. Sainte-Beuve has left us a charming description of the brilliant rise into distinction of the still youthful writer and scholar: 'Proclaimed at the Floral Games the prince of poets, Ronsard, as had been said of Marot, became the poet of princes. Margaret of Savoy, sister of Henry II., was his Margaret of Navarre—not to speak of Diana of Poitiers, who played an important part in introducing the new school. Mary Stuart received him during the short reign of her husband. Later on she remembered him, when seated on the throne of Scotland, as at a still later period she read his poems in her captivity. Queen Elizabeth sent a valuable diamond to the poet who had celebrated her beautiful and royal rival, and who charmed her while she was a prisoner. Charles IX. cherished Ronsard and heaped abbeys and benefices upon him.' There was no writer of his period, as Pasquier has reminded us, who did not address eulogistic verses to him. It was a continual hymn of praise, a veritable worship.

His works were publicly read and explained in the French schools of Flanders, England, Poland, and even at Danzig. And this chorus of laudation lasted during fully fifty years, not only without diminution, but ever increasing with the lapse of time. Towards the end of his life, the poet Desportes enjoyed, it is true, the entire favour of Henry III.; but Desportes, as well as Bertaut, was brought forward under Ronsard's patronage, and had been formed by his example.

I must not omit to add that Ronsard devoted twenty-five years of his life to the composition of an epic poem entitled 'La Franciade,' which was left unfinished at his death.

When our poet died in 1585, his loss was mourned by the whole of France. Funeral orations were pronounced, and statues erected, in his honour. Invested with all sorts of honours, he seemed to have been enshrined in a true Temple of Fame. Fifteen years had scarcely passed away when Malherbe, who reformed everything, who was a grammarian as well as a poet, scrupulously particular, and severe towards him as well as others, pronounced upon the poet, so loudly extolled but a short time before, a judgment which posterity has ratified, in cancelling, verse by verse, the whole of Ronsard. The French Academy and Boileau finished the work of effacing him. But it has been seriously doubted whether the author of the 'Satires' and 'Epistles' ever read his works. Ronsard was pedantic, no doubt, and as the satirist said, 'his muse spoke Greek and Latin,' but he scarcely deserved the severe censures pronounced upon him by Honoré de Balzac, when he declared that the stream of his poetry contained more mud and sand than water, for his lighter compositions are really felicitous in expression, and full of brightness and gaiety. Neither should we forget the honour due to him as a patriot and as a man. Few of Ronsard's fellow countrymen would have had the courage to address words like these to Charles IX.: 'Sire, ce n'est pas tout que d'être Roi de France.'

Few religious thinkers of his time were raised so high above the brawling of the sects as to be able to condemn alike the fanaticism of the Protestants and the intolerance of the Catholics, or as to record his belief that one day both of them would live harmoniously in heaven. Few men showed at that time so much sincerity and perseverance in preaching peace and conciliation as Ronsard did, who applied all the force of his nature to avert the horrors of civil war, provoked by differences of religious belief.

When we come to examine the writings of Ronsard, we discover in them some pearls which will well repay the search. An admirer of the ancients, he imitated instead of translating them, and it was through him that, for the first time, the features of the past seemed to revive in the French language. We owe him this much at any rate. As examples of his best work, I will cite the following passages:

> Quand vous serez bien vieille, au soir, à la chandelle,
> Assise auprès du feu, devisant et filant,
> Direz, chantant mes vers et vous émerveillant,
> Ronsard me célébrait du temps que j'étais belle.
>
> Lors vous n'aurez servante oyant telle nouvelle,
> Déjà sous le labeur à demi sommeillant,
> Qui au bruit de mon nom ne s'aille réveillant,
> Bénissant votre nom de louange immortelle.
>
> Je serai sous la terre et, fantôme sans os,
> Par les ombres myrteux je prendrai mon repos :
> Vous serez au foyer une vieille accroupie,
>
> Regrettant mon amour et votre fier dédain,
> Vivez, si m'en croyez, n'attendez à demain ;
> Cueillez dès aujourd'hui les roses de la vie.

Following the example of my predecessors who have sketched the history of French literature, I will quote some graceful stanzas addressed by Ronsard to a lady, under the title of

LA VIE EST RAPIDE

> Mignonne, allons voir si la rose
> Qui ce matin avait desclose
> Sa robe de pourpre au soleil
> A point perdu, ceste vesprée,
> Les plis de sa robe pourprée
> Et son teint au vostre pareil.
>
> Las ! voyez comme en peu d'espace,
> Mignonne, elle a dessus la place,
> Las ! las ! ces beautés laissé cheoir !
> O vrayment marastre nature,
> Puisqu'une telle fleur ne dure
> Que du matin jusques au soir !
>
> Donc, si vous me croyez, mignonne,
> Tandis que votre âge fleuronne

> En sa plus verte nouveauté,
> Cueillez, cueillez vostre jeunesse :
> Comme à cette fleur, la vieillesse
> Fera ternir vostre beauté.

As an appropriate pendant to the foregoing let me quote the last six lines of an irreproachable sonnet :

> Icy chanter, là pleurer je la vy,
> Icy sourire, et là je fus ravy
> De ses discours par lesquels je desvie :
> Icy s'asseoir, là je la vy danser ;
> Sur le mestier d'un si vague penser
> Amour ourdit les trames de ma vie.

Such was the more graceful aspect of Ronsard's muse, and it would be unjust to overlook the fact that if he did not definitively found the noble language of the poetry towards which his principal efforts were directed, he has, nevertheless, given it that diapason which Malherbe knew so well how to maintain. Henry Martin's estimate of him appears to me to reach the *juste milieu* of criticism : 'He had neither the invention which is the privilege of genius only, nor the taste which was scarcely to be looked for in that epoch of tumultuous transition. But the Muses had given him warmth of colouring, picturesqueness of expression, an inexhaustible abundance of imagery, the instinct of harmony, transformed by labour into the science of rhythm, and something of that sentiment of nature which had been the very life of antique poetry. The variety of the elegiac and lyric modes in which he indulged ravished the ear, while the voluptuous charm of his pictures enervated the heart and the senses. What should induce us to pardon the poet but to condemn the chief of a school, is that while Ronsard triumphs in the middle region of amorous poetry, in the Anacreontic ode, we see his Icarian wings melt whenever he attempts to wing a loftier flight towards the sun of the epic or of the Pindaric ode. But, in the matter of sustained style, he raises himself many degrees above the sphere of Marot.' The critic I have just quoted adds : 'His contemporaries did not judge him thus, but placed him in the poetical empyrean at a height from which he was speedily precipitated by other gods like a thunder-smitten Titan. Fifty years of immoderate glory have been expiated by two centuries of unjust contempt.'

It has been remarked that, in the study of a literary epoch, our principal critics have always had a favourite author. Walter Besant in his 'Early French Writers' has shown a marked predilection for the tender and amiable Clotilde de Surville, whose very existence is a matter of controversy. Payne in England and Campaux in France made an idol of Villon. Villemain has reserved his special admiration for Charles d'Orléans and Montaigne, while Sainte-Beuve—and this is the point I am coming to—has praised, commented upon, explained, and occasionally excused, Ronsard as none of his most enthusiastic and indulgent annotators have done. The more recent of these two critics has even gone so far as to dedicate the following sonnet to the poet's honour :

> A toi, Ronsard, à toi, qu'un sort injurieux
> Depuis deux siècles livre au mépris de l'histoire,
> J'élève de mes mains l'autel expiatoire
> Qui te purifiera d'un arrêt odieux.
>
> Non que j'espère encore au trône radieux,
> D'où jadis tu régnais, replacer ta mémoire,
> Tu ne peux de si bas remonter à la gloire :
> Vulcain impunément ne tomba point des cieux.
>
> Mais qu'un peu de pitié console enfin tes mânes ;
> Que, déchiré longtemps par des rires profanes,
> Ton nom, d'abord fameux, recouvre un peu d'honneur ;
>
> Qu'on dise : Il osa trop, mais l'audace était belle ;
> Il lassa, sans la vaincre, une langue rebelle,
> Et de moins grands depuis eurent plus de bonheur.

Before concluding this notice of Ronsard I will show how he, too, could use the key wherewith, as Wordsworth says, 'Shakespeare unlocked his heart :'

> Je vous envoi un bouquet que ma main
> Vient de trier de ces fleurs épanies :
> Qui ne les eust à ce vespre cueillies,
> Cheutes à terre elles fussent demain.
>
> Cela vous soit un exemple certain
> Que vos beautez, bien qu'elles soient fleuries,
> En peu de temps cherront toutes flaitries,
> Et comme fleurs périront tout soudain.
>
> Le temps s'en va, le temps s'en va, ma Dame,
> Las ! le temps non ; mais nous nous en allons,
> Et tost serons estendus sous la lame :

> Et des amours desquelles nous parlions,
> Quand serons morts, n'en sera plus nouvelle :
> Pour ce aymez-moy, cependant qu'estes belle.

Ronsard's swan-song was pious and pathetic. He dictated two sonnets addressed to Jesus Christ, then turned upon his side and rendered up his last sigh, with a smile upon his lips. The news of his death produced a great sensation in Paris. The funeral ceremony was celebrated in the chapel of the college of Dreux, the court and the parliament being both represented on the occasion. The king sent his musicians, and the bishop of the diocese pronounced the absolution. The classical tendencies of the age found curious expression in one passage of the prelate's discourse. 'Nature,' said he, 'has put on mourning as she did at the death of the god Pan!'

Remi Belleau, the pastoral poet *par excellence*, 'the gentle Belleau' of the Pléiade, was born at Nogent de Rotrou in 1528, and died in Paris in 1577. He made a comedy in verse, 'La Reconnue,' which is one of the earliest of our plays, and is still readable. But a better idea of this poet will be obtained if I quote the following imitation of Anacreon from his pen:

> Si l'or et la richesse
> Retardaient la vitesse,
> La vitesse et le cours
>   De nos beaux jours :
>
> Je l'aurais en réserve,
> Afin de rendre serve [esclave]
> La mort tirant à soi
>   L'argent de moi.
>
> Mais las ! puisque la vie,
> A tous vivants ravie,
> Ne peut se retarder
>   Pour marchander,
>
> Que me sert tant de plaintes,
> Tant de larmes contraintes,
> Et sanglots ennuyeux
>   Pousser aux cieux ?
>
> Puisque la mort cruelle
> Sans merci nous appelle,
> Que nous servirait or [à présent]
>   L'argent et l'or ?

> Avant que mort descendre
> Là-bas, je veux dépendre [dépenser]
> Et rire, à table mis
> De mes amis.

Jean Antoine de Baïf, Ronsard's fellow student, was born in the year 1552 in Venice, where his father had been ambassador from Francis I. to the republic of St. Mark. He was the most fertile writer of the group to which he belonged. He endeavoured to invent a new alphabet consisting of ten vowels, nineteen consonants, eleven diphthongs, and three triphthongs. He instituted the first literary society which was founded in France, endeavoured to introduce four- and five-syllabled verses into our language, and wrote a mass of poetry which is never read. After exhibiting his loyalty to the programme issued by Du Bellay, De Baïf died in 1591. Subjoined is an example of his style :

> LE CALCUL DE LA VIE
>
> Tu as cent ans et davantage :
> Mais calcule de tout ton âge
> Combien en eut ton créancier,
> Combien tes folles amourettes,
> Combien tes affaires secretes,
> Combien ton pauvre tenancier,
>
> Combien tes procès ordinaires,
> Combien tes valets mercenaires,
> Combien ton aller et venir :
> Ajoute aussi tes maladies,
> Ajoute encore tes folies,
> Si tu pouvais t'en souvenir :
>
> Et tout cela qui, sans usage,
> S'en est allé pour ton dommage :
> Si tout cela tu en rabats,
> Tu verras avoir moins d'années
> Que tu ne t'en étais données,
> Et que tout jeune tu t'en vas.

I must deal briefly with the other members of the Pléiade, but in so doing I may succeed perhaps in giving you some idea of the style and general tendencies of the group.

The part which Jodelle played in the movement was that of resuscitating the tragic authors of Greece. Many translations into French had already been made of the plays of

Euripides and Sophocles, as also of the comedies of Terence from the Latin. Jodelle himself had written a version of the 'Plutus' of Aristophanes in 1549. Three years later he ventured to put upon the stage two original tragedies in imitation of the ancients, entitled 'Cleopatra Captive' and 'Dido' respectively. The first was acted before Henry II. by a company of amateurs. The author, who was only twenty, played the part of the Egyptian queen, and his friends Rémi Belleau and Jean de la Péruse sustained the other leading characters. It met with an immense success, and the king presented the dramatist with 500 crowns. It is a curious proof of how men's judgments are frequently blinded by a transitory and factitious enthusiasm that Ronsard allowed himself to be so completely carried away as to declare that Sophocles, Euripides, and Menander were mere schoolboys in comparison with the French author! Listen to this dithyrambic outburst on his part:

> Jodelle le premier d'une plainte hardie
> Françoisement chanta la Grecque tragédie ;
> Puis en changeant de ton, chanta devant nos rois
> La jeune comédie en langage François,
> Et si bien les rima que Sophocle et Ménandre,
> Tant fussent-ils savants, y eussent pu apprendre.

Looking at these dramatic experiments from a calmer and more critical point of view, the plaudits of Jodelle's contemporaries find no echo in our own times. Nearly all the tragedies and comedies of the new school sinned in one important particular. There was no invention of characters. Yet, singularly enough, Jodelle proved the exception to the rule in his 'Eugène,' a comedy written in imitation of the Italians, and played before the king as an afterpiece to 'Cleopatra.' M. Royer, in his 'Histoire Universelle du Théâtre,' says that besides being picturesque in expression it contains two characters, a chaplain and a captain, drawn from life.

In the plays of that period, the situations and the management of the plot are scrupulous reproductions and perfect counterfeits of Greek forms. The action is simple, observes Sainte-Beuve, the personages few in number, the acts very short and intermingled with choruses, the lyric poetry of which is far superior to the dialogue ; and these pieces are written in a style which aims at nobility and gravity, and which only fails to reach them because their language is faulty. Such, in brief, are the tragedies of Jodelle and his contemporaries. The efforts made by himself and by some of the disciples of Ronsard to supersede the mysteries, farces, and foolish productions placed upon the stage by pieces imitated from the antique suggest a passing allusion to the old theatre which was about to disappear.

The authors of the Mysteries had ended by lowering their subjects to the level of their uncultivated audiences. Those representations had degenerated, indeed, into veritable saturnalia, and the disorders which attended some of them provoked the interference of the magistracy of Paris. The last bright days of the Mysteries were seen during the winter of 1540 and 1541, when the Brethren of the Passion played the 'Acts of the Apostles' at the Hôtel de Flandres. It was a truly gigantic composition by the Brothers Gréban, doctors in theology, containing 80,000 lines, and necessitating the co-operation of 500 performers. It embraced the crucifixion of St. Peter, the transport of the emperor Nero to hell, and the roasting alive of St. Thomas upon red-hot bars. The stage directions show that even the vapour of boiling water was introduced upon the stage in order to represent the smoke ascending from the martyr's body. Quite recently it was revived in the Roman amphitheatre at Bourges, where the performance lasted for forty consecutive days!

The king's people complained of the entertainments presented by the Brotherhood, and after some years of vacillation a decree was issued by parliament forbidding the acting of Mysteries taken from the Holy Scriptures, and confining such dramas to 'profane and honest' subjects. And thus in 1548 the religious theatre of the Middle Ages came to an end in France. A similar statute had been passed in England five years previously; and there the disappearance of sacred plays led to the creation of a national drama, and the appearance of such a constellation of dramatic poets, including Marlowe, Massinger, Jonson, Beaumont and Fletcher, Peele, Dekker, Ford, and Webster, with Shakespeare towering head and shoulders above them all, as England never saw before nor has seen since.

France did not proceed so rapidly and so directly along the same career. The Renaissance at first merely ventured to place upon the scene an antique puppet in lieu of the old Catholic drama. And that epoch, otherwise so intelligent, allowed itself to be deluded into accepting Jodelle as a great genius. At the same time it should be added that his vogue was confined to the court and to the educated classes. The great bulk of the public remained completely indifferent to his academic tragedy of 'Cleopatra,' which was above the comprehension of the crowd and not worth studying in their opinion. The dramatist and his associates announced that they had it in contemplation to replace the old farces as well as the Mysteries, and to resuscitate pure comedy as well as tragedy. But their experiments in that direction, with the exception I have mentioned, did not differ essentially from the ancient farces; and the best of them is very inferior to 'Pathelin,' that fine old prototype of French comedy, which remained unsurpassed, as Sainte-Beuve has said, until the days of Molière.

Hallam, who is not less deserving of the epithet 'judicious' than Richard Hooker, says of Jodelle, 'His style is often low and ludicrous, which did not prevent this tragedy ("Cleopatra"), the first fruits of a theatre which was to produce Racine, from being received with vast applause. There is, in reality, amidst those raptures that frequently attend an infant literature, something of an undefined presage of the future, which should hinder us from thinking them quite ridiculous.'

'Call no man happy until he dies' was the exclamation of one of old. Did Jodelle remember it when he lay upon his death-bed, lonely and neglected, miserable and forgotten? He had fallen under the royal displeasure owing to a simple blunder on the part of a mechanist to whom he had entrusted a matter of detail connected with a masque which the poet had been commanded to arrange at the Hôtel de Ville in honour of the Duc de Guise. The bungle excited a roar of laughter, and Jodelle passes into disgrace, oblivion, and poverty. 'Put not your trust in princes' might have served him for an epitaph.

The poets of the time who laboured with him for the

regeneration of our dramatic art were Jean de la Péruse, Charles Toustain, Jean-Jacques de la Taille, Jacques Grévin, Mellin de Saint-Gelais, Jean-Antoine de Baïf, and Remi Belleau. The repertory of these innovators was inconsiderable, each of them contributing three or four pieces at the most, all of which were marked by a total want of originality, and were indebted to the ancients for their form and substance.

Among the dramatic authors of that epoch, I must not omit to mention Pierre de Larivey, who wrote half a dozen comedies, which, if somewhat licentious in language, were vivacious in dialogue, and moral in their general tendency. One of the best of them was dedicated to an Italian gentleman named Nicolò Buonaparte. It was the first mention, I believe, of that name in French literature.

Then came Alexandre Hardy (1560–1630), a most voluminous playwright, who is said to have written, or vamped, 600 tragedies and tragi-comedies; in some of which he introduced scenes of revolting indecency, with what Hood might have called an insolent hardy-hood. All that remain of his profuse and generally worthless productions are forty-one examples, collected and published by himself when he was an old man.

I pass over many undistinguished names, to pause for a moment at that of Robert Garnier, a judge, who was held in the highest estimation by Charles IX. and Henry III.; and a dramatist who was much superior to Jodelle. He adopted classic models, like him selecting Seneca in preference to the great Greek masters, from whom, however, he borrowed the idea of his choruses; while the correctness of his versification, the elevation of his style, and the sustained dignity of his dialogue marked him out as one of the precursors of that classic drama in France which was brought to perfection by Corneille and Racine.

Both Jodelle and Garnier bestowed a new language on tragedy; and some of the choruses of the latter merit the title of odes. Here is a passage in which Cæsar, making a triumphal entry into Rome, thus apostrophises that august city :

      O sourcilleuses tours ! O coteaux décorés !
      O Palais orgueilleux ! O temples honorés !

> O vous, Murs, que les dieux ont maçonnés eux-mêmes,
> Eux-mêmes étoffés de mille diadèmes !
> Ne ressentez-vous point le plaisir en vos cœurs,
> De voir votre César, le Vainqueur des Vainqueurs,
> Par tant de gloire acquise aux nations étranges,
> Accroître votre empire, ainsi que vos louanges ?
> Et toi, fleuve orgueilleux, ne vas-tu pas tes flots
> Aux tritons mariners faire bruire mon los,
> Et au père océan te vanter que le Tybre
> Roulera plus fameux que l'Euphrate et le Tygre ?
> Jà presque tout le monde obéit aux Romains :
> Ils ont presque la mer et la terre en leurs mains :
> Et soit où le soleil, de sa torche voisine
> Les Indiens perleux au matin illumine ;
> Soit où son char, lassé de la course du jour,
> Le ciel quitte à la nuit, qui commence à son tour ;
> Soit où la mer glacée en cristal se resserre ;
> Soit où l'ardent soleil sèche et brûle la terre ;
> Les Romains on redoute, et n'y a si grand roi
> Qui au cœur ne frémisse, oyant parler de moi.

I shall avoid fatiguing you by making further extracts from these authors ; and indeed a complete familiarity with the infancy of our dramatic literature is unnecessary to any one who does not desire to make a special study of it ; and I believe I have said enough on this head to fulfil the purpose I have in view. I shall confine myself hereafter to analysing those dramatic works only which have obtained, and still preserve, the distinction of being French classics.

However open to adverse criticism the theatrical productions of the Pléiade were, they nevertheless left their mark upon the stage, by endowing our dramatic poetry with the Alexandrine verse, and this was the gift of La Péruse, whose 'Médée,' imitated from Seneca, is notable for its rigorous observance of the rule with respect to masculine and feminine rhymes.

Let us now pass on to the consideration of other authors belonging to the same group and the same school. Guillaume de Salluste, Sieur Du Bartas, born about 1544, in the village of Montfort, may be said to have 'lisped in numbers,' for he began composing verses even in childhood. A Protestant in religion, he drew his inspiration from the Bible ; and his 'Muse Chrétienne' was a protest against the pagan tendencies of contemporary literature. It was dedicated to Margaret of Navarre, who is said to have been his godmother. His views were elevated, but his literary faculties did not enable him to soar into the higher regions of song. His 'Uranie' and his 'Judith' were heavy and tedious productions, and his most important work 'The Week' (or 'Creation') was not of such a character as to justify the prodigious success it achieved, or to explain the extraordinary admiration which Goethe conceived for it. 'We are struck,' he writes, 'by the grandeur and variety of the images which his verses call up before us; we render justice to the strength and vivacity of his pictures, and to the wide extent of his knowledge of physics and of natural history.'

The real secret of the popularity of this elaborate poem must be sought for, I think, in the circumstances of the times : Du Bartas was the poet of the French Calvinists, and the trusted servant of Henry IV., just as Milton was afterwards the poet of the English Puritans and the secretary of Cromwell; and at an epoch in which all good Catholics in France affected the light and licentious poetry which pleased the Cavaliers in the days of the Stuarts, Du Bartas presented himself as the exponent of the religious muse, and as a defender of the Christian faith. Be this as it may, 'The Week,' which no doubt inspired the 'Sette Giornate' of Tasso, ran through thirty editions in six years. It was translated into Latin, Italian, Spanish, German, and English; and extorted the praises of so true a poet as Edmund Spenser; while it is worthy of remark that the compound words which Du Bartas introduced into French literature, and which were condemned by the critics as pedantic, were adopted from that time forth by the best English writers : Chapman employed them in his admirable translation of Homer, so warmly eulogised by Keats ; Sir Philip Sidney did the same in his 'Arcadia;' Milton in both his great epics; and Phineas Fletcher in his 'Purple Island.'

In 'The Week,' Du Bartas, having arrived at the creation of man, when—the world having been formed and peopled—nothing remained but to introduce the principal guest, did so in this pleasant fashion :

> Le sage ne conduit la personne invitée
> Dans le lieu du festin, que la salle apprêtée

> Ne brille de flambeaux, et que les plats chargés
> Sur le linge flamand ne soient presque rangés :
> Ainsi notre grand Dieu, ce grand Dieu qui sans cesse
> Tient ici cour ouverte . . .
> Ne voulut convier notre aïeul à sa table
> Sans tapisser plus tôt sa maison délectable
> Et ranger, libéral, sous les pôles astrés
> La friande douceur de mille mets sucrés.

The poet's conceptions of the Supreme Being were as anthropomorphic as those of Murillo himself; and he concludes a description of the person of the Most High in this quaint fashion :

> En bref, l'oreille, l'œil, le nez du Tout-Puissant
> En son œuvre n'oit rien, rien ne voit, rien ne sent
> Qui ne prêche son los.

Sainte-Beuve considers that if the capacity of Du Bartas had equalled his ambition, he would have been our Milton; as Du Bellay is, in some respects, a French Spenser. Such comparisons, however, are generally injudicious and misleading, however plausible and attractive.

In 1584, the poet published a 'Second Week,' or rather the first two days of it; but it met with a frigid reception from the public, and encountered some hostility from the critics, who, finding it very inferior to his former poem, began to cast doubts upon his authorship of that, alleging that he had plagiarised the work from the 'Hexameron' of George Pisides, a Byzantine poet and historian, who lived in the seventh century, and described the creation of the world in a poem bearing that title.

Du Bartas, in any case, had exhausted the capital of his reputation, and being the last of the Pléiade, and one of its most conspicuous members, he had to bear the brunt of all the ridicule and adverse criticism which its eccentricities and its strained neologisms had provoked; and even now, when that group of poets is spoken of, we are apt rather to think of the faults of Du Bartas than of his praiseworthy efforts as the founder of a school. But, whatever may have been his defects as a writer, let us never forget the heroism of his death, as a son of France. 'Commanding a company of cavalry,' De Thou tells us, 'under the orders of Marshal de Matignan, governor of the province (during the League), he succumbed to the heat of the season, the toils of the campaign, and to some wounds which had been badly closed, in the month of July 1590, in the flower of his age, being only forty-six.'

I have yet to speak of another author, Théodore Agrippa d'Aubigné, who was also a soldier and a courtier. Born at Saintonge on February 8, 1550, the future historian made such rapid progress with his education that he could read Greek, Latin, and Hebrew at six years of age. At thirteen he took part in the religious wars, being an ardent Calvinist, like his father, and assisted at the siege of Orleans. He was condemned to death for his participation in these conflicts; fought under the flag of the Prince of Condé, and entered the service of Henry IV., by whom he was greatly admired for his valour, his cheerful spirit, his great intellectual gifts, and the genuine nobility of his character. On the death of that monarch, by whom he was most inadequately requited for his loyal devotion, both as a soldier and a diplomatist, D'Aubigné relinquished the sword for the pen, and dedicated some years of retreat to the composition of a 'Universal History' of his times, from 1550 to 1601, a work remarkable alike for the boldness of its views and the independence of its opinions; which excited so much anger in high places that the last volume was publicly burnt by order of the parliament of Paris. Its author would no doubt have shared the same fate if he had been within reach, but he took refuge in Geneva, where he spent the last ten years of his life in fortifying the principal cities of Switzerland for the defence of their Protestant liberties. 'Threatened men live long,' says the proverb, and it was verified in the case of D'Aubigné, who, after having been four times condemned to death, died in his bed on April 22, 1630, at the advanced age of eighty. One of his sons, Constant, Baron of Surineau, was the father of the lady who married Scarrou, 'l'Empereur du Burlesque,' and then Louis XIV., le Roi-Soleil. Besides his 'Universal History,' D'Aubigné left behind him many other works, among which may be mentioned a satire in seven cantos, entitled 'Les Tragiques,' overflowing with the fiercest invective, and not unworthy of his Roman model; 'La Confession Catholique du Sieur de Sancy,' and 'La

Baron de Fœneste,' which are also biting satires, and his own biography. Henry Martin's critical estimate of this writer is so sound and just that I cannot deny myself the pleasure of quoting it.

'He is far superior,' he observes, 'to Du Bartas, and is too little read nowadays, although much less forgotten than the author of "La Semaine." What a formidable inspiration is that of "Les Tragiques," those vast satires which, combined, enclosed the court of the Medici in a circle of 11,000 verses, written with a pen of brass, dipped in the blood of the martyrs! The impassioned imprecations of the prophets are blended with the bitter and cynical *verve* of Juvenal in that astonishing work, where passion overflows with a too impatient violence all bounds and limitations; and the poet is too little master of himself and of his subject to fulfil the true conditions of art; but where, nevertheless, a thousand gloomy beauties break forth. The savage rudeness of the language intensifies the effect of the idea and the image; for that rudeness involves neither inflation nor obscurity. The expression is as clear and trenchant as steel. "Les Tragiques" are, as it were, the death song and the damnation of the last of the Valois and of their mother.' Although these satires were written in 1577, they were not published until 1616. In the other two I have referred to, irony took the place of anathema.'

Little remains to be said of the remaining poets of the Pléiade. Jean Dorat, the preceptor of Ronsard, was but an indifferent versifier, although he received the title of Poet Royal from Charles X., and was foolishly pronounced to be the modern Pindar by some of his admirers. Pontus de Thiard, at the age of twenty-two, published a volume of 'Amorous Errors,' which he followed up by a collection of lyrical poems. His contemporaries called him the Great Thiard; and the epithet was not altogether undeserved, for he was a great eater and a great drinker, as we learn on the authority of De Thou, and was both tall and corpulent. Forsaking poetry for divinity, he received from Henry III. the bishopric of Chalon-sur-Saône, and sustained with dignity the duties which it entailed.

I make no pretension to completeness in this catalogue of poets, for to name all the rank and file who served under the seven captains of the Pléiade would be tedious and wearisome in the extreme. Some of them, indeed, acquired a certain celebrity during their lifetime, but others have escaped identification even by the erudite.

Jacques Tahureau, a descendant on his mother's side from Bertrand du Guesclin, is better known by his moral and satirical 'Dialogues' than by his somewhat erotic poems, which were collected and published nineteen years after his death; the latter event occurring in 1550, when he was only eight-and-twenty. Olivier de Magny, who was for a time secretary to Henry II., wrote numerous excellent sonnets, odes, and lyric poems, some of which were addressed to Diana of Poitiers; but they were too often disfigured by a gross licentiousness. Jean de la Taille was the author of three or four tragedies, and distinguished himself, like D'Aubigné, on the field of battle, fighting for the Protestant cause. His bravery was so conspicuously exhibited in the fight at Arnay-le-Duc, where he was dangerously wounded, that the king of Navarre publicly embraced him, and confided him to the care of his own surgeon.

I cannot conclude this rapid survey of the poets who were the colleagues and camp-followers of Ronsard better than by quoting what Geruzez has written concerning them.

'It is only right,' he observes, 'to remember that that generous, obstreperous, and fertile school was not unserviceable to the progress of our literature and the development of our language. It provoked a crisis necessary to the growth of poetry. It was needful to make an energetic appeal to superior intellects, still held back by the habitual employment of Latin, which appeared to them to be the only clothing worthy of serious ideas, to make use of the vulgar tongue, which had need of their assistance to fortify and to enrich it. That appeal was listened to. They continued to acquire Latin, and they learned Greek more thoroughly, which was a great resource; but they believed themselves to be less obliged to write in the ancient languages, which were thenceforth merely an exercise, a means and not an end. They aimed at the expansion of the mother tongue, which had been hindered in its advance by the vicinity of the dead languages.'

If the school of Ronsard founded nothing, it gave an impulse to a movement which would lead to an end; and its efforts were not sterile, since they prepared the materials and the implements for the edifice which more favoured hands have been privileged to construct.

Here I close the study of the members of the Pléiade which I have felt it to be my duty to submit to you. The influence of that school made itself felt long after the disappearance of every one of its members; and we shall have from time to time to recur to it when speaking of the poets who immediately succeeded it, and who will form the subject of the next lecture.

And here I may find it a fitting occasion to express my high sense of the value of such an institution as the Public Library in this city.[1] It is, in fact, only by means of the collection of works upon French literature which I have had an opportunity of consulting there that I have found it possible to prepare this series of lectures.

To find in Australia so complete and well selected a collection of books upon this subject may not surprise those foreigners residing here, who live in a certain intellectual atmosphere; but I know a good many Parisians—and why should I not add a good many Londoners also?—who would be greatly astonished by such a fact. But what would they say if they were informed, in addition, that the private libraries, which have been hospitably opened to me, are, relatively speaking, on the same scale as the Public Library, which stands on as high a level as the best institutions of the kind in Europe?

[1] Melbourne.

LECTURE VII

Desportes (1545-1606)—Bertaut (1552-1611)—Régnier (1573-1613)—
Malherbe (1555-1628)—Racan (1589-1670)—Gombauld (1570-1666)
—Maynard (1583-1646)—Malleville (1597-1647).

In the last lecture I pointed out the signal failure of the poets of the Pléiade to effect that revolutionary change in our literature which their demonstrative efforts were intended to promote. They aimed at a sweeping reform, and they produced confusion. Their intention was to nationalise our language and to create a distinctly French school of poetry; but if the mask of the muse was Gallic, her voice spoke alternately in the accents of ancient Greece and Rome. This was especially the case with the last of the group, the author of 'La Semaine;' and it now remains to speak of two poets who, while affiliated to the Pléiade, nevertheless escaped to some extent from its pedantic influences, and marked a period of transition from Ronsard and Du Bartas to Malherbe—I speak of Philippe Desportes and Jean Bertaut. The first of these writers was born at Chartres in 1545, and died at the age of sixty-one in the Abbey of Bonport, which had been bestowed upon him by Henry III. in recompense for one of the poet's sonnets. Never, indeed, was versifier more royally rewarded. The king presented him with 30,000 livres on the publication of his works; and the Duc de Joyeuse and others gave him no less than four valuable benefices. To crown all, Desportes was offered the archbishopric of Bordeaux, which he declined, much to the astonishment of his royal patron, to whom he stated that he was unwilling to undertake the cure of souls. 'But,' remonstrated the king, 'have you not charge of the souls of your monks?' 'No!' replied the poet, 'for they have none!' The income of Desportes is estimated to have been 10,000 crowns, which would represent an immense sum in our days; and he expended a good deal of it in the formation of a magnificent library, which was accessible to all the men of learning who sought to take advantage of it. A man of wide and general erudition himself, his writings bore the impress of scholarship, but were classic in form rather than in substance. His compositions included odes, love songs, elegies, sonnets, ballads, chansons, pastorals, and a versified translation of the Psalms, of which he offered a weak and colourless paraphrase only. It was undertaken probably in order to atone for the youthful indiscretions of his muse, such as his 'Premières Amours,' his 'Amours d'Hippolyte,' his 'Dernières Amours,' and his 'Baisers.' With the latter, by the way, Mademoiselle d'Aubigné, afterwards Madame de Maintenon, was so charmed that she is said to have conceived quite a *tendresse* for its author. Desportes, on the principle that a fond mother generally loves her deformed child better than all the others, seems to have thought very highly of his feeble version of the 'Psalms,' and one day, before sitting down to dinner with a party he had invited, he proposed to read some of them, just as a modern host sometimes invites his guests to whet their appetites with a glass of sherry and bitters. Malherbe, who was present, splenetically exclaimed: 'Let them alone! let them alone! Your soup is better than your Psalms.' The coarse and vulgar gibe was not forgotten by another of the guests, young Mathurin Régnier, the nephew of Desportes, who afterwards ridiculed Malherbe with so much caustic wit in his Ninth Satire as to cause his victim to writhe under the attack.

It is by his earlier poems, however, that Desportes invites the judgment of posterity. And some of these, so elegant in their language, and so fluent in their versification, were on every lip. Charles IX., who cultivated the art himself, was so much charmed with his 'Rodomont' that he presented him with 800 golden crowns; and it is related of the unfortunate Henry of Guise, that a few minutes before he fell under the dagger of the Valois in the château at Blois he was humming the following lines:

> Rozette, pour un peu d'absence,
> Vostre cœur vous avez changé,
> Et, moi, sçachant cette inconstance,
> Le mien autre part j'ai rangé ;
> Jamais plus beauté si légère
> Sur moi tant de pouvoir n'aura :
> Nous verrons, volage bergère,
> Qui premier s'en repentira.
>
> Où sont tant de promesses saintes,
> Tant de pleurs versés en partant ?
> Est-il vrai que ces tristes plaintes
> Sortissent d'un cœur inconstant ?
> Dieux, que vous êtes mensongère !
> Maudit soit qui plus vous croira !
> Nous verrons, volage bergère,
> Qui premier s'en repentira.
>
> Celui qui a gagné ma place
> Ne vous peut aimer tant que moi ;
> Et celle que j'aime vous passe
> De beauté, d'amour et de foi.
> Gardez bien votre amitié neuve :
> La mienne plus ne variera ;
> Et puis nous verrons à l'épreuve
> Qui premier s'en repentira.

Even as late as the reign of Louis XIV., Desportes' celebrated chanson 'O nuit ! jalouse nuit !' written in imitation of Ariosto, but in a different strain of feeling, was still extremely popular. The first lines of this often-quoted freak of fancy run thus :

> O nuict ! Jalouse nuict contre moi conjurée,
> Qui renflammes le ciel de nouvelle clarté,
> T'ai-je donc aujourd'hui tant de fois désirée
> Pour être si contraire à ma félicité !

All the first flowering of the poetical genius of Desportes still retains its primitive grace and freshness, notwithstanding the lapse of so many years. Here, for example, are some charming couplets from a chanson which enjoyed great celebrity in its day :

> Oh, bienheureux qui peut passer sa vie
> Entre les siens, franc de haine et d'envie,
> Parmi les champs, les forêts et les bois,
> Loin du tumulte et du bruit populaire ;
> Et qui ne vend sa liberté pour plaire
> Aux passions des princes et des rois !

> Dans les palais enflés de vaine pompe,
> L'Ambition, la faveur qui nous trompe
> Et les soucis logent communément :
> Dedans nos champs se retirent les fées,
> Reines des bois, à tresses décoiffées,
> Les jeux, l'amour, et le contentement.
>
> Ainsi vivant, rien n'est qui ne m'agrée ;
> J'ois des oiseaux la musique sacrée,
> Quand au matin ils bénissent les cieux,
> Et le doux son des bruyantes fontaines,
> Qui vont coulant de ces roches hautaines,
> Pour arroser nos prés délicieux.

The poem reminds one at once of 'The Old Man' of Claudian, and of the 'Mine be a cot beside the hill' of Samuel Rogers. How easy it is to write in this vein when one is an immensely rich abbot like Desportes, or the friend and favourite of two emperors, like the Roman poet, or a wealthy banker with a perfect *bijou* of a town mansion in Park Lane, like the author of 'Italy'!

Desportes introduced into French poetry something of the mellifluous expression of Ariosto and Tasso. He wrote more purely, as La Harpe observes, than Ronsard and his imitators; he effaced the rust impressed on our versification, and rescued it from the chaos into which it had been plunged. He took care to avoid the *enjambement* and the *hiatus*; but feeble in his ideas and in his style, he was unable, in the succeeding century, to maintain his station upon Parnassus.

La Harpe's opinion of Desportes is concurred in by Sainte-Beuve, who also disputes the statement that he and Bertaut and Passerat effected a reform in French poetry. 'The two first,' he says, 'made no revolution, but continued that of Ronsard; and, rigorously considered, they are writers of a period of decadence much more than of one of regeneration.' Desportes was, as we have said, one of the favourites of fortune; and, although for a time, during the civil wars, his revenues were confiscated by the Royalists, yet they were restored to him by Henry IV., whom he assisted to re-enter Normandy, so that he died a wealthy man. He made few enemies, consisting mainly of those who, like Malherbe, envied him; his nature was kindly, benevolent, and incapable of rancour; and he remained to the last unspoiled by that prosperity which is so much harder to bear, in general, than adversity.

Jean Bertaut was another poet upon whom the sun shone. He was born at Caen in 1552, and the writings of Ronsard so captivated his imagination that he strove, at an early age, to clothe his own thoughts in verse. His ear seemed naturally attuned to melody; his theme was love; his admiration was beauty; and he understood so well the art how to rise in life, that his poems were always addressed to persons of the highest distinction, by whom they were munificently rewarded. Henry III. appointed him his private secretary and reader, and he was very near him when he was assassinated by Jacques Clément. Marie de Médicis made him her almoner, and Henry IV. presented him with the rich abbey of Aubney, and twelve years afterwards gave him the bishopric of Seez, in Normandy, where he died in 1611, after having assisted in the conversion of his sovereign to Roman Catholicism.

Sainte-Beuve remarks that his stanzas, elegies, and chansons appeal to the ear rather than to the eye, and that he possesses the indisputable merit of having given nobility to our language before Malherbe; while Mademoiselle Scudéry ranks him above Ronsard and Desportes in some respects. Here is an elegy of his, which is prized by all people of taste :

>   Les cieux inexorables
>   Me sont si rigoureux,
>   Que les plus misérables,
> Se comparant à moy, se trouveroient heureux.
>
>   Mon lict est de mes larmes
>   Trempé toutes les nuits ;
>   Et ne peuvent ses charmes,
> Lors mesme que je dors, endormir mes ennuys.
>
>   Si je fay quelque songe,
>   J'en suis espouvanté,
>   Car mesme son mensonge
> Exprime de mes maux la triste vérité.
>
>   La pitié, la justice,
>   La constance et la foy,
>   Cédant à l'artifice,
> Dedans les cœurs humains est esteinte pour moi.

> En un cruel orage
> On me laisse périr,
> Et courant au naufrage,
> Je vois chacun me plaindre et nul me secourir.
>
> Félicité passée,
> Qui ne peux revenir,
> Tourment de ma pensée,
> Que n'ay-je, en te perdant, perdu le souvenir.

'Of these couplets,' observes Sainte-Beuve, 'the last more particularly—singular chance!—has survived for two centuries. Our mothers know it still and have sung it. The quality peculiar to our author is a contemplative note, in which love and religion blend together, and each finds in turn its vague and touching expression. Our poet in a "Complaint," from which I must quote a passage, has hit upon the double and charming expression of enduring love and eternal regret:

> Mes plaisirs s'en sont envolez,
> Cédans au malheur qui m'outrage,
> Mes beaux jours se sont escoulez
> Comme l'eau qu'enfante un orage,
> Et s'escoulans ne m'ont laissé
> Rien que le regret du passé.

'To do entire honour to the poet,' adds Sainte-Beuve, 'I will bring forward certainly the most sustained verses he has composed, a rare and natural image, developed in happy fulness. It is taken from an elegy in which he expresses his sadness when he loses sight of his lady, and complains of the inequality of their torments in absence:

> Mais las! pourquoy faut-il que les arbres sauvages
> Qui vestent les costeaux ou bordent les rivages,
> Qui n'ont veines ni sang qu'amour puisse allumer,
> Observent mieux que nous les lois de bien aimer?
>
> On dit qu'en Idumée, es confins de Syrie,
> Où bien souvent la palme au palmier se marie,
> Il semble, à regarder ces arbres bienheureux,
> Qu'ils vivent animez d'un esprit amoureux;
>
> Car le masle, courbé vers sa chère femelle,
> Monstre de ressentir le bien d'estre auprès d'elle:
> Elle fait le semblable, et pour s'entr'embrasser,
> On les voit leurs rameaux l'un vers l'autre avancer.

De ces embrassements leurs branches reverdissent,
Le ciel y prend plaisir, les astres les bénissent,
Et l'haleine des vents soupirans à l'entour
Loue en son doux murmure une si sainte amour.

Que si l'impiété de quelque main barbare
Par le tranchant du fer ce beau couple sépare,
Ou transplante autre part leurs tiges désolez,
Les rendant pour jamais l'un de l'autre exilez,

Jaunissans de l'ennuy que chacun d'eux endure,
Ils font mourir le teint de leur belle verdure,
Ont en haine la vie, et pour leur aliment
N'attirent plus l'humeur du terrestre élément.

Si vous m'aimiez, hélas ! autant que je vous aime,
Quand nous serions absents, nous en ferions de mesme ;
Et chacun de nous deux regrettant sa moitié,
Nous serions surnommez les palmes d'amitié.

The germ of this pretty idea, as a French critic has already pointed out, is to be found in Pliny and in Theophrastus, and they probably borrowed it from the beautiful Eastern tradition which affirms that each man and woman is but half a being, and that it is only by his or her discovery of the complementary moiety, and by union therewith, that a perfected entity can be arrived at and a true marriage accomplished. Marie de France expressed a similar idea with felicitous simplicity in 'Le Lai du Chevrefoil,' observes Henry Martin, and it has been also developed by Goethe and other poets. Sainte-Beuve speaks of the foregoing as 'the most beautiful, perhaps the only really beautiful, page in Bertaut. Besides this, he has only scattered odes. Apart from these two palm trees, the enduring crown of the poet, there would be not enough surviving the wrecks of time to form a volume, however slender, from the salvage. It is enough, at any rate, to find the wherewithal to adorn a eulogy, and to fix an honourable remembrance of his name in the memories of men. For that purpose two or three golden nails suffice.'

At the age of thirty-six the Anacreontic poet merged into the austere prelate who recorded the conversion of the king in sacred verse, translated the writings of St. Ambrose, wrote polemical treatises, and died five years after his assumption of the mitre.

From the school of Ronsard, however, one genuine poet

issued—the first poet of genius, indeed, that France had hitherto produced. This was Mathurin Régnier, who was born at Chartres in 1573. Educated for the Church, he received the tonsure at eleven, and was only twenty when Cardinal de Joyeuse, who had been named Protector of France at the court of Rome, took him to that city, the social life of which at that time was licentious in the extreme. He plunged into it with all the ardour of a youthful and undisciplined nature, *vif de courage*, as he says, *et tout chaud d'espérance*; and seems to have been not unfamiliar with privations. The ten years he spent in Rome showed him so much of the seamy side of human life, and were so fruitful of adventures and experiences, that they probably developed in him those cynical views of character, and that talent for satire, which afterwards found expression in his works. Returning to France, his uncle Desportes provided him with a liberal income, and gave him a few years afterwards a canonry in the cathedral of Chartres. In spite of his ecclesiastical functions the conduct of Régnier was anything but decorous. He was improvident by habit, by no means abstemious in the matter of the bottle, and he often complains that his old cloak is full of patches. Mathurin Régnier lived, in fact, under a reign in which the lavish eccentricities of that of Henry III. were unknown. Besides, the utter carelessness of the poet made it impossible for him to acquire a fortune, or at any rate to keep one. He says himself that, living heedlessly, he just allowed things to take their chance. He was irregular in his morals and in his writings, rather by reason of his thoughtlessness than of his imprudence; and even in the most biting of his satires one perceives the bonhomie of the poet who was surnamed the 'Good Régnier,' because, to use his own expression, he had not wit enough to be wicked.

Satire is so much a national instinct, it existed so long before Régnier, and displayed itself under so many forms, in our *fabliaux* and in our romances, in our farces and in our chansons, that we can scarcely term him the founder of it. Nevertheless it has been said that Régnier founded it in France; which is true in a sense, for he reduced it to rule and measure. Sainte-Beuve has summed up his characteristics in this admirable fashion:

'The mouth of a satyr, but more prone to laugh than to bite; heartiness, good sense, exquisite malice, at times a bitter eloquence, narratives with the smirch of the kitchen, the tavern, and naughty places on them; in his hands, instead of a lyre, some clownish but not discordant instrument; in a word, ugly and abundantly grotesque—such may we picture, in the gross, Mathurin Régnier. Placed at the gateway of our two principal literary centuries, he turned his back upon them and gazed towards the Sixteenth. He stretched out his hands towards those Gallic forefathers, Montaigne, Ronsard, and Rabelais. Where Régnier excelled above all was in his knowledge of life, in his expression of manners and personages, and in his portrayal of interiors. His 'Satires' are a gallery of admirable Flemish portraits. Once known, his poet, his pedant, his coxcomb, can never be forgotten.'

In quite as great a degree as Malherbe, Régnier revived in France the imitation of our old authors. He profited by the abortive efforts of the Pléiade, avoiding and combating at the same time the errors into which, as we have seen, they and their immediate successors fell. When we reflect upon the careless hardihood and the abundant and overflowing vitality of his style, so like that of our greatest essayist, we feel justified in designating him the Montaigne of our poetry. To quote his best passages would be to swell this page into a volume.

I have already referred to the insult offered by Malherbe to Desportes at his own table, and to the way in which Régnier afterwards resented it in a satire, in which the pedantic tone of Malherbe, so provocative of ridicule, was lashed by the younger poet. Here is a sample of his verse:

> Ces rêveurs dont la muse insolente,
> Censurant les plus vieux, arrogamment se vante
> De réformer les vers. . . .
> Qui veulent déterrer les Grecs du monument,
> Les Latins, les Hébreux, et toute l'antiquaille,
> Et leur dire à leur nez qu'ils n'ont rien fait qui vaille.
> Ronsard en son métier n'était qu'un apprentif;
> Il avait le cerveau fantastique et rétif;
> Desportes n'est pas net, Du Bellay trop facile;
> Belleau ne parle pas comme on parle à la ville;
> Il a des mots hargneux, bouffis et relevés,
> Qui du peuple aujourd'hui ne sont pas approuvés.
> Comment! il nous faut donc, pour faire une œuvre grande
> Qui de la calomnie et du temps se défende,
> Qui trouve quelque place entre les bons auteurs,
> Parler comme à Saint Jean parlent les crocheteurs!

And what right have these poets to come along and change everything? Have they any pretension to genius? No.

>Leur savoir ne s'étend seulement
>Qu'à regratter un mot douteux au jugement,
>Prendre garde qu'un ' qui ' ne heurte une diphthongue,
>Épier si des vers la rime est brève ou longue,
>Ou bien si la voyelle, à l'autre s'unissant,
>Ne rend point à l'oreille un vers trop languissant,
>Et laissent sur le verd le noble de l'ouvrage.
>Nul aiguillon divin n'élève leur courage ;
>Ils rampent bassement, faibles d'inventions,
>Et n'osent, peu hardis, tenter les fictions,
>Froids à l'imaginer : car, s'ils font quelquechose,
>C'est proser de la rime et rimer de la prose.

Born, as I have said, in 1553, Régnier, although younger than Malherbe, died in 1613, fifteen years before the latter, leaving no school and no literary posterity worthy of his great talent. For he was not the forefather of Molière and Boileau, much as they owed to him ; and the tribute which the latter writer paid to his genius is as honourable to its author as to its object. 'The celebrated Régnier,' said he, 'is, by universal consent, the poet who before the time of Molière was best acquainted with the manners and the character of men.' Sainte-Beuve indicates points of resemblance between Régnier and La Fontaine. He must surely have been a great man who could thus suggest so many illustrious names without being eclipsed by them.

Some time before his death, it appears, Régnier experienced a return to pious sentiments, and shed tears of penitence. Like his uncle, he composed some devotional sonnets. It was the fashion of the time, our poets terminating the stormiest existences by translating or imitating the Holy Scriptures. All things considered, Régnier closed one epoch as Malherbe opened another ; and without entirely accepting the exalted estimate formed of him by Alfred de Musset, we may certainly adopt without hesitation that of Boileau :

>De ces maîtres savants, disciple ingénieux,
>Régnier seul, parmi nous, formé sur leurs modèles,
>Dans un vieux style encore, a des grâces nouvelles.

His 'literary baggage' comprises sixteen satires, five elegies, three epistles, and numerous odes, stanzas, and epigrams; a collective edition of which was published by the celebrated Elzevir. Nor can I take leave of Régnier without quoting his epitaph upon himself, for it is a portrait from the life:

> J'ai vécu sans nul pensement,
> Me laissant aller doucement
> A la bonne loi naturelle;
> Et si m'étonne fort pourquoi
> La mort osa songer à moi
> Qui ne songeai jamais à elle.

Before François de Malherbe, who was born in 1555, France had not yet acquired a poetic diction of an elevated character. Its advent constituted an epoch in the history of the French language and literature. Malherbe alone revealed all the riches of our versification: beauty of expression, picturesqueness of imagery, rapid movement, variety of metre, cadence—nothing was wanting in his fine odes. No one knew better than himself the effects of harmony; no one was gifted with greater taste. His severity in the choice of his words was extreme, and he commenced that purification of our mother tongue which was continued by the Academy. He is one of those writers, indeed, who have rendered the greatest services to the French language, making it a vehicle of expression alike for the court, the city, and the people. Here are some stanzas addressed to a friend, to console him for the death of his daughter in 1607:

> Ta douleur, du Périer, sera donc éternelle,
> Et les tristes discours,
> Que te met en l'esprit l'amitié paternelle,
> L'augmenteront toujours?
>
> Le malheur de ta fille au tombeau descendue
> Par un commun trépas,
> Est-ce quelque dédale, où ta raison perdue
> Ne se retrouve pas?
>
> Je sais de quels appas son enfance estoit pleine,
> Et n'ai pas entrepris,
> Injurieux amy, de soulager ta peine
> Avecque son mépris.
>
> Mais elle estoit du monde, où les plus belles chose
> Ont le pire destin;
> Et Rose, elle a vécu ce que vivent les roses,
> L'espace d'un matin.

> La mort a des rigueurs à nulle autre pareilles :
>   On a beau la prier ;
> La cruelle qu'elle est se bouche les oreilles,
>   Et nous laisse crier.
>
> Le pauvre en sa cabane, où le chaume le couvre,
>   Est sujet à ses lois ;
> Et la garde qui veille aux barrières du Louvre
>   N'en défend point nos rois.
>
> De murmurer contre elle, et perdre patience,
>   Il est mal à propos ;
> Vouloir ce que Dieu veut est la seule science
>   Qui nous met en repos.

These verses reveal to us another poet who had 'learned in suffering what he taught in song;' for we find in them a softened echo of the pathetic sentiment which breathes through every line of the singularly touching letter which he addressed to his wife in 1599, to apprise her of the death of 'Ma chère fille et la vôtre, notre belle Jordaine.' 'It showed that there was a time in his life when he was neither heartless nor irreligious.' In the same sombre strain of feeling the poet moralised upon the tombs of kings :

> Ils sont rongés des vers :
> Là se perdent ces noms de maîtres de la terre,
> D'arbitres de la paix, de foudres de la guerre ;
> Comme ils n'ont plus de sceptre, ils n'ont plus de flatteurs,
> Et tombent avec eux d'une chute commune,
>   Tous ceux que la fortune
>   Faisait leurs serviteurs.

But among these servants of the great and the fortunate there were few more obsequious than the poet himself, and few more ready to treat with obloquy the corpse of the dead lion. While Henry III. lived, Malherbe fawned upon him in a couplet full of adulation, like the following :

> Henri, de qui les yeux et l'image sacrée
> Font un visage d'or à cette âge ferrée ;

and the poet was rewarded with 500 crowns for his sycophancy. But no sooner had the king joined the 'diet of worms' than he was stigmatised by the same pen as a 'roi fainéant, la vergogne des princes.' It was the same with Marie de Médicis, whom Malherbe extolled during her regency as a ruler of matchless wisdom and goodness, and as a masterpiece of heavenly work. When she was exiled

and disgraced he smeared the Duc de Luynes with the
thickest of honey, and hailed him as the saviour of France.
But when that statesman's day of power came to an end,
the satirist turned upon him the weapons of invective and
lampooned him as

>Une absinthe au nez de barbet
>Que je voudrais voir au gibet;

while before the rising sun of Richelieu the poet prostrated
himself in the dust, and could scarcely find words in his
copious vocabulary sufficiently eulogistic to lavish on 'ce
grand cardinal, grand chef-d'œuvre des cieux!' There was
so much in fact that was thoroughly contemptible in the
character and career of Malherbe, that it is difficult to set
aside the unpleasant impression produced upon the mind
by the knowledge of his conduct as a man, while we are
engaged in picturing his works as a poet. Even his egregious
vanity almost tempts one to depreciate his genius. What
an overweening estimate of himself must he have formed
when, in writing an ode, as the court poet, on the death of
Henry IV., he found occasion to inform his countrymen
that there were only three or four upon whom Apollo would
bestow a laurel crown :

>Au nombre desquels on me range,

adding that they

>Peuvent donner une louange,
>Qui demeure éternellement;

and we find him repeating the same vainglorious boast in a
sonnet to the king :

>Les ouvrages communs durent quelques années,
>Ce que Malherbe écrit dure éternellement.

To find his parallel in English literature, we should have
to fuse Charles Churchill and Alexander Pope into one
being. Malherbe was as unscrupulous as the first and as
cynical as the second; and he was gifted with the splendid
powers of satire which were common to both. Like Pope,
he was a great artificer of language; and Balzac, writing
some time after the death of Malherbe, says: 'Do you
remember that old pedagogue of the court, who was formerly
called the tyrant of words and syllables? I pity a man
who makes so much ado between *pas* and *point*, and who

treats a matter of participles and gerunds as if it were one of two neighbouring peoples jealous about their frontiers.'

Sainte-Beuve considers the immortal glory of Malherbe to have been this: that 'he was the first French writer who possessed the sentiment and the theory of style in poetry, and who comprehended that the choice of terms and ideas is, if not the principle, at any rate the condition of all true eloquence, and that the happy arrangement of words and things is very often more important than the words and things themselves.'

Malherbe's methods of composition were slow and laborious in the extreme. They resembled the work of the diamond cutters in Amsterdam, and were just as tedious and prolonged. Was it not Sydney Smith who said that when Samuel Rogers was about to give birth to a couplet he took to his bed, had the street strawed with tan, muffled the door knocker, and awaited with exemplary patience the arrival of the little stranger? Much the same might have been said of the French poet. He was once commissioned by a high functionary to write some verses on the death of his wife. After three years of gestation the lines saw the light, but in the meantime the widower had married again. On another occasion he served up to Richelieu a dish of verse which had been first cooked years before. It was one of Malherbe's favourite maxims, indeed, that after having written a poem, short or long, the mind required to lie fallow for ten years.

To him must be ascribed the honour of having emancipated the French language from its previous bondage to foreign tongues, and of having bestowed upon it a gravity and a dignity, a harmony and a grace in which it had hitherto been deficient. He was a purist in the matter of grammar and prosody, and he may be said to have died with a correction on his lips; for, an hour before breathing his last, he roused himself for the purpose of reprimanding his nurse, who had used a word which was not pure French. When his confessor remonstrated with him for so doing at such a moment, he said he could not help it, and that he was resolved to defend the purity of the French language to the very death.

Malherbe was a reformer of French prose as well as of

French poetry, and Balzac formed his own style upon that of his predecessor, and may be considered as having perfected the revolution which he commenced. Henry Martin somewhat qualifies the excessive praise bestowed upon Malherbe by earlier critics, and makes the happy remark that his was the task of forging the weapons of which later writers made such a noble use. 'He prepared the way for Corneille and Racine, just as Henry IV. prepared it for Richelieu and Louis XIV.; with this important difference, however, that Henry IV. will never be effaced by his successors, more powerful, perhaps, but not greater than himself.'

It is impossible to speak of Malherbe without recalling to mind the name of Racan, the favourite disciple of him whom Boileau calls the first in France who

> Fit sentir dans les vers une juste cadence,
> D'un mot mis en sa place enseigna le pouvoir,
> Et réduisit la Muse aux règles du devoir.

The Marquis of Raçan, who was born in 1589 and died in 1670, has less power but quite as much natural grace as his preceptor. He was one of the first members of the French Academy founded by Richelieu in 1604, and his 'Bergeries,' a long dramatic pastoral, contains many beautiful passages. The difference between the master and his disciple has been cleverly hit off by Boileau in the following couplet:

> Malherbe d'un héros peut chanter les exploits,
> Racan chanter Phillis, les bergers et les bois.

In the subjoined lines we catch an echo of Malherbe, but they bear at the same time the stamp of individuality:

> Le bien de la fortune est un bien périssable;
> Quand on bâtit sur elle, on bâtit sur le sable;
> Plus on est élevé, plus on court de dangers;
> Les grand pins sont en butte aux coups de la tempête,
> Et la rage des vents brise plutôt le faîte
> Des maisons de nos rois que des toits des bergers.

> O bienheureux celuy qui peut de sa mémoire
> Effacer pour jamais ce vain espoir de gloire
> Dont l'inutile soin traverse nos plaisirs,
> Et qui, loin retiré de la foule importune,
> Vivant dans sa maison, content de sa fortune,
> A selon son pouvoir mesuré ses désirs;

> Il voit de toutes parts combler d'heur sa famille,
> La javelle à plein poing tomber sous la faucille,
> Le vendangeur ployer sous le faix des paniers,
> Et semble qu'à l'envy les fertiles montagnes,
> Les humides vallons et les grasses campagnes
> S'efforcent à remplir sa cuve et ses greniers.

What causes Racan to be still read in our days is the harmonious way in which he depicts his own sentiments; when he speaks of the pleasures of rural life and compares them with the agitations of those people who are engaged in the pursuit of fortune, he shows himself to be a true poet. He was a sincere lover of nature, and holding the vanities of the world and the ambition of men in but light esteem, he produced some of his most telling effects by the antithetical presentation of his affection for the country and his contempt for a city life. Questions of this kind are often propounded in his verse:

> Que sert à ces galants ce pompeux appareil
> Dont ils vont dans la lice éblouir le soleil
> Des trésors du Pactole?
> La gloire qui les suit après tant de travaux
> Se passe en moins de temps que la poudre qui vole
> Du pied de leurs chevaux.

Racan was by no means unacquainted with the life he despised; for in his youth he had been one of the pages of the chamber to Henry IV., and later on he had embraced a military career, had taken part in nearly all the expeditions of Louis XIII., and had commanded a company at the siege of Rochelle. He did not marry until he was nine-and-thirty, and soon afterwards the Duchess of Bellegarde bequeathed him an income of 10,000 livres per annum; whereupon he settled down in his ancestral château of La Roche-Racan, in that garden of France, beautiful Touraine. Tallemant des Réaux describes the poet as having all the appearance of a country farmer, rustic in his manners and stammering in his speech. His imitations of the ancients in his poetry were perfect; and some of them were preferable to those of Malherbe on account of their superior simplicity. When his model died, Racan was so much grieved that he laid aside his pen for twenty years. Towards the close of his life he cultivated the composition of sacred verse, and died at the age of eighty-one. La Fontaine has coupled the names of Malherbe and Racan in his well-known fable of 'The Miller, his Son, and his Ass,' where he says:

> Ces deux rivaux d'Horace, héritiers de sa lyre,
> Disciples d'Apollon, nos maîtres, pour mieux dire.

Before speaking to you of Balzac, 1597–1655, who has been called the Malherbe of French prose, I must glance for a moment at two poets who were contemporary with Malherbe and Racan. Jean Ogier de Gombauld, 1570–1666, in spite of the fact that he was a Huguenot, enjoyed the favour of Marie de Médicis, Henry IV., Louis XIII., and Louis XIV. He was one of the *beaux esprits* of the Hôtel de Rambouillet, and one of the original members of the French Academy. Some of his sonnets and epigrams still survive. The following will serve as examples of his style:

JUGEMENT DES ŒUVRES D'AUTRUI

> Vous lisez les œuvres des autres
> Plus négligemment que les vôtres,
> Et vous les louez froidement.
> Voulez-vous qu'elles soient parfaites,
> Imaginez-vous seulement
> Que c'est vous qui les avez faites.

LE MOYEN DE SE DÉFAIRE DE QUELQU'UN

> Tu veux te défaire d'un homme,
> Et jusqu'ici tes vœux ont été superflus.
> Hazarde une petite somme :
> Prête-lui trois louis, tu ne le verras plus.

There is a good deal of wit and satire in the epigrams of Gombauld; and if the specimens I have quoted should induce you to desire to know more of him, I may refer you, for fuller information, to the 'Historiettes' of Tallemant des Réaux.

François Maynard, 1582–1646, is perhaps better known by his lines on the misery of poets than by anything he ever wrote. They are these:

> Muses, Parnasse est une terre
> Où désormais nos nourrissons,
> Soit dans la paix, soit dans la guerre,
> Feront de petites moissons.

> Mais les vers ont perdu leur prix,
> Et pour les excellents esprits
> La faveur des princes est morte ;
> Malherbe, en cet âge brutal,
> Pégase est un cheval qui porte
> Les grands hommes à l'hôpital.

Maynard was a facile writer, with much lucidity and elegance of expression, simple and natural in the construction of his verses; and although he laboured to secure their high finish, yet he possessed the 'art of concealing art,' so that his most laboured efforts appeared spontaneous. Voltaire includes him among the precursors of the age of Louis XIV. During a visit to Rome, Maynard was honoured with the friendship of Cardinal Bentivoglio and of Urban VIII.; and this is understood to have excited the jealousy of Richelieu, who remained persistently unfriendly to him.

Maynard's own ideas of lucidity of expression are very well set forth in the following epigram :

> Ce que ta plume produit
> Est couvert de trop de voiles ;
> Ton discours est une nuit
> Veuve de lune et d'estoiles.
>
> Mon ami, chasse bien loin
> Cette noire rhétorique ;
> Tes ouvrages ont besoin
> D'un devin qui les explique.
>
> Si ton esprit veut cacher
> Les belles choses qu'il pense,
> Dis-moi, qui peut t'empescher
> De te servir du silence.

After a second journey to Rome, during the regency of Anne of Austria, Maynard, wearying of dancing attendance on the great, and of 'burning incense,' as he says, 'before the idols of the day,' quitted Paris for Aurillac, where he held an appointment, and wrote above the door of his library the following verse :

> Las d'espérer et de me plaindre
> De la cour, des grands et du sort,
> C'est ici que j'attends la mort
> Sans la désirer ni la craindre.

It calls to mind the concluding passage of Leigh Hunt's essay on his books : 'I can help the appreciation of them while I last, and love them till I die; and perhaps, if fortune turns her face once more in kindness upon me before I go, I may chance some quiet day to lay my own beating temples on a book, and so have the death I most envy.'

Boileau quotes the names of Maynard and of Gombauld, *à propos* of the sonnet, that form of composition so difficult to treat, when he says:

> A peine dans Gombault, Maynard et Malleville,
> En peut-on admirer deux ou trois entre mille.

And, speaking of the sonnet, I would venture to remind you that it was imported into France from Italy by Mellin de Saint-Gelais, Joachim du Bellay, and Pontus de Thiard. Malleville, of whom I should not have spoken if his name had not been coupled with the two others by Boileau, was born in 1597 and died in 1647, was an Academician, and cultivated the same kinds of poetry as Maynard.

I now take leave of this branch of my subject; not that I have by any means exhausted it, but because I feel that I ought not to increase my demands upon the attention of my hearers. It is difficult, if not impossible, in studying a literature like the French, to say, 'I will begin here and I will finish there;' but I think I have arrived at a convenient halting place, at which to pause before resuming my journey across the wide field that stretches out before me.

LECTURE VIII

Rabelais (1495-1553)—Amyot (1513-1593)—Montaigne (1533-1592).

I COME now to an author who was one of the founders of French prose. I speak of Rabelais, whom I can neither omit from my course nor discuss except with that reserve which becomes a woman approaching such a theme. Possibly I may be the first of my sex who has studied his works in order to speak of them in a public discourse; but if others have preceded me, they will certainly understand my hesitation and appreciate my embarrassment. Nevertheless, Rabelais fills so large a place in French literature that he cannot and must not be overlooked. I have read his writings both in French and in the wonderful translation of them which exists in English, and will try to communicate to you in what follows the knowledge I have acquired of them.

Nisard has made some remarks upon this enigmatical author, which naturally rise to one's lips on an occasion like this: 'Owing to that mania of critics which induces them to apparel the life of a writer with the character of his works, they have constructed a burlesque and anecdotic biography of Rabelais, of which the last act was his testament: "I possess nothing; I owe a great deal; I give the rest to the poor." They have also placed in his mouth when dying the words, "Drop the curtain; the farce is over." Whatever is authentic and indisputable in the life of Rabelais is insignificant. All that is doubtful is exaggerated. His biography and his writings have been equally misconceived. In his book, one portion is pure fantasy, facetiousness, intellectual libertinage, and farce. Another portion is sheer obscenity, a veritable cesspool, which cannot be qualified as literature. But there is yet a third part—philosophical in spirit, evidently written with a satirical purpose, replete with good sense, elevated in reason, very superior in style, thoroughly original, and displaying far more maturity of judgment than the two others. One must laugh at the first, supposing we are able to comprehend all its *finesses*, but without subjecting it to torture, in order to discover a serious meaning which is not there. We must glide over the second so as not to defile our vision, and it can offer no gratification except to a very coarse or an exceedingly jaded intelligence. Finally, we must perforce admire the third, study it, and extract much profit from it, by retaining its enduring ideas, by meditating on the richness of the style, and by learning by heart those aphorisms of which the good sense and the practical application will last for ever.'

It is in reliance upon the judgment of so excellent a literary critic that I have ventured to undertake a study of Rabelais, by following the advice which he gives for the threefold perusal of his works. That portion which Nisard says should be glided over I shall carefully avoid, confining my attention to the satirical and philosophical aspects of one of the masterpieces of the national literature.

François Rabelais was born at Chinon in what he justly calls 'the garden of France,' fair Touraine, in the year 1495, memorable also as that in which Martin Luther and Raffaelle first saw the light. He was at first a novice in a convent of Benedictines, and the immensity and profundity of his youthful studies are a sufficient refutation of the traditions current with respect to the irregularity of his habits. He was by turns librarian, secretary, doctor, and parish priest. Medicine, mathematics, theology, astronomy, botany, jurisprudence, the natural sciences, and the romances of chivalry—nothing came amiss to him. With Greek, Latin, Hebrew, and Arabic he was as familiar as with his mother-tongue. He contrived to emancipate himself from conventual life just before reaching the age of forty, when he qualified himself for, and obtained, the diploma of a physician, and by way of intellectual recreation acquired a knowledge of the Spanish, Italian, German, English, and Basque languages. Anticipating Cervantes, he conceived the idea of burlesquing the old romances of chivalry, of which he had read so many, and, remembering the legends of Gargantua, the great giant, of whom he must have heard from the lips of his aunt down in Touraine, he selected that popular personage as the hero of a work which stands quite alone in European literature. He began it in 1532, and published it at Lyons, under the title of 'The Chronicles of Gargantua.' In the year following appeared 'Pantagruel,' in which were recorded the exploits of the giant's son, which immediately became so popular that three editions of it were called for in a twelvemonth.

In his advice to the reader occur the following verses, which are pretty widely known and have served as a text for many a modern author:

> Amys lecteurs, qui ce livre lisez,
> Despouillez vous de toute affection ;
> Et le lisant ne vous scandalisez,
> Il ne contient mal ne infection.
> Vray est qu'icy peu de perfection
> Vous apprendrez, sinon en cas de rire.
> Autre argument ne peut mon cueur élire,
> Voyant le deuil qui vous mine et consomme :
> Mieulx est de ris que de larmes escripre ;
> Pour ce que rire est le propre de l'homme.
> Vivez joyeux.

We find him in the same year visiting Rome, in company with his old friend, Cardinal du Bellay, who was negotiating with the Pope for the divorce of Henry VIII. of England from Catherine of Aragon. He revisited that city on his own account in 1536, to obtain absolution for having violated certain ecclesiastical rules, and the absolution was readily granted. At the same time—and here we see the practical side of the great scholar's mind—Rabelais introduced the melon, the artichoke, and the carnation into France.

It was on his second return from Rome, in 1539, that Rabelais prefaced a revised edition of his 'Gargantua' by the following enigmatical words, which many of his commentators have quoted in their anxiety to solve an apparent riddle and to decipher the historical meaning of the work: 'My worthy disciples,—When reading the merry titles of some books of our invention, you are too apt to fancy that nothing but jest and frolic is to be found within. . . . But the frock does not make the monk. . . . That is why the book should be carefully opened and its contents seriously weighed. Then you will find out that the drug inside is much more precious than the box would seem to indicate. . . . The book should be interpreted in a far higher sense than one which you might imagine perchance to have been written in mere gaiety of heart.'

'Certain critics,' observes Nisard, 'wishing to discover the historic sense of Rabelais's work and to explain all its enigmas, have added to his obscurities those of their own contradictions. No doubt Rabelais did not lose sight of the men and abuses of his own times, and he sought to amuse himself and his contemporaries at their expense, but he was far from making war to the knife on the age he lived in;' and Buckle has pointed out that it was to his abstinence from so doing that he was indebted for his immunity from persecution at an epoch in which toleration was practised by no religious party whatever.

In 1546 he published the Third Book, and three years later he issued eleven chapters of the fourth, while the fifth and last was found in manuscript after his death. Cardinal du Bellay had presented him with the living of Meudon, which he held in conjunction with another *cure* of souls, in 1548, but, for some unexplained reason, he resigned them both in 1552, and died in the year following.

To say that Rabelais was one of the greatest humourists the world has ever seen is only to claim for him his rightful due. So also was Shakespeare, but both of them were something far higher than that. They were deep thinkers and serious reasoners, and while they laughed right jovially at the follies and foibles of mankind, they mingled with their mirth philosophical reflections and precepts instinct with practical wisdom.

For the present, however, I must proceed to speak of Rabelais as the king of jesters. We may put aside for the present the speculations which have been indulged in, and the rash conjectures which have been hazarded, with respect to the hidden sense of what I may call the epic of extravagant jocundity, and take the colossal joke just as we find it. Altogether apart from the piquancy of its satire, as directed against the vices and follies of the time, the 'Life of Gargantua and Pantagruel' is one of the most extraordinary books that have ever been written, a monument of its author's deep and varied erudition, no less than an evidence of the wildly capricious flights of his irrepressible imagination. How can one characterise a work in which wisdom and buffoonery, rollicking fun and mordant satire, the jovial laughter of the genial lover of his kind and the sardonic grin of the cynic, the lofty morality of the sage and the rank indecency of Silenus, are so inextricably interwoven? It is a book without ancestry and without posterity. It stands alone as a fantastic, grotesque, amorphous, and phantasmagoric production of the human mind, conceived without a plan, executed in obedience to the dominant impulse of the passing moment, and achieved at a time when the restraints upon freedom of thought and speech were so numerous and powerful, and when so many men were burned alive for expressing themselves far more guardedly concerning abuses in Church and State than ever he did, that it is amazing to reflect upon the extraordinary good fortune which enabled Rabelais to die peaceably in his bed.

Let me endeavour to present you with a brief analysis of the first part of his immortal work.

Grandgousier, whose portrait is painted with a broad and flowing brush, resides at Chinon with his wife Gargamelle. A gigantic son is born to them, whom they name Gargantua; and the first words he utters are 'Drink, drink, drink,' in so tremendous a tone of voice as to be audible for many miles round. It requires 17,913 cows to supply him with milk, and his pretty little under-garment consumes 1,950 yards of the finest linen. As soon as he is old enough to be sent to Paris, he rides thither on a mare as big as six elephants, which was imported in three carricks and a brigantine. This is the best of Rabelais: he is always so accurate in his details. For example, he tells us how Gargantua used to hear from twenty-six to thirty masses when he went to church, and how he used a cartload of rosaries in his devotions; if he had said a barrowful, we might not have believed him. He gave half an hour to study every morning. It was the halfpennyworth of bread to the intolerable deal of sack which he consumed, for he held very strong opinions upon this subject, contending that the legitimate limits of toping were when the cork of the drinker's shoes had swollen half a foot. And he ate—ye gods! how Gargantua did eat! His daily bill of fare reminds one of the *menu* of King Arthur at Caerleon :

> Hogsheads of honey, kilderkins of mustard,
>   Muttons and fatted beeves and bacon swine;
> Herons and bitterns, peacock, swan and bustard,
>   Teal, mallard, pigeons, widgeons, and in fine
> Plum-puddings, pancakes, apple-pie, and custard;
>   And therewithal he drank good Gascon wine,
> With mead, and ale, and cider of his own,
>   For porter, punch, and negus were not known.

Gargantua's education was entrusted in the first instance to Sophists, and the life which his earliest preceptors led him is portrayed in a highly comic vein. When he rose in the morning, the child arranged his hair by means of a German comb, that is to say, with his ten fingers; while his masters taught him that to wash himself, and to be cleanly generally, was sheer waste of time in this world. After a perfunctory toilet he gorged himself with food; and having despatched an enormous breakfast, he went to church, where he heard from six-and-twenty to thirty masses; and Rabelais tells us, in addition, that, for his rosary, he required, as I have said, a whole cartload of beads. His religious exercises accomplished, one little half-hour was devoted to study; and during the whole of this time our hero's heart was in the kitchen. Then followed an immense Pantagruelian dinner; after which he chatted and played with the persons chosen to wait upon him, and then, without troubling himself about anything good or evil, he slept for two or three hours. On awaking, he drank, read a little, and went into the kitchen to see what joints were roasting on the spit, supped, went to bed, and slept until eight o'clock next morning.

His first preceptors were replaced by Ponocrates, who completely reversed his system of education, which Gargantua was sent to finish in Paris. He rode thither on a mare of colossal proportions and as high as six elephants, for nothing less would have sufficed for a youth of such stupendous stature. Some of the incidents of his journey are related in this extravagantly humorous fashion:

Thus merrily they proceeded along the highway, everywhere refreshing themselves with good cheer, until they drew near Orleans; at which place there was an extensive forest about thirty-five leagues long and seventeen broad, or thereabouts. This wood was horribly fertile, and swarming with hornets and horse-flies, so that for the poor mares, horses, and asses, it was a regular scene of torment. But Gargantua's roadster inflicted a summary vengeance for all the outrages sustained by beasts of her species, by a single stroke, for no sooner had she entered the aforesaid forest, and the hornets had commenced a general assault, than she spread forth her tail, and whisked it with such tremendous force that down went the whole of the forest, striking the trees at random, here and there, forward and backward, above and below, to the right hand and the left, far and near; so that the timber fell like grass before the mower's scythe, so that presently neither flies nor trees were visible, but all was open country. Seeing which, Gargantua was very pleased indeed, and without making any boast of it, said to his people 'That's fine!' (*Je trouve beau ce!*) And so that region was thenceforth called Beauce.

Gargantua's impressions of Paris and the Parisians are full of naïveté and sly sarcasm.

'The people,' he says, ' are so foolish, so boobyish,[1] and naturally so inept, that a mountebank, a ragpicker, a mule with his bells, or a player on the hurdy-gurdy, in the middle of a thoroughfare, will draw together more people than a good preacher of the Gospel. And he met with so many obstructions by the way that he was obliged to sit down and rest himself on the towers of Notre-Dame. And being there he took a look at the large bells in the towers, and caused them to ring harmoniously; in doing which, it occurred to him that they would be just the things to hang on the neck of his mare whenever he should send her back to his father, laden with cheeses of Brie, and with fresh herrings. So he carried the bells off to his lodgings.'

A deputation is sent to wait upon Gargantua to solicit restitution of the bells, and its spokesman addresses the jolly giant in the most delightful of dog-Latin. Here is a specimen of it: 'Omnis clocha clochabilis in clocherio clochando clochans clochativo clochare facit clochabiliter clochantes. Parisius habet clochas. . . .'

Of course the reasoning is unanswerable.

But in the meanwhile Grandgousier's kingdom is invaded by King Picrochole (meaning ' bitter bile '), and Gargantua

---

[1] *Tant badault*, whence the modern *badaud*.

is summoned home from Paris, and performs a succession of tremendous exploits in the way of pulling down fortresses and slaughtering his father's enemies, without sustaining any other inconvenience than that of getting his hair so full of bullets and cannon-balls that it takes him a long time to comb them out again. But the whole campaign, its origin, its incidents, and its consequences, as described by Rabelais, constitute a biting satire upon wars in general and upon those who wage them. Sainte-Beuve compares the proceedings of the council held by Picrochole to a scene out of Molière; but if M. Taine had written a commentary upon it he would probably have found in it a sort of prophetic vision of the Napoleonic epic. His captains, having received the king's gracious permission to keep their helmets on in his presence, proceed to submit a plan of operations. Having subdued Grandgousier, he will overrun Spain and Portugal, take ship at Lisbon, rebuild the Pillars of Hercules, rebaptise the Mediterranean by the name of the Picrocholine Sea; and this accomplished, Barbarossa will tender his submission. 'I will be merciful to him,' exclaims Picrochole. 'The north of Africa, Italy, Sicily, Corsica, and Sardinia will succumb to him, and having seized the islands in the Levant, he will bend his course towards the Holy Land.' 'Then will I build the temple of Solomon,' says Picrochole. 'Do nothing rashly, but make haste slowly,' rejoin his sage counsellors, who proceed to map out other conquests, while he generously apportions among them some of the territories he is going to subdue.

All this is excellent fooling, and it is something more and something better. The dreams of world-wide conquest cherished by an Alexander of Macedon, a Charles V., and a Napoleon Bonaparte: are they not as illusory as the visions of Picrochole?—who is afterwards routed and put to flight, together with his lieutenants, and nobody ever knew what had become of them; they did not even find a retreat in a Spanish monastery or upon a lonely rock in the Atlantic. But let us be grateful to the campaign of Gargantua against his father's enemy; for how otherwise would he have known Friar John? and if there had been no Friar John, there would have been no Abbey of Thelema—that miracle of architecture which Rabelais has described so minutely that it is as real as Blois, Chambord, or Chenonceaux, and constitutes 'the noblest dream of the sixteenth century.' No one has been better qualified to appreciate it than Mr. Walter Besant, the virtual founder of the People's Palace in London ; and this is how he speaks of it : 'This Abbey of Thelema is one of the most graceful and most noble fancies that ever entered into the brain of man.' Its inmates are 'composed entirely of young people living together in the freedom of gentlehood, unrestricted by any conventional and useless rules. They are to learn, by watching the wishes and wants of each other, how to live ; they are to be occupied all day in study, in manly exercises, or in the acquirement of womanly accomplishments; they are to be entirely free from the petty cares and anxieties of the ignoble life; they are to live in accordance with the laws of nature, and are therefore to be exempt from disease.'

In depicting the architectural glories, the splendour, the luxury, and the comforts of the Abbey, Rabelais exhibits the imagination of a poet combined with the feeling of an artist; and the scheme of life and conduct which he devised for the Thelemites proved him to be a deep philosophic thinker. Even the rules of the monastery, condensed in one clause, 'Do as thou wilt,' did not imply licence, but were based upon the assumption that, to quote his own words, 'men who are free, well born, well bred, and conversant with honourable company, have naturally an instinct which prompts them to virtuous actions and withdraws them from vice—this is called honour.' The conscience of each is his or her own guide. They live a life of unselfish labour, and their meditations and mutual service conduct them towards the higher life, upon which their thoughts are set. 'Love among them is free, and marriage the natural outcome of their life. All is noble, all is delightful, all is elevated, all is well bred and worthy, and to crown everything, from a Rabelaisian point of view,' observes Mr. Besant, 'there is not a priest in the place.'

Such, in brief, is the substance of the first book of this marvellous compound of riotous and sometimes ribald humour, and of an elevated and ennobling moral philosophy; a book of which, as its author assures us, more copies were sold in two months than were bought of the Bible in nine years.

I will now endeavour, in spite of the difficulty of the undertaking, to give you some idea of the other four books into which the rest of the work is divided. Grandgousier has departed this life, and Gargantua reigns in his stead. It is Pantagruel and Panurge who occupy the entire attention of the reader. Gargantua was getting on in years—to be exact, he was 498 years old—when Pantagruel was born; and the infant was so sturdy, and withal so thirsty, that he had to be fed with the milk of 4,600 cows; and it was boiled in the big bell which still hangs in the belfry at Bourges. As soon as he was old enough he visited all the universities in France; and at Orleans he met with a scholar who addressed him in Latinised French, such as Ronsard and his school were supposed to affect. This is a sample of it. Pantagruel asked him how the students in Paris spent their time, and the scholar replied: 'We transfretate the Sequane at the dilucul and crepuscul; we deambulate by the compites and quadrives of the urb; we despumate the Latial verbocination; and like verisimiler amorabonds, we ceptat the benevolence of the omnijugal, omniform, and omnigenal feminine sex.' Could Shakespeare have read this passage when he made Sir Andrew Aguecheek remark to the clown, in 'Twelfth Night,' 'Thou wast in very gracious fooling last night, when thou spokest of Pigrogromitus, of the Vapians passing the equinoctial of Queubus'?

Arrived in Paris, Pantagruel favours us with his famous catalogue of the Library of St. Victor; quotes the noble and admirable letter addressed to him by his father with respect to his studies and future conduct; and meets for the first time with Panurge, the incomparable and immortal Panurge, a character worthy of Shakespeare, Cervantes, Ariosto, and Molière, and one whom Sainte-Beuve has bracketed with Pathelin, Lazarillo, Falstaff, Sancho Panza, and Sganarelle. Panurge addresses him in thirteen different languages, a reminiscence, no doubt, of an incident which is alleged, on somewhat doubtful authority, to have occurred to Rabelais himself, when pleading for the liberties of the University of Montpellier before Chancellor Duprat in Paris.

Taken into the household of Pantagruel, Panurge turns out to be an evil-doer, a cheat, a drunkard, a vagabond, a libertine, if ever there was one in Paris, but is, nevertheless, says Rabelais, 'one of the best fellows in the world.' To enumerate the pranks he plays, the scrapes he gets into, and the thousand and one irregularities of his character and conduct, would tax my pains and your patience. He loved to whip the pages whom he met in the street carrying wine to their masters. In his coat which contained six-and-twenty little pockets, were sharp penknives for cutting purses; bottles of verjuice, which he threw in people's eyes; burs stuck with goose-feathers, which he dropped on the heads and robes of honest people; little horns and quills full of fleas, which he poured down the necks of young ladies as they knelt in church; hooks and crochets, with which he secretly hooked together men and women at their devotions, especially those who were well-dressed; squibs, with tinder and matches for lighting them; burning-glasses, with which—always in church—he drove people nearly mad; and powder, with which he made ladies sneeze for four consecutive hours without stopping, a thing which mightily amused him.

In one respect Panurge is the precursor of Mephistopheles. He symbolises intellect entirely divorced from conscience. He has nothing ever so faintly resembling a moral sense. He has a mind, but no soul. He is without pity and without shame; and in a mere spirit of reckless gaiety and unbridled mirth, he exclaims with Satan, 'Evil, be thou my good!' In other respects he is the progenitor of all the unprincipled and lying valets who have figured on the stage or in fiction since this brain-child of Rabelais was first born.

But what of the three principal characters who figure in the First Book? Mr. Walter Besant ingeniously suggests that Pantagruel is the personification of wisdom and of science, gathering both from his councillors and applying them to the practical purposes of life. Epistemon, his tutor, represents scholarship and learning; Eusthenes the right application of strength. I do not feel qualified to offer an opinion upon the allegorical nature of this extraordinary book; but one thing appears to me to be sufficiently clear: that it teems with allusions to events and topics which were the theme of common conversation at the time it was written. Contemporary anecdotes and the gossip of the country-side found a place in the narrative, which throws a flood of light upon the ideas of that epoch, an epoch yielding in celebrity to no other; for it was an epoch illustrated in France by men like Erasmus, Brantôme, Des Périers, Marot, and Rabelais himself.

In the third book, Pantagruel, who has conquered Dipsodie, the land of thirsty souls, and has colonised it with 9,876,543,210 Utopians, not reckoning their wives and children, bestows the government of Salmigondin on Panurge, whose prodigality becomes excessive, who grows enthusiastic in praise of debt, and discusses the question, 'To marry or not to marry,' in a succession of chapters as full of learning as of drollery. Chapters XXXIX. to XLIII. contain that delicious bit of comedy in which Judge Bridoise makes the naïve avowal that he has always been in the habit of deciding all cases by a cast of the dice, using large ones for decisions of importance, and small ones for those of minor concern. Nor does he see the slightest impropriety in the proceeding, or any possibility of a miscarriage of justice, except for his vision becoming so enfeebled as to prevent him from accurately counting the spots.

In the fourth book, Pantagruel sets out upon a voyage in quest of the Divine Bottle, in which Rabelais overwhelms with ridicule the travellers' stories which used to be brought home by adventurous navigators in those early days. On the way Panurge quarrels with a sheep-drover named Dindenault, but pretending to be reconciled with him, buys the ram of his flock and flings it into the sea; whereon every one of the sheep leaps after him; and hence the popular proverb, *Sauter comme les moutons de Panurge.* The voyagers touch at many marvellous islands; and their course is continued in the fifth book, which has been left incomplete by its author. Finally they reach the object of their search and consult the Oracle, who has no better answer to return to Pantagruel, who professes to be searching for the truth, than the laconic injunction, 'Drink!' Truly 'a lame and impotent conclusion,' and one worthier of a Silenus than of a man of vast erudition, rare genius, and of a genuinely philosophical habit of mind like François Rabelais.

His influence upon European literature, but more particularly upon that of France and England, has been very great indeed. La Fontaine has borrowed from him more than one of the subjects of his 'Fables,' and more than one picturesque expression. Rodilardus, Raminagrobis, and Grippeminaud are personages of Rabelais. Henry Martin observes that the characters—the beings he has created—are as powerful and as original as his language. In that strange, colossal world, he adds, the whole of our literature has sought for its living types, from La Fontaine and Molière down to Beaumarchais.

'The vogue of his Homeric buffoonery penetrates everywhere, and has left its stamp upon the arts. He communicated a new impulse to the grotesque, and the employment of quaintly fantastic figures, called *Mascarons*, began to multiply in monumental sculpture. There is one quarter of the old city of Angers in which an entire commentary upon Pantagruel seems to have been portrayed in the carvings of its timber gables. What he has done for our language is simply incalculable. In his hands it assumes a grandeur that it never had before or since. . . . What Dante did for Italian, Rabelais has done for French. He has employed and fused all the dialects, and the elements of every century and of each province which the Middle Ages supplied him with, adding thereto a world of technical expressions furnished to him by the arts and sciences. Any other man would have succumbed to this immense variety of erudition. He harmonised it all, his knowledge of antiquity, and above all of the Greek genius, as well as of every modern language, enabling him to envelope and dominate our own.'

To this eloquent appreciation by Michelet I will venture to add that of Sainte-Beuve :

Rabelais's book is a great feast; not one of those noble and delicate feasts of antiquity, where golden chalices, wreathed with flowers, ingenious railleries and philosophical remarks circulate to the sound of the lyre ; not one of those delicious banquets of Xenophon and Plato, celebrated under marble porticoes in the gardens of Scillus or of Athens. It is a smoky orgy, a bourgeois carousal, a Christmas revel. It is moreover, if you will, a prolonged drinking song, the piquant couplets of which are frequently interrupted by a merry refrain and the jingle of glasses. And in these choruses the verve supplies the sense ; and to try and comprehend the latter is to miss its meaning altogether.

An excellent translation of Rabelais was made by Sir Thomas Urquhart, of Cromarty, in Scotland, who died in 1642. It has been everywhere cited as an unprecedented *tour de force*; for the original has been so admirably reproduced as to make an English author of the great French writer. A purified version was published in London, not long ago, and may be consulted by those who wish to shun the grossness of the earlier and more literal translation.

There are many passages in Rabelais which no woman could or should read; and yet to omit any notice of his writings in such a course of lectures as this would be altogether unpardonable. For his place, not only in our own, but in all literature, is simply unique. There never was but one Rabelais; and I doubt if there can ever be another. His learning was prodigious and his jocundity inexhaustible. He was the most exuberant, rollicking, joyous, buoyant, and irrepressible of humourists; and at the same time so wise, reflective, and sagacious in the midst of his buffoonery. He let loose a torrent of vociferous ridicule upon the follies, fanaticisms, and superstitions of the Church, in which he had been a monk and was afterwards a minister, and was just as unsparing of the Protestants; and neither denomination ever forgave him. Yet at the same time his conceptions of the Supreme Being were so pure, so noble, and so elevated, as to anticipate the most exalted notions of God entertained by Spinoza and Novalis. Let us condemn without stint his grossness, coarseness, indecency, and repulsive realism; and let us acknowledge that, if they are explained, they are in no way excused by the licentiousness of the age in which he lived. But, having done this, let us frankly admit how much there was to admire and even, perhaps, to love in François Rabelais. If Voltaire once called his book 'Un ramas des plus grossières ordures qu'un moine ivre puisse vomir;' and if Calvin, Luther, La Bruyère, Fénelon, and Lamartine considered it detestable; let us remember, on the other hand, that Bishop Huet annotated four editions of it, and that it has been praised and defended by Victor Hugo, Michelet, Guizot, Villemain, Sainte-Beuve, Prosper Mérimée, and Jules Janin in France; and by Coleridge, Charles Kingsley, and Walter Besant in England. To me Rabelais appears to resemble nothing so much as that wonderful compound of fun and frolic, of wit and wisdom, of madcap merriment and stinging satire, of which Shakespeare's fools are the immortal type. In the midst of his wildest flights of jovial gaiety, he pauses to indite a masterly treatise on the education of a young prince—an anticipation, indeed, of the 'Télémaque' of Fénelon. When he is pursuing the 'Quest of the Divine Bottle,' he pilots us into that unknown sea in which Jonathan Swift afterwards discovered Lilliput and Brobdingnag and the land of the Houyhnhnms. If there had been no Pantagruel I think there would have been no 'Tristram Shandy' and no 'Baron Munchausen;' and in that Abbey of Thelema, which has been characterised by an English critic as 'one of the most graceful and noble fancies that ever entered into the brain of man,' may we not find the germinal idea of the beautiful institution of which the Princess Ida was the president in Tennyson's 'Princess'?

While Rabelais scoffed at astrologers, alchemists, casuists, and the inventors of new religions, he could sincerely respect, as Mr. Besant has said, 'that gentle, amiable, and pure-minded school of religious and speculative men who gathered principally about the little court of Marguerite—Lefèvre d'Étaples, Roussel, Briçonnet, and their friends—who thought to keep religion free from the clergy, and taught their flocks that a life of personal holiness was the only walk with God.' Beneath the robe of the arch-jester beat the heart of a true philosopher and of a really devout man, whose creed has been thus compendiously expressed: Trust in God as a Being of infinite love and wisdom, and a life of effort on your own part for the good of others, taking the blessings of life as they come, and thanking the Author of all good for the enjoyment they afford.

I continue this lecture with the study of a writer whose talent was equalled by his modesty; whose name, like his works, is imperishable, and who rendered a notable service to moral philosophy. Jacques Amyot was something more than a translator: he was a translator of genius. He has left us a version of Plutarch which has been a real boon to France. 'We ignorant folk,' observes Montaigne, 'should have been lost if this book had not lifted us out of the slough. Thanks to him we now venture to speak and to write, and ladies lord it over their teachers. It is our breviary, by reason of the *naïveté* and purity of its language.' Racine praises Amyot for having combined with the quaintness of the old style a grace which has never been equalled by the moderns, and Henry Martin pronounces him to have been a discreet and able neologist, full of good sense and moderation, who had imbibed all that was sweet and harmonious in our language. Amyot was one of its creators, indeed. He did not translate the 'Lives;' he transfused the spirit of Plutarch into his own picturesque, animated, original, and dramatic narratives, and produced a great literary monument, when he only professed to be an interpreter of the famous Greek biographer. And he possessed that 'capacity for taking infinite pains' which is close akin to genius, for to perfect his work he ransacked the great libraries at Venice and in the Vatican, in order to examine and compare the best Greek and Latin texts of his author, and left no source of information unexplored, no means of elucidation uninvestigated.

His life was a little romance in itself. Born of poor parents at Melun, on October 30, 1513, he seems to have been sent to Paris, where he received a scanty supply of food once a week from home, conveyed to him by one of the boatmen on the Seine; and to provide himself with clothes and books and the means of paying for his lodgings, he performed menial offices for the richer students. By dint of unwearied application and of great natural ability, Amyot became proficient in Greek, Latin, philosophy, and mathematics, took his degree as Master of Arts, and was appointed, at the age of only nineteen, professor of Greek and Latin in the University of Bourges. A translation of a Greek romance and of some of the Lives of Plutarch, which he dedicated to François I., procured for him the abbey of Bellezene. Then occurred his visit to Italy, on his return from whence Henry II. appointed him tutor to his sons, and Amyot completed his translation, which he dedicated to his royal master. When Charles IX. came to the throne, he appointed his late preceptor Grand Almoner, and subsequently Bishop of Auxerre. Henry III. added to these distinctions the commandership of the order of the Holy

Spirit, an honour rarely conferred upon men of plebeian birth. He suffered severely during the Wars of the League, and died, in the hospital at Orleans, of a slow fever at the age of eighty, leaving behind him an immense fortune. Avarice was, indeed, the one blot upon his character. The hardships and privations he had undergone in early life had caused him to be thrifty to excess and eager in the acquisition of money, and there can be no doubt that there was a good deal both of truth and of philosophy in his reply to Charles IX., from whom he was soliciting the gift of another abbey. 'Did you not once assure me,' said the king to the wealthy pluralist, 'that you would limit your ambition to the acquisition of an income of a thousand crowns?' 'Yes, sire,' replied the covetous prelate, 'but then, you know, the appetite grows by what it feeds upon.' Amyot was at Blois when the assassination of the Duc de Guise occurred, and was accused of complicity in it by the Leaguers. The charge was wholly groundless, but if his force of character had been equal to his learning and his understanding, he would probably have obtained such a moral ascendency over his two royal pupils as would have prevented their reigns from being rendered infamous by the massacre of St. Bartholomew and the dastardly murder just referred to.

If I were to follow up the progress of French prose, so disdained by the school of Ronsard, I should have to show how it gained in maturity and strength, to a greater extent than the poetry of the period, at the hands of Nicolas Herberat des Essarts, an officer of the French artillery, who translated from the Spanish the first eight books of 'Amadis de Gaule,' a work nearly approaching that of Amyot. He was a brilliant representative of the prose writers of that epoch, but I cannot aim at completeness as regards any of the subjects upon which I touch. That virtue has to be sacrificed to compression, but I trust it will suffice to present you with a succinct and at the same time just and accurate idea of the men who have won for themselves an honoured name in both branches of our literature.

And here I am called upon to salute the illustrious author of the 'Essays,' Michel Eyquem, Seigneur de Montaigne, the Frenchman of all others whom English men of letters know most familiarly, the writer with whom they are most perfectly at home, the friend who takes us all most unreservedly into his confidence. He was born at the château of that name down in Périgord, on February 28, 1533, where he received a sound classical education, his tutors conversing with him so habitually in Latin that it became like a second mother tongue to him. He learned Greek as a pastime, and at six years of age he entered the college of Guyenne, at Bordeaux, which he quitted at thirteen, after having studied under Buchanan, who afterwards became the historian of his native country, Scotland, and under Muret, the Latin poet and orator of evil notoriety. Having passed his legal examination, Montaigne was appointed, in 1554, counsellor to the parliament of Bordeaux. He was highly esteemed by the celebrated Chancellor de l'Hôpital, while another of his confrères, of whom I shall have occasion to speak hereafter, La Boëtie, blended his name with that of Montaigne in a friendship which the essayist has immortalised in his writings. In 1566 Montaigne married, and published his first work soon afterwards. This was simply a translation he had made at the request of his father; and in 1571 and 1572 he edited the works of his friend La Boëtie. The political agitations of the period caused him to retire to his château, where he calculated upon passing the rest of his days in studious indolence, 'the world forsaking with a calm disdain.' But his mind, a veritable 'runaway horse,' as he terms it, insisted upon being fed, and so we find him sitting down at the age of thirty-nine to begin those 'Essays' which were destined to render him immortal. The first two books were published in 1580, and the third in 1588. Thanks to his natural indifference to what was going on outside of his own library, which, like that of Prospero, was to him 'a dukedom large enough,' he scarcely felt the shock of the calamitous events of the times in which he lived, although he did not always succeed in preserving his château 'virgin of blood and sack' in the midst of the civil wars which were raging around him. But his adopted daughter, Mademoiselle de Gournay, and his friend Charron helped him, by their consolations, to support these slight and transitory misfortunes. He made occasional excursions in France, Germany, Switzerland, Italy, observing much and reflecting more; was twice elected mayor of Bordeaux; was decorated with the Order of St.

Michael by Charles IX.; was honoured by receiving the freedom of the city of Rome, and died in 1592, when he was approaching his sixtieth year.

Although it did not appear until some years later, the work of Montaigne was conceived during the stormy reign of Charles IX., if it be permissible to use the word 'conception' in connection with the 'Essays,' that universal mirror which reflects the thousandfold aspects of human nature, without order and without connection other than the caprice of a vagrant idea. 'How can we analyse Montaigne?' asks Henry Martin. 'One might as well try to sketch the profile of the Alps or the Pyrenees, or to fix the aspect of the ocean and its restless waves.' *Que sais-je ?* What can I know? is the motto of the great doubter, who gave an immortal impetus to the independence of the human mind. His 'Essays' form an epoch not only in the literature but also in the civilisation of France. Putting aside the personal dissimilarities which, after all, have less importance than is generally supposed, one will find that between Rabelais and Montaigne there is all the difference which exists between the two epochs at which their respective works were published—1545 and 1588. To make my meaning better understood by my English readers, I might add that Montaigne stands in the same relation to Rabelais as that which Hooker bears to Jewell on the one side, and Chillingworth to Hooker on the other; for the law which governs those relations is that of progressive scepticism. Such, at least, is the dictum of Buckle, who pithily remarks that, while the writings of Rabelais were only directed against the clergy, those of Montaigne 'were directed against the system of which the clergy were the offspring.' He was no Pyrrhonist, however, and his scepticism was only that of Pliny when he wrote in his 'Natural History'—'Solum certum nihil esse certi, et homine nihil miserius aut superbius.' His was the 'honest doubt,' in which, as Tennyson said, 'there lives more faith' than in 'half the creeds.' A good Catholic, Montaigne was full of tolerance in an age in which toleration was regarded almost as a crime; and among the friends with whom he lived were François de la Noue, surnamed Bras de Fer, and Théodore de Bèze, two of the foremost Huguenots of the time. He extolled the first for the sweetness and beauty of his character, and proclaimed the second to be one of the greatest poets of the century, notwithstanding that his writings had been laid under a ban by Rome.

Lamartine has called Montaigne and Montesquieu the two great Republicans of French thought, and the first of these was undoubtedly the precursor of Descartes. Nor must it be forgotten that the publication of the second series of his 'Essays,' in which he vindicated the principle of religious toleration, and preached compassion, forbearance, prudence, and wisdom, as Bodin and L'Hôpital had done before him, preceded by five years only the promulgation by Henry IV. of the Edict of Nantes. Before Montaigne doubt was almost unknown, and it is to the publication of the works of this sceptic that we owe, in all probability, the issue of that memorable Edict, by which civil and religious rights were conceded to heretics by a Catholic government. Once, if not twice, the king of Navarre was his guest at the old château in Périgord; and may we not imagine the young monarch imbibing from the lips of the philosopher, who was twenty years his senior, those tolerant ideas which were embodied in that document?

No epoch in the history of France defines so clearly the close of the old world and the advent of a new one as that of which the 'Essays' of Montaigne constitute one of the great literary landmarks. Intellectually nurtured on the past, for Athens and Rome were the foster-mothers of his mind, his eyes were firmly fixed on the future. His was the voice that announced principles of political, social, and individual conduct that were to be adopted and applied long after he should have mouldered into dust. Liberty of conscience, freedom to believe; the enfranchisement of the human mind from the slavery of tradition, prejudice, superstition; the overthrow of impostures of all kinds; and the extinction of those false sciences which obstruct the progress of the true ones: these were the objects which seemed to be dearest to his heart. Yet we must not believe, however, that he replied 'No' to the great questions to which previous generations had responded 'Yes.' What he substituted for the latter, as Henry Martin observes, was 'Perhaps.' The attitude of his mind was not one of blank negation, but of a reflective hesitation. He disliked dogmatism, which, according to the witty definition of Douglas Jerrold, is 'only puppyism full-grown.' Dogmatism is the offspring of intellectual conceit and arrogance. Montaigne was humble because he had read much, observed much, and reflected much. Above all, he had pored over the mysteries of his own mind. He held, with Pope, that 'the proper study of mankind is man,' and that the whole of humanity is capable of being read by the introspective examination and analysis of himself. And thus, becoming cognisant of his own weaknesses and imperfections, he learned to be very indulgent towards those of all others.

As one of his critics has pointed out, Montaigne passed through two periods of doubt. In the first—during which he composed his 'Essays'—it was that expressed by Hamlet in the memorable soliloquy beginning 'To be, or not to be;' and this was succeeded, in the second place, by a less placid and dreamy and a more passionate and tragic doubt. Only a few of the essayist's contemporaries were qualified to discern the greatness of the man and the enduring nature of his work. Justus Lipsius surnamed him the 'French Thales;' De Thou, the historian, predicted his immortality; Etienne Pasquier read his writings with delight; and Cardinal du Perron pronounced them to be 'the Breviary of honest people.' But his adopted daughter's womanly intuitions enabled her to predict, with singular foresight, in 1634, that a century would elapse, at the very least, before the generality of people would adequately appreciate Montaigne. Yet, on the other side of the English Channel, there was a young dramatist who was eight-and-twenty when Montaigne passed out of this world, and who, having probably read the 'Essays' in French, afterwards procured a copy of John Florio's translation of them into English, wrote his name upon the title-page, and read the book—the precious volume is now in the British Museum—with what we may well believe to have been affectionate attention and sympathetic admiration. For this same dramatist, William Shakespeare by name, transplanted some of the essayist's flowers into his own garden; as when he borrowed a whole passage from Montaigne's dissertation on cannibals, beginning,

'It is a nation, I would answer Plato, that hath no kind of traffic, no knowledge of letters,' &c., and transformed it into poetry, where the lines commence thus:

> I' the commonwealth I would by contraries
> Execute all things; for no kind of traffic
> Would I admit,—no name of Magistrate;
> Letters should not be known; &c., &c.

So, too, we find Shakespeare, in 'Macbeth,' epitomising Montaigne's antipathy to drugs in the often-quoted sentence, 'Throw physic to the dogs.' And, again, the essayist's expressed aversion to artificial perfumes appears to be revived in Hotspur's vehement outburst against the scented coxcomb with his pouncet-box, in the First Part of 'King Henry the Fourth.' Moreover, Montaigne's observation that none are so old and decrepit as not to believe that they have yet some twenty years of life before them, seems to find an echo in aged Justice Shallow's unconcealed astonishment at the death of 'old Double,' in the Second Part of the same play. Finally, is there not a striking coincidence between the great Frenchman's remark, '*Philosopher, ce n'est autre chose que s'apprester à la mort*,' and Hamlet's 'If it be not to come, it will be now; if it be not now, yet it will come: *the readiness is all*'?

It is impossible to separate Montaigne from his 'Essays;' they are a part of himself; he has incorporated his moral with his mental tissues in those compositions. 'His life,' said his intimate friend Etienne Pasquier, 'was nothing else but *le général de ses escripts*.' Therefore, to understand them, we must first of all understand him. And is there any man in the whole range of literature whom we know so well, unless it be old Sam Pepys perhaps? We live with him. He 'made his toilet in public,' as some one has said; not from the diseased craving for notoriety which induces the little great people of modern society to lay themselves out to be interviewed by newspaper reporters, and to send paragraphs about their movements, their receptions, and their new dresses to society journals; but because he was of such an expansive nature that he enjoyed taking people into his confidence, and conversing with them in a spirit of delightful frankness, and with an unreserve that is always charming because his is such an interesting and engaging personality.

If I were to name another writer who is equally candid both in his essays and his letters, and for whom his readers entertain the same sort of affection they cherish for Michel de Montaigne, it would be Charles Lamb. How accurately we know them both! And how peculiarly applicable to each is the aphorism of Buffon: *Le style, c'est l'homme.* Both loved books with a feeling in which tenderness and reverence were equally blended. The domestic affections of both were not less deep than durable. Although Montaigne's marriage with Mademoiselle Françoise de la Chassaine was one of *convenance*, yet he appears to have been a model husband in times when the yoke of matrimony sat rather lightly, on the shoulders of husbands more particularly. Only one of his letters to his wife has come down to us; and some passages in this are too characteristic to be omitted. 'You are very well aware,' he writes, with his customary frankness, 'that, according to the rules of these modern days, it does not become a gentleman of fashion to be still courting and caressing his wife'—too often, indeed, the husband of the period was courting and caressing somebody else's—'for they say that a sensible man may very well take a wife for himself, but to espouse her is the act of a fool. Well, let them say what they will; I hold, for my part, to the simple fashion of old times, as I do to the cut of my beard. Let you and me, my wife, love each other after the good old French ways.' After the marriage of his only daughter and child he adopted Mademoiselle Marie de Gournay le Jars, who seems to have repaid his fatherly affection with filial gratitude. In one of his essays he tells us that he loves her more than anything in the world. 'If youth can give any presage of the future,' he adds, 'that soul will one day be capable of the highest things; and, among others, of the perfection of that holiest form of friendship to which we do not read of her sex having as yet attained.' No one was so well qualified to speak with authority on the subject of friendship as Montaigne himself. Among the memorable friendships of antiquity, such as those of Harmodius and Aristogiton, of Alexander and Hephæstion, of Agis and Cleombrotus, there are none more close and touching, more perfect and unbroken, than that which united the essayist to Etienne de la Boëtie. When the elder of the two was asked why he loved the younger so fondly, he could only reply, with laconic simplicity, 'Because it was he—because it was I.' That friendship, after a duration of four years, was terminated by the death of La Boëtie; and the grief occasioned by their separation was never effaced from the mind of Montaigne. Eighteen years after its occurrence something brought his departed friend into his mind, and the recollection of what he had lost saddened him for the rest of the day. Such a friendship

> masters Time indeed, and is
> Eternal, separate from fears;
> The all-assuming months and years
> Can take no part away from this.

Let us look in upon Montaigne when he had returned from his public duties at Bordeaux to his picturesque old château in the valley of the Dordogne, where he occupied the round tower originally constructed for the purposes of safety and defence in times of peril and disorder. It is thus that he described his abode:

> From my library, I command at once my whole establishment. I enter it and see below me my garden, my court, my farmyard, and nearly all quarters of my premises. Then I turn over the pages now of one book, and now of another, without order or method, in disconnected snatches. At one time I meditate, at another I make notes and dictate such fancies as you have here. 'Tis the third story of a tower. The first is my chapel, the second is a bedchamber and its dependencies, where I often sit for the sake of being alone. Above this is a large room, which was formerly the most useless part of the house. Here I pass most of the days of my life, and most of the hours of my day: I am never there at night. Connected with it is a cabinet, handsome enough, capable of holding a fire in the winter, with windows very pleasantly arranged. . . . The shape of this room is circular, and there is no flat wall except enough for my table and chair, and its curves present to my view all my books, ranged in five rows of standing presses all round me.

On the rafters of the open ceiling of his library Montaigne had caused to be inscribed upwards of fifty mottoes in Greek and Latin, which might be regarded as expressing the essence of his philosophy. 'All is vanity,' was one of these. 'I do not understand,' 'I hesitate,' 'I examine,' were others, highly significant of his mental attitude towards all questions. As a warning against and a corrective of that intellectual vanity which is one of the mental diseases of our own time, he kept well in view before him sentences like these: 'Woe unto those that are wise in their own eyes,' 'Be not wise in your own conceits,' 'If any man think that he knoweth anything, he knoweth nothing yet as he ought to know;' and, finally, this epitome of sage counsel: 'The final wisdom of man is to make the best of things as they are, and for what remains, to face it with confidence.'

What was the personal appearance of the only French writer who, according to Voltaire, was known outside of France to those who were acquainted with the language in which he wrote? He has obligingly sketched his own portrait for us when he was forty years of age. *Imprimis*, he was rather below the middle height, which he regretted, because he was apt to get jostled in a crowd, and to be splashed with mud by people passing him on horseback. Then, again, he was neither sprightly nor athletic. 'Nevertheless,' said he, 'my figure is strong and well knit, my face not fat but full, my temperament between the cheerful and the melancholic, moderately sanguine and warm, my health sound and vigorous, even now that I am pretty well advanced in age, and it is seldom disturbed by illness.' He could run fairly well, but did not shine in dancing, tennis, and wrestling; he was stupid at music, knew nothing of swimming, fencing, vaulting and leaping; and he added, 'I am so clumsy with my hands that I cannot write well enough for myself to read.' Then, by way of completing the catalogue of his defects, he says: 'I do not know how to fold a letter properly, I cannot mend a pen, or carve at table to any purpose, nor saddle and bridle a horse, nor carry a hawk nor fly her, nor halloo to a hawk, a hound, or a horse.' But he could write essays which have been a source of instruction and delight to ten generations of his countrymen and foreigners in all parts of the civilised world, and 'the rest is all but leather or prunella.'

Montaigne fancied he was of English extraction, and says that his family name (Eyquem) was known on the other side of the Channel in his own day, and was spelt as Egham, Higham, or Ockham. And is he not more closely akin to Robert Burton, the author of the 'Anatomy of Melancholy,' than to any French essayist? Is there not something like an echo of Montaigne, when he was in one of his self-depreciatory moods in what follows? 'I have read many books, but to little purpose, for want of good method. I have confusedly tumbled over divers authors in our libraries with small profit, for want of art, order, memory, judgment. . . . I am not poor; I am not rich; *nihil est, nihil de-est.* I have little, I want nothing. All my treasure is in Minerva's tower.' And there is a strain of pensive reflection and occasionally of meditative melancholy in Montaigne's writings which seems to us rather more English than French, rather more touched by the sombre influences of a northern climate upon the Anglo-Saxon intellect, than by the brightness and hilarity which have always characterised the people of Gascony.

Of the 'Essays' themselves it would be hopeless to attempt to say anything new. Nobody sits down to read them persistently and perseveringly, as he would a poem, a romance, or an historical narrative. They are to be sipped like liqueurs, and not taken in tumblers like *vin ordinaire.* Huet said of them that they constitute 'the handbook for gentlemen in their leisure hours.' This is entirely true; for their author has poured into them, as Burton did into his famous book, and as Robert Southey did into 'The Doctor,' the fruit of such extensive and desultory reading, that same culture — which was formerly the exclusive privilege of 'gentlemen' and scholars—that is so essential to their comprehension and enjoyment; and being thus desultory in their composition, these essays should be read in a desultory fashion also. 'There are, in fact,' as Nisard has observed, 'men who have always been reading Montaigne, and who have never finished him.' With the essayist commences the long and majestic march of our classic literature, and his book is the first in date and glory of all those masterpieces which have been the contribution of France towards the perfecting of human genius.

His essay on 'The Art of Conversation' ranks among the best that proceeded from his pen, and I will quote one passage from it, partly because it illustrates his literary style, and partly because it reveals some of the many aspects of his mental character. 'I engage in argument and discussion,' he remarks, 'with great ease and freedom, since opinions find in me a very bad soil to strike deep into, or to take firm root. No propositions astonish me, and no belief offends me, however opposite it may be to my own. There is no fancy so frivolous or extravagant as not to seem to me a natural product of the human mind.' And here we have an example of that beautiful spirit of toleration by which Montaigne was guided and governed. It was all the more honourable and remarkable when we remember the times in which he lived, and that he was contemporary with, and an eyewitness of, the infamous massacre of St. Bartholomew.

'Contradiction of my opinion, therefore,' he continues, 'neither offends me nor disconcerts me. It only rouses me and puts me on my mettle. We shrink from having our judgment challenged; we ought rather to court and lay ourselves out for it, especially when it comes in the form of argument and not dictation. Whenever we are contradicted we are apt to consider not whether the contradiction be just, but how we are to get the better of it, right or wrong. Instead of opening our arms to it, we thrust out our claws. I could bear to be even roughly handled by my friends—"You are an ass—you are dreaming." I love plain and bold speech between gallant men, and that our words should go along with our thoughts. We must harden our ears and steel ourselves against that overtenderness. . . . For my own part I welcome and embrace truth in whatsoever hands I find it, and submit to it cheerfully; nay, hold out my arms to it in token of submission as soon as I see it approaching in the distance; and provided always it does not take an imperious and dictatorial tone, I take pleasure in being set right, often rather on grounds of civility than conviction, because I love to gratify and encourage the liberty of admonition by my readiness to give way even to my own cost.'

What is so delightful in passages like these is their engaging mixture of philosophical reflection with innocent and agreeable egotism. We are listening to the serious thoughts on familiar subjects of a mind ripened by culture and mellowed by experience; and we are at the same time taken into the confidence of one who is at once the kindliest of instructors and the pleasantest of gossips. Considering the intellectual plane upon which he stands, it is little less than an act of condescension on his part; but Montaigne is too much of a gentleman ever to let us feel that it is so.

To very few writers has it been given, as Sainte-Beuve has observed, to become an inexhaustible and everlasting subject of studies and of comments. Yet such is Montaigne, such has he been, and so he will continue to remain, in all probability, while the language and literature of France shall endure. Not the smallest details of his life are indifferent to us, or devoid of interest, if they be found capable of adding so much as a single new feature to the physiognomy of the great writer who has admitted us into the innermost sanctuaries of his private and domestic life. 'What a pleasure it would be to have such a neighbour as Montaigne!' said Madame La Fayette. 'He is everybody's neighbour,' exclaimed Sainte-Beuve, 'and one can never know too much about his neighbour.' Montesquieu characterised him as a great poet; Etienne Pasquier characterised his 'Essays' as constituting 'a true summary of beautiful and notable sentences;' adding that one may find in them something for every age and for every hour of our lives. M. Villemain praises his inexhaustible memory, his taste, his judgment, and his instinct; and observes that upon every subject which he takes up, he begins by telling us all he knows, and ends—which is still better—by informing us as to what he believes. Speaking of his literary style, the same writer asserts that Montaigne has no superior in the art of painting by words: 'What he thinks, he sees; and by the vivacity of his expressions he brings it vividly before the eyes of everybody else.' And Hallam remarks that 'the fascination of Montaigne's manner is acknowledged by all who read him, and with a worse style or one less individually adapted to his character, he would never have been the favourite of the world.'

Who that has read the ever-delightful letters of Madame de Sévigné can have forgotten the frank outburst of naïve joyfulness excited by having found a volume of Montaigne which she did not know that she had brought with her? 'Ah! l'admirable homme!' she exclaims; 'qu'il est de bonne compagnie! C'est mon ancien ami; mais, à force de m'être ancien, il m'est nouveau. Mon Dieu! que ce livre est plein de bon sens!' More than three hundred years have elapsed since the 'Essays' of Montaigne were first published at Bordeaux; ten generations have come and gone, and the garrulous gossip of the dear old Gascon is as fresh and as full of good sense as ever it was:

> Age cannot wither it, nor custom stale
> Its infinite variety.

Egotism is usually odious, but the egotism of Montaigne is simply adorable, because we feel it to be the outpouring of a rich mind, a good heart, and a most sincere and ingenuous nature. When Henry of Valois told him that he liked his book, the essayist replied 'Then your Majesty must needs like me, for my book contains nothing but a dissertation on myself and my own notions.' And this constitutes its greatest charm—not the less so because the man was very far from perfect. Had he been an example of all the virtues, we could not have liked him half so well. He is allied to us by his weaknesses and frailties; and with what admirable candour, with what entire freedom from reserve, does he unbosom himself to us. 'I leave nothing,' he writes, 'for people to wish for or to guess at concerning myself. If they must be talking of me I would have them do so fairly and truly. I would willingly come back from the other world to give the lie to any one who should make me out to be other than I am, even though it were intended to do me honour.'[1]

There speaks Montaigne! And because he leaves nothing to be wished for or guessed at, his 'Essays' constitute one of the most copious and truthful autobiographies to be found in any literature, ancient or modern. Cicero comes the nearest to him in his 'Letters.' Let us not forget, moreover, that Montaigne was the inventor of the Essay. He opened up a new field of letters. It is his by right of conquest and discovery, and in it he is still supreme. He stands at the head of that splendid cohort of writers whom we admire or venerate under the names of Bacon, Locke, Bolingbroke, Shaftesbury, Pope, Addison, Steele, Dryden, Temple, Defoe, Cowley, Macaulay, Lamb, Hazlitt, Pascal, La Bruyère, Leibnitz, La Rochefoucauld, Vauvenargues, Voltaire, Bonald, Chateaubriand, Lamennais, Sainte-Beuve, and a host of German and Italian essayists, not forgetting Jean Paul and Gasparo Gozzi. What a magnificent family for Father Montaigne to be proud of!

[1] *Essay* 103: 'Of Vanity.'

LECTURE IX

La Boëtie (1530-1563)—Pierre Charron (1541-1603)—Michel de l'Hôpital (1503-1573)—Cujas (1522-1590)—Bodin (1530-1596)—Calvin (1509-1564)—Costar (1603-1660)—Vaugelas (1585-1650)—La Mothe le Vayer (1588-1672)—Le Maistre (1608-1658)—Patru (1604-1681)—Tallemant des Réaux (1619-1692)—Descartes (1596-1650)—Pascal (1623-1662),

ETIENNE DE LA BOËTIE, born at Sarlat in Périgord on November 1, 1530, was the senior by two years of Montaigne, his fervid friendship for whom has caused the names of both to be linked together like those of Tennyson and Hallam. Montaigne's affection for the young scholar, whose life was cut short in the moment of its highest promise, inspired some of the most beautiful and pathetic passages in his essay on Friendship. He who could awaken so deep and durable a sentiment in the mind of so philosophical a thinker, so shrewd an observer of character, and so perfect a gentleman as the Seigneur de Montaigne, must have had rare intellectual gifts and admirable qualities of heart.

Such indeed was La Boëtie, whose name is embalmed for ever in the elegiac prose of the greatest of French essayists, and perhaps few writers have appreciated his sterling worth with so much delicacy of discernment and sympathetic insight as M. Feugère, whose eloquently expressed estimate of him I cannot deny myself the pleasure of quoting.

His most brilliant qualities impressed upon his entire person a severe charm and the stamp of distinction. The equality of a soul governed by duty; a virtue rigorous towards himself and indulgent to others; an unalterable frankness; a piety remote from all superstition, and as exempt from laxity as from stubbornness; much weight and security of judgment; an habitual elevation of views and ideas; an easy and agreeable humour; much knowledge joined to the graces of a lively and fertile imagination; a rare combination of vigour and penetration; a tender attachment to that miserable country which was then being preyed upon openly by enemies at home and abroad; an ardent love for freedom and mankind; a profound aversion to every vice, and more especially to that odious traffic in justice which usurps and dishonours its name; a singular modesty which endeavoured to conceal such an affluence of endowments, and which by veiling augmented their lustre: such were the features of the mind and character of that great and good man, as Montaigne called him. The enthusiasm which dreams of perfection found in the wisdom and rectitude of his sentiments its model and its equilibrium.

Such men as La Boëtie and L'Hôpital are the very salt of the earth, and they preserve mankind from corruption. They are the glory of the country in which they are born, but they are also an honour to the human race. We are proud of them as our countrymen, but we must not refuse to recognise the broader proprietary interest in them which is claimed by the whole of humanity.

Etienne's early years of study were passed, like those of Montaigne, in the college of Bordeaux, where his precocity amazed both the professors and his class-fellows. He acquired a perfect mastery of the language and literature of Greece and Rome, and translated some of the works of Aristotle and Xenophon. He was only eighteen when he wrote his 'Discourse on Voluntary Servitude,' a philosophical protest against the tyranny of kings, called forth by the remorseless way in which the insurrection in Guyenne had been suppressed by royal authority. Appointed counsellor to the parliament of Bordeaux in 1552, he became, a few years later, the colleague of Montaigne in the exercise of similar functions, and then commenced the memorable friendship which continued unbroken until the death of La Boëtie on August 18, 1563.

In the essay already referred to, Montaigne tells us that, in natural parts, he knew of no man comparable with his friend, and that their intimacy, founded on mutual respect and esteem, was 'so perfect, inviolate, and entire, that certainly the like is hardly to be found in story, and among the men of his age there is no sign nor trace of any such thing in use.' Their friendship, he says, was something differentiated from all other friendships. It was free from the slightest taint of self, and the will of each lost itself in the will of the other. 'Our souls,' adds Montaigne, 'have drawn so unanimously together, and we have with so mutual a confidence laid open the very bottom of our hearts to each other's view, that I not only know his as well as my own, but should certainly, in any concern of mine, have trusted my interest much more willingly with him than with myself.' The essayist believes that he and La Boëtie were drawn together 'by some secret appointment of heaven,' so that from that time forward they became so mutually endeared that 'nothing was so dear to them as each other.' And Montaigne, in exalting his friend upon so high a pedestal, seems to have anticipated the great poet of our own times, who, in apostrophising his beloved comrade, exclaimed:

> But thou, that fillest all the room
> Of all my love, art reason why
> I seem to cast a careless eye
> On souls, the lesser lords of doom.

And a somewhat similar sentiment is to be found in La Bruyère, where he says, 'There is a savour in pure friendship unattainable by those of mediocre birth.'[1] La Fontaine has shown his fine conception of friendship in the 'Two Pigeons' and the 'Two Friends of Monomotapa.' In Montaigne and in the Fabulist, friendship has its sweet folly and its delirium, and Montesquieu was probably thinking of this when he said, 'I am enamoured of friendship.'[2] Only one fault is to be found with that admirable essay which has conferred immortality upon La Boëtie, and it is that the author of it seems to imply that woman is incapable of that excellent sentiment. 'Their soul,' he says, 'appears to be insufficiently strong to sustain the strain of a tie so close and durable.'[3] The greatest minds, you see, are mistaken, or at any rate take imperfect views of things. Craving to be excused for making this digression into a domain which is foreign to my subject, I return to the works of La Boëtie.

---

[1] 'Il y a un goût dans la pure amitié où ne peuvent atteindre ceux qui sont nés médiocres.'
[2] 'Je suis amoureux de l'amitié.'
[3] 'Leur âme,' dit-il, 'ne semble assez ferme pour soutenir l'étreinte d'un nœud si pressé et si durable.'

Although enrolled under the flag of the Pléiade, he is scarcely to be regarded as a poet on the strength of the twenty-nine sonnets of his which Montaigne has preserved. He did not possess the lyrical faculty, although Viollet-le-Duc has translated one of his Latin poems, which he pronounces to be a little masterpiece of *esprit*, grace, and facility. La Boëtie, however, will not float down to posterity on a poetical pinnace. But as the example of his versification, and of the language with which he clothes an idea which Montaigne extols as having been derived from no author of ancient or modern times, I will quote the following sonnet:—

> Toi que oyes mes soupirs, ne me sois rigoreux
> Si mes larmes à part toutes miennes je verse,
> Si mon amour ne suit en sa douleur diverse
> Du Florentin transi les regrets langoreux,
> Ne de Catulle aussi, le folâtre amoreux,
> Qui le cœur de sa dame en chatouillant lui perce,
> Ne le savant amour du migregeois[1] Properce;
> *Ils n'aiment pas pour moi, je n'aime pas pour eux.*
> Qui pourra sur autrui ses douleurs limiter,
> Celui pourra d'autrui les plaintes imiter:
> *Chacun sent son tourment et sait ce qu'il endure.*
> Chacun parle d'amour ainsi qu'il l'entendit,
> *Je dis ce que mon cœur, ce que mon mal me dit,*
> Que celui aime peu, qui aime à la mesure!

There are, as Sainte-Beuve has pointed out, some beautiful lines in this sonnet, and the italics are his own. At the same time I am bound to acknowledge that the poet's prose is much more fluent than his verse.

I have already mentioned La Boëtie's 'Discourse on Voluntary Servitude.' It was written during the reign of Henry II., when an insurrection had broken out in the south-western provinces of France, aroused by the intolerable pressure of taxation, and the cruel rigour with which payment was enforced. Even the nobility, the clergy, and the burghers of the large towns and cities made common cause with the unfortunate peasantry. The king expostulated with the insurgents and promised them, if they would lay down their arms and return to their homes, that he would redress their grievances. They did so, and then the royal miscreant despatched the terrible Constable Anne

[1] Semi-Greek.

de Montmorency to pacify the disaffected districts. 'Do not kill or pillage,' said the monarch, with his tongue in his cheek. Brantôme tells us how these instructions were carried out: 'Hang such a one,' were the Constable's commands. 'String that fellow up to a tree. Run your pike through this rascal; shoot down that other. Cut to pieces every one of those villains. Burn down yonder village, and set fire to the country for a quarter of a league around it.' His atrocities culminated in the hideous crimes of which he was guilty to a magistrate named Les-tonal, and his afflicted wife: crimes with the narrative of which I dare not sully my pages.

The city of Bordeaux, although it had made humble submission to the king, and to the infamous miscreant who was the instrument of his vengeance, was treated like a foreign town that had been taken by assault, and during the four or five weeks of its occupation by the Constable, executions, confiscations, and outrages of all kinds were the order of the day.

It was under these circumstances, and in full view of the scaffolds erected for the execution of the victims of Montmorency's ferocity, that La Boëtie wrote his memorable discourse, 'the first war-cry of that abstract republicanism,' as Henry Martin has remarked, 'which has been the answer made to the doctrines of monarchical despotism.' Down in Guyenne was sown some of the seed of that harvest of blood which was reaped during the Reign of Terror 240 years later. The 'Discourse' was a cry of indignation raised from a heart all aflame with anger at the insolence and murderous brutality of armed authority, and all aglow with compassion for the abject misery and helpless submission, and perhaps the cowardice also, of the crushed and bleeding masses.

'What is to be done,' exclaimed La Boëtie, 'when so many men, so many towns, so many cities, so many nations submit to a single tyrant, who possesses no power but that which is given to him, and who could not injure them if they were not willing to endure it? What a misfortune, or what a vice, to see an infinite number of people, not obeying but serving, not being governed but being tyrannised over by a single individual; and he neither a Hercules nor a Samson, but an insignificant little man, and very often the greatest coward, and the most effeminate person in the nation! Poor, miserable people! senseless races, stubbornly clinging to evil, and blind to your own welfare, you live in such a way that you can call nothing your own, neither your property, nor your kinsfolk, nor your children, nor your own lives. And all this ruin befalls you, not from your enemies—although, doubtless, he is your enemy—but from him whose greatness is of your own making; for whom you go forth so courageously to war, and for whose grandeur you do not hesitate to sacrifice your own lives. You plant your cornfields and orchards in order that he may ravage them; you build and furnish your houses that he may pillage them. From such indignities as these, which the very beasts of the field would not put up with, you might deliver yourselves, if you were only willing to do so. He who thus lords it over you, from whom but you does he obtain so many eyes to act as a spy upon you? Who but yourselves give him so many hands wherewith to smite you? What could he do if you were not the receivers of the stolen goods he robs you of; accomplices of the assassin who murders you, and traitors to yourselves? Make up your minds to serve him no longer, and you are free! I would not excite or unsettle you, but would only urge you to uphold him no longer, and you will see him topple over like a huge colossus which has lost its pedestal, and by its own weight tumbles into ruins.... The first cause of voluntary servitude is habit. People say they have been always subjects, they and their fathers before them, and therefore they fancy that they are bound to champ the bit, and they ground their obedience on the length of time they have been owned by those who tyrannise over them; but, of a verity, years do not confer the right to do evil. Rather they aggravate the injury.'[1]

[1] 'Comment se peut-il faire, que tant d'hommes, tant de bourgs, tant de villes, tant de nations, endurent un tyran, seul, qui n'a puissance que celle qu'on lui donne, qui n'a pouvoir de leur nuire, sinon de tant qu'ils ont vouloir de l'endurer?.... Quel malheur, ou quel vice, de voir un nombre infini, non pas obéir, mais servir; non pas être gouvernés, mais tyrannisés d'un seul, et non pas d'un Hercule ni d'un Samson, mais d'un seul petit homme, et le plus souvent du plus lâche et féminin de la nation.... Pauvres gens et misérables, peuples insensés, nations opiniâtres en votre mal et aveugles en votre bien, vous vivez de sorte que vous pouvez dire que rien n'est à vous, ni vos biens, ni vos parents, ni vos enfants, ni votre vie même! Et toute cette ruine vous vient, non pas des ennemis, mais bien certes de l'ennemi et de celui que vous faites si grand qu'il est, pour lequel vous allez si courageusement à la guerre, pour la grandeur duquel vous ne refusez pas de présenter à la mort vos personnes.... Vous semez vos fruits afin qu'il en fasse le dégât; vous meublez et remplissez vos maisons, pour fournir à ses voleries.... De tant d'indignités, que les bêtes mêmes n'endureraient point, vous pouvez vous délivrer si vous essayez seulement de le vouloir! Celui qui vous maîtrise tant, d'où a-t-il pris tant d'yeux dont il vous épie, si vous ne les lui donnez? Comment a-t-il tant de mains pour vous frapper, s'il ne les prend de vous? Que vous pourrait-il faire, si vous n'étiez receleurs du larron qui vous pille, complices du meurtrier qui vous tue et traîtres à

Remembering the date at which this was written, it is surely an audacious and remarkable protest against 'the monstrous faith of many made for one,' and an unflinching arraignment of 'the right divine of kings to govern wrong.' And does it not contain the germs of those revolutionary principles which, formulated by Thomas Paine in his 'Common Sense,' served as the basis of the American Declaration of Independence, and of the great organic changes in France between 1789 and 1793?

La Boëtie's vigorous piece of declamation was followed by a picture of the favourites and parasites of tyranny: 'those devourers of the people, whose names, execrated during their lifetime, are blackened, after their death, by the ink of a thousand pens; their reputations torn to pieces in a thousand books, and their very bones dragged from their graves by posterity.'[1]

This writer, whom Montaigne calls 'the greatest man of his century,' lived almost unknown, and died in the arms of his friend at the age of thirty-two. His last words were very touching. 'Peradventure,' said he, 'I was not born so useless as not to have had the means of rendering some service to the public good, but let that be according as it pleases God.'[2]

Montaigne's letters, written many years after the death of his friend, breathe an enthusiastic admiration for him of whom he never ceased to celebrate the virtue, the justice, the elevation of mind, the purity of morals, the enlightened piety, and the tender affection for his miserable country.

---

vous-mêmes? Soyez résolus de ne servir plus et vous voilà libres! Je ne veux pas que vous le poussiez ni l'ébranliez; mais seulement ne le soutenez plus et vous le verrez, comme un grand colosse à qui on a dérobé la base, de son poids même fondre en bas et se rompre! ... La première raison de la servitude volontaire, c'est la coutume! Ils disent qu'ils ont été toujours sujets, que leurs pères ont ainsi vécu; ils pensent qu'ils sont tenus d'endurer le mors et fondent eux-mêmes, sur la longueur de temps, la possession de ceux qui les tyrannisent; mais, pour vrai, les ans ne donnent jamais le droit de mal faire, ains agrandissent l'injure. ...

[1] 'Ces mange-peuples, dont le nom, exécré durant leur vie, est, après leur mort, noirci de l'encre de mille plumes, la réputation déchirée dans mille livres, et les os même traînés par la postérité!'

[2] 'Par aventure, n'étais-je pas né si inutile, que je n'eusse moyen de faire service à la chose publique! mais qu'il en soit ce qui plaît à Dieu!'

Indeed, allowing for differences of personal temperament, of race, and of period, these tributes to the genius and goodness of La Boëtie, from the pen of the great essayist, bear a singular resemblance in substance, although not in form, to the sentiments expressed towards Arthur Henry Hallam by the author of the finest elegiac poem ever penned in any language, ancient or modern. Indeed, Montaigne might well have written of his departed friend what Tennyson wrote of his more than brother:

> Whatever way my days decline,
>   I felt and feel, though left alone,
>   His being working in mine own;
> The footsteps of his life in mine;
>
> A life that all the Muses deck'd
>   With gifts of grace, that might express
>   All-comprehensive tenderness,
> All-subtilising intellect.

Some years after the publication of Montaigne's 'Essays' there appeared a work in France which, although but seldom read to-day, had a great vogue in the seventeenth century. This was the celebrated 'Treatise on Wisdom,' by Charron, in which we find, for the first time, in a modern language, the attempt to establish a system of independent morals.

Pierre Charron, born in 1541, was the son of a Parisian bookseller and one of a family of twenty-five children. Educated for the law, he acquired both distinction and profit in that profession, with which, however, the innate integrity of his nature caused him to become disgusted, and he relinquished it, after five or six years' successful practice at the bar, for theology, and entered into holy orders. He became so distinguished for his eloquence in the pulpit that he was appointed preacher to Marguerite, wife of Henry IV., and honours and preferments flowed in upon him. While residing at Bordeaux, he acquired the friendship of Montaigne, whose principal disciple he became. Naturally he imbibed much of his master's scepticism, and adopted *Je ne sçay* as his motto. He threw himself with the utmost ardour into the cause of the League, and became one of its most powerful and passionate preachers. He went beyond Montaigne in his doubts, for in his 'Treatise on Wisdom' he declared all religions to be 'strange and revolting to common sense.' His enemies stigmatised him as an atheist, but in this they wronged him. He was a theist pure and simple, and in much that he held and wrote concerning God and immortality he seems to have anticipated the Abbé Lamennais in our own days.

Montaigne, when dying, signified his wish to bequeath his armorial bearings to Charron, and he himself testified his affection for the memory of the great sceptic by constituting Montaigne's brother-in-law his universal legatee.

Of all Charron's writings, the 'Treatise on Wisdom' is by far the most important, and also the most difficult to analyse. It was something more than an endeavour to systematise the opinions of Montaigne. It was, as Buckle has said, 'an attempt made for the first time, in a modern language, to construct a system of morals without the aid of theology. What rendered this book,' continues the same writer, 'in some respects even more formidable than Montaigne's, was the air of gravity with which it was written. Charron was evidently deeply impressed with the importance of the task he had undertaken, and he is honourably distinguished from his contemporaries by a remarkable purity both of language and of sentiment. His work is almost the only one of that age in which nothing can be found to offend the chastest ears.'

Charron has been accused, by Sainte-Beuve among others, of having borrowed largely from Montaigne, and from the writings of his contemporaries; and Hallam goes so far as to say that he was 'often little else than a transcriber;' but Buckle deprecates such statements as too strong and asserts that, 'on the most important subjects, Charron was a bolder and deeper thinker than Montaigne.' Incidentally, he mentions a curious fact, which he found in the 'Memoirs' of Madame de Genlis—namely, that Talleyrand was a great admirer of the 'Treatise on Wisdom,' and presented his favourite copy of it to that lady.

I need not examine Charron's alleged obligations to the

great essayist, to Du Vair, Bodin, Plutarch, and Seneca; nor point out in what respect Montaigne and Charron may be regarded as the precursors of Comte and of Herbert Spencer, and as the first to propound the theory that religion is subject to the law of evolution, although he did not make this statement in so many words, but showed that some such conception was in his mind. It will be found, I think, to underlie the following passage, in which he arrives at certain conclusions based upon the progressive birth and death of religious ideas among mankind, and upon what may be called 'the survival of the fittest' of such ideas. Each being imperfect in itself passes away, and its successor is built up on its ruins, as 'Judaism was on the religion of the Gentile Egyptians, Christianity on Judaism, and Mahommedanism on Judaism and Christianity combined.'

Mr. Buckle's estimate of the 'Treatise on Wisdom' appears to me to be so eminently just and fair that I cannot do better than transcribe it. 'There is about the work of Charron a systematic completeness which never fails to attract attention. In originality he was, in some respects, inferior to Montaigne; but he had the advantage of coming after him, and there can be no doubt that he rose to an elevation which to Montaigne would have been inaccessible.' This is certainly the case in the eloquent passage which follows: 'We should rise above the pretensions of hostile sects, and without being terrified by the fear of future punishment, or allured by the hope of future happiness, we should be content with such practical religion as consists in performing the duties of life,[1] and, uncontrolled by the dogmas of any particular creed, we should strive to make the soul retire inward upon itself, and by the efforts of its own contemplation, admire the ineffable grandeur of the Being of beings, the Supreme Cause of all created things.'

Charron regarded a man's religion as the result of his environment, his race, family, native country, and

---

[1] To know
That which before us lies in daily life,
Is the prime wisdom.
                            MILTON.

particular epoch; and thus anticipated John Dryden when he wrote:

> By education most have been misled,
> So they believe because they so were bred;
> The priest continues what the nurse began,
> And thus the child imposes on the man.

If, as Pope says, 'an honest man's the noblest work of God,' Michel de L'Hôpital is entitled to take high rank in that divine aristocracy. For, great as he was in intellect, he was even greater in the moral elevation of his character. He resembled, indeed, one of Plutarch's men, for he combined a belief in ethical precepts as pure and beautiful as those of Marcus Aurelius with the practice of virtues resembling those of Cato.

Born in the year 1503, he was sent to study the law at Toulouse, when his father was exiled and his property confiscated for political reasons, and the son was thrown into prison. Obtaining his release, he followed his father to Milan, and was there when the city was besieged by Francis I. Young Michel succeeded in escaping to Padua, where he resumed his studies. But the death of the French king brought into power the friends of the elder L'Hôpital, and the young man was actually sent as ambassador to Bologna. Not only so, but on his return from Italy Marguerite de Valois appointed him her chancellor, and Henry III. nominated him president of the parliament. In that capacity he distinguished himself by his unswerving integrity, his strict economy, his stern repression of waste and corruption in all their forms, and in the courageous measures he adopted for purifying the administration of justice.

'Gentlemen,' said he to the judges, in defining their duties, 'take care, when ascending the judgment-seat, not to bring with you any hostility, favour, or prejudice. I see many judges who intermeddle with cases and wish to adjudicate on causes in which their enemies or friends are concerned. I daily observe passionate persons who are the adversaries or the partisans of individuals, sects, and factions, giving judgment for or against them without ever considering the equities of the case. You are judges of a field or a meadow, and not of life, not of morals, not of religion. You think fit to decide upon a cause in favour of the man whom you look upon as the most well to do, or the best Christian, as if it were a question between the litigants of which was the best poet orator, painter, or artisan; in short, you are guided by the profession, the power, worth, or other sufficing circumstance, and not by the matter at issue. If you do not feel sufficiently strong and just to command your passions and to love your enemies as God commands you, do not take upon yourself the office of a judge.'

To imagine the effect of such an harangue as this, uttered by a man of spotless probity, high position, and commanding ability, we should have to project ourselves into an age when might made right, when the strong habitually oppressed the weak, and unjust judges and magistrates were as plentiful as blackberries. He himself, in the course of the same address, found occasion to animadvert upon 'the venality of justice disguised in the form of presents.' And we must remember that it was only about thirty years after this time that one of the greatest lawyers and wisest philosophers that ever occupied the Woolsack in England was fined £40,000 and committed to prison in the Tower for habitually receiving bribes as presents from suitors in his own court.

L'Hôpital married a Protestant wife, and her influence, as well as the breadth and liberality of his own sentiments, caused him to espouse the side of freedom of conscience and to use his utmost efforts to appease the rancour of religious animosities. Had his counsels been followed, France might have escaped those religious wars which were responsible for the shedding of so much blood and so many bitter tears. He offered a strenuous opposition to the establishment of the Inquisition in that kingdom; and when the Guises sentenced to death the Prince of Condé, Michel de L'Hôpital refused to sign the sentence of death. 'I know how to die,' said the brave and upright man, 'but not how to commit an act of dishonour.'

He had been appointed chancellor of France by Francis II., and was continued in that office by Charles IX.; but his policy, which was always patriotic and far-seeing, was thwarted by the parliament, by the king, and by the queen-mother. Then came the infamous crime of St. Bartholomew, and L'Hôpital resigned the great seal and retired to his château at Vignay. Thither, however, he was pursued by a furious populace, and his domestics came to him in fear, and asked if they should arm themselves. 'No!' replied the calm old statesman; 'if the small portal is not wide enough for their admission, throw open the great gates.' The queen-mother having sent a detachment of cavalry for his protection, the commanding officer assured L'Hôpital that he would be forgiven for his former zeal on behalf of the heretics. 'I did not know,' was the rejoinder, 'that I had ever deserved either death or pardon.' His daughter, who was a Protestant, had been saved in Paris by the mother of the Duke of Guise. He himself did not long survive a catastrophe which had surpassed his worst anticipations. He died on March 13, 1573, having expressed the horror and despair with which that frightful event had inspired him in a Latin poem which was published after his death.

He rendered inestimable services to French jurisprudence by filling the chairs of law in the various schools with professors, of whom Cujas may be quoted as the most brilliant type. The enactments which he himself drafted were the models for some of the best legislation of later centuries. Henry Martin has truly said of L'Hôpital that he was dominated by a single passion—devotion to his beloved country. He was the unwavering opponent of civil war, and when the Constable angrily reproached him for interfering in such affairs, L'Hôpital replied 'Lawyers may not know how to wield arms, but at any rate they know when they should be used.' During the minority of Charles IX. the chancellor gave him for a device two pillars, with the legend 'Piety and Justice.' The lesson was quite lost on the royal butcher. The remains of the great statesman, legist, and patriot were laid to rest in the village church of Champmoteux, near his château, and his tomb was restored in 1836 by subscriptions contributed by a very great number of French magistrates. Upon a slab of black marble lies the stately image of L'Hôpital, in his chancellor's robes; and near him is a statue of St. Michael, his patron saint, overthrowing the Dragon as the symbol of violence and injustice.

Among his literary works, which have been collected in five volumes, are his 'Treatise on the Reformation of Justice,' his 'Testament,' his 'Harangues,' and 'Remonstrance,' some Latin poems, and other compositions. But his greatest work was his life: so pure in purpose and noble in act; so loyal to the sense of right, and so elevated in its conception of duty :

> Foremost *legist* of his time,
> Rich in saving common sense,
> And as the greatest only are,
> In his simplicity sublime.

To Jacques Cujaus, or Cujas, the son of a poor clothdresser of Toulouse, where the future jurisconsult was born in 1522, belongs the glory of having completed that restitution of the old Roman law to its original integrity, which had been commenced by Alciat, and of having thus paved the way for the creation of the stately fabric of modern jurisprudence upon that strong and solid foundation. To qualify himself to do this, Cujas acquired, by his own unaided efforts, a knowledge of the dead languages, of ancient history, eloquence, poetry, philosophy, and mathematics, until he became a marvel of erudition. At twenty-five years of age he commenced in his native city a course of lectures upon the 'Institutes' of Justinian, which he continued for seven years; and so remarkable in form and substance were they that they drew law students and scholars from all parts of Europe. 'He may be said to have been the legal educator of the splendid galaxy of men whose attainments in this respect were such that it was said, by an impartial foreigner, that 'if the Roman Jurisprudence were to be lost among all other nations it would be found quite complete among the French.' Spanish and Italian cities competed equally with each other to induce the great legist to settle among them, and he lectured in some of the most famous law schools of his time—in Paris, Turin, Valence, Bourges, &c. He was honoured by Pope Gregory XIII., Charles IX., and Henry III. of France. He secretly embraced the Protestant faith, and was a zealous partisan of religious liberty. The works he left behind him were exclusively legal ones, and are distinguished, it is said, 'not less by the purity, the conciseness, and the elegant limpidity of his style, than by their depth and erudition.' It is remembered of him that he always pursued his studies stretched at full length on the floor of his chamber, which was piled up with the books he wished to consult. He died at Bourges in 1590, with a reputation as a jurisconsult second to none in the whole of Europe.

The expulsion of the Jews from Spain was as deplorable a mistake as the revocation of the Edict of Nantes at a later period. Among the fugitives who crossed the Pyrenees, perhaps, were the grandparents of Jean Bodin, who was born at Angers in 1530. Educated for the law in the university of Toulouse, he found his way to Paris, where he published his 'Method of History,' written for the purpose of giving a philosophical direction to the study both of law and history; and in it he showed himself the forerunner of Francis Bacon, of Vico, and of Herder. In another work he laid down most of the foundation principles of political economy with surprising clearness and force, and demonstrated how the prices of all commodities rise and fall according to the abundance or scarcity of the supply of the precious metals used as currency. He was also an advocate of freedom of exchange, up to a certain point. Being suspected, and probably not without cause, of a leaning to Protestantism, he narrowly escaped assassination in the massacre of St. Bartholomew. Bodin published his celebrated 'Republic' in 1577, in which he put forth some views on political government and liberty of conscience very much in advance of his age, and perhaps of our own; and Jean Reynaud does not hesitate to pronounce him to have been the father of political science in France, while Hallam brackets his name, as a great political philosopher, with that of Montesquieu. In his 'Heptaplomeres,' which is a dialogue on religion between seven persons holding different opinions, he displayed an astonishing hardihood in putting forward heterodox views on questions of religious belief; and yet—strange contradiction!—he published a work on 'Demonomania' which proved him to be as superstitious in some respects as he was audaciously free in his thoughts concerning the dominant beliefs of his time. Accused of heresy in 1590, his library was seized and publicly burnt in the centre of the large square in Laon, where he resided. He died of the plague in 1596.

Henry Martin said that to know Rabelais, Calvin, and Loyola, all three of whom might have met together on a given day in the streets of Paris, is to know the whole of the sixteenth century. I have nothing to do with Calvin as a theologian, but the influence of his language on the prose literature of France has been so very marked that I cannot exclude him from a series of lectures like the present. Of his life I shall say but little. His real name was Jean Chauvin, and his father was a notary at Noyon, in Picardy, where the future reformer was born in the year 1509. He received a good education, and at the age of twelve (!) was appointed chaplain, for the purpose of securing him a stipend. He studied successively in the universities of Paris, Bourges, and Orleans, and was intended for the profession of the law. But on the death of his father, in 1531, Calvin gave himself up to theological studies and pursuits. He had, however, previously embraced the doctrines of the Reformation, and from that time until his death at Geneva, in 1564, he was one of the most combative of the new sect; and his 'Institutes of the Christian Religion,' published anonymously in 1535, was the precursor of a mass of polemical literature from his pen, filling six portly folio volumes. His *magnum opus*, which he dedicated to Francis I., was for Protestantism what the 'Summa' of Thomas Aquinas had been for Roman Catholic theology. It was written with incomparable ability in language which, while owing its parentage to the logical French of the Middle Ages, was the progenitor of the noblest prose writings of the seventeenth century. It conquered for ever a sphere of its own—that of theological controversy and metaphysics. Bossuet, who of course detested his religious principles, pays a generous tribute to the admirable correctness of his style, and the power and eloquence of his language, while reprehending its passionate vehemence and the violence of the abusive epithets which he hurled at his adversaries.

Nisard says of Calvin that he

not only perfected while he enriched the general tongue, but he created a particular language, of which the forms, very variously applied, have not ceased to be the best because they have been from the very first conformable to the genius of our country; I mean the language of polemics. It is the style of serious discussion, more habitually nervous than coloured, which has more of movement than imagery; its object not being to please but to convince: a formidable instrument, by which French society was enabled to conquer one by one all the progressive steps it took, and to transform into facts everything it had conceived by the power of reason.

Another critic has admirably described what Calvin did for the French language in the following words:

That new form of speech, firm, clear, sober, eloquent without emphasis; expressive with simplicity; vigorous without extravagance; logical, before all things, in its rigorous construction; which ignored the grammars of antiquity; was made for instruction, for exposition, for discussion, for demonstration and conviction; has retained the greater part of the Gallic qualities and left the defects to our kindred, the Spaniards; rebellious to classic discipline; but in thus parting with those defects, it has also relinquished some of the gifts of our fathers, and, by an excess of logic, has sacrificed, not altogether the sentiment, but another element of poetry—the free movement of the imagination. Calvin scarcely thought of that which is to-day his undisputed glory. He intended to forge a weapon of combat, and not an instrument of renown for himself.

It was in the month of August 1535 that there appeared at Basle the dogmatic treatise above referred to. It was dedicated to Francis I. of France. This work had no direct effect and did not influence the king; but indirectly its result was immense. It furnished a religious code to the Reformers in France and in a great part of Europe. The dedication to Francis I. is a masterpiece of style, address, reasoning, and even of eloquence; but to speak of it at length would be out of place in a purely literary lecture; and I pass on, merely telling you all that is needful to be known, and all that can interest us, about that prose writer, and indicating the place which he filled during his life, and the influence he exercised upon the writers who came after him.

If the cause of reform had its orators, and the League had its preachers, the Christian pulpit could boast of a popular eloquence which was extremely effective by its pleasantries and its gestures with the crowd. When the political passions and private vices of Henry III. inflamed that oratory, it became powerful as addressed to a still coarse and rough populace. I must content myself with a mere enumeration of the more violent of these 'gospellers' —Boucher, Launay, Prévost; then Rose, Bishop of Senlis, Pelletier, Quincestre, Hamilton, and Cueilly. These are the men who caused Madame de Montpensier, the soul of the League, to boast 'I have done more by the mouth of my preachers than they could do with all their devices, arms, and armies put together,' and caused Henry IV. to exclaim 'All my reverses were inflicted by the pulpit.'

I must also add to the prose writers of this epoch the name of Marshal de Montluc, whose military 'Commentaries' have been compared to those of Cæsar. He belonged to the ultra-Catholic party.

Pierre Costar was a man brimful of Greek and Latin, the friend of Voiture and Balzac, and an imitator of both. Although the son of a hatter, he was received into the inner circle of the frequenters of the Hôtel de Rambouillet, and he belonged, like a great many authors I have cited, and a great many more I have omitted, to an epoch in which letters were cultivated with a perfect frenzy, and for themselves alone.

Whatever other reproaches may be directed against it, this much, at least, may be said on its behalf, that the period was one of great intellectual activity.

To be admitted to pay your court to the famous lady who was the sun of the planetary system revolving around her in that memorable Hôtel, constituted in itself a title of literary nobility before Molière had written his 'Précieuses Ridicules,' and Costar must have been a man of considerable mental gifts in order to enable him to overcome the aristocratic prejudices of that very exclusive set. I am afraid he must have been a bit of a tuft-hunter and a time-server; for it is related of him that he first attracted attention by condemning an ode which had been addressed to Cardinal Richelieu by Chapelain, and afterwards begged his pardon, protesting that he was the best poet in the world for heroic verse. In spite of his *bourgeois* origin, Costar was a perfect gentleman in his manners, except that, in the company of noblemen, his politeness was apt to degenerate into obsequiousness, and this gave rise to a brilliantly cynical *mot*: 'Monsieur Costar is extremely polite,' it was remarked; 'he always has his hat in his hand.' 'Ah!' was the rejoinder, 'he derived that habit from his father!'

He wrote, among other works, 'A Defence of the Writings of M. Voiture,' for which Mazarin rewarded him with a pension. He published also a collection of Letters, as full of classic quotations as Burton's 'Anatomy of Melancholy,' while at the same time their literary style was that of most of the second-rate authors of his period. It was smart, pointed, elegant, and fastidious; but disfigured by an excess of emphasis, which was the besetting sin of the epistolers of his time.

I do not suppose that we are less *spirituel* in France to-day than they were in the eighteenth century, but it is nevertheless worthy of remark that the pungent witticisms of these latter days appear to be either repetitions or revivals, and when we look back upon the exuberant *esprit* of our forefathers, we seem to be drawing upon the store of good things which they accumulated. But at any rate we may flatter ourselves that we know how to make a good use of them.

Claude Favre de Vaugelas, emigrating from Savoy to Paris, was appointed chamberlain to Gaston, Duke of Orleans, and, remaining faithful to him in his disgrace, lost a handsome pension for two lives which Louis XIII. had conferred upon his father. He applied himself thereupon to literary pursuits, and his admirable knowledge of the French language enabled him to become one of the most useful of the compilers of the Dictionary of the Academy, of which he undertook the general direction. Richelieu was so much pleased with his zeal that he restored him his pension, and when Vaugelas waited upon him to thank him, the cardinal remarked with a grim smile, 'Well, you won't forget the word "pension" in the Dictionary, will you?' 'No, Monseigneur,' was the prompt reply, 'nor "gratitude" either.' His 'Remarks on the French Language,' published in 1647, earned for him the title of its 'Oracle.' He published a translation of Quintus Curtius, which Balzac pronounced 'inimitable,' and he wrote some indifferent verses. He died so poor, owing to his noble attachment to his original patron, the Duke of Orleans, that the manuscript of the Dictionary was seized after his death by his creditors, but rescued from their clutches by the Academy, of which he was one of the first members.

La Mothe le Vayer wrote in 1647 a work entitled 'Considerations upon French Eloquence,' in which he oscillated between the old and new schools of French style. He blames Du Vair for making use of strange and barbarous words, and at the same time ridicules those who were beginning to object to the introduction of certain low and common phrases. The conjunction *car* was not employed by some writers, and Le Vayer composed an entire treatise upon that folly. Some French purists condemned the use of quotations from a foreign language, but he approved of it. But altogether, as Hallam remarks, his treatise is of very little value, and is exceedingly diffuse.

Two other French writers are entitled to passing mention, Patru and Le Maistre, both of them famous advocates in their day. The pleas of the first, written with extreme correctness, acquired for him a great reputation at the Bar and among men of letters. Their language is so pure and their style so polished that Hallam does not hesitate to assert that they resemble some of the harangues of Demosthenes. Purely Attic in form, as he observes, they are free from pompous ornament, make no appeal to the emotions of the heart, and contain no bold figures of rhetoric. Perrault also praises his style for its lucidity, simplicity, nice arrangement, and freedom from emphasis; and states that his pleadings still serve as models for correctness of composition in the French language.

La Maistre made his *début* at the Bar in Paris in 1629, when he was only one-and-twenty years of age, and very soon became one of its leaders. A disappointment in marriage led him to renounce a brilliant career, and to retire into the seclusion of Port Royal, where he acquired the surname of Father of the Solitaires. He wrote the lives of some of the Saints, translated the works of some of the Fathers of the Church from the Greek, and furnished Pascal with some of the documents he made use of in his 'Provinciales.'

Another writer of that time whose name has come down to us has an equal right to be mentioned in this place. I allude to Tallemant des Réaux, who is called by some 'the Brantôme of the seventeenth century.' But his position in French literature will be better understood by English readers if I compare his 'Historiettes' to the 'Diary' of Samuel Pepys and the 'Letters' of Horace Walpole; for they appear to me to combine the gossip of the first with the *esprit* of the second. Educated for the magistracy, Gédéon Tallemant married his cousin, Elizabeth de Rambouillet, who brought him an independent fortune, and gave him the *entrée* to the celebrated Hôtel of which he became the chronicler. While his 'Historiettes' record the conversations, they also reflect the prejudices of his hostess. What he tells us respecting the reign of Henry IV. is an echo of the former. What he says to the discredit of Louis XIII. is tinctured with the personal antipathy which the Marquise entertained towards that monarch. Tallemant was also a poet, but we possess only his 'Madrigal of the Lily' and his 'Garland of Julia,' together with some fugitive compositions. He also aspired to the dignity of an historian, and commenced, but never completed, a 'History of the Regency.' His 'Historiettes,' like the suppressed portions of Pepys's 'Diary,' are not altogether suitable for extract; and I may have occasion to return to him when speaking of some of the famous writers of his epoch, for we owe to him much of our knowledge of them. And while he was not a chronicler upon whom implicit reliance can be placed, his book is a valuable one to consult for information concerning the secondary events of the period and the topics which were then discussed in the higher circles of society. Speaking of his personal character, his friend Mancroix says of Tallemant des Réaux, 'He was one of the most honourable and upright men I have ever known.'

Descartes was born in 1596 and died in 1650. Strictly speaking, his life and works belong to the history of philosophy; but he is entitled to be mentioned in this series of purely literary lectures as the author of the 'Discourse on Method,' which is one of the most remarkable literary monuments of the *grand siècle*, and is, in point of date, the first masterpiece of modern French prose. It is, moreover, the only work which he wrote directly in his own language. I would limit myself to a succinct analysis of this 'Discourse,' and to an enumeration of the titles of his different works, were it not that the important place he occupies in modern philosophy and the numerous pages devoted to him in every treatise on our literature by eminent writers—who acknowledge that, in so doing, they are stepping outside of their sphere—compel me to speak of him at greater length than I would do otherwise.

At sixteen years of age Descartes had absorbed all the

knowledge he could acquire at the college of La Flèche, and at nineteen he formed the resolution to efface all he had learned, to discard books, and to study the fundamental principles of the truth which must underlie all science. These considerations impelled him to compose his celebrated 'Discourse,' which, however, he did not publish till 1637, having, in the meantime, embraced the career of arms, and displayed great intrepidity at the battle of Prague in 1620. Disgusted with the atrocities perpetrated by the army in Hungary, he renounced the military profession, travelled through France, Switzerland, and Italy, and finally settled down in Holland, where he gave himself up to philosophical and mathematical pursuits. But his views were regarded as heretical by the ecclesiastical authorities in that country, who accused of atheism the author of what Mr. Lecky calls 'the most sublime of all modern proofs of the existence of the Deity,' publicly burnt his works, and would probably have put him to death if he had not fled to Sweden, where Queen Christina had offered him an asylum. He died in Stockholm in the fifty-fourth year of his age.

As a geometrician Descartes may be said to have been the creator of modern mathematics, while his 'Discourse on Method' has been placed by Bossuet above all the works of his country. It was the first fruit of a genius which had reached its maturity in the very springtime of his life. It was the splendid result of his courageous determination to apply the mathematical method to all philosophical speculation and all scientific research. And its literary workmanship was perfect. He found it to be necessary almost to apologise for using his mother tongue, and he did so, he says, because he trusted 'that they who only employ their simple and native reason will estimate my opinions more fairly than they who only believe in ancient books.' And what an admirable use he made of that language! Descartes was not only a great thinker, but a great writer, and his 'Discours,' which preceded Pascal's famous 'Provinciales' by twenty years, may be likened to Minerva, springing in the fulness of her stature and perfectly equipped from the brain of Jove. The principles upon which he proceeded in his search for truth may best be described in his own words: 'When I set forth in its pursuit,' he writes, ' I found that the best way was to reject everything I had hitherto received, and pluck out all my own opinions, in order that I might lay the foundation of them afresh, believing that by this means I should more easily accomplish the great scheme of life than by building on an old basis, and supporting myself by principles which I had learned in my youth without examining if they were really true.' And this in an age when authority in theology, science, and philosophy was supreme, dogmatic, and fiercely intolerant! And so earnest a truth-seeker was he that he declared he would not sacrifice a single leisure hour for the most honourable employment upon earth.

His 'Discourse on Method' was followed by his 'Meditations,' in which he demonstrated the existence of God and the immortality of the soul; and in 1644 appeared his 'Principles of Philosophy,' in which he predicated of man as an incarnation of thought, declaring that we have no knowledge of our soul except as a thinking substance, and that it would be easier for us to believe that the soul should cease to exist than that it should cease to think. God and man, the order of the universe, the earth, the heavens, and the elements, all find their place in his treatise. Science can point to no work more audacious in its conception; and although, in our own times, most of the hypotheses it contains have been abandoned, its extraordinary grandeur has not been diminished thereby.

The last work printed during his lifetime was a 'Treatise on the Passions;' and the rest of his writings, collected and published after his decease, were of a philosophical or scientific character. Instead of enumerating them it will be more interesting to show the estimation formed by later writers of the services which Descartes has rendered to mankind. Victor Cousin, while tracing his intellectual paternity to Plato, indicates the points of resemblance and of dissimilarity between these two great and original thinkers, and remarks that they possessed in common 'the genius which lifts us, in the first place, above the things of sense, and, by the intermediation of those marvellous ideas which are undoubtedly within us, bears us towards Him who alone can be the substance of them, and who is the infinite and perfect Author of our ideas of infinity and perfection.'

Dugald Stewart pronounces Descartes to have been 'the father of the experimental philosophy of the human mind.' Paul Janet declares that all modern philosophy has originated in him, and that it would be easy to show the transformations which each of his ideas underwent in the minds of Leibnitz, Spinoza, Malebranche, Hume, Locke, Schelling, Kant, and Hegel; and how the 'Discourse on Method' contains the germ of all our modern thinking upon mental philosophy. Henry More, the Cambridge Platonist, extols Descartes as having 'alone of all philosophers at once banished from philosophy all those substantial forms or souls derived from matter, and absolutely divested matter itself of the faculty of feeling and thinking.' Henry Hallam remarks that the single fact of his having first established, both in philosophical and popular belief, the proper immateriality of the soul, were we even to forget the other great contributions which he made to psychology, would declare the influence he had had on human opinion. Mr. Lecky, the historian, points out that it was the proud distinction of Descartes to have

taught for the first time, or almost for the first time in France, the innocence of error and the evil of persecution. Descartes had a far greater confidence in human faculties, but he had also a far greater distrust of the ordinary judgments of experience. He taught men that the beginning of all wisdom is absolute, universal scepticism; that all the impressions of childhood, all the conclusions of the senses, all of what are deemed the axioms of life, must be discarded, and from the simple fact of consciousness the entire scheme of knowledge must be unfolded.

Buckle speaks of Descartes as having been

the author of what is emphatically called Modern Philosophy. He is the originator of that great system and method of metaphysics, which, notwithstanding its errors, has the undoubted merit of having given a wonderful impulse to the European mind, and communicated to it an activity which has been made available for other purposes of a different character. Besides this, and superior to it, there is another obligation which we are under to the memory of Descartes. He deserves the gratitude of posterity not so much on account of what he built up as on account of what he pulled down. His life was one great and successful warfare against the prejudices and traditions of men. He was great as a creator, but he was far greater as a destroyer. . . . He was the great reformer and liberator of European intellect, and was one of those men who, by removing the pressure of tradition, have

purified the very source and fountain of our knowledge, and
secured its future progress by casting off obstacles in the presence
of which progress was impossible.

Elsewhere the same writer calls attention to the similarity
observable between the views of Descartes on the subject of
toleration, and those put forth about the same time by Chillingworth, the English divine, which, it is remarked,

> ought not to excite surprise, for they were but the natural products of a state of society in which the right of private judgment
> and the independence of the human reason were first solidly established. If we examine this matter a little closer (continues
> Buckle), we shall find still further proofs of the analogy between
> England and France. So identical are the steps of the progress
> that the relation which Montaigne bears to Descartes is just the
> same as that which Hooker bears to Chillingworth; the same in
> reference to the difference of time, and also in reference to the
> difference of opinions. . . . And as the generation after Hooker
> brought forth Chillingworth, just so did the generation after
> Montaigne bring forth Descartes.

I would refer my readers, or such of them as may be
interested in this comparison between the intellectual state
of France and England at that epoch, to the author I have
quoted from. It will be found in the first chapter of the
second volume of his 'History of Civilisation in England,'
and is a lucid exposition of the simultaneous development
of intellectual freedom, along two parallel lines, in countries
differently circumstanced, and professing different and
hostile forms of religious belief.

The name of Descartes brings to mind that of Pascal,
the necessary complement of the apostle of pure reason.
These two men represent the entire genius of France. But
what a grievous contrast is presented between their two
lives! How complete was the self-possession of the one, and
with what a sovereign freedom did he use all the gifts
bestowed upon him by God: while the other, alas! buffeted
about by eternal storms, was far from reaching 'those
serene temples of the wise, in which his rival sits with
tranquil majesty'!

I borrow the comparison of the two great writers
textually from Henry Martin, and I put it forward in
advance against any criticism which may be urged against
the desultory and inadequate character of the analysis of

Pascal I am about to offer you. He, even less perhaps than Descartes, cannot be excluded from the programme of my lectures. Those 'Letters to a Provincial,' generally known as 'Les Provinciales,' which in the opinion of the best authorities have definitively fixed the French language, certainly claim a distinct recognition on my part; and I would have analysed them, one by one, were it not that they touch upon questions of faith and doctrine which I am bound to avoid.

I should have greatly wished, at the same time, to invite your admiration of the style and workmanship of these compositions, which Villemain has characterised in these words: 'Conciseness, lucidity, an unusual elegance, a mordant and natural pleasantry, a power of using words which fasten on the memory, secured for them a popular success.' And presently he adds, 'My admiration of the "Provincial Letters" would have been less had they not been written before Molière.'

Pascal anticipated high comedy. He introduced upon the scene many actors—an indifferent person who receives the confidences of all manner of people, of the wrathful and passionate, of men belonging to the party of sincerity, of false men connected with the party which is more ardent than the others, of those who are genuinely disposed to reconciliation but are everywhere repulsed, and of hypocrites who are everywhere welcomed, the whole constituting a veritable 'comedy of manners.'

The first three of the 'Provincial Letters' discuss the question of grace—a thorny subject—of which he upholds the hard and narrow side. And he does so, as Demogeot observes, with characteristic frankness and inflexible logic, although abounding with tortuous ambiguities. But how could I hope to enlist any kind of interest on your part in such a theme as this?

From and after the fourth letter, Pascal discusses the morality of the casuists, whom he attacks, a ground upon which he had the good sense of the public entirely with him; but I am sure you will thank me for sparing you the terrible list of propositions which he puts forth in opposition to those of the Jesuits, and in defence of the Jansenists, for I should only be treading upon the still smouldering ashes of one of the most heated of the many theological controversies by which France has ever been distracted. It is much pleasanter to consider the purely literary qualities of the 'Provincial Letters,' which, in spite of the apparent aridity of the subjects they discuss, are really delightful reading. Although issued anonymously, their success was immediate; and by the time the seventeenth had appeared, it was found necessary to strike off 10,000 copies, each of which, passing rapidly from hand to hand, found at least a dozen readers; so that the aggregate circulation would probably exceed 100,000. In point of eloquence they have been compared to the noblest efforts of Cicero and Demosthenes; and Voltaire has declared that Bossuet produced nothing more sublime than the later ones. They excited the enthusiasm of Madame de Sévigné, who exclaims, 'Could there be a style more perfect, a raillery more fine, more natural, more delicate, more worthy to be the offspring of those Dialogues of Plato which are in themselves so beautiful? . . . What solidity! what strength! what seriousness! what eloquence! what a love for God and for the truth! And what a method of sustaining it, and of making it understood!' That keen and trenchant irony, breaking out at last into withering indignation; that gibing dialectic, weaving itself round and stifling his adversaries within deadly folds unknown to the rhetorical methods of the old school of polemics, caused the objects of the writer's attack to writhe in impotent agony, like the central figure in the matchless group of the Laocoon. Pascal's pen is by turns a poignard and a club. Sometimes he irritates his opponents by a rapid series of slight dagger thrusts, as the Spanish *picador* does the maddened bull in the arena; and sometimes he levels him to the earth by a single blow of his massive bludgeon. His language, strenuous, supple, and brilliant as steel, seems to have been created expressly for the 'Provincials,' as that of Descartes had been for the 'Discourse on Method.' The phraseology of the latter is alternately simple and majestic, but withal a little lengthy. Pascal's phrases are as swift as the flash of a sword; their march is governed by art, and the man of sentiment must be a much better artist than the man of pure reason.

In Pascal there is nothing whatever to add, nothing whatever to retrench, in either the form or substance of the composition. The French language is as much fixed as it is possible for a language to be; that is to say, it has attained the highest perfection of which it is susceptible; and I regret that the topics discussed in these 'Letters,' and the doctrines in controversy, prevent me from quoting some passages, from the Seventh and Ninth Letters more particularly, in order to prove that all that has been said about Pascal as a combatant falls actually short of the truth.

He had also made preparations for a second and more important work: nothing less than a defence of the Christian religion. It was never completed; and the scattered and apparently incoherent fragments of it were not gathered together until after his death. They were first published in 1670, under the title of 'Pascal's Thoughts upon Religion and other Subjects;' and these fragments, 'at once so luminous and sombre,' as Henry Martin has said, continue to possess, and will probably always retain, a certain fascination for all to whom the deeper problems of existence present themes for grave reflection and intellectual speculation; while they also serve to show, in the words of Principal Tulloch, 'the greatness of Pascal's soul, and the depth and power of his moral genius.'

In these 'Thoughts' there are axioms as profound as those of Descartes himself. Take the following as examples: 'The heart has its reasons, which the reason knows not. The heart loves the universal being naturally and itself naturally; it is the heart which feels God and not the reason.' Pascal attributes to the heart, to the sentiment, all that is not demonstrable, and first principles admit of no demonstration. His theory tends to establish, after St. Augustine and St. Thomas Aquinas, three principles of knowledge, the Essence, Reason, and Faith; and then he proceeds to build up, on these corresponding elements, a sort of hierarchy, in which the carnal life occupies the lowest place, the mental life an intermediate position, and the life of the heart—otherwise, that of charity or wisdom—the highest grade.

The philosophy of Pascal, however, is something which lies outside the scope of a lecture of this kind, and I hasten back to its legitimate boundaries. Let me, therefore, quote some of those 'Thoughts' in which he has epitomised so much practical wisdom and shrewd observation with equal point and terseness :

Vanity is so rooted in the heart of man, that a soldier, a hodman, a cook, a porter will be given to boasting, and wishes to have his admirers, as do philosophers themselves. Those who write against glory desire the glory of having written well on the subject; and those who read what has been written desire the glory of having read it; while I, who write this, am not free perhaps from the same craving.[1]

Men are necessarily such fools that it would be a folly of another kind not to be a fool.

Do you wish men to speak well of you? Then never speak well of yourself.

The last thing we discover in writing a book is to know what to put at the beginning.

'This is *my* dog,' say children; 'that sunny seat is *mine*.' There is the beginning and type of the usurpation of the whole earth.

It is the contest that delights us, not the victory. It is the same in play, and the same in search for truth. We love to watch in argument the conflict of opinion; but the plain truth we do not care to look at.

He who would thoroughly know the vanity of man has only to consider the causes and effects of love. The cause is an—I know not what, an indefinable trifle; the effects are monstrous. If the nose of Cleopatra had been a little shorter it would have changed the history of the world.

There are two kinds of men : the righteous, who believe themselves sinners; and sinners, who believe themselves righteous.

If each of us examines his own thought he will always find it occupied with the past and the future. We scarcely think of the present, and if we think of it at all it is only for the sake of the light it may throw on the future. The present is never our object; the past and the present are our means; the future alone is our end.[2]

Thus we never live, but we hope to live, and being always disposed to be happy, it is inevitable that we should never be so, if we aspire to no other beatitude than that which may be enjoyed in this life.[3]

---

[1] 'La vanité est si ancrée dans le cœur de l'homme, qu'un soldat, un goujat, un cuisinier, un crocheteur, se vante, et veut avoir ses admirateurs, et les philosophes même en veulent. Et ceux qui écrivent contre la gloire veulent avoir la gloire d'avoir bien écrit ; et ceux qui le lisent, veulent avoir la gloire de l'avoir lu ; et moi, qui écris ceci, j'ai peut-être cette envie.'

[2] 'Que chacun examine sa pensée, il la trouvera toujours occupée au passé et à l'avenir. Nous ne pensons presque point au présent; et si nous y pensons, ce n'est que pour en prendre la lumière pour disposer de l'avenir. Le présent n'est jamais notre fin : le passé et le présent sont nos moyens; le seul avenir est notre fin.'

[3] 'Ainsi nous ne vivons jamais, mais nous espérons de vivre, et nous

And once we find this great and original thinker striking a note of singular solemnity. It is in the following:

The last act is always tragedy, whatever fine comedy there may have been in the rest of life—we must all die alone.

Love, in the life of Descartes, as Henry Martin has observed, was of so little consequence that history has not taken the trouble to remember that the philosopher was a husband and a father. In the life of Pascal love was an essential event, the mainspring of the drama, and we are indebted to it for one of the most precious of the works of genius which fell from the pen of that great man, or rather from his heart; that is to say, that treatise on the passion of love which miraculously escaped the severity of the Jansenists, and has been recently revealed to France. How, continues Henry Martin, are we to analyse that lay, which seems to have been directed to a metaphysician-poet by the harmonious shades of Petrarch and Raffaelle? 'Man is born to think, but thought does not suffice for his happiness. He must have movement and action; he must have passions, love and ambition being the two principal ones. . . . The greater the intellect the stronger the passions. In a great soul, all is great.' Then follow some sublime words concerning love. 'We are only sent into the world to love,' and he explains in language worthy of Plato, 'that which impels man to transcend the narrow limits of self-love—the ideal of beauty which is a natural instinct, and which he not only realises in himself, but craves for outside of himself.' '*L'homme seul* is imperfect; a second being is essential to his happiness. Therefore it is he loves that which most resembles himself among other beings—woman. . . . Man is born for pleasure: he feels it; any other proof is unnecessary. He obeys his reason, therefore, in cultivating pleasure. . . . Love and reason, far from being antagonistic, are one and the same thing; and one could not wish it should be otherwise.' At the same time we must not understand Pascal as employing the word 'pleasure' in the sense of a vulgar epicureanism, or as asso-

disposant toujours à être heureux, il est inévitable que nous ne le soyons jamais, si nous n'aspirons à une autre béatitude qu'à celle dont on peut jouir en cette vie.'

ciating it with anything that is coarse, sensual, and debasing. The refinement of his mind, the delicacy of his perceptions, and the purity and nobility of his character, combine to discredit any such notion. Were it not so, the following passage would effectually disprove it:

> The first effect of love is to inspire a great respect. We cherish a feeling of veneration for those we love. This is very just. Nor can we recognise anything in the world so great as this. The diversion of love into many channels is as monstrous as injustice in the mind. . . . He who loves seems to be quite a different being from what he was when he loved not. He is raised by that passion to the greatest height his nature is capable of.[1]

We obtain a pretty clear insight into the beautiful mind of Pascal, as well as an accurate knowledge of the elevation of his spirit, from the 'Memoirs' of Nicholas Fontaine, who has preserved some of his conversations with De Saci, his spiritual director at Port Royal. From these we learn that his two favourite authors were Epictetus and Montaigne: the great moralist of classical antiquity and the philosophical sceptic of an epoch near his own. He knew nothing of the Fathers of the Church, and yet he had intuitively divined what was highest and best in the teachings of them all. His conversation on these subjects was so wonderful, indeed, that De Saci looked upon him as another St. Augustine; and when we remember that he died at the early age of thirty-nine, it is with something like a feeling of awe that we contemplate the variety and magnitude of his intellectual gifts.

It only remains to supplement this imperfect notice of his literary works by a short sketch of his life.

Blaise Pascal was born on June 19, 1623, at Clermont Ferrand, of an old and somewhat distinguished family. His parents removed to Paris in 1632, and there the house of Pascal *père* became the rendezvous of men like Descartes, Gassendi, and Hobbes. Blaise was only twelve when he

---

[1] 'Le premier effet de l'amour, c'est d'inspirer un grand respect; l'on a de la vénération pour ce que l'on aime. Il est bien juste; on ne reconnaît rien au monde de grand comme cela. L'égarement à aimer en divers endroits est aussi monstrueux que l'injustice dans l'esprit . . . . il semble que l'on ait une tout autre âme quand on aime que quand on n'aime pas : on s'élève par cette passion et l'on devient toute grandeur!'

had taught himself, without book or teacher, the definitions, axioms, and demonstrations of mathematics, as far as the thirty-second proposition of the first book of Euclid. At sixteen he had written a treatise on conic sections, which had excited the 'mingled incredulity and astonishment' of Descartes ; and at the age of nineteen he invented that famous arithmetical machine, by which elaborate calculations were rendered practicable by mechanical means. His researches with respect to atmospheric pressure enabled him to verify the theories of Galileo and Torricelli, and he laid the foundations of the modern science of pneumatics, as well as of the doctrine of probabilities. Not only so, but he came so near the discovery of the differential and integral calculus that, 'if he had proceeded with his mathematical studies,' Bossuet tells us, 'he would have anticipated Leibnitz and Newton in the glory of their great invention.'

With these multifarious scientific researches and discoveries Pascal combined a prodigious literary activity, enabling him to endow the literature of France with two masterpieces, and with many precious fragments besides. What wonder, then, if his fiery soul,

> Working out its way,
> Fretted the pigmy body to decay,
> And o'erinformed the tenement of clay ?

He was only four-and-twenty when he had an attack of partial paralysis, for which he was attended by Descartes. He recovered sufficiently to admit of his going a good deal into society, and for a time he mingled with the most brilliant of the Frondeurs ; when he seems to have fallen in love with Charlotte, the young and beautiful daughter of the Duc de Roannez, to whom he is supposed to allude in his 'Discourse on the Passion of Love,' when he says, 'Sometimes man fixes his affections on an object far beyond his rank, and the flame burns the more intensely that he is forced to conceal it in his own bosom.' The lady, however, became the Duchesse de la Feuillade, and her life was full of misfortunes.

We are indebted to Pascal for the invention of the wheelbarrow and the truck, destined to lighten so greatly the toil of the labouring classes; and I might continue almost indefinitely the enumeration of all our obligations to him. But I must forbear, and hasten on to his last moments.

Blaise Pascal was fast moving towards the tomb. His soul had completely worn out that feeble body which from the age of eighteen had never known a day that was free from pain. Upon his deathbed he made it a matter of self-reproach that he was surrounded with too many comforts, for his thoughts went out to the many poor creatures who were dying in indigence and wretchedness, with none to minister to their last necessities. He ended by an heroic act of self-sacrifice, in abandoning his house to a poor sufferer attacked by a contagious malady, and went to die under his sister's roof. He expired on August 19, 1662, when not yet forty years of age, and went to seek elsewhere the happiness which had been denied him on earth.

LECTURE X

La Satyre Ménippée (1593)—Jean Passerat (1534-1602)—Louise Labé (1526-1566)—Madame de la Fayette (1634-1693)—Madame de Longueville (1619-1679)—Madame Deshoulières (1634-1694)—Madame de la Sablière (1636-1693).

POLITICAL satire, of which we find but rare examples in the old *fabliaux*, seems to have taken its rise among the ancient guild of lawyers. It was not until the sixteenth century was drawing to a close that such satire began to manifest itself in prose and verse. On its first appearance it was, as might be expected, full of personalities and coarseness. There were successively published 'Fanfreluche et Gaudichon,' an 'Apologie de la Ste.-Barthélemy,' 'La Fortune de la Cour,' ' La Légende du Cardinal de Lorraine,' ' La Légende de Catherine de Médicis,' and many others which have passed away and left no trace behind them. Only one satire was sufficiently imbued with genius to cause it to endure ; only one among them all was so vigorous and trenchant as to influence the current of popular opinion, and to affect the course of national events. This was a composition at once robust and healthy, gay and caustic, pungent and urbane, witty and corrosive. It was, indeed, such a masterpiece of its kind that a critic of some authority (Père Rapin) has compared it to 'Don Quixote,' while M. Nisard has declared that it combines the hostile energy of Aristophanes with the ingenious irony of Socrates. If you could imagine a great political pamphlet in which the lambent wit of Sydney Smith and the delicate humour of Charles Lamb should be blended with the mordant satire of Dean Swift, you would then have something very like the ' Satyre Ménippée.' This creation took its title, as may be readily concluded, from Menippus, the cynic philosopher of Gadara, an enfranchised slave who became an extortionate money-lender, and revenged himself upon those who condemned his usurious practices by writing thirteen satires, not one of which has come down to us.

The 'Satyre Ménippée' was first issued in 1593, by a little group of writers—magistrates and citizens—whom we may proceed to enumerate. There was, first of all, Jacques Gillot, canon of the Ste.-Chapelle in Paris, a man of great erudition, and a collector of all the clever sayings and epigrams current in society at that time, which he published in his 'Chroniques Gillotines,' a complete record of the slanders in circulation against the *Ligue*. Then came Pierre le Roy, the real instigator of the 'Satyre;' he was a canon of the cathedral of Rouen, a man of singular probity, modesty, and worth; who shrank from notoriety as much as some of his colleagues courted it. Nicolas Rapin was as skilful with his sword as with his pen, followed the white plume of Henry of Navarre at Ivry, and was distinguished alike as a lawyer and as a poet. Jean Passerat, professor of rhetoric and also poet, will be spoken of later on. With these were associated Florent Chrestien, the Calvinist, who had been Henry IV.'s tutor, and who was one of the best Greek scholars of his day; Pierre Pithou, equally famous for his integrity and his legal lore; and Gilles Durant, a lawyer by profession, a gentleman by birth, and a poet by choice.

In this group of writers the old national spirit survived which we have already seen animating the works of those who wrote after Poitiers and Agincourt. They hated all foreigners—the Spaniard more particularly—as heartily as Eustache Deschamps and Alain Chartier had execrated the triumphant English. Such were the men who rallied round the worthy Gillot in his house on the Quai des Orfèvres— the same in which Boileau Despréaux was afterwards born, as if its roof had been predestined to cover our best satirists.

Let us take a look at Paris then. The streets were full of broils; the Louvre and the city gates were garrisoned by Spanish troops; fanatical preachers belonging to the League were fulminating from the pulpits of the capital; gibbets were being continually erected; and Mayenne, the fat chief of the League, was striving with might and main to restrain the populace, which growled like a famished hound, and promising day after day victories and victuals which never arrived. There, in a quiet corner, Gillot and his little band kept up a running fire of couplets, epigrams, and pleasant jests, directed against the Lorraines, the League, and the Catholicon of Spain. It required courage to laugh then. People risked their heads in proportion as the prospects of the one party grew more gloomy and those of the other brightened. It is related that a servant having mentioned that her master and mistress exhibited some pleasure in hearing of the battle of Ivry, the indiscreet couple narrowly escaped hanging.

Having thus indicated the men by whom and the place wherein the 'Satyre Ménippée' was written, I will endeavour, before proceeding to analyse it, to give you a slight sketch of the state of France at the time of its appearance. Henry III. had fallen beneath the dagger of the fanatic Jacques Clément (1589), only a few months after the assassination of the Duc de Guise and his brother the cardinal by the king's command. Paris received the news of the death of its king with every demonstration of ostentatious delight. Ministers of religion so far forgot the principles of peace as to extenuate the crime of the assassin, and even to apologise for the criminal, while the Duchesse de Montpensier, sister of the Duc de Guise, who had suborned the assassin, went about Paris proclaiming the news of his death from her carriage windows, distributing green scarves in token of her delight, and causing bonfires to be lit in honour of the murder! But the unhappy Parisians soon made the discovery that they had escaped from the frying-pan into the fire. Henry of Navarre was the next heir to the crown; the League was split up into two factions; Philip of Spain was coquetting with the young Duc de Guise with a view to raise him and the Infanta Isabella to the vacant throne; and at that very time Henry IV., after conquering his kingdom, town after town, and winning the victories of Arques and Ivry, was approaching the walls of Paris. Such, then, was the condition of political affairs when this famous satire made its appearance, not yet as a printed volume, but in the shape of fly-leaves, passing from hand to hand, and even learned by heart by those poor famishing citizens of Paris who, according to the chronicles of the period, were as pallid as statues.

All forms of eulogy have been exhausted, as Lenient observes, with respect to the 'Ménippée.' No better epithet, perhaps, has ever been bestowed upon it than that of the 'king of pamphlets.' 'It is a masterpiece of militant literature in an age when the pen fought as many battles as the sword. Never had the double vocation of our France "to combat and to speak skilfully" been better justified.'

It is time, however, that I should make you acquainted with the general plan of this satire, and, without penetrating to its very core, should at any rate describe its principal features. The basis of the work is the convocation of the States General, which was continually being deferred by the party of the League; and it was the future speeches of the orators in an assembly which had not yet met that our satirists were parodying in anticipation. The writers of the 'Ménippée' are much more nimble and alert than the States themselves, who were framing their resolutions and slowly preparing their orations while parodies of them were actually circulating in the streets of Paris.

The satire commences by a sort of exhibition of mountebanks, such as was very common then and long afterwards. It takes place in the courtyard of the Louvre, where two quacks, one from Lorraine, and the other from Spain—the Cardinals de Pellevé and Plaisance—hold forth from their stage to the gaping crowd on the virtues of a celebrated drug, the Catholicon of Spain, compounded of gold-dust, pensions, promises, and persuasive words, and sublimated in the college of Jesuits at Toledo. Its good qualities are more than fifty in number. It is the universal panacea, by the use of which any one will be enabled to commit every imaginable crime and to be guilty of the most shameful treasons without the slightest remorse of conscience, for the greater welfare and glory of the Church. This first part is full of piquant allusions to the doings of the more prominent leaders of the League.

To the parade of the characters succeeds the solemn procession which is to call down the blessing of God upon the labours of the League. This is a masquerade conceived and described in a spirit of exquisite humour. It is headed by Rose, the rector of the University, formerly Bishop of Senlis, who 'has put off his rector's hat and donned the gown of a master of arts, with a bishop's mantle, a soldier's gorget, a sword at his side, and a halberd in his hand. After him comes an army of *curés*, monks, novices, all equipped in similar style,' and armed according to Paul's injunctions. Then follow the leaders of the League, each described with the fidelity of a caricature : the legate, 'a true mirror of perfect beauty,' being the ugliest man in the world ; Madame de Nemours, mother of the Duc de Mayenne, grandmother of the young Duc de Guise, uncertain whether to appear as queen-mother or queen-grandmother ; the Dowager-Duchess of Montpensier (sister to the Duc de Mayenne), with a green scarf very dirty from long use ; the guards, Italian, Spanish, and Walloon, but no French ; and the rest. And so they all go to church, where they hear a sermon by the rector Rose on continuing the war, ending appropriately with the quotation, 'Blessed are the poor in spirit.'[1] And thus ends the first day.

We now arrive at the gem of the satire, which is a vivid description of the power wielded by the States of the League. The hall in which they are held is tapestried with hangings which depict the horrors and iniquities of civil and religious warfare, as exemplified in profane and sacred history ; the actors in these scenes bear a striking resemblance to the chiefs of the League, while the assassination of the late king by a monk is also graphically portrayed. The battles of Senlis, Arques, and Ivry are also represented, and in one corner a group of peasants singing these words :

> Let us resume the dance,
> Be merry while we may ;
> The springtime shines in France,
> And monarchs pass away.
>
> One King alone remains ;
> The fools are scatter'd far ;
> Fortune rewards our pains,
> And smash'd is every jar.[2]

---

[1] *The French Humourists*, by Walter Besant.
[2] Reprenons la danse, Un roi seul demeure ;
Allons, c'est assez : Les sots sont chassez :
Le printemps commence ! Fortune a ceste heure
Les roys sont passez. Tous aux pots cassez.

At the summons of a herald, who describes the members one by one, they appear and take their places: his sarcastic sketches of each constitute the most caustic portions of the satire. At length the deputies commence the debate. Imagine, if you can, any legislative assembly in Europe abandoning, for one sitting, all the accustomed forms of oratory and usages of discussion, and every speaker in it turning himself inside out, as it were, laying bare all the vices and weaknesses of his character, dissecting his own moral nature with a firm and fearless hand, 'exposing the baseness of his motives, the pitifulness of his ambition, the narrowness of his views, the poverty of his imagination, the extent of his ignorance, and the selfishness of his measures;'—imagine all this, and then picture the delight of a public naturally prone to *persiflage*, to raillery, and to sarcasm, as each of the prominent Leaguers mounted the pillory and opened a window as it were in his bosom! And this, too, at a time when party spirit ran so high; when personal animosities were so bitter and deadly; when the hostilities of opposing factions were fierce, savage, and unappeasable; and when men hated each other for the love of God, and persecuted each other in the sacred name of religion. The speeches put into the mouths of ecclesiastics, nobles, and people of high degree are really magnificent specimens of irony; those of the Duc de Mayenne and the Italian legate more especially so. But after these is heard the voice of one who represents the insignificant and almost impotent *Tiers État*. It is no longer the language of sarcasm or of veiled invective that we are listening to, but that of history, stern, simple, and impressive as a chapter of Tacitus. The accents are those which previously lent so much pathos and poignancy to the heartrending cry of the poor labourers of France, as represented in lines first written in 1422, it is believed, and published in the 'Chronicles' of Monstrelet, which found an echo in the 'Chanson du Pain' of quite recent date.

I must quote a portion of this speech, because it is a document of no little historical value, and faithfully reflects some of the social aspects of the epoch:

O Paris, who art no longer Paris, but a den of wild beasts, a citadel of Spaniards, Walloons, and Neapolitans, an asylum and a secure retreat for thieves, murderers, and assassins: wilt thou never resume thy dignity, and remember what thou hast been and what thou hast become? Wilt thou never, never shake off that frenzy which has caused thee to engender, instead of a legitimate and gracious sovereign, fifty kinglets and fifty tyrants? Behold thyself in fetters, behold thyself beneath the yoke of the Spanish Inquisition, a thousand times more intolerable and more hard to bear by minds born free and frank, like those of France, than the most cruel deaths the Spaniards are capable of devising! Thou couldst not endure thy king,[1] so *debonair*, easy, and familiar, who behaved himself like an ordinary citizen and burgess of the city, which he has enriched and embellished with such sumptuous edifices, surrounded with strong and stately ramparts, and endowed with such honourable privileges and exemptions. What did I say? Thou couldst not endure him! It is far worse. Thou hast chased him from his city, his home, and his bed. Chased, quotha? Thou hast pursued him. Pursued him, quotha? Thou hast assassinated him; thou hast canonised his murderer, and kindled joyful bonfires in celebration of his death.

This harangue, the last of the scenes, is the only one written in a serious vein. Like La Boëtie, the speaker had read the classics of antiquity, and had assimilated their essence; and listening to his words, as Nisard has remarked, 'when he is denouncing the League in the name of those eternal principles which condemn every kind of anarchy, we seem to hear the accents of Demosthenes unmasking Philip, or of Cicero overwhelming Antony, while painting the horrors of civil war. Never have patriotism, probity, and common sense spoken braver or more loyal words.'

Such was the 'Satyre Ménippée,' which consummated the ruin of the League, and left it dead, past all recovery. I have already mentioned the names of those who were principally concerned in its production. Most of them were copious writers at an epoch of great literary fertility, Gillot and Rapin more particularly so; and it is a remarkable circumstance that, with a single exception, each of them is now known and remembered only as one of the contributors to the 'Satyre Ménippée.'

That exception was Jean Passerat, a man of genius and a poet. Placed by his uncle, a canon of the cathedral of Troyes, in the college of that city, his youthful excesses compelled him to take flight, and he was reduced to such a necessitous condition as to beg for work in an iron mine

[1] Henry III.

near Bourges. A worthy monk befriended him and prevailed upon him to return home, where his uncle forgave him, and Jean repaired to Paris and applied himself to study in such good earnest that he was appointed professor of eloquence in the College of France. He wrote and translated many works, chiefly in verse. Singularly enough, love was one of their principal themes, although, like Alain Chartier and Eustache Deschamps, his personal ugliness disqualified him for becoming a lover. He became blind in his latter days, and died in Paris at the age of sixty-eight. As an example of his poetry I will quote the biting satire which he wrote on the Prince d'Aumale and other prominent Leaguers who turned tail at Senlis:

THE BATTLE OF SENLIS[1]

To each of us kind nature gives,
   For firm support, a pair of feet;
And these will ofttimes serve us well,
   Provided we are only fleet.

Thus Prince d'Aumale, a valiant wight,
   By using both his legs with speed,
Though reft of all his best effects,
   Preserved his life in time of need.

He saw the open way, and then,
   While deadly fears oppress'd his mind,
Betook himself to rapid flight,
   And never once did look behind.

[1] SUR LA JOURNÉE DE SENLIS

A chacun nature donne
   Des pieds pour le secourir :
Les pieds sauvent la personne :
   Il n'est que de bien courir.

Ce vaillant Prince d'Aumale
   Pour avoir fort bien couru,
Quoiqu'il ait perdu sa malle,
   N'a pas la mort encouru.

Quand ouverte est la barrière,
   De peur de blâme encourir,
Ne demeurez point derrière :
   Il n'est que de bien courir.

Courir vaut un diadème :
   Les coureurs sont gens de bien :
Trémont, et Balagny même,
   Et Cougy le savent bien.

Bien courir n'est pas un vice :
   On court pour gagner le prix :
C'est un honnête exercice :
   Bon coureur n'est jamais pris.

Souvent celui qui demeure
   Est cause de son méchef :
Celui qui fuit de bonne heure
   Peut combattre derechef.

Il vaut mieux des pieds combattre
   En fendant l'air et le vent,
Que se faire occire ou battre
   Pour n'avoir pris le devant.

Qui a de l'honneur envie
   Ne doit pourtant en mourir :
Où il y va de la vie,
   Il n'est que de bien courir !

> To fly is worth a diadem;
>   The swift of foot are prudent men;
> So thought Tréuront, Cougy too;
>   Balagny[1] also scuttled then.
>
> To run is not so bad a thing,
>   Men do so when a prize they'd gain;
> It is an honest exercise:
>   The nimble runner's rarely ta'en.
>
> For he who stays behind full oft
>   Has cause to rue his sad delay;
> But he who has the chance and flies
>   May live to fight another day.[2]
>
> 'Tis better, then, to use your feet
>   In cleaving through the yielding wind
> Than risk a fatal wound or death
>   By lingering too long behind.
>
> He who for honour's cause would live
>   For honour's sake should never die;
> And so to save one's life, you see,
>   The safest course is—just to fly.[3]

Sainte-Beuve remarks that Jean Passerat was the first poet, after the literary reform of 1550, who reverted to the natural gaiety and rare pleasantry of the older writers. He composed volumes of hexametrical Latin verses, but it is by those he wrote in French, although much fewer in number, that he will be chiefly remembered. The greater part of the verses in this satire are from his pen; and among others this capital quatrain:

> What means the double cross, the League
>   Emblazons on its flag so plain?
> It is to signify thereby
>   They crucify our Lord again?[4]

---

[1] Three conspicuous Leaguers.

[2] Was this the origin of the couplet in Butler's *Hudibras*?—
  'For those that fly may fight again,
    Which he can never do that's slain.'
Or did the French and English poets both borrow it from Erasmus?—
  'That same man that runneth awaie
    Maie again fight another daie.'

[3] There is a curious resemblance between this verse and Falstaff's soliloquy on Honour in the fifth act of *Henry IV.* (first part). Is it a coincidence, or had Shakespeare read *La Journée de Senlis*, which had appeared about four years before the date of his historical play?

[4] Mais dites-moi, que signifie
    Que les ligueurs ont double croix?
  C'est qu'en la Ligue on crucifie
    Jésus-Christ encore une fois.

One cannot study the poetry of the sixteenth century without being conscious of the obligations we owe to Sainte-Beuve for the elucidations it has received from his critical researches and acumen, and my own personal debt to him is very great indeed. He has pointed out how much Passerat had in common with Marot and Villon. All three were 'vexed with the want of pence' which afflicts poets as well as 'public men,' and they could all ask for it with singular address. This is how Passerat approached the Treasurer:

> My verse, as everybody knows,
> Is worthless quite; yet you, Monsieur,
> Could make it full of worth appear,
> If you'd translate it into prose.[1]

The Treasurer replied, 'I will not forget you,' and the poet rejoined:

> I do not doubt your memory is keen;
> But if you send some coin to meet my suit,
> I can assure you it will then be seen
> My memory of you is just as 'cute.[2]

His 'Metamorphosis of a Man into a Bird' is quite a little masterpiece of its kind, making an epoch in the history of our poetry, and conferring honour on the sixteenth century. It is the best known of all his productions, and in it its author shows himself the forerunner of La Fontaine and of Voltaire. Passerat was a great admirer of Rabelais, and wrote voluminous commentaries on his 'Pantagruel,' which were never published. Like him, he died with a pleasantry upon his lips; for while he recommended them to throw flowers upon his grave, he also begged of them to refrain from casting any bad verses on it, because they would lie so heavily on his remains.

Nicolas Rapin and Gilles Durant also wrote some of the verses in the 'Satyre Ménippée;' the last, more particularly,

---

[1] Mes vers, Monsieur, c'est peu de chose :
    Et, Dieu merci, je le sais bien :
    Mais vous ferez beaucoup de rien
    Si les changez en votre prose.

[2] Je crois qu'avez bonne mémoire ;
    Mais si je puis argent tenir,
    Monsieur, vous pouvez aussi croire
    Que j'en aurai bon souvenir.

is remembered by his 'Lamentation on the Dead Ass' (a Leaguer), which is an admirable specimen of frolicsome *badinage*, and proves him to have been a worthy heir to Marot, and the precursor of Voltaire. He was born in 1554 and died about 1615.

The name of Passerat reminds me of how much there still remains to be said with respect to that inexhaustible sixteenth century, which proved to be such a magnificent flowering-time of the human intellect, not in one country of Europe alone, but in all. What a glorious epoch it was in Italy, when the genius of Michael Angelo, Raffaelle, Titian, Leonardo da Vinci, and Andrea del Sarto ; of Ariosto, Tasso, Sannazzaro, Machiavelli, Guicciardini, Bembo, Guarini, and the founders of the lyric drama, shed a transcendent lustre over that lovely land ; when Cervantes, Garcilaso de la Vega, Hurtado de Mendoza, Ercilla, Bermudez, in literature; and Velasquez, Morales 'the divine,' and Coello, in art, were reflecting their renown on Spain ; and when Shakespeare, Spenser, Sidney, Marlowe, Bacon, Massinger, and a perfect constellation of poets and dramatists appeared to glorify ' the spacious times of great Elizabeth ' ! ' In our own country it was the splendid morning of that radiant noon of literature which arrived a century later, and has been universally recognised as *le grand siècle* ; an epoch comparable with those of Pericles, of Augustus, and of Leo X.'

Sainte-Beuve has divided the literary activity of the sixteenth century in France into periods ; and of these I have endeavoured to show you the principal productions, necessarily omitting those of writers of a secondary character, like Roger de Collerye, Jacques Pelletier, and others. I should wander away from the well-defined limits of literary history if I were to endeavour to disentomb from the graveyard of oblivion those authors whose works enjoyed a temporary vogue during their lifetime, but are now hidden beneath three centuries of accumulated dust.

The list of poets whose writings I have already quoted would be incomplete, however, if I were to omit from it the name of Louise Labé, a native of Lyons, where she was born in 1526. She was both the Aspasia and the Lady Jane Grey of her epoch: as beautiful and as enchanting as the first ; as intellectually gifted as both. She knew Greek,

Latin, Spanish, and Italian, was an admirable musician and a splendid swordswoman. Her superb beauty and the loveliness of her hands and feet set all the poets of the city raving. At the age of sixteen she disguised herself in male attire, and served in the army of Francis I. under the name of Captain Joys. At the end of the campaign she married a rich ropemaker, Ennemond Perrin, and hence she became known as La Belle Cordière. Inhabiting a sumptuous mansion in Lyons, their house became the rendezvous of every person conspicuous for wit and talent; and, as she was adored by all her friends, she was naturally hated and defamed by the envious of her sex. But contemporary writers praise her as a model of conjugal fidelity. Her husband, dying in 1565, bequeathed her the whole of his wealth, so as to enable her to continue her brilliant receptions if she wished. She excelled as a prose writer more especially, and exhibited a vigour and an elegance which were extremely rare at that period. Her 'Debate between Folly and Love' is her most striking production of this kind. It is unnecessary to analyse it, because it has served as the foundation of one of La Fontaine's best known fables. An 'Ode to Venus,' some elegies, four-and-twenty sonnets, and an epistle to the ladies of Lyons, compose her poetical 'baggage.' The following sonnet is avowedly an imitation of Sappho:

> I live, I die, I'm burning and I drown;
> I pass from icy chill to torrid heat;
> Life is at once too bitter and too sweet;
> My joys uplift, my sorrows drag me down.
>
> One moment merry, and the next in tears:
> My pleasures turning momently to grief;
> My anguish lasting, and my raptures brief;
> My life now winter and now spring appears
>
> Thus fickle love beguiles me like a dream,
> And when most wretched to myself I seem
> My heart is on a sudden light again;
> Then, when I deem that I am free from pain
>
> And at the very top of my desire,
> Back on me flows a flood of dolours dire

> ¹ Je vis, je meurs; je me brûle et me noie;
> J'ai chaud extresme en endurant froidure;
> La vie m'est et trop molle et trop dure;
> J'ai grands ennuis entremeslés de joie.

I will venture to quote one more sonnet, which is a cry for death when no more happiness is possible for the heart, and nothing remains of the freshness or the joy of life. If La Belle Cordière had never written anything else, this poem alone would have won her the laurel crown. It is needless to add that the composition suffers immensely when translated into another tongue.

> So long as tears may dim my weary eyes,
> Bewailing bygone happiness with thee,
> And sighs and sobs oppress and sadden me,
> So long as my faint voice is choked with cries;
>
> So long as o'er the lute my fingers stray,
> Telling in music of thy matchless grace;
> So long as all thy loveliness to trace,
> I still within my mind can make essay;
>
> I do not, cannot feel the wish to die.
> But when all utterance from my voice shall fly,
> Mine eyes grow dim, my fingers nerveless fall;
>
> When my poor spirit, lodg'd in mortal shell,
> Can no more its unbounded passion tell,
> I'll pray to Death to veil me in his pall.[1]

These are the cries, Sainte-Beuve observes, which cause a poet's name to live, and never fail to find an echo in suc-

> Tout à un coup je ris et je larmoye,
> Et en plaisir maint grief tourment j'endure ;
> Mon bien s'en va, et à jamais il dure ;
> Tout en un coup je sèche et je verdoie.
>
> Ainsi Amour inconstamment me mène :
> Et quand je pense avoir plus de douleur,
> Sans y penser je me treuve hors de peine :
>
> Puis quand je crois ma joie estre certaine,
> Et estre au haut de mon désiré heur,
> Il me remet en mon premier malheur.

[1] Tant que mes yeux pourront larmes espandre,
A l'heur passé avec toi regretter ;
Et qu'aux sanglots et soupirs resister
Pourra ma voix, et un peu faire entendre ;

Tant que ma main pourra les cordes rendre
Du mignard luth, pour tes graces chanter ;
Tant que l'esprit se voudra contenter
De ne vouloir rien fors que toi comprendre ;

Je ne souhaite encore point mourir,
Mais qu'en mes yeux je sentirai tarir
Ma voix cassée et ma main impuissante,

Et mon esprit en ce mortel séjour
Ne pouvant plus montrer signe d'amante,
Prêrai la mort noircir mon plus clair jour.

ceeding generations, so long as spring returns and youth is born into the world. Let us assign a place of honour, then, among the poets of the sixteenth century to La Belle Cordière, to the intellectual queen who held her little court in that fair city which sees the waters of the Saone mingling with those of the Rhone. Her poems, although they appeared at the dawn of the Pléiade, had no relation to, and derived no influence from, that constellation—knowing, indeed, no other inspiration than the planet Venus. She belongs to no school or literary sect, and took counsel only of her own warm loving heart.

Mademoiselle de la Vergne, who was born in 1634, was married in 1655 to the Comte de la Fayette; but as her husband, after bestowing his name upon her—a name which she rendered illustrious—effaced himself and disappeared from her life, we may drop him out of the narrative. In reading her biography, indeed, one cannot help remembering the words of La Bruyère: 'There is here and there a woman who extinguishes or entombs her husband so completely that people cease to mention his name. Is he still living, or does he live no longer? One is in doubt about it.' This was the case with Madame de la Fayette and her husband. In her youth she was admitted to the Hôtel de Rambouillet; but, thanks to the natural soundness and solidity of her mind, she resisted the contagion of bad taste of which that Hôtel was the centre. Not only so, but she became the reformer of the romance—the chivalrous and sentimental romance—in France, and impressed upon it that particular *nuance* which, to a certain extent, reconciles the ideal with observation.[1] And if among her early compositions 'Zayde' is still written in the old romantic style, and if it smacks yet of the 'Astrée' of D'Urfé, and exhibits the same abrupt and extraordinary passions, those incredible resemblances of features, those mistakes so fruitful in adventure, and those resolutions suddenly formed on the sight of a portrait or a bracelet, yet, on the other hand, the 'Princess of Cleves' entirely breaks away from all the commonplaces of the old school. It was in the month of March 1678 that this celebrated romance appeared, and obtained a popularity which it well

[1] Sainte-Beuve, *Portraits de Femmes*.

deserved, but which it has now outlived. Up to that time, as La Harpe has pointed out, no writer of fiction had painted with such fidelity and delicacy the conflict between duty and affection; the reason being, I believe, that she was the heroine of her own story. The book marked an epoch in French literature. 'It was more than an innovation,' as has been happily observed; 'it was almost a revolution;' and the mixture of historical facts with semi-fictitious characters and incidents in the 'Princess of Cleves' almost entitles it to be regarded as the precursor of that school of romance writers which comprehends the honoured names of De Vigny, Dumas, and Sir Walter Scott.

Into that story Madame de la Fayette breathed all the tenderness and poetic feelings of her heart, which still cherished the precious and unfulfilled dreams of her youth. They had found no fulfilment in actual life, and so she transported them into the realm of fiction and watched their realisation in the existence of a creature of her own imagination, La Rochefoucauld stamping the work with the high and authoritative seal of his admiration and approval. It is unnecessary for me to analyse a romance which, in spite of all the praise it receives, is so very rarely read. Enough to say that its language is exquisite and delicious, that its style is purity and transparency itself, and that in it Madame de la Fayette has dethroned Mademoiselle de Scudéry. The writer of it was not popular with the fops and fribbles, the 'poodles' and profligates of her epoch. Her life was too pure, her judgment too sane, and her mind and morality too elevated to please men like Bussy-Rabutin and the graceless courtiers of her time; but she knew how to conciliate the esteem and affection of people like Madame de Sévigné, the Duc de la Rochefoucauld, Bishop Huet, and La Fontaine; and' this was ample compensation for the disparaging opinions entertained of her by the butterflies and bluebottles of the court.

The erudite prelate whose name I have just mentioned had defined the origin and theory of romance. Madame de la Fayette, by her excellent works, had caused that kind of literature, which seems to belong of right to women, and in which they now take the lead, to turn from hyperbolical gallantry and spurious wittiness to sentiment and nature, putting into practice what Bishop Huet had laid down in theory. She had become warmly attached to the Duchess of Orleans, who appointed her one of her maids of honour, and who was the first, according to Voltaire, who brought into the court of Louis XIV. the charm of perfect manners, and of that courtesy which springs from innate kindness and goodness. She was present when the duchess died, and, instead of offering you any extracts from the romances of Madame de la Fayette, which might weary you, I will quote her account of the last hours of the duchess, merely reminding you that she was the daughter of Charles I. of England, that she was unhappily married, and that it was her decease which called forth that masterpiece of pulpit oratory, Bossuet's funeral sermon, in which his utterance of the simple phrase '*Madame se meurt ! Madame est morte !*' sent such a thrill of awe, such a spasm of poignant emotion through the vast congregation, that even his firm voice quivered, and his utterance was interrupted for a while.

'I ascended to her room,' writes Madame de la Fayette. 'She told me she had been sorrowing, and the sad tones in which she spoke would have seemed becoming to the happier hours of other women, they were so full of natural sweetness, and she was so incapable of littleness or anger. . . . She asked me to come near to her, so that her head almost leaned on mine. . . . During her sleep she changed so considerably, that after looking at her I felt surprised, and thought it must be her spirit that was lighting up her countenance. . . . I was wrong, however, in making such a reflection, for I had often watched her sleeping and had never seen her expression less winning. And presently,' she continues, 'Monsieur was standing by her bedside. She embraced him, and said to him with a tenderness and a look capable of softening the most barbarous heart, "Alas! Monsieur, you have long ceased to love me. But that was unjust. I have never been untrue to you." Monsieur appeared to be greatly touched, and all that passed between them afterwards was so inaudible that nothing was heard but the sound of falling tears.'

The principal works of Madame de la Fayette, besides those already mentioned, are the 'History of Henrietta of England,' the 'Countess of Tende,' the 'Princess of Montpensier,' and 'Memoirs of the Court of France' from 1688 to 1689. She survived by thirteen years La Rochefoucauld, the friend of whom she was accustomed to say, 'He has brightened my intelligence, but I have reformed his heart.'

Her affliction at his death was immense, and has been depicted by Madame de Sévigné, in the most touching manner, in many of her letters. 'Poor Madame de la Fayette no longer knows what to do with herself; all accept consolation excepting her.' No one could fill the place which he had occupied in her life. As people approach the evening of existence it is almost impossible to find substitutes for the cherished friends of long years. Nevertheless, Madame de Sévigné, to whom she had been attached from the time of her marriage, still remained to her; and a year before her death Madame de la Fayette wrote her a little note describing her sufferings by day and night, and her resignation to God, concluding in these words, 'Believe me, my dear friend, you are the one person in the world whom I have most truly loved.' At length the end came, and in June 1693, a few days after the fatal event, Madame de Sévigné, writing to Madame de Guitand, thus deplores the death of her old friend: 'Her infirmities during the last ten years had become extreme. I upheld her always, because people said she was foolish not to wish to depart. She had a mortal swoon. What folly it was! Is she not the happiest woman in the world? But I tell those persons who are so precipitate in their judgments, Madame de la Fayette is not foolish, and this I stand to. . . . The poor woman is now abundantly justified. Besides mental suffering, she was affected with polypus of the heart. Was not this enough to account for that feeling of desolation of which she complained? She was right during her life, she was justified after her death, and she was never without that divine reasonableness which was her principal quality.'

'So died and so lived, in a condition at once of melancholy sweetness and of acute suffering, of wisdom according to the world, and of repentance before God, one whose ideal production has enchanted us.'[1]

With the name of the good, sensible, judicious, and serious Madame de La Fayette, upon whom I have been dwelling, another appears to associate itself by all sorts of relations. I will not attempt the portrait of Madame de Longueville, the first portion of whose life was all ambition

[1] Sainte-Beuve, *Portraits de Femmes.*

and gallantry, and the second all devotion and penitence; for what could I hope to add to the admirable monograph of Victor Cousin, who seems to have cherished a Platonic affection for her two hundred years after she had been laid in her grave? Yet I must offer some sort of a biographical sketch of a lady who made so great a figure all through the stormy epoch of the Fronde.

Married, at the age of twenty-three, to the Duc de Longueville, who was twenty-four years her senior, it was not long before—impelled at first by her passion for La Rochefoucauld—she took an important part in the dissensions by which France was then distracted. At that time we find the following description of her: 'She had all the advantages which wit and beauty could bestow, and this in so high a degree and with such a charm of manner that it seemed as if nature had taken pleasure in composing a perfect work in her person and had achieved it, but those qualities shone with diminished lustre by reason of a blemish which is never seen in a person of her merit, which was this, that so far from imposing her will upon those who entertained a particular adoration for her, she transformed her own sentiments so completely that they were no more recognisable as her own.' In other words, she was capable of complete self-effacement.

It is curious to hear La Rochefoucauld—for the words are his—passing such a judgment on the character of a lady who, out of love for him and to serve his ambition, placed at his disposal all her influence, and, what was far more, her delicate, prompt, and ingenious spirit of intrigue. Although there was a certain nonchalance in the character of Madame de Longueville, she had also, in the midst of her natural languor, luminous and surprising flashes of energy. She led away her brother, the Prince de Conti, under the inspiration of the master-passion of her life. She remained in Paris while the city was being blockaded by the royal troops, and was throughout that stormy period the life and soul of the Fronde. The peace, which was signed in her apartments in 1649, did not last long. Wounded by the coldness of the court, she soon plunged into fresh intrigues, reanimated the hatred of the Prince de Conti against the cardinal, and applied herself to detach from his party the

Prince of Condé, whose fraternal tenderness for her knew no bounds. Threatened with arrest, she fled into Normandy, where she hoped to be able to raise the population. Her expectations were deceived, and, after having been reduced to conceal herself and to wander along the coasts of that province for some considerable time, she repaired to Stency, the headquarters of Turenne, where she kept up an active correspondence with all her friends, combating to the utmost the ever-increasing power of Mazarin. There was a reconciliation of the princess and of herself with the court and the cardinal, but it was followed by a fresh rupture, and La Rochefoucauld must have had her in his mind's eye when he wrote the following maxim: 'The intelligence of most women serves rather to justify their folly than their reason.' It was very soon afterwards, however, that the political career of Madame de Longueville came to an end. Insensibly she withdrew from the scene in which she had played so active a part, and left the Prince of Condé to continue the strife which she had commenced.

Later on the troubles were appeased, the Frondeurs were pardoned, she was restored to favour, and she opened her salon to all the political and literary celebrities of the day. Her Hôtel resembled that of Rambouillet. Her grace, amenity, and love of letters caused her to become the object of general homage on the part of all that was most elegant and distinguished in Parisian society. The latter part of her life was spent in retirement and devoted to the education of her children and the fulfilment of her religious duties. She died in 1679, at the age of fifty-nine, and her heart was deposited, by her own directions, in the chapel at Port Royal, which she had defended against the persecutions of the Jesuits with as much ardour as she had displayed in the cause of the Frondeurs in the earlier part of her life. The deeply religious education she had received in childhood, and which had impelled her at the age of fourteen to contemplate entering a convent, seemed to revive within her towards the close of her existence.

She wrote to the Carmelites, with whom she had passed that period in which she was receiving instruction, for advice as to the books she ought to read. 'If,' she said, not without a certain eloquence of the heart and a touch of tender pathos—'if I have had some attachments to the world, of whatever nature you may suppose them to have been, they are now broken and even shattered.' She was then, or was about to place herself, under the spiritual guidance of an able and experienced director of souls—Monsieur Singlin, the friend and disciple of St. Vincent de Paul, who knew how to speak peace to the troubled soul of the poor penitent sinner.

Victor Cousin, who has studied the life and character of the Duchesse de Longueville with such affectionate assiduity, has quoted some of her letters in which she has unconsciously depicted her own mental nature so accurately that I cannot deny myself the pleasure of transcribing a few passages.

On receiving the letter of Monsieur Singlin, which appeared to me very thick, and consequently caused me to hope many things concerning the matter which is uppermost in my mind, I opened it quickly, as my nature always impels me to do with whatever occupies my thoughts (I say this in order to make myself better known), and it causes me to be greatly negligent of, and indifferent to, anything that is not engaging my attention for the moment, thus exercising a complete mastery over me. And thus it is that some people fancy I am violent and impetuous, because they have observed me on some occasions under the influence of passion, or of minor inclinations and propensities; and at others, slow and indolent, and even torpid, if I may use the word, because they have seen that nothing touched me, whether good or evil, for the time being. And this is why they have defined me as if I had been two persons of entirely opposite dispositions, so that they have sometimes said that I was crafty, and sometimes that I had changed my humour, although neither was the case. It merely arose from the different situations in which I found myself. For I was as torpid as a corpse to whatever was not in my head at the moment, and perfectly alive to the smallest matters which concerned me. I never allow this humour to obtain the complete mastery of me.'

This is a bit of self-dissection not altogether unworthy of Montaigne; and she continues in the same strain, with regard to her sudden aversions and changes of humour, concluding as follows: 'A thought has occurred to me in relation to myself; and that is that I find great pleasure, by reason of my self-love, in being directed to write all this, because there is nothing I like so much as to occupy myself and others with what concerns myself, for self-love induces one to prefer speaking evil of oneself rather than be quite silent on such a subject.' La Rochefoucauld could not have analysed self-love more skilfully, or have framed a more sententious maxim than the last. It recalls to mind the explanation offered by a clever woman of the popularity of physicians with her sex: 'It is,' said she, 'because they are the only persons who will listen patiently to us while we are talking of nothing but ourselves.'

The death of the Duc de Longueville, which took place in 1663, permitted the duchess to devote herself entirely to penitence, as there was no longer any impediment in her path. She soon afterwards built herself a small residence at Port Royal des Champs, and divided her time between it and the Carmelite convent, where she had also apartments. The death of her son, the Comte de St. Paul, who was killed while crossing the Rhine, had the effect of completely detaching her from the world. Madame de Sévigné, in one of her immortal letters, under date of June 20, 1672, has related how the afflicting news was communicated to the bereaved mother. Here is the narrative:

> Mademoiselle de Vertus returned two days ago to Port Royal, where she generally remains. They went to find her and M. Arnauld in order to break that terrible news. Mademoiselle de Vertus had only to show herself. Her precipitate return denoted only too well something of an ominous character. In fact, directly she appeared, the duchess exclaimed 'Ah! Mademoiselle, how is Monsieur my brother?' [the Great Condé]. Her thoughts went no further. 'Madame, his wound is going on well.' 'Then there has been a battle! And my son?' They made no answer. 'Ah! Mademoiselle, my son, my dear boy! answer me. Is he dead?' 'Madame, I can find no words in which to reply to you.' 'Ah! my dear son! Did he die on the field of battle? Had he not a single moment? Oh! my God! what a sacrifice!' And then she fell upon her bed, and all that the keenest anguish could inflict, whether by convulsions, by swoonings, by a mortal silence, by stifled sobs, by bitter tears, by piteous appeals to heaven, and by tender and agonising exclamations—she endured them all. She has seen certain people, she has taken a little nourishment, because it is the will of God, but she knows no repose; and her health, which was previously very feeble, is seriously impaired. For my own part, I can only desire to see her die, as I cannot conceive her living after such a loss.

The death of that beloved son, her austerities, and her anguish of mind hastened her decease. She died at the

Carmelites, on April 15, 1679, and one year after her death her funeral oration was pronounced by Roquette, Bishop of Autun (who, by the way, is supposed to have been the original of Molière's Tartuffe).

Madame Deshoulières, born in Paris in 1634, where she died in 1694, was one of the most brilliant women of the most brilliant epoch in the literary history of France. As beautiful as she was accomplished; as elegant in her manners as she was rich in intellectual wealth; learned in philosophy and science, and yet an exemplary wife and mother; enamoured of poetry and excelling in its composition, and yet fulfilling the homely duties of everyday life with a grace and simplicity which were peculiarly her own; her image has floated down the stream of time as one of the most gifted and at the same time most lovable women of the *grand siècle*. She was only thirteen and a half when she was married to a brave officer who was serving in the army of the Great Condé; but they separated at the church door, and did not come together again until she was nearly twenty years of age. In the meantime she had made herself thoroughly mistress of the Latin, Italian, and Spanish languages; and her husband, justly proud of her beauty and her talents, took her to Brussels, where she became an object of universal admiration; the Prince of Condé himself offering her a homage which failed to diminish by one iota her loyal devotion to M. Deshoulières. Nor was their married life without a dash of romance: large arrears of pay were due to her husband from the Spanish government, and so earnestly did she importune the viceroy on his behalf, that that potentate ordered her to be arrested and imprisoned in the fortress of Vilvorden. Placing himself at the head of a trusty band of soldiers, M. Deshoulières managed to procure admittance to her prison, carried her off, after eight months' captivity, and fled with her to France. But the fair student turned even her compulsory seclusion to account, for while it lasted she acquired an intimate knowledge of the Bible and of the Fathers of the Church. In Paris, her literary associates and friends included the two Corneilles, Fléchier, Benserade, Ménage, and La Rochefoucauld, to whom she dedicated an ode. Following the example of the ducal thinker, she, too, wrote some maxims and moral reflections upon 'The immoderate desire of handing one's name down to posterity;' but it is only by some poems, and chiefly by one of an idyllic character, to which I shall presently recur, that she is known to posterity as one of the female poets of her time; although she wrote two tragedies and a comedy, which were represented with success upon the Parisian stage.

Happy in the affection of her husband, her children, and her friends, and in the social consideration she enjoyed, Madame Deshoulières' life was often saddened by the painful privations imposed upon her by her scanty means, especially as the estimation in which she was held compelled her to maintain a certain position. This will no doubt explain a certain note of tender melancholy by which her poetry is distinguished from that of her contemporaries. Another thing worth noting is that Madame Deshoulières acquired in the society of men like La Rochefoucauld, and of women like Madame de la Sablière, a habit of looking at human passions in their *ensemble*, which found expression, quite simply and without affectation, in maxims and moral sentences. Take, for example, a maxim of Madame de Sablé, as versified by Madame Deshoulières:

> L'amour-propre est, hélas! le plus sot des amours;
> Cependant des erreurs il est la plus commune.
> Quelque puissant qu'on soit en richesse, en crédit,
> Quelque mauvais succès qu'ait tout ce qu'on écrit,
>   *Nul n'est content de sa fortune*
>   *Ni mécontent de son esprit.*

Here, too, we have one of La Rochefoucauld's maxims clothed with verse which would be only spoiled in the translation:

> Que chacun parle bien de la reconnaissance,
>   Et que peu de gens en font voir!
> D'un service attendu la flatteuse espérance
> Fait porter dans l'excès les soins, la complaisance!
> A peine est-il rendu, qu'on cesse d'en avoir.
> De qui nous a servis la vue est importune;
>   On trouve honteux de devoir
>   Les secours que dans l'infortune
> On n'avait point trouvé honteux de recevoir.

When occasion required, Madame Deshoulières knew how to barb an epigram. Here are some lines which she addressed in 1687 to Father Bouhours, who had made no mention of herself in his book 'Sur l'Art de bien penser sur les Ouvrages de l'Esprit:'

> In a list of great authors extoll'd in your book,
> My name, I observe, you completely o'erlook;
> A proof, is it not? it was ne'er in your mind.
> But Pascal's is also omitted, I find,
> And he being not a bad scribe on the whole,
> With his own exclusion myself I console.[1]

But what are held to justify the title of the Tenth Muse, bestowed upon Madame Deshoulières during her lifetime, are the Idylls which she wrote; for they are masterpieces of grace, sensibility, and elegance of expression. One of the best known of these was written in 1674, and is entitled 'The Sheep.' It is replete with those reflections which arise in the thoughtful mind when it contrasts the peaceful and apparently happy lives led by the lower animals with the agitated existence of man, with his artificial wants, his unsatisfied desires, and his complete alienation from nature. Here is the poem:

LES MOUTONS
Idylle (1674)

Hélas! petits moutons, que vous êtes heureux!
Vous paissez dans nos champs, sans souci, sans alarmes;
 Aussitôt aimés qu'amoureux,
On ne vous force point à répandre des larmes;
Vous ne formez jamais d'inutiles désirs,
Dans vos tranquilles cœurs l'amour suit la nature,
Sans ressentir ses maux, vous avez ses plaisirs.
L'ambition, l'honneur, l'intérêt, l'imposture,
 Qui font tant de maux parmi nous,
 Ne se rencontrent point chez vous.
Cependant nous avons la raison pour partage,
 Et vous en ignorez l'usage,
Innocents animaux, n'en soyez point jaloux,
 Ce n'est pas un grand avantage.

[1] Dans une liste triomphante
De célèbres auteurs que votre livre chante
 Je ne vois pas mon nom placé:
A moi, n'est-il pas vrai? vous n'avez point pensé.
 Mais aussi dans le même rôle
 Vous avez oublié Pascal,
 Qui pourtant ne pensait pas mal:
 Un tel compagnon me console.

Cette fière raison, dont on fait tant de bruit,
Contre les passions n'est pas un sûr remède :
Un peu de vin la trouble, un enfant la séduit,
Et déchirer un cœur qui l'appelle à son aide
    Est tout l'effet qu'elle produit.
    Toujours impuissante et sévère,
Elle s'oppose à tout, et ne surmonte rien ;
    Sous la garde de votre chien,
Vous devez beaucoup moins redouter la colère
    Des loups cruels et ravissants,
Que, sous l'autorité d'une telle chimère,
    Nous ne devons craindre nos sens.
Ne vaudroit-il pas mieux vivre, comme vous faites,
    Dans une douce oisiveté ?
Ne vaudroit-il pas mieux être, comme vous êtes,
    Dans une heureuse obscurité,
    Que d'avoir, sans tranquillité,
    Des richesses, de la naissance,
    De l'esprit et de la beauté ?
Ces prétendus trésors, dont on fait vanité,
    Valent moins que votre indolence ;
Ils nous livrent sans cesse à des soins criminels ;
    Par eux plus d'un remords nous ronge ;
Sans songer qu'eux et nous passerons comme un songe,
    Il n'est dans ce vaste univers
    Rien d'assuré, rien de solide :
Des choses d'ici-bas la fortune décide
    Selon ses caprices divers.
    Tout l'effort de notre prudence
Ne peut nous dérober au moindre de ses coups.
Paissez, moutons, paissez sans règle et sans science ;
    Malgré la trompeuse apparence,
Vous êtes plus heureux et plus sages que nous.

After the death of her husband, Madame Deshoulières' anxieties on account of her children caused her to address an allegorical poem to Louis XIV., in which she assumes the *rôle* of a shepherdess who has lost the faithful guardian of her flock, and implores for her lambs the favour and protection of the all-powerful Pan.

VERS ALLÉGORIQUES

À ses Enfants (*janvier* 1693)

    Dans ces prés fleuris
    Qu'arrose la Seine,
    Cherchez qui vous mène,
    Mes chères brebis.

J'ai fait, pour vous rendre
Le destin plus doux,
Ce qu'on peut attendre
D'une amitié tendre :
Mais son long courroux
Détruit, empoisonne
Tous mes soins pour vous,
Et vous abandonne
Aux fureurs des loups.
Seriez-vous leur proie,
Aimable troupeau,
Vous de ce hameau
L'honneur et la joie ;
Vous qui, gras et beau,
Me donnez sans cesse
Sur l'herbette épaisse
Un plaisir nouveau ?
Que je vous regrette :
Mais il faut céder :
Sans chien, sans houlette,
Puis-je vous garder ?
L'injuste fortune
Me les a ravis :
En vain j'importune
Le ciel par mes cris ;
Il rit de mes craintes,
Et, sourd à mes plaintes,
Houlette ni chien
Il ne me rend rien.
Puissiez-vous contentes
Et sans mon secours,
Passer d'heureux jours
Brebis innocentes,
Brebis mes amours !
Que Pan vous défende :
Hélas ! il le sait,
Je ne lui demande
Que ce seul bienfait.
Oui, brebis chéries,
Qu'avec tant de soin
J'ai toujours nourries,
Je prends à témoin
Ces bois, ces prairies,
Que si les faveurs
Du dieu des pasteurs
Vous gardent d'outrages,
Et vous font avoir
Du matin au soir
De gras pâturages,
J'en conserverai,
Tant que je vivrai,

> La douce mémoire,
> Et que mes chansons
> En mille façons
> Porteront sa gloire,
> Du rivage heureux
> Où vif et pompeux
> L'astre qui mesure
> Les nuits et les jours,
> Commençant son cours
> Rend à la nature
> Toute sa parure,
> Jusqu'en ces climats
> Où, sans doute las
> D'éclairer le monde,
> Il va chez Téthys
> Rallumer dans l'onde
> Ses feux amortis.

In another charming poem, which takes the form of an epistle addressed to a lady with the object of reconciling her to the loss of her beauty, she reminds her that, while the complexion fades and the features wither, the true loveliness of heart and mind is an enduring possession and never ceases to attract.

ÉPÎTRE CHAGRINE À MADAME ******

> Supportez un peu mieux, Silvie,
>   La perte de votre beauté !
> Ce n'est que par le temps qu'elle vous est ravie.
>   Hé ! bien, est-ce une nouveauté ?
> Devoit-elle durer autant que votre vie ?
> Lorsque cinquante fois on a vu le printemps,
>   N'être plus belle alors n'est pas une infortune ;
>   C'est l'avoir été plus longtemps
>   Que ne le veut la loi commune.
>   Croyez-moi, d'un visage égal
> On doit s'apercevoir qu'on cesse d'être aimable ;
>   Dans une aventure semblable,
>   Le murmure sied toujours mal,
> Si pleine de raison, pour une bagatelle
>   Vous aviez compté vos appas,
> Leur perte vous seroit sans doute moins cruelle ;
>   Vous ne vous en plaindriez pas.
>   La beauté n'est pas éternelle ;
> Et nous nous préparons un facheux avenir,
>   Quand nous ne comptons que sur elle,
>   On ne sait plus que devenir,
>   Lorsque l'on n'a su qu'être belle.

Vous l'éprouvez, Silvie ; et je vous l'ai prédit.
Lorsqu'à votre miroir sans relâche attachée,
    Je ne vous voyois point touchée
    Des plaisirs que donne l'esprit.
    Cette foule de gens frivoles
    Qui, du matin jusques au soir,
    Ne vous disoit que des paroles,
    Fait du bruit chez de jeunes folles
Qui, comme vous, un jour seront au désespoir.

    Plus je vous vois, plus je raisonne,
Plus je crains que l'ennui que votre sort vous donne
Ne vous engage à suivre un usage commun.
    Vous justifirez mes alarmes ;
    Oui, vous emprunterez des charmes
    Pour faire revenir quelqu'un.
    Mais du moins d'une tendre amie,
    Qui dans son goût est tous les jours,
    Par les hommes même affermie,
Écoutez un moment les sincères discours.

Croyez-vous que l'amour s'allume dans une âme
Par le rouge et le blanc qu'on mêle sur le teint ?
    Et tient-on compte à quelque femme
    Des couleurs dont elle se peint ?
Songeons, pour nous guérir de l'erreur où nous sommes,
    Que le fard le plus beau de tous,
Loin de nous attirer les suffrages des hommes,
    Ne leur donne que des dégoûts.

    Mais peut-être me direz-vous
Que si j'avais un teint aussi laid que le vôtre
J'aurois contre le fard un peu moins de courroux,
    Et que j'en mettrois comme une autre.
Point du tout. Je me sens des sentiments meilleurs ;
    Et si la nature en partage
Ne m'avoit pas donné d'assez belles couleurs,
J'aurais assurément respecté son ouvrage.
Et si l'on m'en croyoit, faux braves, faux amis,
    Faux dévots comme fausses prudes,
    Tout à découvert seroient mis,
Et tous perdroient par là les lâches habitudes
Où par un long abus ils se sont affermis.

Some time before her death, Madame Deshoulières wrote some paraphrases of certain of the Psalms, which are really remarkable, and are probably the best of her compositions. There is only one incident in her literary career upon which she had occasion to look back with regret. This was the animosity she exhibited towards Racine, which originated in a gratuitous insult offered to her by Mademoiselle de Champmeslé, the actress, on the first night of the performance of 'Phèdre.' The provocation was no doubt great and exasperating, but the resentment was unworthy of a mind so beautiful and a nature which was generally so admirable as those of Madame Deshoulières.

Marguerite Hessein, who married Antoine Rambouillet, Sieur de la Sablière, and was the sister of that Mademoiselle Hessein who was the friend of Boileau and Racine (both of whom stood in awe of the pungency of her sarcasms), was not less celebrated for her beauty than for her love of letters and her intellectual gifts. To these Boileau has made scornful reference in the satire which he wrote upon women, sneeringly attributing the pallor of her countenance to her sitting up all night with an astrolabe in her hands, watching the path of Jupiter through the heavens; for those were the days in which the 'lords of creation' regarded it as little short of a high crime and misdemeanour that women should apply themselves to those serious studies of which men were supposed to enjoy the monopoly.

Madame de la Sablière was rendered chiefly famous, however, by her friendship for, and her generous hospitality to, La Fontaine. The vivacity of her disposition, the never failing charm of her conversation, and the elegance of her manners, rendered her one of the ornaments of Parisian society in her day; and she drew around her all that was most distinguished in art, literature, and science. Her frailty, it must be regretfully added, was as conspicuous as her beauty; and she sought in her later years to atone by her devotion for the errors of her youth.

Some of her Thoughts and Maxims are occasionally appended to those of La Rochefoucauld, and are of a distinctly religious character, while others resembled those of the Marquise de Sablé. It is only necessary to add that Madame de la Sablière was born in Paris in the year 1636; that she was married at eighteen to a husband as inconstant as that of Madame de Sévigné; and that she died in a religious institution at the age of fifty-seven.

LECTURE XI

'L'Astrée' of D'Urfé (1568-1625)—Balzac (1594-1655)—Voiture (1598-1648)—Mademoiselle de Scudéry (1607-1701)—La Rochefoucauld (1613-1680)—Select Maxims.

I PROPOSE in the present lecture to confine myself exclusively to the prose writers who flourished in France at the beginning of the seventeenth century. These are so numerous as to render the task of making a selection from them extremely difficult. My desire is, however, to make a conscientious study of that interesting period, and to omit nothing of importance, nothing that is worth recalling to mind, of our prose writers since Balzac. This lecture will include Voiture, the frequenters of the Hôtel de Rambouillet, La Calprenède, Mademoiselle de Scudéry, Ménage, Maynard, a faint echo of Malherbe, Segrais, an agreeable poet and a wit, the ingenious Benserade, the energetic and rugged Brébeuf, Bishop Godeau, who mingled rhymes of gallantry with sacred verse, as well as those other writers who knew how to resist the bad taste then in vogue, and who formed a phalanx of enemies to the Hôtel de Rambouillet. I speak of Sarrazin, Scarron the emperor of burlesque, the witty Saint-Evremond, the forerunner of the eighteenth century, Saint-Amant, the fantastic Cyrano de Bergerac, and the moralists and letter writers who bring us down to Pascal and Descartes.

These close the period under consideration, and will lead us on to the examination of Corneille, Rotrou, Racine, Molière, Boileau, La Fontaine, and Regnard.

Before touching upon Balzac, I must make some mention of a highly successful romance written towards the commencement of the seventeenth century by Honoré d'Urfé, entitled 'L'Astrée.' It was, indeed, so often read and re-read at the court, where it was praised by all the intellectual people of the time, that I cannot omit it from my course. This romance, moreover, was long regarded as a model of its kind, and prepared the way for that throng of romance writers who inundated with their compositions the *ruelles* of the 'Précieuses' during the whole of the first half of the century. Mademoiselle de Scudéry professed the highest admiration for a work to which she was largely indebted for the inspiration of her own. It seems that the plot of the story is based upon actual adventures, of which Patru has supplied us with the key. The story of a noble lady, Diana de Chateaumorant, who was successively married to the elder brother of D'Urfé and to himself, and the gallantries and amorous intrigues of Henry IV., furnish the chief materials of the narrative, which is scarcely worth dwelling upon, however. And although its author also composed an epic poem, entitled 'The Savoisiade,' and a pastoral fable called 'The Silvanire,' which he dedicated to Marie de Médicis, yet he contributed nothing durable to our literature, in which he is only known as the precursor of writers who have exaggerated his bad taste and have done nothing for the language. Hence we may dismiss him without further ado, and pass on to speak of Balzac and Voiture.

Jean-Louis Guez, Seigneur de Balzac, who was born at Angoulême in 1594 and died in 1655, enjoys the distinction of having contributed to the restoration of the French language, and of having done for prose that which, as I have already indicated in my study of Malherbe, that great reformer did for our poetry. Balzac naturally possessed an extreme delicacy of temperament, a lively imagination, and a sound judgment. His talent revealed itself very early, and he had scarcely reached his twentieth year, when the Cardinal Duperron, astonished, as Desportes had previously been, by the early verses of Malherbe, exclaimed: 'If the progress of his style equals its fine commencement, he will soon be the master of masters.' Balzac has been praised by Descartes, who commended, in a Latin composition which he addressed to him, the balance, the proportion, and the harmony of the *ensemble* of his letters, and pronounced him superior to other writers in the truth and nobility of his diction. To these praises Balzac modestly replied: 'I shall not dare to appeal to your judgment on my writings, because it is too favourable, and because, perhaps, your affection has got the better of your integrity.' The answer was characteristic of the man, and it is all the more worthy of note, because it offers such a striking contrast to the exaggerated bad taste, the affectation, the satirical mannerisms, the verbal contortions, and far-fetched ideas of Voiture and other writers of the same epoch.

Balzac's works comprise numerous letters, the best of which were addressed to the Marchioness of Rambouillet, some treatises entitled 'The Prince,' 'Aristippus,' his favourite work, and 'The Christian Socrates,' a satire entitled 'Le Barbon,' and many Latin verses. He was one of the most fastidious of writers, and bestowed more pains upon polishing a sentence than other writers would take in writing a whole chapter. He was, in fact, a 'stylist' two hundred years before the phrase came into common use. In that respect, I think, he stands alone among all his contemporaries, and the services he rendered to our language and literature, by proving the harmonious form into which prose writings are capable of being cast, have been somewhat inadequately acknowledged, perhaps, by those who are now using the perfected instrument. Balzac dealt with a phrase as Benvenuto Cellini did with a fragment of silver or ivory: it did not leave his hands until it bore the distinct impress of his artistic touch. And, as Henry Martin has pointed out with characteristic acumen, the sustained eloquence of his noble style has been to Bossuet and Pascal what Malherbe was to Corneille and Racine.

Like Montaigne, the Seigneur de Balzac was a country gentleman, and it was in the seclusion of his château that he composed most of his letters and probably the whole of his wellnigh forgotten treatises. And for that reason there is more of the studious thinker than of the observant man of the world in his writings, which are more remarkable in form than in substance. His correspondence, which appeared in 1624, attracted much attention, and earned for him the title of 'The Great Epistoler.' Some have looked upon him as the father of French rhetoric, and have asserted that all those who have written good prose since his time, or who will do so hereafter, in our mother tongue owe him a lasting obligation; while Geruzez regards him as a connecting link between the two assemblies which have exerted the greatest influence on French literature—namely, the Hôtel de Rambouillet and the French Academy. From his sequestered château near Angoulême he was the oracle of the *salon* of Arthenice and of the learned society founded by Richelieu for the government of the republic of letters. His epistles and dissertations were sent up from his distant and isolated sanctuary for the entertainment of the select circle of Madame de Rambouillet, each member of which contributed to swell the chorus of praise raised in honour of the writer. Richelieu was very enthusiastic on the subject of these letters, and wrote to Balzac, complimenting him on their vigour and on their superiority to the imagination of ordinary men and women, while approving themselves to the good sense of people with elevated minds. When I add that Balzac founded at the Academy the prize for eloquence which was awarded for the first time to Mademoiselle de Scudéry, I have said all that it is necessary to say concerning this accomplished prose writer.

Voiture was born at Amiens in the year 1598, and therefore on the confines of two centuries. His father was a wine merchant having large business transactions with the court, which brought him into intercourse with many important personages. He gave his son an excellent education, sending him to Paris for that purpose, and afterwards to Orleans, where he studied law. His verses and letters began to be talked about while he was yet a youth, but such reputation as he acquired was confined to bourgeois circles, from whence he was led to emerge by the intervention of a gentleman who remarked to him, 'Monsieur, you are much too well bred to remain among the bourgeoisie; I must take you away from them and present you to the Marchioness of Rambouillet, the oracle of merit and politeness.' And from that moment Voiture found himself in his true sphere, and had nothing to do but to follow his genuine vocation, which was that of a fashionable man of wit in a highly select circle. Voiture was more particularly known by his letters; at any rate, his other productions are inferior to them. They are addressed to Madame de Rambouillet and various other persons of both sexes. Notwithstanding they are evidently laboured, they are, in spite of their affectation, the original types and models of the epistolary schools of both France and England. We may trace his influence in the letters of Pope, Walpole, Gray, and Cowper. The art of saying nothing, or something of very small significance, so agreeably that it should interest by the mere method of its presentation, and of addressing a witty compliment to a person in such a way as not only to raise the recipient but the writer in his or her good opinion, was one in which both Voiture and Balzac excelled. Their letters were apt to become wearisome in the long run, and yet they were far from being destitute of ability. Those of Balzac are the more serious and dignified, while, at the same time, they have a more solid foundation of good sense. Of those of Voiture it might almost be said that the writer imagined that a witty composition would suffer by any admixture of good sense. 'Pope,' as Hallam has remarked, 'when addressing ladies, was the ape of Voiture;' and the remarks of his judicious critic on his correspondence generally are so sound that I cannot forbear quoting them. 'It was, unfortunately, thought necessary,' he writes, 'either to affect despairing love, which was to express itself with all possible gaiety, or, where love was too presumptuous, as with the Rambouillets, to pour out a torrent of nonsensical flattery, which was to be rendered tolerable by far-fetched terms of thought. Voiture had the honour of having rendered this style fashionable; but if the bad taste of others had not perverted his own, Voiture would have been a good writer. His letters, especially those written from Spain, are sometimes truly witty and always vivacious. . . . We should also remember that Voiture held his place in good society upon the tacit condition that he should always strive to be witty.' His position in this respect was something intermediate between that of the court fool of earlier times and that of a professional jester, like Theodore Hook, in more recent days. At the present hour, in England at least, where men of wit can find a good market for their wares at a publisher's, society pays humourists, like Mr. Corney Grain or Mr. Grossmith, to supply them with an evening's facetiousness, at which they have only to laugh, and are not called upon to invent repartees.

Voiture, it must be confessed, was a bit of a snob. He was ashamed of his father's occupation, and this gave rise to the *mot* that 'wine, which animates the hearts of most men, depressed that of Voiture.' His wit and talent had built him a bridge across the tremendous chasm which then separated the aristocratic from the trading classes in France, and he did not like to be reminded that he belonged to the latter by the accident of his birth. He dined every day with the elegant and high-bred men and women who frequented the Hôtel de Rambouillet, and he tried to assure himself that within that charmed circle he was 'native and to the manner born.' One must project oneself into the midst of that exclusive society, with its pride of birth, its supreme contempt for the bourgeoisie, and its genuinely sincere belief that it was a superior caste, set apart by nature for the enjoyment of all the pleasures of life, in order to be able to understand and to make a reasonable allowance for the taint of snobbery in Voiture's character. In reading his letters at the present time we do so, as Sainte-Beuve has said, not so much to amuse ourselves by what he has written, as to learn what were the occupations and amusements of that refined, supremely elegant, and fastidious circle which has given the tone to the best society of later days. The familiar footing upon which Voiture was received by Madame de Rambouillet is indicated by the anecdote of his introducing two muzzled bears into her bedroom one morning before she was up. She returned the compliment afterwards when he brought her a sonnet, which he looked upon as the best he had ever written. 'I have read this somewhere before,' she said. The poet assured her that it was fresh from the mint of his own brain; but next morning he was thunderstruck when she showed him in a printed book the very composition, word for word. 'I must have read it there, must have unconsciously impressed it upon my memory, and innocently reproduced it as my own,' said Voiture; and he went about relating this curious psychological phenomenon to every person he met, until the Marchioness laughingly confessed that she had had his sonnet surreptitiously printed, and had interpolated it in the book she showed him.

Upon another occasion the Comte de Guiche mentioned

to Voiture that he had heard he was married, and asked if it was true. The poet denied the soft impeachment, and some time afterwards knocked the Comte up at two o'clock in the morning. 'What the deuce is the matter?' he cried out between sleeping and waking. 'Monsieur,' replied Voiture, with all becoming seriousness, 'you did me the honour, some time ago, to inquire if I was married; I have now come to tell you that I am.'

There is a letter of his, called 'La Berne,' which acquired considerable vogue at the time, and may be quoted as offering a very fair specimen of his style. It was addressed to Mademoiselle de Bourbon, who was indisposed, and Voiture was sent to amuse her, but he was not in the mood, and she complained that she had never found him so dull. The Rambouillets and their friends were disappointed and irritated at his failure to be funny when called upon to do so for so great a lady, and determined to punish him, and to understand what follows it is necessary to explain that to be *berné* or tossed in a blanket was a pleasantry frequently indulged in by those superfine people.

'Mademoiselle,' he wrote to the invalid, 'I was tossed in a blanket on Friday after dinner, because I had not made you laugh in the time allotted me for that purpose, the order having been given by Madame de Rambouillet at the instigation of Mademoiselle her daughter and of Mademoiselle Paulet. They had postponed the execution of the decree until the return of Mademoiselle la Princesse and yourself, but they afterwards thought it best not to defer it any longer, as a punishment ought not to be inflicted on a day set apart for enjoyment. I made a great outcry and some resistance, but the blanket was procured and its corners were held by four of the strongest fellows in the world, and this I may say, Mademoiselle, that no one ever went so high as I did, and that I never supposed fortune could raise me to such an elevation. At every shake of the blanket they sent me out of sight, and I soared to heights never reached by the eagles,' &c. &c. Then follows a burlesque history of what took place, intermingled with dainty compliments regarding the lady to whom he was writing. All this is very frivolous and flimsy, however, but before dismissing Voiture and his blanket, we will do him the justice to quote what Feuillet de Conches has said of Balzac and him in his 'Causeries d'un Curieux:' 'It was with them that our classic literature commenced. The first gave our language numbers and elegance; the second indicated its *finesses*. Descartes has solidified and Pascal has fixed it.'

When the renown of Balzac and Voiture began to pale, the light of De Sévigné was already reddening the eastern sky; but before we reach that famous name, we must linger by the roadside to consider for a while the influence of Spain upon the literary productions of France during the first half of the Age of Louis XIV.; nor will this be a digression, for only thus can we understand the influences that were in operation to bring about the lapse into bad taste which is observable in the literature of the period. Ever since the reign of Charles V., the power of Spain had pressed heavily on the rest of Europe. In France, the League, under Philip II., had threatened to become for the moment the organ of the monarchy, and the ambassadors of that sovereign exercised an enormous effect on the policy of both England and France. James I. had sacrificed Raleigh to the vengeance of Gondomar, and as late as the days of Richelieu Cinq-Mars had been executed for having conspired with the government of his own country against that of Spain.

Henry IV. had rolled back the torrent, but although he had driven the Spaniards from France he was unable to deliver the latter either from their fashions or their ideas. The costume, the pose, the language, all smacked of Spain, and the fashions of the country, as Demogeot has observed, were stronger than Régnier, than Sully, than Henry IV. himself. Francis I., the most French of our kings, donned the black costume of Philip II., *nolens volens*, and when he was growing old grumblingly applied himself to learn Spanish, just as Cato the Censor learned Greek in his old age.

The king's teacher, Antonio Perez, played a prominent part in the literary revolution which had introduced into France the elegant but far-fetched style of the writers of Spain, and you would certainly be filled with amusement did the limits of my lecture permit me to quote a page or two from the correspondence of this same Antonio Perez. To a lady of title for whom he had been unable to procure a pair of dogskin gloves she had asked him for, he replied, 'I am your ladyship's dog, and will willingly sacrifice a portion of my own skin for the purpose required.' And many others of his letters were much to the same effect.

Italy also sent us the author of 'Adonis,' whose arrival in France was heralded by the great reputation he had acquired in his own country.

Marini or Marino composed the epic thus entitled in twenty cantos. It narrates the loves of Venus and Adonis, and overflows with *concetti*, laboured antitheses, *jeux de mots*, and outrageous metaphors. It gave rise to a style of writing called the Marinesque, and it was admired and imitated by Mademoiselle de Scudéry, by Voiture, Balzac, and Malherbe, but was finally suppressed by Boileau and Molière, although, in later times, it seems to have captivated Rousseau.

You will thus perceive that the Hôtel de Rambouillet, of which I have already had occasion to speak, did not invent but adopted the bad taste for which it has been ridiculed. On the other hand, that celebrated reunion purified the language, imparted refinement and delicacy to the manners and sentiments of the time, served the purpose of a public to the writers of the period, pending the formation of a real reading public, and fostered, as Demogeot has said, the literary spirit until it had acquired strength enough to stand alone. It was also to these assemblages and to the Précieuses so much ridiculed at the time that we owe the essentially French art of *causerie*. Three women reigned there successively: Giulia Savelli, wife of the Marquis de Pisani, and correspondent of the just mentioned Antonio Perez, a noble and gracious lady of Italian origin; her daughter, the Marchioness of Rambouillet, who, under the romantic name of Arthenice, the anagram of Catherine, received from Marino his tenderest compliments and most florid madrigals, and who was mystically adored by the ancient Malherbe; and finally, Julie d'Angennes, daughter of Catherine, whose reign extended from the death of Malherbe in 1628 until that of Voiture in 1648. That was the most brilliant period. The Condés, the Contis, the La Rochefoucaulds, the Bussys, and the Grammonts formed the court of the regency queen.

We will study later on the versifiers, letter writers, and grammarians, who succeeded each other in the famous blue salon of the marchioness.

The ambition to construct a national *épopée*, and to endow France with a great epic poem, a task which even Ronsard had failed to accomplish, still agitated many minds, and there had appeared the 'Pucelle' of Chapelain, the 'Alaric' of Scudéry, the 'Clovis' of Desmarets, and several other ponderous compositions, including the 'Saint Louis' of Father Lemoine, which are now completely forgotten. Here and there flashes of light illuminate the cloudy and massive conceptions of the Jesuit, who was the victim of Pascal's raillery, but his poem is nevertheless, in the opinion of Henry Martin, by no means comparable with the old 'Chanson de Roland.'

Akin to these lumbering experiments in epic poetry was a huge romance in prose, which lifted Mademoiselle de Scudéry into sudden notoriety; for that lady, her brother George, and La Calprenède continued the school of the 'Astrée' of D'Urfé with a success much more extensive than durable. We no longer read the long, laboured, and wearisome narratives of Mademoiselle de Scudéry, which were very much inferior to their model, the work we have just named; for this remains the first in talent as it is also the earliest in date of the false kind of romances to which it gave rise; and it is therefore still quoted, as it serves to designate a class of literature and a mode of thought and expression peculiar to a celebrated period. It is a model, as Sainte-Beuve has observed, which was very near passing into general circulation and becoming current coin of the realm. For these reasons it is incumbent upon me to say something of Mademoiselle de Scudéry, both as a woman and as a writer.

She was a native of Havre, where she was born in 1607, in the reign of Henry IV., and she lived to be ninety-four, dying in 1701, towards the end of the reign of Louis Quatorze. Her father was of Italian origin, but married a wife in Normandy, and he dying while Madeleine was still very young left her to the tutelage of an uncle, who gave her an admirable education, which included the Italian and Spanish languages, agriculture, medicine, and the arts of painting and music. Gifted with a powerful imagination, a wonderfully retentive memory, a remarkable gift for conversation, and no little self-reliance, as well as self-esteem, she felt a strong determination to shine, and shine she did. She likewise entertained an exaggerated idea of the importance of her own family, and would talk of the 'downfall of her house,' as if it were an event not less momentous, to quote the malicious words of Tallemant des Réaux, than 'the overthrow of the Greek empire.'

In person she was tall and meagre, with a long face which was really ugly. Her skin was coarse and swarthy; her eyes were black, and so were her finger nails, which gave Madame Cornuel an excuse for saying that Mademoiselle de Scudéry exuded ink through every pore of her skin. It is a merciful dispensation of Providence that those of my own sex to whom beauty is denied are quite unconscious of the fact. Not only was this the case with our Madeleine, but she was also unable to perceive the excessive ugliness of M. Pellisson, another of the Rambouillet set, whom she looked upon as an incomparable Adonis; or perhaps I ought to say Phaon, since she has depicted herself as Sappho in her famous romance of the 'Grand Cyrus.' Her own early years, her education, her extreme aptitude in acquiring knowledge, and above all, her personal charms, are all described beneath a thin veil of fiction in that work. This is the image which presented itself to the lively imagination of Mademoiselle de Scudéry, as she stood before her mirror and limned her own portrait, under the pseudonym of Sappho: 'When you hear me speak of her as the must wonderful, the most charming person in all Greece, you must not suppose that her beauty was absolutely without a flaw. . . . At the same time, she was just as capable of inspiring a powerful passion as the greatest beauties in the world. . . . As to her complexion, it was not of surpassing fairness, but its lustre was always such that you would pronounce it handsome. But Sappho's sovereign claim was this, that her eyes were so beautiful, so loving, and so full of intelligence, that you could neither sustain their gaze, nor detach your own regards from them. . . . What rendered them so very dazzling was the incomparable contrast presented between the white and black of those orbs. Yet there was nothing violent in the contrast,' &c. Think of that tall, gaunt woman, with ink oozing out of every pore of her swarthy Sicilian complexion, delineating her features in this wise! Burns might well exclaim

> O wad some power the giftie gie us
> To see oursels as others see us!

But let us turn to Mademoiselle de Scudéry as a writer, and pay a just tribute of gratitude to that *précieuse* of the seventeenth century, who has invented a phraseology, a language, and an imagery peculiarly her own, even in the portrayal of the Sappho whom she wishes us to accept as a reflected image of herself. On the death of her uncle she quitted Rouen for Paris, where her brother had already established himself as one of the dramatic authors connected with the Hôtel Bourgogne. She appeared to advantage in the best social circles, and made her *début* in the world of letters by writing some romances, with her brother's name on the title-page. 'Ibrahim ou l'illustre Bassa' was thus published in 1641; 'Artamène' or the 'Grand Cyrus' in 1650; and 'Clélie' in 1656. Each of the two latter filled ten volumes! Mademoiselle de Scudéry, in those romances, depicted the manners of the upper classes of her day. She shows us all the centres of conversation rivalling the Hôtel de Rambouillet, and maps out, like a geographical explorer, the regions traversed by the susceptible heart on its voyage down the river of Tenderness. It is difficult to imagine a company of highly educated and singularly accomplished men and women, belonging to the best classes of society in France, and apparently endowed with common sense, dissipating their time and finding the utmost delight in poring over Mademoiselle de Scudéry's 'Carte de Tendre,' and the sailing instructions which accompanied it, wherein the voyager was informed of the whereabouts of such villages as Friendship, Sincerity, Honesty, Generosity, Exactitude, and Goodness; and was admonished to avoid such places as Negligence, Inequality, Tepidity, Levity, and Forgetfulness, because these were all on the road to the Lake of Indifference. All this sentimental trifling is frivolous, forced, far-fetched, and fantastic in the extreme; but at the same time one cannot close one's eyes to the ingenuity, the intellectual effort, the invention, and the misdirected ability which are involved in the composition.

It was like an enormous soap-bubble, and the wits and beauties of the day were absorbed in their admiration of the prismatic colours which glittered on its unsubstantial surface, when Boileau comes, breathes on it, and lo! it is dissolved, like the romances of which it is an episode. It was impossible to survive the ridicule of the 'Tenth Satire' and of 'Lutrin.'

And yet the 'Grand Cyrus' was a remarkable book, and excited the admiration of men like Massillon, Fléchier, and La Fontaine, and of a woman so gifted as Madame de Sévigné. Mademoiselle de Scudéry was an exceedingly acute observer, and in the romance under notice she has really presented us with an invaluable picture of the woman of the seventeenth century—her mental constitution, her moral sentiments, and her daily occupations. Again, the story was read with the greatest interest at the time because, as in 'Coningsby' in our own days, the characters who figured in the romance were nearly all portraits of the most distinguished people of the epoch, including, of course, the elegant frequenters of the Hôtel de Rambouillet. Thus Artamène was no other than the Great Condé; the Duc de Saint-Aignan was Artaban; Conrart was Theodamas; Pellisson, Acante; Bishop Godeau the Magus of Sidon; and the authoress, as we have said, was Sappho. Mademoiselle de Scudéry made herself the echo of all the frivolities and futilities which were then in vogue, and polite society rapturously applauded the faithful painter of its manners, its ideas, and its trivial occupations. After having been one of the favourites of the Hôtel de Rambouillet, and the adopted sister of Julie d'Angennes, Mademoiselle de Scudéry aspired to have a *salon* of her own, where her Saturday evening receptions were attended by all the *beaux esprits* of the day. But as her means were very moderate, she was accustomed to distribute her compliments among those who were capable of making her the most liberal return for them. In order to sell her books, and thus augment her income, it was necessary to secure for them influential patrons. 'She has need to leave no stone unturned,' observes Tallemant, 'and when I think of that I forgive her.' Small presents, gratifications, pensions—these natural proofs of the consideration in which she was held—were by no means indifferent to her. Worldly prudence reminded her that 'solid pudding' was quite as necessary to her wellbeing as 'empty praise.' All this contributed, perhaps, to give a tincture of worldliness to her moral sentiments, and to contract her moral vision within the narrow circle of 'good society.'

Even before the days of Molière, as Sainte-Beuve has remarked, Mademoiselle de Scudéry had made more than one sensible remark on the subject of female wits and *femmes savantes*.

She carefully discusses the question if it would be well for women in general to know more than they do. 'While I may be the declared enemy,' she writes, 'of all women who become blue-stockings, I do not fail to find the other extreme very censurable, and I am often shocked to see many women of quality so grossly ignorant as, in my opinion, to dishonour our sex.' But in her days highly cultured women like herself were extremely rare: and it is related of as *spirituelle* a lady as Madame de Sablé, the friend of La Rochefoucauld, that she could not spell a word properly. 'It is quite certain,' observes Mademoiselle de Scudéry, 'that there are women who speak well and write badly, which is entirely their own fault. . . . It is, in my opinion, an intolerable mistake on the part of every woman to wish to speak well, and at the same time to write badly. . . . Most ladies seem to write as if they did not want to be understood; there is so little connection between their words, and their spelling is so queer.' Her ideas upon female education are worthy of attention even at this moment:

'There is nothing,' she writes, 'more droll than the way in which people ordinarily act with respect to the education of women. They do not want to bring them up to be flirts or coquettes, and yet they allow them to learn carefully everything relating to the intrigues of love, without permitting them to acquire anything which could fortify their virtue and employ their minds. In fact, the only things for which they are found serious fault with, in their early youth, is not being sufficiently nice, not dressing themselves stylishly enough, and not being so attentive as they might be to the lessons of their dancing and singing masters. And do not these things prove what I say? And it is very rarely that a woman can dance with propriety for more than five or six years of her life; yet, nevertheless, she spends ten or twelve years in continually learning what she can only practise during half as many, while that same person who ought to exercise a sound judgment up to the hour of her death, and to be able to converse until she breathes her last sigh, never learns anything whatever which would qualify her to speak more agreeably, or to act with wisdom and discretion.'

Still harping on the same subject, Mademoiselle de Scudéry goes on to say:

What I should like, then, would be this, that it might be said of a person of my own sex, that she knows a hundred things of which she never makes any boast; that she has a very enlightened mind; that she knows well the works of the best authors; that she speaks well, writes accurately, and has some knowledge of the world. But I don't want people to say of her, 'She is a blue-stocking,' for those two characters are totally dissimilar.

Evidently there was a great fund of good sense at the bottom of Mademoiselle de Scudéry's character, in spite of her self-admiration and the sentimental affectations by which her writings are disfigured.

Indeed, her 'Clélie' was as much a story with a purpose as the 'Télémaque' of Fénelon, or the novels of Mrs. Humphry Ward. What is woman's place in modern society? How is she to obtain and to maintain it? These were the questions raised by Mademoiselle de Scudéry in that romance, and discussed with no little perspicacity, piquancy, elevation of purpose, and breadth of outlook. She certainly did not belong to what is irreverently called nowadays the 'shrieking sisterhood,' but she was one of the earliest to contend for the elevation of her sex, and to establish the claims of her sister-woman to worthier treatment than that of becoming either the pretty plaything or the household drudge of her 'lord and master.' The story of 'Clélie,' as M. Saint-Marc Girardin has pointed out, 'is merely the framework or accessory of this great subject of controversy, and in that controversy we meet with all the discussions which have been raised in our own times with respect to the enfranchisement of women.'

When speaking of Balzac, I mentioned the prize for eloquence founded by him and won by Mademoiselle de Scudéry. The subject chosen by himself was 'Praise and Glory,' a theme which she treated so admirably as to extort the plaudits of all that remained of the old Academicians of the time of Richelieu. She was then sixty-four years of age, and up to the end of her life she gathered around her her little circle of courtiers, who used to speak of her as 'the marvel of the age of Louis the Great;' and when she died in 1701, the *savants* and men of letters in Paris vied with each other in pompous eulogies of her talent.

Sainte-Beuve, at the close of his essay on Mademoiselle de Scudéry, connects her name with that of Ninon de l'Enclos, a really wonderful woman, who combined her grace, urbanity, freshness, and vigour of mind with the gift of perpetual youth, which Mademoiselle de Scudéry certainly did not possess; and who passed away about the same time as herself, at nearly the same age, and in the same quarter of Paris—namely, the Marais.

'There comes a time in our lives when La Rochefoucauld pleases us greatly, and when he appears truer, perhaps, than he really is.' It is thus that Sainte-Beuve commences his study of the moralist whom I am about to analyse. Equally well known in the political as in the literary history of his time, a member of one of the most important families in France, and associated with the most famous men and women of an epoch rich in celebrities, a nobleman of perfect manners, a born wit, and a penetrating observer of human character, La Rochefoucauld was predestined by nature to a career of distinction. Born in the year 1613, in the midst of a national crisis, and belonging to a class which Richelieu was doing his utmost to enfeeble and abase, La Rochefoucauld became a *Frondeur* almost as soon as he could walk and talk; so that, when a mere lad, he was implicated in most of the intrigues which vexed the cardinal during the latter years of his life.

After the death of that statesman, the young duke, captivated by the Duchesse de Longueville, flung himself with all the ardour of a lover of seventeen into the cause of the Fronde. Parodying the couplet of a popular poet, he exclaimed:

> To win her heart, to please her lovely eyes,
> I warr'd on kings: I would have fought the skies.[1]

But later on, having had one of his eyes destroyed by a

---

[1] Pour mériter son cœur, pour plaire à ses beaux yeux,
J'ai fait la guerre aux rois, je l'aurait faite aux dieux.

shot from a musket during an engagement in the Faubourg Saint-Antoine, he saw reason to alter the couplet thus:

> For that frail heart, which now before me naked lies,
> I did make war on kings, and I have lost my eyes.[1]

The wars of the Fronde came to an end, however; La Rochefoucauld received the royal pardon, and, disillusioned with respect to Madame de Longueville, he contracted a lifelong friendship with Madame La Fayette, in whose conversation and society he found an enduring charm. His Hôtel in Paris was the rendezvous of all the intellectual people of his day, and the letters of one of his guests, Madame de Sévigné, present us with an animated picture of those who moved in that charmed circle.

The first work published by La Rochefoucauld was his portrait, which appeared in 1658, and although it only covers four pages, reveals to us the moralist 'in his habit as he lived.' His 'Memoirs' were published in 1662, and the first edition of his 'Maxims' three years later.

In the opinion of Voltaire, the last-named work contributed very materially to mould the taste of the nation, and to bestow upon its intellect the qualities of correctness and precision. In point of form, the book is a masterpiece. It is so terse, so piquant, so vigorous, and so accurate in expression. In point of substance, it is one of the most mischievous works ever written. Rousseau called it a sad book. It is, indeed; for it makes self-love the mainspring of human action, and acquiesces in a view of our common nature which is both disheartening and dishonourable. The 'Maxims' are undoubtedly the fruit, and even the matured fruit, of their noble writer's observation and experience of the world. But these excluded from view all that is noblest, purest, and most elevated and elevating in the motives and conduct of our race. Man as depicted by La Rochefoucauld is something intellectually higher, although morally lower, than the animal; for while the instinct of self-love is powerful in the latter, its capacity for self-sacrifice is very great; and the stork who allows herself to

---

[1] Pour ce cœur inconstant, qu'enfin je connais mieux,
J'ai fait la guerre aux rois, j'en ai perdu les yeux.

be burnt to death rather than forsake the nest which contains her callow brood is a nobler creature than the man or woman whose character has been formed in accordance with the 'Maxims' of La Rochefoucauld. Self-love may be, and is, a potent factor of human conduct; but the most beautiful lives ever led upon the earth have been lives of self-effacement, lives which have been lived for others; and the love and reverence of mankind have naturally fastened upon these single-minded and single-hearted benefactors of their race.

And again, I think that the 'Maxims' of La Rochefoucauld, replete as they are with worldly wisdom, perfect as many of them are in point, in felicity of phrase, and conciseness of expression, have tinged French literature, as well as that of other nations, with a tone of cynicism which is greatly to be regretted. They have taught men to look on the seamy side of human nature; to apply the microscope to its defects; to exaggerate its weaknesses and its errors; to overlook its redeeming qualities; to substitute scorn and contempt for pity and compassion; to stab with a sarcasm, where correction was possible by means of a gentle remonstrance or a playful reproof; and to suppress all tendencies to sympathy by habitual indulgence in satire.

I think Thackeray's keenness of insight into all that is meanest, most selfish, hypocritical, and despicable in human nature was just as remarkable as that of La Rochefoucauld. Indeed, it would be easy to collect from the writings of one whom I regard as among the greatest of English moralists a collection of maxims not unworthy to rank with those of my illustrious countryman. But Thackeray's cynicism was only worn as a mask; beneath it were the kindly features of the man who, like Abou Ben Adhem, could exclaim

'Write me as one that loves his fellow-men.'

The creator of Becky Sharp, and of Major Pendennis, and the Crawleys; the writer who transfixed upon his steel pen the innumerable family of Snobs and made them ridiculous for ever, had a heart as large as his intellect, sympathies as broad as the range of his genius; and the caustic humourist, the unflinching anatomist of human folly, pretentiousness, and insincerity, is also overflowing with tenderness, with gentleness, with admiration of goodness, simplicity, and sincerity; and shows us the pathetic and deeply-to-be-compassionated aspects of what is weakest in our fellow-creatures.

To return for a moment, however, to La Rochefoucauld. The publication of his 'Maxims' brings us to the middle of the *grand siècle*. The 'Provinciales' of Pascal had appeared nine years previously; the 'Pensées' would be published five years later; and the 'Caractères' of La Bruyère would see the light almost twenty years after that. The great monuments of French prose literature, and the masterpieces of pulpit oratory which adorned the reign of Louis XIV., were being given to the world by Bossuet, Massillon, Bourdaloue, Fléchier, and the rest; and it is interesting to study at this decisive moment of our literature the writings of that delicate cynic, that polished and smiling misanthrope, who, in the estimation of Voltaire, combined qualities unequalled by any writer in Europe since the renaissance of letters.

And for this purpose, I think I cannot do better than make a selection of the more terse and telling of the 'Maxims,' while quoting, at the same time, kindred thoughts on similar subjects from other authors.

MAXIMS

VIII.

Les passions sont les seuls orateurs qui persuadent toujours. Elles sont comme un art de la nature dont les règles sont infaillibles; et l'homme le plus simple qui a de la passion persuade mieux que le plus éloquent qui n'en a point.

XIX.

Nous avons tous assez de force pour supporter les maux d'autrui.

XXIX.

Le mal que nous faisons ne nous attire pas tant de persécution et de haine que nos bonnes qualités.

XXXI.

Si nous n'avions point de défauts, nous ne prendrions pas tant de plaisir à en remarquer dans les autres.

Charron, dans son livre 'De la Sagesse,' dit la même chose, en d'autres termes : ' L'envie est un regret du bien que les autres possèdent qui nous ronge fort de cœur ; elle tourne le bien d'autrui en notre mal.'

XLI.

Ceux qui s'appliquent trop aux petites choses deviennent ordinairement incapables des grandes.

A ce sujet, Vauvenargues estime ' qu'il serait plus vrai de dire que ceux dont il s'agit *sont nés* incapables des grandes.' Dans une de ses ' Maximes ' il dit : ' Si l'on voit quelques hommes que la spéculation des grandes choses rend en quelque sorte incapables des petites, on en trouve encore davantage à qui la pratique des petites a ôté jusqu'au sentiment des grandes.' Cette Maxime est d'une grande justesse et la vérité qu'elle contient a été exprimée bien des fois. Commynes blâme déjà ce défaut dans Louis XI, et Fénelon dans son ' Télémaque ' dit : ' Un esprit épuisé par les détails est comme la lie du vin, qui n'a plus ni force ni délicatesse.'

XLIX.

On n'est jamais si heureux ni si malheureux qu'on s'imagine.

LXX.

Il n'y a point de déguisement qui puisse longtemps cacher l'amour où il est, ni le feindre où il n'est pas.

Pascal, dans son discours sur ' Les Passions de l'Amour ' dit : ' L'on ne peut presque faire semblant d'aimer, que l'on ne soit bien près d'être amant.'

LXXIV.

Il n'y a qu'une sorte d'amour, mais il y en a mille différentes copies.

LXXXVII.

Les hommes ne vivraient pas longtemps en société, s'ils n'étaient les dupes les uns des autres.

Je rapproche de cette Maxime cette Pensée de Pascal : ' La vie humaine n'est qu'une illusion perpétuelle ; on ne fait que s'entretromper et s'entre-flatter .... L'union qui est entre les hommes n'est fondée que sur cette mutuelle tromperie.' Et ces deux ' Maximes ' de Vauvenargues : ' Les hommes semblent être nés pour faire des dupes, et l'être d'eux-mêmes : '—et : ' Si les hommes ne se flattaient pas les uns les autres, il n'y aurait pas de société.'

LXXXIX.

Tout le monde se plaint de sa mémoire, et personne ne se plaint de son jugement.

La Bruyère, dans ses ' Caractères,' dit ainsi : ' L'on se plaint de son peu de mémoire, content d'ailleurs de son grand sens et de son bon jugement.'

XC.

Nous plaisons plus souvent dans le commerce de la vie par nos défauts que par nos bonnes qualités.

Il y a de Vauvenargues un Maxime qu'on peut juxtaposer à celle-ci : 'On peut aimer de tout son cœur ceux en qui on reconnaît de grands défauts : il y aurait de l'impertinence à croire que la perfection a seule le droit de nous plaire.'

CXXXIX.

Une des choses qui fait que l'on trouve si peu de gens qui paraissent raisonnables et agréables dans la conversation, c'est qu'il n'y a presque personne qui ne pense plutôt à ce qu'il veut dire qu'à répondre précisément à ce qu'on lui dit ; les plus habiles et les plus complaisants se contentent de montrer seulement une mine attentive, au même temps que l'on voit, dans leurs yeux et dans leur esprit, un égarement pour ce qu'on leur dit, et une précipitation pour retourner à ce qu'ils veulent dire, au lieu de considérer que c'est un mauvais moyen de plaire aux autres, ou de les persuader, que de chercher si fort à se plaire soi-même, et que bien écouter et bien répondre est une des plus grandes perfections qu'on puisse avoir dans la conversation.

Ce défaut, si commun parmi nous, a été également noté par La Bruyère dans ses 'Caractères :' 'L'on parle impétueusement dans les entretiens, souvent par vanité ou par humeur, rarement avec assez d'attention : tout occupé du désir de répondre à ce qu'on n'écoute point, l'on suit ses idées, et on les explique sans le moindre égard pour les raisonnements d'autrui.'

CXLIX.

Le refus des louanges est un désir d'être loué deux fois.

Montaigne, dans ses 'Essais,' dit seulement : 'De dire moins de soi qu'il n'y en a, c'est sottise, non modestie.'

Madame de Sablé, de son côté, s'exprime ainsi : 'C'est une force d'esprit d'avouer sincèrement nos défauts et nos perfections ; et c'est une faiblesse de ne pas demeurer d'accord du bien ou du mal qui est en nous.'

CLI.

Il est plus difficile de s'empêcher d'être gouverné que de gouverner les autres.

Amyot nous donne, dans sa traduction de Plutarque, les quelques mots suivants prêtés à Thémistocle qui expriment la même pensée, sous une forme comique : 'Mon fils est le plus puissant homme de la Grèce, pour ce que les Athéniens commandent au demeurant de la Grèce, je commande aux Athéniens, sa mère à moi, et luy à sa mère.'

CCIX.

Qui vit sans folie n'est pas si sage qu'il croit.

Montaigne cite un mot semblable de Caton : 'Les sages ont plus à apprendre des fols, que les fols des sages.' Pascal dit : 'Les hommes sont si nécessairement fous, que ce serait être fou par un autre tour de folie, de ne pas être fou.'

CCXVIII.

L'Hypocrisie est un hommage que le vice rend à la vertu. C'est là une des Maximes les plus universellement connues de La Rochefoucauld. Vauvenargues a une Maxime dans ce sens : ' L'utilité de la vertu est si manifeste que les méchants la pratiquent par intérêt.' Dans un autre endroit, il dit encore : ' Quand le vice veut procurer quelque grand avantage au monde, pour surprendre l'admiration, il agit comme la vertu.'

Massillon dans un de ses sermons de son ' Petit Carême ' dit aussi : ' L'Hypocrisie est du moins un hommage que le vice rend à la vertu, en s'honorant de ses apparences.'

CCCXIV.

L'extrême plaisir que nous prenons à parler de nous-mêmes nous doit faire craindre de n'en donner guère à ceux qui nous écoutent.

Pascal dit : ' Voulez-vous qu'on croie du bien de vous ?—n'en dites pas.'

CCCXLVII.

Nous ne trouvons guère de gens de bon sens que ceux qui sont de notre avis.

CDVIII.

Le plus dangereux ridicule des vieilles personnes qui ont été aimables, c'est d'oublier qu'elles ne le sont plus.

La Bruyère dit plus longuement : ' Une femme coquette ne se rend point sur la passion de plaire, et sur l'opinion qu'elle a de sa beauté ; elle regarde le temps et les années comme quelque chose seulement qui ride et qui enlaidit les autres femmes ; elle oublie du moins que l'âge est écrit sur le visage. La même parure qui a autrefois embelli sa jeunesse, défigure enfin sa personne, et éclaire les défauts de sa vieillesse.' La mignardise et l'affectation l'accompagnent dans la douleur et dans la fièvre. Elle meurt parée et en rubans de couleur.

Saint-Evremond dit : ' Les plus belles passions se rendent ridicules en vieillissant.' Et encore : ' Dieu n'a pas voulu que nous fussions assez parfaits pour être toujours aimables. Pourquoi voulons-nous être toujours aimés ? '

CDLI.

Il n'y a point de sots si incommodes que ceux qui ont de l'esprit.

Molière a dit : ' Un sot savant est sot plus qu'un sot ignorant.' La Bruyère dit : ' Ne pouvoir supporter tous les mauvais caractères dont le monde est plein n'est pas un fort bon caractère : il faut dans le commerce des pièces d'or et de la monnaie.'

Duclos s'exprime ainsi : ' De tous les sots, les plus vifs sont les plus insupportables.'

CDLXXIX.

Il n'y a que les personnes qui ont de la fermeté qui puissent avoir une véritable douceur : celles qui paraissent douces n'ont d'ordinaire que de la faiblesse, qui se convertit aisément en aigreur.

Vauvenargues a une Maxime qu'on peut citer à côté de celle-ci : ' Il n'y a guère de gens plus aigres que ceux qui sont doux par intérêt.'

CDLXXX.

La timidité est un défaut dont il est dangereux de reprendre les personnes qu'on en veut corriger.

Cette Maxime a, sans doute, été inspirée à La Rochefoucauld par sa propre timidité, sur un point au moins ; car on prétend qu'il ne se présenta jamais à l'Académie, reculant devant la nécessité de prononcer le discours de réception.

I have thought it better to allow La Rochefoucauld to speak for himself than to quote long extracts, however good, from his critics and commentators.

As to his life, mixed up, as he was, in all the intrigues of his time, it would be necessary, in order to do justice to it, that I should precede it by a history of the latter part of the reign of Louis XIII., of the minority of Louis XIV., and of the troubles of the Fronde. I prefer to regard him as the thinker rather than as the man of action ; as the man of letters rather than as the politician. Besides which, I shall often have occasion to refer to him in connection with the numerous authors of his own epoch, who have also written maxims, thoughts, characters, and reflections. For La Rochefoucauld had many imitators, among whom I may enumerate Madame de Sablé, the Chevalier de Méré, the Abbé d'Ailly, Domat, Mesdames de Longueville, de la Fayette, de Sévigné, de Grignan, de la Sablière, and Deshoulières, Saint-Evremond, and the Abbé Esprit. All these personages were contemporaries, and met one another at Madame de Sablé's, who is entitled to the distinction of having given the first impulse to this kind of condensed thinking.

La Rochefoucauld is not a moralist for the general reader. His 'Maxims' scarcely descend from the heights of public life, and his *morale* resembles that of tragedy in which the heroes are kings and the events are catastrophes. This is the secret of that grand style, which does not depend upon ornament, but which owes all its beauty to its exactitude. With La Rochefoucauld, the universal principles of morality expressed themselves, for the first time in France, in definite language; for at the time these 'Maxims' appeared, the 'Thoughts' of Pascal had not yet seen the light. In these, which were published four years afterwards, but conceived about the same time, that great genius, leaping backward across the centuries, sought for wisdom and for first principles far remote from the experiences of the present time, to which La Rochefoucauld remained too fondly attached. But the 'Thoughts' of Pascal have done no harm to the book of 'Maxims,' and these two great examples of the art of thinking and writing combined to form La Bruyère, whom we shall have presently to consider.

Let me add that I am indebted for these reflections to Nisard's 'History of French Literature,' and with them I finish this study of La Rochefoucauld.

LECTURE XII

Hôtel de Rambouillet—La Calprenède (1610-1663)—Gilles Ménage (1613-1692)—Isaac de Benserade (1612-1691)—Godeau (1605-1672)—Segrais (1624-1701)—Brébeuf (1618-1661)—Académie Française (1634)—Sarrazin (1605-1654)—Saint-Evremond (1613-1703—) Charles Perrault (1628-1703)—Théophile Viaud (1590-1626)—Saint-Amant (1594-1661)—Cyrano de Bergerac (1620-1655)—Paul Scarron (1610-1660)—Father Bouhours (1628-1702).

IN the course of my studies on Balzac, Voiture, and Mademoiselle de Scudéry I have often mentioned the Hôtel de Rambouillet, of which I now propose to speak more fully.

In a 'Mémoire pour servir à l'Histoire de la Société polie en France,' Roederer tells us that with the dawn of the seventeenth century a select society arose in the heart of the capital, uniting the two sexes by new ties and new affections, blending distinguished men of the court with those of the city, people of the polite world with that of letters, creating delicate and noble manners, in the midst of the most repulsive dissoluteness, reforming and enriching the language, preparing for the outburst of a new literature, and elevating men's minds to the feeling and the need of enjoyments ignored by the vulgar.' It was Catherine de Vivonne, Marquise de Rambouillet, who created this new society, which shone with such brilliancy and exercised so much authority up to the middle of the reign of Louis XIV. That salon of *beaux esprits* was opened in Paris about the year 1600, in the time of Henry IV., in the Hôtel of that name situated in one of those streets of old Paris which have since been swept away in order to admit of the completion of the Louvre.

That celebrated salon was, undoubtedly, the arbiter of taste, the sanctuary of morals, and the academy of elegant diction, during half a century; and if its authority first declined, and then entirely disappeared, in the eighteenth century, which bestowed on it nothing but sarcasm and disdain, the fault rested with the clumsy and exaggerating imitators of its language and its manners.

Living, as we do, in an epoch sufficiently removed from a state of society that has vanished for ever, we can review without prejudice that celebrated reunion, and can pass judgment on it equally exempt from the infatuation of contemporaries and from the contempt of the generations which immediately succeeded it. And this is what I will endeavour to do, with the assistance, and relying on the authority, of our best modern critics.

That society, originally political as well as literary and moral, was organised as a protest of good taste against the barbarisms and the disorderly manners of the court of Henry IV., and it may be worth while to pause for a moment in order to indicate how much was meant by the word 'Court' at that period. It was a sort of Olympus, with the king for its Jupiter, and his ministers, his mistresses, and the great officers of the crown as the minor deities of that lofty realm to which all eyes were turned in homage and adoration. The monarch and his satellites were the observed of all observers. They were regarded as supreme authorities upon all questions of morality, art, letters, religion, speech, manners, social habits, and costume. The nobility conformed to their example, and the *bourgeoisie* imitated the people of title and estate. As to the proletariat, *they* did not count. It was enough for them to toil from daybreak until sundown, like beasts of burden, and to pay in dumb submissiveness whatever taxes were imposed upon them. Hence the overwhelming influence of the court upon society, against which the Hôtel de Rambouillet really instituted a sort of covert revolt, and dared to set up a little *imperium in imperio*.

Men of letters were regarded as a mere *quantité négligeable*, for the king and the great statesman who was his chief minister, Sully, without being altogether indifferent to intellectual pursuits or hostile to literature, had very little leisure to bestow on such matters; while the dilapidated state of the finances, a bequest from previous reigns, imposed a strict economy on the state. Nor was it till long after he had retired from the cares of government that the illustrious economist found time to prepare those invaluable memoirs which he gave to the world under the title of ' Les Économies Royales.'

The literary indifference of Louis XIII. and of his ministers prior to Richelieu is well known. During those two reigns the direction or patronage of letters was not in the hands of the state; and it was the Hôtel de Rambouillet which undertook them prior to the foundation of the Académie Française in 1634. The number of the frequenters of that Hôtel was limited at first. They were received sometimes in one of the cabinets; sometimes in the bedchamber, where they formed a circle in the centre of the room, protected from the draughts by two or three screens; for no fires were ever lighted even in the middle of winter; Madame de Rambouillet being unable to bear the heat of a fire upon the hearth, or even the rays of the sun in summer. The intimate friends of the house, M. de Chaudebonne, his very dear friend the Duc de Guise, the Princesse de Condé, the Cardinal de la Valette, the beautiful Mademoiselle Paulet, surnamed ' the lioness ' on account of her fair hair, and poets like Gombauld, Malherbe, Racan, and others, were received every evening. Conversation very soon became the sole attraction of that society and took rank among the keenest and noblest enjoyments of life, a preference being shown for intellectual themes; for the sentiments of the soul; for love in its purest expression; and for friendship in its most refined and delicate manifestations. The ladies regulated and dominated that conversation, which, beginning with discussions on the lighter kinds of literature, branched out into the torturing of phrases, words, syllables, and even letters, and ended in the distortion of passion. The ideas and language of that superfine society were peculiarly its own. Those who frequented its assemblies were the Initiates; strangers, the Profane. And so, in order to distinguish itself from the mass of the public, the Hôtel de Rambouillet indulged in mannerisms and affectations. The court, as I have already said, was indifferent, the people very ignorant, and there was nothing therefore to check the errant propensities of these amateurs of letters, and keep them within due bounds.

Julie d'Angennes, daughter of the Marchioness, considered it to be 'good form' to resist for twelve years the amorous attentions of the Duc de Montausier, and not to bestow her hand upon him until her beauty had begun to wane; and her sighing suitor, one of the most remarkable men in the court of Louis XIV., presented to the lady of his love what was called 'The Garland of Julia,' a collection of short poems written by some of the most famous pens in Paris.

Each flower, artistically painted, was accompanied by verses appropriate to its form and colour, and the whole of them were panegyrics of the incomparable Julia. M. de Montausier was the author of the little madrigal on the carnation which I am about to read to you as an example of the flowers composing the 'Garland':

> Bien que dans l'empire des fleurs,
> J'espère emporter la couronne
> Dessus toutes mes autres sœurs,
> Au moins si la beauté la donne;
> Devant ton teint vif et vermeil,
> De qui l'effet, plus grand que celui du soleil,
> Des cœurs les plus gelés fond la plus dure glace,
> Mon éclat se ternit et mon lustre s'efface;
> Mais dessus tes cheveux je reprends ma beauté,
> Et j'emprunte de toy ce que tu m'as ôsté.

Thus you will observe how passion was falsified by those great ladies; and now let us see what they did with the language. Molière has taught us how the vulgar armchair was converted by the Précieuses into a 'commodity of conversation,' and also how a mirror was transformed into a 'counsellor of the Graces;' but there was a good number of other expressions which were still more strange and absurd: music became 'the paradise of the ears'; a wig 'the youth of the aged;' our teeth 'the furniture of the mouth'; a fan 'a zephyr;' a glass of water 'an internal bath;' a flower 'a purveyor of perfume;' and women 'visible divinities.'

Geographical and topographical names underwent a similar metamorphosis. For France the Précieuses substituted 'Greece,' for Paris 'Athens,' for the island of Notre Dame 'Delos,' for Tours 'Cæsarea,' for Poitiers 'Argos,' and for Aix 'Corinth.' The name of Louis XIV. was exchanged for that of 'Alexander;' the Great Condé became 'Scipio;' Richelieu 'Seneca;' and Mazarin 'Cato.' Nor, in bestowing these epithets, was there any thought of covert sarcasm. Again, in their own set, Voiture was dignified as 'Valerius,' Sarrazin as 'Sesostris,' and Calprenède as 'Calpurnius.' All this is very ridiculous and extremely affected; but it must be added that the Précieuses were very often in the right, and that our language has been enriched by a good many happy paraphrases which they introduced. 'Hair of a daring blonde' is an agreeable substitute for the vulgar 'carrots;' and phrases like the following, 'to have only the mask of virtue,' 'to clothe ideas with a noble expression,' 'to be sober in speech,' 'to open one's heart,' and scores of others, have become part of the current coin of conversation. Even Molière himself in seven of his comedies has employed in all seriousness something like a hundred of the neologisms which originated in the Hôtel de Rambouillet; and passages might be quoted from Racine and Corneille to show that they too did not disdain to borrow from the vocabulary of the Précieuses.

Nor were the latter killed by the immortal comedy of the greatest French dramatist. On the contrary they were livelier than ever, and their numbers went on increasing, nor should it be forgotten that Molière held up to ridicule only the absurdities of the provincials, who exaggerated the faults of the Parisians, without having either their talent or their high distinction.

Even after the death of the old marchioness in 1667, and that of the Duchess of Montausier in 1671, the renown of the Hôtel de Rambouillet continued to hold a place in the recollections of people belonging to the best society. This rapid sketch may perhaps enable you to understand the important part which that celebrated assemblage played in the literature and even in the civilisation of France. The criticisms of Boileau and of Molière are sometimes understood by us as having demolished the Hôtel de Rambouillet and whatsoever bore the name of Précieuse; but we have been wrong, for that epithet which is to-day a term of reproach has been borne by women like the Longuevilles the La Fayettes, the De Sévignés, and the Deshoulières. The heritage of the Hôtel de Rambouillet devolved upon the

Duchesses of Montausier and Orleans and on Madame de Maintenon, who continued the traditions of its *spirituelle* and refined conversation. Mesdames Cornuel and La Fayette and the Marchionesses of Sablé and Coulanges continued to open their salons to their faithful courtiers; and in short the traditions of elegance and good breeding were prolonged and maintained in the eighteenth century in the little court of the Duchess of Maine and in the salons of Mesdames de Tencin and Geoffrin.

We will now take a rapid survey of some of the authors who adopted the affectations of the Précieuses. La Calprenède (1610-1663) began by narrating such agreeable stories to the ladies of the court of Anne of Austria that she herself wished to see and hear him; and it was not long before the young *improvisatore* committed to paper what he related so well. His first romance, 'Cassandra,' in ten octavo volumes, was successful in spite of its prolixity and bad style. It was followed by 'Cleopatra,' in twenty-three volumes; and by 'Pharamond,' only seven volumes of which had appeared when its author died from the result of an accident, in 1663. La Calprenède was a Gascon, and Boileau thus speaks of him in his 'Art Poétique:'

> Souvent, sans y penser, un écrivain qui s'aime
> Forme tous ses héros semblables à soi-même;
> Tout à l'humeur Gasconne, en un auteur Gascon,
> Calprenède et Juba parlent de même ton.

Juba is the hero of 'Cleopatra.' Its author also wrote for the theatre 'La Mort de Mithridate,' 'Bradamante,' 'Jeanne d'Angleterre,' 'Le Comte d'Essex,' 'La Mort des Enfants d'Hérode,' 'Bélisaire,' and other pieces; all of which justify the censure of Richelieu, who told their author that his verses were *lâches*. 'Cap de Dious,' exclaimed the irascible Gascon, 'Your Eminence ought to know that there is nothing *lâche* in the house of La Calprenède.' In his 'Historiettes' Tallemant des Réaux says of him 'There never was a man who was more of a Gascon than himself;' and this criticism of his coincides with that of Boileau: 'His heroes resemble each other like two drops of water; they all talk "Phœbus" (the name given to the fine jargon of that period), and are every one of them men who are a hundred thousand leagues above all other men.'

Another *coryphée* of the Hôtel de Rambouillet was Gilles Ménage, who was born at Angers on August 15, 1613, and died in Paris on July 23, 1692. He was a man of great erudition, to whom Spanish and Italian were as familiar as Greek and Latin. He was the tutor, the unsuccessful suitor, and afterwards the friend and confidant of Madame de Sévigné, to whom he made the half humorous, half pathetic remark ' I was your martyr; I am now your confessor ! '

He held a little academy of his own at his abode in the cloisters of Notre-Dame, for Mazarin had given him two ecclesiastical benefices, and he made a considerable figure in the world of letters. But he had the misfortune to incur the hostility of Molière, Racine, and Boileau, who resolutely combined to keep him out of the French Academy. By the first of these Ménage was unjustifiably and cruelly caricatured as Vadius in ' Les Femmes Savantes,' and this ' moral assassination,' as one of the dramatist's latest editors [1] terms it, is certainly a blot upon his memory, for no one can read the ' Ménagiana ' without being strongly impressed, as has been happily observed, by ' the profound erudition, the vast range of knowledge, the gaiety of mind, the zealous and enduring friendships, the moderation towards his adversaries, the integrity, the wisdom of thought, and the felicity of expression ' which characterised Gilles Ménage. His generosity towards an avowed enemy was shown by his frankly expressed opinion of ' Les Précieuses Ridicules.' As he quitted the theatre of Le Petit Bourbon, after the first performance of the comedy, on November 18, 1659, Ménage said, as he took the arm of his friend Chapelain, ' Monsieur, you and I approved of all those follies which have just been criticised with so much keenness and good sense, and, believe me, to adopt the words used by St. Remi to Clovis, "we must burn what we have adored and adore what we have burnt." '

And this was what actually happened, for that first representation was followed by a reaction against the tumid and artificial phraseology which it laughed to scorn.

The principal centres of the Précieuses were greatly moved by these satires, and the attacks upon Molière would have been very fierce if he had not taken the precaution when printing the piece to repudiate the idea of assailing the

[1] C. H. Livet.

genuine Précieuses. It was their clumsy imitators—'the mischievous monkeys who deserved to be tossed in a blanket'—upon whom he laid the lash of 'honest satire.' The admiration which Molière, in spite of his indefensible treatment of Ménage, inspired in the mind of the great scholar was charmingly indicated by the following *mot* which he invented: An indifferent poet presented to a princely patron an epitaph he had written on Molière. 'Sir,' said the prince, 'I would much rather he had brought me your own'!

Ménage was the author of many Latin works in prose and poetry, and of others in the Spanish and Italian languages, besides his well-known 'Observations sur la Langue Française,' his 'Origines de la Langue Française,' and his satire entitled 'La Requête des Dictionnaires,' which procured for him the enmity of the Academy. If he was addicted to affectation, it must be remembered at the same time that he enriched his mother-tongue with many words which have since become incorporated with it, such as *sagacité, sécurité, urbanité, prosateur, insidieux, impardonnable, inobservation,* &c.

Isaac de Benserade is another writer of the same period whom I must present to you. He is also one of the representatives of the bad taste of his epoch—a wit and a jester, whose *chansonnettes* and *rondeaux*, although full of affectation, after the manner of Voiture and Balzac, won for him the friendship of the great and the favours of fortune. His conversation was seasoned with pleasantries, which nowadays are offensive to the taste, but they nevertheless excited general admiration in his own time. He excelled more particularly in writing verses for the ballets enacted before Louis XIV., and exhibited a special talent for compositions of gallantry, but there can be very little doubt that the success he achieved was attributable almost exclusively to the address with which he endowed his characters with the inclinations and passions of his auditors, or of those who represented his heroes, and to the flatteries with which the whole were intermingled and surcharged.

Employed as secretary by Mademoiselle de la Vallière, Benserade in all probability indited her love-letters to Louis XIV., and the king, who subsequently proved himself to be such a heartless scoundrel to the duchess, after Montespan had supplanted her in his favour, was lavish in his bounty to the poet-parasite, who did not scruple to prostitute his pen to any purposes that would bring him a lucrative reward, holding it to be the duty of a courtier to fatten on the royal vices. He was not singular in that respect, and was only distinguishable by his literary abilities from the great crowd of obsequious sycophants who grovelled in the dust at the feet of 'Le Roi-Soleil.'

But as the writings of Benserade acquired no little celebrity in their time they must not be overlooked in a review of French literature.

One of his sonnets, entitled 'Job,' helped to excite a bitter but bloodless civil war, in which scores of pens were sharpened and rivers of ink were spilled. It was written after the death of Voiture, and people lauded it to the skies. But some critic was rash enough to pronounce it inferior to the 'Uranie' of the last-named poet, and thereupon belligerent factions descended into the arena, and the feud of the Jobelins and the Uranians divided and distracted polite society. The Prince de Conti was the leader of the first, and M. de Longueville that of the second.

> Pity such difference should be
> 'Twixt Tweedledum and Tweedledee!

But what could be expected from a court which could applaud a ballet written by Benserade to glorify the incident of Louis XIV.'s wig being powdered with gold-dust? And what are we to think of a poet who could thus apostrophise the crowned profligate under the name of Phœbus?

> Soleil de qui la gloire accompagne le cours,
>   Et qu'on m'a vu louer toujours,
> Avec assez d'éclat, quand vostre éclat fut moindre ;
> L'art ne peut plus traiter ce sujet comme il faut,
>   Et vous estes montés si haut,
> Que l'éloge et l'encens ne vous sçauroient plus joindre.

Benserade at such moments reminds us of a fly feebly struggling in a pot of treacle. Of the rest of his literary baggage it will suffice to say that he turned the 'Fables' of Æsop into quatrains and the 'Metamorphoses' of Ovid into rondeaux, and that both are equally ridiculous. He also wrote some poems of feathery levity, but, on the other hand, he published two quarto volumes of tragedies as ponderous as if they had been cast in lead. And they made him an Academician—a distinction denied to Molière. So the poet who besmeared Louis XIV. with the most viscid of honey failed to deserve the epitaph of Piron:

> Ci-gît Piron, qui ne fut rien,
> Pas même académicien.

But a time arrived when Benserade, deserted by his admirers, turned his back upon the world with a sentiment of deep disgust. Weary of everything, he withdrew from society, and died in solitude, neglected and forgotten. Almost alone in his retreat, he amused himself by covering the walls and ceilings with inscriptions in verse, and, like Orlando in the forest, he marred the trees by writing songs upon their bark. As will be remembered, Montaigne adorned the rafters of his château with aphorisms, which posterity has piously preserved; and Benserade seems to have imitated our great essayist in this respect, although in no other. One of these inscriptions, graven on the trunk of a tree when the poet was seventy years of age, is, it seems, touched with a tender melancholy:

> Adieu, fortune, honneurs; adieu, vous et les vôtres!
> Je viens ici vous oublier;
> Adieu, toi-même, amour, bien plus que tous les autres
> Difficile à congédier.

Godeau, Bishop of Grasse and Vence, was born at Dreux in 1605 and died at Vence in 1672. His life naturally falls into two divisions. During the first he was a typical abbé of the period, insinuating in manners, elegant in address, polished in phraseology, and so graceful a versifier as to excite the jealousy of Voiture. Introduced to the brilliant society of the Hôtel de Rambouillet, he became such a favourite as to be called—in reference to his diminutive stature—'Juba's dwarf.' Richelieu presented him with the bishopric of Grasse, to which he added that of Vence. Then a great change came over Godeau. The worldly abbé was transformed into the spiritual prelate, whose life and conversation reflected honour upon his Church. Exemplary in the fulfilment of his episcopal duties, all his leisure hours were devoted to sacred compositions, both in prose and verse, as diffuse in style as they were voluminous in substance. They are only remembered by their titles. Godeau was one of the first members of the French Academy.

There still remains for notice a crowd of second-rate writers associated with this epoch, of whom some passing mention must be made, although their works are known to-day only to diligent students of French literature. Some of them are like flies embalmed in the amber of Boileau's famous satire; and yet they acquired considerable celebrity at the commencement of the seventeenth century, and are entitled to present consideration on account of their bygone notoriety. Segrais, for example, whose 'Eclogues' were accepted as models by André Chénier, and whose poetry in general was spared by Boileau, enjoyed no small popularity during his lifetime; and his attempts to revive the Arcadia of classic times among the apple trees of Normandy was certainly as amusing an instance of antique pastorals in modern masquerade as could be found in so bizarre an epoch and in so highly artificial a state of society.

Jean Regnauld de Segrais was born at Caen in 1624, and died in Paris in 1701. Intended for the Church, he was allured from it by literature; wrote a personal poem entitled 'Athis;' a tragedy on the death of 'Hippolyte,' and a romance named 'Bérénice.' At the age of twenty-four he was appointed secretary to the Duchess of Montpensier; remained with her for twenty years; quarrelled with her; and obtaining a similar post in the household of Madame de la Fayette, assisted that lady with her advice when she was writing 'Zaïde' and 'La Princesse de Clèves.' Both of these were for some time erroneously attributed to Segrais; to the second—originally published in his name, and the precursor of the modern romance—I shall have occasion to return. Declining an offer of the tutorship of the Duc de Maine, one of the king's natural sons, Segrais married a rich heiress and retired to his native city, where his house became the rendezvous of people of culture and refinement, attracted by the charm of his conversation and the vivacity of his reminiscences of the brilliant court of which he had been privileged to form an observant member.

His original poems and his translations from Virgil have alike fallen into oblivion.

Less fortunate than Segrais, Guillaume de Brébeuf (1618–1661), poet, translator, and epigrammatist, fell under the lash of Boileau, who has immortalised one line of his version of 'Pharsalia'[1] in the 'Art Poétique.' On the other hand, let us do the translator of Lucan the justice to remember that Corneille, in speaking of his energetic and vivid verses, declared that he would willingly have given two of his best tragedies to have written them; and that Cardinal Mazarin was charmed with Brébeuf's tumid phraseology.

And here I must close the long list of writers in prose and verse who formed the court of the Marchioness of Rambouillet and of Julie d'Angennes, her daughter, as well as of those who, without belonging to that charmed circle, wrote in the same style, cultivated the same affectations, and followed more or less closely the false theories of taste instituted by that celebrated reunion.

The Précieuses grew old in time, but they never ceased to be Précieuses. At the court Madame de Montespan turned them into ridicule for the king's amusement; and there can be very little doubt that this was really the origin and object of the 'Femmes Savantes' of Molière. For, although our great comedian may be acquitted of having these illustrious examples in his mind when he wrote it, it is quite evident that they gave him the idea of the comedy, which, according to the dramatist, did not refer to them, but to those females who, wishing to imitate them, only succeeded in bringing out their weak points without possessing any of their finer qualities.

As I have said, those celebrated Précieuses declined into 'the portion of weeds and outworn faces.' One by one they disappeared from the scene, and the salons of Mesdames de la Fayette, Cornuel, de Sablé, and de Coulanges successively closed their doors, after that of the famous Marchioness of Rambouillet, in the last years of the seventeenth century.

---

[1] Mais n'allez point aussi, sur les pas de Brébeuf,
Même en une Pharsale, entasser sur les rives
'De morts et de mourants cent montagnes plaintives.'

I make no pretence to completeness in any of the subjects I discuss. I only try to indicate the spirit and the general tendencies of the epoch I study, by analysing the principal works of the period. I have nevertheless dwelt upon that frivolous, yet brilliant, astonishing, and interesting society, the best of its kind in the *grand siècle*, more fully than upon that of previous epochs, and more in detail, perhaps, than is justified by the purely literary scope of my lectures. If I have bestowed a good deal of my time and attention upon some ladies more celebrated by reason of their wit, their intrigues, their beauty, and their conversational powers, than by the literary productions they have bequeathed to us, it is because they formed the germ of a new development. A new branch of literature arose out of the *causeries* of the Hôtel de Rambouillet. That elegant and accomplished coterie may be said to have created in France the art of conversation—bright, vivacious, clever conversation—and out of that oral conversation was born what I may venture to call written conversation—the correspondence, personal memoirs, 'maxims,' 'thoughts,' and 'characters'—which have so richly embellished French literature, and of which each variety has been brought to the highest perfection. For, in numberless instances, are we not delighted by encountering

> What oft was thought, but ne'er so well expressed?

And in the hands of these gifted writers, what a beautiful, highly polished, and expressive language their mother tongue became! bright as steel, flexile as a Toledo blade, lucid as mountain air, transparent as the waters of a spring, and capable of being moulded into all the forms demanded for the service of the poet, the historian, the man of science, the diplomatist, the orator, the preacher, the letter-writer, and the *causeur*.

This is the principal and the enduring glory of these women belonging to the society of the seventeenth century, in the eyes of their posterity. But I have not yet entirely finished with them, as I shall find occasion to speak of them again when I come to analyse the letters of Madame de Sévigné, whom I have detached from the group of her contemporaries in order that I might study her more closely, and make you, if possible, more intimately acquainted with that altogether delightful figure in French literature.

THE FRENCH ACADEMY

Literature is under great obligations, it must be admitted, to that assemblage of distinguished men and women presided over by the Marquise de Rambouillet. The French school of letters came into existence there, and even in England, Pope and Walpole, Gray and Cowper, and perhaps Lady Mary Wortley Montagu, followed in the footsteps of Voiture. We may even trace to those dictators of *bon ton*, who issued their decrees from her ladyship's Hôtel, the art of conversation, the knack of saying clever things, and the charm of narrative which were so successfully cultivated in France in the following century.

At the same time the French language was purified, and numerous new words and ingenious, if frequently affected, expressions were added to its vocabulary. But the traces thus left by that celebrated Hôtel would have been brief in their duration, and would have been long since effaced, if the French Academy had not given them a permanent character, and continued—in regard to the language—that which the Hôtel de Rambouillet had commenced. It was in 1634 that Richelieu, looking upon the French as the most perfect of living languages, conceived the happy idea of making it the successor of the Latin tongue, just as that had replaced the Greek, and of causing it to become the international form of speech, the language of diplomacy, and the speech *par excellence* of European sovereigns and statesmen. To this end it was essential to divest it of all provincialisms, and of everything like popular, scholastic, or judicial jargon, to consolidate its principles, and to stamp upon it the impress of logic, lucidity, and stability. These were the motives which actuated the cardinal in raising a private enterprise to the dignity of a national institution.

Academies had been established in Paris long before 1634, for the idea had been transplanted from Italy by the Italians who enjoyed the favour of Charles IX. and Henry III. The Pléiade of Ronsard was somewhat academic in its character, but it did not long survive its founder; and although it was succeeded by other literary reunions, they were soon swept away in the troubles of the League. But the basic principle was sound and made its way, for we find Margaret of Valois, the first wife of Henry IV., instituting an academy in her own house, in 1607, of which Desportes, Régnier, and Maynard formed part. Another of these academies was organised by Mademoiselle de Gournay, the adopted daughter of Montaigne. According to Pellisson, certain men of letters began to meet at each other's houses weekly in 1629 to discuss public affairs, literature, and the news of the day. Godeau, already spoken of, Boisrobert, Chapelain, Conrart, De Malleville, Gombauld, and some others, were accustomed to hold secret meetings, the object of which each member promised not to divulge. But by an indiscretion of Boisrobert these assemblies came to the knowledge of Richelieu, who authorised his informant to offer the cardinal's protection to each of his friends, with an undertaking to issue letters patent on their behalf, and an assurance of his personal affection to them all. They were twelve in number, and after considerable hesitation it was determined by the vote of the majority to accept the protection of the powerful minister. Conrart undertook to draw up the letters patent of the associated writers, who took the title of the Académie Française, and the king's signature was attached to them on January 2, 1635. The number of members was fixed at forty, and the specific purpose of the Academy was to compose a dictionary of the French language, and to fix the laws of poetry and rhetoric, and thus, as Henry Martin observes, was established the senate of the Republic of Letters, a type of equality in the midst of a society bristling with privileges. In it the prerogatives of rank and birth were alike unknown.

On the fringe of the empire of Arthenice, which we have just finished exploring, were some vassals disposed to insubordination, and outside of it was a camp, or rather a horde, of hostile barbarians, constituting the literary free lances, of which it is time that I should speak. Sarrazin was one of these, and the most conspicuous. A singularly versatile writer, a facile poet, and an able historian, a sound and judicious critic, and as full of cynicism and buffoonery as his friend Scarron—he was, in addition, an adventurer, whose life supplied abundant materials for a romance. Entrusted by M. de Chevigny with a diplomatic mission to the Pope of Rome, Sarrazin repaired to Germany, and dissipated in company with a mistress the 4,000 livres he had received from the minister. When it was all gone he married an ugly woman for the sake of her wealth, abandoned her soon afterwards, and was appointed secretary to the Prince de Conti, to whom he was occasionally so impertinent in his unseasonable fooleries that the prince could only check his exuberant jocularity by threatening to throw him out of the window. One day, incensed beyond measure, his employer struck him over the head with a weapon he held in his hand. The wound threw Sarrazin into a burning fever, from the effects of which he is said to have died. Pellisson caused this epitaph to be engraved upon his tomb:

>Pour écrire en styles divers,
>Ce rare esprit surpassa tous les autres ;
>Je n'en dis plus rien, car ses vers
>Lui font plus d'honneur que les nôtres.

By the side of Sarrazin appeared Saint-Evremond, who was born in 1613, and died in London in the third year of the eighteenth century.

He was the *avant-coureur* of the latter, and much more disposed to rail at than to admire the Précieuses, his sympathies being rather with Ninon than with Julie. Educated for the magistracy, his natural inclinations led him to embrace a military career, and he was only sixteen when he first saw active service. His remarkable abilities, the wonderfully wide range of his knowledge, and the charm of his conversation, secured for him the friendship of Turenne and some of the foremost soldiers and statesmen of his period, but he was an inveterate satirist, and rallying the Prince of Condé on some of his foibles, Saint-Evremond fell into disgrace ; he was shut up in the Bastille for making too free with Cardinal Mazarin, and eventually retired to England, where Charles II. allowed him a moderate pension, which was continued by William III. He was thus enabled to lead a life of lettered ease and elegant epicureanism. His society was courted by all the wits and beauties of his time, and when the beautiful and *spirituelle* Mancini,

Duchesse de Mazarin, took up her abode in England, Saint-Evremond attached himself to her, and became her honoured friend and confidant, as he was the delight of the brilliant circle which she gathered around her. To him might Dryden's couplet be very well applied:

> A man so various that he seem'd to be
> Not one, but all mankind's epitome.

Philosopher, moralist, poet, musician, dramatist, critic, historian, and humourist, his curiosity led him to study all branches of learning, and to write many kinds of books, the best of them having been his treatises on Roman literature and the drama in France, Spain, Italy, and England. But, as has been well observed by M. Gilbert, his distinguishing merit was, that he was, like La Rochefoucauld, the writer for people of quality pre-eminently, throwing over everything he committed to paper the style of a gentleman and the grand air of a man of birth and breeding.

Saint-Evremond has left us a portrait of himself, from which I will quote the opening and concluding passages, both as an example of his antithetical style and as a probably faithful reflex of his character:

> I am a philosopher, as far removed from superstition as from impiety; a voluptuary, who has not less abhorrence of debauchery than inclination for pleasure; a man who has never known want nor abundance, I occupy that station of life which is contemned by those who possess everything, envied by those who have nothing, and only relished by those who make their felicity consist in the exercise of their reason. . . . In religion and in friendship, I have only to paint myself as I am—in friendship more tender than a philosopher; and in religion, as constant and as sincere as a youth who has more simplicity than experience. My piety is composed more of justice and charity than of penitence. I rest my confidence on God, and hope everything from His benevolence. In the bosom of Providence I find my repose and my felicity.

In the same year that Saint-Evremond, in the full possession of his faculties, calmly breathed his last at the age of ninety, died Charles Perrault, one of the masters of style. Born in Paris in 1628, he was sent to the college of Beauvais, where he and a fellow-student, having quarrelled with one of the professors, vowed they would never enter the place again. For nearly four years in succession they devoted five hours a day to reading all kinds of books; and he says in his memoirs 'If I know anything at all, I owe it more especially to those desultory studies.' Articled to a lawyer he becomes

> A clerk foredoom'd his father's soul to cross,
> Who pens a stanza when he should engross.

But his stanzas excite attention, and Colbert gives him a valuable appointment and nominates him a member of that body which afterwards is known as the Academy of Inscriptions and Belles Lettres. Classical studies engage his attention by preference, and he is adventurous enough to place modern writers on the same level as the ancients. This brings Racine and Boileau about his ears, and it requires nothing less than the influence of Arnauld and Bossuet to appease the quarrel which ensues. By way of recreation, perhaps, and in order to unbend his mind, Perrault gathers together and recasts in his own inimitable way the fairy tales which have formed the folklore of the French peasantry from time immemorial. These fascinating stories, which have travelled to us from the cradle of our race in the Far East, received a new life beneath the vitalising touch of Perrault, in whose prose we may find the same charm which attaches to the verse of La Fontaine.

The transparent simplicity of his style is not less to be admired than the perfect good faith with which he appears to narrate the incidents of the various stories, so that he resembles that

> Prevailing poet, whose undoubting mind
> Believed the magic wonders which he sung.

Not improbably English literature is indebted to his 'La belle au bois dormant' for the inspiration of Tennyson's lovely 'Day-Dream.' Perrault has also left us an epic poem, satirised by Boileau, two comedies, his 'Eloges des Hommes Illustres du 17ème Siècle,' an 'Apologue des Femmes,' and numerous other works now wellnigh forgotten, while his 'Fairy Tales' will live as long as there are children in France.

Many writers of that epoch are classed by Henry Martin among the champions of unbridled fantasy and of pure Bohemianism. The most brilliant and daring of these 'chartered libertines' of the mind was Théophile Viaud, whose writings were as licentious as his morals. For his 'Parnasse Satyrique,' a collection of salacious poems, some of the worst of which were written by himself, he was sentenced to be burnt alive, but his punishment was commuted to imprisonment, and eventually to lifelong banishment. But protected and concealed by the Duc de Montmorency, Viaud died in Paris at the age of thirty-six, and one of his latest works was a treatise on the immortality of the soul.

Saint-Amant, another poet of the same school and period, whose 'Moïse Sauvé' was gibbeted by Boileau, was an original and even powerful writer, and had it not been for the grossness of his language, and the irregularity of his life, he might have acquired an honourable place in French literature. As it was, his name occurs amongst those of the first forty members of the French Academy, and he may be said to have sounded the heights and depths of fortune, for, after having been pensioned by the queen of Poland, and sent as special envoy to Stockholm on the coronation of the queen of Sweden, the closing years of his life were clouded by poverty, and were not unfamiliar with actual want, and he has recorded some of his experiences in his sonnet on 'Prodigality:'

> Coucher trois dans un lit, sans drap et sans chandelle,
> Au plus fort de l'hiver, dans la salle aux fagots,
> Où les chats, ruminant le langage des Goths,
> Nous éclairent de l'œil en roulant la prunelle.

Since the 'Satyre Ménippée' the Parisians had had no incentive to laughter. Malherbe's solemnity of tone, and the affectation and strict propriety of the Hôtel de Rambouillet seem to have killed gaiety in France. And to this fact, rather than to his literary qualities, perhaps, we may attribute the success of Saint-Amant, although the former were by no means of an undistinguished character; for as a judicious critic has said, 'he anticipated the romantic school by cultivating antithesis, by his love of colour, of picturesqueness, and of effect, and by his systematic alliance of lyricism with triviality, of the sublime with the grotesque.' He excelled in frolicsome compositions, and more especially in those of a convivial kind. Nor was he without a certain sentiment of nature such as was not often to be met with among his predecessors. There were the possibilities of better things in both his heart and mind, but they were warped and turned awry by the temptations to which he succumbed with such a fatal facility.

The best, as it was the earliest, of his compositions was an ode on Solitude, which exhibited genuine talent, but was wanting in sustained power. He had the gift of imagination, combined with originality, but a total want of self-restraint was visible in his poetry as in his life. He was the Jan Steen of the pen; and where he shone most was in depicting those scenes of reckless revelry in which he was himself the leading spirit. He was an inveterate smoker, the first man of letters in France, perhaps, to use tobacco, and a hard drinker. He is inimitable when he hurls himself in a comic fury against the city of Evreux, where he pretends that he could not find anything to drink:

> O bon ivrogne ! O cher Faret !
> Qu'avec raison tu la méprises ;
> On y voit plus de cent églises,
> Et pas un seul cabaret.

Strange irony of fate ! This Faret was not at all addicted to drink. They were close friends without being boon companions, and his refusal to join in the crapulous habits of Saint-Amant induced the latter afterwards to write

> On fait à sçavoir que Faret
> Ne rime plus à cabaret !

A life of dissipation would have been scarcely compatible with the historical studies which Faret pursued, and with the preparation of the historical works which he produced. Nevertheless his name has always been coupled with that of the bibulous Saint-Amant, as afflicted with the same tippling propensities; and the Academic historian—for Faret was one of the original Forty—has received the brand of Boileau in the well-known couplet:

> Ainsi tel autrefois qu'on vit avec Faret
> Charbonner de ses vers les murs d'un cabaret.

During a visit which he paid to the Eternal City, Saint-Amant composed his 'Rome Ridicule,' in which he revealed his capacity for satire. In his 'Moïse Sauvé' the poet of the cabaret openly attacked the Bible, and it was for this he was pilloried by Boileau. At the same time, that unlucky epic entirely killed his reputation. Its style is deplorable, and the periphrases which he employs are tumid and ridiculous efforts at pomposity. His animals do not browse, they 'shear the rich enamel which flowers on the sward;' his fishes are 'rapid mutes,' and his swallows the 'little precursors of the pleasant season.' Saint-Amant is an independent, like Rabelais, La Fontaine, and Béranger. He belongs to no school, and it is quite possible that, after all, his jocular pieces will be read long after the more familiar authors of the rigid and frigid Hôtel de Rambouillet.[1]

To the same epoch belongs Cyrano de Bergerac (1620–1655), one of the most original and courageous thinkers, and one of the bravest and most daring soldiers, France has given birth to. He compressed into his brief span of life more activity of thought and action than most men find room for in sixty years. As a swordsman his splendid exploits rival anything imagined by Dumas; as a dramatist his 'Pédant Joué' furnished Molière with the materials for two of the most delightful scenes in the 'Fourberies de Scapin;' while Corneille was under still greater obligations to his 'Agrippine.' Few persons are aware, when laughing at the frequent repetition of 'Que diable allait-il faire dans cette galère?' that it is taken bodily from the comedy of De Bergerac. His pen had as fine a point as his sword, and he 'pinked' the pedants, the plagiarists, pretenders, and charlatans of his time with exquisite skill and deadly effect. In religion his enemies accused him of impiety on account of the sentiments he placed in the mouth of one of the characters in 'Agrippine;' but no one can read his letter to a pedant who had accused him of infidelity without perceiving that De Bergerac's views on the most solemn of all questions were at least two hundred and fifty years in advance of his age, and that he lived in an atmosphere of thought immensely

> Above the smoke and stir of this dim spot
> Which men call Earth.

Paul Scarron, the 'Emperor of Burlesque' as Henry Martin calls him, and who was, like Caliban, 'as dispropor-

[1] Jules Sandeau.

tioned in his manners as in his shape,' was born in Paris in 1610, and died there in 1660. It is only necessary to mention that he became a cripple at the age of twenty-eight, and that he was confined to his chair during the rest of his life; only preserving the use of his hands, his tongue, and his stomach; abusing as well as using all three, and finding no other compensations for his long martyrdom than those supplied by scurrility and gluttony. Yet he passed his time gaily. The salon of the palsied jester was the liveliest of all the Parisian circles; and it was at once a bureau of wit, and a dining-room to which each guest brought his contingent of *bons mots* for the mind and food for the body. The Cardinal de Retz, the beautiful Ninon, and Sarrazin came to seat themselves beside that little bed of yellow damask; the Comtes de Lude and Villarceau brought their suppers thither; and the fine gentlemen of the period resorted to the receptions of the lively invalid much as they would go to look at an exotic animal.

The oddest incident in his life was his marriage with Françoise d'Aubigné, whose mother was a near neighbour of Scarron's. She was almost destitute, and when Scarron proposed to the daughter, the mother's consent was given with alacrity. As to Françoise, she was of opinion that a cripple was better than the convent. They were married, and when the notary put the usual question to the bridegroom with respect to the bride's dowry, he gaily replied: 'Her dowry? Two large roguish eyes; a very beautiful bust; a pair of lovely hands; and an abundance of wit.' 'And you?' added the notary, 'what do you bring her?' 'Immensity, immortality,' was Scarron's reply. 'Other names may perish, but that of the wife of Scarron will live for ever!' But he could scarcely have foreseen that the widow whom he afterwards left penniless would become famous in French history, not as La Veuve Scarron, but as Madame de Maintenon, wife of Louis XIV.

As a writer, Scarron is not to be disdained. He is one of our best prose authors. His 'Roman Comique' and his novels will be always read. His comedies, carelessly written, possess the true comic *verve* and contain many happy passages. They are no longer performed, and no wonder; but as M. Geruzez, from whom I borrow these remarks, observes, one may still read them out of curiosity. Scarron was the first to make people laugh at a comedy. Gaiety came in with him; Molière purified while preserving it, adding thereto that portrayal of manners which will make his own works last as long as humanity. Scarron's sprightly piece of buffoonery, 'Don Japhet d'Arménie,' long maintained its place upon the stage. La Harpe has quoted some amusing passages from it. The other comedies abound with genuinely comic passages; some of which I should like to have quoted, did time permit. Independently of his dramatic humour, in which he excelled, Scarron was the inventor of burlesque; and the progenitor therefore of the Offenbachs, the Planchés, and the whole tribe of modern professors of travesty. Burlesque may be defined as the transformation of noble characters and sentiments into ridiculous figures and vulgar passions, effected in such a way as to preserve an obvious resemblance between the originals and their distorted and dishonoured parodies. It drags the images of the gods through the mud, connects ludicrous and debasing associations with all that is purest and most exalted in human attributes and conduct, and disdains no unworthy method of provoking frivolous or mocking laughter. Scarron's travesty of the 'Æneid' was the first work to establish his reputation, and served as a model for all productions of a similar kind in later times. The hero of Virgil's epic, so often in tears, degenerates into a snivelling nincompoop; Jupiter's quarrels with his wife prove him to be a brutal husband; Juno turns out to be a shrewish housewife; Cassandra, an ordinary fortune-teller and compiler of prophetic almanacs; and so with all the rest. Other writers followed the example set them by Scarron, and carried their buffoonery to outrageous lengths; for in 1649 was published 'The Passion of Our Lord Jesus Christ' in burlesque verse! Douglas Jerrold may or may not have been cognisant of the fact when he asked the author of the 'Comic History of England'—'And when are you going to bring out a Comic Bible?'

Scarron's claim to be considered one of our best prose writers may safely rest on his 'Roman Comique;' for its literary style, its characters, its humorous situations, and its faithful pictures of contemporary manners will always cause it to live. Unhappily it was left unfinished; but, as

Geruzez has remarked, the first chapters of it have made us acquainted with physiognomies like those of Destin and L'Etoile Ragotin and Rancune which can never be forgotten.

Scarron's novels are also highly interesting. Molière's Tartuffe might well have taken lessons from Monturar in the ' Hypocrites,' and in the ' Useless Precaution ' we find a first sketch of the dramatist's Agnes.

From what I have said of the coterie of the Hôtel de Rambouillet, and of those who were either exempt from its influence or were opposed to its authority, you may judge whether the courteous champions of the fair Arthenice came off victorious upon all occasions of their entering the poetic lists against their dissolute adversaries; and whether the latter, when the inspiration of the bottle fired them and they discarded all respect for heaven and earth, may not have been capable at times of exhibiting an astonishing vigour in their assaults. The only true poet who establishes the supremacy of the cause of Arthenice, and who has completely survived the period I am speaking of, is Racan, ' the sweet Racan ; ' of whom Henry Martin has justly remarked that, with the single exception of La Fontaine, he has been most keenly alive to the beauties of nature, and has written verses over which the breath of Virgil seems to have passed, while their harmony is like a foretaste of Racine.

A Jesuit Father, Bouhours, remains to be mentioned as having occupied an honourable position among authors of a secondary rank. In his 'Entretiens d'Ariste et d'Eugène ' he proved himself to be an able critic and an elegant writer, and this work is of great value to any one wishing to acquire a good idea of the genius of the French language in the seventeenth century, and of the manner in which it was comprehended by the best writers and the best critics. He compares it with the Greek and Latin, the Spanish and Italian, and pronounces it to be superior to all; because it possesses 'the secret of uniting brevity with clearness and purity with politeness.' The French pronunciation he declares to be ' the most natural and pleasing of any. The Chinese and other Asiatics sing, the Germans rattle, the Spaniards spout, the Italians sigh, the English whistle, the French alone can properly be said to speak; which arises, in fact, from our not accenting any syllable before the penultimate. The French language is best adapted to express the sentiments of the heart, for which reason our songs are so impassioned and pathetic, while those of Italy and Spain are full of nonsense. Other languages may address the imagination, but ours alone speaks to the heart.' Of course this was the language of exaggerated patriotism, and it is interesting to compare with it the dictum of the emperor Charles V. of Germany who said, 'You should pray to your God in Spanish, speak to your mistress in Italian, converse with your friend in French, whistle to your bird in English, and address your horse in German.'

Among the other works written by Bouhours was 'La manière de bien penser,' and a translation into French of the New Testament. He was a punctilious purist, and he is said to have exclaimed, just before taking his departure from this life, 'Je vais ou je vas mourir; l'un et l'autre se dit ou se disent.' I must mention one other anecdote to his honour. As everybody knows, when our illustrious Molière had breathed his last, it was only by the powerful intervention of Louis XIV. that Christian burial was secured for his remains; while Bossuet disgraced himself by defiling the tomb which held all that was mortal of our greatest dramatic genius. Bouhours, on the other hand, although a zealous churchman and fervently religious, addressed an earnest remonstrance, in vigorous verse, to his countrymen, with respect to the ingratitude they displayed towards the mighty dead. It was reserved for the 'Eagle of Meaux'—the enemy of the saintly Fénelon—to exult over the decease of the dramatist, and to represent him as passing from the pleasantries of the theatre to a place of eternal torment. Mankind has grown more charitable since then.

LECTURE XIII

La Bruyère (1645-1696)—Selected 'Characters.'

JEAN DE LA BRUYÈRE, who was born in Paris in the year 1639, and died at Versailles in 1696, was the son of a person occupying a position of trust and responsibility in the municipality of his native city. Educated for the law, he practised at the bar, but, buying a valuable appointment, he filled it from 1673 until 1687. In the meantime, however, his office being one which could be filled by deputy, he spent most of his time in Paris or at Versailles, and at the suggestion of the all-powerful Bossuet he was nominated tutor to the Duc de Bourbon, grandson of the Great Condé. When this young gentleman's education was completed, his preceptor was received into the Condé household, where he enjoyed an annual pension of a thousand crowns, plenty of opportunities for studying human character, and an abundance of leisure for placing his observations on paper. It would require a much more vigorous pencil than my own to depict the strange family into which La Bruyère was admitted upon terms of almost intimacy. Besides, has not Saint-Simon, who knew them so well, delineated their portraits and those of their friends in colours that can never fade? Has he not shown us the old warrior with his failing intellect; Monsieur the Prince, his son, a man of such capricious moods and eccentric habits that at times it appeared as if there was a taint of insanity in his mind; and Monsieur the Duke, La Bruyère's pupil, with his wild, brutal, and terrible propensities, and his ferocious and intolerable humours?

In such a *ménage*, or menagerie, La Bruyère played the part of a comtemplative philosopher. He watched, listened to, and moralised upon what was going on in the Condé household, for the benefit alike of his contemporaries and of posterity. Boileau has characterised him in four lines, which may be thus paraphrased :

> Each overweening worshipper of self
> Lessons so wise and good as these must prize ;
> And by these moral essays he may learn
> All egotistic feelings to despise.

Strange to say, although La Bruyère was the author of a work which has no superior in any language, and is regarded by the best judges as having excelled the famous 'Characters' of his model Theophrastus, yet he found his admission to the Academy vehemently opposed by some of the literary men of his period; but public opinion was on his side, and, receiving the powerful support of Bossuet, Racine, and Boileau, he eventually took his place among the 'Immortals.' Before publishing the work which has given him an enduring place among the master minds of France, he showed it to a friend, who remarked 'It will attract a multitude of readers and make you a host of enemies.'

The prediction was literally fulfilled. There is nothing so painful to the sensitive epidermis of self-love as the application of a rough truth; and hundreds not merely winced but writhed under those uttered by La Bruyère. The sufferers pelted him with epigrams, a few of which have survived; the best of them being one written at the time he was a candidate for a seat among the Forty :

> When La Bruyère comes forward, as now,
> Why raise such a boisterous *haro* ?
> To make up the number of forty,
> You cannot dispense with a zero.

Like La Rochefoucauld with his 'Maxims,' our great moralist repeatedly recast his 'Characters,' retouching them as often as a fresh edition was called for, omitting passages which he had come to look upon as feeble, and adding finishing touches to the portraits he had traced with such consummate ability. The book went through nine editions during the lifetime of the author ; the last, which also received his corrections, appearing in the year in which he died. His death was the result of an attack of paralysis, preceded, a few days before, by total deafness.

The 'Characters' are grouped under different headings, and the work might also be spoken of as a scientific essay on human zoology, embracing, as it does, the whole species and its numerous varieties. He shows us man in his social relations, and man as an individual. He does much more: he exhibits the individual under a number of aspects. He likewise portrays the morals and manners of the times in which he lived, descending from the universal to the particular, and imparting, by a few brilliant touches, dramatic variety and vivacity to the people who were unconsciously sitting to him for their portraits. Voltaire has pronounced the 'Characters' to be something quite unique; Saint-Simon complimented La Bruyère on his inimitable portraiture of the men of his epoch; Vauvenargues extolled his creative genius; Chateaubriand pronounced him to be one of the first writers of the age of Louis XIV.; Sainte-Beuve says of his book that it conferred the greatest honour on the genius of the nation which produced it; and Taine, while denying him the gift of invention, declares that he stamps everything he touches with an ineffaceable mark, the imprint of his own clear and vigorous mind.

In point of literary style, La Bruyère reached perfection. His sentences are frequently models of conciseness, point, antithesis, exquisite balance, and high polish. His maxims and reflections are in prose what so many of Pope's and Dryden's couplets are in verse—'What oft was thought but ne'er so well expressed.' What can be more compact than the following?—'It is very miserable not to have wit enough to talk well nor judgment enough to hold one's tongue.' 'Many people have nothing to recommend them but a name; when you see them close at hand, they are less than nothing; at a distance, they are imposing.' 'Love and friendship exclude each other.' 'Men are much less ashamed of their crimes than of their weaknesses and their vanity.' 'A hundred years hence the world will be just as it is now—the same stage, the same scenery, but with a fresh company of actors.' 'It is better to expose oneself to ingratitude than to miss the relief of misery.'

La Bruyère, when speaking of works of the intellect, observes: 'There are certain things in which mediocrity is insupportable—namely, music, poetry, painting, and public speaking. What a torture to have to listen to a frigid discourse pompously declaimed, or commonplace verses pronounced with all the emphasis of a bad poet!'[1]

Montaigne had previously expressed a somewhat similar idea in his 'Essays:'—'One may play the fool everywhere else, but not in poetry.'[2]

La Bruyère is said to have had Corneille in his mind when he wrote the following:

> Certain poets are addicted in dramatic writing to lengthy passages of pompous verse, which seem powerful, elevated, and replete with great sentiments. The people listen eagerly, with eyes intent and open mouth, believing they are pleased, and the less they understand the more they admire. They have no time to breathe, scarcely enough for exclamations and applause. I used to suppose, in my first youth, that such tirades were clear and intelligible to the actors, the pit, and the gallery; that they were understood by the authors themselves, and that with the entire attention which I gave to their recital I was to blame for not comprehending them. I am undeceived.[3]

Voltaire quotes some fragments of 'Pompey' and of 'Andromeda,' which are perfectly unintelligible. Boileau, before him, had given, as an example of their nonsense, these four lines from 'Tite et Bérénice:'

> Must he die, madam, and so near the term?
> Is your notorious caprice so firm
> That all that's left of one I deem'd so strong
> May my own death forebode ere very long?[4]

---

[1] Il y a de certaines choses dont la médiocrité est insupportable: la poësie, la musique, la peinture, le discours public. Quel supplice que celui d'entendre déclamer pompeusement un froid discours, ou prononcer de médiocres vers avec toute l'emphase d'un mauvais poëte!

[2] On peult faire le sot partout ailleurs, mais non en la poësie.

[3] Certains poëtes sont sujets, dans le dramatique, à de longues suites de vers pompeux qui semblent forts, élevés, et remplis de grands sentiments. Le peuple écoute avidement, les yeux élevés et la bouche ouverte, croit que cela lui plaît, et à mesure qu'il y comprend moins, l'admire davantage; il n'a pas le temps de respirer, il a à peine celui de se récrier et d'applaudir. J'ai cru autrefois, et dans ma première jeunesse, que ces endroits étaient clairs et intelligibles pour les acteurs, pour le parterre et l'amphithéâtre; que leurs auteurs s'entendaient eux-mêmes, et qu'avec toute l'attention que je donnais à leur récital, j'avais tort de n'y rien entendre: je suis détrompé.

[4] Faut-il mourir, Madame, et si proche du terme?
Votre illustre inconstance est-elle encor si ferme
Que les restes d'un feu que j'avais cru si fort
Puissent dans quatre jours se promettre ma mort?

It is related of Baron the actor, who played the character, that he asked the dramatist what was the meaning of the lines, and Corneille, after pondering over them for some time, replied 'I don't very well know, myself, but continue to recite them, for those who don't understand them will admire them.'¹ The same story is repeated of various poets.

Here is a shrewd remark on taste: 'There is in art a point of perfection, as there is one of goodness or of maturity in nature. He who feels and loves it has perfect taste. He who does not feel it, or whose preferences go beyond or fall short of it, is defective in taste. There is, then, a good and a bad taste, and the subject is therefore fairly disputable.'²

'Noodles read a book without understanding it; mediocre minds fancy they comprehend it thoroughly; great minds understand a portion, but not the whole of it: what is obscure, they find to be so; what is clear, they perceive clearly. Superfine wits make a point of finding obscurity where there is none, and of failing to understand what is intelligible enough.'³

In this section of his disquisition on works of the intellect La Bruyère praises Balzac and Voiture for their best qualities, and touches upon their want of sentiment. Sentiment, he observes, took its rise among female writers who far excelled masculine authors in this respect; for that which was the fruit of much labour and research among the latter is the spontaneous gift and natural charm of the woman who takes a pen in her hand. It is their happy

---

[1] C'est du 'Galimatias double,' c'est-à-dire du galimatias que non seulement le public mais même l'auteur ne comprend pas (Du Casse, *Histoire anecdotique de l'ancien théâtre en France*). 'Je ne les entends pas trop bien non plus; mais récitez-les toujours; tel qui ne les comprendra pas, les admirera.'

[2] Il y a dans l'art un point de perfection, comme de bonté ou de maturité dans la nature. Celui qui le sent et qui l'aime a le goût parfait; celui qui ne le sent pas, et qui aime en-deçà ou au-delà, a le goût défectueux. Il y a donc un bon et un mauvais goût; et l'on dispute des goûts avec fondement.

[3] Les sots lisent un livre, et ne l'entendent point; les esprits médiocres croient l'entendre parfaitement; les grands esprits ne l'entendent quelquefois pas tout entier: ils trouvent obscur ce qui est obscur, comme ils trouvent clair ce qui est clair; les beaux esprits veulent trouver obscur ce qui ne l'est point, et ne pas entendre ce qui est fort intelligible.

privilege, he observes, to convey a whole sentiment by a single word, to give a delicate rendering of a delicate thought, and to weave their language into a compact chain of 'linked sweetness long drawn out.' 'If women were always correct,' he observes, 'I would venture to say that the letters of some of them would be perhaps the best written things our language could boast of.'[1]

When La Bruyère penned this eulogy of our female letter-writers, the correspondence of Madame de Sévigné had not yet been published, although it was probably circulating in manuscript. At the same time she was not the only letter-writer among the women of that remarkable epoch, while after her time came many who distinguished themselves in that form of composition, as, for example, Madame de Maintenon, Mdlle. de Scudéry, Madame de Bussy-Lameth, Madame de Bois-Landry, and many others. Why should the literature, history, and biography of France be so rich in correspondence which was never intended, in the first instance, for the public eye? I think the explanation must be sought for in (1) the genius of the people; (2) the habits and feelings of my own sex in the seventeenth and eighteenth centuries; and (3) in the nature of the vehicle employed.

In the first place, we are sociable by nature, communicative in our ideas, somewhat effusive perhaps, eager for news, and eager to receive and quick to acquire new impressions. Secondly, a Frenchwoman craves sympathy, and is generous in bestowing it; her family affections are

[1] Je ne sais si l'on pourra jamais mettre dans les lettres plus d'esprit, plus de tour, plus d'agrément et plus de style que l'on en voit dans celles de Balzac et de Voiture; elles sont vides de sentiments, qui n'ont régné que depuis leur temps, et qui doivent aux femmes leur naissance. Ce sexe va plus loin que le nôtre dans ce genre d'écrire. Elles trouvent sous leur plume des tours et des expressions qui souvent en nous ne sont l'effet que d'un long travail et d'une pénible recherche; elles sont heureuses dans le choix des termes, qu'elles placent si juste, que tout connus qu'ils sont, ils ont le charme de la nouveauté, et semblent être faits seulement pour l'usage où elles les mettent; il n'appartient qu'à elles de faire lire dans un seul mot un sentiment, et de rendre délicatement une pensée qui est délicate; elles ont un enchaînement de discours inimitable, qui se suit naturellement et qui n'est lié que par le sens. Si les femmes étaient toujours correctes, j'oserais dire que les lettres de quelques-unes d'entre elles seraient peut-être ce que nous avons dans notre langue de mieux écrit.

warm and strong, deep and tender; her perceptions are quick, and her power of apprehension is vivid; she excels in the analysis of her own emotions, and is acute in her discernment of those of others who are endeared to her by kindred or friendship; and she possesses, by a natural instinct, the faculty of clothing in appropriate language what she thinks and feels and sees and hears; and all these things make her an excellent correspondent. Lastly, the French language seems to have been specially designed for *causerie*, whether by word of mouth or on paper. Perhaps I ought to say, it has been formed by a sociable, conversational, and communicative race; and, therefore, it has become an admirable medium for the brilliant talk of a hundred salons in Paris, and for the letters preserved in countless volumes of correspondence, from the days of Madame de Sévigné to those of George Sand.

There were no newspapers,[1] in the modern sense of the word, and therefore no 'Causeries du Lundi,' in the days of La Bruyère; but he was nevertheless the Sainte-Beuve of his epoch; and in the essay under notice he has presented us with a critical estimate, in a condensed form, of the more prominent writers of the century in which he lived.

These are exceedingly interesting and instructive, as the judgments of a keen and well-qualified observer. They are generally terse and incisive, and they frequently hit off points of contrast in a masterly manner. Take the following, as a case in point:

I have read Malherbe and Théophile. They are both acquainted with Nature, but with this difference: the first, in a style that is full and uniform, reveals at once all that is most noble and most beautiful, most artless and most simple in Nature; he describes her as an artist, or as an historian. The other, without choice and without exactitude, with a free and unequal pen, sometimes overloads her with descriptions, oppresses her with details, anatomises her; sometimes he makes believe, exaggerates, and violates truth in Nature; making a romance of her.[2]

---

[1] The *Mercure François* first appeared in 1605; the *Gazette de France*, the earliest political newspaper, dates from May 30, 1631. The title of the latter was borrowed from the *Gazetta* of Venice, and was the name of the small coin paid for that journal (1563).

[2] J'ai lu Malherbe et Théophile. Ils ont tous deux connu la nature avec cette différence, que le premier, d'un style plein et uniforme, montre tout à la fois ce qu'elle a de plus beau et de plus noble, de plus

Boileau has also indulged in some sarcasms at the expense of the fool of quality who prefers Théophile to Malherbe,[1] and quotes two lines from one of the tragedies of the former, which have remained ridiculous ever since:

> Lo! here the dagger, with its owner's blood defil'd,
> See how it blushes for the dastard blow it struck![2]

And yet when a poet of genius employs the same simile, in connection with an inanimate object, what an exquisite fitness and beauty we discover in it! As witness that famous scene in Shakespeare's 'King John,' when, speaking of the fire with which Hubert had heated the irons that were to destroy the little prince's eyes, Arthur exclaims:

> There is no malice in this burning coal:
> The breath of heaven has blown his spirit out
> And strew'd repentant ashes on his head.
>
> *Hubert:* But with my breath I can revive it, boy.
> *Arthur:* An if you do, you will but make it blush
> And glow with shame of your proceedings, Hubert.

La Bruyère next proceeds to examine the style, and trace the literary affiliation, of Ronsard, Balzac, Marot, and Rabelais, to condemn the inexcusable nastiness of the last two, and to condense into a few sentences a masterly characterisation of the great work of the Curé of Meudon: 'His book is an inexplicable enigma. It is a chimera. It is the face of a beautiful woman, with the feet and tail of a serpent, or of some other creature still more deformed. It is a monstrous combination of refined ingenious morality and of filthy corruption. Where it is bad, it transcends the very worst of its kind; where it is good, it is exquisite and excellent in the extreme, a banquet of choicest delicacies.'

Speaking of two of Montaigne's hostile critics,[3] La

---

naïf et de plus simple; il en fait la peinture ou l'histoire. L'autre, sans choix, sans exactitude, d'une plume libre et inégale, tantôt charge ses descriptions, s'appesantit sur les détails : il fait une anatomie ; tantôt il feint, il exagère, il passe le vrai dans la nature : il en fait le roman.

[1] Tous les jours à la cour un sot de qualité
Peut juger de travers avec impunité.
A Malherbe, à Racan préférer Théophile. . . .

[2] Ah ! voici le poignard qui du sang de son maître
S'est souillé lâchement ! il en rougit, le traître.

[3] La Mothe le Vayer and Malebranche.

Bruyère agrees with neither; because he tells us, 'one of them does not think enough to be able to enjoy a writer who thinks very much, and the other thinks too subtly to adapt himself to ideas which are entirely natural.' Amyot is praised for his grave, serious, and scrupulous style; and then La Bruyère passes on to speak at great length of the Opera, which may be said to have been born into France almost at the same time as himself, and of the French drama. Corneille is declared to be without a peer in those parts wherein he excels; but if original and inimitable at times, he is also unequal, and prone to be negligent and declamatory. Racine, on the other hand, always maintains the same high level, finding his inspiration in nature, obeying the dictates of good sense; elegant, harmonious, and correct in his versification, and equally capable of grandeur and pathos. He depicts men as they are, while Corneille portrays them as they ought to be. The one is more moral and the other more natural. Both modelled themselves on the classic dramatists, Corneille imitating Sophocles, and Racine Euripides.

After discussing eloquence and sublimity, La Bruyère proceeds to touch upon the modifications of literary style in France just before his own time, he himself, as I take it, being one of its reformers; for, while preserving and amending that of his predecessors, he introduced into it that refined, delicate, and concise spirit which received its full development in the succeeding century. He concludes this important chapter of his 'Characters' by the repetition of an old truth, to which he contrives to impart a new form:

'"Horace or Despréaux has said it before you." Granted, but I have said it in my own way. Cannot I think a true thing after them, and will not others still think it after I have gone?'[1]

Montaigne, in one of his essays, has made a very similar remark, and so has Pascal, who contends that an old idea acquires a character of originality by the novelty of the method of its preservation, while Father Bouhours de-

[1] 'Horace ou Despréaux l'a dit avant vous.' Je le crois sur votre parole; mais je l'ai dit comme mien. Ne puis-je pas penser après eux une chose vraie, et que d'autres encore penseront après moi?

fines the difference between the ancients and the moderns to be this, that the former came first, and the only offence which can be imputed to the latter is that of thinking like the ancients, in many instances without ever having read them. Sheridan has also pointed out the difficulty which so often arises, in our own minds, with respect to ideas of doubtful origin, such as we may have given birth to, or may have unconsciously appropriated. 'Faded ideas,' he observes, 'float in the fancy like half-forgotten dreams, and imagination, in its fullest enjoyments, becomes suspicious of its offspring and doubts whether it has created or adopted.'

In his chapter on Personal Merit, La Bruyère has strung together a number of sententious aphorisms, which denote both the penetrative character of his intellect and the philosophically reflective cast of his mind. I subjoin some of the more striking.

'There are many people whose only worth consists in their name. When you approach them closely, they are less than nothing. At a distance they impose upon you.'[1] The latter clause of this sentence recalls the clever *mot*: 'The height of statues diminishes as we get away from them; that of men, as we approach them.'

'Genius and great talents fail sometimes for want of opportunity. Such and such persons may be extolled for what they have done, such and such for what they might have done.'[2]

La Rochefoucauld has expressed the same idea more concisely and much better, in my opinion: 'Nature makes the merit, and fortune sets it to work.'[3]

'There is nothing so slight, so simple, or so imperceptible, connected with our manners, that it does not betray us. A stupid does not enter a room, nor leave it, nor sit down, nor rise up, nor hold his tongue, nor stand still, in the same way as a man of brains does.'[4]

[1] De bien des gens il n'y a que le nom qui vaille quelque chose. Quand vous les voyez de fort près, c'est moins que rien; de loin ils imposent.
[2] Le génie et les grands talents manquent souvent, quelquefois aussi les seules occasions: tels peuvent être loués de ce qu'ils ont fait, et tels de ce qu'ils auraient fait.
[3] La nature fait le mérite, et la fortune le met en œuvre.
[4] Il n'y a rien de si délié, de si simple et de si imperceptible, où il

Before the days of La Bruyère, a great lady had said of a talkative gentleman 'He is a fool down to the very tone of his voice.'[1]

'He is good who does good to others. If he suffers for doing it, he is doubly good. If he suffers through those to whom he has been kind, his goodness is so great as to be incapable of augmentation, unless it be in proportion to the increase of that suffering; and if it should occasion his death, his goodness reaches its utmost limit: it is heroic, it is perfect.'[2] Centuries before the time of La Bruyère was it not written 'Greater love hath no man than this, that a man lay down his life for his friends'?

Everything that La Bruyère has written is worth reading, and a great proportion of it is also worth remembering. But in the selections I am making I will endeavour to confine myself to those which are general in their application and are true for all time, rather than to quote such as are more limited in their scope, and especially appropriate to the times in which, and the people among whom, the moralist lived. In the chapter on woman he writes: 'Men and women rarely agree as to the merits of a woman. Their interests diverge too much. Women do not please each other by the same charms which please the men. A thousand little devices which kindle a great passion in the other sex merely excite aversion and antipathy among women themselves.'[3]

'A beautiful woman who possesses the qualities of an honourable man is the most delicious companion in the

---

n'entre des manières qui nous décèlent. Un sot ni n'entre, ni ne sort, ni ne s'assied, ni ne se lève, ni ne se tait, ni n'est sur les jambes, comme un homme d'esprit.

[1] Il n'y a pas jusqu'au son de sa voix qui ne soit une sottise.

[2] Celui-là est bon qui fait du bien aux autres; s'il souffre pour le bien qu'il fait, il est très bon; s'il souffre de ceux à qu'il a fait ce bien, il a une si grande bonté qu'elle ne peut être augmentée que dans le cas où ses souffrances viendraient à croître; et s'il en meurt sa vertu ne saurait aller plus loin: elle est héroïque, elle est parfaite.

[3] Les hommes et les femmes conviennent rarement sur le mérite d'une femme: leurs intérêts sont trop différents. Les femmes ne se plaisent point les unes aux autres par les mêmes agréments qu'elles plaisent aux hommes: mille manières qu'allument dans ceux-ci les grandes passions, forment entre elles l'aversion et l'antipathie.

world, for she unites the best qualities of both sexes.'[1] Pope has also told us that

> Heaven, when it strives to polish all it can
> Its last best work, but forms a softer man.

Again, La Bruyère tells us that 'an inconstant woman is one who no longer loves; a frivolous woman, one who already loves another; a volatile woman, one who does not know what she loves or whether she loves at all; and an indifferent woman, one who loves nothing at all.'[2] The proverb of the woman who went through the wood in search of a straight walking-stick and picked a crooked branch at last, finds a piquant illustration in the following : 'To judge of that lady by her beauty, her youth, her pride, and her disdain, no one can doubt that she will be satisfied by nothing less than a hero. Her choice is made: she marries a little deformity without brains.'[3] 'A wife who is addicted both to coquetry and piety is too much for any husband to contend against. She ought to choose either one or the other.'[4]

Piety was so often synonymous with hypocrisy in those days that a *fausse dévote* became an object of suspicion, if not of aversion, among men of enlightened minds. Every woman in fashionable society had her 'spiritual director,' whose influence in the household was dangerously great, and was in many instances shockingly misused; and hence the sarcasm which envenoms the point of the following: 'If, Hermas, I marry an avaricious woman, she will not ruin me; if a gambler, she may enrich herself; if a bluestocking, she may instruct me; if a prude, no one will run away with her; if a shrew, she will exercise my patience; if a coquette, she will try to please me; if a light o' love, she

---

[1] Une belle femme qui a les qualités d'un honnête homme, est-ce qu'il y a au monde d'un commerce plus délicieux? l'on trouve en elle tout le mérite des deux sexes.

[2] Une femme inconstante est celle qui n'aime plus; une légère, celle qui déjà en aime un autre; une volage, celle qui ne sait si elle aime et ce qu'elle aime; une indifférente, celle qui n'aime rien.

[3] A juger de cette femme par sa beauté, sa jeunesse, sa fierté et ses dédains, il n'y a personne qui doute que ce ne soit un héros qui doive un jour la charmer. Son choix est fait: c'est un petit monstre qui manque d'esprit.

[4] C'est trop contre un mari d'être coquette et dévote; une femme devroit opter.

may perhaps grow to be fond of me; but if I marry a pietist, tell me, Hermas, what can I expect from one who would fain deceive God, and who likewise deceives herself?'[1]

Of women generally, La Bruyère asserts that they run into extremes, and that they are either better or worse than men.[2] Probably so, in virtue of the impressionability of their natures and the ductility of their characters; but if there have been Messalinas, and Borgias, and Brinvilliers, there have been hosts of women—numbers of them leading obscure and unrecorded lives—of whom it might be truly said that God 'made them a little lower than the angels.' And inasmuch as the truest nobility of character is usually associated with unfeigned humility, with an utter unconsciousness of its own simple grandeur and beautiful purity, and with a delicate sensibility that shrinks from anything like publicity, it may be regarded as perfectly certain that in countless households there have been mothers and wives, sisters and daughters, who have led saintly lives in the best sense of the word—lives of unobtrusive but continual beneficence, of complete self-forgetfulness, of patient and heroic self-suppression, and of lofty self-sacrifice, without suspecting that in so doing they were fulfilling anything more than one of the ordinary duties of their daily lives.

In the same chapter La Bruyère touches upon a question which was never more in evidence than at the present hour —the right and natural qualifications of woman to receive such an education as shall render her the intellectual equal and companion of man.

'By what law, by what edicts, by what rescripts,' he asks, ' are they interdicted from opening their eyes and reading, from retaining what they read, and from rendering an account of it in their conversation, or in their works? Have they not, on the contrary, accustomed themselves to the habit of knowing nothing either by the weakness of their dispositions, or by the idleness of their minds,

---

[1] Si j'épouse, Hermas, une femme avare, elle ne me ruinera point; si une joueuse, elle pourra s'enrichir; si une savante, elle s'aura m'instruire; si une prude, elle ne sera point emportée; si une emportée, elle exercera ma patience; si une coquette, elle voudra me plaire; si une galante, elle le sera peut-être jusqu'à m'aimer; si une dévote (fausse dévote), répondez, Hermas, que dois-je attendre de celle qui veut tromper Dieu, et qui se trompe elle-même?

[2] Les femmes sont extrêmes; elles sont meilleures ou pires que les hommes.

or by the care of their beauty, or by a certain levity which prevents them applying themselves to prolonged study, or by the talent and genius which they exhibit for those works only which lie close at hand, or by the distractions arising out of the details of domestic life, or by a natural dislike to painful and serious occupations, or by the exercising of a curiosity totally distinct from that which satisfies the mind, or by a complete aversion to the exercise of the memory? But to whatever cause men may attribute this ignorance of women, they may be thankful that they have this advantage, at least, over the sex which governs them in so many other ways.

'A learned woman is regarded as a beautiful weapon, artistically chiselled, admirably polished, and elaborately wrought; a cabinet ornament which is exhibited to the curious, but is not intended for use, either in war or in the chase, any more than a circus-horse, although very highly trained.

'If learning and wisdom are united in the same person, I do not trouble myself as to his or her sex. I simply admire; and if you tell me that a prudent woman scarcely cares about being learned, or that a learned woman is scarcely prudent, you have already forgotten what I have just written, namely, that women are only repelled from the sciences by certain defects; the natural conclusion on your part being that, the fewer they possess of these defects, the wiser they will become, so that a prudent woman would only be the better qualified to become learned; while a learned woman, being what she is in virtue of her capability of overcoming many defects, is only the more prudent.'[1]

[1] Pourquoi s'en prendre aux hommes de ce que les femmes ne sont pas savantes ? Par quelles lois, par quels édits, par quels rescrits leur a-t-on défendu d'ouvrir les yeux et de lire, de retenir ce qu'elles ont lu, et d'en rendre compte ou dans leur conversation ou par leurs ouvrages ? Ne se sont-elles pas au contraire établies elles-mêmes dans cet usage de ne rien savoir, ou par la foiblesse de leur complexion, ou par la paresse de leur esprit, ou par le soin de leur beauté, ou par une certaine légèreté qui les empêche de suivre une longue étude, ou par le talent et le génie qu'elles ont seulement pour les ouvrages de la main, ou par les distractions que donnent les détails d'un domestique, ou par un éloignement natural des choses pénibles et sérieuses, ou par une curiosité toute différente de celle qui contente l'esprit, ou par un tout autre goût que celui d'exercer leur mémoire ? Mais à quelque cause que les hommes puissent devoir cette ignorance des femmes, ils sont heureux que les femmes, qui les dominent d'ailleurs par tant d'endroits, aient sur eux cet avantage de moins.

On regarde une femme savante comme on fait une belle arme : elle est ciselée artistement, d'une polissure admirable et d'un travail fort recherché ; c'est une pièce de cabinet, que l'on montre aux curieux, qui n'est pas d'usage, qui ne sert ni à la guerre ni à la chasse, non plus qu'un cheval de manège, quoique le mieux instruit du monde.

Si la science et la sagesse se trouvent unies en un même sujet, je ne m'informe plus du sexe, j'admire ; et si vous me dites qu'une femme sage ne songe guère à être savante, ou qu'une femme savante n'est guère sage,

If La Bruyère speaks thus of women, it is because in his time, and even a century before it, there were those whose intellectual accomplishments rendered them worthy of the highest admiration. In France there had been Margaret of Valois, distinguished alike as a writer and as a stateswoman; and in England there had been Lady Jane Grey, who perished on the scaffold at seventeen :

> Most gentle, most unfortunate,
> Crowned but to die—who in her chamber sate
> Musing with Plato, though the horn was blown,
> And every ear and every heart was won,
> And all in green array were chasing down the Sun!

And there were also the three daughters of Chancellor More, Margaret, Elizabeth, and Cecilia, who inherited the learning of their father, and with it his sweetness of nature and purity of character.

In Italy there had been Vittoria Colonna, 'the model of matrons and the mirror of feminine virtues,' whose genius as a poetess was extolled by Ariosto in the well-known lines :

> Vittoria è 'l nome ! e ben conviensi a nata
> Fra le vittorie, ed a chi, o vada, o stanzi,
> Di trofei sempre, e di trionfi ornata,
> La vittoria abbia seco, o dietro, o innanzi.

Equalling her in fame was Veronica Gambara, whose house in Bologna became the rendezvous of the intellectual sovereigns of her own epoch ; while, at the same time, Italy could boast of a constellation of brilliant women, comprising Gaspara Stampa, Laura Terracina, Leonora Faletti, Claudia della Rovere, Laura Battiferri degli Ammanati, Isotta Brembati, Tullia d' Aragona, Lucia Bertana, and Tarquinia Molza ; the last of whom is one of the interlocutors in Tasso's dialogue on Love.

Contemporary with La Bruyère in France were Madame de Sévigné, her daughter Madame de Grignan, and Madame de la Fayette, of whom Segrais tells us that, three months

vous avez déjà oublié ce que vous venez de lire, que les femmes ne sont détournées des sciences que par de certains défauts ; concluez donc vous-mêmes que moins elles auroient de ces défauts, plus elles seroient sages, et qu'ainsi une femme sage n'en seroit que plus propre à devenir savante, ou qu'une femme savante, n'étant telle que parce qu'elle auroit pu vaincre beaucoup de défauts, n'est que plus sage.

after she had begun to learn Latin, she knew more of it than her masters, Ménage and Père Papin. One day, in fact, when both of them were puzzled as to the meaning of a certain passage, their pupil told them that neither of them understood it, and immediately proceeded to translate it accurately.

Upon this subject of female education Montaigne differed from La Bruyère. 'If ladies of quality will be persuaded by me,' writes the essayist, 'they will content themselves with setting out their proper and natural treasures; they conceal and cover up their own beauties under others that are none of theirs. It is a great folly to put out their own lights and shine by a borrowed lustre.... What need have they of anything but to live beloved and honoured?' He adds that with the natural gifts they possess, and their great power to charm, they can 'command magisterially, and rule both the regents and the schools.'[1] At the same time, he would not debar women of rank from the study of poetry, history, and moral philosophy.

We shall see, later on, when we come to speak of 'Les Femmes Savantes,' how Molière treated this question.

Sir Thomas Overbury contended that a woman's 'greatest learning is religion;' while Nicholas Breton, in his 'Characters upon Essaies, Moral and Divine,' appeared to be very much of the same opinion as Montaigne, and to consider that a woman's power to charm and bless springs mainly from the qualities of her heart. Hence, mental culture plays a very important part in his enumeration of the excellences combined in the character of a good wife; a portion of which deserves quotation as a choice example of condensed expression and epigrammatic style: 'Her voice is music, her countenance meekness, her mind virtuous, and her soul gracious. She is her husband's jewel, her children's joy, her neighbours' love, and her servants'

---

[1] Si les dames bien nées me croient, elles se contenteront de faire valoir leurs propres et naturelles richesses: elles cachent et couvrent leurs beautés soubs des beautés estrangères (Montaigne parle là des femmes savantes).... Que leur faut-il, que d'être aimées et honorées? elles n'ont et ne scavent que trop pour cela.... Avecques cette science elles commandent à la baguette et régentent les régents de l'eschole.

honour. She is poverty's prayer and charity's praise, religion's love and devotion's zeal. She is a care of necessity and a course of thrift, a book of housewifery and a mirror of modesty. In sum, she is God's blessing, earth's honour, and heaven's creature.'

Tennyson's ideas upon this subject found eloquent expression in 'The Princess,' where he points out that the intellectual and moral development of woman must proceed *pari passu* with that of man, and that they must 'rise or sink together, dwarf'd or god-like, bond or free,' so that

> In the long years liker must they grow;
> The man be more of woman, she of man;
> He gain in sweetness and in moral height,
> Nor lose the wrestling thews that throw the world;
> She mental breadth, nor fail in childward care,
> Nor lose the childlike in the larger mind;
> Till at the last she set herself to man,
> Like perfect music unto noble words.

Finally, we have the shrewd, practical, worldly, and common-sense view of the subject set forth by Alphonse Karr in 'Les Femmes,' where he writes with equal brevity and wit: 'The education which we give to our daughters renders it more easy for them to charm ten lovers than to enchain one husband. We teach them how to make traps to catch birds with, but not how to construct cages to keep them in.'[1]

In a chapter treating of the sentiments of the heart, La Bruyère asserts that there is a liking in pure friendship to which those who are born in a mediocre rank of life cannot attain. 'Love,' he says, 'is born abruptly, without reflection, by temperament or by weakness; a beautiful feature fixes and determines us. Friendship, on the contrary, is contracted gradually, by lapse of time, by habit, by long communion. How much ability, goodness of heart, mutual service and kindness among friends, go to make up, in many years, an attachment far less strong than is some-

---

[1] L'éducation qu'on donne aux filles leur rend plus facile de charmer dix amants que d'enchaîner un mari. On leur enseigne à faire des trébuchets pour prendre les oiseaux, mais non à faire des cages pour les retenir.

times created in a moment by the sight of a beautiful face or of a pretty hand.'[1]

'So long as love endures,' he goes on to say, 'it is self-subsistent and is sometimes sustained by what, it might be supposed, would extinguish it—by caprice, by harshness, by separation, by jealousy. Friendship, on the contrary, stands in need of assistance: it perishes for want of attentions, of confidence, of kindnesses.'[2]

La Rochefoucauld, in one of his Maxims, asserts that 'love, like fire, cannot subsist without continual movement; and it ceases to exist the moment it ceases to hope or to fear.'[3] But both of these writers overlooked the essential difference between masculine and feminine love. There is always an element of selfishness in the first; while the second, more often than otherwise, is capable of entire self-effacement and uncalculating self-sacrifice. Exclusive possession is the demand of the stronger sex; accompanied in many instances by an irritable jealousy and an irritating suspicion, if his domestic chattel is not entirely subservient to his transitory whims, and does not adapt herself to all his wayward moods. Woman's affection is larger, broader, and more expansive. From the husband, when he is worthy of it, it extends without diminution to her children, her family, her friends, and to those disinherited children of fortune whose privations and sorrows appeal to the tenderest emotions of her sensitive and sympathetic heart. Then, again, as Byron has said:

> Man's love is of man's life a thing apart,
> 'Tis woman's whole existence.

---

[1] L'amour naît brusquement, sans autre réflexion, par tempérament ou par foiblesse: un trait de beauté nous fixe, nous détermine. L'amitié au contraire se forme peu à peu, avec le temps, par la pratique, par un long commerce. Combien d'esprit, de bonté de cœur, d'attachement, de services et de complaisance dans les amis, pour faire en plusieurs années bien moins que ne fait quelquefois en un moment un beau visage ou une belle main.

[2] Tant que l'amour dure, il subsiste de soi-même, et quelquefois par les choses qui semblent le devoir éteindre, par les caprices, par les rigueurs, par l'éloignement, par la jalousie. L'amitié au contraire a besoin de secours : elle périt faute de soins, de confiance et de complaisance.

[3] L'amour, aussi bien que le feu, ne peut subsister sans un mouvement continuel, et il cesse de vivre dès qu'il cesse d'espérer ou de craindre.

Man has a thousand aims, ambitions, aspirations, occupations to absorb his thoughts, to engage his energies, and to interest and stir him deeply during his waking hours. It is woman's privilege, and not unfrequently her glory, to rise

> To her peculiar and best altitudes
> Of doing good and of enduring ill,—
> Of comforting for ill, and teaching good,
> And reconciling all that's ill and good
> Unto the patience of a constant hope.

'We are so constituted,' says La Bruyère, 'that we wish to make all the happiness or, if this cannot be so, all the unhappiness of the person we love.'[1] La Rochefoucauld, who discovers the mainspring of all human actions in egoism and self-love, says something of the same kind: 'There are none of the passions in which self-love reigns so powerfully as in love itself, and one is often more inclined to sacrifice the peace of a beloved object than to lose one's own.'[2] And again: 'If we are to judge of love by most of its effects, it bears a greater resemblance to hatred than to friendship.'[3]

Shakespeare, who 'knew all things with a most learned quality,' has portrayed the revulsion from affection to aversion as the result of jealousy, in the great scene between Othello and Iago, in the third act of the tragedy:

> All my fond love thus do I blow to heaven.
> 'Tis gone.
> Arise, black vengeance, from thy hollow cell!
> Yield up, O love, thy crown and hearted throne
> To tyrannous hate! Swell, bosom, with thy fraught,
> For 'tis of aspics' tongues!

The worldly wisdom of La Bruyère nowhere asserts itself more powerfully than in the following passage from the same chapter we have just been quoting: 'To live with our enemies as if they might one day become our friends, to live with our friends as if they may one day be our enemies, is not altogether in the nature of hatred, nor

---

[1] L'on veut faire tout le bonheur, ou, si cela ne se peut ainsi, tout le malheur de ce qu'on aime.

[2] Il n'y a point de passions où l'amour de soi-même règne si puissamment que dans l'amour, et l'on est souvent plus disposé à sacrifier le repos de ce qu'on aime qu'à perdre le sien.

[3] Si l'on juge de l'amour par la plupart de ses effets, il ressemble plus à la haine qu'à l'amitié.

according to the rules of friendship. It is not a moral but a political maxim.'[1] And its justification is to be sought for in experience, and also in the fact so pithily expressed by Alphonse Karr: 'Too many friends, not enough friendship' ('Trop d'amis, pas assez d'amitié'). Acquaintances are, in innumerable instances, mistaken for friends; they are taken into our confidence; we treat them as if it were impossible they should ever be our enemies; a rupture occurs, and they prove themselves to be our greatest adversaries. On the other hand, we conceive hasty and possibly groundless prejudices against this or that person; we take no pains to conceal them; we arouse in their minds a feeling of hostility or dislike; and a day arrives, perhaps, when we make the discovery that their friendship would have been well worth cultivating, and that we have suffered in many ways by neglecting to live with them as if future friendly relations were possible or probable.

'Men,' says La Bruyère, 'are less ashamed of their crimes than of their weaknesses and vanity.'[2] Rousseau has almost repeated the observation in his 'Confessions,' where he says: 'It is not what is criminal that costs so much to avow, as what is ridiculous and foolish.'[3]

In his chapter on 'Society and Conversation' the moralist presents us with a fine specimen of his skill in character-drawing. It is the following:

Arrias has read everything, seen everything. He wishes to persuade himself so. He is a universal man, and he gives himself out as such. He prefers to prevaricate rather than keep silent or appear ignorant of anything. The conversation at table turns upon a great personage at a northern court. He cuts in, and takes the words out of the mouths of those who are about to relate what they know of him. He finds his way about that region as if he were a native of it. He discusses the manners of the court, the women of the country, its laws and its customs; relates the gossip which has

---

[1] Vivre avec ses ennemis comme s'ils devoient un jour être nos amis, et vivre avec nos amis comme s'ils pouvaient devenir nos ennemis, n'est ni selon la nature de la haine, ni selon les règles de l'amitié; ce n'est point une maxime morale, mais politique.

[2] Les hommes rougissent moins de leurs crimes que de leurs foiblesse et de leur vanité. Tel est ouvertement injuste, violent, perfide, calomniateur, qui cache son amour ou son ambition, sans autre vue que de la cacher.

[3] Ce n'est pas ce qui est criminel qui coûte le plus à dire, c'est ce qui est ridicule et honteux.

reached him, is greatly amused by it, and is the first to explode with laughter at the humour of it. Some one ventures to contradict him, and proves very clearly that he is stating things which are untrue. Arrias is not disconcerted, but he is indignant with the person interrupting him. 'I advance nothing,' he exclaims, 'I relate nothing, but what I have received from original sources. My information came from Sethon, our ambassador in that court, who returned to Paris a few days ago. I knew him intimately; I questioned him closely, and he concealed nothing from me.' Then he resumes the thread of his discourse more confidently than before, when one of the guests remarks to him : 'It is Sethon himself who has been speaking to you, and who has just arrived from the embassy.'[1]

As a companion picture to the foregoing take the following, from the 'Lettres Persanes' of Montesquieu:

I was, the other day, in the company of a man on the best of terms with himself. In a quarter of an hour he had settled three moral questions, four historical problems, and five points in physical science. I have never met with so universal a dogmatist. His mind was never clouded by the slightest doubt. We gave up the sciences, and spoke of the news of the day. I wanted to trip him up, so I said to myself 'I must take him on my own ground. I will take refuge in my own country.' So I talked about Persia: but I had scarcely uttered four words before he had given me the lie twice, upon the authority of MM. Tavernier and Chardin. 'Good heavens!' I said to myself, 'what a man this is! In a minute he will know the streets of Ispahan much better than I do.' My resolution was soon taken: I held my tongue, I let him talk, and he is dogmatising still.[2]

[1] Arrias a tout lu, a tout vu, il veut le persuader ainsi ; c'est un homme universel, et il se donne pour tel : il aime mieux mentir que de se taire ou de paroître ignorer quelquechose. On parle à la table d'une grande cour du Nord : il prend la parole, et l'ôte à ceux qui alloient dire ce qu'ils en savent ; il s'oriente dans cette région lointaine comme s'il en était originaire ; il discourt des mœurs de cette cour, des femmes du pays, de ses lois et de ses coutumes, il récite des historiettes qui y sont arrivées ; il les trouve plaisantes, et il en rit le premier jusqu'à éclater. Quelqu'un se hasarde de le contredire, et lui prouve nettement qu'il dit des choses qui ne sont pas vraies. Arrias ne se trouble point, prend feu au contraire contre l'interrupteur : ' Je n'avance,' lui dit-il, ' je ne raconte rien que je ne sache d'original. Je l'ai appris de *Sethon*, ambassadeur de France dans cette cour, revenu à Paris depuis quelques jours, que je connois familièrement, que j'ai fort interrogé, et qui ne m'a caché aucune circonstance.' Il reprenait le fil de sa narration avec plus de confiance qu'il ne l'avait commencée, lorsque l'un des convives lui dit : ' C'est Sethon à qui vous parlez, lui-même, et qui arrive de son ambassade.'

[2] Je me trouvai l'autre jour dans une compagnie, où je vis un homme bien content de lui. Dans un quart d'heure il décida trois questions de morale, quatre problèmes historiques, cinq points de phy-

Few writers have been more successful in condensing a whole volume of worldly wisdom into a few words than La Bruyère. Take the following as an example: 'It is a great misery not to possess sufficient intelligence to talk well, nor enough judgment to keep silence. This is the principle of all impertinence.'[1] The first Lord Lytton tells us of a groom who married a rich lady, and dreaded the ridicule of the guests who assembled at her table. 'Wear a black coat and hold your tongue,' was the advice given to him by a clergyman. He took the hint, and passed for an exceedingly sagacious and reflective gentleman.

'Ridicule,' said La Bruyère, 'is often intellectual poverty.'[2] It frequently springs from an inability to comprehend what is mocked, and, at other times, from envy of the person who is derided, or from an instinctive aversion to the lofty and noble sentiments which are made the subjects of ridicule or sarcasm.

'I know of no principle,' wrote Sydney Smith, 'which it is of more importance to fix in the minds of young people than that of the most determined resistance to the encroachments of ridicule.' Bishop Earle defined a man addicted to ridicule and detraction to be one who has lost all good himself and is loth to find it in another. D'Alembert declared that 'the fear of ridicule stifles more talents and virtues than it corrects vices and defects;' and Bernardin de Saint-Pierre asserted that even in his time ridicule had acquired so much power in France as to have become the most formidable weapon that could be wielded. It has been largely instrumental in obliterating the sentiment of

---

sique. Je n'ai jamais vu un décisionnaire si universel; son esprit ne fut jamais suspendu par le moindre doute. On laissa les sciences, on parla des nouvelles du temps: je voulus l'attraper, et je dis en moi-même: il faut que je me mette dans mon fort; je vais me réfugier dans mon pays. Je lui parlai de la Perse: mais à peine eus-je dit quatre mots, qu'il me donna deux démentis fondés sur l'autorité de MM. Tavernier et Chardin. Ah! mon Dieu! dis-je en moi-même, quel homme est-ce là? Il connoîtra tout à l'heure les rues d'Ispahan mieux que moi! Mon parti fut bientôt pris; je me tus, je le laissai parler, et il décide encore.

[1] C'est une grande misère que de n'avoir pas assez d'esprit pour bien parler, ni assez de jugement pour se taire. Voilà le principe de toute impertinence.

[2] La moquerie est souvent indigence d'esprit.

reverence from the human mind in all civilised countries. Not only may it be said that *Rien n'est sacré pour un sapeur,* but nothing possesses any sacredness in the eyes of the comic writer, the caricaturist, the composer of opera-bouffes, burlesques, and parodies.

The founders of religions, the great personages of history, the saviours and martyrs of mankind, the gods of Olympus, and the monarchs and warriors who have shaped the destinies of our race, have been all dragged down from their pedestals, exhibited under the most ludicrous and contemptible aspects, and associated with mean, sordid, and degrading surroundings, for the purpose of exciting that noisy laughter which an English poet has described as bespeaking 'the vacant mind.'

But then, to come back to La Bruyère, 'Derision is often intellectual indigence,' and the time is gone by, I fear, when Emile de Girardin's words were true of the two nations: 'The Frenchman, with his *esprit*, jeers at everything and believes in nothing. The Englishman, with his good sense, jeers at nothing and believes in everything.'

'It is deep ignorance,' our moralist goes on to say, 'which inspires the dogmatic tone. He who knows nothing believes he can teach others what he has yet to learn himself. He who knows a great deal scarcely imagines that what he says can be unknown to others, and speaks more diffidently.'[1]

'Dogmatism,' said Douglas Jerrold, with the perfection of wit, 'is puppyism full-grown.' Rousseau has remarked that 'the people who know little talk a good deal, and the people who know very much say little. It is only natural to believe that an ignorant man should consider what he knows to be important and should proclaim it to all the world, whereas the educated man does not open his store of knowledge so readily. He would have too much to say, and as he sees that there is still more to be said after him, he holds his tongue.'[2]

---

[1] C'est la profonde ignorance qui inspire le ton dogmatique. Celui qui ne sait rien croit enseigner aux autres ce qu'il vient d'apprendre lui-même; celui qui sait beaucoup pense à peine que ce qu'il dit puisse être ignoré, et parle plus indifféremment.

[2] Les gens qui savent peu parlent beaucoup, et les gens qui savent

A little knowledge, moreover, breeds conceit; a great deal almost compels humility.

Speaking of material prosperity, La Bruyère says that 'one must be thirty years old to think about a fortune, which is not acquired at fifty; we begin to erect the edifice in our old age, and we die before the painters and glaziers are out of the house.'[1] He adds that there are only two ways of getting on in the world—by your own industry, and by the imbecility of others; and that the scorn with which the successful man looks down upon his inferiors has its origin in the same feeling which prompts us to abase ourselves before our worldly superiors. Lord Lytton has said that we are democrats to those above and aristocrats to those below us.

That La Bruyère was a humorist as well as a philosopher will be very apparent upon reading his amusing sketch of a near-sighted and absent-minded man. It is a composite portrait, no doubt, but not the less diverting on that account:

> Menalcas descends his staircase, opens the door to go out, and closes it again. He perceives that he has not taken off his night-cap, and a closer examination of his face shows him that he is only half-shaved. He observes that his sword is upon his right side, that his stockings are down at heels, and that his shirt is visible above his waist-band. As he walks along the street he meets with a violent blow in his stomach or on his face, and cannot imagine from whence it proceeds, until, lifting up his eyes, he discovers that he has come in contact with the shaft of a cart or with a plank which a workman is carrying on his shoulders. He has been seen jostling against a blind man, tripping him up by inadvertence, so that both of them came tumbling down together. It has frequently happened to him to find himself brought face to face with a prince, whom he scarcely recognised, and had scarcely time enough to plant himself against a wall, so as to allow him to pass. He looks in every direction, he is confused, he cries out, he gets excited, he calls for his valets, one after the other; everything gets lost or goes astray with him; he asks for his gloves, which he holds in his hands, like the lady who demanded her mask, which was on her face all the time. He enters a room, and passes under the chandelier, which

---

beaucoup, parlent peu. Il est naturel de croire qu'un ignorant trouve important tout ce qu'il sait, et le dit à tout le monde; mais un homme instruit n'ouvre pas aisément son répertoire: il aurait trop à dire, et comme il voit encore plus à dire après lui, il se tait.

[1] Il faut avoir trente ans pour songer à sa fortune; elle n'est pas faite à cinquante; l'on bâtit dans sa vieillesse, et l'on meurt quand on en est aux peintres et aux vitriers.

catches his wig and holds it suspended in the air. All the courtiers look at him and laugh, and Menalcas laughs more loudly than all the rest, looking around the assembly to see who it is that is showing his ears for want of a peruke. If he goes into the city, and proceeds in a certain direction, he begins to fancy that he has lost his way, is disturbed in his mind, and asks the passers-by where he is, and they tell him that he is in no other than his own street; whereupon he re-enters the house, and precipitately quits it, in the belief that he has been deceived. Descending the steps of the Palace, he finds a carriage drawn up at the bottom which he mistakes for his own, enters it, and the coachman drives away, and believes he is taking his master home. Menalcas springs from the door, walks across the court-yard, mounts the staircase, proceeds through the ante-chamber, the chamber, and the cabinet. All seems familiar to him, nothing new or strange; he sits down and feels himself perfectly at home. The master arrives, Menalcas rises to receive him, treats him with the utmost civility, begs of him to be seated, and believes he is discharging the duties of a host. He converses, woolgathers, and revives the conversation. The master of the house begins to feel a little bored and is somewhat astonished. Menalcas is not less so, but he is too well-bred to tell him what he thinks. He has to do with a troublesome visitor, a flâneur, who will eventually retire, he hopes; so he practises patience, and when the evening arrives, he is scarcely undeceived.[1]

[1] Ménalque descend son escalier, ouvre sa porte pour sortir, il la referme; il s'aperçoit qu'il est en bonnet de nuit; et, venant à mieux s'examiner, il se trouve rasé à moitié, il voit que son épée est mise du côté droit, que ses bas sont rabattus sur ses talons, et que sa chemise est par-dessus ses chausses. S'il marche dans les places, il se sent tout d'un coup rudement frapper à l'estomac ou au visage; il ne soupçonne point ce que ce peut être, jusqu'à ce qu'ouvrant les yeux et se réveillant, il se trouve au devant un timon de charrette, ou derrière un long ais de menuiserie que porte un ouvrier sur ses épaules.
On l'a vu une fois heurter du front contre celui d'un aveugle, s'embarrasser dans ses jambes, et tomber avec lui chacun de son côté à la renverse. Il lui est arrivé plusieurs fois de se trouver tête pour tête à la rencontre d'un prince et sur son passage, se reconnoître à peine, et n'avoir que le loisir de se coller à un mur pour lui faire place. Il cherche, il brouille, il crie, il s'échauffe, il appelle ses valets l'un après l'autre : on lui perd tout, on lui égare tout ; il demande ses gants, qu'il a dans ses mains, semblable à cette femme qui prenoit le temps de demander son masque lorsqu'elle l'avoit sur son visage. Il entre à l'appartement, et passe sous un lustre où sa perruque s'accroche et demeure suspendue : tous les courtisans regardent en riant; Ménalque aussi rit plus haut que les autres, il cherche des yeux dans toute l'assemblée où est celui qui montre ses oreilles, et à qui il manque une perruque. S'il va par la ville, après avoir fait quelque chemin, il se croit égaré, il s'émeut, et il demande où il est à des passants, qui lui disent précisément le nom de sa rue ; il entre ensuite dans sa maison, d'où il sort précipitamment, croyant qu'il s'est trompé. Il descend du palais, et trouvant au bas du grand degré un carrosse qu'il prend pour le

All this is conceived and related in a spirit of elegant comedy, and the whole scene is enacted before our eyes;

sien, il se met dedans : le cocher touche et croit ramener son maître dans sa maison ; Ménalque se jette hors de la portière, traverse la cour, monte l'escalier, parcourt l'antichambre, la chambre, le cabinet ; tout lui est familier, rien ne lui est nouveau ; il s'assied, il se repose, il est chez soi.

Le maître arrive : celui-ci se lève pour le recevoir ; il le traite fort civilement, le prie de s'asseoir, et croit faire les honneurs de sa chambre ; il parle, il rêve, il reprend la parole : le maître de la maison s'ennuie, et demeure étonné ; Ménalque ne l'est pas moins, et ne dit pas ce qu'il en pense : il a affaire à un fâcheux, à un homme oisif, qui se retirera à la fin, il l'espère, et il prend patience : la nuit arrive qu'il est à peine détrompé. Une autre fois il rend visite à une femme, et se persuadant bientôt que c'est lui qui la reçoit, il s'établit dans son fauteuil, et ne songe nullement à l'abandonner : il trouve ensuite que cette dame fait ses visites longues, il attend à tous moments qu'elle se lève et le laisse en liberté ; mais comme cela tire en longueur, qu'il a faim, et que la nuit est déjà avancée, il prie à souper : elle rit, et si haut qu'elle le réveille. Lui-même se marie le matin, l'oublie le soir, et découche la nuit de ses noces, et quelques années après il perd sa femme, elle meurt entre ses bras, il assiste à ses obsèques, et le lendemain, quand on lui vient dire qu'on a servi, il demande si sa femme est prête et si elle est avertie.

C'est lui encore qui entre dans une église, et prenant l'aveugle qui est collé à la porte pour un pilier, et sa tasse pour le bénitier, y plonge la main, la porte à son front, lorsqu'il entend tout d'un coup le pilier qui parle, et qui lui offre des oraisons. Il s'avance dans la nef, il croit voir un prie-dieu, il se jette lourdement dessus : la machine plie, s'enfonce, et fait des efforts pour crier ; Ménalque est surpris de se voir à genoux sur les jambes d'un fort petit homme, appuyé sur son dos, les deux bras passés sur ses épaules, et ses deux mains jointes et étendues qui lui prennent le nez et lui ferment la bouche ; il se retire confus, et va s'agenouiller ailleurs.

Il tire un livre pour faire sa prière, et c'est sa pantoufle qu'il a prise pour ses Heures, et qu'il a mise dans sa poche avant que de sortir. Il n'est pas hors de l'église qu'un homme de livrée court après lui, le joint, lui demande en riant s'il n'a point la pantoufle de Monseigneur ; Ménalque lui montre la sienne, et lui dit : 'Voilà toutes les pantoufles que j'ai sur moi ;' il se fouille néanmoins, et tire celle de l'évêque de ——, qu'il vient de quitter, qu'il a trouvé malade auprès de son feu, et dont, avant de prendre congé de lui, il a ramassé la pantoufle, comme l'un de ses gants qui étoit à terre : ainsi Ménalque s'en retourne chez soi avec une pantoufle de moins. Il a une fois perdu au jeu tout l'argent qui est dans sa bourse, et voulant continuer de jouer, il entre dans son cabinet, ouvre une armoire, y prend sa cassette, en tire ce qu'il lui plaît, croit la remettre où il l'a prise : il entend aboyer dans son armoire qu'il vient de fermer ; et étonné de ce prodige, il l'ouvre une seconde fois, et il éclate de rire d'y voir son chien, qu'il a serré pour sa cassette. Il joue au trictrac, il demande à boire, on lui en apporte ; c'est à lui à jouer, il tient le cornet d'une main et un verre de l'autre, et comme il a une grande soif, il avale les dés et presque le cornet, jette le so that we are witnesses of a really delicious little series of verre d'eau dans le trictrac, et inonde celui contre qui il joue. Et dans une chambre où il est familier, il crache sur le lit et jette son chapeau à terre, en croyant faire tout le contraire. Il se promène sur l'eau, et il demande quelle heure il est : on lui présente une montre ; à peine l'a-t-il reçue, que ne songeant plus ni à l'heure ni à la montre, il la jette dans la rivière, comme une chose qui l'embarrasse. Lui-même écrit une longue lettre, met de la poudre dessus à plusieurs reprises, et jette toujours la poudre dans l'encrier. Ce n'est pas tout : il écrit une seconde lettre, et, après les avoir cachetées toutes deux, il se trompe à l'adresse ; un duc et pair reçoit l'une de ces deux lettres, et en l'ouvrant y lit ces mots : ' Maître Olivier, ne manquez, sitôt la présente reçue, de m'envoyer ma provision de foin.' . . . Son fermier reçoit l'autre, il l'ouvre, et se la fait lire ; on y trouve : ' Monseigneur, j'ai reçu avec une soumission aveugle les ordres qu'il a plu à Votre Grandeur ' . . . Lui-même encore écrit une lettre pendant la nuit, et, après l'avoir cachetée, il éteint sa bougie : il ne laisse pas d'être surpris de ne voir goutte, et il sait à peine comment cela est arrivé. Ménalque descend l'escalier du Louvre, un autre le monte, à qui il dit : ' C'est vous que je cherche ; ' il le prend par la main, le fait descendre avec lui, traverse plusieurs cours, entre dans les salles, en sort ; il va, il revient sur ses pas ; il regarde enfin celui qu'il traîne après soi depuis un quart d'heure : il est étonné que ce soit lui, il n'a rien à lui dire, il lui quitte la main, et tourne d'un autre côté. Souvent il vous interroge, et il est déjà loin de vous quand vous songez à lui répondre ; ou bien il vous demande en courant comment se porte votre père, et comme vous lui dites qu'il est fort mal, il vous crie qu'il en est bien aise. Il vous trouve quelque autre fois sur son chemin : ' Il est ravi de vous rencontrer ; il sort de chez vous pour vous entretenir d'une certaine chose ; ' il contemple votre main : ' Vous-avez là,' dit-il, ' un beau rubis ; est-il balais ? ' Il vous quitte et continue sa route : voilà l'affaire importante dont il avait à vous parler. Se trouve-t-il en campagne, il dit à quelqu'un qu'il trouve heureux d'avoir pu se dérober à la cour pendant l'automne, et d'avoir passé dans ses terres tout le temps de Fontainebleau ; il tient à d'autres d'autres discours ; puis revenant à celui-ci : ' Vous avez eu,' lui dit-il, ' de beaux jours à Fontainebleau ; vous y avez sans doute beaucoup chassé.' Il commence ensuite un conte qu'il oublie d'achever ; il rit en lui-même, il éclate d'une chose qui lui passe par l'esprit, il répond à sa pensée, il chante entre ses dents, il siffle, il se renverse dans une chaise, il pousse un cri plaintif, il bâille, il se croit seul. S'il se trouve à un repas, on voit le pain se multiplier insensiblement sur son assiette : il est vrai qui ses voisins en manquent, aussi bien que de couteaux et de fourchettes, dont il ne les laisse pas jouir longtemps. On a inventé aux tables une grande cuillère pour la commodité du service : il la prend, la plonge dans le plat, l'emplit, la porte à sa bouche, et il ne sort pas d'étonnement de voir repandu sur son linge et sur ses habits le potage, qu'il vient d'avaler. Il oublie de boire pendant tout le dîner ; s'il s'en souvient, et qu'il trouve que l'on lui donne trop de vin, il en flaque plus de la moitié au visage de celui qui est à sa droite, il boit le reste tranquillement, et ne comprend pas pourquoi tout le monde éclate de rire de ce qu'il a jeté à terre ce qu'on lui à versé de trop.

Il est un jour retenu au lit pour quelque incommodité : on lui rend visite ; il y a un cercle d'hommes et de femmes dans sa ruelle qui l'entre-

contretemps, of mutual deceptions, and entertaining mis-

tiennent, et en leur présence il soulève sa couverture et crache dans ses draps. On le mène aux Chartreux ; on lui fait voir un cloître orné d'ouvrages, tous de la main d'un excellent peintre ; le religieux qui les lui explique parle de Saint *Bruno*, du chanoine et de son aventure, en fait une longue histoire, et la montre dans l'un de ses tableaux : Ménalque, qui pendant la narration est hors du cloître, et bien loin au-délà, y revient enfin, et demande au père si c'est le chanoine ou Saint Bruno qui est damné. Il se trouve par hasard avec une jeune veuve ; il lui parle de son défunt mari, lui demande comment il est mort ; cette femme, à qui ce discours renouvelle ses douleurs, pleure, sanglotte, et ne laisse pas de répandre tous les détails de la maladie de son époux, qu'elle conduit depuis la veille de sa fièvre, qu'il se portait bien, jusqu'à l'agonie : ' Madame,' lui demande Ménalque, qui l'avoit apparemment écoutée avec attention, 'n'aviez-vous que celui-là ?' Il s'avise un matin de faire tout hâter dans sa cuisine, il se lève avant le fruit, et prend congé de la compagnie : on le voit ce jour-là en tous les endroits de la ville hormis en celui où il a donné un rendez-vous précis pour cette affaire qui l'a empêché de dîner, et l'a fait sortir à pied, de peur que son carrosse ne le fît attendre. L'entendez-vous crier, gronder, s'emporter contre l'un de ses domestiques ? Il est étonné de ne le point voir : ' Où peut-il être ?' dit-il ; ' que fait-il ? qu'est-il devenu ? qu'il ne se présente plus devant moi, je le chasse dès à cette heure.' Le valet arrive, à qui il demande fièrement d'où il vient ; il lui répond qu'il vient de l'endroit où il l'a envoyé, et il lui rend un fidèle compte de sa commission. Vous le prendriez souvent pour tout ce qu'il n'est pas : pour un stupide, car il n'écoute point, et il parle encore moins ; pour un fou, car outre qu'il parle tout seul, il est sujet à de certaines grimaces et à des mouvements de tête involontaires ; pour un homme fier et incivil, car vous le saluez, et il passe sans vous regarder, ou il vous regarde sans vous rendre le salut ; pour un inconsidéré, car il parle de banqueroute au milieu d'une famille où il y a cette tache, d'exécution et d'échafaud devant un homme dont le père y a monté, de roture devant des roturiers qui sont riches et qui se donnent pour nobles. De même il a dessein d'élever auprès de soi un fils naturel sous le nom et le personnage d'un valet ; et quoiqu'il veuille le dérober à la connoissance de sa femme et de ses enfants, il lui échappe de l'appeler son fils dix fois le jour. Il a pris aussi la résolution de marier son fils à la fille d'un homme d'affaires, et il ne laisse pas de dire de temps en temps, en parlant de sa maison et de ses ancêtres, que les Ménalque ne se sont jamais mésalliés. Enfin il n'est ni présent ni attentif dans une compagnie à ce qui fait le sujet de la conversation. Il pense et il parle tout à la fois, mais la chose dont il parle est rarement celle à laquelle il pense ; aussi ne parle-t-il guère conséquemment et avec suite : où il dit non, souvent il faut dire oui, et où il dit oui, croyez qu'il veut dire non ; il a, en vous répondant si juste, les yeux fort ouverts, mais il ne s'en sert point : il ne regarde ni vous ni personne, ni rien qui soit au monde. Tout ce que vous pouvez tirer de lui, et encore dans le temps qu'il est le plus appliqué et d'un meilleur commerce, ce sont ces mots : *Oui vraiment ; C'est vrai ; Bon ; Tout de bon ? Oui-da ! Je pense qu'oui ; Assurément ; Ah ! ciel !* et quelques autres monosyllabes qui ne sont pas même placés à propos.

Jamais aussi il n'est avec ceux avec qui il paroît être : il appelle sérieusement son laquais *Monsieur* ; et son ami, il l'appelle la

understandings. But La Bruyère has not yet done with his absent-minded creation.

Another time he visits a lady, and presently falls into the delusion that he himself is the host; so he drops into an easy chair and makes himself a fixture there. He begins to find that his supposed visitor makes her call a very long one, and is continually expecting that she will rise and leave him free; but as she stays on, and he is getting hungry, and the night is already far advanced, he invites her to supper. She laughs, and that so heartily that it arouses him from his hallucination.

He himself gets married one morning, forgets all about it by the evening, and returns to his solitary couch.[1] Some years afterwards, he loses his wife, who dies in his arms. He follows her to the grave, and next day when he is told that dinner is prepared he asks whether his wife is ready, and if she has been notified of the fact.

It is he also who, entering a church and taking the blind man, who stands propped against the porch, for a pillar, and his cup for a holy-water basin, dips his fingers into it, carries them to his forehead, and suddenly hears the pillar speak and offer up prayers on his behalf. Advancing up the nave he fancies he sees a *prie-dieu*, drops heavily upon it, when the machine bends, collapses, and endeavours to cry out. Menalcas is surprised to find himself kneeling on the legs of a very little man, pressing on his back, his two arms passed over his shoulders, and his two clasped hands compressing his nose and closing his mouth. He withdraws confused, and goes to kneel elsewhere.

He puts his hand into his pocket for a prayer-book, and finds he has mistaken a slipper for a missal and has pocketed it accordingly.

It must be confessed that here the comedy broadens into farce, and that La Bruyère must have had in his mind some of those diverting *turlupinades* invented in the previous century by that merry trio of journeymen-bakers, Gauthier-Garguille, Gros-Guillaume, and Turlupin; which so de-

Verdure; il dit *Votre Révérence* à un prince du sang, et *Votre Altesse* à un Jésuite. Il entend la messe: le prêtre vient à éternuer; il lui dit: *Dieu vous assiste!* Il se trouve avec un magistrat: cet homme grave par son caractère, vénérable par son âge et par sa dignité, l'interroge sur un évènement et lui demande si cela est ainsi; Ménalque lui répond: *Oui, mademoiselle.* Il revient une fois de la campagne: ses laquais en livrées entreprennent de le voler et y réussissent; ils descendent de son carrosse, lui portent un bout de flambeau sous la gorge, lui demandent la bourse, et il la rend. Arrivé chez soi, il raconte son aventure à ses amis, qui ne manquent pas de l'interroger sur les circonstances, et il leur dit: *Demandez à mes gens, ils y étoient.*

[1] This is an adventure attributed to the Comte de Brancas, and related with some fantastic variations by Tallemant des Réaux and by the Duchesse d'Orléans, mother of the Regent.

lighted Richelieu, when they gave a private performance at the Palais Cardinal, that he issued orders for their enrolment in the theatrical company of the Hôtel de Bourgogne, whose entertainments, he declared, had such a depressing effect upon him that he was determined to enliven them by the introduction of some genuine fun.

Menalcas has scarcely quitted the church when a livery servant runs after him, and smilingly inquires if he has not got Monseigneur's slipper. Menalcas shows him his own, and says: 'These are the only slippers I have about me.' He fumbles in his pockets, however, and produces one belonging to the Bishop of ——, whom he had just left. He had found him indisposed and sitting before the fire, and, on taking his leave, had picked it up, supposing it to be a glove he had dropped. So Menalcas returned home with one slipper the less.

On one occasion, losing at play all the money he had in his purse and wishing to continue the game, he entered his cabinet, opened a closet, and took from a chest what coin he required, then put it back again as he thought, and was astonished to hear a dog yelping in the closet he had closed. Opening it for the second time he roared with laughter to see that he had locked up his dog instead of his money-box....

Another time he wrote two letters, and then, after having sealed them, he forgot which was which, so that each was misdirected. A duke received the one commencing thus: 'Master Oliver, as soon as this reaches you, don't fail to send me a stock of hay.' His farmer received the other, which began thus: 'Monseigneur, I bow with blind submission to the orders Your Highness has been good enough to send me.'[1]

Finding himself by chance with a young widow, recently bereaved, he speaks to her of her late husband, and inquires the cause of his death. The lady, whose grief is revived by this conversation, weeps, sobs, and dwells with painful iteration upon all the details of his illness, from his first attack of fever until his final agony. 'Madame,' inquires Menalcas, who has been apparently listening attentively, 'was he the only husband you had?'

And so La Bruyère continues to string together all the instances of absent-mindedness he had ever heard of, and to draw upon his imagination for the possible exemplifications of its effects, much after the fashion of the modern American humorist when he describes a man, on retiring to rest, as blowing himself out and putting his candle to bed.

It is, however, in his aphoristic sayings that we find La

[1] This blunder is related by Madame de Sévigné, in a letter dated June 2, 1672, as having been perpetrated by the Comte de Brancas.

Bruyère at his best. He was not a deep thinker, perhaps, but he was an acute and philosophical observer, with a good deal of humour and no cynicism. Unambitious, yet highly placed, his opportunities for the study of human character and conduct were all that he could desire; and what he thought and felt he clothed in language which was at once vigorous and picturesque, concise and expressive. Among the many eminent critics who have analysed his writings, we do not think there is one whose estimate of him is sounder or more judicious than that of Chateaubriand, who has written as follows: 'La Bruyère is one of the finest writers of the age of Louis Quatorze. No one has known how to give more variety to his style, more diversity of form to his language, more movement to his ideas. He descends from the highest eloquence to familiarity, and passes from pleasantry to reasoning without offending good taste or his readers. Irony is his favourite weapon. As philosophical as Theophrastus, his vision embraces a much greater number of objects, and his remarks are more original and more profound. Theophrastus conjectures, La Rochefoucauld divines, and La Bruyère shows us what is passing at the bottom of our hearts.'

More recently the great moralist found a most discerning and sympathetic critic in Sainte-Beuve, whose sentiments towards the acute and original thinker of the seventeenth century were touched by the warmth of personal affection, as in the following passage: 'It has been agreed to recognise in La Bruyère the portrait of a philosopher, who, seated in his closet and always accessible, in spite of his deep studies, bids you enter, because you bring him something more precious than gold or silver—the opportunity for conferring an obligation upon you.' In fact, the moralist fulfilled the divine injunction 'To do good and to distribute, forget not.' For he distributed, with a lavish hand, his treasures of wisdom: the fruits of his observation and reflection; the mental wealth which he felt that he held in trust for the benefit of his fellow-creatures. And his benefactions in this respect will endure as long as the language in which his thoughts were clothed.

Let me endeavour to string together some of the pearls which dropped from his eloquent and facile pen:

The glory or merit of certain men is to have written well, and that of some others is not to have written at all.[1]

There is no such painful business in the world as that of making a great name. Life ends before the work is scarcely sketched.[2]

We ought to work in order to render ourselves worthy of employment. The rest concerns us not. It is the affair of other people.[3]

Modesty is to merit what shade is to the figures in a picture. It gives them strength and relief.[4]

Women excel men in their capacity for affection; men exceed women in their capacity for friendship.[5]

A man is more faithful to another's secret than his own; a woman, on the contrary, keeps her own secret better than another's.[6]

It costs women little to say what they do not feel; it costs men still less to say what they do feel.[7]

An insensible woman is one who has not yet seen the man she is to love.[8]

Love and friendship mutually exclude each other.[9]

Hatred is not so far from friendship as antipathy.[10]

Time which fortifies friendships weakens love.[11]

Liberality consists less in giving much than in giving seasonably.[12]

The beginning and the end of love are best denoted by the embarrassment occasioned when the two persons are alone with each other.[13]

---

[1] La gloire ou le mérite de certains hommes est de bien écrire; et de quelques autres, c'est de n'écrire point.

[2] Il n'y a point au monde un si pénible métier que celui de se faire un grand nom; la vie s'achève, que l'on a à peine ébauché son ouvrage.

[3] Nous devons travailler à nous rendre très dignes de quelque emploi; le reste ne nous regarde point, c'est l'affaire des autres.

[4] La modestie est au mérite ce que les ombres sont aux figures dans un tableau; elle lui donne de la force et du relief.

[5] Les femmes vont plus loin en amour que la plupart des hommes; mais les hommes l'emportent sur elles en amitié.

[6] Un homme est plus fidèle au secret d'autrui qu'au sien propre: une femme, au contraire, garde mieux son secret que celui d'autrui.

[7] Il coûte peu aux femmes de dire ce qu'elles ne sentent point: il coûte encore moins aux hommes de dire ce qu'ils sentent.

[8] Une femme insensible est celle qui n'a pas encore vu celui qu'elle doit aimer.

[9] L'amour et l'amitié s'excluent l'un l'autre.

[10] Il n'y a pas si loin de la haine à l'amitié que de l'antipathie.

[11] Le temps, qui fortifie les amitiés, affaiblit l'amour.

[12] La libéralité consiste moins à donner beaucoup qu'à donner à propos.

[13] Le commencement et le déclin de l'amour se font sentir par l'embarras où l'on est de se trouver seuls.

One should laugh before feeling happy for fear of dying without having laughed at all.[1]

To be infatuated with one's self, and to be strongly persuaded that one has a great deal of intelligence, is an accident which scarcely ever occurs except to a person who has very little or none at all.[2]

Politeness does not always inspire goodness, equity, amiability, and gratitude. It supplies at least the appearance of them, and enables man to show himself externally what he ought to be internally.[3]

It is often easier and more useful to adapt ourselves to other people than to make them adjust themselves to us.[4]

You believe him to be your dupe. If he pretends to be so, who is the greater dupe—you or he?[5]

The wise man often shuns the world for fear of being bored.[6]

Nothing better enables us to understand the insignificance of the gift which God considers he is bestowing upon men in abandoning to them great wealth and large possessions, than in observing the uses which are made of them, and the sort of persons upon whom they are conferred.[7]

He is rich who receives more than he consumes; he is poor whose expenditure exceeds his income.[8]

---

[1] Il faut rire avant que d'être heureux, de peur de mourir sans avoir ri.

[2] Etre infatué de soi, et s'être fortement persuadé qu'on a beaucoup d'esprit, est un accident qui n'arrive guère qu'à celui qui n'en a point, ou qui en a peu.

[3] La politesse n'inspire pas toujours la bonté, l'équité, la complaisance, la gratitude. Elle en donne du moins les apparences, et fait apparaître l'homme au dehors comme il devrait être intérieurement.

[4] Il est souvent plus court et plus utile de cadrer aux autres, que de faire que les autres s'ajustent à nous.

[5] Vous le croyez votre dupe; s'il feint de l'être, qui est plus dupe, de lui, ou de vous?

[6] Le sage quelquefois évite le monde, de peur d'être ennuyé.

[7] Rien ne fait mieux comprendre le peu de chose que Dieu croit donner aux hommes, en leur abandonnant les richesses, l'argent, les grands établissements et les autres biens, que la dispensation qu'il en fait, et le genre d'hommes qui en sont le mieux pourvus.

[8] Celui-là est riche, qui reçoit plus qu'il ne consume: celui-là est pauvre, dont la dépense excède la recette.

We meet with the same idea in Gibbon's 'Autobiography:' 'I am indeed rich, since my income is superior to my expense and my expense is equal to my wishes.' And again in the sententious remark of Mr. Wilkins Micawber: 'Annual income twenty pounds, annual expenditure nineteen pounds nineteen and six; result, happiness. Annual income twenty pounds, annual expenditure twenty pounds eight and six; result, misery. The blossom is blighted, the leaf is withered, the god of day goes down upon the dreary scene, and in short you are for ever floored, as I am.'—*David Copperfield.*

Children would be, perhaps, dearer to their fathers, and reciprocally, fathers to their children, if no heirship intervened.[1]

It is difficult to decide whether irresolution renders a man more unhappy or more contemptible,[2] or whether it is better to take the wrong side rather than take no side at all.

If poverty is the mother of crime, ignorance is its father.[3]

The man who says he was not born happy may at least become so by conferring happiness on his friends and neighbours.[4]

If life is miserable, it is hard to bear; if it is happy, it is horrible to lose. They both amount to the same thing.[5]

People hope to be old, and they fear old age; that is to say, they love life and shun death.[6]

Death comes but once, and makes itself felt at every moment of our lives. It is harder to apprehend than to undergo.[7]

A long illness seems to be interposed between life and death, in order that death may become a solace to those who die and to those who remain.[8]

Children have neither a past nor a future; and—what rarely happens to us—they enjoy the present.[9]

Party-spirit lowers the greatest men to the level of the common people.[10]

Men almost despise the virtues of the heart, and idolise the talents of the body and the mind.[11]

All the intelligence in the world is useless to the man who has none; he has no views, and is incapable of profiting by other people's.[12]

---

[1] Les enfants peut-être seraient plus chers à leurs pères, et réciproquement les pères à leurs enfants, sans le titre d'héritiers.

[2] Il est difficile de décider si l'irrésolution rend l'homme plus malheureux que méprisable: de même s'il y a toujours plus d'inconvénient à prendre un mauvais parti qu'à n'en prendre aucun.

[3] Si la pauvreté est la mère des crimes, le défaut d'esprit en est le père.

[4] L'homme qui dit qu'il n'est pas né heureux pourrait du moins le devenir par le bonheur de ses amis ou de ses proches.

[5] Si la vie est misérable, elle est pénible à supporter; si elle est heureuse, il est horrible de la perdre. L'un revient à l'autre.

[6] L'on espère de vieillir, et l'on craint la vieillesse; c'est à dire, l'on aime la vie, et l'on fuit la mort.

[7] La mort n'arrive qu'une fois, et se fait sentir à tous les moments de la vie; il est plus dur de l'appréhender que de la souffrir.

[8] Une longue maladie semble être placée entre la vie et la mort, afin que la mort même devienne un soulagement et à ceux qui meurent et à ceux qui restent.

[9] Les enfants n'ont ni passé ni avenir; et, ce qui ne nous arrive guère, ils jouissent du présent.

[10] L'esprit de parti abaisse les plus grands hommes jusques aux petitesses du peuple.

[11] Les hommes comptent presque pour rien toutes les vertus du cœur, et idolâtrent les talents du corps et de l'esprit.

[12] Tout l'esprit qui est au monde est inutile à celui qui n'en a point; il n'a nulles vues, et il est incapable de profiter de celles d'autrui.

Everybody declares that a coxcomb is a coxcomb; nobody dares to say the same thing to his face. He dies without knowing it, and without any one having his revenge.[1]

The generality of men spend the first part of their lives in making the second miserable.[2]

Hatreds are so enduring and so inveterate, that the greatest sign of death in an invalid is his reconciliation with an enemy.[3]

An amorous old man is the greatest deformity in nature.[4]

We rarely repent of saying too little, but very often of speaking too much. It is a trite and trivial maxim, which everybody knows and nobody practises.[5]

There is in some men a certain mediocrity of mind which helps to render them sagacious.[6]

The condition of actors was infamous among the Romans, and honourable among the Greeks. What is it among ourselves? We repute them as the Romans did, and we associate with them like the Greeks.[7]

An intellectual expression in men is what regularity of features is with women: it is a kind of beauty to which the vainest may aspire.[8]

Those who, without knowing us, think badly of us do no wrong to us. It is not ourselves whom they attack, but a phantom of their own imagination.[9]

Vices arise from a depravity of the heart, faults from a vice of temperament, ridicule from a defect of the intellect.[10]

One of the marks of mental mediocrity is to be always prating.[11]

---

[1] Tout le monde dit d'un fat qu'il est un fat; personne n'ose le lui dire à lui-même; il meurt sans le savoir, et sans que personne se soit vengé.

[2] La plupart des hommes emploient la première partie de leur vie à rendre l'autre misérable.

[3] Les haines sont si longues et si opiniâtres, que le plus grand signe de mort dans un homme invalide, c'est la réconciliation.

[4] C'est une grande difformité dans la nature qu'un vieillard amoureux.

[5] L'on se repent rarement de parler peu, très-souvent de trop parler; maxime usée et triviale, que tout le monde sait, et que tout le monde ne pratique pas.

[6] Il y a dans quelques hommes une certaine médiocrité d'esprit qui contribue à les rendre sages.

[7] La condition des comédiens était infâme chez les Romains, et honorable chez les Grecs; qu'est-elle chez nous? On pense d'eux comme les Romains, on vit avec eux comme les Grecs.

[8] L'air spirituel est dans les hommes ce que la régularité des traits est dans les femmes; c'est le genre de beauté où les plus vains puissent aspirer.

[9] Ceux qui, sans nous connaître assez, pensent mal de nous, ne nous font pas de tort; ce n'est point nous qu'ils attaquent, c'est le fantôme de leur imagination.

[10] Les vices partent d'une dépravation du cœur; les défauts, d'un vice de tempérament; le ridicule, d'une défaut d'esprit.

[11] L'une des marques de la médiocrité de l'esprit est de toujours conter.

Talent, taste, intelligence, good sense, are things distinct but not incompatible. Between good sense and good taste there is the difference between cause and effect.[1]

Next to a spirit of discernment the greatest of rarities are diamonds and pearls.[2]

The first thing that happens to men after renouncing pleasures, either from convenience, or weariness, or from a set purpose, is to denounce them in others. We have a lingering attachment to them, and are jealous of those who are taking up what we have laid down.[3]

In the closing chapter of his work La Bruyère deals with the freethinkers of his time, and takes us into the inner sanctuary of his nature, as it were. His belief in God seems to have been a conviction forced upon him by the contemplation of the external universe, and an assurance arising from an internal instinct; or, perhaps it would be more correct to say, an intuition.

'What could be more discouraging,' he exclaims, 'than to doubt whether one's soul is not as material as a stone or a reptile, and if it be not corruptible like those vile creatures! Is there not more force and grandeur in the idea which the mind receives of a Being superior to all other beings, who has made the whole of them, and to whom the whole of them are related; of a Being supremely perfect, who is pure, who is without beginning and without ending; of whom our own soul is the image, and—if I may venture so to speak—a spiritual portion, immortal like Himself?'

The chapter is full of passages of great eloquence and beauty, and it is, throughout, a sustained plea for a pure and virtuous life; not merely as the best preparation for that which may or must follow, but because virtue itself, altogether apart from future recompense, is desirable for her own sake; La Bruyère evidently holding with Tennyson that

---

[1] Talent, goût, esprit, bon sens, choses différentes, non incompatibles. Entre le bon sens et le bon goût il y a la différence de la cause à son effet.

[2] Après l'esprit de discernement, ce qu'il y a au monde de plus rare, ce sont les diamants et les perles.

[3] La première chose qui arrive aux hommes après avoir renoncé aux plaisirs, ou par bienséance, ou par lassitude, ou par régime, c'est de les condamner dans les autres. Il entre dans cette conduite une sorte d'attachement pour les choses mêmes que l'on vient de quitter: l'on aimerait qu'un bien qui n'est plus pour nous ne fût plus aussi pour le reste du monde: c'est un sentiment de jalousie.

Because right is right, to follow right
Were wisdom in the scorn of consequence.

The moralist's last words are especially concise and impressive: 'Extremes are vicious and are of human origin. All compromise is just and proceeds from God.'

I see that I have expatiated upon La Bruyère at much greater length than I intended to do. Many other chapters remain, from which abundant quotations could be made. That on the Great, for example, teems with ideas as profound as they are just. La Bruyère knew the Great. He lived in the midst of them, and had been made to suffer by them; and the shafts he levels at them are very sharp-edged.

At the same time, these things possess very little interest for us who live in an epoch when the great, in his sense of the word, no longer exist.

I will quote nothing from the chapter on the Sovereign or the Republic, nor from that upon Judgments. They are excellent to read, but are not well adapted for analysis in public lectures. In the chapter on Fashion, and on Some Usages, a choice of quotations would be equally difficult to make. The eccentricities and absurdities characterised by La Bruyère belong so entirely to the seventeenth century that it would be impossible for a nineteenth century audience to feel any interest in them.

I must likewise pass over, without touching upon, the chapter on the Pulpit. As to the last of the 'Characters,' that entitled Thinkers, our Christian philosopher believed it to be his duty to write it in order to atone for, and to counterbalance, his attacks upon religious hypocrites and the spiritual directors of women. La Bruyère seems to have considered that sceptical opinions had already made a sufficiently notable progress in his century, and that he should now endeavour to arrest their course.

As I have already mentioned, La Bruyère found considerable difficulty in obtaining admission to the Academy, where Fontenelle had been received, in preference to himself, in 1691. One of his most strenuous opponents was Benserade, the wit, poet, and court sycophant, whom the moralist has pilloried for ever, under the name of Theobald, in his immortal 'Characters.' Many others were permitted to occupy a *fauteuil* before La Bruyère, and it was generally supposed that he had withdrawn his candidature, when, in the month of May 1693, he was elected in succession to La Chambre, and that, too, without the personal canvass which is customary on such occasions; for towards the end of his discourse, he made the following remarks: 'I will not disguise from you that I have sufficiently prized the distinction with which you have honoured me, to wish to obtain it in all its bloom and in all its integrity. I wished to be able to owe it to your own selection only; and I value that choice so highly that I have not ventured to offend it, nor even to infringe upon its freedom, by any importunate solicitation. Besides, I entertained a proper distrust of myself, and was reluctant to ask you to prefer me to others whom you might elect.'

La Bruyère's discourse at his election is worth reading by every one who would like to know the opinion then entertained by men of letters of the writers whose works are now recognised as classics. He was not obliged to submit his speech, as has since become the custom, to a committee appointed for that purpose, and therefore he felt himself perfectly free to speak of his contemporaries in such a way as he would probably not have been permitted to do by the other Academicians, if they had been previously consulted. The opening passages of his discourse at his reception were devoted, as was customary, to the praise of Cardinal Richelieu, as the founder of the Academy; and then he paid homage to the illustrious writers with whom he was thenceforth to be associated. First of all, he alluded to Segrais, who had revived Virgil in France, and had infused into our language the grace and richness of the Latin; had written romances which *do* come to an end; and had banished prolixity and incredibility, to substitute for them the probable and the natural. Then, proceeding to speak of La Fontaine, he declared him to be more equal in his poetical compositions than Marot, and superior in style to Voiture, while exhibiting the naïveté of both; adding that 'he instructed by his pleasantries; persuaded men to virtue by endowing animals with speech; raised the smallest subjects to the level of the sublime;' that he was 'a writer unique in his kind, who, whether as inventor or translator, surpassed his models; and was himself a model very hard to imitate.'

Of Boileau, he observed that 'he excelled Juvenal and equalled Horace; appearing to create the thoughts of others, and to make everything he touched his own. Upon what he borrowed elsewhere, he bestowed all the charm of novelty and all the merit of originality. His strong and harmonious verse, wrought by genius, though perfected by art, full of life and poetry, will be read when our language itself grows old, and will be found among its latest débris. As a critic he is sound, judicious, and impartial; and whatever he has condemned as bad assuredly is bad.' We next come to Racine, an author 'praised, applauded, and admired, whose verses fly from place to place, and have passed into a proverb; who dominates and rules the scene and has taken entire possession of the stage.' La Bruyère is not the man to bid him stand aside; but he places another monarch near his throne, and we can fancy with what alert attention the Academicians listened, as the great moralist instituted a comparison between the famous dramatist and his twin star. 'Some will not allow Corneille, the great Corneille, to be preferred; while others refuse to admit him on a footing of equality.' It was thus that La Bruyère spoke of the great writers, his fellow-members of the Academy, during the first half-century of its existence. Bossuet, Fénelon, and Fléchier were equally extolled by him; and it is interesting to note that posterity has ratified his judgment of all the more illustrious of his colleagues; and what a splendid galaxy of human intellect, at the time of its most splendid bloom in France!

Three years after his reception La Bruyère passed away in the manner I have already described. Studious by habit, and taciturn like most men addicted to meditation and reflection, he was very little known outside the Hôtel of the Condés and the walls of the Academy; and a pretty anecdote is related in connection with his social obscurity. He used to haunt a small book-shop in the Rue Saint-Jacques, where the little daughter of the bookseller attracted his kindly notice. One day he said to her father: 'Should you be willing to print this?'—at the same time drawing from his pocket the manuscript of his 'Characters'— 'I don't know whether it will pay you; but if it should, you can give the profits to my little friend.' Michallet, the bookseller, closed with the offer there and then; the book met with a very large sale, and he gained so much by it that he was enabled to give his daughter such a handsome dowry that her hand was sought in marriage by a financier, who afterwards became one of the farmers-general. As to La Bruyère, he was so wisely indifferent to money, that he was perfectly content to vegetate upon his pension of 120*l.* a year.

I have already quoted some of the judgments pronounced upon this deep thinker, vigilant observer, and admirable writer, by later critics.

He was the forerunner of Montesquieu, with his 'Persian Letters;' while, as Sainte-Beuve has pointed out, the Duclos, the Chamforts, the Rulhières, the Meihans, and the Rivarols have all dipped their pens in La Bruyère's ink-bottle; and we may hail him, as the same judicious writer has observed, as a classic whom all the world has agreed to recognise.

LECTURE XIV

Madame de Sévigné (1626–1696).

AMONG all the clever letter-writers of the seventeenth century Marie de Rabutin-Chantal, Marquise de Sévigné, bears away the palm; and among all the women who brightened French society by the sparkle of their wit, and purified and elevated it by the sweetness, the elegance, and the genuine goodness of their private lives, there is not one whom we can take so entirely to our hearts as the châtelaine of Les Rochers. What an ever-widening circle of friends and admirers she has made all over Europe—nay, in all parts of the civilised world, during the last two centuries or more! How intimately we seem to know her, and knowing her so well, how fond we naturally become of her, and how entirely we enter into the feelings of Madame de la Fayette, who, when lying on her deathbed, addressed her in these simple and touching words, 'I think I have loved you better than any other human being.' Dr. Young has told us in his gloomy 'Night Thoughts' that

> Heaven's Sovereign saves all beings but Himself
> That hideous sight, a naked human heart.

But Madame de Sévigné, in her letters, has laid her own heart entirely bare, and the revelation is an altogether delightful one. We are very thankful, indeed, that she lived in an age when the penny post, the electric telegraph, the telephone, and the phonograph were quite unknown, for these, combined with the fever, the wild rush, and the incessant excitement of modern life, have pretty well killed the beautiful art of letter-writing—an art born of much leisure, refined culture, and sustained and sincere warmth of feeling. It is scarcely too much to assert that the twentieth century will never produce another Madame de Sévigné. She belongs to an epoch and a condition of society separated from our own by a deep and impassable chasm produced by the tremendous agency of political, social, and scientific convulsions which even now have by no means spent their force.

Born in Paris in the year 1626, she lost her father when she was only eighteen months old, and her mother when she was only seven years and a half. On her first bereavement, her maternal grandmother took the child under her wing, and when her mother died her uncle, the Abbé de Coulanges, charged himself with the education of his niece.

Ménage, the Vadius of 'Les Femmes Savantes,' was one of her tutors, and Chapelain, the epic poet, was the other. They taught her Latin, Spanish, and Italian. The abbé was more than a father to her, and a beautiful friendship sprang up between uncle and niece, which endured unbroken for fifty years. As for Ménage, he fell in love with his charming pupil, but his romantic passion was not reciprocated; and as he observed to her many years afterwards, 'I was once your martyr; I am now your confessor.' Her cousin, Bussy-Rabutin, seems also to have been enamoured of the youthful beauty and she of him; but nothing came of it, and eventually a marriage was arranged for her with the Marquis de Sévigné, who was wealthy, noble, handsome, and of agreeable manners; but he had one very serious fault: 'he loved everywhere, but never anything so amiable as his own wife.' In a word, he was tainted with the fashionable vice of the period. She was only eighteen when she married. She loved and esteemed her husband, who was unworthy of her; but in spite of his neglect, and of the temptations to which she was incessantly exposed in an age of general licentiousness, she 'wore the white flower of a blameless life' untainted by the slightest spot of evil. While the marquis was leading a career of folly and dissipation in Paris, his wife was fulfilling every duty devolving upon her as the mother of two children, a son and a daughter, in a sequestered château far away from the capital. Among the reigning beauties at whose feet the marquis knelt was the too famous Ninon de l'Enclos, who seemed to possess the gift of eternal youth, for in later years she fascinated not only the son but the grandson of the marquis. After her, this volatile adorer of the royal favourite transferred his affections to Madame de Gondran; but this discreditable intrigue involved him in a duel, in which he fell mortally wounded. Thus perished, at the early age of twenty-seven, the Marquis de Sévigné, whose name was destined to be rendered immortal by the genius of his wife.

In the early years of their married life she had been introduced by her husband to the salon of Madame de Rambouillet, and she shone upon that brilliant society like a vision of radiant youth and winsome beauty. Mademoiselle de Scudéry thus describes her under the name of the Princesse Clarinte in 'Clélie:' 'She has blue eyes, full of life and expression. She dances with marvellous grace; her voice is sweet and melodious; and she sings in a passionate manner. . . . She wins the hearts of all women, as well as those of men. She writes as she speaks—that is to say, in the most courteous and agreeable manner. I have never seen so much charm united with so much brightness of intellect, such innocence and virtue. Nobody else has ever known the art of being graceful without affectation, witty without malice, gay without folly, modest without constraint, and virtuous without severity.'

When one woman pens such a eulogium on another, we must perforce admit that the object of it was a person of the rarest excellence and attractiveness. Among the many compliments paid to her at this time, there were few more graceful than the quatrain written by the abbé de Montreuil on seeing Madame de Sévigné playing at blindman's buff, which has been thus rendered into English by Tennyson:

> Your right is to enthrall,
> You charm in every way;
> But surely, most of all,
> You charm us all to-day.
> Your blindfold eyes we see,
> And deem you 'Love'—none other;
> Your blindfold eyes we free;
> And lo! you are 'Love's mother.'

Hers was more than a superficial beauty. It was 'the mind, the music breathing from the face.' Many countenances are masks. That of Madame de Sévigné resembled some perfectly transparent medium, illuminated by the warmth of her pure and generous heart, and by the glowing light of her brilliant intellect. Hence it was a beauty which mellowed, but did not fade. Listen to the description of her given by her cousin, Emmanuel de Coulanges, to whom she had gone upon a visit in 1677—that is to say, when she was fifty-one years of age. 'We hold her at last, that incomparable mother-beauty. She is more beautiful, more incomparable than ever. Do you think that she came to us tired? Do you think she stayed in bed to rest after her fatigue? Nothing of the sort. She did me the honour to land at my door more beautiful, fresher, more radiant than I can describe; and since then she has been in a continual state of activity, which does not in the least injure her health. She is well in body. As for her soul, it is, by my faith, altogether with you (her daughter), and if it chances to revert to its beautiful shrine for a while, it is only to speak of this rare countess in Provence.'

At sixty years of age she received and declined an offer of marriage from the Duc de Luynes. But her heart was so full of her two children that it had no room for another inmate. She was the most devoted of mothers, and at the same time the truest and most unchanging of friends, as is abundantly attested, not merely by the language of her correspondence, but by the facts of her busy and beneficent life. Madame de Sévigné possessed, indeed, the happy art of converting her disappointed suitors into attached and faithful friends.

Her daughter, whom Bussy-Rabutin calls 'the prettiest girl in France,' was married in 1669 to the Comte de Grignan, and six years after their marriage they took up their abode in Provence, where her husband filled the post of Lieutenant-General. It was then that Madame de Sévigné commenced that correspondence with her daughter which has rendered the mother immortal. Other letters, in themselves sufficiently remarkable, have come down to us, but they do not bear that stamp of ineffable grace, tenderness, effusive candour, unselfish affection, freshness of feeling, maternal solicitude, sympathy, vivacity, and exquisite naturalness which constitutes the charm of the letters she wrote to Madame de Grignan. 'There seems to have been love enough in this woman,' writes Miss Thackeray, 'to make half a dozen daughters happy; perhaps, poor lady, there was too much for the happiness of one.'

When Madame de Sévigné sat down to write to her friends, the nerve currents which flowed to her pen came mostly from her brain; the words she indited to her daughter rushed warm and impetuous from her heart. It was the adoring and adorable mother who was conversing, not corresponding, with her child.

The letters remain, for all time, models of that form of composition. Perfectly unstudied and spontaneous, they have all the sparkle, the purity, the limpidity, and the ebullience of a transparent mountain spring. And as the stream into which it presently expands reflects every object on its banks, and mirrors on its placid surface the changing aspects of the heavens above, and is now bright with the rejoicing sunshine, and now dark with the shadows of accumulating clouds; now gives back the image of a stately forest, and anon reveals the counterpart of a fringe of meadow-sweet; so the letters of Madame de Sévigné reflect the varying moods and emotions of her own mind and heart, and also the passing events of the period at which they were written. Each is a page of contemporary history, as well as of domestic biography, and the whole forms a precious and highly interesting chapter in the annals of France. They constitute, moreover, an historical portrait gallery embellished by the likenesses of some of the most famous personages of the epoch in which the writer of them lived. Watch the procession as it passes by, and let us ask Monsieur de Lamartine to act as herald and announce the men and women who figure in the pageant. He does so in the following order:

The Princ de Condé; the Duc de Rohan; the Comte de Rude; Ménage, perpetually amorous of her and perpetually repulsed; the Cardinal de Retz; Montmorency; Brissac; Bellièvre; Montrésor; Chateaubriand; De Chaulnes; Caumartin; D'Hacqueville; Carbinelli; the two Arnaults, the fathers of Jansenism, and Pascal their apostle; D'Humières; D'Argenteuil, her cousin Bussy, who was also in love with her, always importunate and often perfidious; Sablonnière; Montrose, the Scotchman, the heroic martyr of a king proscribed; the Duchesse de Longueville, the animating spirit of the Fronde, which was defeated in spite of all her efforts; the Duchesse de Lesdiguières; the Duchesse de Montbazon; the

Princesse de Coulanges, sister of the Abbé of the same name; Mesdames de Laverdan, De Maintenon, De la Vallière, De Montespan, and De la Vergne; Henriette d'Angennes, afterwards Comtesse d'Olon, celebrated for her beauty and for her wildness; Madame de la Fayette, the friend of the great Duc de la Rochefoucauld, the author of the 'Maxims;' La Rochefoucauld himself, the fastidious judge and supreme arbiter of elegance and fashion; De Vardes, Turenne, Bossuet, Corneille, Fénelon, Racine, Molière, La Fontaine, Boileau. What a splendid company! What a galaxy of wits, beauties, warriors, statesmen, and men and women of genius! Shall we ever look upon their like again?

But it is time that I should allow Madame de Sévigné to speak for herself; and who can speak so charmingly as she does in these interesting letters? Here is a handful of gems taken at random from a heap:

To M. de Pomponne.[1]

Monday, December 1, 1664.

I must tell you a little story, which is quite true, and which will amuse you: the king, for some short time past, has dabbled in poetry; MM. de Saint-Aignan and Dangeau teaching him how to do it. The other day, he wrote a little madrigal, of which, however, he did not think much. One morning, he said to the Marshal de Gramont: 'Monsieur le Maréchal, may I beg of you to read this little madrigal, and tell me whether you have ever met with such a silly one. Because it is known that I have taken to versification of late, I am pestered with things of this kind.' After reading it, the marshal said to the king, 'Sire, your Majesty's judgment is always perfectly correct. This is really the most foolish and ridiculous madrigal I ever read.' The king laughingly rejoined, 'Must not the man who wrote it have been a coxcomb?' 'Sire, there is no other epithet which would fit him.' 'Ah! well,' said the king, 'I'm delighted you have been so candid with me on the subject of these verses; for I wrote them.' 'Ah, Sire! what an act of treason has your Majesty led me into! Pray return them to me! I read them so hastily.' 'No, Monsieur le Maréchal, first impressions are always the most natural.' The king laughed heartily at this escapade, and everybody looks upon it as the most cruel trick that could be played upon an old courtier. For my own

---

[1] Simon Arnauld, Marquis of Pomponne, was one of the ablest and most upright statesmen of his period. He shone alike as a diplomatist and as a Minister of Foreign Affairs. In the latter capacity he concluded the Treaty of Nimègue. His highly cultivated intellect rendered him one of the most welcome guests in the Hôtel de Rambouillet, and Saint-Simon, who was the reverse of a flatterer, eulogises the sweetness and elevation of his character, the sincerity of his piety, the charming simplicity of his manners, the wide range of his attainments, and the unwavering justice and probity of his actions.

part, being fond of moralising, I wish the king would do this sort of thing often, in order that he might find out how very far he is from ever knowing the real truth.¹

I have already made a passing reference to the Abbé Coulanges ; but he had a nephew, the Marquis de Coulanges, to whom many of Madame de Sévigné's letters were addressed, and among them the one I am about to quote. But, before doing so, something must be said of her cousin and correspondent. He was a type of the gay, frivolous, *insouciant* man of pleasure and *chansonnier* of the period. Appointed one of the counsellors of the parliament of Paris, his confidence failed him in the first cause he had to plead, which related to a certain pond belonging to a man named Crappan, and he thus addressed the august tribunal: 'Pardon me, gentlemen, I am floundering in Crappan's pond, and am your very humble servant.' That settled his career as one of the *noblesse de robe*, and he sold his appointment and accompanied the Duc de Chaulnes to Rome, where a punning epigram which he wrote on the Pope Innocent XII. was in everybody's mouth. It was as follows:

> Son nom, ses armes sont des pots.
> Une carafe était sa mère.

The Pope's family name was Pignatelli, signifying small

---

[1] Il faut que je vous conte une petite historiette, qui est très-vraie, et qui vous divertira. Le roi se mêle depuis peu de faire des vers; MM. de Saint-Aignan et Dangeau lui apprennent comment il s'y faut prendre. Il fit l'autre jour un petit madrigal, que lui-même ne trouva pas trop joli. Un matin il dit au maréchal de Gramont : 'M. le maréchal, lisez, je vous prie, ce petit madrigal, et voyez si vous en avez jamais vu un si impertinent : parce qu'on sait que depuis peu j'aime les vers, on m'en apporte de toutes les façons.' Le maréchal, après avoir lu, dit au roi : 'Sire, votre Majesté juge divinement bien de toutes choses ; il est vrai que voilà le plus sot et le plus ridicule madrigal que j'aie jamais lu.' Le roi se mit à rire, et lui dit : 'N'est-il pas vrai que celui qui l'a fait est bien fat ?' 'Sire, il n'y a pas moyen de lui donner un autre nom.' 'Oh bien,' dit le roi, 'je suis ravi que vous m'en ayez parlé si bonnement ; c'est moi qui l'ai fait.' 'Ah ! sire, quelle trahison ! Que votre Majesté me le rende ; je l'ai lu brusquement.' 'Non, M. le maréchal ; les premiers sentiments sont toujours les plus naturels.' Le roi a fort ri de cette folie, et tout le monde trouve que voilà la plus cruelle petite chose que l'on puisse faire à un vieux courtisan. Pour moi, qui aime toujours à faire des réflexions, je voudrais que le roi en fît là-dessus, et qu'il jugeât par là combien il est loin de connaître jamais la vérité.

earthen pots. He had three of these on his shield, and his mother was one of the Caraffe of Naples.

Among the innumerable verses, good, bad, and indifferent—mostly the latter—which he wrote, the following octave, on the origin of nobility, is one of the best:

> From Adam we have all been born,
>   The proof of it's well known to all;
> As likewise that our sire and dam
>   Both held the plough-tail in their hands;
> But, growing weary of the toil
>   Of turning up the stubborn glebe,
> One, in the morning, dropped the stilt,
>   The other in the afternoon.[1]

It is curious that the aristocratic poetaster of the seventeenth century should have repeated the same sentiment which animated John Ball, the democratic leveller of the fourteenth century, when he encouraged the English peasants to revolt against the lords of the soil:

> When Adam delved and Eve span,
> Who was then the gentleman?

But it had also found expression at a still earlier period in the old German proverb:

> So Adam reutte, und Eva span;
> Wer was da ein eddelman?

And now I pass on to the letter already spoken of—a letter overflowing with vivacity and affection. This is perhaps the best known of her letters:

To Monsieur de Coulanges.

December 15, 1670.

I am going to tell you something most astonishing, most surprising, most wonderful, most miraculous, most triumphant, most bewildering, most unprecedented, most singular, most extraordinary, most incredible, most unexpected, most important, most insignificant, most rare, most common, most notorious, most secret until now, most

---

[1] D'Adam nous sommes tous enfants,
   La preuve en est connue,
Et que tous nos premiers parents
   Ont mené la charrue;
Mais las de cultiver enfin
   La terre labourée,
L'un a dételé le matin,
   L'autre l'après-dînée.

brilliant, most enviable; in short, something unexampled, with one exception, in all the bygone ages; and even that example is not altogether analogous; something we cannot believe in Paris, and how can it be credited at Lyons? a thing which makes everybody cry, 'Lord have mercy on us!' a thing which fills Madame de Rohan and Madame de Hauterive with joy; a thing, in fine, which is to come off next Sunday; when those who behold it will fancy they see double. I cannot bring myself to divulge it. Can you guess it? I give you three chances. Do you give it up? Well, then, I must tell you, M. de Lauzun is to be married on Sunday, at the Louvre. To whom? I give you four, I give you ten, I give you a hundred guesses. Madame de Coulanges says: 'Ah! this is very hard to guess. Is it Madame de la Vallière?' Nothing of the kind, madame. 'Is it Mdlle. de Retz?' Not at all. How provincial you are! 'Ah!' you rejoin, 'we are really very stupid: it is Mdlle. Colbert.' Farther off than ever. 'Then it must be Mdlle. de Créquy.' No; you are no nearer than before. Then I must tell you, after all. He is to marry on Sunday at the Louvre, with the king's permission, mademoiselle, mademoiselle, mademoiselle de ——, mademoiselle? Guess the name, he marries mademoiselle. He does indeed! upon my word! I swear it! Yes, *the* mademoiselle, the great mademoiselle, mademoiselle, daughter of the late monsieur,[1] mademoiselle, grand-daughter of Henry the Fourth, Mademoiselle d'Eu, Mademoiselle de Dombes, Mademoiselle de Montpensier, Mademoiselle d'Orléans; mademoiselle, cousin-german to the king; mademoiselle, destined to the throne; mademoiselle, the only match in France worthy of monsieur. There's a fine topic for discourse! If you cry out; if you exclaim 'You are beside yourself;' if you say that we have lied, that it is false, that we are making fun of you, that it is a good joke, and that it is too silly for belief; if, in short, you call us hard names, we shall think you are quite right, we should do the same. Farewell; the letters you will receive by this post will tell you whether we are speaking the truth or otherwise."[2]

[1] Gaston of France, Duke of Athens, brother of Louis XIII.
[2] Je m'en vais vous mander la chose la plus étonnante, la plus surprenante, la plus merveilleuse, la plus miraculeuse, la plus triomphante, la plus étourdissante, la plus inouïe, la plus singulière, la plus extraordinaire, la plus incroyable, la plus imprévue, la plus grande, la plus petite, la plus rare, la plus commune, la plus éclatante, la plus secrète, jusqu'à aujourd'hui, la plus brillante, la plus digne d'envie; enfin une chose dont on ne trouve qu'un exemple dans les siècles passés : encore cet exemple n'est-il pas juste; une chose que l'on ne peut pas croire à Paris, comment la pourrait-on croire à Lyon? Une chose qui fait crier miséricorde à tout le monde; une chose qui comble de joie Madame de Rohan et Madame d'Hauterive; une chose enfin qui se fera dimanche, où ceux qui la verront croiront avoir la *berlue*; une chose qui se fera dimanche, et qui ne sera peut-être pas faite lundi. Je ne puis me résoudre à la dire; devinez-la; je vous le donne en trois. *Jetez-vous votre langue aux chiens ?* Eh bien! Il faut donc vous la dire: M. de Lauzun épouse dimanche au Louvre, devinez qui? Je vous le

To Monsieur de Coulanges.

December 19, 1670.

What is called falling from the clouds, or from a pinnacle, happened last night at the Tuileries; but I must go further back. You have already shared in the joy, the transport, and ecstasies of the princess and her happy lover. It was just as I told you: the affair was made public on Monday. Tuesday was passed in talking, astonishment, and compliments. Wednesday mademoiselle made a deed of gift to Monsieur de Lauzun, investing him with certain titles, names, and dignities, necessary to be inserted in the marriage contract, which was drawn up that day. She gave him then, till she could give him something better, four duchies: the first was that of Count d'Eu, which entitles him to rank as first peer of France; the dukedom of Montpensier, which title he bore all that day; the dukedom de Saint-Fargeau; and the dukedom of Châtellerault, the whole valued at twenty-two millions of livres. The contract was then drawn up, and he took the name of Montpensier. Thursday morning, which was yesterday, mademoiselle was in expectation of the king's signing the contract, as he had said he would; but, about seven o'clock in the evening, the queen, monsieur, and several old dotards that were about him, had so persuaded his majesty that his reputation would suffer in this affair that after sending for mademoiselle and Monsieur de Lauzun into his presence, he declared to them, before the prince, that he absolutely forbade them to think any further about this marriage. Monsieur de Lauzun received this order with all the respect, all the submission, all the firmness, and, at the same time, all the despair that could be expected in so great a reverse of fortune. As for

donne en quatre, je vous le donne en dix, je vous le donne en cent. Madame de Coulanges dit: Voilà qui est bien difficile à deviner! c'est Madame de la Vallière. Point du tout, madame. C'est donc mademoiselle de Retz? Point du tout; vous êtes bien provinciale. Vraiment, nous sommes bien bêtes, dites-vous: c'est mademoiselle Colbert. Encore moins. C'est assurément mademoiselle de Créquy. Vous n'y êtes pas. Il faut donc à la fin vous le dire: il épouse, dimanche, au Louvre, avec la permission du roi, mademoiselle, mademoiselle, mademoiselle de ——, mademoiselle, devinez le nom; il épouse mademoiselle, ma foi! par ma foi! ma foi jurée! Mademoiselle, la grande mademoiselle, mademoiselle, fille de feu monsieur; mademoiselle, petite-fille de Henri IV., mademoiselle d'Eu, mademoiselle de Dombes, mademoiselle de Montpensier, mademoiselle d'Orléans, mademoiselle, cousine germaine du roi; mademoiselle, destinée au trône; mademoiselle, le seul parti de France qui fût digne de monsieur. Voilà un beau sujet de discourir. Si vous criez, si vous êtes hors de vous-même, si vous dites que nous avons menti, que cela est faux, qu'on se moque de vous, que voilà une belle raillerie, que cela est bien fade à imaginer; si enfin vous nous dites des injures, nous trouverons que vous avez raison; nous en avons fait autant que vous. Adieu; les lettres qui seront portées par cet ordinaire vous feront voir si nous disons vrai ou non.

mademoiselle, being under no restraint, she gave full vent to her
feelings, and burst forth into tears, cries, lamentations, and the most
violent expressions of grief; she keeps her bed all day long, and
takes nothing within her lips but a little broth. What a fine dream
is here! What a glorious subject for a tragedy, or a romance, but
especially for an eternity of talk and argument! This is what we
do day and night, morning and evening, without staying or stopping.
We hope you do the like, 'E fra tanto vi bacio le mani.'[1]

The other letters which follow were addressed by
Madame de Sévigné to her daughter, Madame de Grignan,
of whom it is fitting to say a few words in this place. She
was an only daughter, as her brother Charles was the only
son of his parents; and her mother, who regarded her as the
prettiest girl in France—and she certainly was one of the
prettiest—lavished upon her a wealth of affection which was
never adequately reciprocated. Married at three-and-twenty
to the Comte de Grignan, a man who was nearly forty, who
had already buried two wives, and whose debts swallowed
up the whole of his wife's handsome dowry, the Comtesse

---

[1] Ce qui s'appelle tomber du haut des nues, c'est ce qui arriva hier
au soir aux Tuileries; mais il faut reprendre les choses de plus loin.
Vous en êtes à la joie, aux transports, aux ravissements de la princesse
et de son bienheureux amant. Ce fut donc lundi que la chose fut
déclarée, comme je vous l'ai mandée. Le mardi se passa à parler, à
s'étonner, à complimenter; le mercredi, mademoiselle fit une donation
à M. de Lauzun, avec dessein de lui donner les titres, les noms et les
ornements nécessaires pour être nommé dans le contrat de mariage qui
fut fait le même jour. Elle lui donna donc, en attendant mieux, quatre
duchés: le premier, c'est le comté d'Eu, qui est la première pairie de
France et qui donne le premier rang; le duché de Montpensier, dont il
porta hier le nom toute la journée; le duché de Saint-Fargeau, le duché
de Châtellerault: tout cela estimé vingt-deux millions. Le contrat fut
fait ensuite, où il prit le nom de Montpensier. Le jeudi matin, qui était
hier, mademoiselle espéra que le roi signerait le contrat, comme il l'avait
dit; mais, sur les sept heures du soir, sa majesté étant persuadée par la
reine, monsieur et plusieurs barbons, que cette affaire faisait tort à sa
réputation, il se résolut de la rompre et après avoir fait venir mademoiselle et M. de Lauzun, le roi leur déclara, devant M. le prince, qu'il
leur défendait de plus songer à ce mariage. M. de Lauzun reçut cet
ordre avec tout le respect, toute la soumission, toute la fermeté et tout
le désespoir que méritait une si grande chute. Pour mademoiselle,
suivant son humeur, elle éclata en pleurs, en cris, en douleurs violentes,
en plaintes excessives; et tout le jour elle n'a pas sorti de son lit,
sans rien avaler que des bouillons. Voilà un beau songe, voilà un beau
sujet de roman ou de tragédie, mais surtout un beau sujet de raisonner
et de parler éternellement: c'est ce que nous faisons jour et nuit, soir
et matin, sans fin, sans cesse; nous espérons que vous en ferez autant:
E fra tanto vi bacio le mani.

seems to have been of a cold, reserved, and unsympathetic nature, 'with an irritable temper and expensive habits.' She reminds one, indeed, of a sandy plain, which absorbs all the rain that falls upon its surface without exhibiting any sign of fertility in its turn. Her mother's cousin, Bussy-Rabutin, said of her, 'She has ability, but hers is a crabbed intellect, and her pride is insupportable. She will make as many enemies as her mother has made friends and admirers.' Bussy, it will be remembered, was one of these. And the opinion formed of her by the Duc de Saint-Simon was equally unfavourable. But either Madame de Sévigné was blinded by maternal affection to the faults of her daughter, or, knowing them, she resolutely closed her eyes and treated them as non-existent. At any rate, nothing could diminish the warmth and tenderness of the love for Madame de Grignan which breathes throughout her letters to her during a period of nearly twenty years; and we must be grateful to the recipient of that correspondence for having so carefully preserved what was destined to become one of the masterpieces of French literature. And if the affection of the mother for her unresponsive daughter had been less ardent and less enduring, those letters might never have been written, and Madame de Sévigné might have missed immortality, and many generations of cultivated readers in all parts of the civilised world would have been deprived of a personal source of instruction and delight; while the very knowledge we possess of Madame de Grignan's character communicates an accent of pathos to the correspondence which her mother addressed to her.

To Madame de Grignan.

Friday, February 20, 1671.

I declare to you I cannot express how desirous I am of hearing from you. Consider, my dear, I have not had a letter of yours since that from La Palice : I know nothing of the rest of your journey to Lyons, nor of your route to Provence. I am very certain that there are letters for me, but then I await them, and they don't come. I have nothing left to comfort and amuse me but in writing to you. You must know that Wednesday night last, after I came from M. de Coulanges', where we had been making up our packets for the post, I began to think of going to bed; that is nothing very extraordinary, you'll say, but what follows is more so; about three o'clock in the morning I was wakened with a cry of 'thieves! fire!' and it seemed so near, and grew so loud, that I had not the least doubt of its being in the house; I even fancied I heard them talking about my little grand-daughter. I imagined she was burnt, and with that idea got up without any light, and trembling in such a manner that I could scarcely stand. I ran directly to her room, which is the same that was yours, and found everything very quiet; but I presently saw Guitaut's house all in flames; the fire had caught that of Madame de Vauvineux. The flames cast a horrible light all over our court-yard and over Guitaut's, all was outcry, hurry, and confusion, and the beams and joists falling down made a dreadful noise. I immediately ordered our doors to be opened and sent my people to give their assistance. Monsieur de Guitaut sent me a casket containing his chief valuables, which I locked up in my cabinet, and then went into the street to gaze like the rest. There I found Monsieur and Madame Guitaut almost naked; Madame de Vauvineux, the Venetian ambassador, and all his people; with little Vauvineux whom they were carrying fast asleep to the ambassador's house, with a great quantity of rich movables and plate. Madame de Vauvineux had removed all her goods. As for our house, it was quite isolated, but I was greatly concerned for my poor neighbours. Madame Guêton and her brother gave some excellent directions, but we were all in great consternation; the fire was so fierce that there was no approaching it, nor any hope of extinguishing it until it had burnt poor Guitaut's house entirely down. He was really a melancholy object; he was anxious to save his mother, who was in the midst of the flames on the third floor, but his wife clung to him and violently held him back. He was in the greatest distress at being unable to save his mother, and from fear of hurting his wife, who was near five months *enceinte*. At last he begged me to hold her, which I did, and he went in search of his mother, whom he found quite safe after having run through the flames. He then endeavoured to save some papers, but found it impossible to get near the place where they were. At length he came back to us in the street where I had induced his wife to sit down. Some Capuchins full of charity and zeal had worked so well that they had succeeded in arresting the spread of the fire. Water was thrown upon the burning buildings and at last 'the conflict ceased for want of combatants;' that is to say, after several of the best apartments were entirely consumed. It was looked upon as a piece of good fortune that any part of the house was saved, though as it is poor Guitaut will lose at least ten thousand crowns; for they propose to rebuild the room, that was painted and gilded. M. Le Blanc, who owned the house, lost several fine pictures besides tables, looking-glasses, tapestry, and other valuable pieces of furniture. They are greatly concerned about some letters, which I take to be those of the prince. Well, by this it was nearly five o'clock in the morning, and time to think of getting Madame de Guitaut to rest; I offered her my bed; but Madame Guêton put her into hers, for she had several apartments in her house ready furnished. We had her bled, and sent for Boucher, who is apprehensive of a miscarriage from the violence of the fright. She is still at Madame Guêton's, where everybody goes to see her. You will ask me, perhaps, how the fire originated, but that nobody can tell. There was not a spark in the room where it first broke out; but surely, could any one have thought of being merry at such a melancholy time, what pictures might not have been drawn of us as we then appeared? Guitaut had nothing on but his shirt and a pair of drawers; his wife was bare-legged, and had lost one of her slippers; Madame de Vauvineux was in a short under-petticoat, without any night-gown on; all the footmen and the neighbours were in their night-caps. The ambassador in his night-gown and long peruke duly maintained the importance of a *serenissimo*, but his secretary was a most admirable figure. You talk of the chest of Hercules, but this was quite another thing; we had a full view of it: it was white, fat, plump, and quite bare, for the string that should have tied his shirt had been lost in the engagement. So much for the melancholy news of our quarter. Let me beg of Deville to take his rounds every night, after the family are in bed, to see that the fire is out everywhere, for one cannot be too careful to prevent accidents of this kind. I hope the waters have done you good; in a word I wish you every happiness, and implore God to preserve you from all evil.[1]

[1] Je vous avoue que j'ai une extraordinaire envie de savoir de vos nouvelles: songez, ma chère bonne, que je n'en ai point eu depuis la Palice; je ne sais rien du reste de votre voyage jusqu'à Lyon, ni de votre route jusqu'en Provence; je suis bien assurée qu'il me viendra des lettres; je ne doute point que vous ne m'ayez écrit; mais je les attends, et je ne les ai pas: il faut se consoler, et s'amuser en vous écrivant. Vous saurez, ma petite, qu'avant hier, mercredi, après être revenue de chez M. de Coulanges, où nous faisons nos paquets les jours d'ordinaire, je songeai à me coucher. Cela n'est pas extraordinaire; mais ce qui l'est beaucoup, c'est qu'à trois heures après minuit j'entendis crier Au voleur! au feu! et ces cris si près de moi, et si redoublés, que je ne doutai point que ce fût ici; je crus même entendre qu'on parlait de ma pauvre petite-fille; je ne doutai point qu'elle ne fût brûlée. Je me levai dans cette crainte, sans lumière, avec un tremblement qui m'empêchait quasi de me soutenir. Je courus à son appartement qui est le vôtre, je trouvai tout dans une grande tranquillité; mais je vis la maison de Guitaut toute en feu; les flammes passaient par-dessus la maison de Madame de Vauvineux: on voyait dans nos cours, et surtout chez M. de Guitaut, une clarté qui faisait horreur: c'étaient des cris, c'était une confusion, c'était un bruit épouvantable, des poutres et des solives qui tombaient. Je fis ouvrir ma porte, j'envoyai mes gens au secours. M. de Guitaut m'envoya une cassette de ce qu'il a de plus précieux; je la mis dans mon cabinet, et puis je voulus aller dans la rue pour bayer comme les autres; j'y trouvai M. et Madame de Guitaut quasi nus, Madame de Vauvineux, l'ambassadeur de Venise, tous ses gens, la petite de Vauvineux qu'on portait tout endormie chez l'ambassadeur, plusieurs meubles et vaisselles d'argent qu'on sauvait chez lui. Madame de Vauvineux faisait démeubler. Pour moi, j'étais comme dans une île, mais j'avais grande pitié de mes pauvres voisins. Madame Guêton et son frère donnaient de très-bons conseils; nous étions tous dans la consternation; le feu était si allumé qu'on n'osait en approcher, et l'on n'espérait la fin de cet embrasement qu'avec la fin de la maison de ce

To Madame de Grignan.
April 26, 1671.

This is Sunday, April 26, and this letter will not go out till Wednesday, but it is not so much a letter as an account just brought me by Moreuil, expressly for you, of what passed at Chantilly with regard to poor Vatel. I wrote to you last Friday, that he had stabbed himself; and I now give you the whole particulars of the affair. The king arrived there on Thursday night. The chase, the lanterns, the

pauvre Guitaut. Il faisait pitié; il voulait aller sauver sa mère qui brûlait au troisième étage; sa femme s'attachait à lui, et le retenait avec violence; il était entre la douleur de ne pas secourir sa mère, et la crainte de blesser sa femme, grosse de cinq mois. Enfin il me pria de tenir sa femme, je la fis; il trouva que sa mère avait passé au travers de la flamme, et qu'elle était sauvée. Il voulut aller retirer quelques papiers; il ne put approcher du lieu où ils étaient. Enfin il revint à nous dans cette rue où j'avais fait asseoir sa femme. Des capucins, pleins de charité et d'adresse, travaillèrent si bien qu'ils coupèrent le feu. On jeta de l'eau sur les restes de l'embrasement, et enfin le combat finit faute de combattants, c'est-à-dire après que le premier et le second étage de l'antichambre et de la petite chambre et du cabinet, qui sont à main droite du salon, eurent été entièrement consumés. On appela bonheur ce qui restait de la maison, quoiqu'il y ait pour Guitaut pour plus de dix mille écus de perte; car on compte de faire rétablir cet appartement, qui était peint et doré. Il y avait aussi plusieurs beaux tableaux à M. le Blanc, à qui est la maison; il y avait aussi plusieurs tables, miroirs, miniatures, meubles, tapisseries. Ils ont un grand regret à des lettres; je me suis imaginé que c'étaient des lettres de M. le prince. Cependant, vers les cinq heures du matin, il fallut songer à madame de Guitaut; je lui offris mon lit; mais madame Guêton la mit dans le sien, parce qu'elle a plusieurs chambres meublées. Nous la fîmes saigner; nous envoyâmes quérir Boucher; il craint bien que cette grande émotion ne la fasse accoucher devant neuf jours. Elle est donc chez cette pauvre madame Guêton; tout le monde la vient voir, et moi je continue mes soins, parce que j'ai trop bien commencé pour ne pas achever.

Vous m'allez demander comment le feu s'était mis à cette maison; on n'en sait rien, il n'y en avait point dans l'appartement où il a pris. Mais si on avait pu rire dans une si triste occasion, quels portraits n'aurait-on pas faits de l'état où nous étions tous? Guitaut était nu en chemise avec des chausses; madame de Guitaut était nu-jambes, et avait perdu une de ses mules de chambre; madame de Vauvineux était en petite jupe sans robe de chambre; tous les valets, tous les voisins, en bonnets de nuit. L'ambassadeur était en robe de chambre et en perruque, et conserva fort bien la gravité de la sérénissime. Mais son secrétaire était admirable. Vous parlez de la poitrine d'Hercule; vraiment celle-ci était bien autre chose; on la voyait tout entière; elle est blanche, grasse, potelée, et surtout sans aucune chemise, car le cordon qui la devait attacher avais été perdu à la bataille. Voilà les tristes nouvelles de notre quartier. Je prie M. Deville de faire tous les soirs une ronde pour voir si le feu est éteint partout; on ne saurait trop avoir de précaution pour éviter ce malheur. Je souhaite que l'eau vous ait été favorable; en un mot, je vous souhaite tous les biens, et prie Dieu qu'il vous garantisse de tous les maux.

moonlight, the promenade, and the collation served in a place strewed with jonquils, were everything that could be wished. They sat down to supper, but the *rôti* was wanting at some of the tables because they had been obliged to provide many more dinners than were expected. This troubled Vatel, and he was heard to say several times, 'I have lost my honour! I cannot bear this disgrace! My head is giddy,' said he to Gourville; 'I have not had a wink of sleep these twelve nights. I wish you would assist me in giving orders.' Gourville did all he could to comfort and assist him; but the want of the *rôti* (which however did not happen at the king's table, but at some of the other twenty-five) was always uppermost in his mind. Gourville mentioned it to the prince, who was so good as to go to Vatel's apartment, and say to him, 'It is all right, Vatel; nothing could be finer than his majesty's supper.' 'Your highness's goodness,' replied he, 'overwhelms me; I know the *rôti* was wanting at two tables.' 'Not at all,' said the prince; 'do not worry yourself, all is right.' Midnight came, the fireworks did not succeed, they were enveloped in cloud; they had cost sixteen thousand francs. At four o'clock in the morning, Vatel went everywhere about, and found all fast asleep; he met one of the under-purveyors who had arrived with only two loads of fish. 'Is that all?' said he. 'Yes, sir,' replied the man, not knowing that Vatel had despatched other people to all the sea-ports. Vatel waited for some time; no other purveyors arrived, his head became inflamed; he fancied there was no more water to be had; and finding Gourville: 'Sir,' said he, 'I cannot survive this disgrace. My honour and my reputation are at stake.' Gourville laughed at him: Vatel went up to his room, and placing the hilt of his sword against the door, ran himself through the heart at the third stroke, after giving himself two wounds which were not mortal; and then fell dead. At that moment the fish arrived from all parts; Vatel was inquired for to distribute it, they ran to his room, knocked at his door, broke it open, and found him bathed in his blood. The prince was hastily sent for, and was greatly distressed. The duke wept, for the success of his visit to Burgundy depended upon Vatel. The prince related the incident to his majesty with very great concern: it was looked upon as occasioned by a too scrupulous sense of honour; and some blamed while others praised his courage. The king said he had put off this excursion to Chantilly for five years, because he was sensible of the trouble it would give; and he told the prince that he ought to have had but two tables, and to have dispensed with the rest, vowing he would never suffer the prince to do the like again; but this was too late for poor Vatel. However Gourville endeavoured to supply the loss of Vatel, and did so. They dined luxuriously, refreshed themselves at intervals; they supped; they walked, they hunted; all was perfumed with jonquils; all was enchantment. Yesterday, which was Saturday there was a repetition of it all; and in the evening the king set out for Liancourt, where he had ordered a *media-noche* (midnight entertainment); he is to remain there to-day. This is what Moreuil

z

gave me to send to you; I do not care a straw for the rest, as I know nothing about it. M. D'Hacqueville, who was present, will no doubt tell you all about it; but as his handwriting is not so legible as mine, I invariably write myself, and I send you the fullest particulars, because, under similar circumstances, I should myself like to receive a circumstantial account.[1]

[1] Il est dimanche 26 avril; cette lettre ne partira que mercredi; mais ce n'est pas une lettre, c'est une relation que Moreuil vient de me faire, à votre intention, de ce qui s'est passé à Chantilly touchant Vatel. Je vous écrivis vendredi qu'il s'était poignardé; voici l'affaire en détail. Le roi arriva le jeudi au soir; la chasse, les lanternes, le clair de la lune, la promenade, la collation dans un lieu tapissé de jonquilles, tout cela fut à souhait. On soupa, il y eut quelques tables où le rôti manqua, à cause de plusieurs dîners à où l'on ne s'était point attendu. Cela saisit Vatel, il dit plusieurs fois: Je suis perdu d'honneur; voici un affront que je ne supporterai pas. Il dit à Gourville: La tête me tourne, il y a douze nuits que je n'ai dormi; aidez-moi à donner des ordres. Gourville le soulagea en ce qu'il put. Le rôti qui avait manqué, non pas à la table du roi, mais aux vingt-cinquièmes, lui revenait toujours à la tête. Gourville le dit à M. le prince. M. le prince alla jusque dans sa chambre, et lui dit: 'Vatel, tout va bien; rien n'était si beau que le souper du roi.' Il répondit: 'Monseigneur, votre bonté m'achève; je sais que le rôti a manqué à deux tables.' 'Point du tout,' dit M. le prince: 'ne vous fâchez point: tout va bien.' La nuit vient, le feu d'artifice ne réussit pas, il fut couvert d'un nuage; il coûtait seize mille francs. A quatre heures du matin, Vatel s'en va partout, il trouve tout endormi, il rencontre un petit pourvoyeur qui lui apportait seulement deux charges de marée; il lui demanda: 'Est-ce là tout?' 'Oui, monsieur.' Il ne savait pas que Vatel avait envoyé à tous les ports de mer. Vatel attend quelque temps; les autres pourvoyeurs ne viennent point; sa tête s'échauffait, il croit qu'il n'aura point d'autre marée; il trouve Gourville, il lui dit 'Monsieur, je ne survivrai pas à cet affront-ci.' Gourville se moqua de lui. Vatel monte à sa chambre, met son épée contre la porte, et se la passe au travers du cœur; mais ce ne fut qu'au troisième coup, car il s'en donna deux qui n'étaient point mortels; il tombe mort. La marée cependant arrive de tous côtés: on cherche Vatel pour la distribuer, on va à sa chambre; on heurte, on enfonce la porte; on le trouve noyé dans son sang; on court à M. le prince, qui fut au désespoir. M. le duc pleura; c'était sur Vatel que tournait tout son voyage de Bourgogne. M. le prince le dit au roi fort tristement: on dit que c'était à force d'avoir de l'honneur en sa manière; on le loua fort, on loua et blâma son courage. Le roi dit qu'il y avait cinq ans qu'il retardait de venir à Chantilly, parce qu'il comprenait l'excès de cet embarras. Il dit à M. le prince qu'il ne devait avoir que deux tables, et ne point se charger de tout le reste. Il jura qu'il ne souffrirait plus que M. le prince en usât ainsi; mais c'était trop tard pour le pauvre Vatel. Cependant Gourville tâche de réparer la perte de Vatel; elle fut réparée: on dîna très-bien, on fit collation, on soupa, on se promena, on joua, on fut à la chasse; tout était parfumé de jonquilles, tout était enchanté. Hier, qui était samedi, on fit encore de même; et le soir, le roi alla à Liancourt, où il avait commandé *media-noche*; il y doit demeurer aujourd'hui. Voilà ce que Moreuil m'a dit, pour vous mander. Je jette mon bonnet par-dessus le moulin, et je ne

To Madame de Grignan.
April 27, 1671.

Monsieur and madame de Villars are about to leave me, and they send you thousands of compliments; they want a copy of your picture which hangs over my mantelpiece, to take with them to Spain. My little girl has been all day in my room, arrayed in her beautiful lace, and does the honours of the house; a house that reminds me continually of you, and where you were a prisoner for nearly a year. It is a house that every one comes to see, every one admires, and that no one will occupy. I supped the other evening with the Marchioness d'Uxelles, Madame la Maréchale d'Humières, Mesdames d'Arpajon, de Beringhen, de Frontenac, d'Outrelaise, Raimond, and Martin; you were not forgotten. I entreat you, my dear child, to send me a true account of your health, and of all your plans and of what you wish me to do. I am very uneasy about your condition, and am afraid you are not sufficiently so yourself. I foresee a thousand vexations, and a train of thought runs through my head, that is not good for me by day or night. I am beset with countless worries, and thoughts course through my mind which make day and night alike miserable.[1]

April 29.

Since I began this letter, my darling, I have made a pretty little excursion. I set out from Paris yesterday morning, and went to dine at Pomponne, where I found our good friend, who expected me. I was unwilling to go without taking my leave of him. I found in him a wonderful deepening of spirituality, and his mind seems to grow more pure the nearer he approaches death. He scolded me very seriously, carried away by the warmth of his zeal and friendship for me; he told me I was foolish not to have yet thought of my conversion; that I was a pretty pagan. He said that I had made an idol of you in my heart; that this sort of idolatry was just as dangerous as any other, although, perhaps, I

sais rien du reste. M. d'Hacqueville, qui était à tout cela, vous fera des relations sans doute ; mais comme son écriture n'est pas si lisible que la mienne, j'écris toujours ; et si je vous mande cette infinité de détails, c'est que je les aimerais en pareille occasion.

[1] Monsieur, Madame de Villars, et la petite Saint-Gerand sortent d'ici, et vous font mille et mille amitiés. Ils veulent la copie de votre portrait qui est sur ma cheminée, pour la porter en Espagne. Ma petite enfant a été tout le jour dans ma chambre, parée de ses belles dentelles, et faisant l'honneur du logis ; ce logis qui me fait tant songer à vous, où vous étiez il y a un an comme prisonnière ; ce logis que tout le monde vient voir, que tout le monde admire, et que personne ne veut *louer*. Je soupai l'autre jour chez le marquis d'Uxelles, avec madame la maréchale d'Humières, mesdames d'Arpajon, de Beringhen, de Frontenac, d'Outrelaise, Raimond et Martin. Vous n'y fûtes point oubliée. Je vous conjure, ma fille, de me mander sincèrement des nouvelles de votre santé, de vos desseins, de ce que vous souhaitez de moi. Je suis triste de votre état, je crains que vous ne le soyez aussi ; je vois mille chagrins, et j'ai une suite de pensées dans ma tête, qui ne sont bonnes ni pour la nuit ni pour le jour.

might look upon it as less criminal; and that I ought to think of my own salvation. He said all this so powerfully that I had not a word to say. At length, after a grave but very agreeable conversation of six hours, I took my leave of him, and came here, where I found May in all its glory. The nightingale, the cuckoo, and the linnet, have already 'opened the spring in our woods.' I walked alone the whole evening, finding much food for melancholy thought, which I shall withhold from you. . . . I have reserved a part of this afternoon for writing to you in the garden, where I am almost deafened by three or four nightingales perched over my head. I shall return in the evening to Paris, where I shall make up my packet and send it to you.

I must confess, my dear, that there is a degree of warmth yet wanting in my love for you. I ought to have set out with the galley-slaves when I met them, instead of being content to write to you by them. I reproach myself for so doing. How agreeable a surprise would it have been to you to have met me at Marseilles in such good company! And so you propose going thither in a litter. What a whim! I have noticed that you were only fond of litters when they were unattainable; how you are changed! I am entirely at one with your detractors, and the only credit I can allow you is to believe that you never could have been brought to make use of such a conveyance, if you had not left me, or if M. de Grignan had remained in Provence. How sorry I am for this misfortune! Pray take care of yourself, my dearest, and think how the Guisarde beauty, by getting about too soon after a favourable accouchement, was so seriously injured that for three days she was lying at the point of death. Let that be a warning to you. Madame de la Fayette is always apprehensive for your life; she makes no scruple of allowing you the first place in my own heart, on account of your perfections; and when she is in a good humour she says she does it without the least pain, but that being settled and approved, she thinks she is justly entitled to the second place in my love, and it is hers, although La Troche is dying with envy. I go on always in the old way, and my way leads me also to Brittany. It is certain we shall lead very different lives; mine will be greatly troubled by the States, who will come to torment me at Vitré, towards the end of July, greatly to my annoyance. Your brother will be gone before that. My dear child, you wish time to fly more quickly until we meet again. You know not what you do; you will be disappointed. Time will obey you only too exactly, and when you want to stop him you will find you are no longer his mistress. I was formerly guilty of the same fault as you, and have had reason to repent it; for though he has been more lenient to me than to many others, yet he has left too many marks of his passage by the loss of a thousand little enjoyments which he has taken away from me. So you find that your comedians require some intelligence to be able to repeat the verses of Corneille. Some of them are, indeed, ravishingly fine. I amused myself agreeably yesterday evening with a volume of his works that I brought with me. But are you not greatly pleased with five or six of the Fables of La Fontaine in that volume I sent you? We were quite delighted with them the other day at Monsieur de la Rochefoucauld's, and learnt that of the Monkey and the Cat by heart, and that of the Pumpkin and the Nightingale is worthy of a place in the first volume. How foolish I am to write about such trifles! Well, this idleness at Livry will be the death of you. The note you wrote Brancas is admirable; he wrote you a whole quire of paper the other day. It was a rhapsody, but tolerably good. He read it to Madame de Coulanges and myself, and I told him to finish it by Wednesday, and send it to me. 'Not I, indeed,' said he; 'she shall not see a line of it; it is such wretched stuff.' 'But,' said I, 'what do you take us for? We have heard you read it; we know what it is.' 'That may be, but she shan't see it, for all that.' He was never so foolish as now.... What do you think, my dear, of the infinite length of this letter? I could find it in my heart to write till this time to-morrow. Be careful of yourself, my darling. This is the constant burden of my song. Beware of a fall, and keep your bed now and then. Inasmuch as I have given my little one a nurse, as in the time of Francis the First, I think you should pay attention to my advice. Do you suppose I will not come and see you this year? I had, indeed, made other arrangements, and all for your sake too; but your litter has upset everything. How can I help making an excursion this year, if it is never so little your wish? Alas! I may well say that I have no fixed abode, except where you are. Your picture hangs in triumph over my mantelpiece. You are at present adored in Provence, in Paris, at Court, and at Livry; in short, child, you must certainly become ungrateful, for how can you return all this? I embrace you and love you, and shall ever tell you so, because it will be ever the same. I would embrace that rogue Grignan, too, but that I am angry with him.

Poor Paul[1] died about a week ago: our garden is all in mourning for him.[2]

[1] The gardener at Livry.

[2] Depuis que j'ai écrit ce commencement de lettre, j'ai fait hier, ma chère bonne, un fort joli voyage. Je partis assez matin de Paris; j'allai dîner à Pomponne; j'y trouvai notre bonhomme qui m'attendait; je n'aurais pas voulu manquer à lui dire adieu. Je le trouvai dans une augmentation de sainteté qui m'étonna: plus il approche de la mort, plus il s'épure. Il me gronda très-sérieusement; et transporté de zèle et d'amitié pour moi, il me dit que j'étais folle de ne point songer à me convertir; que j'étais une jolie païenne; que je faisais de vous une idole dans mon cœur; que cette sorte d'idolâtrie était aussi dangereuse qu'une autre, quoiqu'elle me parût moins criminelle; qu'enfin je songeasse à moi. Il me dit tout cela si fortement, que je n'avais pas le mot à dire. Enfin, après six heures de conversation très-agréable, quoique très-sérieuse, je le quittai, et vins ici, où je trouvai tout le triomphe du mois de mai.

> Le rossignol, le coucou, la fauvette,
> Dans nos forêts ont ouvert le printemps.

Je m'y suis promenée tout le soir toute seule; j'y ai trouvé mes tristes pensées: mais je ne veux plus vous en parler..... J'ai destiné une

To Madame de Grignan.

Paris : January 13, 1672.

For heaven's sake, my dear child, what are you talking about ? What pleasure can you find in thus abusing your person and understanding, and depreciating your own goodness, and in concluding that one must have a great deal of good nature to think of you ? Although surely you do not think all this, yet it wounds and angers me. You really make me angry with you, and though

partie de cette après-dîner à vous écrire dans ce jardin, où je suis étourdie de trois ou quatre rossignols qui sont sur ma tête. Ce soir je m'en retourne à Paris, pour faire mon paquet et vous l'envoyer.

Il est vrai, ma fille, qu'il manqua un degré de chaleur à mon amitié, quand je rencontrai la chaîne des galériens ; je devais aller avec eux vous trouver, au lieu de ne songer qu'à vous écrire ; je m'en fais des reproches à moi-même. Que vous eussiez été agréablement surprise à Marseille, de me trouver en si bonne compagnie ! Mais vous y allez donc en litière : quelle fantaisie ! J'ai vu que vous n'aimiez que quand elles étaient arrêtées : vous êtes bien changée. Je suis entièrement du parti des médisants : tout l'honneur que je vous puis faire, est de croire que jamais vous ne vous fussiez servie de cette voiture, si vous ne m'aviez point quittée, et quo M. de Grignan fût demeuré dans sa Provence. Que je suis fâchée de ce malheur ! Conservez-vous, ma très-chère ; songez que la Guisarde beauté ayant voulu se prévaloir d'une heureuse couche, s'est blessée rudement, et qu'elle a été trois jours prête à mourir : voilà un bel exemple. Madame de la Fayette craint toujours pour votre vie : elle vous cède sans difficulté la première place auprès de moi, à cause de vos perfections ; et quand elle est douce, elle dit que ce n'est pas sans peine ; mais enfin cela est réglé et approuvé : cette justice la rend digne de la seconde, elle l'a aussi ; la Troche s'en meurt. Je vais toujours mon train et mon train aussi pour la Bretagne. Il est vrai que nous ferons des vies bien différentes : je serai bien troublée dans la mienne par les états, qui me viendront tourmenter à Vitré sur la fin du mois de juillet ; cela me déplaît fort. Votre frère n'y sera plus en ce temps-là. Ma fille, vous souhaitez que le temps marche pour nous revoir ; vous ne savez ce que vous faites ; vous y serez attrapée : il vous obéira trop exactement, et quand vous voudrez le retenir, vous n'en serez plus la maîtresse. J'ai fait autrefois les mêmes fautes que vous, je m'en suis repentie, et quoique le temps ne m'ait pas fait tout le mal qu'il fait aux autres, il ne laisse pas de m'avoir ôté mille petits agréments, qui ne laissent que trop de marques de son passage.

Vous trouvez donc que vos comédiens ont bien de l'esprit de dire des vers de Corneille. En vérité, il y en a de bien transportants ; j'en ai apporté ici un tome qui m'amusa fort hier au soir. Mais n'avez-vous point trouvé jolies les cinq ou six fables de La Fontaine, qui sont dans un des tomes que je vous ai envoyés ? Nous en étions ravis l'autre jour chez M. de la Rochefoucauld ; nous apprîmes par cœur celle *Du Singe et du Chat.* Et la *Citrouille*, et le *Rossignol*, cela est digne du premier tome. Je suis bien folle de vous écrire de telles bagatelles : c'est le loisir de Livry qui vous tue. Vous avez écrit un billet admirable à Brancas ; il vous écrivit l'autre jour une main tout entière de papier : c'était une rapsodie assez bonne ; il nous la lut à madame de Coulanges

I ought not, perhaps, to answer things that are only said in joke, yet I cannot help scolding you before I go any further. It is very rich, your saying that you are afraid of the wits. Alas! my dear, if you knew how insignificant they are when you come near them, and how much they are taken up with their own persons at times, you would very soon take the right measure of them. Do you remember how tired you used to be of them sometimes? Do not let distance magnify objects too much; it is one of its usual effects.

We sup every evening at Madame Scarron's.[1] She has a most engaging wit, and is surprisingly sagacious. These conversations sometimes show us what a far cry it is from the morality of Christ to the morality of statesmen. It is interesting to hear her discussing the terrible troubles of a certain country which she knows well; and the vexations that Heudicourt undergoes at a time when his position appeared to be so dazzling; the continual rage of little Lauzun; the gloomy chagrin and depressing *ennui* of the ladies at St. Germain's, from which the most envied of them are not always exempt. It was pleasant to hear her conversing on all this; and these discourses sometimes carried us far afield, from one moral reflection to another, sometimes of a religious and sometimes of a political kind. We very often spoke of you: she is fond of your wit and manners; and whenever you return hither, you need not fear to be out of favour. . . .

But listen while I tell you of the king's goodness, and of the pleasure it is to serve so amiable a master. He sent for Marshal Bellefonds into his closet the other day, and thus addressed him: 'Monsieur le Maréchal, I wish to know why you want to leave

et à moi. Je lui dis: Envoyez-le-moi donc tout achevé pour mercredi. Il me dit qu'il n'en ferait rien, qu'il ne voulait pas que vous la vissiez; que cela était trop sot et trop misérable. Pour qui nous prenez-vous? vous nous l'avez bien lu. Tant y a que je ne veux pas qu'elle le lise. Voilà toute la raison que j'en ai eue; jamais il ne fut si fou. Que dites-vous, ma chère enfant, de l'infinité de cette lettre? Si je voulais, j'écrirais jusqu'à demain. Conservez-vous, c'est ma ritournelle continuelle; ne tombez point, gardez quelquefois le lit. Depuis que j'ai donné à ma petite une nourrice comme celle du temps de François 1er, je crois que vous devez honorer tous mes conseils. Pensez-vous que je n'aille point vous voir cette année? J'avais rangé tout cela d'une autre façon, et même pour l'amour de vous; mais votre litière me dérange tout: le moyen de ne pas courir cette année, si vous le souhaitez un peu? Hélas! c'est bien moi qui dois dire qu'il n'y a plus de pays fixe pour moi, que celui où vous êtes. Votre portrait triomphe sur ma cheminée; vous êtes adorée présentement en Provence, et à Paris, à la cour, et à Livry. Enfin, ma fille, il faut bien que vous soyez ingrate: le moyen de rendre tout cela? Je vous embrasse et vous aime, et vous le dirai toujours, parce que c'est toujours la même chose. J'embrasserais ce fripon de Grignan, si je n'étais fâchée contre lui.

Maître Paul mourut il y a huit jours; notre jardin en est tout triste.

[1] Afterwards Madame de Maintenon and wife of Louis XIV.

me. Is it devotion? Is it from an inclination to retire, or is it on account of your debts? If it is the latter, I myself will take care of them, and inform myself of the state of your affairs.' The Maréchal was sensibly touched by this goodness. 'Sire,' answered he, 'it is my debts; I am overwhelmed by them, and cannot bear to see some of my friends, who have assisted me with their fortunes, likely to suffer on my account, without having it in my power to satisfy them.' 'Well, then,' said the king, 'they shall have security for what is owing them. I now give you a hundred thousand francs on your house at Versailles, and a grant of four hundred thousand more, as a security in case of your death. The hundred thousand francs will enable you to pay off the arrears, and so now you remain in my service.' That heart must be very insensible, indeed, that could refuse the most implicit obedience to such a master, who enters with so much goodness and condescension into the interests of his servants. Accordingly the marshal made no further resistance; he is now reinstated in his place and loaded with favours. This is all strictly true.

Not a night passes at St. Germain's without balls, plays, or masquerades. The king shows an assiduity to divert madame that he never did for the others. Racine has written a comedy, entitled 'Bajazet,' which they say carries everything before it. Certainly it does not go on *emperando*, as the others did. Monsieur de Tallard says that it as much exceeds the best piece of Corneille's as Corneille's does one of Boyer's. This is something like praise; we must not hide the truth. We shall judge of it by our ears. I want to go, therefore, to the play.

I have been at Livry. Ah! my dear child, how well did I keep my word with you, and how tenderly I thought of you! It was delightful weather, though very cold; but the sun shone, every tree was hung with pearls and crystals, which made a pleasing diversity. I walked a great deal. The next day I dined at Pomponne. How can I tell you all that passed during a stay of five hours? However, I was not at all tired with my visit. Monsieur de Pomponne will be here in four days. I should be very much vexed if I was to be obliged to apply to him about your Provence affairs; I am persuaded he would not hear me. You see I give myself airs of knowledge. But really nothing comes up to M. d'Uzès; I never saw a man of better understanding, nor one more capable of giving sound advice. I wait to see him, that I may inform you of what he has done at St. Germain's.

You desire me to write you long letters. I think, my dear, you ought to be contented; I am sometimes frightened at their immensity. It is your flatteries that give me confidence.[1]

[1] Eh! mon Dieu, ma fille, que dites-vous? Quel plaisir prenez-vous à dire du mal de votre personne, de votre esprit; à rebaisser votre bonne conduite; à trouver qu'il faut avoir bien de la bonté pour songer à vous? Quoique assurément vous ne pensiez point tout cela, j'en suis blessée, vous me fâchez, et quoique je ne dusse peut-être pas répondre à des choses que vous dites en badinant, je ne puis m'empêcher de vous

To Madame de Grignan.

Paris: March 16, 1672.

You speak of my departure. Alas! my dear, I languish in that pleasing hope; nothing now prevents it but my aunt, who is dying of grief and the dropsy. It breaks my heart to witness her sufferings, and to listen to her tender and moving language; her courage, patience, and resignation are altogether admirable. Monsieur d'Hacqueville and I watch her from day to day; he sees my inmost heart, and knows how grieved I am not to be at liberty just now. I am entirely guided by him, and all will be

en gronder, préférablement à tout ce que j'ai à vous mander. Vous êtes bonne encore quand vous dites que vous avez peur des beaux esprits. Hélas! ma chère, si vous saviez qu'ils sont petits de près, et combien ils sont quelquefois empêchés de leurs personnes, vous les remettriez bientôt à hauteur d'appui. Vous souvient-il combien vous en étiez quelquefois lasse? Prenez garde que l'éloignement ne vous grossisse les objets; c'est un effet assez ordinaire.

Nous soupons tous les soirs avec madame Scarron. Elle a l'esprit aimable et merveilleusement droit; c'est un plaisir que de l'entendre raisonner sur les horribles agitations d'un certain pays qu'elle connaît bien. Les désespoirs qu'avait cette d'Heudicourt dans le temps que sa place paraissait si miraculeuse; les rages continuelles de Lauzun, les noirs chagrins ou les tristes ennuis des dames de Saint-Germain, et peut-être que la plus enviée [madame de Montespan] n'en est pas toujours exempte : c'est une plaisante chose que de l'entendre causer de tout cela. Ces discours nous mènent quelquefois bien loin, de moralité en moralité, tantôt chrétienne, et tantôt politique. Nous parlons très-souvent de vous; elle aime votre esprit et vos manières; et quand vous vous retrouverez ici, vous n'aurez point à craindre de n'être pas à la mode. . . . . .

Mais écoutez la bonté du roi, et songez au plaisir de servir un si aimable maître. Il a fait appeler le maréchal de Bellefonds dans son cabinet, et lui a dit: 'Monsieur le maréchal, je veux savoir pourquoi vous me voulez quitter : est-ce dévotion? est-ce envie de vous retirer? est-ce l'accablement de vos dettes? Si c'est le dernier, j'y veux donner ordre, et entrer dans le détail de vos affaires.' Le maréchal fut sensiblement touché de cette bonté. 'Sire, dit-il, ce sont mes dettes; je suis abîmé; je ne puis voir souffrir quelques-uns de mes amis qui m'ont assisté, et que je ne puis satisfaire.' 'Eh bien!' dit le roi, 'il faut assurer leur dette : je vous donne cent mille francs de votre maison de Versailles, et un brevet de retenue de quatre cent mille francs, qui servira d'assurance, si vous veniez à mourir; vous payerez les arrérages avec les cent mille francs; cela étant, vous demeurerez à mon service.' En vérité, il faudrait avoir le cœur bien dur pour ne pas obéir à un maître qui entre avec tant de bonté dans les intérêts d'un de ses domestiques : aussi le maréchal ne résista pas; et le voilà remis à sa place et comblé de bienfaits. Tout ce détail est vrai.

Il y a tous les soirs des bals, des comédies et des mascarades à Saint-Germain. Le roi a une application à divertir madame, qu'il n'a jamais eue pour l'autre. Racine a fait une tragédie qui s'appelle *Bajazet*, et qui en lève la paille; vraiment elle ne va pas *emperando* comme

decided between this and Easter. If her illness increases as much as it has done since I came hither, she will die in our arms; but if she should obtain some little relief and be likely to linger for any time, I will set out as soon as M. de Coulanges comes back. Our poor abbé is in despair, as well as myself; but we shall see how things turn out in the month of April. I have nothing else in my head. You cannot wish to see me more than I do to embrace you; so restrain your ambition, and do not hope to equal me in that respect.

My son tells me they are miserable in Germany, and don't know what they are doing. He was much grieved at the death of the Chevalier de Grignan. You ask me, my dear child, if I am as fond of life as ever. I must own to you that it has its mortifications, and these are very acute, but death is still more displeasing to me. I look upon it as so great a misfortune to be obliged to end all one's pursuits by that, that I should desire nothing better than to come back again. I find myself in an embarrassing position. I was brought into life without my own consent; I must leave it again, and that overwhelms me; for how shall I leave it? In what manner? By what door? When will it be? And what disposition shall I be in? Am I to suffer a thousand and one pangs which will make me die in desperation? Shall I lose my senses? Shall I die by an accident? How shall I stand with God? What shall I have to offer to Him? Will fear and necessity impel me to turn towards Him? How am I sure that I shall have no other sentiment but that of fear? Yet what have I to hope? Am I worthy of entering into Paradise, or am I deserving of hell?

les autres. M. de Tallard dit qu'elle est autant au-dessus des pièces de Corneille, que celles de Corneille sont au-dessus de celles de Boyer: voilà ce qui s'appelle louer; il ne faut point tenir les vérités captives. Nous en jugerons par nos yeux et par nos oreilles.

J'ai été à Livry. Hélas! ma chère enfant, que je vous ai bien tenu parole, et que j'ai songé tendrement à vous! Il y faisait très-beau, quoique très-froid; mais le soleil brillait; tous les arbres étaient parés de perles et de cristaux : cette diversité ne déplaît point. Je me promenai fort: je fus le lendemain dîner à Pomponne : quel moyen de vous redire ce qui fut dit en cinq heures ? Je ne m'y ennuyai point. M. de Pomponne sera ici dans quatre jours; ce serait un grand chagrin pour moi si jamais j'étais obligée à lui aller parler pour vos affaires de Provence : tout de bon, il ne m'écouterait pas ; vous voyez que je fais un peu l'entendue. Mais, de bonne foi, rien n'est égal à M. d'Uzès ; c'est ce qui s'appelle les grosses cordes ; je n'ai jamais vu un homme, ni d'un meilleur esprit, ni d'un meilleur conseil: je l'attends pour vous parler de ce qu'il aura fait à Saint-Germain.

Vous me priez de vous écrire de grandes lettres ; je pense que vous devez en être contente ; je suis quelquefois épouvantée de leur immensité : ce sont toutes vos flatteries qui me donnent cette confiance. Je vous conjure de vous conserver dans ce bienheureux état, et ne passer point d'une extrémité à l'autre. De bonne foi ; prenez du temps pour vous rétablir, et ne tentez point Dieu par vos dialogues et par votre voisinage.

Dreadful alternative! Alarming uncertainty! Nothing is so foolish as to leave one's salvation in doubt. Yet nothing is more natural, and the silly life I lead is so easy to comprehend. I lose myself in these thoughts, and I find death so terrible that I hate life more for leading me thither than for the thorns with which it is bestrewed. You will tell me that I wish to live for ever? Not at all; but if I had been consulted in the matter, I should much have liked to die in my nurse's arms; it would have spared me many vexations, and would have secured heaven for me very surely and easily. But let us talk of something else.

I am distressed that you should have received 'Bajazet' from any hand but mine. It is that rascal Barbin, who hates me because I do not write 'Princesses of Cleves and Montpensier.' You have formed a very true and just judgment of 'Bajazet,' and you will have seen that I am of your opinion; I wish I could send you Champmeslé[1] to enliven it a little. The character of Bajazet wants life, and the manners of the Turks are very badly portrayed; they do not make so much fuss about marrying; the dénouement is not well prepared; and there are no reasons for such a deal of slaughter. Nevertheless, the piece contains some agreeable passages, but nothing perfectly fine, nothing that thrills one; none of those speeches of Corneille's which make one quiver. Far be it from us, my child, to compare Racine with him; we must always be sensible of the difference between them. There are frigid and feeble scenes in Racine's plays, and he will never excel 'Alexandre' and 'Andromaque.' In the opinion of many people, and in my own, if I might venture to quote myself, 'Bajazet' is inferior to both of these. Racine's plays are written for Champmeslé, and not for posterity. If ever he ceases to be youthful and to be amorous, the same thing will not happen. Long live, then, our old friend Corneille! and let us forgive his bad verses for the sake of those divine and sublime beauties that transport us, and of those masterly strokes which are inimitable. Despréaux has said far more before me; and in a word, it is the verdict of good taste: let us abide by it.

Here is a *bon mot* of Madame de Cornuel's, which has highly diverted the parterre. M. Tambonneau, the son, has quitted the long robe, and has put a belt round his waist. With his gentility he wants to go to sea; I do not know what the land has done to him; however, somebody told Madame de Cornuel that he was going to sea. 'Alas!' said she, 'has he been bitten by a mad dog?' As this was said without malice, it made people laugh extremely.

Madame de Courcelles[2] is greatly embarrassed. They have rejected all her petitions; but she says she is still in hopes that she

---

[1] The famous actress who played the leading character in it.

[2] One of the loveliest women of the time, who was prosecuted by her husband—a worthless scamp—on a charge of adultery, in order to enable him to get hold of her fortune.

will have some favour shown her, as men are to be her judges. Our coadjutor will show her no mercy, just now; you tell me he is at present occupied like St. Ambrose. It seems to me that you ought to be content that your daughter was made after his *image and likeness*, without having your son like him too : but without offence to the coadjutor's beauty, where did the little rogue get his pretty small mouth, and all the rest of his winsomeness ? I find after all he resembles his sister ; this resemblance puzzles me a good deal. I love you fondly, my dear daughter, for not being *enceinte* ; content yourself then with being uselessly handsome, with the pleasure of not being continually dying . . . Ah! my dear, I can well understand how people like you employ their time and thoughts among your provincials : I should find them just as you do, and pity you all my days for passing so many of the best years of your life among them. I am so little desirous of shining at your court in Provence, and judge it so well by what I know of that of Brittany, that for the same reason that, in less than three days after being at Vitré, I wished for nothing so much as to return to my Rocks, so I solemnly declare to you the sole object of my desire is to pass the summer with you at Grignan, and nowhere else. My St. Laurence wine is at Adhémar's; I shall have it to-morrow ; it is a long time since I thanked you for it *in petto*, which is very obliging. M. de Laon is very well pleased at the manner in which he has been made a cardinal. I am told that M. de Montausier, in talking to the dauphin about the dignity of cardinal, told him that it depended entirely upon the Pope, and that if he had a mind to raise a groom to the purple he could do so. Just at that instant in came Cardinal Bonzi ; the dauphin, seeing him, asked him if it was true that the Pope could make a groom a cardinal. His eminence was a little surprised at first, till guessing the affair, he made answer, that doubtless the Pope might make choice of whom he pleased for that dignity; but that he had never heard of his Holiness taking a cardinal from his stables. I had the whole of this story from the Cardinal de Bouillon.[1]

---

[1] Vous me parlez de mon départ : ah ! ma chère fille, je languis dans cet espoir charmant. Rien ne m'arrête que ma tante, qui se meurt de douleur et d'hydropisie : elle me brise le cœur par l'état où elle est, et par tout ce qu'elle dit de tendre et de bon sens. Son courage, sa patience, sa résignation, tout cela est admirable. M. d'Hacqueville et moi, nous suivons son mal jour à jour : il voit mon cœur, et la douleur que j'ai de n'être pas libre tout présentement. Je me conduis par ses avis; nous verrons entre ci et Pâques. Si son mal augmente, comme il a fait depuis que je suis ici, elle mourra entre nos bras: si elle reçoit quelque soulagement, et qu'elle prenne le train de languir, je partirai dès que M. de Coulanges sera revenu. Notre pauvre abbé est au désespoir, aussi bien que moi ; nous verrons donc comme cet excès de mal se tournera dans le mois d'avril. Je n'ai que cela dans la tête : vous ne sauriez avoir tant d'envie de me voir que j'en ai de vous embrasser: bornez votre ambition, et ne croyez pas me pouvoir jamais égaler là-dessus.

Mon fils me mande qu'ils sont misérables en Allemagne, et ne savent

To Madame de Grignan.

Paris, August 28, 1675.

My dear child,—If I had the means of sending letters to you every day, I could easily contrive to write them. I sometimes do write daily, although I do not send the letters away. The pleasure of writing is reserved for you alone. If I write to others it is because I am bound to do so. I am now going to speak to you again of M. de Turenne. Madame d'Elbeuf, who is spending some few days with the Cardinal, her brother, invited me to dine with them yesterday, and to talk over their affliction. Madame de la Fayette

ce qu'ils font. Il a été très-affligé de la mort du chevalier de Grignan. Vous me demandez, ma chère enfant, si j'aime toujours bien la vie : je vous avoue que j'y trouve des chagrins cuisants ; mais je suis encore plus dégoûtée de la mort : je me trouve si malheureuse d'avoir à finir tout ceci par elle, que, si je pouvais retourner en arrière, je ne demanderais pas mieux. Je me trouve dans un engagement qui m'embarrasse : je suis embarquée dans la vie sans mon consentement ; il faut que j'en sorte, cela m'assomme ; et comment en sortirai-je ? Par où, par quelle porte ? Quand sera-ce ? En quelle disposition ? Souffrirai-je mille et mille douleurs, qui me feront mourir désespérée ? Aurai-je un transport au cerveau ? Mourrai-je d'un accident ? Comment serai-je avec Dieu ? Qu'aurai-je à lui présenter ? La crainte, la nécessité feront-elles mon retour vers lui ? N'aurai-je aucun autre sentiment que celui de la peur ? Que puis-je espérer ? Suis-je digne du paradis ? Suis-je digne de l'enfer ? Quelle alternative ! Quel embarras ! Rien n'est si fou que de mettre son salut dans l'incertitude ; mais rien n'est si naturel, et la sotte vie que je mène est la chose du monde la plus aisée à comprendre. Je m'abîme dans ces pensées, et je trouve la mort si terrible que je hais plus la vie parce qu'elle m'y mène, que par les épines qui s'y recontrent. Vous me direz que je veux donc vivre éternellement ; point du tout ; mais si on m'avait demandé mon avis, j'aurais bien aimé à mourir entre les bras de ma nourrice—cela m'aurait ôté bien des ennuis, et m'aurait donné le ciel bien sûrement et bien aisément : mais parlons d'autre chose.

Je suis au désespoir que vous avez eu *Bajazet* par d'autres que par moi. C'est ce chien de Barbin qui me hait, parce que je ne fais pas des Princesses de Clèves et de Montpensier. Vous en avez jugé très-juste et très-bien de Bajazet, et vous aurez vu que je suis de votre avis. Je voulais vous envoyer la Champmeslé pour vous réchauffer la pièce. Le personnage de Bajazet est glacé ; les mœurs des Turcs y sont mal observées, ils ne font point tant de façons pour se marier ; le dénouement n'est point bien préparé ; on n'entre point dans les raisons de cette grande tuerie. Il y a pourtant des choses agréables, mais rien de parfaitement beau, rien qui enlève, point de ces tirades de Corneille qui font frissonner. Ma fille, gardons-nous bien de lui comparer Racine, sentons-en toujours la différence ; les pièces de ce dernier ont des endroits froids et faibles, et jamais il n'ira plus loin qu'*Alexandre* et qu'*Andromaque* ; *Bajazet* est au-dessous, au sentiment de bien des gens, et au mien, si j'ose me citer. Racine fait des comédies pour la Champmeslé : ce n'est pas pour les siècles à venir : si jamais il n'est plus jeune, et qu'il cesse d'être amoureux, ce ne sera plus la même chose. Vive donc notre vieil ami Corneille ! Pardonnons-lui de méchants vers, en faveur des divines

came too. We did exactly what we had intended, for there was
not a dry eye the whole evening. Madame d'Elbeuf had a portrait
of the hero divinely painted. His suite arrived about eleven o'clock.
All these poor creatures were in tears, and already in deep mourning. Three gentlemen from among them came forward, whom
the sight of this portrait almost killed. There were heart-breaking
cries—no one could say one word: his valets, his lackeys, his
trumpeters—all were weeping, and made the others weep too.
The first who was able to speak answered our sad questions, and
gave us the narrative of his death. He had wished to go to confession, and upon withdrawing for that purpose had given his orders
for the evening. He was to take the Communion the following day,
Sunday, which was the day he thought he should give battle. He
mounted his horse on the Saturday at two o'clock after having
eaten, and as he had a great many followers, he left them all
thirty feet off from the height which he wished to reach, and said

et sublimes beautés qui nous transportent; ce sont des traits de maître
qui sont inimitables. Despréaux en dit encore plus que moi; et, en un
mot, c'est là bon goût, tenez-vous-y.

Voici un bon mot de Madame Cornuel, qui a fort réjoui le parterre :
M. Tambonneau le fils a quitté la robe, et a mis une sangle autour de
son ventre et de son derrière ; avec ce bel air, il veut aller servir sur la
mer : je ne sais ce que lui a fait la terre. On disait donc à Madame
Cornuel qu'il s'en allait à la mer: 'Hélas ! dit-elle, est-ce qu'il a été
mordu d'un chien enragé ? ' Cela fut dit sans malice, c'est ce qui a fait
rire extrêmement. . . . .

Je ne saurais vous plaindre de n'avoir point de beurre en Provence,
puisque vous avez de l'huile admirable et d'excellent poisson. Ah! ma
fille, que je comprends bien ce que peuvent faire et penser des gens
comme vous, au milieu de votre Provence. Je les trouverai comme
vous et je vous plaindrai toute ma vie de passer avec eux de si belles
années de la vôtre. Je suis si peu désireuse de briller dans votre cour
de Provence, et j'en juge si bien par celle de Bretagne, que par la même
raison qu'au bout de trois jours, à Vitré, je ne respirais que les Rochers,
je vous jure devant Dieu que l'objet de mes désirs c'est de passer l'été à
Grignan avec vous : voilà où je vise, et rien au delà. Mon vin de Saint-
Laurent est chez Adhémar, je l'aurai demain matin ; il y a longtemps
que je vous en ai remercié *in petto*; cela est bien obligeant. M. de Laon
aime bien cette manière d'être cardinal. On assure que l'autre jour M.
de Montausier, parlant à M. le Dauphin de la dignité des cardinaux, lui
dit que cela dépendait du pape, et que s'il voulait faire cardinal un palefrenier, il le pourrait. Là-dessus le cardinal de Bonzi arrive ; M. le
Dauphin lui dit: ' Monsieur, est-il vrai que si le pape voulait, il ferait
cardinal un palefrenier ? ' M. de Bonzi fut surpris ; et, devinant l'affaire,
il lui répondit : ' Il est vrai, monsieur, que le pape choisit qui il lui plaît,
mais nous n'avons pas vu jusqu'ici qu'il ait pris des cardinaux dans son
écurie.' C'est le cardinal de Bouillon qui m'a conté ce détail. . . . . .

Écrivez un peu à notre cardinal, il vous aime : le faubourg vous
aime ; madame Scarron vous aime, elle passe ici le carême, et céans
presque tous les soirs. Barillon y est encore, et plût à Dieu, ma belle,
que vous y fussiez aussi ! Adieu, mon enfant, je ne finis point ; je vous
défie de pouvoir comprendre combien je vous aime.

to young d'Elbeuf, 'My nephew, stay here: you do nothing but hover round me and make me conspicuous.' M. Hamilton, who was near the spot whither he was going, said, 'My lord, come this way; they are firing in the direction towards which you are going.' 'Sir,' said he to him, 'you are right; I have no wish whatever to be killed to-day; that will be the best way.' He had scarcely turned his horse when he saw Saint-Hilaire, hat in hand, who said to him, 'My lord, cast your eyes on that battery which I have just raised.' M. de Turenne turned, and in one instant, without having time to stop, his arm and his body were shattered by the same shot which carried off the arm and hand that held Saint-Hilaire's hat. This gentleman, who was still looking at him, did not see him fall; the horse carried him on to where he had left little d'Elbeuf. He had not yet fallen, but he was bent head downwards on his saddle. At that moment the horse stops, the hero falls into the arms of his men; twice he opens wide both eyes and mouth, and then remains motionless for ever. He was dead—one half of his heart carried off. There were screams and tears. M. Hamilton stopped the noise, and removed little d'Elbeuf, who had thrown himself on the body, refusing to leave it, and was swooning with anguish. They cover the body with a cloak, and carry it on a litter noiselessly. A carriage comes and conveys him to his tent. M. de Lorges, M. de Roze, and many others thought they should die of grief; but they had to control themselves, and to think of the great matters which had now devolved upon them. There was a military service performed in the camp, where tears and lamentations betokened true mourning, besides which all the officers wore crape scarves; all the drums, too, were covered with crape, and only beat one roll, trailing bayonets and arms reversed. One cannot realise the tears of a whole army without feeling deep emotion. . . . When the corpse left the army, a new despair began, and wherever it passed one heard only wailings. At Langres they went to meet him in mourning apparel to the number of two hundred or more, followed by the populace, and all the clergy fully robed. A solemn service took place in the town, and in one moment they had all agreed to share the expense, which amounted to 5,000 francs, for they followed the corpse to the next town, and wished to pay for everything. What do you say to these natural signs of a feeling founded upon extraordinary merit? He is to arrive at Saint-Denis to-night or to-morrow. All his people go to meet him two leagues away. What do you say to our manner of diverting ourselves? We dined, as you may imagine, and did little else but sigh up to four o'clock.

The Cardinal Bouillon spoke of you, and remarked that you would have made one of our melancholy party if you had been here. I am well assured, indeed, of the grief you will feel. He will answer your letter and that of M. de Grignan, and begs me to give you a thousand kind remembrances, as also does the good d'Elbeuf, who, like her son, has lost everything. What a fine idea of mine to undertake to relate to you what you must already know; but I was struck by the originality of these narratives, and it was a great pleasure to let you see how we forget M. de Turenne in this part of the country. . . . . . .

M. de Barillon supped here last night. The conversation turned upon M. de Turenne, at whose death he is greatly afflicted. He dwelt upon the solidity of his virtues, his love of truth, how much he prized virtue for its own sake, and found it his best reward, and he ended by saying that no one could love and esteem M. de Turenne without being the better man for it. His company and conversation inspired such a hatred of duplicity and double dealing, as raised all his friends above the level of other men. Among these friends the chevalier was particularly distinguished. That great man showed a more than common esteem and affection for him, and he on his side was one of his adorers. . . . Let us continue to speak of M. de Turenne; about whom it would be shameful to keep silent. Listen to what the little cardinal said of him yesterday. You are well acquainted with Pertuis, and with his adoration of and attachment to M. de Turenne. As soon as he heard of his death, he wrote to his majesty as follows: 'Sire, I have lost M. de Turenne. I feel that I cannot bear up against this calamity; therefore, being no longer in a condition to serve your majesty, I beg to resign my government of Courtrai.'

The Cardinal de Bouillon prevented the letter from being delivered to the King; but fearing he might come in person, he informed his majesty of the effect Pertuis's grief had had on him. The king appeared to enter fully into his sorrow, and told the Cardinal de Bouillon that he esteemed Pertuis all the more highly, that he could not think of his retirement, as he was far too honest a man not to discharge his duty in whatever situation he might be placed. Such is the sorrow inspired by the death of the hero, who, it seems, had an income of forty thousand livres per annum; and M. Boucherat says, that after all his debts and legacies have been paid, there will not remain more than ten thousand livres per annum; that is, two hundred thousand francs for the whole of his heirs. This is how he has enriched himself during fifty years of service. Adieu, my dearest child; I embrace you a thousand times, and with a tenderness not to be expressed.[1]

---

[1] Si l'on pouvait écrire tous les jours, je m'en accommoderais fort bien; je trouve même quelquefois le moyen de le faire, quoique mes lettres ne partent pas, mais le plaisir d'écrire est uniquement pour vous; car à tout le reste du monde, on voudrait avoir écrit, et c'est parce qu'on le doit. Vraiment, ma fille, je m'en vais bien vous parler encore de M. de Turenne. Madame d'Elbeuf, qui demeure pour quelques jours chez le cardinal de Bouillon, me pria hier de dîner avec eux deux, pour parler de leur affliction. Madame de La Fayette y vint. Nous fîmes bien précisément ce que nous avions résolu; les yeux ne nous séchèrent pas. Madame d'Elbeuf avait un portrait divinement bien fait de ce héros, dont tout le train était arrivé à onze heures; tous ces pauvres gens étaient en larmes, et déjà tout habillés de deuil. Il vint trois gentilshommes qui pensèrent mourir en voyant ce portrait; c'étaient des cris qui faisaient fendre le cœur; ils ne pouvaient prononcer une parole; ses valets de chambre,

To Madame de Grignan.

Paris: July 29, 1676.

Here is a change of scene, which will appear as agreeable to you as it does to all the world. I was on Saturday at Versailles with the Villars; and this is how they pass their time. You know the queen's toilette, the mass, the dinner; but there is no need to

ses laquais, ses pages, ses trompettes, tout était fondu en larmes, et faisait fondre les autres. Le premier qui fut en état de parler répondit à nos tristes questions; nous nous fîmes raconter sa mort. Il voulait se confesser, et en se cachotant il avait donné les ordres pour le soir, et devait communier le lendemain dimanche, qui était le jour qu'il croyait donner bataille. Il monta à cheval le samedi à deux heures, après avoir mangé; et comme il avait bien des gens avec lui, il les laissa tous à trente pas de la hauteur où il voulait aller, et dit au petit d'Elbeuf: 'Mon neveu, demeurez là; vous ne faites que tourner autour de moi, vous me feriez reconnaître.' M. d'Hamilton, qui se trouve près de l'endroit où il allait, lui dit: 'Monsieur, venez par ici; on tire du côté où vous allez.' 'Monsieur,' lui dit-il, 'vous avez raison; je ne veux point du tout être tué aujourd'hui; cela sera le mieux du monde.' Il eut à peine tourné son cheval, qu'il aperçut Saint-Hilaire, le chapeau à la main, qui lui dit: 'Monsieur, jetez les yeux sur cette batterie que je viens de faire mettre là.' M. de Turenne revint; et dans l'instant, sans être arrêté, il eut le bras et le corps fracassé du même coup qui emporta le bras et la main qui tenaient le chapeau de Saint-Hilaire. Ce gentilhomme, qui le regardait toujours, ne le voit point tomber; le cheval l'emporte où il avait laissé le petit d'Elbeuf, il n'était point encore tombé; mais il était penché le nez sur l'arçon: dans ce moment, le cheval s'arrête; le héros tombe entre les bras de ses gens; il ouvre deux fois de grands yeux et la bouche, et demeure tranquille pour jamais; songez qu'il était mort, et qu'il avait une partie du cœur emportée. On crie, on pleure; M. d'Hamilton fait cesser le bruit et ôter le petit d'Elbeuf, qui s'était jeté sur le corps, qui ne le voulait pas quitter, et se pâmait de crier. On couvre le corps d'un manteau, on le porte dans une haie; on le garde à petit bruit; un carrosse vient, on l'emporte dans sa tente; ce fut là où M. de Lorges, M. de Roye et beaucoup d'autres, pensèrent mourir de douleur; mais il fallut se faire violence, et songer aux grandes affaires qu'on avait sur les bras. On lui a fait un service militaire dans le camp, où les larmes et les cris faisaient le véritable deuil; tous les officiers avaient pourtant des écharpes de crêpe; tous les tambours en étaient couverts; ils ne battaient qu'un coup; les piques traînantes et les mousquets renversés; mais ces cris de toute une armée ne se peuvent pas représenter, sans que l'on en soit tout ému. Ses deux neveux étaient à cette pompe, dans l'état que vous pouvez penser. M. de Roye tout blessé s'y fit porter; car cette messe ne fut dite que quand ils eurent repassé le Rhin. Je pense que le pauvre chevalier [de Grignan] était bien abîmé de douleur. Quand ce corps a quitté son armée, ç'a été encore une autre désolation; et partout où il a passé on n'entendait que des clameurs; mais à Langres ils se sont surpassés; ils allèrent au-devant de lui en habits de deuil au nombre de plus de deux cents, suivis du peuple; tout le clergé en cérémonie; il y eut un service solennel dans la ville, et en un moment se cotisèrent tous pour cette

be stifled, while their majesties are dining, for at three, the king, the queen, monsieur, madame, mademoiselle, all the princes and princesses, Madame de Montespan, and all her train, all the courtiers, and all the ladies—in a word, the whole court of France, retire to that fine suite of rooms of the king's, which you know. It is divinely furnished; we do not know there what it is to feel the heat; we pass from one room to another without being in the least crowded. A game at *reversis* decides the grouping and determines its arrangement. The king and Madame de Montespan keep the bank . . . monsieur, the queen, and Madame de Soubise, Dangeau, and Langlée, with their companies, are at different tables. A thousand louis d'or are laid upon the cloth, and these are the only counters. I saw Dangeau play, and noticed how awkward others appeared in comparison with him. He thinks of nothing but his play, wins where others lose; he neglects nothing; profits by everything, never allows his attention to be diverted; and, in short, his politic conduct leads to fortune, so that his account book shows him to have been a winner of two hundred thousand francs in ten days, and one hundred thousand crowns in a month. He

dépense, qui monte à cinq mille francs, parce qu'ils reconduisirent le corps jusqu'à la première ville, et voulurent défrayer tout le train. Que dites-vous de ces marques naturelles d'une affection fondée sur un mérite extraordinaire? Il arrive à Saint-Denis ce soir ou demain; tous ses gens l'allaient reprendre à dieux lieues d'ici; il sera dans une chapelle en dépôt, on lui fera un service à Saint-Denis, en attendant celui de Notre-Dame, qui sera solennel. Voilà quel fut le divertissement que nous eûmes. Nous dînâmes comme vous pouvez penser, et jusqu'à quatre heures nous ne fîmes que soupirer. Le cardinal de Bouillon parla de vous, et répondit que vous n'auriez point évité cette triste partie si vous aviez été ici; je l'assurai fort de votre douleur: il vous fera réponse et à M. de Grignan; il me pria de vous dire mille amitiés, et la bonne d'Elbeuf, qui perd tout, aussi bien que son fils. Voilà une belle chose de m'être embarquée à vous conter ce que vous saviez déjà; mais ces originaux m'ont frappée, et j'ai été bien aise de vous faire voir que voilà comme on oublie M. de Turenne en ce pays-ci.

M. de la Garde me dit l'autre jour que dans l'enthousiasme des merveilles que l'on disait du chevalier, il exhorta ses frères à faire un effort pour lui dans cette occasion, afin de soutenir sa fortune, au moins le reste de cette année; et qu'il les trouva tous deux fort disposés à faire des choses extraordinaires. Ce bon la Garde est à Fontainebleau, d'où il doit revenir dans trois jours pour partir enfin, car il en meurt d'envie, à ce qu'il dit; mais les courtisans ont bien de la glu autour d'eux.

Vraiment l'état de madame de Sanzei est déplorable; nous ne savons rien de son mari; il n'est ni vivant, ni mort, ni blessé, ni prisonnier: ses gens n'écrivent point. M. de la Trousse, après avoir mandé le jour de l'affaire qu'on venait de lui dire qu'il avait été tué, n'en a plus écrit un mot ni à la pauvre Sanzei, ni à Coulanges. Nous ne savons donc que mander à cette femme désolée. . . .

M. de Barillon soupa hier ici; on ne parla que de M. de Turenne; il en est très-véritablement affligé. Il nous contait la solidité de ses

was good enough to say I was his partner in the bank, by which means I secured a very pleasant and comfortable seat. I bowed to the king in the way you taught me; and he returned my salutation as if I had been young and handsome. The queen talked to me of my illness as if it had been an *accouchement*, and also spoke of you. Monsieur the duke bestowed on me a thousand of those unmeaning caresses, of which he is so liberal. M. de Lorges attacked me in the name of the Chevalier de Grignan; and, in short, *tutti quanti*. You know what it is to receive a compliment from every one who passes by you. Madame de Montespan talked to me of Bourbon, and begged me to tell her about Vichy, and whether I had found any benefit there. She said that Bourbon, instead of removing the pain from one of her knees, had made them both bad. I found her back rather flat, as Madame de la Meilleraye had told me; but seriously it is quite surprising how she retains her beauty and her figure, which is not half so large as it was; and her complexion, eyes, and lips are quite as fine as ever they were. She was dressed in French lace; her hair fell in a thousand curls very low upon her cheeks; she wore on her head black ribbons; her hair was braided with the pearls which had once belonged to the Maréchale de L'Hôpital; and she wore superb diamond earrings;

vertus: combien il était vrai, combien il aimait la vertu pour elle-même, combien par elle seule il se trouvait récompensé; et puis finit par dire qu'on ne pouvait pas l'aimer, ni être touché de son mérite, sans en être plus honnête homme. Sa société communiquait une horreur pour la friponnerie et pour la duplicité, qui mettait tous ses amis au-dessus des autres hommes; dans ce nombre on distingua fort le chevalier comme un de ceux que ce grand homme aimait et estimait le plus, et aussi comme un de ses adorateurs. Bien des siècles n'en donneront pas un pareil; je ne trouve pas qu'on soit tout à fait aveugle en celui-ci, au moins les gens que je vois; je crois que c'est se vanter d'être en bonne compagnie. . . . Mais disons encore un mot de M. de Turenne: voici ce qui me fut conté hier. Vous connaissez bien Pertuis et son adoration et son attachement pour M. de Turenne; dès qu'il eut appris sa mort, il écrivit au roi, et lui manda: 'Sire, j'ai perdu M. de Turenne; je sens que mon esprit n'est point capable de soutenir ce malheur; ainsi, n'étant plus en état de servir Votre Majesté, je lui demande la permission de me démettre du gouvernement de Courtrai.' Le cardinal de Bouillon empêcha qu'on ne rendît cette lettre; mais, craignant qu'il ne vînt lui-même, il dit au roi l'effet du désespoir de Pertuis. Le roi entra fort bien dans cette douleur, et dit au cardinal de Bouillon qu'il en estimait davantage Pertuis, et qu'il ne voulait pas que Pertuis songeât à se retirer, le croyant trop honnête homme pour ne pas toujours faire son devoir, en quelque état qu'il pût être. Voilà comme sont ceux qui regrettent ce héros. Au reste, il avait quarante mille livres de rente de partage; et M. Boucherat a trouvé que, toutes ses dettes et ses legs payés, il ne lui restait que dix mille livres de rente; c'est deux cent mille francs pour tous ses héritiers, pourvu que la chicane n'y mette pas le nez. Voilà comme il s'est enrichi en cinquante années de service. . . . Adieu, ma chère enfant; je vous embrasse mille fois avec une tendresse qui ne peut se représenter.

three or four hair-pins, but no head-dress. In a word, her triumphant beauty excited the admiration of all the ambassadors. Knowing that people complained of her preventing all France from seeing the king, she has restored him to the nation, as you perceive; and you could scarcely believe the delight which this has occasioned to everybody, nor how charming the court has become. This charming confusion without confusion, of all that is most select, lasts from three o'clock until six. If any couriers arrive, the king retires to read his letters, and then returns. There is always music of a soft and delicate kind, to which he listens, and which has an admirable effect. He converses with the ladies who are accustomed to have that honour. They leave off play at the hour I mentioned, without the trouble of a settlement, because there are no marks or counters. The pools are not less than five, six, or seven hundred louis; the larger ones a thousand or twelve hundred.... They talk incessantly and remember nothing they say. 'How many hearts have you?' 'I have two, I have three, I have one, I have four.' 'Then there are only three or four left in the pack.' Dangeau is delighted with this chatter, because he finds out how the game lies, and plays accordingly. In fact, I was charmed to notice his great ability. He really knows the inside of the cards, and all the other suits.

At six they take the air in chariots. The king and Madame de Montespan, the prince and Madame de Thianges, and Mademoiselle d'Heudicourt, upon the front seat; that is to say, they are in Paradise, as it were, or in the glory of Niquée.[1] You know how these chariots are made; they do not sit face to face in them, but all look the same way. The queen was in another with the princesses; the whole court followed in different equipages, according to their own fancies. They afterwards went in gondolas upon the canal, where there was music; they came back at ten when the comedy began, and at twelve they concluded the day with the Spanish entertainment of *media-noche*.[2] Thus we passed the Saturday. But we came back in the afternoon. If I were to tell you how often I was spoken to about you, how many inquired after you, how many asked questions without waiting for a reply, how many I neglected to answer, how little they cared about me, and how much less I cared about them, you would recognise *l'iniqua corte, au naturel*. Yet it was never so agreeable, and one greatly wishes it may continue so. Madame de Nevers is very handsome, very modest, very naïve. Her beauty reminds me of you. M. de Nevers is always the most agreeable of *robins*,[3] and his wife loves him passionately. Madame de Thianges is a more regular beauty than her sister. M. du Maine is incomparable, his

---

[1] An allusion to Niquée, in *Amadis de Gaule*, whom the fairy Tirphée placed upon a magnificent throne.

[2] This was the name given by the Spaniards to a sumptuous supper partaken of—as the word implies—at midnight, after one of the fast-days of the Church.

[3] A *robin* is a man of more pretension than worth.

wit is astonishing, and you cannot imagine the things he says. Madame de Maintenon, Madame de Thianges, *Guelfs* and *Ghibelines*[1]—just imagine how all are brought together. Madame paid me a thousand little attentions on account of the good Princess of Tarento. Madame de Monaco was at Paris.

The prince paid a visit the other day to Madame de la Fayette: the prince, *alla cui spada ogni vittoria è certa.*[2] How is it possible not to be flattered by such a compliment, especially as he does not throw himself at the heads of the ladies? He talks of the war, and awaits intelligence like other people. One trembles a little for what may arrive from Germany. At the same time, it is stated that the Rhine is so swollen by the snows melting on the mountains that the enemy is more embarrassed than ourselves. Rambure was killed by one of his own soldiers, who was thoughtlessly discharging his musket. The siege of Aire continues. We have lost some lieutenants in the guards and some soldiers. Schomberg's army is perfectly safe; Madame de Schomberg has renewed her liking for me. The baron is profiting by the excessive favours of his general. 'Le petit Glorieux'[3] has no more to do than the rest. He can only be bored, and if he is in want of a wound he can only inflict it on himself. . . . Such is my dreadful budget of news, which will either bore or amuse you very much. It cannot be indifferent to you. I wish you may be in the humour you are sometimes, when you say, 'But you won't talk to me. How I wonder at my mother, who would rather die than say a single word to me!' Oh! if you are not satisfied now it is not my fault, any more than it is your own that I was not present at the death of Ruyter.[4]

There are parts of your letters that are perfectly heavenly. You give me a good account of the marriage. Nothing could be better. Judgment controls it, but it is a little late. Keep me in the kind remembrances of M. de la Garde, and ever in the friendship of M. de Grignan. Our harmony of views on the subject of your departure renews our friendship.

You find that my pen is always ready to speak of the wonders of the Grand Maître.[5] I do not altogether deny it; but I fancied you would know I was joking when I said that he wished for promotion, and aimed at really becoming a Marshal of France, as was the practice formerly. But be it as you will on this subject:

[1] Two famous factions—one siding with the Pope, the other with the Emperor.

[2] Whose sword is certain of victory.

[3] A nickname bestowed on Schomberg, one of the four greatest soldiers of their time—Condé, Turenne, Schomberg, and Marlborough.

[4] Admiral van Ruyter had been killed in a naval engagement with Admiral Duquesne, off the coast of Sicily, in the previous April; and even the heartless Louis XIV. had the grace to say, on hearing of his death, 'I cannot help regretting the loss of a great man, although an enemy.'

[5] A post in the royal household, corresponding to that of the Lord Chamberlain in the English court.

the world is very unjust. It has been so in regard to the Brinvilliers also.[1] Never have so many crimes been treated so leniently. She was not even put to the question.[2] Hopes were held out to her of a pardon, so that she believed she should escape execution, and when mounting the scaffold, she said, 'Are you really in earnest?' At last her ashes are dispersed by the winds,[3] and her confessor asserts that she is a saint. The first president thought he chose this doctor as a proper person to attend her, and it happened to be the very same they had fixed upon. Have you ever observed people who play tricks with cards? They shuffle them incessantly, invite you to pick out any one you please, as it is all the same to them. You select one, as you fancy, of your own accord, and it happens to be the very card they wanted you to take. The application is perfectly just. The Marshal de Villeroi said the other day, 'Penautier will be ruined by that affair.' The Marshal de Grammont replied, 'He must give up keeping a table.' Such are the epigrams that are flying about! I suppose you know it is believed that one hundred thousand crowns have been distributed in order to smooth matters over. Innocence would scarcely indulge in such profusion. One cannot write all one knows—it would occupy a whole evening. Nothing could be more amusing than all you tell me about that horrible woman. You may rest perfectly satisfied that it is impossible for her to be in Paradise—so evil a soul must be separate from others. 'To assassinate is the surest way.' We are quite of your opinion. It is a bagatelle in comparison with the slow murder of her father during eight months, and all the time receiving all his kindnesses and caresses, which she requited by continually doubling the dose.

Tell the archbishop [of Arles] what the first president recommended me to do for my health. I have shown my hands and almost my knees to Langeron, so that he may tell you how I am. I use a kind of liniment, which, I am assured, will cure me. I am not going to be cruel enough to plunge myself into bullock's blood until the dog-days are over. It is you, my child, who will cure me of all my ailments. If M. de Grignan could only comprehend the pleasure he affords me by approving of your journey, it would console him in advance for the six weeks he will be deprived of your society.

Madame de La Fayette is on good terms with Madame de Schomberg, and the latter makes a very great deal of me, as her husband does of my son. Madame de Villars is seriously thinking of going to Savoy, and will look you up on the way. Corbinelli[4]

---

[1] The notorious poisoner, who, being a marchioness and a fascinating woman, excited a good deal of sympathy in 'society.'

[2] It was still customary at that time to subject suspected criminals to the torture thus called, for the purpose of extorting a confession of guilt.

[3] After her execution, the body of Brinvilliers was cast into a fierce fire, and the ashes were scattered to the four winds of heaven.

[4] Giovanni Corbinelli was the grandson of Giacomo Corbinelli, who was related to Catherine de Médicis and accompanied her to France,

adores you. He is irrepressible and takes the most admirable care of me. The Very Good[1] entreats you not to doubt the delight it will give him to see you. He is convinced that the remedy is necessary for me, and you know the friendship he entertains for me. Livry[2] is often uppermost in my thoughts, and I tell them that I am beginning to stifle here, so that they may approve of my journey.

Adieu, my dearest, my best-beloved. You entreat me to love you. Ah ! I will love you dearly. It shall not be said that I refuse you anything.[3]

where he became the tutor of the Duc d'Anjou. Giovanni was a man of letters, and the gifts of his intellect attracted to him the friendship of the Cardinal de Retz, the Duc de la Rochefoucauld, Madame de Sévigné and her daughter, Bussy-Rabutin, and others. He died in 1716, at the age of 101.

[1] The Bien-Bon was an epithet of endearment applied by Madame de Sévigné to her maternal uncle, guardian, lifelong friend and adviser, the Abbé de Coulanges : one of the most beautiful characters it would be possible to meet with in history or fiction. He might be described as a compound of Fénelon, George Herbert of Bemerton, and Goldsmith's village pastor.

[2] Livry, about twelve miles from Paris on the outskirts of the forest of Bondy, was the place in which Madame de Sévigné passed her girlhood. It is thus spoken of in a letter written forty years after those early days : 'I came here yesterday and found the place in all the triumph of the month of May. The nightingale, the cuckoo, and the thrush, have opened the spring time in our forest.'

[3] Voici, ma bonne, un changement de scène qui vous paraîtra aussi agréable qu'à tout le monde. Je fus samedi à Versailles avec les Villars : voici comme cela va. Vous connaissez la toilette de la reine, la messe, le dîner ; mais il n'est plus besoin de se faire étouffer pendant que leurs majestés sont à table ; car à trois heures le roi, la reine, monsieur, madame, mademoiselle, tout ce qu'il y a de princes et de princesses, madame de Montespan, toute sa suite, tous les courtisans, toutes les dames, enfin ce qui s'appelle la cour de France, se trouve dans ce bel appartement du roi que vous connaissez. Tout est meublé divinement, tout est magnifique. On ne sait ce que c'est que d'y avoir chaud ; on passe d'un lieu à l'autre sans faire la presse en nul lieu. Un jeu de reversi donne la forme, et fixe tout. C'est le roi et madame de Montespan que tient la carte ; monsieur, la reine et madame de Soubise ; Dangeau et compagnie ; Langlée et compagnie. Mille louis sont répandus sur le tapis, il n'y a point d'autres jetons. Je voyais jouer Dangeau ; et j'admirais combien nous sommes sots auprès de lui. Il ne songe qu'à son affaire, et gagne où les autres perdent ; il ne néglige rien, il profite de tout, il n'est point distrait : en un mot, sa bonne conduite défie la fortune ; aussi les deux cent mille francs en dix jours, les cent mille écus en un mois, tout cela se met sur le livre de sa recette. Il dit que je prenais part à son jeu, de sorte que je fus assise très-agréablement et très-commodément. Je saluai le roi, ainsi que vous me l'avez appris ; il me rendit mon salut, comme si j'avais été jeune et belle. La reine me parla aussi longtemps de ma maladie que si c'eût été une couche. Elle me parla aussi de vous. M. le duc me fit mille de ces caresses à quoi il ne pense pas. Le

I have quoted this long letter, almost without abridgment, partly because it offers such an animated picture of

maréchal de Lorges m'attaqua sous le nom du chevalier de Grignan, enfin *tutti quanti*. Vous savez ce que c'est que de recevoir un mot de tout ce que l'on trouve en son chemin. Madame de Montespan me parla de Bourbon, et me pria de lui conter Vichy, et comment je m'en étais trouvée ; elle me dit que Bourbon, au lieu de guérir un genou, lui a fait mal aux deux. Je lui trouvai le dos bien plat, comme disait la maréchale de la Meilleraye ; mais, sérieusement, c'est une chose surprenante que sa beauté ; et sa taille n'est pas de la moitié si grosse qu'elle était, sans que son teint, ni ses yeux, ni ses lèvres, en soient moins bien. Elle était tout habillée de point de France ; coiffée de mille boucles ; les deux des tempes lui tombaient fort bas sur les deux joues ; des rubans noirs sur sa tête, des perles de la maréchale de l'Hôpital, embellies de boucles et de pendeloques de diamants de la dernière beauté, trois ou quatre poinçons, une boîte point de coiffe, en un mot, une triomphante beauté à faire admirer à tous les ambassadeurs. Elle a su qu'on se plaignait qu'elle empêchait toute la France de voir le roi ; elle l'a redonné, comme vous voyez ; et vous ne sauriez croire la joie que tout le monde en a, ni de quelle beauté cela rend la cour. Cette agréable confusion, sans confusion, de tout ce qu'il y a de plus choisi, dure jusqu'à six heures depuis trois. S'il vient des courriers, le roi se retire pour lire ses lettres, et puis revient. Il y a toujours quelque musique qu'il écoute, et qui fait un très-bon effet. Il cause avec les dames qui ont accoutumé d'avoir cet honneur. Enfin on quitte le jeu à l'heure que je vous ai dit ; on n'a du tout point de peine à faire les comptes ; il n'y a point de jetons ni de marques ; les poules sont au moins de cinq, six ou sept cents louis, les grosses de mille, de douze cents. . . . On parle sans cesse, et rien ne demeure sur le cœur. ' Combien avez-vous de cœurs ? J'en ai deux, j'en ai trois, j'en ai un, j'en ai quatre : il n'en a donc que trois, que quatre ; ' et de tout ce caquet Dangeau est ravi : il découvre le jeu, il tire ses conséquences, il voit ce qu'il y a à faire ; enfin j'étais ravie de voir cet excès d'habileté. Vraiment c'est bien lui qui sait le dessous des cartes, car il sait toutes les autres couleurs. On monte donc à six heures en calèche, le roi, madame de Montespan, monsieur, madame de Thianges et la bonne d'Heudicourt sur le strapontin, c'est-à-dire comme en paradis, ou dans *la gloire de Niquée*. Vous savez comme ces calèches sont faites ; on ne se regarde point, on est tourné du même côté. La reine était dans une autre avec les princesses, et ensuite tout le monde attroupé, selon sa fantaisie. On va sur le canal dans des gondoles, on y trouve de la musique, on revient à dix heures, on trouve la comédie ; minuit sonne, on fait *media-noche* ; voilà comme se passa le samedi. Nous révînmes quand on monta en calèche.

De vous dire combien de fois on me parla de vous, combien on me demanda de vos nouvelles, combien on me fit de questions sans attendre la réponse, combien j'en épargnai, combien on s'en souciait peu, combien je m'en souciais encore moins, vous reconnaîtriez au naturel *l' iniqua corte*. Cependant elle ne fut jamais si agréable, et l'on souhaite fort que cela continue. Madame de Nevers est fort jolie, fort modeste, fort naïve ; sa beauté fait souvenir de vous. M. de Nevers est toujours le plus plaisant *robin* ; sa femme l'aime de passion. Mademoiselle de Thianges est plus régulièrement belle que sa sœur, et beaucoup

contemporary events and personages, painted by a true
artist, who was probably unconscious of her gift, and partly

> moins charmante. M. du Maine est incomparable ; l'esprit qu'il a est
> étonnant ; les choses qu'il dit ne se peuvent imaginer. Madame de
> Maintenon, Madame de Thianges, *Guelfes* et *Gibelins*, songez que tout
> est rassemblé. Madame me fit mille honnêtetés, à cause de la bonne
> princesse de Tarente. Madame de Monaco était à Paris.
> M. le Prince fut voir l'autre jour Madame de La Fayette ; ce prince,
> *alla cui spada ogni vittoria è certa.* Le moyen de n'être pas flatté d'une
> telle estime, et d'autant plus qu'il ne la jette pas à la tête des dames ?
> Il parle de la guerre, il attend des nouvelles comme les autres. On
> tremble un peu de celles d'Allemagne. On dit pourtant que le Rhin est
> tellement enflé des neiges qui fondent des montagnes, que les ennemis
> sont plus embarrassés que nous. Rambures a été tué par un de ses
> soldats, qui déchargeait très-innocemment son mousquet. Le siège
> d'Aire continue ; nous y avons perdu quelques lieutenants aux gardes
> et quelques soldats. L'armée de Schomberg est en pleine sûreté.
> Madame de Schomberg s'est remise à m'aimer ; le baron en profite par
> les caresses excessives de son général. '*Le petit glorieux*' n'a pas plus
> d'affaires que les autres ; il pourra s'ennuyer ; mais s'il a besoin d'une
> contusion, il faudra qu'il se la fasse lui-même : Dieu les conserve
> dans cette oisiveté ! Voilà, ma bonne, d'épouvantables détails ; ou ils
> vous ennuieront beaucoup, ou ils vous amuseront ; ils ne peuvent point
> être indifférents. Je souhaite que vous soyez dans cette humeur où
> vous me dites quelquefois : ' Mais vous ne voulez pas me parler ; mais
> j'admire ma mère, qui aimerait mieux mourir que me dire un seul
> mot.' Oh ! si vous n'êtes pas contente, ce n'est pas ma faute ; non
> plus que la vôtre, si je ne l'ai pas été de la mort de Ruyter. Il y a des
> endroits dans vos lettres qui sont divins. Vous me parlez très-bien du
> mariage, il n'y a rien de mieux ; le jugement domine, mais c'est un peu
> tard. Conservez-moi dans les bonnes grâces de M. de la Garde, et tou-
> jours des amitiés pour moi à M. de Grignan. La justesse de nos pensées
> sur votre départ renouvelle notre amitié.
> Vous trouvez que ma plume est toujours taillée pour dire des
> merveilles du grand-maître, je ne le nie pas absolument : mais que je
> croyais m'être moquée de lui, en vous disant l'envie qu'il a de parvenir,
> et qu'il veut être maréchal de France à la rigueur, comme du temps
> passé : mais c'est que vous m'en voulez sur ce sujet ; le monde est bien
> injuste.
> Il l'a bien été aussi pour la Brinvilliers ; jamais tant de crimes n'ont
> été traités si doucement : elle n'a pas eu la question, on avait si peur
> qu'elle ne parlât, qu'on lui faisait entrevoir une grâce, et si bien entre-
> voir, qu'elle ne croyait point mourir ; elle dit en montant sur l'écha-
> faud : ' C'est donc tout de bon ? ' Enfin elle est au vent, et son confes-
> seur dit que c'est une sainte. M. le premier président (de Lamoignon)
> avait choisi ce docteur comme une merveille ; c'était celui qu'on voulait
> qu'elle prît. N'avez-vous point vu ces gens qui font des tours de cartes ?
> Ils les mêlent incessamment, et vous disent d'en prendre une telle que
> vous voudrez et qu'ils ne s'en soucient pas ; vous la prenez, vous croyez
> l'avoir prise, et c'est justement celle qu'ils veulent : à l'application, elle
> est juste. Le maréchal de Villeroi disait l'autre jour : ' Pénautier sera
> ruiné de cette affaire.' Le maréchal de Gramont répondit : ' Il faudra

as an illustration of the moral obtuseness of even the best men and women of the period. In some of the noblest qualities of her sex Madame de Sévigné was irreproachable, and yet the artificial glamour of a corrupt if splendid court seems to have blinded her to its unmitigated profligacy. Here is the king and his titular mistress sitting down to gamble at one table, while his neglected and insulted queen is left to amuse herself with some of the courtiers at another. Then, when they ride out to take the air, Madame de Montespan travels with her royal protector, and the queen follows in a second carriage. And, again, we find a new candidate for dishonour appearing upon the scene—the widow Scarron, who has secretly resolved to supplant the reigning favourite, and, instead of continuing governess to the illegitimate children of Madame de Montespan, is bent on becoming the governess of the king himself! Verily a nest of unclean birds.

qu'il supprime sa table.' Voilà bien des épigrammes. Je suppose que vous savez qu'on croit qu'il y a cent mille écus répandus pour faciliter toutes choses ; l'innocence ne fait guère de telles profusions. On ne peut écrire tout ce qu'on sait ; ce sera pour une soirée. Rien n'est si plaisant que tout ce que vous dites sur cette horrible femme. Je crois que vous avez contentement ; car il n'est pas possible qu'elle soit en paradis ; sa vilaine âme doit être séparée des autres. *Assassiner est le plus sûr*; nous sommes de votre avis ; c'est une bagatelle en comparaison d'être huit mois à tuer son père, et à recevoir toutes ses caresses et toutes ses douceurs, où elle ne répondait qu'en doublant toujours la dose.

Contez à M. l'archevêque (d'Arles) ce que m'a fait dire M. le premier président pour ma santé. J'ai fait voir mes mains et quasi mes genoux à Langeron, afin qu'il vous en rende compte. J'ai d'une manière de pommade qui me guérira, à ce qu'on m'assure ; je n'aurai point la cruauté de me plonger dans le sang d'un bœuf, que la canicule ne soit passée. C'est vous, ma fille, qui me guérirez de tous mes maux. Si M. de Grignan pouvait comprendre le plaisir qu'il me fait d'approuver votre voyage, il serait consolé par avance de six semaines qu'il sera sans vous.

Madame de La Fayette n'est point mal avec Madame de Schomberg. Cette dernière me fait des merveilles, et son mari à mon fils. Madame de Villars songe tout de bon à s'en aller en Savoie ; elle vous trouvera en chemin. Corbinelli vous adore, il n'en faut rien rabattre ; il a toujours des soins de moi admirables. Le '*bien-Bon*' vous prie de ne douter de la joie qu'il aura de vous voir ; il est persuadé que ce remède m'est nécessaire, et vous savez l'amitié qu'il a pour moi. Livry me revient souvent dans la tête, et je dis que je commence à étouffer, afin qu'on approuve mon voyage.

Adieu, ma très-aimable et très-aimée ; vous me priez de vous aimer ; ah ! vraiment je le veux bien : il ne sera pas dit que je vous refuse quelque chose.

Madame de Sévigné sees all this gilded vice and varnished depravity, she understands the crafty intrigues and diplomatic devices of 'the Guelfs and Ghibelines' at court, she is not unacquainted with the miseries of the people, and she is an eye-witness of the scandalous profusion of the royal expenditure; but I am sorry to admit that she has not a word to say even in mild deprecation of the unblushing licentiousness of the king, or of the recklessness with which he is dissipating the revenues wrung in part from the miseries of his starving people, or of the sufferings which his brave army might be at that moment undergoing in Holland, invaded upon what is now admitted to have been an unjustifiable pretext.[1]

I am indebted to M. Suard, perpetual secretary of the French Academy, for the following pages, in which he has detached from their setting some of the most sparkling of the gems in these matchless letters. It seems to me, he writes, that even those who are most fond of this extraordinary woman have not yet sufficiently recognised the entire superiority of her spirit. I find in it all kinds of *esprit* —reasonable or frivolous, pleasant or sublime. She takes all tones with an inconceivable facility. I cannot forego the wish to justify my admiration of her by quoting some of the most piquant passages which present themselves to my memory, or to my eyes, as I turn over her letters at random. It is in her narratives and her pictures more particularly that the grace, the suppleness, and the vivacity of her mind shine with the greatest brilliancy. There is nothing, perhaps, comparable with this story concerning the Archbishop of Rheims, Monseigneur de Tellier:

The Archbishop returned very quickly from St. Germain's. It was like a whirlwind. If he believed himself to be a great personage, his people believed him to be still more so. He passed through Nanterre—tra la, la la. They met a man on horseback. 'Look out! look out!' The poor fellow wanted to draw his horse on one side, but the beast was restive; so the carriage with the six horses turned both the hack and his rider topsy-turvy, and passed right over him. Very much so, in fact, for the carriage itself was upset, and turned upside down. At the same time the equestrian and his steed, instead of having the pleasure of being crushed,

---

[1] See the *Histoire de la Vie et de l'Administration de Colbert* by Clément.

escaped by a miracle; and the man, having remounted his horse, fled with all speed, while the lacqueys and the coachman and the Archbishop himself cried out lustily 'Stop that rascal! Stop him! Thrash him soundly!' And the prelate in telling the story used to say, 'If I had caught hold of the scoundrel I'd have broken his arms and cut off his ears!'[1]

Here is a picture of another kind:

Madame de Brissac had the colic to-day. She was in bed, looking so handsome, and with her hair dressed 'up to the nines.' I wish you could have seen how she carried on about her pains, and how she rolled her eyes, and how she wept and waved her arms and wrung her hands, and how she tried to win our compassion. I was overcome with pity and wonder. I thought her performance so fine, that I must have appeared to be startled by it; which I believe they would willingly suppose to be the case. But just think what must have been the impression made upon the Abbé Bayard, Saint-Hérem, Montjeu, and Planci by this scene.[2]

Listen to her for a moment, while she announces the sudden death of M. de Louvois, and observe how her tone becomes more elevated, yet without any straining after effect:

He is no more; that superb and powerful minister, whose egoism filled so large a space, and who was the central figure of so many affairs. What interests to unravel, what intrigues to follow out, what

[1] L'archevêque de Rheims revenait fort vite de Saint-Germain; c'était comme un tourbillon; s'il se croit grand seigneur, ses gens le croient encore plus que lui. Il passait au travers de Nanterre, tra, tra, tra : ils rencontrent un homme à cheval : 'Gare! gare!' Ce pauvre homme veut se ranger, son cheval ne le veut pas, et enfin le carrosse et les six chevaux renversent cul par-dessus tête le pauvre homme et le cheval, et passent par-dessus, et si bien par-dessus, que le carrosse fut versé et renversé: en même temps l'homme et le cheval, au lieu de s'amuser à être roués, se relèvent miraculeusement, remontent l'un sur l'autre, et s'enfuient, et courent encore, pendant que les laquais et le cocher et l'archevêque même se mettent à crier 'Arrête, arrête ce coquin ! qu'on lui donne cent coups!' L'archevêque, en racontant ceci, disait : 'Si j'avais tenu ce maraud-là, je lui aurais rompu les bras et coupé les oreilles.'

[2] Madame de Brissac avait aujourd'hui la colique : elle était au lit, belle et coiffée à coiffer tout le monde : je voudrais que vous eussiez vu ce qu'elle faisait de ses douleurs, et l'usage qu'elle faisait de ses yeux, et des cris, et des bras, et des mains, qui traînaient sur sa couverture, et la compassion qu'elle voulait qu'on eût. Chamarée de tendresse et d'admiration, j'admirais cette pièce et la trouvais si belle, que mon attention a dû paraître un saisissement, dont je crois qu'on me saura fort bon gré; et songez que c'était pour l'abbé Bayard, Saint-Hérem, Montjeu et Planci, que la scène était ouverte.

negotiations to complete! 'O my God! a little while longer! I would fain humble the Duke of Savoy, and crush the Prince of Orange. Give me another moment!' 'No, you will not have an instant—not a single instant.'¹

Is not this last passage worthy of Bossuet? It seems to me that nothing could be more sublime, and yet withal nothing more simple.

When the Prince de Longueville was killed at the crossing of the Rhine they did not know how to break the news to the duchess, his mother, who idolised him. Nevertheless, they were bound to tell her something had happened. 'How is my brother?' she said. 'Her thought dared go no further,' adds Madame de Sévigné. Is not the phrase admirable? The picture which she presently draws of that tender mother's anguish makes one shudder: 'That liberty of interrupting happiness which death takes ought to console us for not being among the number of the happy. It makes death less bitter.' ²

The letters of Madame de Sévigné teem with reflections of this kind, striking by their truth, energetically expressed, delicate, original, and often intermingled with pleasant and original passages.

She says somewhere of an old lady of her acquaintance who was just dead: 'When she was at the point of death, last year, I said, in noting her sad convalescence and her decrepitude, "*Mon Dieu!* she will die two deaths, quite close to each other." Was I not right? One day, Patris having recovered from a serious illness when eighty years old, and his friends congratulating him and conjuring him to get up, "Alas!" was his reply, "is it worth the trouble of dressing oneself?"' ³

---

¹ Il n'est donc plus, ce ministre puissant et superbe, dont le moi occupait tant d'espace, était le centre de tant de choses! Que d'intérêts à démêler, d'intrigues à suivre, de négociations à terminer! . . . 'O mon Dieu! encore quelque temps: je voudrais humilier le duc de Savoie, écraser le prince d'Orange: encore un moment! . . . Non, vous n'aurez pas un moment, un seul moment.'

² Cette liberté que prend la mort d'interrompre la fortune doit consoler de n'être pas au nombre des heureux; on en trouve la mort moins amère.

³ Quand elle fut près de mourir l'année passée, je disais, en voyant sa triste convalescence et sa décrépitude : Mon Dieu! elle mourra deux

'One has only to leave the human mind to itself,' she says elsewhere, 'and it knows very well where to find its little consolations. One can fancy that one is content.'[1] 'Long illnesses use up pain, and prolonged hopes use up joy.' 'One does not mistake the shadow for the substance for any length of time. One must *be*, if one would *appear* to be. The world in the long run is not unjust.'

She everywhere exhibits a strong tendency towards devotion, and great lukewarmness in regard to practice. '*Mon Dieu!*' she exclaimed in reference to the famous Cardinal de Retz, 'what a happy man he is! I could envy him sometimes with respect to his frightful tranquillity concerning all the duties of life. One ruins oneself when one tries to fulfil them.'[2]

Her devotion was gentle and humane. 'We speak sometimes of the opinion of Origen and of our own. We have great difficulty in getting the idea of an eternity of torments in our head, unless submission comes to our assistance.'[3]

What touching reflections are these upon time, old age, and death:

Death seems to me so terrible, that life is more odious to me because it leads to it, than because of the thorns we encounter on the way. I find the conditions of life very hard. It seems to me that I have been dragged, in spite of myself, to that fatal point at which I must suffer old age. I see it; I am there; and I could wish, at any rate, to go no further; not to advance another step along the path of infirmities, of pains, of loss of memory, and of disfigurements, such as are ready to affront me. But I hear a voice which says: 'You must march on, in spite of yourself'; or rather, if you refuse, you must die; and this is another extremity which nature abhors.' I looked at a clock, and I took pleasure in

---

fois bien près l'une de l'autre. Ne disais-je pas vrai ? Un jour Patris étant revenu d'une grande maladie à quatre-vingts ans, et ses amis s'en réjouissant avec lui et le conjurant de se lever : ' Hélas !' leur dit-il, 'est-ce la peine de se rhabiller ? '

[1] Il n'y a qu'à laisser faire l'esprit humain ; il saura bien trouver ses petites consolations ; c'est la fantaisie d'être content.

[2] Mon Dieu, qu'il est heureux! que j'envierais quelquefois son épouvantable tranquillité sur tous les devoirs de la vie ! On se ruine quand on veut s'acquitter.

[3] Nous parlons quelquefois de l'opinion d'Origène et de la nôtre ; nous avons de la peine à nous faire entrer une éternité de supplices dans la tête, à moins que la soumission ne vienne au secours.

thinking, 'This is how it is when one wishes those hands to move, nevertheless they turn imperceptibly and everything comes to an end.'¹

Sometimes expressions of considerable hardihood escaped her, which one may look upon as affected when taken separately, but looked at in their proper place they appear quite natural—natural, that is to say, in a woman of a very lively imagination and of a highly cultivated mind. 'I know no more pleasures,' she says somewhere; 'it is all very well for me to stamp my foot, nothing springs up but a sad and monotonous life.' One sees she has been reading Plutarch's 'Life of Pompey,' who boasted that in some corner of Italy he had only to stamp his foot and legions would issue from the soil, ready to obey his commands.²

When she wished to intimate that the credit of a minister was on the wane, Madame de Sévigné said that 'his star paled.' Is not the image a happy and brilliant one, and yet free from any affectation? Her style is not invariably simple, but it is always natural; and this quality makes itself especially felt by a negligent *abandon* which pleases, and by a rapidity which draws you along. One everywhere feels what she somewhere says, 'I could write until to-morrow. My thoughts, my pen, my ink, all fly.'³ Does she sometimes wish to relate a pleasant story with a gaiety that is somewhat free in a woman, what adroitness in the turn of the phrase, what delicacy in its expression! She makes us understand everything without pronouncing it.

---

[1] La mort me paraît si terrible, que je hais plus la vie parce qu'elle y mène, que par les épines qui s'y rencontrent.

Je trouve les conditions de la vie assez dures : il me semble que j'ai été traînée malgré moi à ce point fatal où il faut souffrir la vieillesse ; je la vois, m'y voilà, et je voudrais bien au moins ménager de n'aller pas plus loin, de ne point avancer dans ce chemin des infirmités, des douleurs, des pertes de mémoire, des défigurements, qui sont près de m'outrager. Mais j'entends une voix qui dit : Il faut marcher malgré vous ; ou bien, si vous ne le voulez pas, il faut mourir, ce qui est une autre extrémité où la nature répugne.

Je regardais une pendule, et prenais plaisir à penser : voilà comme on est quand on souhaite que cette aiguille marche : cependant elle tourne sans qu'on la voie, et tout arrive à la fin.

[2] Je ne connais plus les plaisirs ; j'ai beau frapper du pied, rien ne sort qu'une vie triste et uniforme.

[3] J'écrirais jusqu'à demain ; mes pensées, ma plume, mon encre, tout vole.

What shines most brilliantly in the letters of Madame de Sévigné is her inexhaustible fund of tenderness for her daughter, which expresses itself under a thousand different forms always full of sensibility, always interesting. But these are precisely the passages least suitable for quotation, because they are ordinarily expressions and *tournures* of extreme simplicity, which can scarcely be detached from the accessory ideas and circumstances surrounding them. Sometimes, nevertheless, the sentiment is embellished by the imagination. This tenderness for her daughter often borrows very ingenious turns without ceasing to be natural. 'Do you know what I do with my telescope?' she writes to Madame de Grignan. 'I incessantly direct it towards the distant horizon, and the troubles which encompass me disappear, and I wish to think only of you.' 'I regret,' she says in another place, 'that my life should be passing away without you; and to meet you again, I would fain throw away the rest of it, as though I had plenty of time to spare.' Many times she repeats this idea: 'I am quite content with the flight of time, which carries me along with it, so that it bring me again to you.' And in another place she says: 'I am so wretched at finding myself quite alone, that contrary to my ordinary ideas I wish that time would gallop, so as to bring me nearer to the hour of meeting you again, and in order to efface a little my too vivid impressions. . . . Is it, then, this continual thought that makes you say there is no absence? I acknowledge that from this point of view there is none. But what do you call that which one feels when the presence is so dear to us? The opposite must of necessity be very bitter.' 'My heart is at rest when it is near you. That is its natural condition, and the only one which can please it.' 'It seems to me that in losing you I have been despoiled of all that I had to love. . . . I should be ashamed if during the whole week I had done anything else but weep. . . . I don't know where to get away from you,' she says elsewhere.[1]

---

[1] Savez-vous ce que je fais de ma lunette? Je ne cesse de la tourner du côté dont elle éloigne; les importuns qui m'environnent disparaissent, et je veux ne penser qu'à vous. Je regrette ce que je passe de ma vie sans vous, et j'en précipite les restes pour vous retrouver, comme si j'avais bien du temps à perdre. Je suis bien aise que

Writing to the president de Monceau she observes: 'I have been received with open arms by Madame de Grignan —with so much joy, tenderness, and gratitude, that it seems to me as if I had not yet come sufficiently early nor sufficiently from afar.'[1]

I feel some reluctance in animadverting on the faults of so amiable and uncommon a woman, but, for the sake of the truth, it must be acknowledged that Madame de Sévigné, with so much intellect, and that intellect such a fine one, shared also the follies of her epoch and her rank. She was childishly proud of her high birth. She dwelt with rapture upon the history of the house of Rabutin, which the Comte de Bussy proposed to write, and she believed all Europe would feel an interest in that important record. She was intoxicated, like everybody else at that time, with the grandeur of Louis XIV. That prince spoke to her one day, after the representation of 'Esther' at St. Cyr, and on that occasion her vanity burst forth with infantine joy. The passage is curious: 'The king, addressing himself to me, said, " Madame, I am assured that you have been pleased." Without betraying astonishment, I replied, "Sire, I am charmed. I want words to express what I feel." The king said, "Racine has a good deal of talent." I replied, "Sire, he has plenty of it; but, in truth, these young people have a good deal also. They enter into the subject as if they had never done anything else." "Ah!" he answered, " that is also true." And then his majesty turned away and left me the object of envy. Monsieur and madame

le temps coure et m'entraîne avec lui, pour me redonner à vous. Je suis si désolée de me retrouver toute seule, que, contre mon ordinaire, je souhaite que le temps galope, et pour me rapprocher celui de vous revoir, et pour m'effacer un peu ces impressions trop vives.... Est-ce donc cette pensée si continuelle qui vous fait dire qu'il n'y a point d'absence? J'avoue que, par ce côté, il n'y en a point. Mais comment appelez-vous ce que l'on sent quand la présence est si chère? Il faut, de nécessité, que le contraire soit bien amer. Mon cœur est en repos quand il est près de vous; c'est son état naturel, le seul qui peut lui plaire.... Il me semble, en vous perdant, qu'on m'a dépouillée de tout ce que j'avais d'aimable... Je serais honteuse, si, depuis huit jours, j'avais fait autre chose que pleurer.... Je ne sais où me sauver de vous.

[1] J'ai été reçue à bras ouverts de Madame de Grignan, avec tant de joie, de tendresse et de reconnaissance, qu'il me semblait que je n'étais pas venue encore assez tôt ni d'assez loin.

la princesse came and spoke a word to me, Madame de Maintenon gave me a glance, and I replied to all, for I was in luck.'[1]

It is in these places that the woman of genius is eclipsed for the moment by the gossip. We know that Louis XIV. one day danced a minuet with Madame de Sévigné. After the minuet, finding herself near her cousin, the Comte de Bussy, she said to him : 'It must be confessed that we have a great king.' 'No doubt, my cousin,' replied Bussy. ' What he has just done is truly heroic.'

It cannot be denied that of all human follies there is none more foolish than the folly of vanity.

Were I to consult my own inclinations, I should like to present the portrait of Madame de Sévigné, as Queen Elizabeth of England is said to have ordered her own to be painted, without any shadows. But Cromwell was no doubt right when he said to Sir Peter Lely : ' I desire you will use all your skill to paint my picture truly like me and not flatter me at all, but portray all those roughnesses, pimples, warts, and everything as you see in me, otherwise I will never pay you one farthing for it.' And in delineating the character of Madame de Sévigné, I feel compelled by a strict regard to truth not to omit the pimples and the warts by which it was disfigured.

During one of her sojourns in Brittany a scarcity of food and the misery it engendered provoked a rising of the unhappy peasants. The terms employed by Madame de Sévigné, when speaking of the punishments inflicted upon these poor creatures, are more than cruel—they are frivolous and foolish. Her heart had been hardened by the atmosphere of the court, so that it had become indifferent to the suffer-

---

[1] Le roi s'adressa à moi, et me dit : 'Madame, je suis assuré que vous avez été contente.' Moi, sans m'étonner, je répondis : ' Sire, je suis charmée, ce que je sens est au-dessus des paroles.' Le roi me dit : 'Racine a bien de l'esprit.' Je lui dis : 'Sire, il en a beaucoup, mais en vérité ces jeunes personnes en ont beaucoup aussi ; elles entrent dans le sujet comme si elles n'avaient jamais fait autre chose.' 'Ah ! pour cela,' reprit-il, ' il est vrai.' Et puis sa majesté s'en alla, et me laissa l'objet de l'envie. Monsieur et madame la princesse me vinrent dire un mot ; madame de Maintenon, un éclair : je répondis à tout, car j'étais en fortune.

ings of people belonging to the lower orders of society. Her sensibilities were easily excited by the slightest ailments of her daughter, or even by anything that occasioned pain or inconvenience to her favourite dogs; and yet she could find amusement in the gibbets upon which the king's soldiery strung up the wretched peasants, who were dragged at the heels of the hangman, and were ignorant of the very language in which their tyrants addressed them. This want of compassion and sympathy for the miserable cultivators of the soil in France shows how deep was the gulf which separated the privileged few from the starving multitude, and helps to illustrate the causes which were even then at work to bring about the terrible convulsion of 1789, when 'the sins of the fathers were visited upon the children, even unto the third and fourth generation.' As Lamartine has said, with stern historical justice, 'In order to really believe in the sensibility of Madame de Sévigné, one must tear out these pages from the volume. The letter-writer who could borrow from the sight of such horrors ornaments of style for the amusement of her daughter might be a mother, but she ceases to be a woman.' In this particular, however, Madame de Sévigné was only typical of the class to which she belonged. That class looked upon these unhappy peasants in much the same light as it did on the cattle on the farms, and regarded the judicial murder of the poor creatures who had been goaded to insurrection by intolerable wrongs much as the highest ladies in imperial Rome—ladies who were otherwise tender-hearted and compassionate, perhaps —regarded the tearing to pieces of Christian martyrs by wild beasts in the arena of the Colosseum, or as the flower of female society in Madrid watches the cruel and often atrocious incidents of a bull-fight at the present day.

Madame de Sévigné died on April 10, 1696, in the arms of the daughter whom she loved so tenderly, and surrounded by her grandchildren. She was buried in the chapel of the Château de Grignan, that is to say, her body was laid to rest there; but, as it has been truly said, her soul is enshrined within her Letters. Visitors to her tomb are shown the grotto of Roche-Courbierre, at the entrance of which so many of those letters were written; and an old fig tree trained against its walls is said to be a survival of her own days. 'It is not very far,' as we are reminded by Lamartine, 'from the grottoes of Vaucluse, immortalised by her favourite poet, Petrarch, whose life, like her own, had been absorbed by one emotion only. Madame de Sévigné, who was almost a poet herself, was in fact the Petrarch of French prose. Like him, her life revolved around a single name, a unique object; and like him, she knew how to communicate to a thousand hearts the throbbings of her own.'

The judgment of posterity has confirmed the title of her 'Letters' to rank with the 'Fables' of La Fontaine, the 'Femmes Savantes' of Molière, and the 'Provinciales' of Pascal. She built a literary monument more enduring than bronze or marble, without apparently having been in the slightest degree conscious of the beauty and permanence of the work upon which she was engaged. While she was opening her heart and emptying her memory of all its little store of remembered words and incidents, without premeditation, without correction, and without reserve, she was unknowingly creating a literary style as distinctive and original as that of Montaigne, of Saint-Simon, or of Bossuet. While she was sitting down to gossip on paper, with the friends she loved and the daughter she adored, in the freest and fullest familiarity of close and affectionate intercourse, she was, in total ignorance of the future, taking into her confidence a multitudinous host of human beings belonging to a greater number of generations than we may venture to estimate.

The renown of warriors, of statesmen, of poets, and of sacred orators, it has been eloquently observed, 'has undergone the vicissitudes of posterity, and finds itself partly obscured by the cloudy medium of distance; but the person and letters of Madame de Sévigné have not been bereft by lapse of time of a single heart-throb or a solitary page. The human heart will always be the human heart, more tender than critical; and the tenderness of a mother for her child, expressed in its natural simplicity with the stamp of genius upon it, moves us quite as deeply as the destinies of an empire.' It is this which assures immortality to these letters, occupying, as they do, the first place among the masterpieces of human genius. Madame de Sévigné is the classic author of the fireside.

LECTURE XV

La Fontaine (1621-1695).

THERE are some men of letters for whom we entertain a personal affection, independently of the admiration excited by their works. Sometimes the feeling is inspired by the moral beauty, sweetness, simplicity, and loveableness of their characters; and sometimes we cherish a warm regard for them, not merely in spite but by reason of their very foibles and weaknesses; for these appear to bring them nearer to ourselves. Shakespeare seems to have been personally beloved by most of his contemporaries; and the epithet 'gentle,' so often applied to him by those who were privileged to enjoy his friendship, lets us partly into the secret of their liking for him. The genuine nobility, the simple dignity, the beautiful integrity, and the exquisite humanity which breathe through the life and letters of Sir Walter Scott have endeared him to the hearts of millions of English-speaking people. We have a kindly feeling for the warm-hearted, thoughtless, thriftless Oliver Goldsmith, notwithstanding all the infirmities of his character; the poet Cowper excites the tenderest sympathies of our nature; and we love Charles Lamb, not so much because he is one of the most delightful essayists in the English language, as because his inconspicuous life was one of heroic self-sacrifice for his afflicted sister, fulfilled with a sublime unconsciousness that he was discharging anything more than an ordinary duty.

Jean de la Fontaine, the immortal fabulist, was one of these writers who has conciliated the personal regard of a dozen generations of his countrymen, notwithstanding the fact that his character was as full of faults as an egg is full of meat. In the Walhalla of our literary worthies he is the *bonhomme par excellence.* Nobody dreams of disputing his title to that unique distinction. And, curiously enough, he was what every one detests—an egotist; yet his very egotism, like that of Montaigne and of the author of the 'Religio Medici,' has made us exceedingly fond of him. He tells us of all his surroundings, his furniture, his likes and dislikes, his amusements and his ailments, not forgetting his rheumatism; and why are we never displeased at it? Saint-Marc Girardin, who was the first to propound the question, has also answered it. It is because La Fontaine knew how to *expand* and take us into his confidence in such a way as both to attract and to charm. He could speak of his very defects with so much naïveté that what would have been repulsive in another man was seductive in him.

La Fontaine was the only one of all our writers, without even excepting Molière or Voltaire, who combined in perfection Latin culture with *l'esprit gaulois.* He was racy as the soil. He was as much the product of its generous elements, and of the bland atmosphere and the genial sunshine of the pleasant land which gave him birth, as the wines of Burgundy and of the Bordelais. 'It is,' observes the late Hippolyte Taine, 'because there is a France that there are, as it seems to me, a La Fontaine and Frenchmen. The temperate climate has helped to make the race; the variety and amenity of the landscape have produced the typical Frenchman. Nature, neither harsh nor austere, neither lavish nor niggardly, and easily amenable to culture, has been instrumental in rearing a human being who is neither dull nor ardent—except when excited—and is rather delicate than robust.' And it was a Frenchman,[1] I believe, who first propounded the theory that as is the soil of a country, such are its flora and fauna; and that as are the flora and fauna of a country, such are the human beings dwelling on its surface. M. Taine, with his gift of subtle analysis, has defined with great felicity, and detailed with equal lucidity, the relations subsisting between the natural features of France and the salient characteristics of its people, as exemplified in so strikingly representative a man as the author of the 'Fables.' 'Intelligence,' as he observes, 'shines and sparkles in that old Gallic race; its spirit is

[1] M. Tremaux.

nimble, accurate, shrewd, mischievous, prone to irony, and apt to be amused by the mistakes of others. The soil and the skies of France have left their impress on the mind and body of the Frenchman. Thus it is,' he adds, 'that nature reproduces herself in his mental constitution and character, and the poetical objects outside of him become the poetical images of his inner mind.'

In the preceding lectures we considered the earliest productions of this Gallic nation, when it just began to speak in stammering accents in our *chansons de geste* of the twelfth century; and again in our *fabliaux*, and in the romances of 'Renard' and 'La Rose' in the thirteenth century. The qualities of their style have been noted; and I have endeavoured, however slightly, to indicate how these early singers and story-tellers succeeded on the instant and without effort in acquiring a correct expression, and in immediately arriving at a clear description of the object they wished to depict, without enveloping it in metaphors. If they did not attain any great elevation, yet, on the other hand, they never deviated from the right path, everywhere maintaining that just, measured, and sprightly diction—that language which La Fontaine will renew, polished by classic culture, for the people who will once more recognise it. Racy of the soil, and redolent of the bland climate of France, the *esprit gaulois* has manifested itself from the twelfth century onwards in a series of literary productions which have served as models to English and Italian writers, and have remained an abundant storehouse which our truly national poets—La Fontaine, Molière, Voltaire, and sometimes Béranger—have always ransacked with success.

In order to speak to you of La Fontaine, it seems to me that I must do as he did when he went to the Academy—namely, 'take the longest way thither.' For, in order to reach the Academy at the age of sixty-three, or to explain to us the sayings and doings of his animals, he always follows the most roundabout road he can find, like a true story-teller of the old stock. I will imitate him to-day, and without going back to the Deluge, or wandering off and losing my way in any of the numerous by-paths which offer their allurements to every student of his graceful compositions, I will nevertheless, before analysing his work, say somewhat of the man, somewhat of his *genre*, and somewhat of the writer; but with such due restraint as befits a short lecture in which the listeners expect condensed information and not diffusive disquisition.

Jean de la Fontaine, born in 1621 at Château-Thierry in Champagne, displayed in very early life characteristics strangely at variance with the sober and serious manner of the times. He was *gaulois*, very much *gaulois* indeed; easy-going, pleasure-loving, thoughtless, thriftless, impulsive, volatile, and *insouciant*. His education was a superficial one; but happening to hear an ode by Malherbe recited, he felt the poetic instinct stirring within his own mind. He had picked up a fair knowledge of Latin at school and at the Oratory, where he was actually studying for the Church —fancy La Fontaine a priest!—and a friend gave him a copy of Horace. Thence he was led to read and enjoy Virgil, and presently he was fascinated by Plato and Plutarch, although not in the original Greek. So thoroughly did he master the great writers of classic antiquity that he is said to have been only excelled in this respect by Archbishop Fénelon.

Arrived at years of discretion—no! he never attained to these—but having grown to manhood, his invincible idleness, his careless habits, and the irregularity of his conduct were a source of no little anxiety to his father, who lost no time in providing him with a wife, a certain youthful beauty named Marie Héricart; at the same time resigning his own appointment as one of the crown rangers of the state forests in favour of the young scapegrace. La Fontaine was as little adapted for a life of humdrum domesticity as a bird of the air is adapted to acquire the habits of a goldfish in a glass bowl. And yet there was much that was gay and attractive in the home life of the period. The conditions of existence were comparatively easy among the *bourgeoisie* of France at that time. People dined jovially, were not in a hurry to despatch the wine and fruit, and had leisure even for a spirited song and a merry story after dinner. Perhaps these were a trifle improper, but the author of the 'Contes et Nouvelles,' to which I need not again refer, was not likely to find fault with them on that account. That La Fontaine spent forty years of his life in the country, sometimes at the Château-Thierry, sometimes at Limoges, and often, we may believe, at the magnificent mansion of Vaux le Vicomte, on the Seine, about thirty miles from Paris, where he was the guest of Fouquet, the farmer-general, who had befriended the poet and given him a handsome pension, is a proof that a rural life must have offered many attractions even to a man of so light and lively a disposition as the great fabulist.

The most amusing trait in his character was his absent-mindedness. This clung to him through life. While a mere youth his father sent him to Paris on important business, and anxiously awaited his return. Jean fell in with some old schoolfellows, went to the theatre, and forgot all about his errand. In later years Louis XIV. consented to accept a volume of his 'Fables,' and to hear him read the poetical preface to them. When La Fontaine reached the court he found he had left the volume at home. The king, much amused, presented him with a purse of gold. Returning to Paris from Versailles, the poet put the money under the cushion of the carriage and thought no more about it. Meeting in society with a nice young fellow of his own name, La Fontaine remarked to his homonym, 'I think I have seen your face somewhere before.' The surmise proved to be perfectly correct, for the young man happened to be his own son.

La Fontaine was fortunate in his friends and protectors; Molière, Racine, and Boileau were the most intimate of the former. Fouquet, the Duchess dowager of Orléans, the Duc de Bouillon, the Great Condé, and Madame de la Sablière were among the kindest and truest of the latter. The lady last named gave him a home for twenty years; and when she died M. d'Hervart met him as he was leaving the house and said to him, 'My dear La Fontaine, I was looking for you to ask you to make your home with me.' 'I was just on my way to you,' was the naïve reply of the poet; and there he abode, and was looked after, like the overgrown child he was, by Madame d'Hervart, who, whenever she found his clothes becoming shabby, used to have them quietly removed from his chamber and new ones placed in their stead, while he remained quite unconscious of the change. He died under their roof in the seventy-fourth year of his age; and his epitaph, written by his own hand, compendiously describes his character and career :

> Poor Jean is gone. As he came, he went;
> He ate up his lands as well as his rent;
>   For silver or gold his care was small;
> For his time a fair division he found,
> Spending one half in slumber sound,
>   And the rest in doing nothing at all.

La Fontaine's life was spent in complacent dependence upon others. He was not at all particular as to the source of the bounty upon which he subsisted, or the channels through which it reached him. He was untroubled by any delicacy of feeling in this respect. His judgment of his own foibles and failings was indulgent to excess. He was the Harold Skimpole of his epoch. 'Responsibility!' said that gentleman; 'I am the last man in the world for such a thing. I never was responsible in my life. I can't be.' And one might almost fancy La Fontaine echoing the very words of the light-hearted Harold and exclaiming to his noble and wealthy patrons, 'I almost feel as if *you* ought to be grateful to *me* for giving you the opportunity of enjoying the luxury of generosity. I know you like it. For anything I can tell, I may have come into the world expressly for the purpose of increasing your stock of happiness. I may have been born to be a benefactor to you, by sometimes giving you an opportunity of assisting me in my little perplexities. Why should I regret my incapacity for details and for worldly affairs when it leads to such pleasant consequences? I don't regret it, therefore.'[1] Would any one but a Harold Skimpole or a Jean de La Fontaine have set out to defend a lawsuit affecting some property; have forgotten all about it on the road; and when judgment was entered against him by default, have exclaimed, 'I'm heartily glad of it. I always hated business'?

Our easy-going fabulist was by no means free from the defects of his epoch. He was one of the most obsequious flatterers of the king. He emulated and excelled the adulation heaped upon his sovereign by the *entourage* of that imposing personage. He adored Madame de Montespan; wrote verses on the lapdog of the dowager duchess of Orleans; and after the revocation of the Edict of Nantes, he did not scruple to speak in terms of palliation of that great

---

[1] *Bleak House.*

blunder, which was certainly 'worse than crime.' Yet La Fontaine was at bottom one of the most inveterate enemies of and scoffers at 'the right divine of kings to govern wrong.' No one has spoken more disrespectfully of the great people of the court, and he seemed to feel a particular pleasure in gibing at them. In his Fables such phrases as 'devourers of the people,' 'thieves,' 'persons who have good heads and no brains,' and so forth, are continually occurring. Hence we may conclude with M. Taine that if the poet sometimes donned the livery of a valet he was not a lackey at heart. It seems to me that there was a sort of dual personality in La Fontaine. His intellect and his instincts composed the one, which was robust, independent, and healthy; a soft and flexile temperament and a plastic and impressionable disposition constituted the other; and this made him, under the pressure of worldly circumstances, a man of easy virtue and of time-serving expedients. But his good qualities must have greatly outweighed the defects of his character, or he would never have won the endearing and enduring epithet of *Le bonhomme*.

His own nature was so kindly that he could never bring his mind to believe in the doctrine of eternal punishment; and once, during a serious illness, when a worthy abbé was enlarging on the terrors of divine wrath, an old woman who was nursing La Fontaine called his ghostly adviser aside and said, 'Tut, tut, sir! God will never have the heart to damn *him*.' One of the poet's dearest friends said of him, 'I do not think he ever told a lie in all his life.' Let me add that while La Fontaine was never known to do any person an evil turn he was no less abstinent from calumny and detraction. Very late in life—somewhere about the age of seventy, in fact —he seems to have become acquainted with the New Testament for the first time; and there is something deliciously naïve in his recommendation of it to a young priest. 'It is a very good book, I assure you,' said the poet, 'a really excellent book!'

And now let us glance at La Fontaine as a man of letters. By common consent he is regarded as the greatest French poet of the seventeenth century. Some, indeed, consider him to be the best that France has ever produced. Voltaire has pronounced his genius to be perfectly unique; and the philosopher of Ferney was originally prejudiced against him. He had never read his Fables; and protested they were poor stuff, in an argument on the subject with Frederick II. Then he applied himself to their perusal for the purpose of cutting them up; and reading page after page with increasing interest and admiration, he at length exclaimed, throwing down the volume in a pet, 'Why, the book is nothing but a collection of masterpieces.' And he afterwards declared that the Fables would go down to posterity, because they are adapted to all men and to all ages. Hippolyte Taine said of him: 'He is our Homer, because he is, to begin with, as universal as Homer. Gods and men, animals and landscapes, eternal nature and the society of the time, all are in his little book.' 'His Fables are divine,' was the pithy eulogy of Madame de Sévigné. 'The most original of our writers,' observes La Harpe, 'he is also the most natural. He does not compose; he talks to us.' 'The simplicity of La Fontaine,' remarks Vauvenargues, 'imparts grace to his good sense, and his good sense lends a piquancy to his simplicity.' 'It may be said,' writes Bernardin de Saint-Pierre, 'that La Fontaine has given a landscape to each fable, and that, in that landscape, he has represented all the powers of nature in full activity.' Charles Nisard has charmingly remarked that La Fontaine is the milk of our childhood, the bread of our maturer years, and the last substantial diet of our old age.' 'He is the familiar genius of each fireside; and if a man has only two books in his house the "Fables" of La Fontaine will be one of them.' Lastly, let me quote the affectionate tribute to his genius rendered by Archbishop Fénelon:

'We rank La Fontaine,' he says, 'in right of his delightful talent, not among the writers of modern date, but among the great names of antiquity. If you hesitate to admit this, reader, open the book—what think you? It is Anacreon whose sportive genius is there. It is Horace, whether fancy-free, or in the ardour of passion, who strikes the lyre. Like Terence, he paints to the very life, in his stories, the characters and the dispositions of men; there breathes throughout his work the exquisite taste and polish of Virgil. Ah! when will the cleverest of the human race match the admirable talk he puts into the mouths of his animals?'

La Fontaine's was an intellect which ripened slowly and produced its best fruit late in life—long past the age of sixty, in fact. But we must not conclude that the periods of his youth and of his prime were dissipated in idleness. Indolent he was, no doubt; but there is an indolence which is full of industry. It is that of the man who observes, reflects, accumulates impressions, and is storing away, in the hive of his mind, the precious honey he has been gradually gathering at the very time he appeared to be idling away his hours among the wayside flowers and under the blossoming trees. If he loitered in 'the primrose paths of dalliance,' plucking here a nosegay, and picking up there a pebble, it was in order that he might polish this into a gem, and weave that into a garland which should bloom with immortal freshness and fragrance.

There was an English poet [1] who was as indolent as La Fontaine, and of whom we recall a pleasant picture, standing with his arms behind him, taking a bite from the sunny side of a peach growing on a tree trained as an espalier to a southern wall. Yet this idler, who was as taciturn as the fabulist himself, was quietly absorbing, in his laziest moods, all those aspects and influences of nature which are reflected from the pages of his 'Seasons.' And thus it was with the greater French writer, who exemplified, in a remarkable degree, the truth of Wordsworth's quatrain:

> One impulse from a summer wood
> May teach us more of man,
> Of moral evil and of good,
> Than all the sages can.

It certainly did in the case of La Fontaine. Not only so, but his good genius seems to have conferred upon him the gift of the Fairy Fine-ear; for he may be said to have listened to and interpreted the language of all organic life. Nay, he could read the mind of every creature of the animal and vegetable kingdom; for who, nowadays, would be rash enough to deny the possession of a mind even to the flower or the tree, when a living naturalist [2] has published a treatise on 'The Sagacity and Morality of Plants'? What distinguishes La Fontaine above all other fabulists, as Marmontel says, is that he has actually heard what he relates, and has seen, and is still looking at, what he describes. And each

---

[1] James Thomson.
[2] J. E. Taylor, F.L.S.

of his animals, I might add, possesses an individuality of his own.

Saint-Marc Girardin says of La Fontaine that 'he respected trees almost as much as an Englishman does;' and he was known to spend whole days and even nights in the woods, watching the habits of their occupants; for he was a naturalist as well as a poet. If he had not been the first of fabulists, he might have written another 'Spectacle de la Nature,' like Pluche, or a 'Palingénésie Philosophique,' like Charles Bonnet. Perhaps he might have emulated the two Hubers or Sir John Lubbock; for we are told that, upon one occasion, 'when he was a guest of a certain lady, he was absent from dinner, and did not make his appearance until nightfall. His excuse was, that he had been attending an ant's funeral—he had followed the corpse to the place of burial, and afterwards accompanied the mourners home.'

His study of the emotions and the intelligence of 'our poor relations' conducted La Fontaine to conclusions which were, in some respects, two centuries in advance of his time; for he held not only that animals have souls, but that man is differentiated from them by his possession of a spirit, which he regarded as a divine endowment. His fable of 'The Two Rats' is, indeed, an eloquent confutation of the Cartesian theory of the animal-machine, a masterly vindication of the reasoning powers of the brute creation, and a concise statement of his views with respect to the spirit 'of which man only is the temple;' while in 'The Owl and the Mice' he shows us the bird ratiocinating in a way which could not be excelled if Aristotle himself were the teacher.

La Fontaine began his career as an author by the composition of some poems and stories which, for the most part, are not worth reading or remembering; and it was not until the year 1668, when he was approaching fifty, that the first six books of his 'Fables' made their appearance. Ten years later five more books were published, and the twelfth was not given forth until 1694, when he was 73 years of age. In this work we may find all he thought and felt; for into it he poured out both mind and heart. As Madame de Bouillon has felicitously observed, 'His Fables were self-engendered in his own brain, and were borne by it just as an apple tree bears apples.' And how various they are in matter and in manner!

To quote the words of Bernardin de Saint-Pierre : 'He has sung all sorts of them in all sorts of tones.' He is the moral poet *par excellence*, and also the poet of sentiment. There is in his verses an indescribable flavour of the antique and the Attic, which is peculiarly their own; and time, instead of aging them, only adds to their beauty.

As I have already had occasion to point out, La Fontaine had a strong sentimental regard for nature, such as was very rare among the poets of his generation. Most of his verses were composed in the open air—that is to say, the ideas occurred to him there; and he afterwards bestowed upon them that polish which he thought necessary for their adequate expression. He was as fond of sylvan solitudes as the American Thoreau, and complained of those who mutilated what he called 'the innocent forest.' Tradition says that he sometimes passed the whole night writing fables or other poems in a cave in the wood of Ferté-Milon, near his birthplace, which still bears the name of 'Le Cabinet du Fabuliste.' Once, in the forest of Vassy, La Fontaine was so completely oblivious of the flight of time, that he was lost for a day and a night, and search parties had to be organised to find him out and bring him home.

'This,' said Alexandre Dumas the younger, when speaking of his father, 'is a great baby, whom I had when I was a boy.' There was very much of the 'great baby' about La Fontaine. Indeed, the epitaph which Pope wrote upon John Gay, who is perhaps the best of English fabulists, is singularly applicable to La Fontaine :

>Of manners gentle, of affections mild ;
>In wit a man, simplicity a child.

It has been said that a knowledge of the 'Fables' of La Fontaine is indispensable to every foreigner desirous of learning French. It is not only his language that is acquired, but an acquaintance with the whole of the society of the seventeenth century skilfully epitomised. Like a man relating what he has seen, the people he has met, and the usages by which he has been most impressed, La Fontaine shows us the world of France as he beheld it : the king and his court, the clergy and the courtiers, the priest, the monk, the tradesman, the magistrate, the doctor, the professor, the artisan, and the peasant. He observes them in the palace, in the streets of the city, and in the fields of labour. He does not give you human portraits, as Chaucer does in his prologue to the 'Canterbury Tales,' but, seeking out their animal analogues, he sets them before you, visible realities, vocal and active, and living so veritable a life, as neither Hesiod nor Æsop, neither Bidpai nor Phædrus, neither the unknown authors of 'Reynard the Fox' nor Guillaume Haudent of Rouen, some of whom were his models, ever did before him. It is true his natural history is often at fault, but did not Cuvier himself blunder when he made the memorable declaration, 'Il n'y a pas d'homme fossile'?

I will not attempt to lead you through the menagerie of La Fontaine, or to expatiate on the qualities and characters of the animals whom he has so dramatically portrayed. Taine has done this so admirably and so completely, in his monograph on the subject, that it would be almost impertinent and certainly presumptuous on my part to attempt to follow in his footsteps. It will be better to quote some of the best of the fabulist's compositions as an example both of his genius and of his varied versification; for as, to borrow his own words, his Fables constitute 'an ample comedy in a hundred different acts,' so his vehicle is as various in form, and as changeable in what may be called its modality, as are the metre and rhythms of the 'Ingoldsby Legends.'

The fable which follows is particularly interesting for many reasons. Its groundwork is supposed to have been originally written in Latin by Philelphus, a great Italian scholar of the fifteenth century. Jean Raulin, who was one of the monks of Cluny, introduced it bodily into one of his sermons; and Guillaume Haudent translated it into French in 1547, entitling it 'The Confession of the Ass, the Fox, and the Wolf.' This is said to be even more humorous than La Fontaine's version of the same, which is subjoined:

THE ANIMALS IN THE PLAGUE [1]

One of those scourges which Heaven's righteous wrath
    Invented for the crimes of earth,
      The Plague, if one must call
    The visitation by its hideous name,
    Down on the animal world in fury came,
    Death day by day to some, sore pains to all.

[1] Translated by the Rev. W. L. Collins.

The love of life no more had power to move;
   Food lost its relish; wolf nor fox
   Prowl'd round the innocent flocks;
        The turtle dove
Fled from her sickening mate; there was no love,
   And therefore no more joy.
The lion held a council and spake out:
   'My friends,' said he, 'this pest the gods employ
To punish our misdeeds, I make no doubt;
   Wherefore it seems to me
'Twere fit the greatest sinner of us all
   Should sacrifice himself in expiation,
So to avert Heaven's wrath and save the nation.
   You that read history know that, in such case,
   These acts of self-devotion find their place.
   Let each examine then, as truth compels,
      Without equivocation,
   The tale his several conscience tells,
      And so make revelation.
   As for myself, I candidly confess
      To satisfy my greediness
   I have devour'd sheep not a few,
Who never did me harm; nay, now and then
   I ate the shepherd too;
   I will devote myself, I say again,
   If needful; but I think the rest are bound
   To make a clean confession first, all round.
   Our earnest wish, I hope and trust, is
   The guiltiest should pay this debt of justice.'
'Sire,' said the fox, 'you have too good a heart—
      Such scruples show it;
But, as for eating sheep—why, for my part,
   I see no sin in that. The stupid brutes!
      You do them too much honour, if they know it;
   As for the shepherd, if your taste he suits,
   Why, I can safely say, by nature's laws,
   He well deserves to reap the righteous fruits
   Of man's preposterous claim to hold dominion
   Over us free-born beasts. That's my opinion.'
So spake the fox; the flatterers hummed applause.
   It was not safe to probe too close the offences
      Of the great nobles there,
      Tiger or bear,
Against whose life there might have been complaints;
   All for their deeds found very fair pretences,
   Down to the very dogs that chased a hare—
To hear them talk, they were four-footed saints.
   The Ass in turn advanced to make confession:
      'I mind me once,' said he,
    'When that the devil of hunger took possession
      Of poor unhappy me.

                    I passed a grassy mead
            Belonging to some monks, and in my need
            (It was so tempting) I just took one bite—
            A mouthful—I confess it was not right.'
            All with one voice cried out upon the thief;
              A wolf who had some smattering of law
            Against the prisoner straight took up his brief;
              'A mangy, thick-skinned brute as e'er I saw!
              From him, my lords, no doubt,
              Has all this public misery come about;
              Rank felony! to eat another's grass.'
            Plainly the righteous victim was the Ass;
            No expiation short of death! and straight
                    The wretch went to his fate.

    As you have power or weakness at your back,
    The court whitewashes you, or brands you black.[1]

         [1] LES ANIMAUX MALADES DE LA PESTE
            Un mal qui répand la terreur,
            Mal que le ciel en sa fureur
         Inventa pour punir les crimes de la terre,
         La peste (puisqu'il faut l'appeler par son nom),
         Capable d'enrichir en un jour l'Achéron,
            Faisoit aux animaux la guerre.
         Ils ne mouroient pas tous, mais tous étoient frappés :
            On n'en voyait point d'occupés
         A chercher le soutien d'une mourante vie ;
            Nul mets n'excitoit leur envie ;
            Ni loups ni renards n'épioient
            La douce et l'innocente proie ;
            Les tourterelles se fuyoient ;
            Plus d'amour, partant plus de joie.
         Le lion tint conseil, et dit : Mes chers amis,
            Je crois que le ciel a permis
            Pour nos péchés cette infortune.
            Que le plus coupable de nous
         Se sacrifie aux traits du céleste courroux ;
         Peut-être il obtiendra la guérison commune.
         L'histoire nous apprend qu'en de tels accidents
            On fait de pareils dévoûments.
         Ne nous flattons donc point ; voyons sans indulgence
            L'état de notre conscience.
         Pour moi, satisfaisant mes appétits gloutons,
            J'ai dévoré force moutons.
         Que m'avoient-ils fait ? nulle offense ;
         Même il m'est arrivé quelquefois de manger
            Le berger.
         Je me dévoûrai donc, s'il le faut ; mais je pense
         Qu'il est bon que chacun s'accuse ainsi que moi ;
         Car on doit souhaiter, selon toute justice,
            Que le plus coupable périsse.
         Sire, dit le renard, vous êtes trop bon roi ;

Thus, in playful language and under the innocent form of an apologue, La Fontaine would write a mordant satire on the rulers of France. Beneath the image of the lion we may discover the moral lineaments of the king devouring both sheep and shepherds, or, in other words, preying upon the very vitals of the people, so that he might squander twenty-five millions of money, according to its present value, upon the palace of Versailles, expending considerably more than a million sterling per annum upon the maintenance of the royal household, and lavishing the revenues of the nation upon shameless mistresses and insatiable parasites; while the whole tribe of crafty and cringing courtiers, symbolised by the cunning fox, applauded the extortions and despised ' the stupid brutes' who were the helpless victims of them. Then came the tiger and the bear, representing the farmers-general and the privileged classes generally, the latter numbering two hundred and seventy thousand—themselves exempt from

> Vos scrupules font voir trop de délicatesse.
> Eh bien, manger moutons, canaille, sotte espèce,
> Est-ce un péché? Non, non. Vous leur fîtes, seigneur,
>   En les croquant, beaucoup d'honneur ;
>   Et quant au berger, l'on peut dire
>   Qu'il étoit digne de tous maux,
> Étant de ces gens-là qui sur les animaux
>   Se font un chimérique empire.
> Ainsi dit le renard ; et flatteurs d'applaudir.
>   On n'osa trop approfondir
> Du tigre, ni de l'ours, ni des autres puissances,
>   Les moins pardonnables offenses ;
> Tous les gens querelleurs, jusqu'aux simples mâtins,
> Au dire de chacun, étoient de petits saints.
> L'âne vint à son tour, et dit : J'ai souvenance
>   Qu'en un pré de moines passant,
> La faim, l'occasion, l'herbe tendre, et, je pense,
>   Quelque diable aussi me poussant,
> Je tondis de ce pré la largeur de ma langue ;
> Je n'en avois nul droit, puisqu'il faut parler net.
> A ces mots on cria haro sur le baudet.
> Un loup, quelque peu clerc, prouva par sa harangue
> Qu'il falloit dévouer ce maudit animal,
> Ce pelé, ce galeux, d'où venoit tout leur mal.
> Sa peccadille fut jugée un cas pendable.
> Manger l'herbe d'autrui ! quel crime abominable !
>   Rien que la mort n'étoit capable
> D'expier son forfait. On le lui fit bien voir.
>
>   Selon que vous serez puissant ou misérable,
> Les jugements de cour vous rendront blanc ou noir.

taxation, but empowered to levy feudal imposts and to exact feudal services of the most cruel and oppressive character, some of them so infamous that I may not even name them. Last of all, we arrive at the poor miserable ass, typical of the oppressed and helpless people, sacrificed alike in peace and war. They were, indeed, beaten with many stripes, impoverished beyond all belief, subsisting miserably upon black bread, water, roots, and even grass. In many instances they had lost the very look, nay, even the very voice, of human beings, and resembled wild animals rather than men and women, seeking refuge in caves, because they were too poor to rent even the wretched hovels in which the starving peasants ordinarily found shelter.[1] Pathetically patient and weighed down by a dumb sorrow and a hopeless suffering was that poor, dejected ass, the French people, for whom neither royal lion, nor fiscal tiger, nor noble wolf, nor sacerdotal fox had any compassion whatsoever.

Had La Fontaine lived a little later, we might have imagined that he had the last hours of Louis XV. in his mind when he wrote the fable of the 'Lion who had grown old.' Brief as it is, it is pregnant with philosophical reflection, and one of the expressions in it has given rise to the proverbial phrase, *Le coup de pied de l'âne*. The following is only offered as a paraphrase :

THE LION GROWN OLD

The lion, the terror of forests,
Grown old, and grieving o'er his vanished might,
By scornful subjects was at length attacked,
Who gained in strength as he grew weak.
The horse approaching struck him with his hoofs.
He felt the wolf's sharp fangs, the bullock's horn ;
The wretched beast, dejected, sad,
Could scarcely roar in his decrepitude.
Awaiting his release, he made no moan,
Until he saw the ass draw near his den.
' Alas ! ' he cried, ' 'tis time that I should die,
For to endure indignity like this
Is twice to suffer death.'[2]

[1] See La Bruyère's famous description of them.

[2] LE LION DEVENU VIEUX

Le lion, terreur des forêts,
Chargé d'ans et pleurant son antique prouesse,
Fut enfin attaqué par ses propres sujets,
Devenus forts par sa foiblesse.

After he has done with the monarch of the beasts, La Fontaine proceeds to portray his courtiers—the tiger, the bear, the wolf, and the other members of the quadruped aristocracy—and then he introduces us to the inferior animals, who wear no embroidered suits nor plumes of feathers. But, like the earlier fabulists, he seems to look upon the fox as superior, if not in intelligence, at any rate in craft and tact, to all the rest. As a courtier, indeed, none can approach him, as witness the following fable of

THE LION, THE WOLF, AND THE FOX

A lion old and impotent with gout,
Would have some cure for age found out.
Impossibilities, on all occasions,
With kings are rank abominations.
This king, from every species—
   For each abounds in every sort—
Call'd to his aid the leeches.
   They came in throngs to court.
From doctors of the highest fee,
To nostrum quacks without degree;
Advised, prescribed, talk'd learnedly;
   But with the rest
Came not Sir Cunning Fox, M.D.
Sir Wolf the royal couch attended,
   And his suspicions there express'd.
Forthwith his majesty, offended,
Resolved Sir Cunning Fox should come,
And sent to smoke him from his home.
He came, was duly ushered in,
And, knowing where Sir Wolf had been,
   Said, ' Sire, your royal ear
   Has been abused, I fear,
By rumours false and insincere;
To wit, that I've been self-exempt
From coming here, through sheer contempt.
But, sire, I've been on pilgrimage,
   By vow expressly made,
   Your royal health to aid;

Le cheval s'approchant lui donne un coup de pied;
Le loup, un coup de dent; le bœuf, un coup de corne.
  Le malheureux lion, languissant, triste, et morne,
  Peut à peine rugir, par l'âge estropié.
Il attend son destin, sans faire aucunes plaintes,
Quand voyant l'âne même à son antre accourir:
Ah! c'est trop, lui dit-il: je voulois bien mourir;
Mais c'est mourir deux fois que souffrir tes atteintes.

And on my way met doctors sage,
In skill the wonder of the age,
  Whom carefully I did consult
About that great debility
Term'd in the books senility,
  Of which you fear, with reason, the result.
You lack, they say, the vital heat,
By age extreme become *effete*.
Drawn from a living wolf, the hide
Should warm and smoking be applied.
The secret's good, beyond a doubt,
For natures weak and wearing out.
Sir Wolf here won't refuse to give
His hide to cure you, as I live.'
The king was pleased with this advice.
Flay'd, jointed, served up in a trice,
Sir Wolf first wrapp'd the monarch up,
Then furnished him whereon to sup.

Beware, ye courtiers, lest ye gain,
By slander's arts, less power than pain;
For in the world where ye are living,
A pardon no one thinks of giving.[1]

---

[1] LE LION, LE LOUP, ET LE RENARD

Un lion, décrepit, goutteux, n'en pouvant plus,
Vouloit que l'on trouvât remède à la vieillesse.
Alléguer l'impossible aux rois, c'est un abus.
  Celui-ci parmi chaque espèce
Manda des médecins : il en est de tous arts.
Médecins au lion viennent de toutes parts ;
De tous côtés lui vient des donneurs de recettes.
  Dans les visites qui sont faites,
Le renard se dispense, et se tient clos et coi.
Le loup en fait sa cour, daube, au coucher du roi,
Son camarade absent. Le prince tout à l'heure
Veut qu'on aille enfumer renard dans sa demeure,
Qu'on le fasse venir. Il vient, est présenté ;
Et sachant que le loup lui faisoit cette affaire :
Je crains, sire, dit-il, qu'un rapport peu sincère
  Ne m'ait à mépris imputé
  D'avoir différé cet hommage ;
  Mais j'étois en pèlerinage,
Et m'acquittois d'un vœu fait pour votre santé.
  Même j'ai vu dans mon voyage
Gens experts et savants ; leur ai dit la langueur,
Dont votre majesté craint à bon droit la suite.
  Vous ne manquez que de chaleur ;
  Le long âge en vous l'a détruite :
D'un loup écorché vif appliquez-vous la peau
  Toute chaude et toute fumante ;
  Le secret sans doute en est beau
Pour la nature défaillante.

The fox, as he has a prescriptive right to do, occupies an important position and plays a leading character in these tales. He is, according to tradition, a jester, bantering and sarcastic, and repaying services by insults, but he is so clever that, wicked as he is, he compels us to admire him. We have heard him exclaim to the lion in 'The Animals sick with the Plague:' 'Your scruples denote your excessive delicacy. But to eat such low-bred, foolish things as sheep, can this be wrong? No, no, sire. In devouring them you do them a very great honour!' Here is a courtier of the first water—a creature who knows how to flatter kings without going too far. And now let us see how Master Reynard comports himself towards his comrades. 'The Fox and the Goat' will tell us this:

THE FOX AND THE GOAT

A fox once journey'd, and for company
A certain bearded, horned goat had he,
Which goat no further than his nose could see;
The fox was deeply versed in trickery.
  These travellers did thirst compel
  To seek the bottom of a well;
  There having drunk enough for two,
  Says fox: 'My friend, what shall we do?
  'Tis time that we were thinking
  Of something else than drinking.
  Raise you your feet upon the wall,
  And stick your horns up straight and tall,
  Then up your back I'll climb with ease,
  And draw you after, if you please.'
  'Yes, by my beard!' the other said,
  ''Tis just the thing. I like a head
  Well stocked with sense, like thine.
    Had it been left to mine,

Messire loup vous servira,
S'il vous plaît, de robe de chambre.
Le roi goûte cet avis-là.
  On écorche, on taille, on démembre
Messire loup. Le monarque en soupa,
  Et de sa peau s'enveloppa.

Messieurs les courtisans, cessez de vous détruire;
Faites, si vous pouvez, votre cour sans vous nuire:
Le mal se rend chez vous au quadruple du bien.
Les daubeurs ont leur tour d'une ou d'autre manière:
  Vous êtes dans une carrière,
  Où l'on ne se pardonne rien.

I do confess,
I never should have thought of this.'
So Reynard clamber'd out,
And leaving there the goat,
Discharged his obligations
By preaching thus on patience:
'Had Heaven put sense thy head within,
To match the beard upon thy chin,
Thou would'st have thought a bit
Before descending such a pit.
I'm out of it; good-bye!
With prudent efforts try
Yourself to extricate.
For me—affairs of state
Permit me not to wait.'

Whatever way you wend,
Consider well the end.[1]

[1] LE RENARD ET LE BOUC

Capitaine renard alloit de compagnie
Avec son ami bouc des plus haut encornés ;
Celui-ci ne voyoit pas plus loin que son nez ;
L'autre étoit passé maître en fait de tromperie.
La soif les obligea de descendre en un puits.
 Là, chacun d'eux se désaltère.
Après qu'abondamment tous deux en eurent pris,
Le renard dit au bouc : Que ferons-nous, compère ?
Ce n'est pas tout de boire, il faut sortir d'ici.
Lève tes pieds en haut, et tes cornes aussi ;
Mets-les contre le mur ; le long de ton échine,
 Je grimperai premièrement ;
 Puis sur tes cornes m'élevant,
 A l'aide de cette machine
 De ce lieu-ci je sortirai ;
 Après quoi je t'en tirerai.
Par ma barbe, dit l'autre, il est bon ; et je loue
 Les gens bien sensés comme toi.
 Je n'aurois jamais, quant à moi,
 Trouvé ce secret, je l'avoue.
Le renard sort du puits, laisse son compagnon,
 Et vous lui fait un beau sermon
 Pour l'exhorter à patience.
Si le ciel t'eût, dit-il, donné par excellence
Autant de jugement que de barbe au menton,
 Tu n'aurois pas, à la légère,
Descendu dans ce puits. Or, adieu ; j'en suis hors.
Tâche de t'en tirer, et fais tous tes efforts ;
 Car, pour moi, j'ai certaine affaire
Qui ne me permet pas d'arrêter en chemin.

En toute chose il faut considérer la fin.

This keen courtier, this embodiment of craft, this imp of mischief, plays a thousand and one scurvy tricks upon all the other animals, including the wolf, whom he beguiles into descending into the well, under the pretence that the full moon that he sees reflected in the water is a cheese, whose weight in the bucket that comes down draws the lighter animal to the top.

> He cried: ' My comrade, look you here:
> See what abundance of good cheer!
> A cheese of most delicious zest!
> Which Faunus must himself have press'd,
> Of milk by heifer Io given.
> If Jupiter were sick in heaven,
> The taste would bring his appetite.'

What eloquence does our crafty friend employ in order to extricate himself from the unpleasant position his gluttony has placed him in! It is Io's cow that has given the milk; Jupiter himself would relish such a cheese, and the rogue drags in all Olympus for the purpose of inducing the wolf to come down in one bucket, while he is drawn to the surface in the other. La Fontaine's fox, observes Taine, ' resembles Panurge, who had sixty-three methods of getting what money he wanted, the most frequent and the most honourable being by theft furtively perpetrated; larcenist, card-sharper, guzzler, vagrant, and rapscallion—if there was one in Paris—he remained " the best fellow in the world," and was always scheming some device to outwit the constables and evade the watch. Another peculiarity was noticeable both in Master Reynard and in Panurge, and this is that each was always ready for dinner, having an urgent necessity for a repast, sharp teeth, empty stomach, dry throat, and clamorous appetite. But in a great number of points shall we be struck by the resemblance between the heroes of Rabelais and those of La Fontaine.'

The fabulist at the same time portrayed the sufferings of the people in moving accents and with penetrating power. And, as we know, that brilliant epoch of Louis XIV. was a terrible one for the poor. We obtain a painful glimpse of it in ' Death and the Woodman,' a composition which reveals to us La Fontaine's goodness of heart:

DEATH AND THE WOODMAN

A poor wood-chopper, with his faggot load,
   Whom weight of years as well as load oppress'd,
   Sore groaning in his smoky hut to rest,
Trudged wearily along his homeward road.
At last his wood upon the ground he throws,
And sits him down to think o'er all his woes.
To joy a stranger, since his hapless birth,
What poorer wretch upon this rolling earth?
   No bread sometimes, and ne'er a moment's rest;
Wife, children, soldiers, landlords, public tax,
All wait the swinging of his old worn axe,
   And paint the veriest picture of a man unblest.
On Death he calls. Forthwith that monarch grim
Appears, and asks what he should do for him.
'Not much, indeed; a little help I lack
To put these faggots on my back.'

      Death ready stands all ills to cure,
        But let us not his cure invite.
      Than die, 'tis better to endure—
        Is both a manly maxim and a right.[1]

The ant is the type of economy and order. It is the careful, thrifty, and circumspect manager; and the fable which brings these qualities into the highest relief, by contrasting them with the disorder and improvidence of

---

[1] LA MORT ET LE BÛCHERON

Un pauvre bûcheron, tout couvert de ramée,
Sous le faix du fagot aussi bien que des ans
Gémissant et courbé, marchoit à pas pesants,
Et tâchoit de gagner sa chaumine enfumée.
Enfin, n'en pouvant plus d'effort et de douleur,
Il met bas son fagot, il songe à son malheur.
Quel plaisir a-t-il eu depuis qu'il est au monde?
En est-il un plus pauvre en la machine ronde?
Point de pain quelquefois, et jamais de repos:
Sa femme, ses enfants, les soldats, les impôts,
    Le créancier, et la corvée,
Lui font d'un malheureux la peinture achevée.
Il appelle la Mort. Elle vient sans tarder,
Lui demande ce qu'il faut faire.
C'est, dit-il, afin de m'aider
A recharger ce bois; tu ne tarderas guère.

      Le trépas vient tout guérir;
      Mais ne bougeons d'où nous sommes:
      Plutôt souffrir que mourir,
      C'est la devise des hommes.

other insects, is that of 'The Grasshopper and the Ant,' which I will now read to you:

THE GRASSHOPPER AND THE ANT

A grasshopper gay
Sang the summer away,
And found herself poor
By the winter's first roar.
Of meat or of bread,
Not a morsel she had !
So a-begging she went
To her neighbour the ant,
   For the loan of some wheat,
   Which would serve her to eat
Till the season came round.
  'I will pay you,' she saith,
  'On an animal's faith,
Double weight in the pound
Ere the harvest be bound.'
   The ant is a friend
   (And here she might mend)
   Little given to lend.
'How spent you the summer?
   Quoth she, looking shame
   At the borrowing dame.
'Night and day to each comer
   I sang, if you please.'
   'You sang! I'm at ease;
For 'tis plain at a glance,
Now, ma'am, you must dance.'[1]

[1] LA CIGALE ET LA FOURMI
  La cigale, ayant chanté
    Tout l'été,
Se trouva fort dépourvue
Quand la bise fut venue :
Pas un seul petit morceau
De mouche ou de vermisseau.
Elle alla crier famine
Chez la fourmi sa voisine,
La priant de lui prêter
Quelque grain pour subsister
Jusqu'à la saison nouvelle.
Je vous paierai, lui dit-elle,
Avant l'oût, foi d'animal,
Intérêt et principal.
La fourmi n'est pas prêteuse :
C'est là son moindre défaut.
Que faisiez-vous au temps chaud ?
Dit-elle à cette emprunteuse.
Nuit et jour à tout venant
Je chantois, ne vous déplaise.
Vous chantiez ! j'en suis fort aise.
Eh bien ! dansez maintenant.

The goat is a lady with a white paw, neat, dainty, original, and capricious, equally useless and vain. The distinctive characteristics of that agile animal are hit off in a masterly fashion by La Fontaine, and it is a pleasure to see how he sets her in motion and causes her to act according to his will. The fable is a little jewel of its kind:

THE TWO GOATS

Since goats have browsed, by freedom fired,
To follow fortune they've aspired;
To pasturage they're wont to roam
Where men are least disposed to come.
If any pathless place there be,
   Or cliff or pendant precipice,
'Tis there they cut their capers free:
   There's nought can stop these dames, iwis.
   Two goats, thus self-emancipated—
The white that on their feet they wore
Look'd back to noble blood of yore—
   Once quit the lowly meadows, sated,
And sought the hills, as it would seem:
   In search of luck, by luck they met
Each other at a mountain stream.
   As bridge a narrow plank was set,
On which, if truth must be confest,
Two weasels scarce could go abreast,
And then the torrent, foaming white,
As down it tumbled from the height,
Might well those Amazons affright.
But maugre such a fearful rapid,
Both took the bridge, the goats intrepid!
   I seem to see our Louis Grand
      And Philip advance
      To the Isle of Conference
      That lies 'twixt Spain and France,
Each sturdy for his glorious land.
Thus each of our adventurers goes,
Till foot to foot, and nose to nose,
Somewhere about the midst they meet,
And neither will an inch retreat.
For why? they both enjoyed the glory
Of ancestors in ancient story.
   The one, a goat of peerless rank
   Which, browsing on Sicilian bank,
   The Cyclops gave to Galatea;
   The other famous Amalthæa,
   The goat that suckled Jupiter,
   As some historians aver.

For want of giving back, in troth,
A common fall involved them both—
A common accident, no doubt,
On Fortune's changeful route.[1]

The cat is a hypocrite like the fox. Everybody knows how that sleek personage, with her placid demeanour, behaves herself. 'She is velvety and mottled, with a long tail, a humble countenance, an air of modesty, and a glittering eye.' She sees everything, without appearing to look at anything. The pious creature always moves with the utmost precaution, with a noiseless footfall and eyes half-closed.

[1] LES DEUX CHÈVRES

Dès que les chèvres ont brouté,
  Certain esprit de liberté
Leur fait chercher fortune : elles vont en voyage
  Vers les endroits du pâturage
  Les moins fréquentés des humains.
Là, s'il est quelque lieu sans route et sans chemins,
Un rocher, quelque mont pendant en précipices,
C'est où ces dames vont promener leurs caprices.
Rien ne peut arrêter cet animal grimpant.
  Deux chèvres donc s'émancipant,
  Toutes deux ayant patte blanche,
Quittèrent les bas prés, chacune de sa part :
L'une vers l'autre alloit pour quelque bon hasard.
Un ruisseau se rencontre, et pour pont une planche ;
  Deux belettes à peine auroient passé de front
    Sur ce pont :
D'ailleurs, l'onde rapide et le ruisseau profond
Devoient faire trembler de peur ces amazones.
Malgré tant de dangers, l'une de ces personnes
Pose un pied sur la planche, et l'autre en fait autant.
Je m'imagine voir, avec Louis le Grand,
  Philippe Quatre qui s'avance
  Dans l'île de la Conférence.
  Ainsi s'avançoient pas à pas,
  Nez à nez, nos aventurières,
  Qui, toutes deux étant fort fières,
Vers le milieu du pont ne se voulurent pas
L'une à l'autre céder. Elles avoient la gloire
De compter dans leur race, à ce que dit l'histoire,
L'une, certaine chèvre, au mérite sans pair,
Dont Polyphème fit présent à Galatée ;
  Et l'autre, la chèvre Amalthée
  Par qui fut nourri Jupiter.
Faute de reculer, leur chute fut commune :
  Toutes deux tombèrent dans l'eau.

  Cet accident n'est pas nouveau
  Dans le chemin de la fortune.

She never asks for what she wants openly, like the dog, for example, but fawns upon you with a soft flattering purr, and with an air that is at once caressing and reserved. When the gentle creature becomes portly with age, she puts on an air of goodness and sanctity. Enveloped in her robe of fur, she basks in the sun by day and on the hearthrug at night, passing her paws over her moustache with the calm gravity of a philosopher. She is fastidious and precise, possesses a miraculous address, and never moves in any direction, like the sage and discreet person she is, without first carefully ascertaining the way. La Fontaine has depicted her in many of his Fables. I have selected one in which a young mouse relates to his mother his first encounter with his smooth enemy :

THE COCKEREL, THE CAT, AND THE MOUSE

A youthful mouse, not up to trap,
Had almost met a sad mishap.
The story hear him thus relate,
   With great importance, to his mother :—
' I pass'd the mountain bounds of this estate,
   And off was trotting on another,
Like some young rat with nought to do
But see things wonderful and new,
When two strange creatures came in view :
The one was mild, benign, and gracious ;
The other—turbulent, rapacious,
With voice terrific, shrill, and rough,
And on his head a bit of stuff
That looked like raw and bloody meat—
Raised up a sort of arms and beat
The air, as if he meant to fly,
And bore his plumy tail on high.'
A cock, that just began to crow,
   As if some nondescript,
   From far New Holland shipp'd,
Was what our mouseling pictured so.
' He beat his arms,' said he, ' and raised his voice,
   And made so terrible a noise,
That I who, thanks to Heaven, may justly boast
   Myself as bold as any mouse,
Scud off (his voice would even scare a ghost).
   I cursed himself and all his house ;
For, but for him, I should have stayed,
   And doubtless an acquaintance made
With her who seem'd so mild and good.
Like us in velvet cloak and hood,

She wears a tail that's full of grace,
A very sweet and humble face—
No mouse more kindness could desire—
And yet her eye is full of fire.
I do believe the lovely creature
A friend of rats and mice by nature.
Her ears, though, like herself, they're bigger,
Are just like ours in form and figure.
To her I was approaching, when,
Aloft on what appear'd his den,
The other scream'd—and off I fled.'
'My son,' his cautious mother said,
'That sweet one was the cat,
The mortal foe of mouse and rat,
Who seeks by smooth deceit
Her appetite to treat.
So far the other is from that,
    We yet may eat
    His dainty meat;
Whereas the cruel cat,
Whene'er she can, devours
No other meat than ours.'

Remember, while you live,
It is by looks that men deceive.[1]

[1] LE COCHET, LE CHAT, ET LE SOURICEAU

Un souriceau tout jeune, et qui n'avoit rien vu,
    Fut presque pris au dépourvu.
Voici comme il conta l'aventure à sa mère :
'J'avais franchi les monts qui bornent cet état,
    Et trottois comme un jeune rat
    Qui cherche à se donner carrière,
Lorsque deux animaux m'ont arrêté les yeux :
    L'un doux, bénin et gracieux,
Et l'autre turbulent et plein d'inquiétude ;
    Il a la voix perçante et rude,
    Sur la tête un morceau de chair,
Une sorte de bras dont il s'élève en l'air
    Comme pour prendre sa volée,
    La queue en panache étalée.'
Or, c'étoit un cochet dont notre souriceau
    Fit à sa mère le tableau
Comme d'un animal venu de l'Amérique.
'Il se battoit,' dit-il, 'les flancs avec ses bras,
    Faisant tel bruit et tel fracas,
Que moi, qui grâce aux dieux de courage me pique,
    En ai pris la fuite de peur,
    Le maudissant de très-bon cœur.
    Sans lui j'aurois fait connaissance
Avec cet animal qui m'a semblé si doux :
    Il est velouté comme nous,
Marqueté, longue queue, une humble contenance,

After the upper and the lower came the middle classes of the animal kingdom : the monkey, the type of the charlatan, who chatters incessantly, lies, blabs, fidgets, invents, and is perpetually in motion ; and then the melancholy owl, with his sad-coloured plumage and gloomy expression, a grumbling, reflective, and slightly philosophical personage ; a man of the study. And next chanticleer, with his stern regard and his 'martial walk.' He is jealous, violent, uncivil, not very gallant, turbulent, and always picking a quarrel with other people.

There are other characters exquisitely drawn and taken likewise from the middle classes: the nightingale; the swallow, caracoling in the air, skimming the surface of the water, attentive to his prey, snapping flies on the wing ; the house-bearing turtle ; the gnawing rat ; the lady weasel, with her long corsage and pointed nose ; the frogs perpetually playing the part of a dupe, with their great round eyes ; the timid hare, which is afraid lest its long ears should be mistaken for horns ; the ducks with their waddling gait, their boobyish look, and contented disposition, who are frisky when it rains and express their satisfaction by nasal quacking; and finally the mule, who believes himself to be a person of great importance and who gives himself all the airs of a magistrate.

Why, the Fables of La Fontaine are as good as a popular treatise on zoology, and may have inspired—who knows ?— 'L'esprit des bêtes' of Alphonse Toussenel, if not the 'Etudes sur les facultés mentales des animaux, comparées

> Un modeste regard, et pourtant l'œil luisant.
> Je le crois fort sympathisant
> Avec messieurs les rats ; car il a des oreilles
> En figure aux nôtres pareilles.
> Je l'allois aborder, quand d'un son plein d'éclat
> L'autre m'a fait prendre la fuite.'
> 'Mon fils,' dit la souris, 'ce doucet est un chat,
> Qui, sous son minois hypocrite,
> Contre toute ta parenté
> D'un malin vouloir est porté.
> L'autre animal, tout au contraire,
> Bien éloigné de nous mal faire,
> Servira quelque jour peut-être à nos repas.
> Quant au chat, c'est sur nous qu'il fonde sa cuisine.'

> Garde-toi, tant que tu vivras,
> De juger des gens sur la mine.

à celles de l'Homme,' for which we are indebted to the pen of the late J. C. Houzeau.

A few words, often a couple only, suffice La Fontaine for the portraiture of his personages. 'A mere sketch,' observes Taine, 'is enough for a Fable. It is a little poem in itself and resembles a miniature epic. It must not be dwelt upon long. If this is done, as it is by the Indians (Pilpay), by the fabulists of the Middle Ages, by Chaucer and Dryden, the animal effaces the man, or the man effaces the animal; and at each instant the one is visible through the other.' How many other portraits might I not present to you did time permit: Don Porceau, the pig, with his lazy life, wallowing in fat and filth; and Jeannot Lapin, the hare, a sprightly comrade, who gaily nibbles the herbage in the evening; with his quick eye and his ear alert; who is brusque, giddy, and a gourmand, with no other thought than that of browsing, running about, and doubling on his pursuers.

There is in these middle-class folk an entire class of society—people who are duped and defeated and who sometimes take their revenge. But I can only make this passing allusion to them.

With the reading of one of the best Fables of La Fontaine I will conclude my study of him, which is certainly incomplete, although I have striven to execute it as conscientiously as possible.

THE TWO DOVES

Two doves once cherish'd for each other
The love that brother hath for brother,
But one, of scenes domestic tiring,
To see the foreign world aspiring,
Was fool enough to undertake
A journey long, o'er land and lake.
'What plan is this?' the other cried;
'Wouldst quit so soon thy brother's side?
This absence is the worst of ills;
Thy heart may bear, but me it kills.
Pray let the dangers, toil, and care,
　Of which all travellers tell,
　Your courage somewhat quell.
Still, if the season later were—
O wait the zephyrs! Hasten not—
　Just now the raven on his oak
　In hoarser tones than usual spoke.
My heart forebodes the saddest lot—

The falcons, nets—Alas, it rains!
    My brother, are thy wants supplied—
    Provisions, shelter, pocket-guide,
And all that unto health pertains?'
These words occasion'd some demur
In our imprudent traveller.
But restless curiosity
Prevail'd at last; and so said he—
'The matter is not worth a sigh;
Three days at most will satisfy,
And then returning, I will tell
You all the wonders that befell,—
With scenes enchanting and sublime
Shall sweeten all our coming time.
Who seeth nought hath nought to say,
My travels' course, from day to day,
Will be the source of great delight.
    A store of tales I will relate—
    Say where I lodged at such a date,
And saw there such and such a sight:
You'll think it all occurr'd to you.'
On this, both, weeping, bade adieu;
Away the lonely wanderer flew.
A thunder-cloud began to lower!
He sought, as shelter from the shower,
The only tree that graced the plain,
Whose leaves ill turn'd the pelting rain.
The sky once more serene above,
On flew our drench'd and dripping dove,
And dried his plumage as he could.
Next, on the borders of a wood,
He spied some scatter'd grains of wheat,
Which one, he thought, might safely eat,
For there another dove he saw.
He felt the snare around him draw!
This wheat was but a treacherous bait
To lure poor pigeons to their fate.
The snare had been so long in use,
With beak and wings he struggled loose:
Some feathers perish'd while it stuck;
But, what was worst in point of luck,
A hawk, the cruellest of foes,
Perceived him clearly as he rose,
Off dragging, like a runaway,
A piece of string. The bird of prey
Had bound him, in a moment more,
Much faster than he was before,
But from the clouds an eagle came,
And made the hawk himself his game.
By war of robbers profiting,

The dove for safety plied the wing,
And, lighting on a ruin'd wall,
Believ'd his dangers ended all.
A roguish boy had there a sling
   (Age pitiless,
   We must confess)
And by a most unlucky fling
Half kill'd our hapless dove;
Who now, no more in love
   With foreign travelling,
   And lame in leg and wing,
Straight homeward urged his crippled flight,
Fatigued, but glad, arrived at night,
In truly sad and piteous plight.
The doves rejoin'd, I leave you all to say,
What pleasure might their pains repay.

Ah, happy lovers, would you roam?
Pray let it not be far from home.
To each the other ought to be
   A world of beauty ever new;
In each the other ought to see
   The whole of what is good and true.
Myself have loved; nor would I then,
For all the wealth of crowned men,
Or arch celestial, paved with gold,
The presence of those woods have sold,
And fields, and banks, and hillocks which
Were by the joyful steps made rich,
And smiled beneath the charming eyes
Of her who made my heart a prize—
To whom I pledged it, nothing loth,
And seal'd the pledge with virgin oath.
Ah, when will time such moments bring again?
To me are sweet and charming objects vain—
   My soul forsaking to its restless mood?
   O, did my wither'd heart but dare
To kindle for the bright and good,
   Should I not find the charm still there?
   Is love, to me, with things that were?[1]

Well might Molière exclaim 'Our *beaux esprits* had better bestir themselves, for the *bonhomme* will outstrip us all.'

[1] LES DEUX PIGEONS
Deux pigeons s'aimoient d'amour tendre:
L'un d'eux, s'ennuyant au logis,
Fut assez fou pour entreprendre
Un voyage en lointain pays.
L'autre lui dit: Qu'allez-vous faire?
Voulez-vous quitter votre frère?
L'absence est le plus grand des maux:

Paradoxical as it may sound, La Fontaine was not the author of his own Fables. He wove the admirable metrical

> Non pas pour vous, cruel ! Au moins, que les travaux,
>   Les dangers, les soins du voyage,
>   Changent un peu votre courage.
> Encor, si la saison s'avançoit davantage !
> Attendez les zéphyrs : qui vous presse ? un corbeau
> Tout à l'heure annonçoit malheur à quelque oiseau.
> Je ne songerai plus que rencontre funeste,
> Que faucons, que réseaux. Hélas ! dirai-je, il pleut :
>   Mon frère a-t-il tout ce qu'il veut,
>   Bon soupé, bon gîte, et le reste ?
>   Ce discours ébranla le cœur
>   De notre imprudent voyageur :
> Mais le désir de voir et l'humeur inquiète
> L'emportèrent enfin. Il dit : Ne pleurez point ;
> Trois jours au plus rendront mon âme satisfaite :
> Je reviendrai dans peu conter de point en point
>   Mes aventures à mon frère ;
>   Je le désennuierai. Quiconque ne voit guère
>   N'a guère à dire aussi. Mon voyage dépeint
>   Vous sera d'un plaisir extrême.
>   Je dirai : J'étois là ; telle chose m'avint :
>   Vous y croirez être vous-même.
> A ces mots, en pleurant, ils se dirent adieu.
> Le voyageur s'éloigne ; et voilà qu'un nuage
> L'oblige de chercher retraite en quelque lieu.
> Un seul arbre s'offrit, tel encor que l'orage
> Maltraita le pigeon en dépit du feuillage.
> L'air devenu serein, il part tout morfondu,
> Sèche du mieux qu'il peut son corps chargé de pluie ;
> Dans un champ à l'écart voit du blé répandu,
> Voit un pigeon auprès ; cela lui donne envie ;
> Il y vole, il est pris : ce blé couvroit d'un lacs
>   Les menteurs et traîtres appâts.
> Le lacs étoit usé ; si bien que, de son aile,
> De ses pieds, de son bec, l'oiseau le rompt enfin :
> Quelque plume y périt ; et le pis du destin
> Fut qu'un certain vautour à la serre cruelle
> Vit notre malheureux, qui, traînant la ficelle
> Et les morceaux du lacs qui l'avoit attrapé,
>   Sembloit un forçat échappé.
> Le vautour s'en alloit le lier, quand des nues
> Fond à son tour un aigle aux ailes étendues.
> Le pigeon profita du conflit des voleurs,
> S'envola, s'abattit auprès d'une masure,
>   Crut pour ce coup que ses malheurs
>   Finiroient par cette aventure ;
> Mais un fripon d'enfant (cet âge est sans pitié)
> Prit sa fronde, et du coup tua plus d'à moitié
>   La volatile malheureuse,
>   Qui, maudissant sa curiosité,
>   Traînant l'aile et tirant le pied,

garment in which the stories are arrayed; but the stories themselves are, for the most part, derived from the far East, and are of wonderful antiquity.

Let me, with the aid of the researches of scholars like Professor Max Müller, and MM. H. Regnier,[1] A. Delbouille,[2] and L. Mellerio,[3] trace the genealogy of a single Fable as a case in point. I will take that of 'La Laitière et le Pot au Lait.' Well, we go back to Bonaventure Despériers, a Burgundian poet, who was private secretary to Margaret of Navarre, and whom Charles Nodier associates with Rabelais and Clément Marot as one of the three great writers of the first half of the sixteenth century. Despériers relates just such a story of *une bonne femme qui portoit une potée de lait au marché.* But where did he find it? In the writings of Prince Don Juan Manuel of Spain, who, in the early part of the fourteenth century—for he died in 1347—related the adventures of a farmer's wife who built up a fabric of future opulence on a pot of honey she was carrying to market. And where in his turn did this princely writer get the incident

> Demi-morte et demi-boiteuse,
> Droit au logis s'en retourna :
> Que bien, que mal, elle arriva
> Sans autre aventure fâcheuse.
> Voilà nos gens rejoints ; et je laisse à juger
> De combien de plaisirs ils payèrent leurs peines.
>
> Amants, heureux amants, voulez-vous voyager?
> Que ce soit aux rives prochaines.
> Soyez-vous l'un à l'autre un monde toujours beau,
> Toujours divers, toujours nouveau :
> Tenez-vous lieu de tout, comptez pour rien le reste.
> J'ai quelquefois aimé ; je n'aurois pas alors,
> Contre le Louvre et ses trésors,
> Contre le firmament et sa voûte céleste,
> Changé les bois, changé les lieux
> Honorés par les pas, éclairés par les yeux
> De l'aimable et jeune bergère
> Pour qui, sous le fils de Cythère,
> Je servis, engagé par mes premiers serments.
> Hélas ! quand reviendront de semblables moments !
> Faut-il que tant d'objets si doux et si charmants
> Me laissent vivre au gré de mon âme inquiète !
> Ah ! si mon cœur osait encor se renflammer !
> Ne sentirai-je plus de charme qui m'arrête ?
> Ai-je passé le temps d'aimer ?

[1] *Œuvres de La Fontaine.*
[2] *L'Histoire des Fables.*
[3] *Un précurseur inédit de La Fontaine.*

from ? The Saracens had brought it into Spain from Arabia, where it had formed part of a collection of fables entitled 'Kalila and Dimnah,' the dreamer of dreams of wealth to come being a farmer with a crock of butter and honey, which he was about to dispose of. But where did the writer of these Arab fables get his idea from ? It is to be found in the 'Pantchatantra,' perhaps the oldest collection of its kind in the world, for it is written in Sanscrit, and describes how a certain Brahmin, named Svabhavakripane, who is going to found a rich family, by a hasty gesture overturns a pot of rice, by the sale of which he expects to commence his career of prosperity.

And so poor little Perrette is the lineal descendant of a Brahmin with a name of six syllables, who flourished centuries ago in far-off India ! 'Is there anything whereof it may be said, See, this is new? It hath been already of old time, which was before us.'

LECTURE XVI

Molière (1622-1673)—'Les Précieuses Ridicules'—'L'Ecole des Femmes'

'LIFE is a comedy to the man who thinks, and a tragedy to the man who feels.' In that epigram, by the late Lord Beaconsfield, is condensed the biography of Jean-Baptiste Poquelin, better known to the whole world as Molière, whose life naturally falls into two divisions, the first beginning in 1643 and ending in 1662. It was the period of comedy. It covered the whole of his career as a strolling player; and it corresponded with the immature period of Shakespeare's development as an actor and a dramatist. The future glory of French literature and the French theatre was the light-hearted thinker and observer, wandering with his company from town to town and from city to city, studying character and acquiring experience; familiar with the vicissitudes inseparable from such an existence, and quite unconscious, in all probability, of the possession of that genius which was destined to raise him, in the eyes of an ever-widening posterity, far above the king who patronised and the statesmen and ecclesiastics who tolerated him because he was a special favourite of their royal master, whose will was absolute and whose word was law.

The second period of Molière's life began with his marriage and ended with his death. It was the tragic section of his existence—the epoch of feeling, of labour, of glory, and of suffering. Study his face as it stands revealed to us in the canvas of Mignard, and what a sad and serious expression it wears! It resembles that of Andrea del Sarto, as portrayed by his own pencil in that noble collection of portraits by artists, which forms one of the treasures of the Uffizi in Florence. For both men were alike in their domestic histories. To the French dramatist might be applied the words which Swinburne wrote of the Tuscan painter: 'His life was corroded by the poisonous solvent of love and his soul burnt into dead ashes.' To Molière, Armande Béjart, his beautiful but vain, capricious, and pleasure-loving young wife, was just such a cause of sorrow, affliction, and anxiety as Lucrezia della Fede proved to be to that divine artist who enriched the world by giving it his exquisite Madonna del Sacco, his Dispute of St. Augustin, and fifty other masterpieces. But of the marriage of the greatest dramatist of France I must speak hereafter.

Jean-Baptiste Poquelin, the eldest child of a prosperous upholsterer carrying on business at the Maison des Singes or Cygnes, in the Rue St. Honoré, Paris, was born there early in the month of January 1622, for he was baptised on the fifteenth of that month. The old shop, with its penthouse roof, the timber-framed façade above it, and the massive pillar at the corner, on which were carved a number of monkeys swarming up an orange tree, was demolished in 1802, and nothing but a tablet remains to mark the site of a building which should have been religiously preserved as one of the most precious relics of the seventeenth century. His mother, Marie Cressé—whose father signed his name with a 'de'—seems to have been a somewhat superior woman; and from her Jean-Baptiste inherited a modest independency, as also, perhaps, his intellectual qualities, since these are almost invariably derived from the mother's side. He was educated at one of the best schools of the day, where the illustrious Gassendi was one of his instructors; studied the law, and was, it is said, called to the bar. At the age of fifteen his father had transferred to him his own appointment as valet-de-chambre tapissier to the king; wishing him, no doubt, to follow up the business in which he himself had prospered so well. But the young man had other views, and as soon as he was of age, and had come into his heritage, he made a retrocession of the patent, dropped the name of Poquelin, and assumed that which he was destined to render immortal. He seems to have been drawn towards the theatre partly by a strong liking for it, and partly by a youthful fancy he had conceived for an actress named Madeleine Béjart. She was four years older than himself;

but Arthur Pendennis was by no means the first to fall in love with the mature charms of an attractive Miss Fotheringay. In what relation Molière afterwards stood to Madeleine is not at all clear. Enough to say that he joined the strolling company to which she and her brothers belonged; that some young fellows of good family also associated themselves with it, and that Jean-Baptiste, being the only one among them with money in his purse, became its manager and treasurer. If it had contained a Scarron, its adventures might have supplied material for another 'Roman Comique.' Once, it seems, the whole company were sued by the tradesmen who had supplied them with wearing apparel, candles, and other necessaries, and, failing to satisfy their creditors, the players were cast into prison. Molière, however, gave his bond for the full amount, and it took him fourteen years to liquidate the obligation thus assumed.

After seven years of vagrancy—shall I call it?—we find Molière and his company at Lyon; and there he composed the first of his comedies, 'L'Etourdi,' which was presently followed by 'Le Dépit Amoureux.' They were both of them essays, and not achievements. They stand halfway between the old conventional pieces founded upon the Italian *commedie dell' arte* and the immortal masterpieces which were afterwards to issue from his creative mind. At Pézenas, where the *Etats généraux* of Languedoc used to hold their sittings, Molière played the first of these comedies before the Prince de Conti, who was so much delighted with it that he induced the author to remain there while the session lasted, namely, from the beginning of November 1655 to the end of February 1656. Life was then, as I have said, a comedy to the budding dramatist; and he was never so happy as when seated in the barber's shop kept by Goodman Gély, listening to the gossip of the place, telling farcical stories, playing practical jokes, mystifying the provincial folk by assumptions of eccentric character, and, above all, studying human nature. The big armchair in which he used to sit has been carefully preserved, and is now one of the most precious relics enshrined in the museum of the Théâtre Français.

Molière was fond of making excursions into the country villages round about Pézenas; in one of the latter Gignac, a municipal benefactor, had diverted the water of a spring into a fountain, and had caused to be inscribed above it the Latin pentameter, ' *Quæ fuit ante fugax, arte perennis erit.*' [1] One day when some bystanders were debating the meaning of these mystic words, Molière strolled up and was immediately appealed to, as a man of learning, to interpret the line. He did so in an impromptu couplet :

> Avide observateur, qui voulez tout savoir,
> Des ânes de Gignac c'est ici l'abreuvoir.

We need not follow the manager and his company from place to place during the next two or three years; but let us meet him and them—they were eleven in number—at the guard-room of the old Louvre, in Paris, on October 24, 1658. It is a day for ever to be remembered by Molière; for his lucky star is in the ascendant, and he is to appear 'before their majesties and the whole court'! Just think of it! What an assemblage for these histrionic vagabonds to play before—Louis XIV., Anne of Austria, Cardinal Mazarin, and a crowd of titled notabilities ! The play is the 'Nicomède' of Corneille ; but 'there's pippins and cheese to come.' After the drama Molière came forward, made an adroitly diplomatic speech, and asked for permission to perform one of his own little pieces. It was graciously accorded, and he presented the 'Docteur Amoureux,' a one-act comedy, which has since perished. It was 'a hit, a palpable hit ; ' the dramatist playing the title rôle, and the young king and his court laughing consumedly.

It was the turning point of Molière's fortune. His company received the title and privileges of the 'Troupe de Monsieur,' the king's brother, and was assigned the joint occupancy of the Hôtel de Petit Bourbon, with the Italian company already in possession of it. He was now thirty-six—the same age at which Shakespeare began to put forth his strength, and the *mezzo del cammin di nostra vita*, wherein Dante met with Virgil. Up to this time Molière had been an undistinguished fragment of nebulæ in a firmament glittering with such stars as Bossuet, Pascal, La Fontaine, Racine, and Pierre Corneille. But the time was close at hand when he was to shine with a lustre equal to that of the brightest star in that brilliant constellation.

[1] ' That which was once apt to flow away by art will be rendered perennial.'

He looked around him, and saw that the artificial society of the period and the characters it produced offered an almost boundless field for satire; and with a courage bordering on audacity he selected the superfine society of the Hôtel de Rambouillet, of which I have already endeavoured to present you with a picture, as the subject of his first purely Parisian comedy, 'Les Précieuses Ridicules.' Its success was immediate and immense; it was so great, indeed, that it was well perhaps for the mental balance of the dramatist that his next play but one, 'Don Garcie de Navarre,' was a failure. Temporarily depressed he may have been, but not disheartened; for he wrote his successful 'Ecole des Maris' in 1661, and his equally successful 'Ecole des Femmes' in 1662; and now we arrive at the parting of the ways. We have done with the comedy of Molière's life, and enter upon its more serious passages.

On January 23, 1662, Molière, being then forty years of age, and in relatively affluent circumstances, was married, in the church of St. Germain l'Auxerrois, to Armande-Grésin-Claire-Elisabeth Béjart, who was then verging on her twentieth year. Armande was born about the same time that Molière entered the company to which her alleged brother and two sisters belonged. Her putative father died shortly before her birth. As soon as she was old enough, Molière undertook to instruct her in the art of acting; and when she grew up into a beautiful and attractive young woman, and was qualified by the gifts of nature, by her own vivacity and intelligence, and by the instruction she had received, to shine as the *ingénue* of the troupe, the teacher fell in love with his pupil. All the strength of his earnest and affectionate nature was concentrated in that passion. And Armande? Well, she was grateful, she was ambitious, and she had a worldly wisdom which had been prematurely ripened in the hothouse atmosphere of the theatre. A marriage with the manager of the company would give her an elegant home, a position of predominance among her colleagues, a 'voice potential' in the distribution of parts, and, above all—was she not a woman and an actress?—the means of procuring beautiful costumes wherewith to heighten the charms of her person, and intensify the admiration she had already excited among the gallants of the court. So she became Mademoiselle Molière, as it was the custom to call the wives of actors. The first fruit of their union, a son, was born in the year 1664, and the king, in order to mark the high esteem in which he held the actor-dramatist, stood godfather to the child, while the Duchess of Orleans was his godmother. Nothing, indeed, in the reign of Louis XIV. did him so much honour as his keen discernment and steadfast appreciation of the genius of Molière, and the unswerving loyalty which he exhibited towards him. Yes, the 'loyalty' of a sovereign towards his suzerain in the great realm of human intellect. When the wretched little insects of a day, who buzz and flutter in the sunshine of royalty, objected to sit down at the same table in the palace as Molière because he was a comedian, the king, courteously addressing him as Monsieur de Molière, invited him to breakfast at his own table, carved a fowl for him, and, turning to the high personages who were privileged to be present at the *petit lever*, said, in his most impressive manner, ' You see, I am making Molière eat something, for my *valets de chambre* don't find him good enough company for them.' Thenceforth the titled lackeys, whose very names have since passed into oblivion, were competitors for the honour of the comedian's company; but he had better occupation for his leisure hours than to partake of their entertainments or to listen to their chatter. His genius had expanded, and his life had become a conflict. It was, as I have said, no longer the comedy of the thinker, but the tragedy of the man who felt, and felt deeply, that he was living in a world of shams, falsehoods, hypocrisies, affectations, follies, frivolities, and vanities. It was as if the jocund Touchstone had been suddenly transformed into the melancholy and moralising Jaques, and had exclaimed, like him :

> Give me leave
> To speak my mind, and I will through and through
> Cleanse the foul body of the infected world,
> If they will patiently receive my medicine,

which the 'infected world' certainly did not, but made wry faces continually, and hated the physician by whom it was administered.

First of all, Molière held up to ridicule the servilities of the whole tribe of obsequious courtiers and ennobled bores, in 'Les Fâcheux;' and while the beribboned and perfumed marquises writhed and wriggled beneath the lash of the satirist, the king laughed joyously at the fidelity of the portraits, and the cause of the dramatist was consequently won. He had now reached the meridian of his greatness, and produced the three works which are admittedly his masterpieces—'Tartuffe,' 'Le Festin de Pierre,' and 'Le Misanthrope.' Of the first, a competent critic has remarked that, 'no other study had ever come from the hands of Molière so pitilessly or so carefully worked out. There is no laugh in his eyes as he elaborates the gloomy picture, though there may be a stern smile about his lips. The pencil is as sharp in his hand as the point of a dagger. . . . The laughing genius of the stage has turned all at once into a stern teacher, almost a prophet. It is as if a sudden revelation of the darker side of human character had burst upon him.'

'Tartuffe,' or rather the first three acts of it, was presented before the king on May 12, 1664, to whom it proved to be 'highly diverting,' and he saw 'nothing to object to' in it. But imagine the electric light suddenly turned into a huge dark barn, filled with owls, bats, and other nocturnal birds of prey; and then picture to yourselves the scene of wild confusion, the clamour, and the uproar which would ensue! So was it in Paris, when Molière flashed the light of his genius upon the vast crowd of religious hypocrites who then flourished in that city. They were literally furious, and they were so powerful and so importunate that even the king bowed before the storm they raised, and issued an order suppressing the public performance of 'Tartuffe.' Secretly he admired and enjoyed it; and it is worthy of remark that it was represented afterwards privately and in its entirety, three times, before members of the royal family, and that Molière could scarcely comply with all the invitations which he received to read the play at the houses of people of the highest distinction. By all who were making a trade and a cloak of religion the dramatist was as bitterly hated as he was feared; so that Despréaux was quite right when, speaking of the bigots in a poetical epistle which he addressed to Louis XIV. in 1665, he said:

Pour eux, un tel ouvrage est un monstre odieux ;
C'est offenser les loix, c'est s'attaquer aux cieux . . .
Leur cœur qui se connoît et qui fait la lumière,
S'il se moque de Dieu, craint Tartuffe et Molière.

In the early part of 1665 'Le Festin de Pierre' was presented for the first time at the theatre of the Palais Royal. Incredible to relate, it was a failure, nor did it find its way into print until the year 1819! Yet it is scarcely a less wonderful work than 'Faust;' and Don Juan, as the incarnation of a diabolical cynicism and of utter unbelief, is not unworthy to stand side by side with Mephistopheles. An English critic,[1] referring to Don Juan and Tartuffe, has said: 'They stand before the world the most finished and terrible pictures of the pretended worshipper and the heartless and cynical scoffer which have ever been exhibited. Such blighting and terrible art was not in the nobler and grander imagination of Shakespeare, and we know no other with whom to compare the Frenchman in these his highest efforts. They have remained since then, for all the educated world, the chief impersonations of the hypocrite who insults God and the profligate who defies him. What can all description, all denunciation, do to stigmatise an impostor that will be half so effectual as to call him a Tartuffe? and what other model of heartless and dauntless vice is so instantly understood as Don Juan?'

And now I must revert for a while to the domestic history of Molière before proceeding to speak of 'Le Misanthrope.' The later years of his married life constitute the most pathetic chapter of his biography. The wife he adored, so radiant in her youth and beauty, so fond of admiration, so susceptible of flattery, so fascinating on the stage, and so full of wit and sparkle in private conversation, was naturally an object of attention and of homage on the part of all the *jeunesse dorée* of her time; in comparison with whom, her middle-aged husband, with his contemplative habits, his somewhat melancholy temperament, and his necessary servitude to his pen, appeared to signal disadvantage. Nor did the splendour of his genius compensate, in her eyes, for the absence of those qualities of manner and address which made her obsequious adorers so agreeable to listen to and

[1] Mrs. Oliphant.

so pleasant to flirt with. But whether her indiscretions were as harmless as those of Lady Teazle, under similar circumstances, is not at all clear. One thing, however, is very certain, and that is, that Molière was made completely miserable by the follies of his wife, whom he loved with a devotion worthy of a better object. She was a born coquette, and he a man too great, in every sense, to adapt himself to the variable caprices of a spoiled beauty, surrounded by temptations which she had neither the strength of mind nor the moral principle to resist; while she resented, as a personal affront, any advice, remonstrance, or reproof.

Walking one afternoon in the garden of his country house at Auteuil, Molière unburdened his mind on the subject of his domestic unhappiness to his old friend and schoolfellow, Chapelle. He had tried, he said, to feel or feign indifference to her heartless conduct; but, he went on to say, with touching candour, 'her presence made me forget all my resolutions, and the first words she said in her own defence left me so convinced that my suspicions were without foundation that I begged her pardon for having been so credulous. However, my kindness has had no effect on her. I determined then to live with her as if she were not my wife; but, if you knew what I suffer, you would pity me. My passion has risen to such a height that it goes the length of entering with sympathy even into her concerns; and when I consider how impossible it is for me to overcome my love for her, I say to myself that she may have the same difficulty in subduing her inclinations, and I feel accordingly more disposed to pity than to blame her.'

After their separation, although living under the same roof, they met only at the theatre; and the thought of her was present in the mind of Molière in writing some of the pieces in which they were to play together. This was certainly the case in 'Le Misanthrope,' in which the author acted Alceste, and his wife Célimène, upon whom he had bestowed all the coquetry of Armande. Listen to the heart of Molière speaking with the voice of Alceste:

> Non, l'amour que je sens pour cette jeune veuve
> Ne ferme pas mes yeux aux défauts qu'on lui treuve . . .
> J'ai beau voir ses défauts, et j'ai beau l'en blâmer,
> En dépit qu'on en ait, elle se fait aimer;
> Sa grâce est la plus forte . . .

One day in conversation with two of his most intimate friends, Mignard, the painter, and Rohaut, the philosopher, Molière complained that he was the unhappiest of men; and when Rohaut exhorted him to call philosophy to his aid, the dramatist replied, with a sad smile, 'I should not know how to be a philosopher, with a wife so winsome as mine.'

But something more than unrequited affection found expression in 'Le Misanthrope,' for, as a Russian commentator, M. Alexander Vesselowsky, has pointed out, 'the rancorous hatred of Molière's adversaries, their incessant complaints to the king, the intrigues which surrounded him and poisoned his life, the storm which burst over his head after the first representation of "Tartuffe," revealed to Molière the malevolence of his environments. The germs of "Le Misanthrope" date from that epoch.' And its central character, which, as I have said, is a bit of self-portraiture, has been well described as 'a sad and noble figure of heroic mould, claiming all our sympathies.'

Between the year 1666, in which 'Le Misanthrope' was first produced, and 1673, when the curtain fell upon the chequered drama of his own troubled life, Molière wrote no fewer than eleven plays; and among these were 'Le Médecin malgré lui,' 'Le Bourgeois Gentilhomme,' 'George Dandin,' 'L'Avare,' 'Les Femmes Savantes,' and 'Le Malade Imaginaire;' any one of which would have made the reputation of an ordinary dramatist. Molière seemed to find, in this fever of productivity, a temporary forgetfulness of his domestic misery; but he could not altogether keep it out of his comedies, any more than Byron could prevent his conjugal troubles from obtruding themselves upon the attention of the readers of 'Childe Harold,' of 'Don Juan,' and others of his poems. Here is an illustration of it in 'George Dandin,' Armande playing Angélique:

George Dandin. Quoi qu'on en puisse dire, les galants n'obsèdent jamais que quand on le veut bien. Il y a un certain air doucereux qui les attire, ainsi que le miel fait les mouches; et les honnêtes femmes ont des manières qui les savent chasser d'abord.

Angélique. Moi! les chasser! et par quelle raison? Je ne me scandalise point qu'on me trouve bien faite; et cela me fait du plaisir.

George Dandin. Oui! mais quel personnage voulez-vous que joue un mari pendant cette galanterie?
Angélique. Le personnage d'un honnête homme qui est bien aise de voir sa femme considérée.
George Dandin. Je suis votre valet, ce n'est pas là mon compte.

Molière seems to have tried to bring about a better understanding with his wife in the year 1670. It was that in which he wrote 'Le Bourgeois Gentilhomme.' They had been estranged for four years, and perhaps the actor-dramatist was conscious that his life was rapidly wearing away beneath the heavy strain imposed upon him by his duties as manager, playwright, and principal comedian. He was sad and solitary, and his large heart craved for sympathy and affection. Was there no tender place in her own for the man who had developed all her natural gifts, and heightened them by his own artistic instruction? He would appeal to her love of admiration: he would draw her portrait, with the fondness of a lover, and the tenderness and indulgence of a husband. And he did so in a comedy that will live for ever. The canvases of Claude, Poussin, Mignard, and Le Brun may fade and perish in the course of time; but while the French language endures 'Le Bourgeois Gentilhomme' will endure; and so long as this continues to entertain and delight successive generations, will the portrait of Lucile, that is to say of Mademoiselle Molière, as portrayed by the dramatist, retain its freshness of colour and its charm of drawing. Cléonte, the lover of Lucile, piqued by her conduct, orders his valet to belittle her to the utmost of his power, in order to make his master thoroughly disgusted with her, and thus the dialogue proceeds:

Covielle. Elle, monsieur! voilà une belle mijaurée, une pimpesouée bien bâtie, pour vous donner tant d'amour! Je ne lui vois rien que de très-médiocre, et vous trouverez cent personnes, qui seront plus dignes de vous. Premièrement, elle a les yeux petits.
Cléonte. Cela est vrai, elle a les yeux petits; mais elle les a pleins de feu, les plus brillants, les plus perçants du monde, les plus touchants qu'on puisse voir.
Covielle. Elle a la bouche grande.
Cléonte. Oui; mais on y voit des grâces qu'on ne voit point aux autres bouches; et cette bouche, en la voyant, inspire des désirs, est la plus attrayante, la plus amoureuse du monde.
Covielle. Pour sa taille, elle n'est pas grande.
Cléonte. Non; mais elle est aisée, et bien prise.

Covielle. Elle affecte une nonchalance dans son parler et dans ses actions.

Cléonte. Il est vrai; mais elle a grâce à tout cela, et ses manières sont engageantes, ont je ne sçay quel charme à s'insinuer dans les cœurs.

Covielle. Pour de l'esprit . . .

Cléonte. Ah ! elle en a, Covielle, du plus fin, du plus délicat.

Covielle. Sa conversation . . .

Cléonte. Sa conversation est charmante.

Covielle. Elle est toujours sérieuse.

Cléonte. Veux-tu de ces enjouements épanouis, de ces joies toujours ouvertes ? et vois-tu rien de plus impertinent que des femmes qui rient à tout propos ?

Covielle. Mais, enfin, elle est capricieuse autant que personne du monde.

Cléonte. Oui, elle est capricieuse, j'en demeure d'accord; mais tout sied bien aux belles; on souffre tout des belles.

Some sort of reconciliation between the husband and wife took place in 1671. 'Les Femmes Savantes' was written in the year following, and proved a comparative failure; and in 1673 he produced his 'Malade Imaginaire,' an expansion of a piece he had concocted when he was only a strolling player and young in the business of dramatic authorship. Mrs. Oliphant makes an ingenious suggestion concerning this comedy, which is worth quoting. 'Along with this germ of a story,' she writes, in allusion to the earlier play, 'was there, perhaps, a forlorn fancy of cheating sickness out of its depression by laughing at that as he had laughed at everything else—and a sick and melancholy desire to be thought less really than fancifully ill by those about him, by the friends who would fain have persuaded him to give up the theatre, and by the young wife, who perhaps would be less indisposed towards her husband were he less suffering?'

Be this as it may, he was seriously ill, and much nearer death than any one had reason to suppose. 'Two months before his death,' writes M. Louis Moland in his invaluable study of Molière and his works, M. Despréaux went to see him and found him much troubled by his cough, and so exhausted by it that his end seemed approaching. Molière, though naturally of cold and reserved manners, received him with great friendliness, which encouraged M. Despréaux to say to him, 'My poor M. Molière, you seem to be in a very sad condition; the continual efforts of your mind, and exertion of your lungs on the stage, ought to induce you at least to give up acting. Is there no one in your company, except yourself, who can play the first parts?' (Boileau might just as well have asked himself, ' Is there no one in my household capable of relieving me of the work of composing my "Satires"?') 'Content yourself with writing,' his visitor went on to say, 'and leave acting to one of your comrades. This will make you more respected by the public, who will then consider your actors as your hired servants, and thus the actors themselves, at present not too submissive to you, will better feel your superiority.' 'Ah, Monsieur,' cried Molière, 'how can you speak so? It is a point of honour with me not to give up.' 'A pleasant point of honour' (the satirist continues to himself), 'which consists in blackening his face daily to produce the moustache of Sganarelle, and in giving his back to all the beatings of comedy. What! this man, the first man of our time, both for talent and for truly philosophical sentiments—this ingenious censor of all human follies—cherishes a greater folly than that which he ridicules daily! This shows what men are.'

Nothing of the sort, good Nicolas Boileau-Despréaux. It was your judgment which was at fault. Molière had a nobler motive in persevering to the tragic end than you had any conception of, as will presently be seen.

On February 17, the fourth performance of 'Le Malade Imaginaire' was announced. Feeling worse than usual, Molière sent for his wife and Baron, one of the leading members of his company, and told them how painfully he suffered, and how apprehensive he was that the end was very near. With tears in their eyes they begged him to close the theatre that afternoon. 'How can you ask me to do that,' he plaintively replied, 'when there are fifty poor fellows depending upon it for their daily bread? What will they do if we do not play? I should reproach myself if I were the means of depriving them of their bread for a single day while it is absolutely in my power to procure it for them.' So he issued his orders for the company to be punctually at their posts, and the representation took place. As he lay back in the easy chair in the eighteenth scene of the third act, conscious of his critical condition and feigning to be dead, could he have listened without a pang to the words he had put into the mouth of Argan's wife on hearing of her husband's demise? 'Quelle perte est-ce que la sienne? et de quoi servoit-il sur la terre? .... Viens, Toinette; prenons auparavant toutes ses clefs.' For must he not have felt that his own removal—he, himself, 'mouchant, toussant, crachant toujours'—would occasion a sense of relief to his still youthful and fascinating widow?

In the third interlude, where Molière, as Bachelierus, had to exclaim 'I swear!' in response to the interrogations of the president, a convulsive shudder was observed to run through the actor's frame, yet none of the audience imagined that they were listening to the words of a dying man, or that they were looking for the last time upon the face of a great actor, and the greatest glory of the dramatic literature of France. He was carried home in a chair as soon as the curtain fell, still wearing the costume of *le malade imaginaire*, and feeling his end approaching he sent Baron for his wife. She was probably in her dressing-room at the theatre, which was close to their house, and divesting herself of the costume she had worn as Angélique. When she reached home Molière had breathed his last sigh, supported in the arms of two religious sisters.

In a book which the whole of Christendom agrees to venerate it is written: 'Greater love hath no man than this, that a man lay down his life for his friends.' Molière laid down his for the sake of the fifty poor dependents who looked to him for their daily bread. It was a sublime act of self-sacrifice, closing and consecrating a life which had been loyally dedicated to labour and to duty, to the purification of society by the exposure of its vices and its follies, and to the making of human life brighter, better, and happier by the dissemination of mirth and laughter. Think of the millions of men and women whose cares he has lightened, and over whose hearts he has shed the sunshine of his own lambent wit and benignant humour! Is not such a man a benefactor to his race? And yet only 'maimed rites' were accorded to his mortal remains when they were laid in the burial-ground of St. Eustache. We can forgive much to Mademoiselle Molière for the sake of that fine outburst of indignation which broke from her lips on that occasion:

'Quoi! l'on refusera la sépulture à un homme qui a mérité des autels!' She appreciated him at last.

And so he passed away. 'Passed away'? He can never pass away. He lives, and will for ever live, in the hearts of his countrymen, and in the admiration and affection of the whole civilised world. To quote all the epitaphs and eulogies which his decease called forth would be impossible, yet one I must cite, because it is from the pen of dear old Jean de la Fontaine :

> Sous ce tombeau gisent Plaute et Térence ;
> Et cependant le seul Molière y gît ;
> Leurs trois talents ne formaient qu'un esprit,
> Dont le bel art réjouissoit la France.
> Ils sont partis, et j'ai peu d'espérance
> De les revoir. Malgré tous nos efforts,
> Pour un long temps, selon toute apparence,
> Térence et Plaute et Molière sont morts.

Having thus endeavoured to compress into a few pages the principal incidents in the life of our great comedian, I will now proceed to say something of his works, beginning with 'Les Précieuses Ridicules.'

The affected language, the kind of upper-class slang current at the Hôtel de Rambouillet and in the principal literary *salons* of the period, and written in the interminable romances of Mademoiselle de Scudéry, the standing jest of the time, is what Molière exposes and castigates in this comedy. Until then the epithet Précieuse had been taken seriously. A Précieuse was a superior woman, exquisite in her tastes, refined in her ideas, scrupulous and fastidious in her judgments, and exceedingly delicate in her sentiments. But after Molière's caricature of the name it became a byword, and was thenceforth associated with ridiculous ideas. At the same time the dramatist, as I shall hereafter have occasion to remark, when speaking of that famous Hôtel, denied all intention of treating the queens of society with disrespect. It was only the exaggerations of provincial pretenders, he alleged, that he made fun of. I am afraid there was more of worldly policy than of candour in this ingenious assertion. Be this as it may, the blow struck home, and we are indebted to this comedy for the suppression of that tedious affectation by which conversation had been previously rendered forced and unnatural.

'Les Précieuses Ridicules' really consists of one act divided into nineteen scenes. Two gentlemen, La Grange and Du Croisy, have been rejected by Madelon and Cathos, both of them affected young ladies, and they resolve to be avenged on their scorners. Gorgibus, the father of Madelon and uncle of Cathos, asks for an explanation of their summary dismissal of the two gentlemen who have aspired to their hands. Madelon tells her father that marriage is impossible where the suitor blurts out his proposal in such a matter-of-fact way, and with such an utter absence of romance.

A lover to be agreeable (she remarks) should know how to utter fine sentiments, how to breathe soft, tender, and passionate thoughts, and to make his suit according to rule. In the first place, he must see his lady-love at church, in the park, or at some public ceremony; or else he must meet his fate by being introduced to her through a relation or friend, and leave her presence pensive and melancholy. For some time he conceals from the beloved object the devotion he feels for her, but he pays her several visits, in the course of which he always introduces the subject of love-making so as to give opportunity for discussion by the company. At last the day comes for his making his proposal, which should be done in the side-walk of some garden, when others are at a distance. This proposal is followed by a display of anger, as shown by our blushes, which keeps the would-be lover for some time at a distance. He finds by degrees some mode of appeasing us, and then again paves the way for a fresh declaration of love, and for drawing forth that avowal which causes so much trouble. Then come a series of exciting adventures: rivals who thwart an established affection; persecution of fathers; jealousies arising from misconceptions, complaints, despair, runaway matches, and the necessary results. This is how love affairs should be carried on according to good manners, which ought always to be followed in true gallantry. But to come point-blank to a matrimonial engagement, to make love only with a marriage contract, and to take romance by the wrong end! Once more, dear father, nothing could be more tradesman-like than such a proceeding, and I feel quite upset at the mere notion.

Gor. What devilish nonsense is this? This is nothing but high-flying rubbish.'

[1] Il faut qu'un amant, pour être agréable, sache débiter les beaux sentiments, pousser le doux, le tendre et le passionné, et que sa recherche soit dans les formes. Premièrement, il doit voir au temple, ou à la promenade, ou dans quelque cérémonie publique, la personne dont il devient amoureux... Il cache un temps sa passion à l'objet aimé, et cependant lui rend plusieurs visites où l'on ne manque jamais de mettre sur le

And now her cousin, Cathos, strikes in and exclaims:

How is it possible to receive people who are utterly innocent of all proprieties? I wouldn't mind wagering that they have never seen the Map of True Love, and that *billets doux*, Tender Attentions, Polite Notes, and Sonnets are unknown regions to them. Cannot you see how their whole bearing shows this, and that they have not the air about them which prepossesses one at once in their favour? The idea of coming love-making in plain breeches, a hat without any feathers, a head with undressed locks, and a coat without any ribbons on it! Good gracious! What lovers are these?[1]

Presently the two young ladies, unwilling to be known in Paris by two such provincial names as Cathos and Madelon, renounce them in favour of Aminte and Polixène, as more romantic and poetical, and announce their intention of having nothing to say to admirers whose ruffs are not well made, and whose clothes are not strictly in the fashion.

In the scenes that follow, we shall see how the rejected lovers revenge themselves upon the *précieuses ridicules*. Marotte, their ladies'-maid, comes to tell them that a footman is at the door, asking if they will receive his master, and this is the dialogue which ensues:

Mad. Learn, you stupid creature, not to speak in such a vulgar way. Say, Here is an indispensable who desires to know whether it is convenient to you to be visible.

Mar. By our Lady! I don't understand Latin, and I ain't never learnt flossophy out of Cyrus like you.

tapis une question galante qui exerce les esprits de l'assemblée. Le jour de la déclaration arrive, qui se doit faire ordinairement dans une allée de quelque jardin, tandis que la compagnie s'est un peu éloignée, et cette déclaration est suivie d'un prompt courroux qui paraît à notre rougeur, et qui, pour un temps, bannit l'amant de notre présence. Ensuite il trouve moyen de nous apaiser, de nous accoutumer insensiblement aux discours de sa passion, et de tirer de nous cet aveu qui fait tant de peine. Après cela viennent les aventures, les rivaux qui se jettent à la traverse d'une inclination établie, les persécutions des pères, les jalousies conçues sur de fausses apparences, les plaintes, les désespoirs, les enlèvements, et ce qui s'en suit. Voilà comme les choses se traitent dans les belles manières. . . .

Gorgibus. Quel diable de jargon entends-je ici? Voici bien du haut style.

[1] Je m'en vais gager qu'ils n'ont jamais vu la carte de Tendre, et que Billets-doux, Petits-soins, Billets-galants et Jolis-vers sont des terres inconnues pour eux.

Mad. Impertinent creature! Who can put up with such insolence? And who is the master of this footman?

Mar. He said he was called the Marquis de Mascarille.

Mad. Oh, my dear, a Marquis! a Marquis! Yes, go and tell him that we will see him. No doubt he's a wit that has heard us spoken of.

Ca. Unquestionably, my dear.

Mad. We must receive him downstairs, and not in our own room. Let us arrange our hair properly, and maintain our reputation. Come here quickly and hold to us the counsellor of the Graces.

Mar. Truly, I can't tell what sort of an animal that is. If you want me to understand you, you must talk like a Christian.

Ca. Bring the looking-glass, you stupid creature, and take care not to defile it with the image of your own face.[1]

Both of them then withdraw, to reappear when Mascarille, the valet of La Grange in the disguise of a fine gentleman, has been introduced with much ceremonial, and awaits their return.

Mas. (*after having bowed to them*). You'll be doubtless surprised, ladies, at the boldness of my visit, but your reputation brings this infliction on you. Merit has such potent charms for me, that I run everywhere after it.

Madelon. If you pursue merit, it is not on our grounds that you must hunt.

Cathos. To find merit here, you must have brought it with you.

Mas. Ah, I engage to prove the contrary. Fame told the truth in relating your worth, and you are going to make a clean sweep of all the gallants of Paris.

Mad. Your courtesy pushes the liberality of its praises somewhat too far, and my cousin and I must not take too seriously the sweetness of your flattery.

Ca. My dear, we should call for chairs.

Mad. Almanzor.

Almanzor. Madame.

Mad. Convey to us quickly the conveniences of conversation.[2]

---

[1] *Madelon.* Ajustons un peu nos cheveux au moins, et soutenons notre réputation. Vite, venez nous tendre ici dedans le conseiller des grâces.

Marotte. Par ma foi, je ne sais point quelle bête c'est là; il faut parler chrétien si vous voulez que je vous entende.

Cathos. Apportez-nous le miroir, ignorante que vous êtes, et gardez-vous bien d'en salir la glace par la communication de votre image.

[2] *Mascarille* (après avoir salué). Mesdames, vous serez surprises, sans doute, de l'audace de ma visite; mais votre réputation vous attire cette méchante affaire, et le mérite a pour moi des charmes si puissants que je cours partout après lui.

Madelon. Si vous poursuivez le mérite, ce n'est pas sur nos terres que vous devez chasser.

Mascarille, anxious to sustain his character as a gallant gentleman, feigns to be charmed by the powerful artillery of their killing glances, and begs to know if he is quite safe there.

Ca. What are you afraid of?
Mas. Some robbery of my heart, some attempt upon my freedom. I see there a pair of eyes which look like two very naughty boys, who would play with liberty and treat a heart no better than a Turk would a slave. Why the deuce do they put themselves on their murdering guard as soon as they see any one approach them? Ah, in truth I distrust them, and must either run away or get good security that they will not do me any harm.
Mad. You need not be afraid; our eyes have no evil designs and your heart may repose in the assurance of their harmlessness.
Ca. But, my dear sir, I hope you will not be inexorable to the advances of the easy-chair which has been stretching out its arms to you for a quarter of an hour; pray yield to its desire to embrace you.

Then they proceed to speak of Paris, the great storehouse of wonders, the centre of good taste, wit, and gallantry, outside of which there is no salvation for people of fashion. Mascarille proposes to establish, under their roof, an academy of wits, and says, ' I promise you that there shall not be a

Cathos. Pour voir chez nous le mérite, il a fallu que vous l'y ayez amené.
Mascarille. Ah! je m'inscris en faux contre vos paroles. La renommée accuse juste en contant ce que vous valez, et vous allez faire pic, repic et capot tout ce qu'il y a de galant dans Paris.
Madelon. Votre complaisance pousse un peu trop avant la libéralité de ses louanges, et nous n'avons garde, ma cousine et moi, de donner de notre sérieux dans le doux de votre flatterie.
Cathos. Ma chère, il faudroit faire donner des sièges.
Madelon. Hola! Almanzor.
Almanzor. Madame.
Madelon. Vite, voiturez-nous ici les commodités de la conversation.
Cathos. Que craignez-vous?
Mascarille. Quelque vol de mon cœur, quelque assassinat de ma franchise. Je vois ici des yeux qui ont la mine d'être de fort mauvais garçons, de faire insulte aux libertés, et de traiter une âme de Turc à More. Comment, diable! D'abord qu'on les approche, ils se mettent sur leur garde meurtrière. Ah! par ma foi, je m'en défie, et je m'en vais gagner au pied, ou je veux caution bourgeoise qu'ils ne me feront point de mal. . . .
Madelon. Ne craignez rien : nos yeux n'ont point de mauvais desseins, et votre cœur peut dormir en assurance sur leur prud'homie.
Cathos. Mais de grâce, Monsieur, ne soyez pas inexorable à ce fauteuil qui vous tend les bras il y a un quart d'heure; contentez un peu l'envie qu'il a de vous embrasser.

rhyme made in Paris which you shall not know by heart before any one else. As for myself, you shall see what I am. I scribble a little when I am in the mood; and you will find my compositions—a couple of hundred songs, as many sonnets, and upwards of a thousand madrigals, without reckoning riddles and portraits—circulating in some of the best houses in the city.'

Apropos (he presently adds) let me repeat to you some extempore verses that I made yesterday at a Duchess's, a friend of mine, where I was paying a visit, for I am tremendously strong in impromptus.
Ca. I think they are the very touchstone of wit.
Mas. Listen then.
Mad. So we will, with all our ears.

Mas. Oh! oh! quite off my guard was I
And no harm thinking,
While you I view
Slyly your eyes my heart surprise—
'Stop thief, stop thief, stop thief!' I cry.

Ca. My goodness! that may rank among the finest pieces of gallantry.
Mas. What I do has the touch of a gentleman; there's nothing of the pedant about it.
Mad. Oh no! It's thousands of miles from that.
Mas. Did you mark the beginning—*Oh, oh!* Because it is extraordinary—*Oh, oh!* Like a man who bethinks himself all at once—*Oh, oh!* Taken by surprise—*Oh, oh!*
Mad. I find that *Oh, oh!* admirable.
Mas. It is nothing.
Ca. Good gracious! What do you say? One cannot think too highly of such things.
Mad. No doubt. I would rather have made that *Oh, oh!* than have composed an epic poem.
Mas. Egad, you have good taste.
Mad. Well, I don't think that it is very bad.
Mas. But don't you also admire *Quite off my guard was I*? *Quite off my guard was I.* I paid no special attention to it; quite a natural way of speaking. *Quite off my guard was I. And no harm thinking*—innocently, without malice, like a poor sheep; *While you I view*—that is to say, while I amuse myself with considering, with observing, with contemplating you. *Slyly your eyes.* What do you think of that word *Slyly*? Isn't it well chosen?
Ca. Excellently.
Mas. Slyly, cunningly—it seems as if it were a cat coming to catch a mouse. *Slyly*.
Mad. Nothing could be better.

Mas. My heart surprise, snatch it away, force it from me; *Stop thief, stop thief, stop thief!* Would not you think it was a man crying out, and running after a thief to seize him—*Stop thief, stop thief, stop thief!*

People of quality knowing everything without ever having learned anything, Mascarille has composed some music for his quatrain, and he sings it. He also offers to take the young ladies to the theatre, where he expects them to applaud a new piece he has taken under his own patronage. For his own part, he is in the habit of crying out 'Bravo!' before the candles are lighted.

He invites the credulous pair to admire the details of his dress—the trimmings, his ribbon, the perfume of his gloves, which is 'awfully nice'—showing that our own fashionable slang is borrowed from the Hôtel de Rambouillet—his

---

[1] Je vous promets qu'il ne se fera pas un bout de vers dans Paris, que vous ne sachiez par cœur avant tous les autres. Pour moi, tel que vous me voyez, je m'en escrime un peu, quand je veux ; et vous verrez courir de ma façon, dans les belles ruelles de Paris, deux cents chansons, autant de sonnets, quatre cents épigrammes et plus de mille madrigaux, sans compter les énigmes et les portraits. . . . Mais, à propos, il faut que je vous die un impromptu que je fis hier chez une duchesse de mes amies que je fus visiter ; car je suis diablement fort sur les impromptus.

Madelon. Nous y sommes de toutes nos oreilles.

Mascarille (récitant)—

Oh! oh! je n'y prenais pas garde :
Tandis que, sans songer à mal, je vous regarde,
Votre œil en tapinois me dérobe mon cœur.
Au voleur! au voleur! au voleur! au voleur!

Cathos. Ah! Mon Dieu! voilà qui est poussé dans le dernier galant. . . .

Mascarille. Avez-vous remarqué ce commencement? *Oh! Oh!* voilà qui est extraordinaire. *Oh! Oh!* comme un homme qui s'avise tout d'un coup. *Oh! Oh!* la surprise, *Oh! Oh!*

Madelon. Oui, je trouve ce *Oh! Oh!* admirable . . . et j'aimerais mieux avoir fait ce *Oh! Oh!* qu'un poème épique.

Mascarille. Tudieu! vous avez le goût bon . . . mais n'admirez-vous pas aussi *Je n'y prenais pas garde? Je n'y prenais pas garde*, je ne m'aperçevois pas de cela ; façon de parler naturelle, *je n'y prenais pas garde. Tandis que, sans songer à mal*, tandis qu'innocemment, sans malice, comme un pauvre mouton, *je vous regarde*, c'est-à-dire je m'amuse à vous considérer, je vous observe, je vous contemple; *votre œil en tapinois* . . . . que vous semble de ce mot *tapinois*? n'est-il pas bien choisi? . . . *tapinois*, en cachette, il semble que ce soit un chat qui vienne de prendre une souris, *tapinois* . . . *me dérobe mon cœur*, me l'emporte, me le ravit ; *au voleur! au voleur! au voleur! au voleur!* ne diriez-vous pas que c'est un homme qui crie et court après un voleur pour le faire arrêter? *au voleur! au voleur! au voleur! au voleur!*

feathers, which are 'dreadfully beautiful,' and the odour of his powdered wig, which he gives them to smell, with that perfection of impudence characteristic of the valets of Molière.

And now the Viscount de Jodelet is announced. This is no other than Du Croisy's valet, arrayed like his comrade, and, being an intimate friend of the Marquis de Mascarille, they embrace effusively. They had become acquainted with each other in the army, where both had performed deeds of wondrous prowess, and they brag of them, after the manner of Pistol and Bobadil. The ladies are enchanted. 'For my part,' cries Cathos, 'I've a tremendous liking for swordsmen.'

Mad. I love them too, but I like wit to temper bravery.
Mas. Do you remember, Vicomte, that half-moon that we carried against the enemy at the siege of Arras?
Jod. What do you mean by a half-moon? Why, man, it was a whole moon.
Mas. I think you are right.
Jod. I ought, in truth, to remember it well enough, for I was wounded there in the leg by the bursting of a hand-grenade, the marks of which I still carry about me. Feel a little, if you please, and you will see what a wound it was.
Ca. (*after touching the spot*). It is true there is a terrible scar.
Mas. Give me your hand a moment, and feel this—there—just in the back of my head. Have you found it?
Mad. Yes, I feel something.
Mas. It is a musket-shot that I received in my last campaign.
Jod. (*uncovering his chest*). Here is where a shot went right through me at the attack on Gravelines.
Mas. They are honourable marks which show what one is.
Ca. We make no doubt what you are.

The *précieuses ridicules* are overjoyed to find themselves thus associated with noblemen who are the representatives of wit and valour, and when the marquis and the viscount propose a dance, musicians are sent for and a few friends hastily invited. Alas! we are approaching the end of the comedy, for, just as they are about to set to partners, who should appear upon the scene but La Grange and Du Croisy, each armed with a stout cudgel, with which they belabour their valets, and at the same time order them to lay aside their borrowed finery. Then turning to the disconcerted victims of the hoax, La Grange addresses them thus: 'And now, ladies, in the condition in which they are, you can carry on your flirtations with them as long as you please. We leave you full liberty for that, and my friend and I assure you that we shall not be jealous in the slightest degree.'

The *précieuses* are thoroughly confounded, and the curtain falls as Gorgibus drives the fiddlers out of the house, and addresses his daughter and his niece in these words : ' As for you, you idle wenches, I hardly know why I don't do as much for you. We shall become the common talk and ridicule of everybody, and this is what you have brought on yourselves by your fooleries. Go and hide yourselves, you wretches ; never let me see you again. And as for you, who are the occasion of their disgrace, with your stupid folly, your mischievous amusements for idle minds, with your romances, verses, songs, sonnets, and sonatas, may you all go to the devil ! '

But this charming little comedy, excellent as it is, merely depicts, like the rest of those belonging to the same group, ridiculous people in general, whereas in the 'Ecole des Femmes' we shall find individual characters portrayed. I have chosen this instead of the 'Ecole des Maris,' because it exhibits in a higher degree Molière's knowledge of human nature, as well as his wit and humour. The last-named comedy has been pronounced superior to the former in point of construction ; but as my object is to exhibit the dramatist as a student and explorer of character, I have selected the work in which the two characters of Arnolphe and Agnes have been conceived and delineated by the hand of a master, and more especially because they have left deep and lasting traces on the national language and literature.

L'Ecole des Femmes.

Arnolphe, otherwise M. de la Souche, has ideas of his own on the subject of female education. They are not his ideas exclusively, and one reason why this comedy possesses an enduring interest is that many husbands to this day indulge in the same dreams as Arnolphe. I believe it is Moland who has said that there is the germ of an Arnolphe in every old bachelor. In a word, if husbands nowadays have relinquished the idea of shutting up their wives, they still debate the question whether it is not desirable to keep them in a condition of intellectual inferiority, and Arnolphe's notions on the subject are not obsolete, I am assured, even in this last decade of the nineteenth century.

Arnolphe is a sceptic and a scoffer. He has no belief in female virtue, for he knows, as he thinks, ' the artful tricks and subtle contrivances' of womankind and how easily men are duped by their cleverness. He is not going to be imposed upon in this way, and so he has taken the precaution to educate a young lady to become his wife, and he informs his friend Chrysalde how he has succeeded in his experiment, and how simple, ignorant, and unworldly his Agnes is.

' I want no lofty mind,' he exclaims, ' for a woman who knows how to write understands more than she should do. I intend that mine shall have so little of the sublime, that she shall not even know what a " rhyme " is ; and if she were playing at Basket, and were to be asked in her turn, " What's put into it ? " I would have her answer, " A cream tart." In a word, I would have her extremely ignorant; it is enough, to speak plainly, if she knows how to say her prayers, to love me, to sew and to spin.' [1]

In order to arrive at the desired result, he has watched over his future wife from her earliest childhood.

' I had her brought up,' he goes on to say, ' in a little out-of-the-way convent, in strict accordance with my views—that is to say, enjoining them to bring her up as much like a fool as possible. Thank Heaven, the result answered my utmost expectations ; and when grown up, I found her so simple-minded that I could not be sufficiently thankful for having found a wife entirely to my mind. I brought her home, and, as my house is continually open to a hundred kinds of people, as it is necessary to take precautions, I have kept her apart in this other house, where no one comes to visit me ; and that her good disposition may not be spoilt, I only have persons about her who are as foolish as herself.' [2]

[1] Je prétends que la mienne, en clartés peu sublime,
Même ne sache pas ce que c'est qu'une rime ;
Et, s'il faut qu'avec elle on joue au corbillon,
Et qu'on vienne à lui dire à son tour : Qu'y met-on ?
Je veux qu'elle réponde : Une tarte à la crème ;
En un mot, qu'elle soit d'une ignorance extrême :
Et c'est assez pour elle, à vous en bien parler,
De savoir prier Dieu, m'aimer, coudre et filer.

[2] Dans un petit couvent, loin de toute pratique,
Je la fis élever selon ma politique ;
C'est-à-dire, ordonnant quels soins on emploierait
Pour la rendre idiote autant qu'il se pourrait.

As might have been anticipated, these extreme precautions are the cause of all his misfortunes. It is unnecessary to follow the intrigue through all its developments. Suffice it to say that every one of Arnolphe's prudent devices is turned against himself, and that Agnes falls in love with a young man, the son of one of Arnolphe's friends, who, knowing him only as M. de la Souche, innocently confides to him the whole story of his love affair. Agnes, reproached by her tutor, thus describes how she first made the acquaintance of Horace:

> I was sitting on the balcony, working in the cool air, when I saw a well-made young man pass under the trees close by, and when he saw me looking at him, he immediately bowed to me very respectfully, and, not to be outdone in civility, I returned him a curtsy. He immediately bowed to me again, and I took care to make him another curtsy. Then he bowed a third time, and I instantly returned a third curtsy. He walked to and fro, making me every time that he passed the most beautiful bow possible, and I, looking at him earnestly all the while, made him as many curtsies; so that, if night had not come on, I should still have continued, being unwilling to give way, or that he should think me less civil than he was.[1]

Arnolphe endeavours to impress upon the young lady the impropriety of her conduct, and makes her promise to close the door against the youthful gallant, and, if he should knock, to fling a stone at him from the window. She obeys these injunctions literally; only, when she throws a stone at her adorer, there happens to be a *billet doux* attached to it. Arnolphe thinks it is high time to rescue his ward from exposure to the attentions of rivals by marrying her, and he addresses this solemn homily to her on the subject:

> Dieu merci, le succès a suivi mon attente;
> Et grande, je l'ai vue à tel point innocente
> Que j'ai béni le ciel d'avoir trouvé mon fait,
> Pour me faire une femme au gré de mon souhait.

[1] J'étais sur le balcon à travailler au frais,
Lorsque je vis passer sous les arbres d'auprès
Un jeune homme bien fait, qui, rencontrant ma vue,
D'une humble révérence aussitôt me salue :
Moi, pour ne point manquer à la civilité,
Je fis la révérence aussi de mon côté.
Soudain il me refait une autre révérence ;
Moi, j'en refais de même une autre en diligence ;
Et lui d'une troisième aussitôt repartant,
D'une troisième aussi j'y repars à l'instant.

Matrimony, Agnes, is no joke; serious duties are required of a wife, and I do not intend to lift you to that position merely for your own freedom and pleasure. Your sex is made only for dependence; all the power is on the side of the beard. They are two parts of the same body, yet these parts are by no means equal—one is the superior, the other subordinate. The one is in all cases subject to the other which governs, and that obedience which the soldier shows to his general, the servant to his master, a child to his father, the lowest monk to his superior, does not come near the tractableness, the submission, the humility, and the profound respect which a wife should have for her husband, her chief, her lord and master. When he looks at her in a serious manner, she should turn her eyes on the ground at once, and never presume to look him in the face until he favours her with a gracious glance. This is what our wives nowadays do not understand; but do not be corrupted by the example of other people. Take care not to imitate those wretched coquettes whose pranks are talked about everywhere. Beware of being captured by the assaults of the evil spirit—that is to say, hearken to no young coxcomb.

Consider, Agnes, that in making you half of myself I am giving my honour into your keeping, and this honour is delicate and easily offended. You must understand that there is no trifling on such a matter as this, and that in hell there are boiling cauldrons in which wives who lead bad lives are plunged for ever. What I am telling you is no idle tale, and you must lay these lessons well to heart. If you follow them sincerely, and avoid being a coquette, your soul will be as white and spotless as a lily, but if you lose your honour, it will become as black as a coal—you will appear a hideous creature to every one, and at last, being the devil's own property, you will go and boil for ever in hell, from which may the goodness of heaven preserve you.[1]

> Il passe, vient, repasse, et toujours, de plus belle,
> Me fait à chaque fois révérence nouvelle.
> Et moi, qui tous ces tours fixement regardais,
> Nouvelle révérence aussi je lui rendais ;
> Tant que, si sur ce point la nuit ne fût venue,
> Toujours comme cela je me serais tenue,
> Ne voulant point céder, et recevoir l'ennui
> Qu'il me pût estimer moins civile que lui.

[1] Le mariage, Agnès, n'est pas un badinage :
A d'austères devoirs le rang de femme engage ;
Et vous n'y montez pas, à ce que je prétends,
Pour être libertine et prendre du bon temps.
Votre sexe n'est là que pour la dépendance :
Du côté de la barbe est la toute-puissance.
Bien qu'on soit deux moitiés de la société,
Ces deux moitiés pourtant n'ont point d'égalité :
L'une est moitié suprême, et l'autre subalterne ;
L'une en tout est soumise à l'autre qui gouverne ;
Et ce que le soldat, dans son devoir instruit,
Montre d'obéissance au chef qui le conduit,

Horace, on the other hand, preaches no such sermons as these to the tender-hearted and susceptible girl, and his ardent protestations of affection find opportunities for expression in spite of the vigilant precautions of Arnolphe, who is mortified by the discovery that the young lady whom he has been so carefully educating for himself has baffled all his tactics.

In this comedy the plot is of very little moment, and the play ends with the marriage of Horace and Agnes, the fathers of the bride and bridegroom arriving just in time to bless a union which they had previously agreed upon. What is most worthy of admiration in 'L'Ecole des Femmes' is the dramatic power with which Molière has drawn and contrasted the two characters of Arnolphe and Agnes: the former an egotist and cynic who entertains a very mean opinion of the feminine nature and has no

> Le valet à son maître, un enfant à son père,
> A son supérieur le moindre petit frère,
> N'approche point encor de la docilité,
> Et de l'obéissance, et de l'humilité,
> Et du profond respect où la femme doit être
> Pour son mari, son chef, son seigneur et son maître.
> Lorsqu'il jette sur elle un regard sérieux,
> Son devoir aussitôt est de baisser les yeux,
> Et de n'oser jamais le regarder en face
> Que quand d'un doux regard il lui veut faire grâce.
> C'est ce qu'entendent mal les femmes d'aujourd'hui ;
> Mais ne vous gâtez pas sur l'exemple d'autrui.
> Gardez-vous d'imiter ces coquettes vilaines
> Dont par toute la ville on chante les fredaines,
> Et de vous laisser prendre aux assauts du malin,
> C'est-à-dire d'ouïr aucun jeune blondin.
> Songez qu'en vous faisant moitié de ma personne,
> C'est mon honneur, Agnès, que je vous abandonne,
> Que cet honneur est tendre, et se blesse de peu,
> Que sur un tel sujet il ne faut point de jeu ;
> Et qu'il est aux enfers des chaudières bouillantes
> Où l'on plonge à jamais les femmes mal vivantes.
> Ce que je vous dis là ne sont pas des chansons,
> Et vous devez du cœur dévorer ces leçons.
> Si votre âme les suit, et fuit d'être coquette,
> Elle sera toujours, comme un lis, blanche et nette ;
> Mais s'il faut qu'à l'honneur elle fasse un faux bond,
> Elle deviendra lors noire comme un charbon ;
> Vous paraîtrez à tous un objet effroyable,
> Et vous irez un jour, vrai partage du diable,
> Bouillir dans les enfers à toute éternité :
> Dont veuille vous garder la céleste bonté.

confidence except in his own astuteness and in what he believes to be his own superior knowledge of the other sex; while Agnes is the very embodiment of subtle ingenuity.

They can never grow old and never cease to charm, for each is a leaf taken from the book of nature; while they are also the typical combatants in that battle which is for ever being waged between old heads and young hearts—between the dictates of a selfish and worldly policy and the generous impulses of a warm and disinterested affection.

In the case of Arnolphe the suspicion of distrust with which he professes to regard all womankind does not extinguish the sentiment of love, and he becomes quite tragical when he rails at his evil fate and discovers that he is likely to be fooled ' by a simple girl and a scatter-brained young idiot.' In spite of his egotism, of his ridiculous theories, and of his no less ridiculous methods of reducing them to practice, we cannot help being touched, at the end of the comedy, by his mental sufferings. For here, as M. Moland has observed, ' comic truth reaches those supreme limits which it ought not to transgress. It is poignant without ceasing to be pleasant, and it offers us one of those great moral lessons which one can only receive from life itself.'

How strange it is to love (Arnolphe observes in a soliloquy), and that men should be subject to such weakness on account of these traitresses! Every one knows their imperfection: they are made up of extravagance and indiscretion; their mind is wayward and their understanding weak; nothing is more frail, nothing more unsteady, nothing more false; and yet, for all that, in the world we do everything for these creatures. (*To Agnes.*) Well, let us make it up. Go, little traitress, I forgive you all, and am fond of you again. Learn by this how much I love you, and, seeing I'm so good, love me in return.

Ag. I should like to gratify you with all my heart. What would it cost me if I could do it?

Ar. My dear life, you can if you will! (*He sighs.*) Only listen to that loving sigh, behold this dying look; look at my person, and have done with this young fop and the love he offers you. He must certainly have cast some spell over you, for you would be a hundred times happier with me. Your great wish is to be fine and gay, and I promise you that you always shall be so. I shall be caressing you day and night; I will fondle you, kiss you, devour you! You shall do all you like. Can I say more? (*Aside*) *How far will my infatuation carry me?* (*Aloud*) Nothing really can be equal to my love. What proof of it would you have me give you, you ungrateful girl? Would you like to see me weep?

Shall I beat myself? Shall I tear my hair out? Or kill myself? You have only to speak the word, cruel creature, and I am ready to do it to convince you of my love.

Ag. Stop! All your talking does not touch my heart. Horace would do more by two words than you with all your discourse.[1]

The dictates of the young heart are more powerful than all the arguments of the old head, and love triumphs all along the line.

Such is 'L'Ecole des Femmes' in so far as I have been able to present it within the time at my disposal.

[1] *Ar.* Chose étrange d'aimer, et que, pour ces traîtresses,
Les hommes soient sujets à de telles faiblesses!
Tout le monde connaît leur imperfection;
Ce n'est qu'extravagance et qu'indiscrétion;
Leur esprit est méchant, et leur âme fragile;
Il n'est rien de plus faible et de plus imbécile,
Rien de plus infidèle: et, malgré tout cela,
Dans le monde on fait tout pour ces animaux-là.
Hé bien! faisons la paix. Va, petite traîtresse,
Je te pardonne tout et te rends ma tendresse;
Considère par là l'amour que j'ai pour toi,
Et, me voyant si bon, en revanche aime-moi.

Agnès. Du meilleur de mon cœur je voudrais vous complaire:
Que me coûterait-il, si je le pouvais faire?

Ar. Mon pauvre petit bec, tu le peux si tu veux.
Ecoute seulement ce soupir amoureux,
Vois ce regard mourant, contemple ma personne,
Et quitte ce morveux et l'amour qu'il te donne.
C'est quelque sort qu'il faut qu'il ait jeté sur toi,
Et tu seras cent fois plus heureuse avec moi.
Ta forte passion est d'être brave et leste,
Tu le seras toujours, va, je te le proteste;
. . . .
Enfin, à mon amour rien ne peut s'égaler.
Quelle preuve veux-tu que je t'en donne, ingrate?
Me veux-tu voir pleurer? veux-tu que je me batte?
Veux-tu que je m'arrache un côté de cheveux?
Veux-tu que je me tue? Oui, dis si tu le veux,
Je suis tout prêt, cruelle, à te prouver ma flamme.

Agnès. Tenez, tous vos discours ne me touchent point l'âme:
Horace avec deux mots en ferait plus que vous.

LECTURE XVII

Molière: Le Misanthrope—Les Femmes Savantes

WE have now arrived at that period in the Literature of France beyond which I do not propose to extend the present series of Lectures. I had intended to speak of Racine in this lecture; but as it would be impossible to treat Racine properly in a single discourse, I have resolved to say something further of Molière, preferring to aim at comparative completeness as regards the one, rather than to deal incompletely with both. I will now endeavour to analyse the 'Misanthrope,' that masterpiece of French comedy—of the comedy of all nations, indeed, the typical creation of Molière.

The personages are these: Alceste, his friend Philinte, Oronte who makes love to Célimène, Célimène, her cousin Eliante, her friend Arsinoé, and Acaste and Clitandre, two marquises, who are equally smitten with Célimène. Alceste is the personification of a ridiculous fellow who sets himself up as a defender of truth and justice, and only succeeds in provoking laughter and drawing down upon himself the dislike of his contemporaries. He is rude and uncompromising in his frankness; Rochefoucauld's maxim that 'society could not endure for an instant if some men were not the dupes of others' is unknown to him. In pushing his sincerity to extremes, Alceste awakens our laughter; but his sincerity compels our sympathy and esteem. Célimène is a young widow, very much sought after, very coquettish, a woman of the world, and perfect mistress of her own house, making not only all the concessions to the manners and usages of the times which are required of her, but even going beyond them. If Alceste shows himself surly and maladroit through excess of candour, Célimène has always for everybody the same demeanour, the same smiles, and for nearly everybody the same wittily severe reflections as soon as they have turned their backs. She amuses herself with the attentions of Alceste, just as she does with the homage offered to her by the crowd of other admirers who throw themselves at her feet. The unhappy man suffers both by her coquetries and her worldly insincerities; but her beauty enchains him, and as often as he recoils a step or two backward it is only to be drawn still nearer to her, until at length——. But I am going to unravel the plot before the curtain is up. The first scene is a typical one. Célimène is absent from it, and the character of Alceste is developed in a conversation with his friend Philinte:

Al. I would have you be sincere and, like a man of honour, not let slip a single word that does not come from the heart.

Phi. When a man comes and receives you with an effusion of delight, you should in reason pay him back in the same coin, answer his eagerness as far as you can, and return him offer for offer and oaths for oaths.

Al. No; I can't put up with that base method which most people of quality affect, and I hate nothing so much as the contortions of all those great protestation-makers, those affable dealers in empty words, who attack every one with civilities, and treat with the same air the man of worth and the blockhead. What good does it do you that a man swears to you eternal friendship, faith, zeal, esteem, tender regards, and makes a speech praising you to the skies, when he runs to do the same to the first scoundrel he meets? No, no, there is not a soul with any good disposition who can desire an esteem so degraded, and the highest praise has but a poor relish when one sees that it is shared with all the world. Esteem must be founded on some preference, and to esteem all the world is to esteem no one. Since you give in to these vices of the age, I cannot count you as one of my friends. I refuse the vast complaisance of a heart which makes no difference in merit. I desire to be distinguished from others, and, to cut the matter short, a friend to all mankind is no friend of mine.[1]

[1] *Alceste.* Je veux qu'on soit sincère, et qu'en homme d'honneur
On ne lâche aucun mot qui ne parte du cœur.
Philinte. Lorsqu'un homme vous vient embrasser avec joie,
Il faut bien le payer de la même monnoie,
Répondre, comme on peut, à ses empressements,
Et rendre offre pour offre, et serments pour serments.
Alceste. Non, je ne puis souffrir cette lâche méthode
Qu'affectent la plupart de vos gens à la mode;

I abridge the magnificent scene of the *début* in which Alceste exhibits his misanthropy to Philinte, whose calm rejoinders only have the effect of exciting him. Oronte, one of Célimène's admirers, and consequently the rival of Alceste, pays her a visit, and finding her absent from home, overwhelms our misanthrope with the most effusive protestations of friendship. He is received at the sword's point by Alceste, who says: 'Sir, you do me too much honour. But friendship demands a little more reserve; and it is assuredly a profanation of the name to make such incessant professions of it, for it should spring from judgment and choice, and be preceded by a closer acquaintance, as it is just possible that our temperaments are such that we should both repent of our bargain.'[1]

> Et je ne hais rien tant que les contorsions
> De tous ces grands faiseurs de protestations,
> Ces affables donneurs d'embrassades frivoles,
> Ces obligeants diseurs d'inutiles paroles,
> Qui de civilités avec tous font combat,
> Et traitent du même air l'honnête homme et le fat.
> Quel avantage a-t-on qu'un homme vous caresse,
> Vous jure amitié, foi, zèle, estime, tendrésse,
> Et vous fasse de vous un éloge éclatant,
> Lorsqu'au premier faquin il court en faire autant?
> Non, non, il n'est point d'âme un peu bien située,
> Qui veuille d'une estime ainsi prostituée,
> Et la plus glorieuse a des régals peu chers,
> Dès qu'on voit qu'on nous mêle avec tout l'univers :
> Sur quelque préférence une estime se fonde,
> Et c'est n'estimer rien qu'estimer tout le monde.
> Puisque vous y donnez, dans ces vices du temps,
> Morbleu! vous n'êtes pas pour être de mes gens ;
> Je refuse d'un cœur la vaste complaisance
> Qui ne fait de mérite aucune différence ;
> Je veux qu'on me distingue, et, pour le trancher net,
> L'ami du genre humain n'est point du tout mon fait.

[1] *Alceste.* Monsieur, c'est trop d'honneur que vous me voulez faire ;
Mais l'amitié demande un peu plus de mystère,
Et c'est, assurément, en profaner le nom,
Que de vouloir le mettre à toute occasion.
Avec lumière et choix, cette union veut naître ;
Avant que nous lier, il faut nous mieux connaître,
Et nous pourrions avoir telles complexions,
Que tous deux du marché nous nous repentirions.

Oronte, however, continues just as obsequious as before, and asks his opinion of a sonnet which he has just written.

Alceste declines, but being pressed by the poet, he listens, and Oronte commences thus:

Or. It is a sonnet. (*Reads.*) Hope———It is a lady who had flattered my passion with some hope. Hope———These are none of your long pompous verses, but soft, tender, languishing verselets. (*At each pause he looks at Alceste.*)
Al. We shall see.
Or. Hope———I don't know whether the style may seem sufficiently clear and easy, and whether you will be satisfied with the choice of words.
Al. We shall see presently, sir.
Or. Besides, you must know that I only took a quarter of an hour to make them.
Al. Let us see, sir; the time has nothing to do with it.

> *Or.* Hope for a while allays, 'tis true,
>   And rocks to sleep our tedious pain,
>   But poor gain, Phyllis, must accrue
>   When nothing marches in its train.

Philinte. I am charmed already with this little bit.
Al. (*to Philinte*). What! have you the face to admire this?

> *Or.* You show'd, indeed, great complaisance—
>   Less had been better, on my word;
>   Why should you be at that expense,
>   When hope was all you could afford?

Phi. In what polite terms these things are expressed!
Al. (*aside to Philinte*). Oh, you vile flatterer, to praise such stupid things!

> *Or.* But if an endless expectation
>   Push to the last extreme my passion,
>   Death must be my reliever.
>   Nor to prevent this, serves your care;
>   Fair Phyllis, 'tis downright despair
>   When we must hope for ever.[1]

---

[1] *Oronte. Sonnet.* C'est un sonnet. *L'Espoir* . . . C'est une dame,
    Qui, de quelque espérance, avait flatté ma flamme.
  L'Espoir . . . Ce ne sont point de ces grands vers pompeux,
    Mais de petits vers doux, tendres, et langoureux.
Alceste. Nous verrons bien.
Oronte.   *L'Espoir* . . . Je ne sais si le style
    Pourra vous en paraître assez net et facile,
    Et si du choix des mots vous vous contenterez.
Alceste. Nous allons voir, monsieur.
Oronte.   Au reste, vous saurez

Philinte praises the poetry, but Oronte is determined upon extorting from Alceste his opinion of it, and the latter replies: 'It is always a delicate question, sir, and where genius is concerned we like those who flatter us. But, as I was saying the other day to some one who shall be nameless, when I saw some of her verses: " A man of the world should always keep the whip hand over those tendencies to scribble which beset every one of us, tempting us to make a parade of our weaknesses, for this ambition to shine causes us to cut a very poor figure."'[1] Alceste nevertheless goes on to pick the sonnet to pieces:

Al. Frankly, it is a very good one to lock up in your desk. You have followed bad models, and your expressions are not at all natural. ... This figurative style that people are so fond of has neither the virtue of good taste nor of truth; it is nothing but a playing upon words, pure affectation, and it is not thus that nature speaks. The bad taste of the age in this respect is horrible; that of our forefathers, unpolished as they were, was much better; and

	Que je n'ai demeuré qu'un quart d'heure à le faire.
Alceste.	Voyons, monsieur; le temps ne fait rien à l'affaire.
Oronte.	L'espoir, il est vrai, nous soulage,
	Et nous berce un temps notre ennui;
	Mais, Philis, le triste avantage,
	Lorsque rien ne marche après lui.
Philinte.	Je suis déjà charmé de ce petit morceau.
Alceste.	Quoi! vous avez le front de trouver cela beau?
Oronte.	Vous eûtes de la complaisance;
	Mais vous en deviez moins avoir,
	Et ne vous pas mettre en dépense
	Pour ne me donner que l'espoir.
Philinte.	Ah! qu'en termes galants ces choses-là sont mises!
Alceste.	Morbleu, vil complaisant, vous louez des sottises!
Oronte.	S'il faut qu'une attente éternelle
	Pousse à bout l'ardeur de mon zèle,
	Le trépas sera mon recours.
	Vos soins ne m'en peuvent distraire:
	Belle Philis, on désespère,
	Alors qu'on espère toujours.

[1] *Alceste.* Monsieur, cette matière est toujours délicate,
Et sur le bel esprit nous aimons qu'on nous flatte.
Mais un jour, à quelqu'un dont je tairai le nom,
Je disais, en voyant des vers de sa façon,
Qu'il faut qu'un galant homme ait toujours grand empire
Sur les démangeaisons qui nous prennent d'écrire;
Qu'il doit tenir la bride aux grands empressements
Qu'on a de faire éclat de tels amusements;
Et que, par la chaleur de montrer ses ouvrages,
On s'expose à jouer de mauvais personnages.

I value all that people admire much less than an old ballad that I will repeat to you.

> Had Royal Henry given to me
> His Paris large and fair,
> And I straightway must quit for aye
> The love of my own dear,
> I'd say, Pardie, my liege Henry,
> Take back your Paris fair;
> Much mo love I my dear, truly,
> Much mo love I my dear.

The versification is not rich, and the style is antiquated. But don't you see that this is infinitely better than all those gewgaws so abhorrent to good sense, and that pure love is speaking here?

> Had Royal Henry given to me
> His Paris large and fair,
> And I straightway must quit for aye
> The love of my own dear,
> I'd say, Pardie, my liege Henry,
> Take back your Paris fair;
> Much mo love I my dear, truly,
> Much mo love I my dear.

That is what a heart can say that is really smitten. (*To Philinte, who laughs.*) Yes, Mr. Laugher, in spite of all the wits, I value this more than the florid pomp and tinsel which every one cries up.[1]

---

[1] *Alceste.*   Franchement, il est bon à mettre au cabinet;
   Vous vous êtes réglé sur de méchants modèles,
   Et vos expressions ne sont point naturelles.
. . . .
   Ce style figuré, dont on fait vanité,
   Sort du bon caractère et de la vérité;
   Ce n'est que jeu de mots, qu'affectation pure,
   Et ce n'est point ainsi que parle la nature.
   Le méchant goût du siècle, en cela, me fait peur;
   Nos pères, tous grossiers, l'avaient beaucoup meilleur;
   Et je prise bien moins tout ce que l'on admire,
   Qu'une vieille chanson, que je m'en vais vous dire.
      Si le roi m'avait donné
         Paris, sa grand'ville,
      Et qu'il me fallût quitter
         L'amour de ma mie,
      Je dirais au roi Henri,
         Reprenez votre Paris,
      J'aime mieux ma mie, ô gué,
         J'aime mieux ma mie.
   La rime n'est pas riche, et le style en est vieux:
   Mais ne voyez-vous pas que cela vaut bien mieux

As a matter of course, our misanthrope makes a mortal enemy of the poet thus criticised; and this enemy is so embittered against him that he is the means of causing him to lose an important lawsuit.

We have seen how he speaks to his friends or to those who wish to become so; and now let us observe how he addresses Célimène:

Madame, may I speak plainly to you? I am by no means satisfied with the way you are behaving. My anger rises when I think of it, and I feel that we must break off our connection. Yes, I should deceive you if I spoke otherwise; sooner or later we must certainly part. I might promise you the contrary a thousand times, but I should not have it in my power to do it.[1]

Célimène replies to his ill-humour in a bantering strain, and asks him whether she can help people admiring her, and whether he thinks she ought to drive them away with a stick. Alceste replies:

No; it is not a stick, madame, that you need, but a heart less easy and melting at their love sighs. I know that your charms accompany you everywhere, but the reception you give them retains those whom your eyes attract; and your gentleness to those who surrender to you finishes in every heart the work which your charms had begun. The too lively hope you inspire them with fixes their assiduous attendance about you; and a more reserved complaisance on your part would drive away that swarm

>   Que ces colifichets dont le bon sens murmure,
>   Et que la passion parle là toute pure?
>   Si le roi m'avait donné
>   Paris, sa grand'ville,
>   Et qu'il me fallût quitter
>   L'amour de ma mie,
>   Je dirais au roi Henri,
>   Reprenez votre Paris,
>   J'aime mieux ma mie, ô gué,
>   J'aime mieux ma mie.
>   Voilà ce que peut dire un cœur vraiment épris.
>   Oui, Monsieur le rieur, malgré vos beaux esprits,
>   J'estime plus cela que la pompe fleurie
>   De tous ces faux brillants, où chacun se récrie.

[1] *Alceste.* Madame, voulez-vous que je vous parle net?
De vos façons d'agir je suis mal satisfait:
Contre elles dans mon cœur trop de bile s'assemble,
Et je sens qu'il faudra que nous rompions ensemble:
Oui, je vous tromperais de parler autrement;
Tôt ou tard nous romprons indubitablement:
Et je vous promettrais mille fois le contraire,
Que je ne serais pas en pouvoir de le faire.

of admirers. But, however, tell me, madame, by what chance that Clitandre of yours has the good luck to please you so much. On what foundation of merit and sublime virtue do you base the honour of your esteem for him? Is it for his beautifully kept finger-nails that he has gained your evident regard? Did you yield, like all the fashionable world, to the surpassing beauty of his fair wig? Or is it his large knee ornaments which make you like him? Has his profusion of ribbons charmed you? Or is it by the allurement of his large rhingrave that he has gained your heart, while he was acting the part of your slave? Or have his manner of laughing and his effeminate voice found the secret of touching you?[1]

In the fourth scene of the second act we listen to a running fire of scandals launched in rapid succession by Célimène, and replied to by Clitandre and Acaste. Her raillery is guarded; she converses without impetuosity, and maintains the tone and diction of the well-bred woman of the world which she is:

Acaste. And Géralde, madame?
Cél. Oh, the tedious romancer! One never hears him leave his grand society. He's head over ears with great people, and never speaks of any one less than a duke, a prince, or a princess. Grand folks turn his head, and all his discourse turns upon nothing but horses, equipages, and dogs; he thee's and thou's

[1] *Alceste.* Non, ce n'est pas, madame, un bâton qu'il faut prendre,
  Mais un cœur à leurs vœux moins facile et moins tendre.
  Je sais que vos appas vous suivent en tous lieux;
  Mais votre accueil retient ceux qu'attirent vos yeux,
  Et sa douceur, offerte à qui vous rend les armes
  Achève sur les cœurs l'ouvrage de vos charmes.
  Le trop riant espoir que vous leur présentez
  Attache autour de vous leurs assiduités;
  Et votre complaisance, un peu moins étendue,
  De tant de soupirants chasseroit la cohue.
  Mais, au moins, dites-moi, madame, par quel sort
  Votre Clitandre a l'heur de vous plaire si fort?
  Sur quels fonds de mérite et de vertu sublime
  Appuyez-vous en lui l'honneur de votre estime?
  Est-ce par l'ongle long qu'il porte au petit doigt,
  Qu'il s'est acquis chez vous l'estime où l'on le voit?
  Vous êtes-vous rendue, avec tout le beau monde,
  Au mérite éclatant de sa perruque blonde?
  Sont-ce ces grands canons qui vous le font aimer?
  L'amas de ses rubans a-t-il su vous charmer?
  Est-ce par les appas de sa vaste rhingrave
  Qu'il a gagné votre âme en faisant votre esclave?
  Ou sa façon de rire, et son ton de fausset,
  Ont-ils de vous toucher su trouver le secret?

people of the highest rank, and the word 'sir' is quite obsolete with him.

Cli. They say that he is most intimate with Bélise.

Cél. Oh, the stupidity of the woman, and her dry conversation! I suffer a perfect martyrdom when she comes to see me. One has to rack one's brain all the time to find out what to say to her, and the barrenness of her ideas lets the conversation drop at every turn. In vain do you invoke the aid of all your commonplace subjects to attack the stupid silence; the fine weather or the rain, the cold or the heat, are matters one soon exhausts with her. At the same time, her visits, insupportable enough in themselves, are drawn out to an unconscionable length, and one may ask what o'clock it is, and yawn twenty times, she no more thinks of moving than if she were a log of wood.[1]

Taine has remarked, when comparing Sheridan's 'School for Scandal' with the 'Misanthrope,' that Molière brings upon the scene the perversities of the world without magnifying them, while in the English comedy they are rather caricatured than portrayed. Célimène is the only censorious person in the 'Misanthrope;' whereas in the 'School for Scandal' all the characters are addicted to backbiting, and with so much animosity that they descend to buffoonery—a remark which I think errs on the side of severity. Sheridan's comedy is, in the estimation of Taine, one of the most bril-

---

[1] *Acaste.* Et Géralde, madame?
Célimène.   Oh l'ennuyeux conteur !
    Jamais on ne le voit sortir du grand seigneur.
    Dans le brillant commerce il se mêle sans cesse,
    Et ne cite jamais que duc, prince, ou princesse.
    La qualité l'entête ; et tous ses entretiens
    Ne sont que de chevaux, d'équipage, et de chiens.
    Il tutaye, en parlant, ceux du plus haut étage,
    Et le nom de monsieur est chez lui hors d'usage.
Clitandre. On dit qu'avec Bélise il est du dernier bien.
Célimène. Le pauvre esprit de femme et le sec entretien !
    Lorsqu'elle vient me voir, je souffre le martyre,
    Il faut suer sans cesse à chercher que lui dire ;
    Et la stérilité de son expression
    Fait mourir à tous coups la conversation.
    En vain, pour attaquer son stupide silence,
    De tous les lieux communs vous prenez l'assistance ;
    Le beau temps et la pluie, et le froid et le chaud,
    Sont des fonds qu'avec elle on épuise bientôt.
    Cependant sa visite, assez insupportable,
    Traîne en une longueur encore épouvantable ;
    Et l'on demande l'heure, et l'on bâille vingt fois,
    Qu'elle grouille aussi peu qu'une pièce de bois.

liant of fireworks; and he remarks that its author compels us to admire and applaud the vivacity of the action and the charm of the dialogue, and to admit that, 'after all, next to great inventive faculty, animation and wit are the most agreeable gifts in the world.' But I am wandering away from the 'Misanthrope.' The scene from which I have just quoted concludes with a sensible speech from Eliante:

Love for the most part is not governed by these rules, and we always find lovers extolling their choice. Their passion never sees anything to be blamed, and everything becomes lovable in the person beloved. They reckon blemishes as perfections, and know how to give them pleasing names. The pale vies with the jasmine in fairness; the deepest black is an adorable brunette; the lean has shapeliness and ease of deportment; the stout has a stateliness full of majesty; the slattern by nature, who has few charms, is termed a negligent beauty; the giantess becomes a goddess in their eyes; the dwarf an epitome of all the wonders of heaven; the haughty has a soul worthy of a diadem; the cheat has wit; the fool is all good-nature; the chatterbox has a pleasant humour; and the dumb preserves a decent modesty. It is thus that the ardent lover loves even the very faults of the person he loves.[1]

In the third act there is a scene between Célimène and Arsinoé which is a perfect gem. The latter, seating herself, after the usual interchange of compliments commences thus:

Ar. It is not at all necessary. Friendship, madame, ought above all to display itself in those things which may be of most

[1] L'amour, pour l'ordinaire, est peu fait à ces lois,
Et l'on voit les amants vanter toujours leur choix.
Jamais leur passion n'y voit rien de blâmable,
Et dans l'objet aimé tout leur devient aimable;
Ils comptent les défauts pour des perfections,
Et savent y donner de favorables noms.
La pâle est aux jasmins en blancheur comparable;
La noire à faire peur, une brune adorable;
La maigre a de la taille et de la liberté;
La grasse est, dans son port, pleine de majesté;
La malpropre sur soi, de peu d'attraits chargée,
Est mise sous le nom de beauté négligée;
La géante paroît une déesse aux yeux;
La naine, un abrégé des merveilles des cieux;
L'orgueilleuse a le cœur digne d'une couronne;
La fourbe a de l'esprit; la sotte est toute bonne;
La trop grande parleuse est d'agréable humeur;
Et la muette garde une honnête pudeur.
C'est ainsi qu'un amant, dont l'ardeur est extrême,
Aime jusqu'aux défauts des personnes qu'il aime.

importance to us. And as nothing can possibly be more important than honour and decorum, I come to show the kindliness my heart feels for you by telling you of something which touches your honour. Yesterday I was calling on some people of distinguished virtue, and the conversation turned on you, and your conduct, madame, with its great display, unhappily did not meet with commendation. This crowd of people whose visits you admit, your easy manners and the talk they give rise to, found more critics than was desirable, and the censure was more severe than I should have wished. You may well suppose which side I took. I did all I could in your defence. I strongly excused you on the ground of your good intentions, and offered to be answerable for your good principles. But you know there are certain things in life which one cannot excuse, even with the strongest desire to do so, and I was obliged to own that your way of living did you a certain amount of harm; that in the eyes of the world it had an ill appearance; that all sorts of ill-natured stories are being told about you, and that if you chose uncharitable judges would have less to find fault with. Not that I believe that decency is in any way outraged—Heaven forbid such a thought! But people easily give credit to the shadow of a fault, and it is not enough to live well, as far as regards ourselves. I believe, madame, that you are too sensible not to take in good part this useful advice, and that you will attribute it to the secret promptings of a zeal which attaches me thoroughly to your interests.

Cél. Madame, I must thank you greatly for the advice you have given me, and far from taking it ill, I desire at once to acknowledge the favour by telling you something that equally touches your honour. And as I see that you prove yourself my friend by telling me of the reports people spread about me, I shall in my turn follow so kind an example by acquainting you with what people say of you. I was paying a visit the other day, and found there some people of rare merit, who, speaking of the care which those must take who lead a virtuous life, turned the conversation on you. There your prudishness and your displays of zeal were by no means referred to as a good model; your affectation of an outward gravity, your endless discourses about wisdom and honour, your affectation and outcries at the shadow of an indecency, through an ambiguous word, which yet may have been meant innocently; the high esteem you are held in by yourself, and the eye of pity you cast on every one else; your frequent lectures and your bitter censures upon things that are innocent and pure; all this, madame, if I may speak frankly to you, was blamed by common consent. What is the good, they said, of that modest look and that quiet exterior which all the rest belies? She's most punctual at her devotions, but she beats her servants and does not pay them their wages. She makes a great show of zeal in all places of devotion, but she paints and wishes to appear handsome. She has nude figures in pictures covered over, but she likes the reality. For my part I undertook your defence against them all, and positively assured them that it was all scandal. But the whole run of their opinion was against me, and their conclusion was that you would do well to trouble less about the actions of others and to take a little more pains with your own; that one ought to look a long time into one's self before thinking of condemning others; that we should add the weight of an exemplary life to the corrections we desire to make in our neighbours, and that it would be still better for us to leave this matter to those in whose hands Heaven has placed it. I believe that you also are too reasonable, madame, not to take this advice in good part, and that you will attribute it to the secret promptings of a zeal which attaches me thoroughly to your interests.[1]

[1] *Ar.* Madame; l'amitié doit surtout éclater
Aux choses qui le plus nous peuvent importer;
Et comme il n'en est point de plus grande importance
Que celles de l'honneur et de la bienséance,
Je viens, par un avis qui touche votre honneur,
Témoigner l'amitié que pour vous a mon cœur.
Hier j'étois chez des gens de vertu singulière,
Où sur vous du discours on tourna la matière;
Et là, votre conduite avec ses grands éclats,
Madame, eut le malheur qu'on ne la loua pas.
Cette foule de gens dont vous souffrez visite,
Votre galanterie, et les bruits qu'elle excite,
Trouvèrent des censeurs plus qu'il n'auroit fallu,
Et bien plus rigoureux que je n'eusse voulu.
Vous pouvez bien penser quel parti je sus prendre;
Je fis ce que je pus pour vous pouvoir défendre;
Je vous excusai fort sur votre intention,
Et voulus de votre âme être la caution.
Mais vous savez qu'il est des choses dans la vie
Qu'on ne peut excuser quoiqu'on en ait envie;
Et je me vis contrainte à demeurer d'accord
Que l'air dont vous vivez vous faisoit un peu tort;
Qu'il prenoit dans le monde une méchante face;
Qu'il n'est conte fâcheux que partout on n'en fasse;
Et que, si vous vouliez, tous vos déportements
Pourroient moins donner prise aux mauvais jugements.
Non que j'y croie au fond l'honnêteté blessée;
Me préserve le ciel d'en avoir la pensée!
Mais aux ombres du crime on prête aisément foi,
Et ce n'est pas assez de bien vivre pour soi.
Madame, je vous crois l'âme trop raisonnable
Pour ne pas prendre bien cet avis profitable,
Et pour l'attribuer qu'aux mouvements secrets
D'un zèle qui m'attache à tous vos intérêts.

Cél. Madame, j'ai beaucoup de grâces à vous rendre.
Un tel avis m'oblige; et, loin de le mal prendre,
J'en prétends reconnoître à l'instant la faveur
Par un avis aussi qui touche votre honneur;
Et comme je vous vois vous montrer mon amie,
En m'apprenant les bruits que de moi l'on publie,
Je veux suivre, à mon tour, un exemple si doux,
En vous avertissant de ce qu'on dit de vous.

From this point, the development of the intrigue proceeds apace; but I must not indulge in further quotations. Célimène, thanks to her slanders and the uncomplimentary pen-portraits of two of her admirers which have fallen into their hands owing to the good offices of her friend Arsinoé, finds herself deserted by them. Alceste alone persists in his affection for the coquette, whom he would fain lead with him into some solitude, far from the haunts of men, which she declines. Eliante marries Philinte, and everybody appears satisfied, except Alceste, who makes his exit with these bitter

> En un lieu, l'autre jour, où je faisois visite,
> Je trouvai quelques gens d'un très rare mérite,
> Qui, parlant des vrais soins d'une âme qui vit bien,
> Firent tomber sur vous, madame, l'entretien.
> Là, votre pruderie et vos éclats de zèle
> Ne furent pas cités comme un fort bon modèle ;
> Cette affectation d'un grave extérieur,
> Vos discours éternels de sagesse et d'honneur,
> Vos mines et vos cris aux ombres d'indécence
> Que d'un mot ambigu peut avoir l'innocence,
> Cette hauteur d'estime où vous êtes de vous,
> Et ces yeux de pitié que vous jetez sur tous,
> Vos fréquentes leçons et vos aigres censures
> Sur des choses qui sont innocentes et pures ;
> Tout cela, si je puis vous parler franchement,
> Madame, fut blâmé d'un commun sentiment.
> A quoi bon, disoient-ils, cette mine modeste,
> Et ce sage dehors que dément tout le reste ?
> Elle est à bien prier exacte au dernier point ;
> Mais elle bat ses gens, et ne les paye point.
> Dans tous les lieux dévots elle étale un grand zèle ;
> Mais elle met du blanc, et veut paraître belle.
> Elle fait des tableaux couvrir les nudités ;
> Mais elle a de l'amour pour les réalités.
> Pour moi, contre chacun, je pris votre défense,
> Et leur assurai fort que c'étoit médisance ;
> Mais tous les sentiments combattirent le mien,
> Et leur conclusion fut que vous feriez bien
> De prendre moins de soin des actions des autres,
> Et de vous mettre un peu plus en peine des vôtres ;
> Qu'on doit se regarder soi-même un fort long temps
> Avant que de songer à condamner les gens ;
> Qu'il faut mettre le poids d'une vie exemplaire
> Dans les corrections qu'aux autres on veut faire ;
> Et qu'encor vaut-il mieux s'en remettre, au besoin,
> A ceux à qui le ciel en a commis le soin.
> Madame, je vous crois aussi trop raisonnable
> Pour ne pas prendre bien cet avis profitable,
> Et pour l'attribuer qu'aux mouvements secrets
> D'un zèle qui m'attache à tous vos intérêts.

words upon his lips: 'Betrayed on all sides, overwhelmed with injustice, I am going to escape from a gulf where vice reigns triumphant, and to seek some retired corner of the earth where one can be free to live as an honourable man.'[1]

And so ends this masterpiece of the French theatre, which will hand the name of Molière down to remotest posterity.

Another of the best comedies of the great dramatist, 'Les Femmes Savantes,' has been embroidered, it is said, on the simple canvas of the 'Précieuses Ridicules.' But while this only ridiculed the jargon and affectation current in some of the Parisian salons, the comedy of 'Les Femmes Savantes' is a more keen, serious, and elaborate satire on the pedantry of certain ladies of the time and their pretensions to intellectual superiority, as well as on pedantry and ignorance in general. Philaminte, Bélise, and Armande, the wife, sister, and eldest daughter of Chrysale, a simple and honest citizen of Paris, are the blue-stockings of the comedy. The character of each of these women is stamped by Molière with the mark of a perfect individuality. Each is ridiculous in her own way; but in the three we have presented to us admirable types of those women who cultivate the sciences in order to make a parade of their erudition, without having any affection for science for its own sake, and who make use of it in order to overwhelm by their own superiority all who come near them, while denying them, at the same time, the possession of average common sense.

The other personages are Henriette, a younger daughter of Chrysale, a modest little maiden, lacking the simplicity of Agnes in the 'Ecole des Femmes,' but endowed with natural good sense and ability; Trissotin, a pseudo-philosophic and pedantic writer, a sort of literary Tartuffe; Vadius, who knows Greek as well as any man in France, a kind of classic plagiarist; Clitandre, who is in love with Henriette; and Martine, a servant, who has never learned her grammar.

---

[1] Trahi de toutes parts, accablé d'injustices,
Je vais sortir d'un gouffre où triomphent les vices ;
Et chercher sur la terre un endroit écarté,
Où d'être homme d'honneur on ait la liberté.

Armande has at first been courted by Clitandre, but now that that philosopher in petticoats has coquettishly thrown him over, and she perceives that he is paying her sister those attentions which were previously addressed to herself, she is vainly endeavouring to win him back again. Clitandre, from the second scene of the first act, explains himself very candidly on the subject in the presence of the two sisters, and gives them to understand that, after having suffered the contempt of Armande, he has sought for gentler treatment from the affection of Henriette. Left to themselves, Clitandre and Henriette fall into confidential talk, and Henriette advises her adorer to gain over her mother, as the consent of her father is sure to be obtained, the only barriers to their union being her mother and her aunt Bélise, who together rule her father, and to neither of these has Clitandre rendered himself acceptable. There now appears upon the scene Bélise, the elderly blue-stocking, whom Clitandre forthwith begins to try to win over to his cause. Over and above her pedantry and her passion for Greek, this mature spinster cherishes the ridiculous belief that she excites a tender passion—discreet, it is true, and restrained by all the rules of propriety—in the hearts of all the young men who approach her; and when Clitandre acquaints her with his affection for her niece, the foolish old woman imagines he is explaining his sentiments towards herself. And she cautions him against being too demonstrative, and against his opening his heart too much to her. However ardent his passion for her, he must not speak it in words. His eyes must declare the flame which consumes him, and not his lips. Baffled in this direction, Clitandre approaches Ariste, the brother of Chrysale, a man of sterling good sense, who laughs at the follies of his sister Bélise, and of his sister-in-law Philaminte, and is annoyed at seeing his brother so completely led by the nose by these two women. Ariste promises Clitandre his assistance, and talks to his brother on the subject, who shows that he is not unfavourable to the union. In steps Bélise, however, who declares that Clitandre is not in love with Henriette, but with herself.

Ariste. With you?
Bélise. Yes, with me!
Aris. Ah, sister!

Bél. What does that 'Ah' mean? And what is there surprising in what I say? I have sufficient attractions, I think, to be able to say that I have not one heart only in subjection to my empire; and Dorante, Damis, Cléonte, and Lycidas plainly show that I have some charms.
Aris. These men love you?
Bél. Yes, with all their hearts.
Aris. Have they ever told you so?
Bél. No one ever took that liberty; they have hitherto so much revered me that they have never said a word to me of their love; but the dumb interpreters have all done their duty in offering me their hearts and devoting their service to me.
Aris. Why, Damis is seldom or never here.
Bél. That's to show me a more submissive respect.
Aris. Dorante is always affronting you with satirical speeches.
Bél. Those are the transports of a jealous rage.
Aris. Cléonte and Lycidas have both of them taken wives.
Bél. That was done through a despair to which I had reduced their love.
Aris. In truth, my dear sister, all this is entirely imagination.
Chr. (to Bélise). You ought to lay aside these idle fancies.
Bél. Ah, idle fancies! So these are what you call fancies! Idle fancies, I! Very good idle fancies! I amuse myself greatly with fancies, brothers. I was not aware that I had any idle fancies.[1]

[1]
Ariste.	Haï, ma sœur!
Bélise.	Qu'est-ce donc que veut dire ce haï? Et qu'a de surprenant le discours que je fai? On est faite d'un air, je pense, à pouvoir dire Qu'on n'a pas pour un cœur soumis à son empire; Et Dorante, Damis, Cléonte, et Lycidas Peuvent bien faire voir qu'on a quelques appas.
Ariste.	Ces gens vous aiment?
Bélise.	Oui, de toute leur puissance.
Ariste.	Ils vous l'on dit?
Bélise.	Aucun n'a pris cette licence; Ils m'ont su révérer si fort jusqu'à ce jour, Qu'ils ne m'ont jamais dit un mot de leur amour. Mais pour m'offrir leur cœur et vouer leur service, Les muets truchemens ont tous fait leur office.
Ariste.	On ne voit presque point céans venir Damis.
Bélise.	C'est pour me faire voir un respect plus soumis.
Ariste.	De mots piquants, partout, Dorante vous outrage
Bélise.	Ce sont emportemens d'une jalouse rage.
Ariste.	Cléonte et Lycidas ont pris femme tous deux.
Bélise.	C'est par un désespoir, où j'ai réduit leurs feux.
Ariste.	Ma foi, ma chère sœur, vision toute claire.
Chrysale.	De ces chimères-là vous devez vous défaire.
Bélise.	Ah! chimères! ce sont des chimères, dit-on. Chimères, moi! Vraiment, chimères est fort bon! Je me réjouis fort de chimères, mes frères; Et je ne savais pas que j'eusse des chimères.

Chrysale is quite willing to bestow his daughter upon Clitandre, who is a young man of high character and the son of a man who was his own dearest friend. He will see his wife on the subject, and in the meantime the matter may be regarded as settled.

And here ensues a deliciously comic scene. Martine, the ungrammatical, receives her dismissal from her mistress on account of a fresh lapse in the unfortunate servant's syntax :

SCENE V.—Chrysale, Martine.

Martine. I'm very unlucky! Alas! that's a true saying, If you want to drown a dog, say he is mad. Another's service is no inheritance.

Chrysale. What's the matter, Martine? What ails you?

Mar. What ails me?

Chr. Yes.

Mar. What ails me is that I'm turned off to-day, sir.

Chr. Turned off?

Mar. Yes. Madame has turned me away.

Chr. I don't understand that. How is it?

Mar. They threaten me with a sound beating if I don't go away.

Chr. No, you shall stay. I am satisfied with you. My wife is often a little hot-headed; and I will not——

But all is changed, for there now appear upon the scene Philaminte and Bélise in addition to Chrysale and Martine.

Philaminte (seeing Martine). What! do I see you, you hussy? Quick, be off, you jade; go, leave this place, and never come into my sight again!

Chrysale. Gently.

Phi. No, there's an end of it.

Chr. Eh?

Phi. I'll have her gone.

Chr. But what has she done, that you choose to act in this manner——

Phi. What, do you uphold her?

Chr. By no means.

Phi. Do you take her part against me?

Chr. Good gracious me! No; I only ask what her crime is.

Phi. Am I one to turn her away without just cause?

Chr. I don't say that; but we must, with regard to our servants——

Phi. No, but I tell you she shall go out of our house.

Chr. Well, yes. Does any one say anything to you to the contrary?

Phi. I'll have no resistance to my desires.

Chr. We're agreed.

Phi. Oh, impudence! to call language founded on reason, and polite custom, jargon.

Mar. One always speaks well when one makes oneself understood, and all your fine terms are not of no use.

Phi. There now! She keeps to her own style still, '*are not of no use.*'

Bél. Oh, unteachable animal! Shall we never be able to teach you to speak suitably, with all the pains we incessantly take? *Not* put with *No* makes a recidivation, and it is, as I have told you, one negative too much.

Mar. Good gracious! I aren't no scollard like you. I speaks just as they do in our parts.

Phi. Now, can this be endured?

Bél. What a dreadful solecism!

Phi. It is enough to destroy any sensitive ear.

Bél. Your mind, I must own, is very dense. *I* is singular, *are* is plural. Will you go on all your life offending grammar in this way?

Mar. Who talks of offending Gammer or Gaffer?

Phi. Oh, heavens!

Bél. You take grammar in a wrong sense. I have already told you where the word comes from.

Mar. I don't care whether it comes from Pontoise, Mantes, or Versailles; it's all the same to me.

Bél. What a country clod, to be sure! Grammar teaches us the rules of the Nominative case, and the Verb, as well as of the Adjective and Substantive.

Mar. I must tell you, madame, I don't know those people.

Phi. What a martyrdom!

Bél. These are the names of words, and you ought to take notice how they must agree with each other.

Mar. What does it matter whether they agree with each other or quarrel?

Phi. (*to Bélise*). Oh, heavens! let us put an end to this style of conversation. (*To Chrysale.*) Won't you send her away from me then?

Chr. Yes, yes. (*Aside.*) I must yield to her fancies. Go, and don't provoke her, Martine; leave us.

Phi. What! you are afraid of offending the hussy? You speak in a very obliging tone.

Chr. I? not at all. (*Roughly.*) Go, be gone! (*More mildly.*) Go away, my poor girl.

Phi. And, if you were a reasonable husband, you would take my part against her, and join in my anger.

Chr. (*turning towards Martine*). So I do. Yes, my wife is quite right in sending you away, you hussy, and your crime is unworthy of pardon.

Mar. What is it that I have done, then?

Chr. (*aside*). Indeed I don't know.

Phi. She's in a temper still to make very light of it.

Chr. Has she incurred your displeasure by breaking a looking-glass or some china?

Phi. Do you suppose I should turn her away or put myself in a passion for so small a matter?

Chr. (*to Martine*). What does this mean? (*To Philaminte.*) It's something serious, then?

Phi. Undoubtedly. Am I an unreasonable woman?

Chr. Has she through carelessness allowed some silver ewer or dish to be stolen?

Phi. Oh, that would be nothing.

Chr. (*to Martine*). Oh, oh! Plague on you, you hussy! (*To Philaminte.*) What, have you surprised her in some dishonesty?

Phi. Worse than all that.

Chr. Worse than all that?

Phi. Worse.

Chr. (*to Martine.*) What the deuce? The wretch! (*To Philaminte.*) What, has she committed——

Phi. She has, with unparalleled insolence, after thirty lessons about it, insulted my ear with the impropriety of a vulgar, rough word which Vaugelas decisively condemns.

Chr. Is that——

Phi. What! In spite of my remonstrances, continually to strike at the foundation of all the sciences—grammar, which even rules over kings, and with a high hand makes them obey its laws!

Chr. I thought she had been guilty of a much greater offence.

Phi. What, don't you think this crime unpardonable?

Chr. Yes, indeed.

Phi. I very much wish you'd excuse her.

Chr. I'll take care not to.

Bélise. It certainly is a pity. All the principles of construction are destroyed by her, yet she has been instructed in the laws of language a hundred times.

Mar. All you preach is fine and good, I believe, but I can't talk your jargon, not I.

Scene VII.—Philaminte, Chrysale, Bélise.

Chrysale. You are satisfied, I hope, now she's gone; but I don't approve of her going in this manner. She's a girl fit for her work, and you turn her out of my house for a trifling cause.

Phi. Would you have me keep her always in my service, to torture my ears incessantly? To break every law of custom and reason, by a barbarous mass of faulty language, of lame expressions, mixed at times with sayings picked up from the market gutters?

Bélise. It is true that it throws one into a perspiration to hear her talk. She pulls Vaugelas to pieces every day, and the least blunders of her gross ignorance are either pleonasm or cacophony.

Chr. What does it matter if she fails in the laws of Vaugelas, so long as she does not fail in the kitchen? For my part, I had much rather that in picking her herbs she made the nouns and the verbs agree wrongly and repeated some outrageous word a hundred times, than have her burn my meat or oversalt my broth. I live by good soup and not by fine language. Vaugelas does not teach how to make good soup; and Malherbe and Balzac, so learned in fine words, would possibly have been fools in the kitchen.

Phi. How terribly this gross conversation shocks me! And how unworthy it is of any one who calls himself a man, to be continually bent on material cares, instead of raising himself towards spiritual ones! Is this body, this rag, of sufficient importance or value to deserve a single thought? And ought we not to leave that far behind?

Chr. Ay, but my body is myself, and I'll take care of it. A rag, if you please, but my rag is dear to me.

Bél. The body, together with the mind, brother, makes a figure; but if you believe all the learned world in the case, the mind ought to have precedence over the body, and our greatest care, our first concern, should be to feed it with the juice of science.

Chr. In truth, if you think of feeding your mind, it's with very airy food, according to what every one says, and you have no care, no solicitude for——

Phi. Ah! the word 'solicitude' seems rough to my ear; it sounds strangely of antiquity.

Bél. It is true the word is of high date.

Chr. Will you let me speak? I must be plain, pull off the mask, and discharge my spleen. People call you mad, and I'm heartily troubled——

Phi. How now?

Chr. (*to Bélise*). It is to you that I'm speaking, sister. The least solecism in speech provokes you, but you make strange ones yourself in conduct. Your eternal books don't please me, and except a big Plutarch that I put my bands in, you ought to burn all this useless lumber, and leave science to the learned men of the city; and to be in the right, you should remove from the garret upstairs that long telescope which is enough to frighten people, and a hundred trifles the sight of which is offensive. It would be better not to trouble about what is being done in the moon, but to look a little after what is being done in your house, where everything is topsy-turvy. It is not right, for a great many reasons, that a wife should study and know so much. To form the minds of her children to good manners, to make her household go well, to have an eye over her servants, and to regulate her expenditure with economy, ought to be her study and philosophy. Our fathers were very sensible on this point when they said that a wife always knew enough when her genius enabled her to distinguish between a doublet and a pair of breeches. Their wives did not read, but they lived well; their households were all their learned discourse, and their books a thimble, thread, and needles, with which they worked at their daughters' wedding outfits. But the women of this age are far from such manners; they must write and turn authors.

No science is too profound for them; and in my house more than in any other place, the profoundest secrets are conceived, and everything is known but what ought to be known. They know the motions of the moon, the polar star, Venus, Saturn, and Mars, which do not concern me, and with all this vain knowledge which they go so far to look for, they do not know how my dinner is being cooked, which I need. My servants, too, aspire after learning in order to please you, and they do nothing less than what they ought to do. Reasoning is the business of all the house, and reasoning drives reason out of it. One burns the joint while she reads some history, another is spouting poetry when I want something to drink. In short, I perceive they follow your example, and though I have servants I am not served. One poor girl remained to me, the only one who was not infected with these senseless airs, and she's dismissed with a great outcry, because she does not speak according to Vaugelas. I tell you, sister, for it is to you, as I said, that I address myself, all this way of going on displeases me. I don't like all your Latin scholars coming to my house, and especially this Monsieur Trissotin.. He it was who lampooned you in verse, and his discourses are foolish trash. After he has spoken, one asks what it has all been about, and for my part I believe that he's got a tile loose.

Phi. Good heavens, what meanness both of soul and language?

Bél. Can there be a duller assemblage of corpuscles? or a mind composed of more vulgar atoms? Is it possible that I'm of the same blood? I hate myself for being of your race, and I leave the place in confusion.[1]

[1] *Martine.* Me voilà bien chanceuse! Hélas! l'on dit bien vrai,
Qui veut noyer son chien, l'accuse de la rage;
Et service d'autrui n'est pas un héritage.

Chrysale. Qu'est-ce donc? Qu'avez-vous, Martine?

Martine. Ce que j'ai?

Chrysale. Oui.

Martine. J'ai que l'an me donne aujourd'hui mon congé, Monsieur.

Chrysale. Votre congé?

Martine. Oui, Madame, me chasse.

Chrysale. Je n'entends pas cela. Comment?

Martine. On me menace,
Si je ne sors d'ici, de me bailler cent coups!

Chrysale. Non, vous demeurerez; je suis content de vous.
Ma femme bien souvent a la tête un peu chaude;
Et je ne veux pas, moi . . .

Scène VI.—Philaminte, Bélise, Chrysale, Martine.

Philaminte (*apercevant Martine*). Quoi! je vous vois, maraude!
Vite, sortez, friponne; allons, quittez ces lieux;
Et ne vous présentez jamais devant mes yeux.

Chrysale. Tout doux.

Philaminte. Non, c'en est fait.

Chrysale. Hé!

Philaminte. Je veux qu'elle sorte.

Chrysale. Mais, qu'a-t-elle commis pour vouloir de la sorte? . . .

In the following scene Chrysale timidly announces to Philaminte his intention of giving Henriette to Clitandre,

Philaminte. Quoi ! vous la soutenez ?
Chrysale. En aucune façon.
Philaminte. Prenez-vous son parti contre moi ?
Chrysale. Mon Dieu ! non ;
Je ne fais seulement que demander son crime.
Philaminte. Suis-je pour la chasser sans cause légitime ?
Chrysale. Je ne dis pas cela ; mais il faut de nos gens . . .
Philaminte. Non ; elle sortira, vous dis-je, de céans.
Chrysale. Hé, bien ! oui. Vous dit-on quelque chose là-contre ?
Philaminte. Je ne veux point d'obstacle aux désirs que je montre.
Chrysale. D'accord.
Philaminte. Et vous devez, en raisonnable époux,
Etre pour moi contre elle, et prendre mon courroux.

Chrysale (se tournant vers Martine).

Aussi fais-je. Oui, ma femme avec raison vous chasse,
Coquine, et votre crime est indigne de grâce.
Martine. Qu'est-ce donc que j'ai fait ?
Chrysale (bas). Ma foi, je ne sais pas.
Philaminte. Elle est d'humeur encore à n'en faire aucun cas.
Chrysale. A-t-elle, pour donner matière à votre haine,
Cassé quelque miroir ou quelque porcelaine ?
Philaminte. Voudrois-je la chasser ? et vous figurez-vous
Que pour si peu de chose on se mette en courroux ?
Chrysale (à Martine). Qu'est-ce à dire ? (*à Philaminte*) L'affaire est donc considérable ?
Philaminte. Sans doute. Me voit-on femme déraisonnable ?
Chrysale. Est-ce qu'elle a laissé, d'un esprit négligent,
Dérober quelque aiguière ou quelque plat d'argent ?
Philaminte. Cela ne seroit rien.
Chrysale (à Martine). Oh ! oh ! peste, la belle !
(*à Philaminte*). Quoi ! l'avez-vous surprise à n'être pas fidèle ?
Philaminte. C'est pis que tout cela.
Chrysale. Pis que tout cela ?
Philaminte. Pis.
Chrysale (à Martine). Comment ! diantre, friponne ! (*à Philaminte*). Euh ! a-t-elle commis ? . . .
Philaminte. Elle a, d'une insolence à nulle autre pareille,
Après trente leçons, insulté mon oreille
Par l'impropriété d'un mot sauvage et bas,
Qu'en termes décisifs condamne Vaugelas.
Chrysale. Est-ce là ?
Philaminte. Quoi ! toujours, malgré nos remontrances,
Heurter le fondement de toutes les sciences,
La grammaire, qui sait régenter jusqu'aux rois,
Et les fait, la main haute, obéir à ses lois !
Chrysale. Du plus grand des forfaits je la croyois coupable.
Philaminte. Quoi ! vous ne trouvez pas ce crime impardonnable ?
Chrysale. Si fait.
Philaminte. Je voudrois bien que vous l'excusassiez !

but his wife cuts him short by informing him without any ceremony that she has already fixed upon a husband for her

Chrysale. Je n'ai garde.
Bélise. Il est vrai que ce sont des pitiés.
Toute construction est par elle détruite ;
Et des lois du langage on l'a cent fois instruite.
Martine. Tout ce que vous prêchez est, je crois, bel et bon ;
Mais je ne saurois, moi, parler votre jargon.
Philaminte. L'impudente ! appeler un jargon le langage
Fondé sur la raison et sur le bel usage !
Martine. Quand on se fait entendre, on parle toujours bien,
Et tous vos biaux dictons ne servent pas de rien.
Philaminte. Hé bien ! ne voilà pas encore de son style ?
Ne servent pas de rien !
Bélise. O cervelle indocile !
Faut-il qu'avec les soins qu'on prend incessamment,
On ne te puisse apprendre à parler congrûment ?
De *pas* mis avec *rien* tu fais la récidive ;
Et c'est, comme on t'a dit, trop d'une négative.
Martine. Mon Dieu ! je n'avons pas étugué comme vous,
Et je parlons tout droit comme on parle cheux nous.
Philaminte. Ah ! peut-on y tenir ?
Bélise. Quel solécisme horrible !
Philaminte. En voilà pour tuer une oreille sensible.
Bélise. Ton esprit, je l'avoue, est bien matériel !
Je n'est qu'un singulier, *avons* est un pluriel.
Veux-tu toute ta vie offenser la grammaire ?
Martine. Qui parle d'offenser grand'mère ni grand-père ?
Philaminte. O ciel !
Bélise. Grammaire est prise à contre-sens par toi,
Et je t'ai déjà dit d'où vient ce mot.
Martine. Ma foi,
Qu'il vienne de Chaillot, d'Auteuil ou de Pontoise,
Cela ne me fait rien.
Bélise. Quelle âme villageoise !
La grammaire, du verbe et du nominatif,
Comme de l'adjectif avec le substantif,
Nous enseigne les lois.
Martine. J'ai, madame, à vous dire
Que je ne connois point ces gens-là.
Philaminte. Quel martyre !
Bélise. Ce sont les noms des mots ; et l'on doit regarder
En quoi c'est qu'il les faut faire ensemble accorder.
Martine. Qu'ils s'accordent entre eux, ou se gourment, qu'importe ?
Philaminte (à *Bélise*).
Hé ! mon Dieu ! finissez un discours de la sorte.
(à *Chrysale*).
Vous ne voulez pas, vous, me la faire sortir ?
Chrysale. Si fait. (à part) A son caprice il me faut consentir.
Va ; ne l'irrite point ; retire-toi, Martine.
Philaminte. Comment ! vous avez peur d'offenser la coquine ?
Vous lui parlez d'un ton tout-à-fait obligeant.
(*d'un ton ferme.*) (*d'un ton plus doux*).
Chrysale. Moi ? point. Allons, sortez. Va-t'en, ma pauvre enfant.

younger daughter—namely, Monsieur Trissotin—Trissotin !
who is his own pet aversion ! Trissotin ! who is always

Scène VII.—Philaminte, Chrysale, Bélise.

Chrysale. Vous êtes satisfaite, et la voilà partie ;
Mais je n'approuve point une telle sortie :
C'est une fille propre aux choses qu'elle fait,
Et vous me la chassez pour un maigre sujet.
Philaminte. Vous voulez que toujours je l'aie à mon service,
Pour mettre incessamment mon oreille au supplice,
Pour rompre toute loi d'usage et de raison,
Par un barbare amas de vices d'oraison,
De mots estropiés, cousus, par intervalles,
De proverbes traînés dans les ruisseaux des halles ?
Bélise. Il est vrai que l'on sue à souffrir ses discours ;
Elle y met Vaugelas en pièces tous les jours ;
Et les moindres défauts de ce grossier génie
Sont ou le pléonasme, ou la cacophonie.
Chrysale. Qu'importe qu'elle manque aux lois de Vaugelas,
Pourvu qu'à la cuisine elle ne manque pas !
J'aime bien mieux, pour moi, qu'en épluchant ses herbes,
Elle accommode mal les noms avec les verbes,
Et redise cent fois un bas et méchant mot,
Que de brûler ma viande ou saler trop mon pot.
Je vis de bonne soupe, et non de beau langage.
Vaugelas n'apprend point à bien faire un potage ;
Et Malherbe et Balzac, si savants en beaux mots,
En cuisine, peut-être, auroient été des sots.
Philaminte. Que ce discours grossier terriblement assomme !
Et quelle indignité, pour ce qui s'appelle homme,
D'être baissé sans cesse aux soins matériels,
Au lieu de se hausser vers les spirituels !
Le corps, cette guenille, est-il d'une importance,
D'un prix à mériter seulement qu'on y pense ?
Et ne devons-nous pas laisser cela bien loin ?
Chrysale. Oui, mon corps est moi-même, et j'en veux prendre soin !
Guenille, si l'on veut ; ma guenille m'est chère.
Bélise. Le corps avec l'esprit fait figure, mon frère ;
Mais, si vous en croyez tout le monde savant,
L'esprit doit sur le corps prendre le pas devant ;
Et notre plus grand soin, notre première instance,
Doit être à le nourrir du suc de la science.
Chrysale. Ma foi, si vous songez à nourrir votre esprit,
C'est de viande bien creuse, à ce que chacun dit :
Et vous n'avez nul soin, nulle sollicitude
Pour . . .
Philaminte. Ah ! *sollicitude* à mon oreille est rude ;
Il pue étrangement son ancienneté.
Bélise. Il est vrai que le mot est bien collet monté.
Chrysale. Voulez-vous que je dise ? il faut qu'enfin j'éclate,
Que je lève le masque, et décharge ma rate.
De folles on vous traite, et j'ai fort sur le cœur . . .
Philaminte. Comment donc ?
Chrysale (à Bélise). C'est à vous que je parle, ma sœur.

spouting Latin and mouthing poetry. Consequently there is nothing more to be said. Philaminte is imperious, and

> Le moindre solécisme en parlant vous irrite ;
> Mais vous en faites, vous, d'étranges en conduite.
> Vos livres éternels ne me contentent pas,
> Et, hors un gros Plutarque à mettre mes rabats,
> Vous devriez brûler tout ce meuble inutile,
> Et laisser la science aux docteurs de la ville ;
> M'ôter, pour faire bien, du grenier de céans,
> Cette longue lunette à faire peur aux gens,
> Et cent brimborions dont l'aspect importune ;
> Ne point aller chercher ce qu'on fait dans la lune,
> Et vous mêler un peu de ce qu'on fait chez vous,
> Où nous voyons aller tout sens dessus dessous.
> Il n'est pas bien honnête, et pour beaucoup de causes,
> Qu'une femme étudie et sache tant de choses.
> Former aux bonnes mœurs l'esprit de ses enfants,
> Faire aller son ménage, avoir l'œil sur ses gens,
> Et régler la dépense avec économie,
> Doit être son étude et sa philosophie.
> Nos pères, sur ce point, étoient gens bien sensés,
> Qui disoient qu'une femme en sait toujours assez,
> Quand la capacité de son esprit se hausse
> A connoître un pourpoint d'avec un haut-de-chausse.
> Les leurs ne lisoient point, mais elles vivoient bien ;
> Leurs ménages étoient tout leur docte entretien ;
> Et leurs livres, un dé, du fil et des aiguilles,
> Dont elles travailloient au trousseau de leurs filles.
> Les femmes d'à présent sont bien loin de ces mœurs ;
> Elles veulent écrire, et devenir auteurs ;
> Nulle science n'est pour elles trop profonde,
> Et céans beaucoup plus qu'en aucun lieu du monde :
> Les secrets les plus hauts s'y laissent concevoir,
> Et l'on sait tout chez moi, hors ce qu'il faut savoir.
> On y sait comme vont lune, étoile polaire,
> Vénus, Saturne et Mars, dont je n'ai point affaire ;
> Et dans ce vain savoir, qu'un va chercher si loin,
> On ne sait comme va mon pot, dont j'ai besoin.
> Mes gens à la science aspirent pour vous plaire,
> Et tous ne font rien moins que ce qu'ils ont à faire.
> Raisonner est l'emploi de toute ma maison,
> Et le raisonnement en bannit la raison !
> L'un me brûle mon rôt, en lisant quelque histoire ;
> L'autre rêve à des vers, quand je demande à boire :
> Enfin, je vois par eux votre exemple suivi,
> Et j'ai des serviteurs, et ne suis point servi.
> Une pauvre servante au moins m'étoit restée,
> Qui de ce mauvais air n'étoit point infectée ;
> Et voilà qu'on la chasse avec un grand fracas,
> A cause qu'elle manque à parler Vaugelas.
> Je vous le dis, ma sœur, tout ce train-là me blesse ;
> Car c'est, comme j'ai dit, à vous que je m'adresse.
> Je n'aime point céans tous vos gens à latin,

Chrysale is willing to do anything for the sake of peace and quietness, while Ariste vainly exhorts him to be a man and to assert his independence. 'Insist upon your wife deferring to your wishes,' he exclaims; 'pluck up your courage and say, I will have it so! Can you without a feeling of shame consent to sacrifice your daughter to the foolish fancies of your family and bestow all your wealth upon a nincompoop merely because he can chatter half-a-dozen words of Latin?'[1]

The second scene in the third act is one of the best in the whole comedy, and it is so inimitable that I must quote it almost in its entirety.

It passes between Trissotin, the literary Tartuffe; Henriette, who is only there by chance; Philaminte, Bélise, and Armande, the three blue-stockings, who go into ecstatic raptures at the mere mention of the name of their poet; and L'Epine, the little valet of the household, who, happening to tumble down, is upbraided by the learned ladies for ignoring the law of gravitation. Philaminte is all anxiety to hear the latest composition of the poet, and adjures him to serve up his delightful repast as quickly as possible, to which he replies:

To satisfy such hunger as you show me, a course of only eight verses seems to me little enough, and I think I should not do wrong if I added to the epigram, or rather madrigal, the relish of a sonnet, in which a certain princess found some delicacy of taste. It is seasoned with Attic salt throughout, and you'll find it very pleasant in flavour, I think.

Ar. Oh, I don't doubt it.

   Et principalement ce Monsieur Trissotin;
   C'est lui qui, dans des vers, vous a tympanisées;
   Tous les propos qu'il tient sont des billevesées.
   On cherche ce qu'il dit après qu'il a parlé;
   Et je lui crois, pour moi, le timbre un peu fêlé.

Philaminte. Quelle bassesse, ô ciel! et d'âme et de langage!
Bélise. Est-il de petits corps un plus lourd assemblage?
   Un esprit composé d'atomes plus bourgeois?
   Et de ce même sang se peut-il que je sois?
   Je me veux mal de mort d'être de votre race;
   Et, de confusion, j'abandonne la place.

---

[1] Quoi! vous ne pouvez pas, voyant comme on vous nomme,
Vous résoudre une fois à vouloir être un homme,
A faire condescendre une femme à vos vœux,
Et prendre assez de cœur pour dire un Je le veux!
Vous laisserez, sans honte, immoler votre fille
Aux folles visions qui tiennent la famille,
Et de tout votre bien revêtir un nigaud,
Pour six mots de latin qu'il leur fait sonner haut.

Phi. Let us give attention at once.

Bél. (*interrupting Trissotin as often as he begins to read*). I feel my heart leap for joy beforehand. I love poetry to distraction, and especially when the verses are gallantly turned.

Phi. If we talk continually he can say nothing.

Tris. So——

Bél. (*to Henriette*). Silence, niece.

Ar. Now let him read.

Tris. A SONNET TO THE PRINCESS URANIE, ON HER FEVER.[1]

>> Asleep your prudence sure must be,
>>> Magnificently thus to treat,
>>> And sumptuously lodge in state,
>> Your most pernicious enemy.

Bél. Oh! what a lovely beginning!

Ar. What a charming turn it has!

Phi. He alone possesses the talent of making smooth verses.

Ar. We must give the palm to *prudence asleep.*

Bél. Lodge her enemy is full of charms to me.

Phi. I like *sumptuously* and *magnificently.* Those two adverbs are joined so admirably.

Bél. Now let's listen to the rest.

Tris.
>> Asleep your prudence sure must be,
>>> Magnificently thus to treat,
>>> And sumptuously lodge in state,
>> Your most pernicious enemy.

Ar. Prudence asleep!

Bél. Sumptuously lodge her enemy!

Phi. Sumptuously! Magnificently!

Tris.
>> Whate'er is said, the serpent send
>>> From your apartment rich and great;
>>> Where insolently the ingrate
>> Your precious life attempts to end.

Bél. Ah! gently! Let us take breath.

Ar. Pray give us time to admire.

Phi. On hearing these verses, one feels something run at the very bottom of one's heart, so that one feels faint.

Ar.
>> Whate'er is said, the serpent send
>>> From your apartment rich and great.

How finely said is *Apartment rich and great!* And with what wit is the metaphor introduced!

Phi. Whate'er is said is admirable for taste. In my opinion, it is an invaluable passage.

Bél. I am of your opinion. *Whate'er is said* is a happy expression.

Ar. I wish I had written it.

Bél. It's worth a whole piece.

Phi. But do you really understand the refinement of it, as I do?

Ar. and *Bél.* Oh! oh!

[1] Quoted from the works of Charles Cotin, 1663.

Phi. Whate'er is said, the serpent send.
Though they should take the fever's part, don't regard it, but laugh at their babbling, *Whate'er is said, the serpent send, Whate'er is said, Whate'er is said.* This *Whate'er is said* says a great deal more than any one thinks; for my part, I don't know if every one is like me, but I understand a million of words beneath it.

Bél. It is true. It says more things than it seems to do.

Phi. (*to Trissotin*). But when you wrote that charming *Whate'er is said*, did you yourself comprehend all its force? Did you really imagine all that it says to us? And did you then think you were putting so much wit into it?

Tris. Aha, aha!

Ar. I have likewise *the ingrate* running in my head: the ingrate of a fever, unjust, uncivil, to treat people ill who entertained it.

Phi. In short, both the quatrains are admirable. Pray let us come quickly to the triplets.

Ar. Ah, once more *Whate'er is said*, if you please.

Tris. Whate'er is said, the serpent send.

Phi., Ar., and *Bél. Whate'er is said!*

Tris. From your apartment rich and great.

Phi., Ar., and *Bél. Apartment rich and great.*

Tris. Where insolently the ingrate.

Phi. Ar., and *Bél.* That 'ingrate' of a fever!

Tris. Your precious life attempts to end.

Phi. Your precious life!

Ar. and *Bél.* Ah!

Tris.   Who, not respecting your high rank,
       Your noble blood has basely drank.

Phi., Ar., and *Bél.* Ah!

Tris.   And hourly plays some cruel prank.
       The next time to the bath you go,
       There take it without more ado,
       And with your own hands drown it so.

Bél. (*to Henriette*). What! no emotion during the reading? You make a strange figure there, niece.

Hen. Every one here below, aunt, makes what figure they can; and one cannot be a wit at will.

Tris. Perhaps my verses annoy you.

Hen. No; I don't listen.

Phi. Now let us hear the epigram.

Tris. It is, *On a carriage of an amarant colour, presented to a lady of his acquaintance.*[1]

Phi. His titles have always something uncommon in them.

Ar. The novelty of them prepares one for a hundred strokes of wit.

Tris. Love has so dearly sold to me his band,

Bél., Ar., and *Phi.* Ah!

Tris.   Already it has cost me half my land.
       And when this lovely carriage you behold,
       Wherein there lies embossed so much gold,

---

[1] Also from Cotin's works.

>   That it amazeth all the country round,
>   And makes my Lais' triumph far resound——
>
> *Phi.* Ah, 'My Lais!' There's erudition!
> *Bél.* The disguise is pretty, and is worth a million.
> *Tris.* And when this lovely carriage you behold,
>   Wherein there lies embossed so much gold,
>   That it amazeth all the country round,
>   And makes my Lais' triumph far resound,
>   No longer say that it is amarant,
>   But much, much rather say 'tis of my rent.
> *Ar.* Oh! oh! oh! oh! That was quite unexpected.
> *Phi.* No one but he can write with so much taste.
> *Bél.*   No longer say that it is amarant,
>   But much, much rather say 'tis o' my rent.
>   Thus may be declined 'My rent, of my rent, to my rent' (*à ma rente*).¹

---

¹ *Philaminte.* Servez-nous promptement votre aimable repas.
Trissotin.   Pour cette grande faim qu'à mes yeux on expose
                Un plat seul de huit vers me semble peu de chose;
                Et je pense qu'ici je ne ferais pas mal
                De joindre à l'épigramme, ou bien au madrigal,
                Le ragoût d'un sonnet qui, chez une princesse,
                A passé pour avoir quelque délicatesse.
                Il est de sel attique assaisonné partout,
                Et vous le trouverez, je crois, d'assez bon goût.
Armande.   Ah! je n'en doute point.
Philaminte.   Donnons vite audience.
Bélise (*interrompant Trissotin chaque fois qu'il se dispose à lire*).
                Je sens d'aise mon cœur tressaillir par avance.
                J'aime la poésie avec entêtement,
                Et surtout quand les vers sont tournés galamment.
Philaminte.   Si nous parlons toujours, il ne pourra rien dire.
Trissotin.   So . . .
Bélise (*à Henriette*). Silence, ma nièce.
Armande.   Ah! laissez-le donc lire.
Trissotin.   Sonnet à la princesse Uranie, sur sa fièvre.
                    Votre prudence est endormie,
                    De traiter magnifiquement
                    Et de loger superbement
                    Votre plus cruelle ennemie.
Bélise.   Ah! le joli début!
Armande.   Qu'il a le tour galant!
Philaminte.   Lui seul des vers aisés possède le talent,
Armande.   A *prudence endormie* il faut rendre les armes.
Bélise.   *Loger son ennemie* est pour moi plein de charmes.
Philaminte.   J'aime *superbement* et *magnifiquement*;
                Ces deux adverbes joints font admirablement.
Bélise.   Prêtons l'oreille au reste.
Trissotin.   Votre prudence est endormie,
                    De traiter magnifiquement
                    Et de loger superbement
                    Votre plus cruelle ennemie.

There is another scene in this same act in which Vadius joins the personages previously on the stage; and in it

Armande.	Prudence endormie !
Bélise.	Loger son ennemie !
Philaminte.	Superbement et magnifiquement !
Trissotin.	Faites-la sortir, quoi qu'on die,
	De votre riche appartement,
	Où cette ingrate insolemment
	Attaque votre belle vie.
Bélise.	Ah ! tout doux ! laissez-moi, de grâce, respirer.
Armande.	Donnez-nous, s'il vous plaît, le loisir d'admirer.
Philaminte.	On se sent, à ces vers, jusques au fond de l'âme
	Couler je ne sais quoi qui fait que l'on se pâme.
Armande.	*Faites-la sortir, quoi qu'on die,*
	De votre riche appartement.
	Que *riche appartement* est là joliment dit !
	Et que la métaphore est mise avec esprit !
Philaminte.	*Faites-la sortir, quoi qu'on die.*
	Ah ! que ce *quoi qu'on die* est d'un goût admirable !
	C'est, à mon sentiment, un endroit impayable.
Armande.	De *quoi qu'on die* aussi mon cœur est amoureux.
Bélise.	Je suis de votre avis, *quoi qu'on die* est heureux.
Armande.	Je voudrois l'avoir fait.
Bélise.	Il vaut toute une pièce.
Philaminte.	Mais en comprend-on bien, comme moi, la finesse ?
Armande et Bélise.	Oh ! Oh !
Philaminte.	*Faites-la sortir, quoi qu'on die.*
	Que de la fièvre on prenne ici les intérêts.
	N'ayez aucun égard, moquez-vous des caquets ;
	Faites-la sortir, quoi qu'on die,
	Quoi qu'on die, quoi qu'on die.
	Ce *quoi qu'on die* en dit beaucoup plus qu'il ne semble.
	Je ne sais pas, pour moi, si chacun me ressemble :
	Mais j'entends là-dessous un million de mots.
Bélise.	Il est vrai qu'il dit plus de choses qu'il n'est gros.
Philaminte (à Trissotin).	
	Mais, quand vous avez fait ce charmant *quoi qu'on die*,
	Avez-vous compris, vous, toute son énergie ?
	Songiez-vous bien vous-même à tout ce qu'il nous dit ?
	Et pensiez-vous alors y mettre tant d'esprit ?
Trissotin.	Haï ! Haï !
Armande.	J'ai fort aussi *l'ingrate* dans la tête.
	Cette ingrate de fièvre, injuste, malhonnête,
	Qui traite mal les gens qui la logent chez eux.
Philaminte.	Enfin, les quatrains sont admirables tous deux.
	Venons-en promptement aux tiercets, je vous prie.
Armande.	Ah ! s'il vous plaît, encore une fois *quoi qu'on die.*
Trissotin.	*Faites-la sortir, quoi qu'on die,*
Philamante, Armande et Bélise.	*Quoi qu'on die !*
Trissotin.	*De votre riche appartement,*
Philaminte, Armande et Bélise.	*Riche appartement !*
Trissotin.	*Où cette ingrate insolemment*

Molière soundly chastises the pedantry of his own age, and of all times, and elevates comedy to a height never reached

Philaminte, Armande et Bélise. Cette *ingrate* de fièvre !
Trissotin.   Attaque votre belle vie.
Philaminte. Votre belle vie !
Armande et Bélise. Ah !
Trissotin.   Quoi ! sans respecter votre rang,
          Elle se prend à votre sang,
Philaminte, Armande et Bélise. Ah !
Trissotin.   Et nuit et jour vous fait outrage !
          Si vous la conduisez aux bains,
          Sans la marchander davantage,
          Noyez-la de vos propres mains.
Philaminte. On n'en peut plus.
Bélise.   On pâme.
Armande.   On se meurt de plaisir.
Philaminte. De mille doux frissons vous vous sentez saisir.
Armande.   *Si vous la conduisez aux bains,*
Bélise.   *Sans la marchander davantage,*
Philaminte. *Noyez-la de vos propres mains.*
          De vos propres mains, là, noyez-la dans les bains.
Armande. Chaque pas dans vos vers rencontre un trait charmant.
Bélise. Partout on s'y promène avec ravissement.
Philaminte. On n'y sauroit marcher que sur de belles choses.
Armande. Ce sont petits chemins tout parsemés de roses.
Trissotin. Le sonnet donc vous semble . . .
Philaminte.   Admirable, nouveau ;
          Et personne jamais n'a rien fait de si beau.
Bélise (à Henriette).
          Quoi ! sans émotion pendant cette lecture !
          Vous faites là, ma nièce, une étrange figure !
Henriette. Chacun fait ici-bas la figure qu'il peut,
          Ma tante ; et bel esprit, il ne l'est pas qui veut.
Trissotin. Peut-être que mes vers importunent madame.
Henriette. Point. Je n'écoute pas.
Philaminte.   Ah ! voyons l'épigramme.
Trissotin. Sur un carrosse de couleur amarante donné à une dame de ses amies.
Philaminte. Ses titres ont toujours quelque chose de rare.
Armande. A cent beaux traits d'esprit leur nouveauté prépare.
Trissotin. · L'amour si chèrement m'a vendu son lien,
Philaminte, Armande et Bélise. Ah !
Trissotin. Qu'il m'en coûte déjà la moitié de mon bien.
          Et quand tu vois ce beau carrosse
            Où tant d'or se relève en bosse
          Qu'il étonne tout le pays,
          Et fait pompeusement triompher ma Laïs . . .
Philaminte. Ah ! ma Laïs ! Voilà de l'érudition.
          L'enveloppe est jolie, et vaut un million.
Trissotin. Et quand tu vois ce beau carrosse
            Où tant d'or se relève en bosse

before. Vadius is introduced by Trissotin as one who has a perfect knowledge of the ancient authors, and understands Greek perfectly.

> *Phi.* (*to Bélise*). Greek! good heavens! Greek! He understands Greek, sister!
> *Bél.* (*to Armande*). Ah! niece, Greek!
> *Ar.* Greek! oh, how delightful!
> *Phi.* What! does monsieur understand Greek? Ah, pray let me embrace you, for Greek's sake! (*Vadius embraces both Bélise and Armande.*)
> *Hen.* (*to Vadius, who would embrace her too*). Excuse me, sir, I don't understand Greek.[1]

It is believed that under the name of Vadius, implying shallowness, perhaps Molière was satirising Ménage, who combined with an extensive knowledge of the languages and literature of antiquity a liberal measure of pedantry. He also was one of the frequenters of the Hôtel de Rambouillet, and was in love with all its beautiful disciples, one after another. Trissotin and Vadius begin by smearing each other with the thickest of honey:

> *Tris.* Your verses have beauties which all others lack.
> *Vad.* Venus and all the Graces reign in all yours.
> *Tris.* You have a free expression, and a fine choice of words.
> *Vad.* We see everywhere that you have the *Ethos* and the
>   *Pathos*.

>   Qu'il étonne tout le pays,
>   Et fait pompeusement triompher ma Laïs,
>   Ne dis plus qu'il est amarante,
>   Dis plutôt qu'il est de ma rente.
> *Armande.*   Oh! oh! oh! celui-là ne s'attend point du tout.
> *Philaminte.* On n'a que lui qui puisse écrire de ce goût.
> *Bélise.*   *Ne dis plus qu'il est amarante,*
>   *Dis plutôt qu'il est de ma rente.*
>   Voilà qui se décline, ma rente, de ma rente, à ma rente.
>
> [1] *Trissotin.* Il a des vieux auteurs la pleine intelligence,
>   Et sait du grec, madame, autant qu'homme de France.
> *Philaminte.* Du grec, ô ciel, du grec! il sait du grec, ma sœur!
> *Bélise.*   Ah! ma nièce, du grec!
> *Armande.*   Du grec! quelle douceur!
> *Philaminte.* Quoi! monsieur sait du grec? Ah! permettez, de grâce,
>   Que, pour l'amour du grec, monsieur, on vous embrasse.
>   (*Vadius, après avoir embrassé les trois pédantes, veut aussi embrasser Henriette, qui se récuse:*)
> *Henriette.* Excusez-moi, monsieur, je n'entends pas le grec.

Tris. We have heard eclogues from you in a style that surpasses Virgil and Theocritus for sweetness.

Vad. Your odes have a noble, gallant, and tender air, which leaves your own Horace far behind.

Tris. Is there anything so amorous as your lays?

Vad. Can one find anything to equal your sonnets?

Tris. Anything more charming than your rondeaux?

Vad. Anything so full of wit as all your madrigals?

Tris. At ballads especially you are admirable.

Vad. And I think you adorable in *bouts-rimés*.

Tris. If France could only know your worth!

Vad. If the age did but render justice to men of wit!

Tris. You'd ride through the streets in a gilt carriage.

Vad. We should see the public erect statues to you. H'm— (*to Trissotin*). Here's a ballad, and I desire that you'll frankly——

Tris. (*to Vadius*). Have you seen a certain little sonnet on the Princess Uranie's fever?

Vad. Yes; it was read to me yesterday in company.

Tris. Do you know the author?

Vad. No; but I know very well that, not to flatter him, his sonnet's worth nothing.[1]

The little rift within the lute widens apace, and when

[1]
Trissotin.	Vos vers ont des beautés que n'ont point tous les autres.
Vadius.	Les Grâces et Vénus règnent dans tous les vôtres.
Trissotin.	Vous avez le tour libre, et le beau choix des mots.
Vadius.	On voit partout chez vous l'*ithos* et le *pathos*.
Trissotin.	Nous avons vu de vous des églogues d'un style Qui passe en doux attraits Théocrite et Virgile.
Vadius.	Vos odes ont un air noble, galant et doux, Qui laisse de bien loin votre Horace après vous.
Trissotin.	Est-il rien d'amoureux comme vos chansonnettes?
Vadius.	Peut-on rien voir d'égal aux sonnets que vous faites?
Trissotin.	Rien qui soit plus charmant que vos petits rondeaux?
Vadius.	Rien de si plein d'esprit que tous vos madrigaux?
Trissotin.	Aux ballades surtout vous êtes admirable.
Vadius.	Et dans les bouts-rimés je vous trouve adorable.
Trissotin.	Si la France pouvoit connoître votre prix,
Vadius.	Si le siècle rendoit justice aux beaux esprits,
Trissotin.	En carrosse doré vous iriez par les rues.
Vadius.	On verroit le public vous dresser des statues. (*à Trissotin*) Hom! c'est une ballade, et je veux que tout net Vous m'en . . .
Trissotin (*à Vadius*).	Avez-vous vu certain petit sonnet Sur la fièvre qui tient la princesse Uranie?
Vadius.	Oui; hier il me fut lu dans une compagnie.
Trissotin.	Vous en savez l'auteur?
Vadius.	Non; mais je sais fort bien Qu'à ne le point flatter, son sonnet ne vaut rien.
Trissotin.	Beaucoup de gens pourtant le trouvent admirable.
Vadius.	Cela n'empêche pas qu'il ne soit misérable.

. . . .

Vadius wants to read a ballad of his own composition, the wounded vanity of Trissotin prompts him to reply:

Tris. A ballad, in my opinion, is an insipid thing; it is no longer in fashion, it savours of antiquity.
Vad. A ballad, however, charms a great many people.
Tris. That doesn't hinder its displeasing me.
Vad. It may be none the worse for that.
Tris. It has a wonderful attraction for pedants.
Vad. And yet we see it does not please you.
Tris. You foolishly attribute your qualities to others. (*They all rise.*)
Vad. You very impertinently cast yours on me.
Tris. Be off, you schoolboy, you paper-blotter!
Vad. Be off, you pitiful rhymer, a shame to your profession!
Tris. Go, you second-hand verse-maker. You impudent plagiarist!
Vad. Go, you pedant——
Phi. Oh, gentlemen, what are you going to do?
Tris. (*to Vadius*). Go, go and restore all the shameful thefts which the Greeks and Latins claim back from you!
Vad. Go, go and do penance on Parnassus for having lamed Horace in your verses.
Tris. Remember your book, and the little impression it made.
Vad. Remember your bookseller reduced to the workhouse.
Tris. My fame is established; it is in vain that you endeavour to tear it to pieces.
Vad. Yes, yes, I send you back to the author of the Satires.
Tris. And I send you to him too.

The quarrel ends by the following threats:

Vad. My pen shall teach you what sort of man I am.
Tris. And mine shall make you know your master.
Vad. I defy you in verse or prose, Greek or Latin.
Tris. Well, well, we shall meet alone at Barbin's.[1]

Trissotin.	La ballade, à mon goût, est une chose fade :
	Ce n'en est plus la mode ; elle sent son vieux temps.
Vadius.	La ballade pourtant charme beaucoup de gens.
Trissotin.	Cela n'empêche pas qu'elle ne me déplaise.
Vadius.	Elle n'en reste pas pour cela plus mauvaise.
Trissotin.	Elle a pour les pédants de merveilleux appas.
Vadius.	Cependant nous voyons qu'elle ne vous plaît pas.
Trissotin.	Vous donnez sottement vos qualités aux autres.
Vadius.	Fort impertinemment vous me jetez les vôtres.
Trissotin.	Allez, petit grimaud, barbouilleur de papier.
Vadius.	Allez, rimeur de balle, opprobre du métier.
Trissotin.	Allez, fripier d'écrits, impudent plagiaire.
Vadius.	Allez, cuistre . . .
Philaminte.	Eh! messieurs, que prétendez-vous faire ?
Trissotin.	Va, va restituer tous les honteux larcins
	Que réclament sur toi les Grecs et les Latins.

Philaminte is more and more bent upon Henriette marrying Trissotin, while Chrysale, on the other hand, who plucks up a good deal of courage only to find it evaporating at the sound of his wife's voice, wishes her to marry Clitandre, and enters into a solemn engagement to that effect with both of them.

The fourth act contains, among other fine scenes, a capital passage at arms between the rival lovers, in which Trissotin gets the worst of it, and is stigmatised as a pedantic dunce by Clitandre in the well-known line 'A learned blockhead is worse than an ignorant one.' As to Clitandre, he never ceases to be the pleasant companion, full of good sense, bright in intellect, hating pedants, and knowing how to make merry over them. We now approach the *dénouement*. Chrysale has undergone some severe heart-quakes in consequence of his wife's terrible temper, and Henriette is on the point of being married to Trissotin, when Ariste reappears as the bearer of very bad news—invented for the occasion. Chrysale and his family are ruined, Henriette is dowerless, our pseudo-philosopher promptly beats a retreat, and Clitandre marries Henriette.'

I feel that in the analysis of four comedies only I have rendered very inadequate justice to the greatest of French dramatists.

It only remains to submit a few words by way of epilogue. When Louis XIV. asked Boileau who was the greatest man of genius in France, the unhesitating reply of the famous critic was—Molière. No one in his own country

Vadius.	Va, va-t'en faire amende honorable au Parnasse D'avoir fait à tes vers estropier Horace.
Trissotin.	Souviens-toi de ton livre, et de son peu de bruit.
Vadius.	Et toi, de ton libraire à l'hôpital réduit.
Trissotin.	Ma gloire est établie; en vain tu la déchires.
Vadius.	Oui, oui, je te renvoie à l'auteur des *Satires*.
Trissotin.	Je t'y renvoie aussi.
. . . . .	
Vadius.	Ma plume t'apprendra quel homme je puis être.
Trissotin.	Et la mienne saura te faire voir ton maître.
Vadius.	Je te défie en vers, prose, grec et latin.
Trissotin.	Eh bien ! nous nous verrons seul à seul chez Barbin.¹

¹ A well-known bookseller in Paris.

has ever approached him; and, as Chamfort finely expressed it, the throne which he occupied has remained vacant ever since. In twenty years he composed thirty-one comedies, half of which are incomparable masterpieces, while the other half contain enough material to set up a dozen minor dramatists in business. 'Molière could not have written a bad piece if he had tried,' said Racine. 'Molière is so great,' exclaimed Goethe, 'that every time I re-read his works I experience fresh astonishment. I have known and loved him from my youth upward, and have been learning from him all my life.' 'Once upon a time,' said a famous English actor, 'the god of comedy, feeling the impulse to write, assumed a human form, and dropped down by chance on France,' where he bore the name of Jean-Baptiste Poquelin, —otherwise Molière.

www.ingramcontent.com/pod-product-compliance
Lightning Source LLC
Chambersburg PA
CBHW051846300426
44117CB00006B/281